NOBLE UNDERTAKING

Volume 1: The Continental Congress and the American Revolution, 1774–78

BRIAN DEMING

BROOKLINE
books

Havertown, Pennsylvania

Brookline Books is an imprint of Casemate Publishers

Published in the United States of America and Great Britain in 2025 by
BROOKLINE BOOKS
1950 Lawrence Road, Havertown, PA 19083
and
47 Church Street, Barnsley, S70 2AS, UK

Copyright 2025 © Brian Deming

Hardback Edition: ISBN 978-1-955041-39-3
Digital Edition: ISBN 978-1-955041-40-9

A CIP record for this book is available from the British Library

All rights reserved. No part of this book may be reproduced or transmitted in any form or by any means, electronic or mechanical including photocopying, recording or by any information storage and retrieval system, without permission from the publisher in writing.

Printed and bound in the United Kingdom by CPI Group (UK) Ltd, Croydon, CR0 4YY

Typeset in India by Lapiz Digital Services, Chennai.

For a complete list of Brookline Books titles, please contact:

CASEMATE PUBLISHERS (US)
Telephone (610) 853-9131
Fax (610) 853-9146
Email: casemate@casematepublishers.com
www.casematepublishers.com

CASEMATE PUBLISHERS (UK)
Telephone (0)1226 734350
Email: casemate@casemateuk.com
www.casemateuk.com

Front cover image: The Declaration of Independence, July 4, 1776, by John Trumbull. (Image courtesy of the Architect of the Capitol)

(All maps by Declan Ingram)

The Publisher's authorised representative in the EU for product safety is Authorised Rep Compliance Ltd., Ground Floor, 71 Lower Baggot Street, Dublin D02 P593, Ireland.
http://www.arccompliance.com

How difficult the task to quench out the fire and the pride of private ambition, and to sacrifice ourselfs and all our hopes and expectations to the publick weal. How few have souls capable of so noble an undertaking.

Abigail Adams to John Adams, July 16, 1775

Contents

Introduction		vii
Maps		ix
1	Eyes of Millions Are Upon Us	1
2	Excited No Terror	11
3	Eats Little, Drinks Little, Sleeps Little, Thinks Much	19
4	A State of Nature	25
5	We Will Never Submit	36
6	Too Saucy & Provoking	50
7	The Great Jehovah and the Continental Congress	60
8	No Harum Starum Ranting Swearing Fellow	70
9	Perfidious Double-Faced Congress	82
10	Spirited Manifesto	89
11	Their Rights as Dear as Our Own	99
12	The Child Was Not Yet Weaned	107
13	To Begin the World Over Again	116
14	Motives of Glory as Well as Interest	127
15	We Cannot Make Events	133
16	Knaves Imposing upon Fools	140
17	Comfort and Cheer the Spirits	150
18	Boots and Spurs	157
19	Singular and Delicate	165
20	Perfidy & Tyranny	173
21	The Most Silent Man in France	185
22	Too Many Members to Keep Secrets	191
23	Excrement of Expiring Genius & Political Phrenzy	200
24	Our Little Handfull	207
25	Dismal & Melancoly	213
26	Violent, Seditious, Treasonable	223
27	Great and Interesting Consequences	231
28	Worst of All Possible Places	236

29	Laying the Foundation of Future Evils	244
30	A Great Expenditure of Liquor, Powder &c	251
31	A Painful Dilemma	259
32	The Wretched Spectator of a Ruin'd Army	266
33	Marks of Deliberation & Design	272
34	Calculated to Deceive	278
35	Women Running, Children Crying, Delegates Flying	286
36	A Dead Weight on Us	292
37	Very Curious and Extraordinary	299
38	Essential to Our Very Existence	305
39	Men Cursing, Women Shrieking, Children Squalling	310
40	We Must Change Our Mode of Conduct	317
41	Too Important to Be Trifled With	324
42	My Heart Is Full, My Eyes Overflow	330
43	A Most Shameful Deficiency	340
44	I Schall Be Laughed At	346
45	Fire Cake & Water	353
46	Most Wicked, Diabolical Baseness	362
47	Ridiculous, Undeserved and Unmerited	372
48	You Damned Poltroon	378
49	The Sluttish Manner of Washing Our Linnen	383
50	Preventing Every Wish of My Heart	387

Endnotes	394
Acknowledgments	443
Bibliography	444
Index	461

Introduction

This is the story of the Continental Congress from 1774, before the United States became a nation, to 1778, when, as a new nation fighting for independence from Great Britain, it secured an ally, France.

Beginning as a convention of delegates groping for an honorable way to mend ties with Great Britain, the Continental Congress evolved into an assembly saddled with the task of ushering in a new nation while managing a war. This book examines the crises that bombarded Congress over those eventful years and explains how this collection of mostly well-off men with much to lose came to lead a rebellion.

When people think of the Continental Congress, if they think of it at all, they tend to dimly recollect something about the Founding Fathers gathering in Philadelphia and bravely declaring American independence. Then the story of Congress fades. We remember perhaps that Congress's Continental dollar was pathetic, and that its framework for governing, the Articles of Confederation, was fatally flawed.

As I embarked on this project, I wanted to know more. How did the delegates to Congress work together? How did Congress pay for the war? How did Congress manage the military? How did Congress initiate diplomacy? What was debated? How did Congress acquire and wield its authority? How did delegates live and manage their private lives?

In looking for answers to these and other questions, I discovered an amazing story. Congress fumbled and failed often before succeeding in what mattered most: securing independence from Great Britain, preserving the fragile union, and achieving an honorable and favorable peace. This book examines the critical first years of that journey, which ended with a peace treaty in 1784.

Many names are familiar: George Washington, Benjamin Franklin, John Adams, Samuel Adams, John Hancock, Thomas Jefferson, and Patrick Henry. All served in Congress at one time or another during this period. Other names, prominent then, but not so well remembered now, include Robert Morris, Richard Henry Lee, and Henry Laurens. This book examines their roles in building a new nation. It also reminds readers that among the delegates were those, like Joseph Galloway, who resisted the Patriot cause and eventually cast his lot with Loyalists.

Many historians, in referring to the Continental Congress, prefer the more specific terms First Continental Congress, Second Continental Congress, and Confederation

Congress, depending on the period. The First Continental Congress met in September and October 1774. The Second Continental Congress came together on May 10, 1775, and met until March 1, 1781, when the Confederation Congress came into being under the nation's first constitution, the Articles of Confederation.

However, the distinction between the First, Second, and Confederation Congress is lost on most people because each body was made up of many of the same men, had about the same authority, and functioned under similar rules.

The official name of the Continental Congress was never the First, Second, or Confederation Congress, or even the Continental Congress. It was just "The Congress" or, after Confederation, "the United States in Congress Assembled." Here I generally used the term *Congress*.

This book takes the story to about the midpoint of the Revolution. Another volume, *Noble Undertaking: Volume 2: The Continental Congress and the American Revolution, 1778–84*, takes readers to the end of the war.

After the war, the Congress limped on, giving way eventually to a government under the Constitution, a blueprint for a "more perfect union," as if the original union were perfect, and that such a perfect union could be made more so.

Alas, as this book shows, that union improvised in those early years was woefully imperfect, as was the Continental Congress, which surprisingly won independence while laying the groundwork of a new and inspiring republic. This all makes the story of the Continental Congress in the emerging nation worth telling.

Readers will note that in quotes from letters and other documents of the time, I have, in most cases, preserved the original spelling and punctuation.

Maps

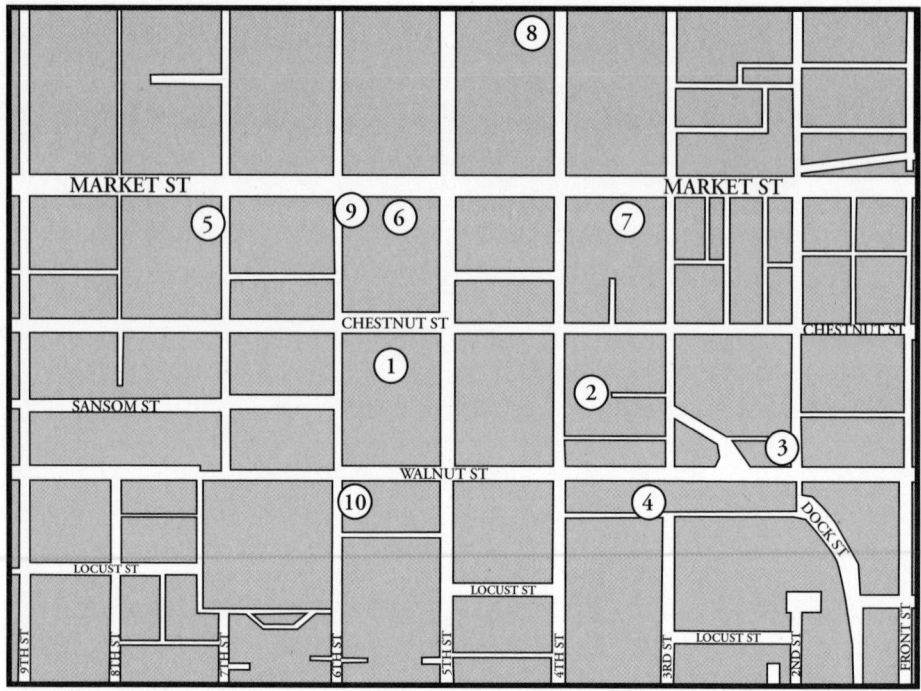

The Philadelphia neighborhood around what was the Pennsylvania State House, the building we now know as Independence Hall.

1. The former Pennsylvania State House (now Independence Hall). Meeting place of the Second Continental Congress.

2. Carpenters' Hall. Meeting place of the First Continental Congress.

3. City Tavern. Site of tavern where delegates to Congress first came together on arriving in Philadelphia and a favored gathering spot on special occasions. A replica of the original tavern now stands here.

4. Site of James Wilson's home. Location of so-called Fort Wilson riot on October 4, 1779.

5. Declaration House. Site of house where Thomas Jefferson drafted Declaration of Independence. In 1776, it was the home of Jacob Graff, a bricklayer. A replica of the house has been built on the site.

6. Site of President's House. Headquarters of British General William Howe during the British occupation of Philadelphia. Later home of Benedict Arnold when he was military commander of the city after the Americans retook the city but before Arnold's betrayal. In 1780, financier Robert Morris bought and enlarged the house. It was the executive mansion for Presidents Washington and John Adams before the federal government left Philadelphia and moved to Washington, DC. Mary Lawrence Masters built the house, completed in 1772, for her daughter, who married the grandson of William Penn, founder of the Pennsylvania colony. The last remnants of the house were demolished in the 1950s.

7. Site of Benjamin Franklin's house. Franklin's wife, Deborah, moved into the new three-story brick house in 1765 while her husband was overseas. She was dead by the time he returned to America in 1775 and stepped foot in the home for the first time. Franklin died in the house in 1790. The house was demolished in 1812.

8. Site of College Hall, a two-story brick building where Congress met briefly while the State House was being cleaned and repaired following the British evacuation of the city.

9. Site of Galloway house. Joseph Galloway and his wife, Grace, lived at a house on this site. Galloway, a delegate to the First Continental Congress, became a Loyalist. He left Philadelphia with his daughter when the British evacuated the city. Grace, left behind, was evicted from the house by Pennsylvania authorities.

10. Site of New Jail, also known as the Walnut Street Jail. American soldiers were imprisoned here, as well as in the State House, during the British occupation.

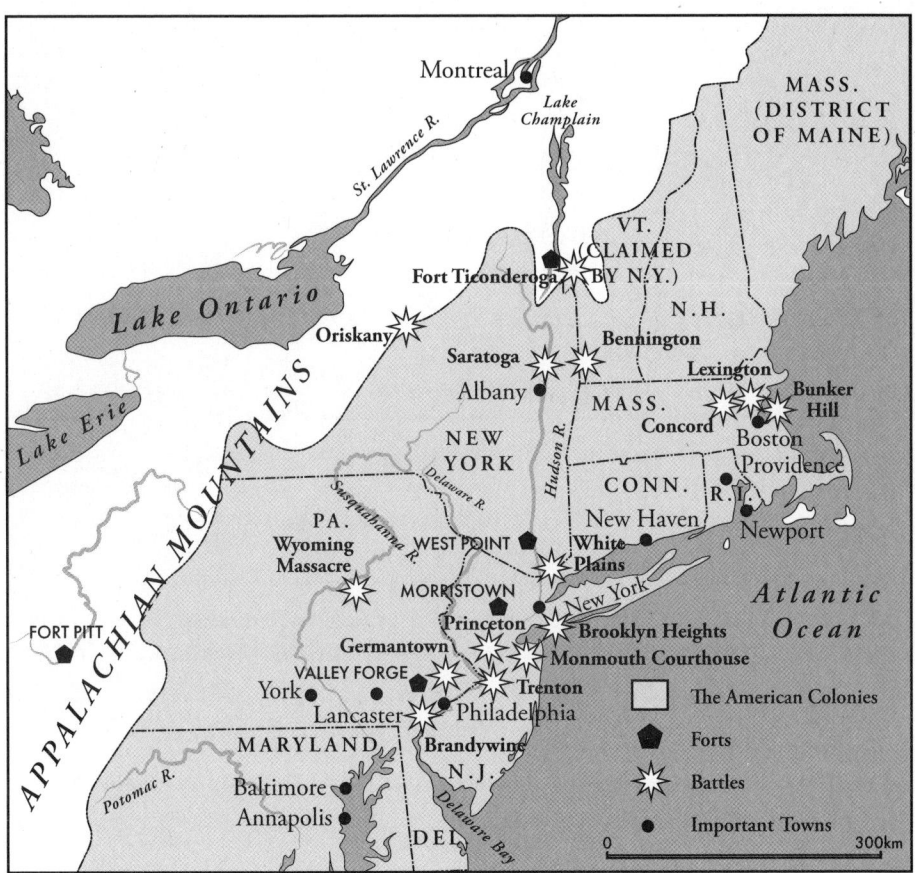

Important battles, towns, and military posts in the North.

Important battles, towns, and military posts in the South.

CHAPTER I

Eyes of Millions Are Upon Us

In Philadelphia, on September 5, 1774, on a brisk, damp morning, 43 men gathered in the spacious City Tavern on the west side of Second Street, between Walnut and Chestnut.[1] They came for a meeting—a congress—to sort out a crisis straining ties between the Great Britain and its colonies along the Atlantic seaboard. Britain, with its awesome navy, had closed Boston Harbor to punish Boston for the event we call the Boston Tea Party: the dumping of tea chests into the harbor on December 16, 1773, by Americans enraged about a tax on tea.

The closing of the port threw many Bostonians out of work and paralyzed the local economy. Everyone in the region suffered, whether they agreed with the protest or not.

The British had also imposed other measures that irritated and angered Americans up and down the coast.

How would the colonies respond?

That was the grave and important business of the newly arrived delegates to what historians would come to call the First Continental Congress. The "Eyes of Millions are upon Us," wrote one delegate to his wife in Connecticut. The task ahead, he declared, "is as arduous, & of as great Consequence, as ever men undertook, & engaged in."[2]

On this particular morning, their arduous task was just figuring out where to meet in the coming days, weeks, months—no one knew how long. The City Tavern, the "most genteel"[3] tavern in America, comprised three stories plus a basement. Many American taverns of the time were cramped dens managed by poor widows eking out a living.[4] This one was convivial, elegant, and spacious, with features that included, according to advertisements, a coffee room "well attended and properly supplied with English and American papers and magazines."[5] Behind the tavern's brick Georgian façade, business hummed: people bought entertainment tickets, sealed real estate deals, delivered lost dogs, and reported runaway servants. Civic boards met there, as did the Jockey Club, the St. George's Society,[6] and the radicals raising a fuss against British authority.

The delegates, as they arrived this morning, went directly upstairs to a long gallery suitable for dancing and banquets.[7] The room had accommodated functions of more than 200 people; it was plenty big enough for the dozens of delegates who strolled in that morning.[8]

Though a fine place for entertaining, the tavern wouldn't suit a solemn congress. Anyway, two other halls had been offered. One was the Pennsylvania State House, the center of government for the colony and the place where the elected Pennsylvania Assembly met. We know it as Independence Hall.

The speaker of the Pennsylvania Assembly, Joseph Galloway, had leveraged his considerable influence to make the room normally occupied by the Assembly available to the Congress. Those lawmakers graciously agreed to vacate the space and meet in an upstairs room while the Congress was in town.[9] The overture was generous and sensible.

The other building offered was Carpenters' Hall, a new brick Georgian building and the pride of a guild made up chiefly of master carpenters. The guild, akin to an association of contractors, intended the two-story building as a venue for meetings and functions, and as a place for members to exhibit their workmanship and conduct business. The ground floor contained two large rooms separated by a corridor. Upstairs were three rooms and a passageway. The tenant for all that space upstairs was the Library Company of Philadelphia, which used one room for its books and another as a small museum for displaying artifacts, specimens, and scientific instruments.[10]

The delegates on that damp morning trooped out of the tavern to inspect both the State House and Carpenters' Hall. Both were within an easy walk, but Carpenters' Hall was closest. At Carpenters' Hall, set back behind a veil of trees, delegates glanced at the meeting room on the east side of the ground floor, a space barely sufficient to accommodate delegates plus chairs and some tables.[11] They thought the library upstairs would be handy. They liked the passageway on the ground floor, a place where "a gentleman may walk,"[12] presumably to unwind or discreetly meet outside the assembly room. They soon pronounced the building acceptable.[13]

A delegate raised an objection. As a "piece of respect"[14] to Speaker Galloway, shouldn't they at least look at the other building?

The concern was ignored. Delegates accepted Carpenters' Hall by a wide majority.

Galloway was dumbfounded. He later grumbled that the State House was clearly "a much more proper Place" for the Congress. Delegates, he speculated, had schemed against him. The matter had been "privately settled by an Interest made out of Doors."[15]

The Congress was off to a sour start. Factions were already forming. Among the dozen colonies represented that fall in Philadelphia, wide differences prevailed in terms of population, stature, and willingness to challenge the mother country.

Leaning toward confrontation were Virginia, Massachusetts (which included the district of Maine), Connecticut, and South Carolina. They were populous, long-established, and seethed about what they considered British misrule. They

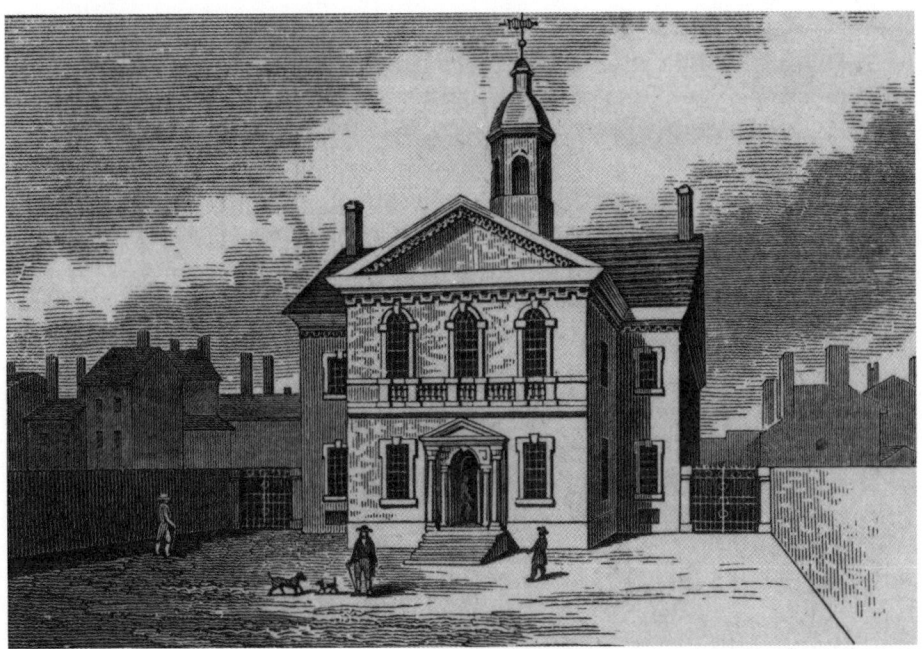

The First Continental Congress met in Carpenters' Hall, a brick building designed to accommodate meetings and provide exhibit space for a carpenters' guild. The 1771 structure near Third and Chestnut is part of Philadelphia's Independence National Historical Park. (Image courtesy of the Miriam and Ira D. Wallach Division of Art, Prints and Photographs: Print Collection, The New York Public Library)

pulled in their wake their smaller neighbors—New Hampshire and Rhode Island in New England; North Carolina in the South. Georgia was unrepresented at the Congress. Remote and tiny, with 17,000 white people, the colony wanted nothing to do with the meeting. Georgia at that time was asking British authorities to help with troublesome indigenous tribes. It was not a time to poke the British monarch, King George III.[16]

The Middle Atlantic colonies, meanwhile, leaned toward conciliation. New York and Pennsylvania, which dominated the region that also included Delaware, New Jersey, and Maryland, had little taste at first for knocking heads with Britain. Indeed, New York of all colonies was friendliest toward royal rule. Pennsylvania, meanwhile, caught up with its own political infighting, had stood aloof from the squabble that so consumed colonies north and south. Also, Quakerism in Pennsylvania—with its emphasis on respect for authority and pacifism—tamped down the impulse to rebel.

***

We think of these delegates as revolutionaries, but most were not. They were by and large well-heeled, well-established, prominent men with no wish to upend their comfortable world. Some, such as Thomas Cushing of Massachusetts and Henry Middleton of South Carolina, were among the richest men in their respective colonies.[17] The social order had treated them well. Most delegates dearly wanted to move the colonies not forward to nationhood, but backward to a time, roughly a decade earlier, when they were snug in the British imperial nest but left mostly to themselves. Britain held the reins, but loosely.

Then, all seemed promising for the 13 British colonies hugging the Atlantic coast between Canada and Florida.

In 1763, after a long war, France and Great Britain signed a peace treaty that made the British monarch master of Canada, Florida, and nearly all of North America from the Atlantic to the Mississippi River. The treaty meant that the French, the previous rulers of Canada and lands west of the colonies to the Mississippi, no longer would hover so dangerously near the Americans, who now could breathe easier and contemplate settlements in the west. The British took control of what is now the province of Quebec, including Quebec City and Montreal, along with the Great Lakes basin. Florida, a former Spanish colony, was also a new prize for the British, who would split that thinly populated territory into two remote colonies: East Florida, administered from St. Augustine, and West Florida, with Pensacola as its capital.

Unfortunately, peace in 1763 spawned new issues that frayed the bonds linking the mother country and the colonies across the Atlantic.

The British wanted more taxes from America to support their far-flung empire. It seemed only fair. The cost of the long conflict with France had been huge, and the British fought in part to defend the American colonists, who now could feel more secure with the removal of the French threat.

British authorities—the king hand in hand with Parliament—thus tightened long-established but poorly enforced tax laws, especially those involving the collection of duties on goods brought into the colonies, such as molasses from the West Indies. American merchants no longer could easily evade taxes through smuggling and bribery.

Americans complained, but British authorities held firm, made tax collection more rigorous, and then laid the groundwork for the Stamp Act, a more aggressive plan to reach into American pockets. This act was designed to reap taxes from legal documents, but also newspapers, dice, and playing cards. Americans threw a fit, even before the act was put into place. British authorities backed down; Parliament removed the taxes.

But the British authorities soon tried another tax scheme with the Townshend duties, which imposed taxes on tea and other goods. Resistance in America, especially in Boston, led authorities to dispatch troops to the town, leading to brawls in the streets between British soldiers—Redcoats—and feisty Boston workers. In March 1770, soldiers on King Street (now State Street), facing a mob of taunting and jeering

Bostonians hurling chunks of ice and snowballs, raised their guns and fired. That bloody result, the Boston Massacre, left five civilians dead. Bostonians gathered in somber funeral processions to beatify the martyrs in the cause of American liberty.

In the wake of this catastrophe, the British retreated and evacuated their troops from Boston. Most of the taxes were lifted. However, significantly, the tax on tea remained. British lawmakers were determined to make a point. The colonists had long argued that, because they had no representation in Parliament in London, Parliament had no business taxing them. Parliament insisted that it did have that authority. The tax on tea stayed in place to make it clear to Americans: Parliament was supreme, no matter what the colonists thought.

Most Americans paid the tax, reasoning that taxation without representation was, after all, not such a big deal. The fire of resistance flickered. Stalwart colonial leaders stoked the embers, reminding Americans about this continuing injustice and other pressing issues. But both sides were eager to mend fences, and Americans were weary of the bickering.

Then came the troubles of the British East India Tea Company. The British government had long cultivated and coddled the famous and sprawling company and came to depend on taxes collected on imports of East India tea, shipped from Asia and bought eagerly by Britons. The company hit a rough patch, however, brought on by bad management and the British public's habit of buying smuggled untaxed tea. Company warehouses filled up with unsold taxed tea. Tax revenue plummeted.

As part of a complicated plan to rescue the company, Parliament authorized the shipment of surplus tea to America for sale at rock-bottom prices. The tax on tea would remain in place. But even with the tax, Americans would have a bargain. It seemed a perfect solution. The surplus tea would be sold, the British government would reap extra revenue, and Americans, who shared the English tea habit, would pay less to satisfy their craving.

But when word of the plan reached America, it inflamed the old dispute by reminding Americans that Parliament continued to tax them without their consent. To many Americans, the tea scheme was nothing but a sneaky way to cement Parliament's claim of absolute taxing authority. Furthermore, the plan would give the East India Company a monopoly on the sale of tea in America, an alarming issue to American merchants. Would other British companies be given similar monopolies over other products bound for America?[18] Protests erupted in the four ports where the tea was to be shipped. In New York, Philadelphia, and Charleston, authorities backpedaled and arranged for the controversial tea to be sent back to England or stored. But in Boston, there was no compromise. There, protesters seized two tea ships. Their leaders demanded the tea be sent back, but the authorities wouldn't budge, and a standoff ensued. Patience at an end, crews of rebellious Americans, clumsily disguised as Mohawks,[19] boarded the ships, smashed the tea chests, and dumped the tea into the harbor.

This Tea Party was too much for Parliament, and indeed for much of the British public, who regarded the Americans as ungrateful and spoiled while long-suffering Britons paid the bill for defending the colonies.

Parliament responded with several measures that angry Americans came to call the Coercive or Intolerable Acts. The first of these was the Boston Port Act, which shut down the port of Boston until the colonists reimbursed the East India Company for the loss. This was meant to punish Boston and force Bostonians to pay for the destruction of the tea. Other Intolerable Acts forced drastic changes to the Massachusetts government, gutting cherished democratic institutions, diminishing local control, and bolstering royal authority. One act gave the royal governor of Massachusetts the authority, under certain circumstances, to transfer a trial from America to Britain. From the British perspective, this law was a reasonable measure to protect British officials trying to enforce unpopular laws. But to many Americans, the law was a license for British authorities in America to harass or even murder Americans without fear of facing impartial justice.[20] Another act gave governors in America the authority to house the king's troops in any uninhabited building. This was unnerving to Americans, who, remembering the Boston Massacre, dreaded standing armies in their midst.

Another act that raised hackles was the Quebec Act, which Americans lumped in with the other Intolerable Acts, though it had nothing to do with events in Massachusetts. Parliament crafted the Quebec Act to appease the French-speaking Catholic majority in Canada, while keeping them firmly under the British thumb. The act offered religious freedom to Catholic Canadians while withholding from them the right to elect their own lawmakers: the king would appoint members of the colony's legislative council.[21] Meanwhile, under this act, the boundaries of Quebec would extend south to the Ohio River.

The Quebec Act may have had the dubious distinction among the Intolerable Acts of irritating the most Americans.[22] The overwhelming majority of Americans were Protestant, and many of them feared Catholicism. Those Americans were horrified that Parliament would extend the borders of Quebec, thereby opening the gates for priests and their followers to enter lands just west of the Protestant colonies, thus hampering Protestant settlement of those lands. Americans were appalled that the British Parliament would work in favor of French-speaking Catholics and against the interests of fellow English-speaking Protestants.

Americans were also alarmed that Parliament denied colonists in Canada the right to elect their own lawmakers. If Parliament could impose on Canada a government with no elected legislature, it could do the same in the other American colonies. To Americans, these implications of the Quebec Act were ominous.

When the news of the Tea Party got around, many Americans were initially disgusted with the lawlessness in Boston and irked with the men who raided the tea ships. But when word arrived in America about the Boston Port Act, opinion came down solidly on Boston's side. Americans saw the closing of the port as a thuggish overreaction. As a Virginian wrote in his diary, Parliament had "declared war against the town of Boston and rather worse, for they have attacked and blocked up their harbor. ... This is but a Prelude to destroy the Liberties of America. The other Colonies, cannot look on the affair but as a dangerous alarm."[23]

After the British clamped down on the port, Boston officials asked for help to ease the suffering in the town. Americans responded: money and goods poured in.

Meanwhile, Massachusetts fractured. People outside Boston friendly to the royal government were harassed and threatened. These people, initially called Tories and later Loyalists,[24] fled to Boston for safety. Meanwhile, many Bostonians outspoken in their opposition to the British now found themselves under suspicion by the British authorities, who were supported by British soldiers. These Americans—Patriots, as they came to be called—left for the countryside. Thus Boston, once a hive of radical resistance, became a haven for Loyalists and the center of British control. The Massachusetts countryside, up to now cautious and conservative relative to Boston, churned with rebellious activity. Almost everywhere outside Boston, royal authority vanished. Control passed to the Patriots.

Leaders of the Patriots tried to rally like-minded leaders outside the colony to immediately strike back at Britain through nonimportation, or—to use a term not yet coined—a boycott, of British-made goods.

Patriot leaders in the other colonies scotched that idea. No boycott would happen without talking first. A congress was necessary, many felt, to debate issues face to face. Others figured a boycott would have more clout if it emerged unanimously from a congress.[25]

Still others, openly or secretly, favored a congress because they distrusted the Massachusetts radicals. While most people sympathized with Boston's plight, many were wary that Massachusetts hotheads calling for a boycott were pushing America toward catastrophe. A congress was an opportunity for cool deliberation.[26]

Massachusetts Patriots were at first unenthused or doubtful about a congress. It would take too long to organize, and action was needed now. Also, they feared that, instead of unity and vigor, such a meeting would produce division, or watered-down resolutions that amounted to nothing, and no boycott.

But with the other colonies unwilling to join a boycott now, a congress was the best Massachusetts could hope for. Virginia often gets credit for coming up with the idea of the Congress. But the notion seems to have emerged from several colonies at about the same time.[27] Indeed, before the crisis in Boston came to a head, the idea had been simmering for months among Patriot factions sharing news and ideas through committees of correspondence, groups assigned to maintain regular contact by letter with like-minded groups in other colonies. The First Continental Congress came together with amazing speed in an era when a letter normally took nine days to get from New York to Boston. On May 10, the news first arrived in Boston that the port would be closed. Before the end of July, Patriot leaders from 12 colonies had agreed to meet in Philadelphia.[28]

***

The task of choosing delegates was delicate. Would that be possible under the noses of British authorities? Would royal appointees of one sort or another disrupt or block the process? In two colonies, Rhode Island and Connecticut no one stood in the way. The governor in each colony was not appointed by the king, but elected by the people, as were the lawmakers, making both colonies virtually independent. In Rhode Island, the legislature appointed delegates to the Congress with no fuss. In Connecticut, the House of Representatives gave the job of selecting delegates to its committee of correspondence.[29]

Elsewhere, the selection of delegates required stealth or outright defiance. Revolutionary gatherings served the purpose in Maryland, Delaware, New Hampshire, New Jersey, and North Carolina.[30] In South Carolina, the lieutenant governor repeatedly suspended the assembly to thwart efforts to elect delegates. Then, early one morning on the day of a new session, lawmakers outfoxed the lieutenant governor by meeting before he was aware of what was going on. The lawmakers quickly confirmed a slate of delegates and authorized money for their expenses.[31]

In Massachusetts, the governor, learning that the colony's House of Representatives was about to select delegates to the Congress, tried to intervene. He sent over a man with an official proclamation to call a halt to the session and disperse the assembly. But the man found the door to the assembly room locked. As he stood outside, shouting out the proclamation, the House inside went ahead and picked the delegates anyway. The governor might have attempted some further action—such as stopping the chosen delegates from leaving the colony—but he did not. Indeed, the four Massachusetts delegates eventually departed like lords in grand style. From Boston, delegates rolled away in a coach drawn by four horses, with two white servants in front and four Black servants behind, all in view of five Redcoat regiments encamped on Boston Common.[32]

In Virginia, the governor dissolved the House of Burgesses, hoping that by dismissing the lawmakers, the movement to select delegates to the Congress would collapse. But Virginians responded by organizing meetings in each county, where people ranted about Parliament, promised support for Boston, and talked of boycotting British imports. These meetings sent off delegates to a special meeting in the capital, Williamsburg, where—under the governor's nose—they chose a tough-minded team to attend the Congress.[33]

In Pennsylvania, the governor wanted no part of the Congress, and neither did the elected Assembly. Led by the Quaker Party, the Assembly at first was unwilling to appoint a delegation to the Congress, even though the meeting would be held right there in Philadelphia, Pennsylvania's capital city. Guiding the Quaker Party was Assembly Speaker Galloway. He had risen high in Pennsylvania society and politics thanks to his considerable skills as an attorney and his choice of a bride, the daughter of one of the richest men in that colony. Aloof and prickly, Galloway was unlikeable and not actually a Quaker. But he was well respected and had been elected speaker of the Assembly every year since 1766.[34] Galloway was no different from most Americans in being frustrated with British policies toward America. But he had more faith than most Americans in British institutions and was disturbed by the messy and violent disorder whipped up by radicals against British authority. So, when radicals in Pennsylvania demanded that delegates be sent to the Congress, Galloway and his Quaker Party balked. Radicals, taking matters in their own hands, called for an outdoor meeting.

Thousands attended on a pleasant June evening in Philadelphia, and out of that meeting, and in defiance of the governor and elected lawmakers, plans emerged for a convention to pick delegates to the Congress. Suddenly, Galloway changed his mind. He recognized that he and his allies were unlikely to prevent a Pennsylvania delegation from attending the Congress. If the colony was going to send a delegation anyway, it was best that it be attuned to his way of thinking. He called the Assembly together for a special meeting where lawmakers chose a delegation, with Galloway as its leader. In a way, both sides won: Pennsylvania would have a delegation at the Congress, as the radicals wanted; but that delegation would oppose the boycott, as the moderates wanted.[35]

Meanwhile, in New York, with many merchants opposed to nonimportation and cool to the notion of a congress, Patriots were unable to organize a colony-wide convention to pick delegates. Nevertheless, delegates were chosen in various counties in meetings of dubious legitimacy. At least one of the meetings may have been a farce. A skeptic later howled that the meeting in Kings County to choose a delegate actually attracted just two people. One was a certain

Joseph Galloway, delegate to the First Continental Congress from Pennsylvania, led a losing effort to find a compromise to mend relations between Great Britain and the American colonies. Galloway would eventually side with the British and end his days in exile. (Image courtesy of the Miriam and Ira D. Wallach Division of Art, Prints and Photographs: Print Collection, The New York Public Library)

Simon Boerum; the other was his friend. They elected Boerum unanimously.[36] In New York City, the squabble over selection of delegates produced fistfights and mayhem. On one day, a public meeting by one faction would "unanimously" support resolutions that would be promptly rejected "unanimously" the next day at a meeting of the opposing faction. The radical faction, afraid that the chaos would result in New York City having no representation at the Congress, finally gave in, concluding that a moderate delegation was better than none. Somehow they managed to get a concession: a statement that those moderate delegates "at present" favored a boycott.[37]

Colonies could send as many delegates as they pleased. New Hampshire and Rhode Island each sent just two, while New York dispatched nine.[38] Some delegates straggled in—North Carolina's two delegates were more than a week late.[39]

As the Congress came together, Galloway stepped up as the leading moderate, and the Pennsylvania and New York delegations would work hardest to head off conflict with London. Galloway felt the best approach would be for the Congress to dispatch "Commissioners" to London, so that by having "these Gentlemen at the Scene of Action, we shall be no longer misled by News-paper Accounts and private Letters, but shall proceed on solid information and Principles of Safety." Galloway thought that "in all Probability the Measures of the present Congress will be deemed illegal & unconstitutional."[40]

CHAPTER 2

Excited No Terror

We are astonished, looking back, that American Loyalists did not raise the alarm and rally to either oppose the Congress or pack the gathering with like-minded delegates. But most Loyalists were unaccountably passive. One later remarked that the Congress at first "raised our curiosity, but excited no terror."[1]

Likewise, we wonder why British authorities did not throw more roadblocks in the way of the Congress. But such steps would likely have failed and raised tensions further. The Congress would have found a way to meet secretly, and blatant attempts to stop the meeting by, for example, seizing delegates would only have conceded the Patriots' point—that authorities were bent on depriving Americans of cherished liberties, such as the right to assemble.

The various governors might have been wiser to back off altogether and let representative assemblies openly select delegates. In the view of Galloway, the governors, by denying their assemblies the chance to pick delegates, irritated allies and gave enemies "the choice of men who would act as they wished."[2] Indeed, the most radical delegations at the Congress were from Massachusetts and Virginia, where the royal governors tried to stop the selection of delegates.

At least one royal governor, New Jersey's William Franklin, had urged royal authorities to endorse the Congress so that royally approved delegates could be sent. He was worried about where this Congress, heavily influenced by radical forces, might lead.[3] Would it not be better to approve it and then infuse it with royal influence?: "[A] Congress if properly authorized by His Majesty ... would be productive of the most beneficial Consequences to the British Empire in general, more especially if they were assisted by some Gentlemen of Abilities, Moderation and Candour from Great Britain commissioned by His Majesty for that Purpose."[4]

Unfortunately for Galloway and his allies, too few moderates seized the opportunity to influence the deliberations in Philadelphia. For example, Connecticut's William Samuel Johnson, a moderate with doubts about the wisdom of a boycott, could have been Galloway's ally. Johnson was duly nominated to represent Connecticut at the Congress. However, unwilling to take part in a meeting dominated by radicals, he turned down the nomination, thus helping to tilt the Congress in the radicals' favor.[5]

***

As the Congress came together, there was no sure sign that it would amount to much. A similar meeting during the Stamp Act crisis had generated nothing of consequence. The groundwork for this Congress in 1774 gave no indication that Americans were intent on war or independence—quite the opposite. The instructions given to delegates from the various colonies underscored a hope that differences could be patched up. From Massachusetts, the most radical of the colonies, instructions expressed the "ardently desired" hope to re-establish the "union & harmony between Great Britain and the Colonies."[6]

The five delegates from South Carolina had the farthest to travel and went by ship. Three of these delegates slipped out of Charleston without much ado. The other two, Christopher Gadsden and Thomas Lynch, were honored with what should have been a splendid sendoff. Hundreds of residents escorted them to the wharf. But there, as the delegates boarded the *Sea Nymph*, a cannon salute went awry. Three men suffered severe burns, and one died.[7]

For the Massachusetts delegates, the journey to Philadelphia was part triumphal procession and part sightseeing jaunt. Passing through Connecticut, they met up with other delegates, and at town after town local Patriots guided them to the nearest tavern for refreshment.

Near New Haven, the local constable, sheriff, and justices of the peace rode out 7 miles from town to meet the delegates, and then, with a parade of carriages and riders, escorted them into town where, as church bells tolled, townspeople gaped from crowded windows and doorways. That evening, cannons boomed in celebration.[8]

Among the New England delegates on this journey were John Adams, 38, of Massachusetts, and Silas Deane, 36, of Connecticut. They were meeting for the first time, but they had already traveled parallel paths. Both had risen from modest beginnings: Adams was a farmer's son; Deane's father was a blacksmith. Both were favored with elite education: Adams at Harvard; Deane at Yale. Both were schoolteachers for a time before training in the law. Deane tried law, but veered into trade, becoming a successful merchant. He also married, giving him some wealth and more status, first to a wealthy widow, Mehitabel Webb, who was five years older and the mother of six with a flourishing store. Then, after her death, he married Elizabeth Saltonstall, the daughter of the governor. His activities related to disenchantment with Britain began at least as early as 1769, when he was named to a committee in Wethersfield, Connecticut, charged with enforcing nonimportation measures. He was elected to the province's General Assembly in 1772, and from there was appointed as a delegate to the Congress in Philadelphia.[9]

Adams became an attorney and stuck with it. Along the way, he married Abigail Smith, daughter of a minister, and gained something more precious than wealth or status: a brilliant and capable partner in life.

He was a rising attorney in Boston when he was drawn onto Boston's political stage. He was conservative by nature, with a distaste for the brawls and rioting associated with the Patriots in Boston. When, after the Boston Massacre, the accused officers and soldiers came to him to represent them on charges of murder, Adams did not flinch. He took on their defense and won acquittals for all but two, and those two were free to go after being branded on the thumbs. Always in sympathy with the Patriots' cause, if not their tactics, his passion for public service waxed and waned until after the Tea Party, when he plunged into the political maelstrom on the Patriot side for good.

Both Adams and Deane would serve the new nation at great personal sacrifice with courage and initiative, sometimes clumsily, sometimes brilliantly. Both would take on key diplomatic posts. One would become president of the United States and live into his nineties. The other died at 51 under murky circumstances, his reputation destroyed. Adams and Deane were among the few Congress delegates who described in detail their impressions on their way to Philadelphia.

Adams, in his diary, sneered at New Yorkers:

> I have not seen one real Gentleman, one well bred Man since I came to Town. At their Entertainments there is no Conversation that is agreable. There is no Modesty—No Attention to one another. They talk very loud, very fast, and Altogether. If they ask you a Question, before you can utter 3 Words of your Answer, they will break out upon you, again—and talk away.[10]

Deane, meanwhile, was out of sorts on the trip, recovering from a bout of dysentery and annoyed by his fellow Connecticut delegate Roger Sherman. Deane wrote to his wife: "Mr. Sherman (wish to Heaven he were well in New Haven) is against our sending our carriages over the ferry this evening, because it is Sunday; so we shall have a scorching sun to drive forty miles in, to-morrow."[11]

Later, in Trenton, Deane found himself "sick, worn out with the heat and dust, headache and anxiety of mind," and in the same room with Sherman: "I turn'd and turn'd, and groan'd, while Judge Sherman, who lodged in the same chamber, snored in concert."[12]

Down the road, there was more torment: "The Weather extreme hot, The Roads sandy, and my illness together allmost sunk Me. The Country has nothing lively, or agreeable."[13]

As the delegates approached Philadelphia after many days—the Massachusetts men had been 19 days[14] on the road—a welcoming committee met them 5 miles from town.[15] All soon gathered with other delegates at the City Tavern for a supper "as elegant as ever was laid upon a table."[16]

By September 1, some 25 delegates had arrived in sultry Philadelphia. The number of delegates at the First Continental Congress eventually came to 56.[17] All but two were over 30 years old. Five were over 60.

Among the delegates were a surveyor, a carpenter, three millers, nine merchants, and nine planters or farmers. More than half of the delegates—at least 30—were lawyers.[18] One-third of the delegates had attended college, 12 in the British Isles, making the level of education among delegates at least equal to that of members of the British House of Commons. One delegate was a native of Wales. All the rest were born in the colonies.[19]

Many were born to privilege, but some started out humbly indeed and worked with amazing diligence to rise in society. Take Sherman of Connecticut. He apprenticed as a cobbler, but then studied in his spare time for the law and was admitted to the bar. He came to hold various offices, prospered as a merchant, took a seat in the colonial legislature, found time to write a series of almanacs and a tract about money, and served as treasurer for Yale College. He also had lots of children. His first wife had seven; his second had eight.[20]

Probably every delegate from South Carolina, North Carolina, Virginia, and Maryland owned enslaved people. South Carolina's Henry Middleton had 800, while at least four of the Virginians owned 200 or more. Some delegates from the Middle Atlantic colonies also owned slaves. None of the New England delegates, as far as we know, were slave owners.[21]

Delegates found accommodations in private homes and rented houses, but also in taverns.[22] Philadelphia had more than 100 drinking establishments, and many had guestrooms. Three South Carolina delegates—Henry Middleton and brothers Edward and John Rutledge—along with their wives and a few slaves—crowded into rooms at Frye's Tavern, perhaps the largest tavern in town. South Carolina's other two delegates, Gadsden and Lynch, lodged at the boardinghouse of Mary House, a 42-year-old widow, at Fifth and Market.[23] The Massachusetts men found rooms at Sarah Yard's boarding house, a stone building across from City Tavern. They later shifted to Jane Port's at Arch near Second for a few days, then back again to Sarah Yard's.[24]

Deane settled into a house with a lieutenant in the British regiment stationed in Philadelphia. The man was married to the daughter of the house's owner, a "genteel and sensible" widow. The lieutenant and his wife made for an interesting couple. Deane described her as a "Daughter of Liberty," meaning she was an ardent opponent of the British policies that her husband was duty-bound to uphold.[25]

**

Philadelphia, extending just eight blocks east to west and 14 blocks north to south,[26] had 38,000 inhabitants, making it the largest city in British North America, though tiny compared to London, with its population of 750,000.[27]

Philadelphia's history is inextricably linked to William Penn and the Quakers. Penn, the son of an English admiral, planted Philadelphia in the American wilderness as a haven for the religious sect. While in his twenties, Penn became involved with the Religious Society of Friends, which emerged in England in the mid-1600s and became known as the Quakers for the trembling members sometimes exhibited at their gatherings.

The English Quakers lived simply, dressed plainly, rejected religious rituals, refused to take oaths, embraced pacifism, but otherwise shook up the norms of Anglican England. In their eagerness to demonstrate their beliefs, they could be outrageous, as in the case of the young Quaker woman who strolled naked through the marketplace in Oxford in 1654.[28] The Quakers quickly became obnoxious to authorities, and many landed in jail.

Troubled by the persecution of the Quakers, Penn first advocated for them and then became a Quaker himself. He also became interested in the American colonies, and after the death of his father, made a deal with King Charles II, who had been in debt to the elder Penn. To settle that debt, Penn accepted title to vast tracts of land in America. That land became Pennsylvania. Penn planned Philadelphia as the colony's capital.

When laying out the town in the 1680s, Penn envisioned a "greene country towne, which will never be burnt and always wholesome."[29] Neat, spacious estates would line broad, straight streets extending 2 miles[30] from the banks of the Schuylkill River in the west to the banks of the Delaware River in the east. His town, built on a grid pattern with broad avenues and wide spaces, was an innovation.[31] Philadelphia would stand apart from the typical cramped American colonial towns with their meandering streets and narrow alleys.

Penn thought his colonists would take advantage of this ample space and spread out inland, away from the riverbanks. But the Quakers and other settlers who flocked to the town didn't share Penn's vision. Sacrificing space for convenience, they clustered near the Delaware River, where commerce bustled. By the 1720s, the population had reached 5,000, but the heart of the city was still just two blocks from the Delaware.[32] Over the following decades, the population boomed and development pushed westward. By 1751, the town had streetlights and paid constables. By 1768, it had a system for picking up garbage and cleaning the streets, services not yet regular in London and Paris. Visitors from Europe who strolled on the brick sidewalks along the tree-lined and paved streets were impressed.[33]

The Quakers, by 1770, accounted for only about one-seventh of Pennsylvania's population.[34] But their influence remained, especially in Philadelphia. Quaker ways charmed, amused, and mystified the delegates. Deane found Philadelphians "affable & Clever." The marketplace, however, disappointed him: "There was not a Fowl, nor a Fish in the Whole market. Water melons look'd tolerable. & was the only Fruit worth buying. There were only a few Miserable Pears, & peaches, & plumbs."[35]

Adams toured the modern town hospital featuring rows of beds on each side of a central aisle. Townspeople were especially proud of this model of efficiency, yet Adams saw only "a dreadful scene of human wretchedness." His visit took him below ground to the cells for the insane—"some furious, some merry, some melancholy"—where he came upon one of his former clients, a man "I once saved at Taunton Court from being whipped and sold for horse stealing."[36]

***

Galloway was likely correct in assuming that some behind-the-scenes scheming took place even before the Congress's first official day of business. Galloway's opponents in Pennsylvania had made a point of letting arriving delegates know that Galloway could not be trusted and did not share the more radical views of most Pennsylvanians.[37] It didn't help Galloway to be the political enemy of John Dickinson, the darling of many delegates and one of the most famous men in America. He was not a delegate, but his influence was evident.

In the days leading to the start of the Congress, and during the three weeks after, many delegates called on Dickinson, who in turn took time to visit delegates at their lodgings. Dickinson was a lawyer famous throughout America for his "letters," essays circulated in the 1760s that established him as an early voice of American discontent.

Dickinson had a privileged childhood on Maryland's eastern shore, where his father owned slaves and grew tobacco on a sprawling estate. The family later lived in Delaware. Young Dickinson was educated at home by tutors, then apprenticed for two years with a lawyer in Philadelphia, and subsequently crossed the Atlantic for further legal study in London at the prestigious Middle Temple. After three years, he returned as one of the best-trained lawyers in America. He opened a law practice, got himself elected to the Delaware Assembly, and soon found himself speaker. With his father's death leaving him with ample property in Pennsylvania, Dickinson shifted his focus and won election to the Pennsylvania Assembly. There he linked up with the Quaker Party and became for a while an ally of Galloway.[38]

The Quaker Party was at odds with the descendants of William Penn. Unlike most other colonies, Pennsylvania was a proprietary colony: its governor was appointed not by the king, but by the proprietor, the Penn family. Those Penn descendants had rejected Quakerism in favor of Anglicanism and imposed policies that annoyed or appalled many Quakers and other Pennsylvanians. Dickinson found common ground with the Quaker Party in its frustration with the Penn family. He parted ways with the faction, however, when it made plans to urge Parliament to strip the colony from the Penns and make it a royal colony, with the governor appointed by the king.

Dickinson attacked the scheme, warning that royal rule could be worse than life under the Penns. Now political enemies, Dickinson and Galloway traded not just harsh words, but blows as well. One day, on the State House steps, Galloway grabbed Dickinson by the nose and smacked him with his cane. Dickinson, stick in hand, reciprocated with a knock to the head.[39]

Dickinson shot to fame throughout the colonies during the Stamp Act crisis in 1765, when he became one of the first Americans to openly contemplate American independence. Responding to British attempts to rein in Americans, Dickinson cautioned that policies to discourage American independence might very well bring it about: "Evils are frequently precipitated by imprudent attempts to prevent them. In short, we can never be made an independent people except by *Great Britain* herself; and the only way for her to do it is to make us frugal, ingenious, united, and discontented."[40]

Colonial leaders recognized Dickinson's talent as an able writer and legal thinker. At age 34, he was the chief author of the petition to the king that emerged from the Stamp Act Congress.[41]

A few years later, Dickinson took up his pen again to produce a dozen essays titled *Letters from a Pennsylvania Farmer*, which appeared first in installments in a Philadelphia newspaper but eventually were republished in 21 of the 25 American newspapers. The pamphlet containing those collected essays was a colonial bestseller.[42]

In attacking the Townshend duties, Dickinson as the "Pennsylvania Farmer" flayed the notion that Parliament had the right to levy any taxes on Americans. He argued that, if Parliament could take "money out of our pockets without our consent ... our boasted liberty is but sound and nothing else."[43] His tone was calm. His aim was reform, not revolution: "The cause of liberty is a cause of too much dignity, to be sullied by turbulence and tumult." He warned Americans "against those who may at any time endeavor to stir you up, under pretenses of patriotism, to any measures disrespectful to our Sovereign, and our mother country."[44] Although not a Quaker, he possessed a Quaker mindset: he had a duty to speak out.[45]

Later, Dickinson gained more fame as the author of the "Liberty Song," a favorite ballad among Patriots before the Revolution. The tune, "Hearts of Oak," was recent, coming out in 1759 with lyrics celebrating British military achievements against the French. Dickinson's words were:

> Come join hand in hand, brave Americans all,
> And rouse your bold hearts at fair Liberty's call;
> No tyrannous acts shall suppress your just claim,
> Or stain with dishonor America's name.[46]

The song, however, was no call for independence. Indeed, it offered a toast to the king:

> This bumper I crown for our sovereign's health,
> And this for Britannia's glory and wealth;
> That wealth, and that glory immortal may be,
> If she is but just, and we are but free.[47]

In 1770, at age 37, Dickinson married. His bride, Mary Norris, had, according to a niece, "solid judgment, good sense, a most affectionate disposition, the tenderest sensibility of heart, and elevated piety."[48] That piety was rooted in Quaker pacifism and respect for authority. Dickinson's mother was a devout Quaker too. John Adams later speculated that Dickinson's wife and mother pestered him with advice steeped in Quaker notions, creating unbearable tension in the family, making Dickinson's life miserable and skewing his political thinking. Reflecting years later, Adams said: "If I had such a wife, such a mother, I believe I should have shot myself."[49] But Dickinson was not Adams. He had a mind of his own and generally followed the Quaker path because that was what he too believed.

Though he read the Bible often, and was raised in a Quaker household, he never formally joined any Quaker meeting or, for that matter, any other church. None offered a doctrine or philosophy that he could wholly embrace. Late in life, Dickinson wrote: "I cannot, and probably never shall be united to any religious Society, because each of them as a society, holds Principles which I cannot adopt."[50] When preparing to wed his pious Mary, he insisted on a civil ceremony, not a ceremony of the Society of Friends. Mary agreed, but her meeting disowned her for it. She later apologized and was accepted back.[51]

Steeped in Quaker culture, Dickinson remained sympathetic with Quakerism, becoming more so as time went on. He came to use "thee" and "thou"; he eschewed oaths; he adopted the Quaker practice of referring to the names of months and days of the week by number; and he would embrace such Quaker causes as prison reform and opposition to theaters. In 1774, he may have owned slaves, but by 1777 he was no longer a slave owner and would come to be an abolitionist.[52]

When John Adams first saw Dickinson, then 42, at the time of the Congress, he was astonished to see a man so thin and pallid: "He is a Shadow—tall, but slender as a Reed—pale as ashes. One would think at first sight that he could not live a Month. Yet upon a more attentive Inspection, he looks as if the Springs of Life were strong to last many Years."[53]

Indeed, Dickinson usually appeared ill and weary, and was often sick, but he would live to 76.[54] Adams came to regard Dickinson as "a very Modest Man, and very ingenious, as well as agreeable. He has an excellent Heart, the Cause of his Country lies near it."[55]

Dickinson would make his mark in the Continental Congress, but for the moment he was on the outside looking in. Even though Dickinson was clearly the American best suited to play the lead in the momentous meeting, he was for now offstage. Galloway and his allies outmaneuvered Dickinson to block him from being included in Pennsylvania's delegation.[56]

CHAPTER 3

Eats Little, Drinks Little, Sleeps Little, Thinks Much

Dickinson—so much a part of the movement pushing back against British authority—was thus curiously absent in Carpenters' Hall as Congress came together for the first time. But other illustrious men were very much present, a few famous on both sides of the Atlantic.

One was Samuel Adams. More than anyone else on the American side, Samuel Adams deserved the credit—or blame—for the crisis at hand. He was the soul of the Patriot faction in Boston. No one doubted that he pulled the strings that set the Tea Party in motion.

Favored with a Harvard education and ushered into his father's business selling malt to brewers, Adams was soon on the path to a comfortable life as a businessman and merchant. But he had no head for money and the business went bust. Adams then went to work as a tax collector, and soon fell behind in his collections. Because his pay was based on the money he gathered, his wife and two children made do with few frills. Adams's house was rickety, his clothes shabby.

His passion, besides singing, was politics. With opinions too extreme and uncompromising for many, he likely

Samuel Adams, delegate from Massachusetts to the First Continental Congress, was assumed to have played a key role in orchestrating the Boston Tea Party, the event that led to the calling of the Congress. He was a master political organizer and propagandist, but a poor businessman, and was much less wealthy than most of his colleagues in Philadelphia. John Hancock commissioned John Singleton Copley to create this portrait in 1772 when Hancock and Adams were political allies in Boston. The portrait is in the Museum of Fine Arts in Boston. (Image via Wikimedia Commons)

would have failed at that, too, but for the blunders of Parliament, the king, and the royal governor. With every stumble, they did Adams a favor. A master organizer and propagandist, Adams rose in influence and prominence, working best behind the scenes. He eventually became clerk of the Massachusetts House of Representatives and a leading force among the elected lawmakers butting heads with the royal governor.

The trip to Philadelphia was Adams's first outside Massachusetts. Among the delegates he might have been the poorest, though rich enough to have two servants in his Boston household.[1] To ensure a good impression among the well-heeled delegates, Adams's Boston friends had sent him off with a new suit and some spending money. Adams was 51 the year of the Congress. But the tremor in his hands gave people the impression he was older.

Moderate Galloway quickly found him "equal to most men in popular intrigue and the management of a faction. He eats little, drinks little, sleeps little, thinks much and is most decisive and indefatigable in the pursuit of his objects."[2]

***

Of all the delegates to the First Continental Congress, only one matched Samuel Adams in his determination to resist British policies. That was Richard Henry Lee of Virginia. Before coming to Philadelphia, Adams and Lee had never met, but they were not strangers. They had been corresponding for more than a year,[3] sharing news and opinions about the crisis. They were the most radical of the radicals at the Congress. In Philadelphia, they formed the core of an alliance linking Massachusetts and Virginia, the two colonies that would lead the drive to independence.

As beneficiary of a family dynasty built on cozy connections with royal governors, as well as on trade in furs, tobacco, and the enslaved, Lee, like many delegates to the Continental Congress, was an unlikely rebel. He was one of nine siblings, including an older brother also named Richard, who died young.[4] Much of Lee's boyhood was spent at Stratford Hall, the family estate along the Potomac in tidewater Virginia, where playmates included children of plantation slaves. Like other children of his class, he was tutored at home—Greek, Latin, reading, writing, but also dancing and music. Like some especially privileged children of his class, he was sent to England to complete his education.[5]

While in England, 18-year-old Lee learned of the deaths of his parents, his mother in January 1750 and his father months later in November. Those deaths left family affairs in the hands of Philip Lee, Richard Henry's oldest surviving brother. Philip expected his younger sibling to immediately return to Virginia.[6]

But Richard Henry dawdled. He was in love. That love blossomed into an engagement with a young woman whose family had business connections with the Lees. While this seemed a promising match, Philip demanded that the engagement be severed. Richard Henry obeyed and ended the romance. But he did not immediately return to Virginia. Instead, he toured the European continent, finally reappearing in Virginia when he was 21.[7]

Soon after moving back in at Stratford Hall, where Philip ruled, Richard Henry immersed himself in the books of the family library as he contemplated a career in law and politics.

People who influenced Richard Henry's thinking included an older sister, Hannah, whom he respected highly. Likely thanks to her, he came to support giving landowning widows and unmarried women the right to vote.[8]

While the siblings squabbled over inheritance and family issues, they were politically aligned. It was thus natural that when Philip stepped out of the House of Burgesses, Virginia's lower legislative house, Richard Henry Lee ran for election to take his place. Another brother and two cousins were also elected that year, 1757, making the Lees a potent force in Virginia politics.[9]

Working with various Lees in the House of Burgesses, Richard Henry dedicated himself to promoting his family's political interests. At the same time, working with Philip at Stratford Hall, Richard Henry labored to build up the family's tobacco business.[10] Politics dovetailed nicely with business for the Lees, enabling them to pull the right levers in government to establish Stratford Hall as an important center for the inspection and transport of tobacco, generating more wealth for the family.

Richard Henry was still living at Stratford Hall when he married 19-year-old Anne Aylett. Two children were born before Lee and his family finally moved out. Lee built an elegant home, called Chantilly, on nearby land leased from Philip.[11] From the bay window of its parlor, visitors could enjoy a spectacular view of the Potomac.

At Chantilly, Anne gave birth to two more children. As Lee provided for his growing family, he found time to indulge in such passions as hunting and entertaining, both of which led to unfortunate consequences. While shooting geese in the winter of 1768, his gun blew up in

Richard Henry Lee, delegate from Virginia, made the motion in Congress to declare independence. He and Samuel Adams led the radical faction in Congress pushing for the break with Great Britain. His brothers Arthur and William carried out diplomatic assignments in Europe. Arthur and another brother, Francis Lightfoot, also served as delegates to Congress from Virginia. (Image of portrait by Charles Willson Peale courtesy of the National Portrait Gallery, Smithsonian Institution)

his hands, taking away four fingers. For the rest of his life, he wore a black silk glove to cover his damaged left hand. Meanwhile, lavish entertaining made it easy for him to indulge in rich foods and wine, leading to gout, causing such painful swelling in his feet that eventually—years hence—he would be unable to wear shoes.[12]

The family relied on the work of enslaved Black people, essential for cultivating, harvesting, and preparing tobacco for shipment. We know the Lees had dozens of slaves—he inherited 40, and possessed 63 when he died. Even so, he was critical of the slave trade, though this criticism had nothing to do with morality. He feared slave rebellions and felt the institution inhibited advancements in agriculture.[13]

The Lees lived well. Because of that and the cost of supporting a growing family, the family's finances were precarious. Thus, when the British Parliament began contemplating what became the Stamp Act, the lure of potential extra income enticed Lee to seek the post of stamp distributor. Lee didn't get the appointment and conveniently pivoted when he became suddenly aware of how much his fellow Virginians loathed the act. Protesting the measure, he led a procession featuring effigies of several British officials, including the man who got the job Lee had wanted. Lee's fellow marchers were mainly his own slaves.[14]

Meanwhile, Lee found himself on the losing side of assorted political tussles in Virginia. These defeats made him more radical. After first railing against corruption in Virginia, he soon recognized Britain as the real target of his disaffection, especially after Parliament passed, in addition to the Stamp Act, other acts that Lee and other Virginians opposed. The Proclamation of 1763, barring white settlements—at least temporarily—west of the Appalachian Mountains, derailed schemes of Lee and his brothers to speculate in western lands. Another act, affecting currency, hindered the ability of tobacco planters such as Lee to finance their crops.[15]

As tobacco prices slid, Lee's criticism of British policies sharpened. When Britain imposed the Townshend duties, Lee joined the chorus of outrage in Virginia and pushed for a boycott of British-made goods.[16]

In 1769, Lee became a widower with four children, the oldest 11. The same year he married again, this time another Anne—Anne Gaskins Pinckard, a widow. In the coming years, she would add five more children to Lee's brood. As the family grew, machinations in England dimmed Lee's prospects, both as a Virginia tobacco planter and a land speculator.[17]

When news of the Boston Tea Party reached Virginia, he was sympathetic. He backed a measure that effectively closed the courts, making it impossible for lawsuits brought by British merchants to go forward. The measure was a lifeline for large and small tobacco planters saddled with debts.[18]

The final straw for Lee, as for many other Virginians, may have been the Quebec Act, which seemed to shut the door forever on acquisition of land to the west.[19] Prominent and outspoken, he was a natural choice as one of seven delegates from Virginia to attend the Congress in Philadelphia.

Nine of the delegates to the First Continental Congress had met before at the Stamp Act Congress.[20] A few were related to each other—the Adamses of Massachusetts were cousins; William Livingston of New Jersey and New York's Philip Livingston, James Duane, and John Jay were related by either blood or marriage; and South Carolina's John and Edward Rutledge were brothers.[21] But few delegates, before they arrived in Philadelphia, knew any from other colonies. So it is surprising that the Congress swiftly completed its first order of business: choosing a chairman.

They picked Virginia's Peyton Randolph because it seemed fitting to give this honor and responsibility to a delegate from the largest and oldest colony. Furthermore, Randolph had been speaker of Virginia's House of Burgesses and thus had some experience in such a role. It would prove to be a wise choice. It helped as well that Randolph made a good impression. Deane of Connecticut was dazzled. He wrote to his wife: "[Randolph] seems designed by nature for the business. Of an affable, open and majestic deportment—large in size, though not of proportion, he commands respect and esteem by his very aspect, independent of the high character he sustains."[22]

Educated as a lawyer in London,[23] Randolph lived in a fine townhouse in Williamsburg, where he ate well, dressed fashionably, and would have been at ease among the English aristocracy. His family was long established in Virginia, and he married a woman with a pedigree no less distinguished.

The royal governor of Virginia had such confidence in Randolph that he appointed him the colony's attorney general, a position Randolph held while also serving as an elected member of the House of Burgesses.[24] Randolph was speaker of the House of Burgesses as the once-amicable relationship between the governor and lawmakers turned chilly. Between 1766 and 1774, Randolph earned lasting respect among those lawmakers for cobbling together compromises between assertive and cautious factions as the colony pushed against royal authority.

With the position of chairman taken care of, delegates turned to the task of appointing someone to record the activities of the Congress. The secretary's job went to Charles Thomson, a radical and foe of Galloway. Thomson was also "the Sam. Adams of Phyladelphia—the Life of the Cause of Liberty, they say,"[25] as John Adams recorded in his diary.

Thomson had hoped to be a delegate to the First Continental Congress, but Galloway had taken pains to make sure that he, like Dickinson, was left out of the delegation.[26] Now, as secretary, Thomson would have a perch in Carpenters' Hall in the middle of the Congress as its first employee. Thomson would have no vote, but his appointment was, like the decision to meet in Carpenters' Hall, "mortifying to the last Degree To Mr. Galloway and his Party."[27] Galloway, surprised at the choice, figured that this, like the decision on the hall, had been settled by his foes "out of Doors."[28]

Thomson, 45, had risen far since arriving in America as a 10-year-old orphan. His Irish father, a widower, died on board the ship that carried Charles and five siblings to America.[29] Charles rose to become a schoolmaster, a Greek and Latin instructor, and then a merchant. He would remain in his post in Congress—that is, through the entire period of the First Continental Congress, the Second Continental Congress, and the Confederation Congress—for nearly 15 years.[30]

Then came the question of "what Title the Convention should assume."[31] They agreed on the term "Congress"—it was never officially the Continental Congress.

What should Randolph's title be? They agreed on "president." Today, the title suggests power, but in this period it was not so weighty. A president was someone who presides—he was merely the meeting's presiding officer.

Then delegates presented their credentials—documents from their respective colonies asserting that they were properly chosen. The papers were read and swiftly approved. Before the end of the first day, delegates started to sort out the rules by which they would function. Those discussions resumed in earnest the next day.

CHAPTER 4

A State of Nature

Most delegates to the First Continental Congress loved to hear themselves talk. Among these were a few worth listening to. One was Patrick Henry, another Virginia delegate.

Henry, 38, son of a Scottish immigrant, failed as a shopkeeper in his teens, but managed to marry well. Thanks to his bride's dowry, he found himself at the age of 18 the owner of six enslaved people and a 200-acre farm. After struggling as a tobacco farmer, he turned to shopkeeping again—and failed again. To support his wife and two children, and to keep debt collectors at bay, Henry took a part-time job tending a tavern, where he also entertained guests with his fiddle.[1]

Then, with little education and not much preparation, Henry managed to snare a license to practice law, where he finally found success, thanks in large part to his impressive voice, like that of a gospel preacher. That talent led him into politics. Within five years of leaving his tavern job behind, Henry entered Virginia's House of Burgesses, where he quickly raised eyebrows for inflammatory remarks attacking the Stamp Act, thereby establishing himself as a radical. He continued to champion the cause of liberty while continuing to own enslaved Black people, a contradiction that troubled him, but not enough to sell or set his slaves free.[2] "I am drawn along," he wrote, "by the general inconvenience of living without them."[3] Henry's oratorical skill was a key reason he was chosen to attend the Congress.[4] Connecticut's Deane, after hearing Henry a few times, described him as "the completest speaker I ever heard." Deane wrote to his wife: "[I]n a letter I can give you no idea of the music of his voice, or the highwrought yet natural elegance of his style and manner."[5]

At the first opportunity, Henry took center stage at the Congress. Recognizing the significance of the meeting and the precedents that would be established early on, Henry pointed out the injustice of giving colonies with small populations the same voting power in Congress as colonies with large populations. Virginia, as it happened, was the most populous colony.

When another delegate countered that small colonies had as much at stake as the large ones, Henry thundered: "Fleets and Armies and the present State of Things shew that Government is dissolved. Where are your Land Marks? your Boundaries

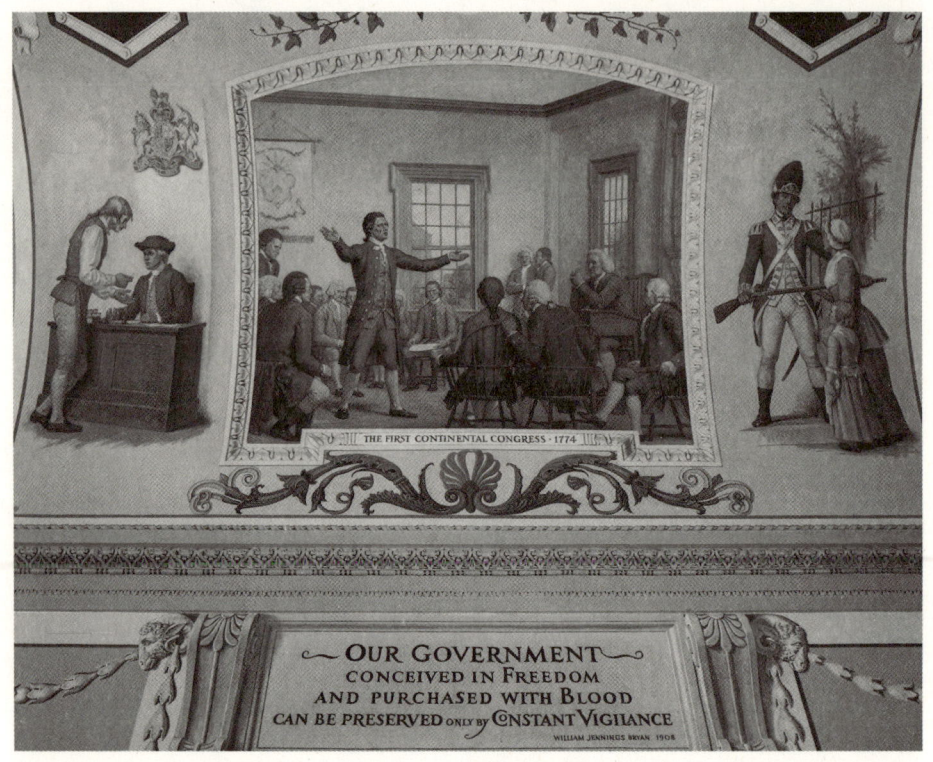

This mural by Allyn Cox shows Patrick Henry speaking in Carpenters' Hall. Fifty-six delegates attended the First Continental Congress. Henry, from Virginia, argued that more populous colonies, such as Virginia, should have more weight in Congress than those with fewer people. Nevertheless, delegates determined that each colony should have equal voting power in Congress. The mural can be seen on the first floor of the U.S. Capitol's House wing. (Image courtesy of the Architect of the Capitol)

of Colonies. We are in a State of Nature, Sir." He was making a point about fairness—"one of the greatest Mischiefs to Society was an Unequal Representation"[6]—but also about setting aside local identities in favor of a loftier one. "The distinctions between Virginians, Pennsylvanians, New Yorkers, and New Englanders are no more. I am not a Virginian, but an American."[7]

This was mostly bunk. In fact, local distinctions were sharp and strong. Henry himself remained very much a Virginian, and arguably more Virginian than American, as he would later demonstrate. Still, his words resonated, and he had a point: plainly it was unfair for thinly populated colonies to have equal standing in Congress with the more populous ones. Benjamin Harrison, another Virginia delegate—"uncommonly large," and "rough in his dress, & speech"[8]—roared in agreement, threatening that the colony might not attend another such gathering if Virginia was to suffer "such a disrespect" of having no greater weight than the smallest colonies.[9]

At some point in the debate, Henry plunged into a related issue that would be especially thorny in coming years. If the population is the measure of representation, how should enslaved people be counted? Counting them like everyone else would be an immense advantage to Southern colonies, where slavery was concentrated. Not counting slaves at all toward representation would give an advantage to Northern colonies. Henry was willing to concede the issue in favor of the North: "Slaves are to be thrown out of the question, and if the freemen can be represented according to their numbers I am satisfied."[10]

Over two days, Congress wrestled with the question. In the end, delegates cast aside Henry's argument and agreed that Congress would count one vote per colony, no matter the population.[11] Delaware, the smallest colony represented at the Congress and with a population—white and Black—of about 36,000, would have the same power in Congress as Virginia, with at least 12 times as many people.[12]

The solution was not fair, but there was no easy alternative: "*Resolved*, That in determining questions in this Congress, each Colony or Province shall have one Vote.—The Congress not being possess'd of, or at present able to procure proper materials for ascertaining the importance of each Colony."[13]

That same day, Tuesday, September 6, was a busy one. Other rules were passed: no one could speak more than twice on the same point without permission; the proceedings would be secret until a majority of the delegates agreed to make them public; and a proper expression of thanks was approved for the Library Company of Philadelphia for the use of its books.[14]

At about 2pm,[15] around the time we imagine delegates slouching in their seats, news seeped into Carpenters' Hall that made them sit up straight. Something awful had happened in Boston, so they were told. John Adams recorded in his diary: "Received by an express an Intimation of the Bombardment of Boston. ... God grant it may not be found true."[16] All afternoon, throughout Philadelphia, muffled bells tolled.[17]

That news may explain why delegates suddenly felt the need for divine guidance. A suggestion came forth that a clergyman be called upon to deliver a prayer the next day. An objection soon followed. Delegates were all Christian Protestants, but of various sects—Episcopal, Quaker, Anabaptist, Presbyterian, and Congregationalist.[18]

Samuel Adams, a devout Congregationalist, stepped up to propose Jacob Duché, a local Episcopal minister. Adams assured delegates that he "could hear a Prayer from a Gentleman of Piety and Virtue, who was at the same Time a Friend to his Country."[19] The gesture was a deft stroke. Massachusetts desperately and urgently needed all the colonies behind it in this crisis. There was nothing to be gained by a quarrel over a prayer. Unity required compromise.

By giving in on this point, and by otherwise keeping a low profile, Samuel Adams and the other Massachusetts delegates shrewdly punctured the common opinion that they were extremists bent on yanking America headlong into disaster. Delaware's

Caesar Rodney, for one, was reassured: "[T]he Bostonians who (we know) have been Condemned by many for their Violence, are Moderate Men, when compared to Virginia, South Carolina, and Rode Island."[20]

The uproar over the rumors about Boston continued. Breathless tales varied, but all painted dreadful images. Delegates were horrified. John Adams wrote to his Abigail: "We have received a confused Account from Boston, of a dreadfull Catastrophy. … Our Deliberations are grave and serious indeed."[21] Deane corresponded to his Elizabeth: "All is in confusion … the people run as in the case of extremity, they know not where nor why."[22]

Amid this crackling tension, Duché opened the next session, reading from Psalm 35 ("Plead my cause, O Lord, with them that strive with me; fight against them that fight against me") and then launched into a 10-minute prayer "with such fervency, purity and sublimity of style and sentiment … that even Quakers shed tears." It was, wrote Deane, "worth riding one hundred miles to hear."[23]

For the moment, Boston got nothing from Congress except prayers. There was no call to arms. Still imagining Boston in ashes, Congress did nothing except draw up some committees: one to craft a statement of the rights of the colonies, how those had been violated, and the best way to restore those rights; and another to look at laws related to manufacturing and trade in the colonies.[24]

With those committees at work—one with 22 members, the other with 11—Congress came together as a whole only occasionally. As the committees shouldered their tasks, fresh reports came in from New England. It seemed Duché's prayer had worked a miracle: all was quiet in Boston. No flames; no bombardment; no catastrophe of any kind. Deane wrote: "[T]he bells of the city are now ringing a peal of joy."[25]

It turned out that a few turbulent events outside Boston had launched a wave of wild tales. The trouble had started with a quiet mission of British troops in Boston to retrieve gunpowder from a stone tower near Cambridge, a few miles west of Boston. The troops completed the early-morning task without incident and returned to Boston. But when people in and around Cambridge became aware of what the soldiers had done, many became indignant. The whole operation was downright sneaky, if not hostile, even though it was the king's gunpowder and belonged to the British military. Locals gathered, grumbled, and threatened Loyalists and others viewed as too close to the British authorities. Reports were retold, embellished, and spiced—as they were relayed north, west, and south—with increasingly harrowing details. It turned out that most of those details were fantasy, as delegates in Philadelphia later learned.

Delegates, now calm, took to enjoying themselves. On September 8, the day he learned that "no blood had been spill'd" in Boston, John Adams dug in to a "most sinfull Feast. … Every Thing which could delight the Eye, or allure the Taste, Curds and Creams, Jellies, Sweet meats of various sorts, 20 sorts of Tarts, fools, Trifles, floating islands, whippd Sillabubs &c. &c.—Parmesan cheese, Punch, Wine, Porter, Beer &c &c."[26]

Delegate Deane's thoughts dwelled on the British officer in the household where he stayed:

> The officer here is much to be pitied. His commission is his principal dependence. He loves his country; he loves his young wife, who is very deserving ... yet [he] is ordered to be ready to march in the afternoon to Boston. This is really affecting ... As we have all dined and supp'd together on a free footing at the same table, he seems the nearer to us.[27]

Soon other news trickled into Philadelphia. The delegates learned that those same shocking but false reports of destruction, battle, or something else in Boston also penetrated to western Massachusetts and Connecticut. The response had been stunning. Thousands of militiamen—part-time soldiers—had grabbed their guns and set off east fully prepared to take on British Regulars, thoroughly trained and well-equipped professional troops. "[I]n different parties upward of 50,000 men well-armed, actually on their march to Boston for the relief of the inhabitants," wrote Delaware delegate Rodney. "[E]very farmer who had a cart or waggon (& not able to bear arms) were with them loaded with provisions, ammunition, baggage &c ... [V]ast numbers more were preparing to march."[28]

Upon hearing the mere rumor of trouble in Boston, the New England countryside had produced an army. When the truth was known, the farmers all turned around and went back home, but the episode astonished the men in Philadelphia. For delegates wondering about how bold they dared to be in confronting British authorities, here was a clear signal from the people. Virginia delegate Richard Henry Lee read the sign. To his brother, William, he wrote: "[T]hese people ... are most firmly resolved to dye rather than to submit."[29]

Thus, many delegates were primed for some spirited action when a rider galloped into town on September 16. The papers in his saddlebag were the Suffolk Resolves, statements drawn up at a meeting of towns near Boston. The opening words crackled with provocation: "the streets of Boston are thronged with military executioners," "our coasts are lined and harbours crouded with ships of war," "the charter of the colony ... is mutilated and, in effect, annihilated," and "murderous law is framed to shelter villains from the hands of justice."[30]

After this hair-raising introduction, the resolutions themselves were measured—prepare for war, but do not incite it. People were "not to engage in any routs, riots, or licentious attacks upon the properties of any person whatsoever."[31]

The resolutions called for widespread civil disobedience in Massachusetts. They advised people to ignore the orders of royal judges and to withhold taxes normally turned over to royal authorities. The resolutions condemned anyone who accepted positions as councilors for the royal governor as "obstinate and incorrigible enemies to their country."[32]

Congress had to respond. Did it support policies of civil disobedience and war preparation or condemn them? A vote damning the Resolves would signal that Massachusetts was on its own in this conflict.

But Congress endorsed the Resolves. Congress "most thoroughly approve the wisdom and fortitude, with which opposition to these wicked ministerial measures has hitherto been conducted, and they earnestly recommend to their brethren, a perseverance in the same firm and temperate conduct as expressed in the resolutions determined upon."[33]

Every delegation in Congress stood behind the Suffolk Resolves, even the moderate men of Pennsylvania and New York. Galloway would later suggest that he was aghast at the Suffolk Resolves, calling them "a complete declaration of war against Great-Britain."[34] But there is no record of a peep of protest from Galloway at the time.

With Congress firmly and unanimously backing the Resolves, Massachusetts delegates were jubilant. John Adams gushed in his diary: "This was one of the happiest Days of my Life. ... This Day convinced me that America will support the Massachusetts or perish with her."[35]

***

Delegates for the most part kept their activities secret from outsiders, such as one young medical student from Rhode Island. He was intensely curious about Congress and dazzled just to be near such an illustrious group: "My Blood thrilled thro' my Veins at the agreeable, Pleasant View of so many Noble and Sage Patriots, met in the great Cause of Liberty."[36]

A delegate gave the medical student a tour of Carpenters' Hall. The young man tried to pry out information on the goings-on in the hall, but got nowhere: "I have been at our Delegate's Lodgings several times; but have learned Nothing of their Proceedings, except what they have made public."[37]

Congress worked six days a week from 10 in the morning to 4:40 in the afternoon. In the evening, the chatter went on less formally and more candidly in Philadelphia taverns and dining rooms.[38]

Like other men at other out-of-town meetings writing to wives back home, Deane assured his wife that, along with all the gabbing and gorging, delegates were engaged in serious toil: "I am really hurried, and have many more engagements than I wish for, though they are agreeable. Am engaged to dine out every day this week. ... You will begin to suspect that we do nothing else, but I assure you it is hard Work."[39]

Within and outside Carpenters' Hall, delegates sized up each other. Deane and John Adams both left musings about their early encounters with colleagues over their first weeks in Philadelphia. Adams called Caesar Rodney of Delaware "the oddest looking man in the world. He is tall—thin and slender as a Reed—pale—his Face not bigger than a large Apple." Edward Rutledge: "Speaks through his nose—a wretched Speaker in Conversation."[40] Of John Rutledge he commented: "There is no Keenness in his Eye. No Depth in his Countenance. Nothing of the profound, sagacious, or sparkling in his first appearance."[41] Deane was astonished at the passion of South Carolina's Christopher Gadsden: "[H]e is for taking up his Firelock, & marching direct to Boston, nay he affirmed this Morning, that were his Wife, and all his Children in Boston, & they were there to perish, by the sword, it would not alter his Sentiment."[42]

***

After the vote on the Suffolk Resolves, talk centered on nonimportation from Britain and its counterpart, nonexportation to Britain. The most extreme measure contemplated by delegates—to register America's abhorrence with the Intolerable Acts—was to stop or restrict the import of British goods and perhaps to also restrict sales of American goods to Britain.

Some delegates were supremely confident that an American boycott would instantly bring British authorities around. One was Annapolis lawyer Samuel Chase, whose ruddy complexion earned him the schoolyard nickname Bacon-Face: "A total nonimportation and nonexportation to Great Britain and the West Indies must produce a national bankruptcy in a very short space of time."[43]

The Massachusetts delegates pushed hard for an agreement to stop both imports and exports. Delegates generally agreed about imports; the sticking point was exports. Maryland, Virginia, and the Carolinas depended on exports of rice and tobacco.[44] A pause in exports to Britain would mean the Southern colonies would bear more than their share of the burden to address a crisis centered in the North. A fissure between North and South was already opening. To close it, a compromise was crafted. Congress decided to cut off imports starting December 1, while exports would stop the following year in September if the Intolerable Acts were still in place.[45]

The radical faction in Congress now seemed in full command. With endorsements from Congress of the Suffolk Resolves—and their call to peacefully challenge British authority in Massachusetts—and calls for a ban on imports and eventually exports, Samuel Adams and his allies had gotten most of what they wanted.

But the moderate Galloway was still in the game, and he was not fighting alone. Among the prominent moderates who shared his wariness about Samuel Adams and like-minded delegates were New Yorkers James Duane and John Jay.

Son of an Irish immigrant who prospered as a merchant in New York City,[46] Duane parlayed a legal education into a highly successful law practice. That made him rich. His marriages made him even richer and gave him sturdy political connections with the cream of New York's landed aristocracy. His first wife was Maria Livingston, daughter of Robert Livingston, who commanded wealth and power in the Hudson

River Valley. After she died, Duane married Gertrude Schuyler, daughter of Philip Schuyler, owner of vast tracts around Albany. Duane's landholdings included 36,000 acres near Schenectady with 235 tenant farmers.[47]

His position as a large landowner conveniently dovetailed with his conservative outlook. He agreed with the notion that those who own the country ought to govern it. He also found appealing the idea of an American peerage and recoiled at the thought of America without a king.[48]

From the start of the dispute with Britain, he consistently and courageously called for restraint. In 1770, he vigorously prosecuted a writer of provocative pamphlets critical of the royal lieutenant governor.[49] John Adams called Duane a "very sensible" man, with "a sly, surveying Eye," "a plodding Body" and a "a very effeminate, feeble Voice."[50]

Jay and Duane were kin in more ways than one. They shared conservative values and family connections. Jay, of Huguenot and Dutch ancestry, grew up in Rye, New York, where his father, a merchant, also had a farm. He was raised in the Anglican Church and grew to be among the most openly religious of the Founding Fathers.[51]

Jay was a child of "very grave disposition,"[52] according to his father when the boy was just six. At age 14, Jay entered King's College (now Columbia University) in New York City.[53] He was a diligent student, but got himself into hot water over an incident involving a dining table that some students deliberately broke. When asked by the school's president if he knew who did the deed, Jay could have fibbed, like other boys, and said he had no clue. But instead, he said, "Yes." When asked who, Jay responded: "I do not choose to tell you, sir."[54] Jay gave a lawyerly defense: none of the college statutes required students to tattle on fellow students. He was briefly suspended.[55]

He indeed became a lawyer, focusing at first on collecting commercial debts. In 1774, aged 28, he married Sarah Livingston and thus into the rich and influential Livingston clan. When troubles between America and Britain boiled up, Jay was slow to join the revolutionaries. He was drawn into the fray only after the Boston Tea Party when he landed on a committee to draft a response to Britain's measures punishing Boston. Jay's committee called for a meeting of representatives from all the colonies to thrash out a united response. This led to the appointment of Jay as one of five delegates to represent New York at the Congress.[56]

He was an odd choice. The youngest of the New York delegates, he had no experience in politics, so why did this political novice, mostly aloof from the crisis to this point, accept the assignment? He likely thought of himself quite the opposite of a rebel. His purpose in going to Philadelphia was to look for a way to peacefully resolve the dispute with Britain, not to blow it up into a war.[57]

Unlike some of the other New York delegates, who enjoyed a loud sendoff with cannon salutes and crowds escorting them to the edge of town, Jay slipped away unnoticed.[58]

So Galloway had these potential allies on his side when, amid the talk of imports and exports, he introduced a distraction that might have taken the Congress—and British America—in a new direction. He presented a blueprint for a new relationship between Britain and America. Under this plan, each colony would be represented in an American Grand Council, which would be like a parliament for America. The British Parliament would still have to approve the measures of this American parliament and the king would decide who presided over it. But it would be nearly like representation in Parliament.[59]

Galloway's proposal didn't come out of the blue. Delegates, fixated on the issue of America's relationship with Parliament, had consumed many hours behind the scenes in debate about Parliament's rule over the American colonies. All delegates agreed that Parliament did not have total authority in America. But what power did it have? Could Parliament regulate trade in the colonies? After much wrangling, delegates could not agree.[60] Galloway and maybe half the others thought Parliament could regulate colonial trade. Radicals thought otherwise.

Galloway's plan was a way around this impasse. The American Grand Council would be like a third house of Parliament, alongside the House of Commons and the House of Lords. Members, elected by colonial assemblies, would serve three-year terms. The Council would have the authority to veto bills coming from London pertaining to America. Meanwhile, the American Council would have no say in laws pertaining only to Britain,[61] but would have equal authority with Parliament over such issues as taxation and trade regulation applying to America: related laws would have to be approved by both.[62] If Congress could agree on this plan, or something like it, and present it to Parliament, a new, more hopeful relationship could emerge.

The idea was enticing—"almost a perfect plan," according to South Carolina's Edward Rutledge.[63] Here was a map for a fresh start with Britain.

Galloway's plan was actually similar to a scheme devised by Americans, including Benjamin Franklin, back in 1754. That scheme went nowhere, and neither did this one. Delegates talked about the plan for one day, set it aside, and then weeks later dismissed it.

The reasons delegates never adopted the idea are unclear. In opposing the proposal, some delegates argued that Congress had no authority to agree to such a plan. Others said the plan would take away some rights that colonial legislatures now had. Supporters of the plan answered these arguments: delegates could take the plan to their respective colonies for review and authorization; and the plan, if put into place, might actually expand the rights and authority of colonial lawmakers.[64] What were the possible unstated reasons to dismiss the plan? Perhaps delegates figured that taking up the plan would again lead to endless debate about the limits of Parliament's authority, and with events moving fast and action needed, the prospect of pushing the plan looked arduous, protracted, and likely futile. They also may have taken for granted that Parliament would toss it aside. Indeed, when America's friends in

Parliament later saw the plan, they were intrigued but unenthused.[65] Presumably, America's enemies in Parliament would have given it short shrift.

As the Congress continued its work, a rider from Massachusetts brought in a letter from the Boston Committee of Correspondence. That committee reported more alarming news from Boston: British authorities were fortifying the town, and citizens might soon be held hostage by British troops for leverage against the Patriot faction in the countryside. The committee asked for Congress's advice on whether people—especially those sympathetic to the Patriots—should leave the town or stay. "[I]f the Congress advise to quit,—they obey—if it is judged that by maintaining their ground they can better serve the public cause, they will not shrink from hardship & danger."[66] The Boston Committee, unwilling to bow to royal authority, was kneeling before Congress. Congress was being asked to govern.

Delegates recognized that they, sitting in Philadelphia, were in a poor position to assess conditions in Boston. They advised that, if the provincial government—the revolutionary government set up outside Boston in defiance of royal authority—should determine such an evacuation necessary, then Congress would recommend that "all America" contribute toward compensating Bostonians for their costs.[67]

Congress also seized the moment to explicitly indicate America's support for Boston and Massachusetts should there be war: "Resolved, That this Congress approve of the opposition by the Inhabitants of the Massachusetts-Bay, to the execution of the late acts of Parliament; and if the same shall be attempted to be carried into execution by force, in such case, all America ought to support them in their opposition."[68]

This was momentous. This was straightforward assurance that, should war break out, Congress would stand by the Massachusetts rebels. Galloway and Duane, recognizing the implications, were so appalled that they asked that their opposition to the resolution be recorded in the minutes. When that was denied, they traded written statements certifying that neither had supported the resolution, which they felt smacked of treason.[69]

The bitter differences between moderates and radicals were set aside on October 14 when Congress produced a statement listing grievances and rights. Duane was a key contributor.[70] Much would be restated more elegantly in the Declaration of Independence less than two years hence. The statement proclaimed,

> That the inhabitants of the English Colonies in North America, by the immutable laws of nature, the principles of the English constitution, and the several charters or compacts, have the following Rights: ... That they are entitled to life, liberty, & property, and they have never ceded to any sovereign power whatever, a right to dispose of either without their consent.[71]

The statement promised that "to restore harmony"[72] between Great Britain and America, the Intolerable Acts, along with several offensive acts dating back to 1764, needed to be repealed, and Britain needed to end the practice of keeping standing armies in the colonies in peacetime. Until those changes were made, America would make good on its threat to stop importing and consuming goods from Britain, and would restrict exports to Britain.[73]

Through the weeks of debate, moderates pushed back against more extreme delegates—especially those from Massachusetts and Virginia. But even moderates found themselves cornered and conceded on fundamental issues. During the course of the debates, Galloway made an astonishing assertion—that all the acts of Parliament made since the colonial ancestors reached American shores "are Violation of our Rights," and acknowledged that his own "arguments tend to an independency of the Colonies."[74]

***

An election in October in Pennsylvania changed the political dynamics of the colony as well as the Congress. Voters put the influential writer John Dickinson back in Pennsylvania's colonial Assembly, which promptly named him as a delegate to Congress.[75] Dickinson was likely well acquainted with most of what was going on behind closed doors at Carpenters' Hall. Historians point to evidence that suggests that even before being named a delegate, he had a hand in drafting key documents of the Congress.[76]

John Dickinson, despite his prominence before the Revolution as a voice of American discontent, resisted calls for independence. He represented Pennsylvania in Congress from 1774–76 and Delaware in 1779. He was later president of Pennsylvania's Supreme Executive Council, a role similar to that of governor, and represented Delaware at the convention that drafted the U.S. Constitution. This portrait, by James Barton Longacre, is a copy done about 1835 of a portrait by Charles Willson Peale. (Image courtesy of the National Portrait Gallery, Smithsonian Institution)

Welcoming Dickinson into Carpenters' Hall, Congress quickly gave their newest colleague an assignment. Unhappy with a draft of an appeal to the king, delegates asked him to write a new one.[77]

CHAPTER 5

We Will Never Submit

By late October, delegates were weary and frazzled. John Adams groused: "In Congress, nibbling and quibbling as usual. ... These great wits, these subtle critics, these refined geniuses, these learned lawyers, these wise statesmen, are so fond of showing their parts and powers, as to make their consultations very tedious."[1]

In letters home, delegates fretted about their businesses, families, and farms. "The black bull should be fatted and the other two year old you may fat or not as is most convenient," wrote Rhode Island's Samuel Ward to a family member (probably daughter Mary). "The Sheep should have the Range of the fattening Pasture or the other farm."[2]

About this time, Congress put the finishing touches to a landmark resolution that would come to demonstrate that Congress, with no money, no power to tax, and no army of soldiers or bureaucrats, was already in its own way the national government.

The long resolution, comprising 14 Articles of Association, touched on such topics as sheep breeding, horse racing, and dress at funerals. Congress wanted Americans to raise more sheep so that the country didn't have to rely so much on British-made woolen cloth. Meanwhile, horse racing, along with cockfighting and such "species of extravagance and dissipation," were discouraged. As for funerals, Congress wanted people to cut back on lavish spending, which was the fashion. For example, it called for a halt to the practice of giving mourners gloves and scarves.[3]

Mainly, however, the Association, or Continental Association as it became known, set out the details of the agreed-upon boycott—that is, the nonimportation of British goods, the nonexportation to Britain of American goods, and the nonconsumption of British products in America—and proposed a plan for enforcing it.

To keep all colonies on board, the proposed restrictions on trade were not as rigorous as most delegates hoped. A compromise had to be worked out on exports. The majority of the South Carolina delegates had pleaded that exports of rice and indigo, the province's main crops, be allowed to continue. Over this, four of the five South Carolina delegates walked out of Carpenters' Hall and thus shattered the façade of unanimity that Congress so wanted to preserve. This may be why John

Adams, in his frustration, scribbled out his impression of one of those delegates, Edward Rutledge: "excessively vain, excessively weak, and excessively variable and unsteady; jejune, inane and puerile."[4] The South Carolina delegates were persuaded to return after a compromise was found: exports could continue on rice, but indigo exports would stop.

As for imports, delegates were steadfast in calling for a ban on all goods from Britain, as well as "East-India tea" from anywhere in the world, and certain other products, such as wine from Madeira. Furthermore, delegates called for a ban on imports of enslaved people after December 1.[5] From that time "we will wholly discontinue the slave trade, and will neither be concerned in it ourselves, nor will we hire our vessels, nor sell our commodities or manufactures to those who are concerned in it."[6]

The ban reflected some moral qualms about slavery that pecked at the consciences of some delegates. But mostly it was about applying economic pressure on the many British merchants who profited from the slave trade; a ban would pinch them, and they in turn, delegates hoped, would pinch Parliament.

It was one thing for Congress to call for a ban of imports; it was another to enforce it. This had been tried before, and had failed. During the days of the Stamp Act, agreements to stop imports fell apart as merchants gave in to the lure of big profits powered by strong consumer demand. Later on, during the protests over the Townshend duties, some town governments pressured people to stop consuming British products. Results were better, but still disappointing. Outside New England, calls for boycotts went largely ignored.[7]

This time, Patriot leaders tried a different approach. The Continental Association called on every county, city, and town to create a committee to "attentively ... observe the conduct of all persons touching this association." That is, to snoop into other people's business. In addition, violations of the boycott were to be published so that "all such foes to the rights of British-America may be publicly known, and universally contemned as the enemies of American liberty."[8] Alleged violators would be shamed and ostracized. There was no suggestion of due process of any kind.

All delegates present signed the Association, including even Galloway. He later claimed that he did so because he felt to do otherwise would put himself in physical danger and hoped by signing to prevent Congress from doing something "more violent."[9]

Shortly after the Association was passed, Peyton Randolph of Virginia fell ill—too ill to continue as president. Called upon to fill that role was South Carolina's Henry Middleton, a wealthy planter with little to say. Deane pronounced him "very modest,"[10] while John Adams found him "silent and reserved."[11]

Before adjourning and ending the First Continental Congress, delegates also prodded each colony to get its militia in order. Some delegates already viewed war as inevitable,[12] but this Congress was not ready to form an army, or to even help colonies gear up for battle.

Congress wrapped up its work by setting the time and place of the next Congress—May 10, 1775, in Philadelphia—"unless the redress of grievances, which we have desired, be obtained before that time,"[13] and by dotting the i's and crossing the t's on messages to all and sundry, including to the king and the British people, but not Parliament. The letters summarized all the old arguments in the squabble, but also betrayed American fears and prejudices, and demonstrated that the long-simmering differences with Britain went beyond the matter of tea in Boston Harbor.

The petition to the king, chiefly the handiwork of Dickinson, repeated the common view that the king himself was blameless. All this trouble was the fault of the king's ministers:

> [T]hose designing and dangerous men, who daringly interposing themselves between your royal person and your faithful subjects ... by abusing your majesty's authority, misrepresenting your American subjects and prosecuting the most desperate and irritating projects of oppression, have at length compelled us, by the force of accumulated injuries too severe to be any longer tolerable, to disturb your majesty's repose by our complaints.[14]

As the king was still sacrosanct, the letter scrupulously incorporated the usual groveling folderol: "That your majesty may enjoy every felicity through a long and glorious reign over loyal and happy subjects, and that your descendants may inherit your prosperity and dominions 'til time shall be no more, is and always will be our sincere and fervent prayer."[15]

In a message to the British people, Congress gave a warning, but also a promise: "We will never submit to be hewers of wood or drawers of water for any ministry or nation in the world. Place us in the same situation that we were at the close of the [French and Indian War, ending in 1763], and our former harmony will be restored."[16]

Congress, in its address to the British people, also railed at Parliament for giving freedom of worship to Catholic Canadians. Parliament, by this act, had anchored in Canada "a religion that has deluged your country in blood, and dispersed impiety, bigotry, persecution, murder and rebellion through every part of the world."[17]

Meanwhile, in its letter to the French-speaking Catholic Canadians of Quebec, Congress prudently left out references to Catholic bigotry, persecution, and murder. Instead, the letter asserted that Parliament, after all, gave Canadians nothing: "[W]hat is offered to you by the late act of Parliament? Liberty of conscience in your religion? No. God gave it to you."[18]

This letter, reminding Canadians that they, as British subjects, were entitled to all the rights of British subjects, warned that the promises coming from London were phony: "The Crown and its Ministers are empowered, as far as they could be by Parliament, to establish even the *Inquisition* itself among you."[19]

In lecturing Canadians on how miserable they were under British authority, Congress also betrayed American fear of attack from the north, should matters come to blows: "Unhappy people! Who are not only injured, but insulted. Nay more!— ... [A]n insolent Ministry ... will engage you to take up arms, and render yourselves the ridicule and detestation of the world, by becoming tools, in their hands, to assist them in taking that freedom from *us*, which they have treacherously denied to *you*."[20]

Before closing as "your sincere and affectionate friends and fellow-subjects," Congress invited the Canadians to send delegates to its next gathering, "to unite with us in one social compact, formed on the generous principles of equal liberty."[21]

In yet another message—this one to their fellow Americans in the 12 colonies taking part in the Congress—delegates reminded the people that the success of the boycott depended on them: "Your own salvation, and that of your posterity now depend upon yourselves ... Against the temporary inconveniences you may suffer from a stoppage of trade, you will weigh in the opposite balance, the endless miseries that you and your descendants must endure from an established arbitrary power."[22]

Delegates also authorized messages to the other British colonies on the North American continent—to Nova Scotia and St. John's (Prince Edward Island) to the north, and to Georgia, East Florida, and West Florida to the south.

On Wednesday, October 26, the Congress ended. That evening the remaining delegates gathered at the City Tavern, and in the following days they headed for home. John Adams lingered in "the happy, the peaceful, the elegant, the hospitable, and polite City," taking time to watch arguments in a case before the Pennsylvania Supreme Court concerning a will.[23]

The Congress had achieved its main mission—an agreement on restricting trade and establishing a method to enforce those restrictions—and remained united in doing so. Galloway later reported that the Congress was a stew of disagreement about resolutions adopted, giving historians the impression of much rancor behind the scenes. But no other delegate made a similar claim. Indeed, one of Galloway's moderate colleagues said that Galloway himself during the Congress quietly went along with almost everything, concealing his dissent so well "that no member knew of it besides himself."[24]

***

"[I]t is not very likely that I shall ever see this Part of the World again."[25] So confided John Adams in his diary as he was leaving Philadelphia. Did he think he would not be a part of the next Congress, or did he think the storm would pass and there would be no Congress?

Certainly, among delegates there was wishful thinking that somehow—perhaps through a change of mind or a change of ministers on the other side of the Atlantic—harmony would be restored between Britain and America.

Dickinson believed that Americans, through Congress, had effectively put Britain on the spot: "Colonists have now taken such Ground, that Great Britain must relax, or inevitably involve herself in a Civil War." He pondered the possibility of fresh thinking in London: "A new Ministry of such a Character, that England & America both can trust, may do great Things ... Why should nations meet with hostile Eyes, because Villains & Ideots have acted like Villains & Ideots?"[26]

Moderate Galloway grumbled that the measures of Congress were too "warm & indiscreet" and will only widen the gap between America and Britain.[27] Other delegates were quite pleased. "God bless the Congress! Surely they were inspired!"[28] wrote North Carolina's William Hooper. Connecticut's Deane was so proud of the Congress that he pushed to have "the whole doings of the Congress" translated for the benefit of French and German speakers on both sides of the Atlantic.[29]

Rhode Island's Ward ruminated about an annual Congress no matter the British response: "[S]hould the Ministry be disposed to make any new Attempts upon Us Nothing would so effectually prevent their taking Place as our continuing firmly united & being ever on our Guard."[30]

What was the public's reaction to the Congress? Predictably, many Loyalists were appalled. Some regarded the proceedings as the product of a nefarious plot cooked up in New England years before. An Anglican clergyman in New Jersey wrote:

> [T]hey have altogether neglected the work they were sent upon; that the powers delegated to them by their constituents, for the good of the colonies, were prostituted to the purposes of private ambition; and that all their proceedings as far as we can judge, were instigated and directed by the New-England republicans, to the utmost confusion of the Colonies, the disgrace of their constituents, and their own infamy.[31]

However, many Americans, probably most, approved of Congress's actions and obeyed its call to enforce the ban on British products. In Maryland, for example, according to a newspaper report, all the people were "in Motion, forming County Meetings, choosing *Committees of Observation* to carry into effectual Execution, without Fear, Favor or Partiality, the Measures recommended by the Grand Continental Congress."[32]

In the various colonies, unauthorized gatherings of one sort or another, similar to the assemblies that selected delegates to the Congress, passed judgment on the work of Congress. In the end, 11 colonies gave their assent to the Association with its call for nonconsumption, nonimportation, and eventually, nonexportation. Even in the outliers, New York and Georgia, scattered committees forged ahead on their own to enforce the Association's measures.[33] For example, a Committee of Inspection sprouted in New York City to take on the task of enforcing nonimportation there.[34]

Such committees for enforcing guidelines of the Association sprang up almost everywhere. They appeared in at least 51 of 61 counties in Virginia and at least 11 of 16 counties in Maryland. Meanwhile, Massachusetts had at least 160 town committees.[35] Committees could include many dozens of people, often community leaders, but others too. The size of these committees of "safety" or "observation" varied widely, averaging 21 in Virginia but ranging from 20 to 200 in Maryland. Some frontier hamlets, where the volume of imports would have been tiny, had committees made up of more than 150, nearly every man in the community. The number of Americans serving on committees of this kind may have come to ten thousand or so.[36] If such committees proved unwieldy, no one seemed to care. The attitude seemed to be, the more the merrier.

But not everyone was enthusiastic. In the colony of New York, committees outside Albany and New York City were rare. More communities in New York ignored the Association than in all other colonies added together.[37]

In Philadelphia, the town's chief committee handling enforcement divided the city into districts and then assigned a subcommittee for each. The subcommittees in turn would each assign two or three members to sit each day at a coffeehouse or some other location, make observations, and gather reports about incoming shipments.[38]

One Massachusetts preacher, looking back after the war started, recalled how the Association stimulated civic involvement, engaging people otherwise overlooked for community duties: "[T]he public eye stimulated them to exertion in their department; they naturally improved others, that were still their inferiors; each one acquired a degree of importance, which was new to him; and by this means, whole communities and societies were cemented together."[39]

We see in the example of little Sutton, Massachusetts, just south of Worcester, how one town embraced the Association and wrestled with its myriad implications. Townspeople gathered and voted "to adopt the Association of the Continental Congress" and choose a Committee of Inspection to see that the Association "be duly observed." Among their other resolutions was one stating that, when a majority of the inspectors "upon due Tryal" found anyone guilty of violating the Association by, for example, buying and drinking the forbidden tea, that the inspectors "shall cause a notification thereof forth with to be posted up at the several Taverns, Mills and Smiths in this Town, that all the Inhabitants may know and avoid all dealings with Him or Her."[40]

Determined to root out violators, the town called on its citizens to snitch on each other.[41] Once caught, however, such violators were to be treated not so much like criminals, but rather as sinners, who could be forgiven if convincingly remorseful:

> [I]f there should appear any symptoms of sorrow and hopes of Repentance, the publication of it [the violation] in the News, may be suspended until the next Town meeting, in order that the offender may have opportunity for Consideration, and space to repent, which if he manifests at such meeting to the satisfaction of the Town, and promises a Reformation, the Town may then restore such offender to Fellowship.[42]

At the same meeting, the town tied itself in knots over what to do about townspeople who dared say "hello" to a proven and unrepentant violator. Such a person should be shunned, like the violator. However, if upon Trial, it should appear to the Committee that such person did no more than to help in case of absolute sickness or some casualty, in which a Building or the Life of some person or creature was in danger of immediately perishing, or spake nothing to offender other than to demand, or pay a Debt or Tax, or about the Things of the Eternal World, or to convince him or her of his or their error in transgressing as above, or if he only spake a word inadvertently, and desisted upon being Reminded of the state of such Offender, he shall not be adjudged as being guilty of Criminal dealing with such Offender.[43]

Some Americans bravely howled in protest of the boycott, the actions of Congress, and the Association. A pamphleteer called the boycott a remedy "ten thousand times worse than the disease." It is, he wrote, like lopping off an arm because of a sore finger.[44]

Another pamphleteer—after charging that Congress "either ignorantly misunderstood, carelessly neglected, or basely betrayed the interests of all the Colonies"—ranted about the widespread meddling by those enforcing the Association's rules: "If I must be enslaved, let it be by a King at least, and not by a parcel of upstart lawless Committee-men. If I must be devoured, let me be devoured by the jaws of a lion, and not gnawed to death by rats and vermin."[45]

In North Carolina, four counties, in messages to the royal governor, denounced the Association. The letter from Anson County, signed by 227 people, expressed "a disapprobation and abhorence of the many lawless combinations and unwarrantable practices actually carrying on by a gross tribe of infatuated anti-Monarchists in the several Colonies in these Dominions."[46]

Others were equally horrified, but reluctant to speak out. In Virginia, a newcomer from Britain hoping to prosper in America wrote in his journal about visiting a tavern and hearing the resolves of Congress—"full of duplicity and false representation"—being read: "I am obliged to act the hypocrite and extol these proceedings as the wisest productions of any assembly on Earth, but in my heart I despise them and look upon them with contempt."[47]

The activities of committees went beyond watching for imports and scolding tea-drinkers. Entertainment of various kinds was discouraged or outlawed as wasteful, immoral, or frivolous. The committee in Portsmouth, New Hampshire, discouraged cards and billiards. That in Wilmington, North Carolina, condemned dancing and discouraged horse racing.[48] The Wilmington committee argued that nothing will "so effectually tend to convince the British Parliament that we are in earnest in our opposition to their measures, as a voluntary relinquishment of our favorite amusements."[49]

By early March 1775, the Wilmington committee's tactics had evolved from suggestion to intimidation. Its members drew up an oath to "Strictly Observe every part of the Association recommended by the Continental Congress" and then went as a body—all 25 members—door to door to demand a signature from each householder. Eleven brave residents stood up to the committee and refused to sign. They were declared pariahs to be held "unworthy of the rights of freemen & as Inimical to the Liberties of their country."[50]

Local militia apparently went further to enforce the Association dictates. A visitor to Wilmington witnessed a confrontation involving local militiamen and a group of men who had refused to sign the oath. She recorded seeing the militiamen holding the men prisoners in the middle of a road. A standoff ensued, the prisoners remaining obstinate. The militiamen lacked the nerve to kill the prisoners, but still would not let them go. The prisoners remained on the street, apparently for hours, until after 2am, when they were finally allowed to return to their homes.[51]

Many committees encouraged manufacturing of, for example, blankets, rugs, stockings, gunpowder, nails, paper, glass, firearms, and buttons. The push to foster American manufacturing inspired novel thinking. Out of Virginia, a report suggested an alternative rum made from pumpkins instead of molasses from imported sugar.[52]

For good or ill, Congress now had more authority in America than the king. The royal governor of New Hampshire confessed: "So great is the present delusion, that most people receive them [orders from Congress] as matters of obedience, not of considerate examination, whereon they may exercise their own judgment."[53]

In Virginia, the royal governor complained that committees of inspection had popped up in every county, officiously overseeing "the conduct of every inhabitant without distinction." Congress and the so-called "laws of Congress" were being given "marks of reverence which they [the people] never bestowed on their legal Government or the laws proceeding from it."[54] Galloway, in January 1775, growled that the American colonies were now governed by "the barbarian Rule of ambitious Fools and impolitic Madmen."[55]

The Association worked. Americans enforced Congress's boycott. But that boycott failed to alter British policy. Americans had believed the boycott would prompt British merchants to complain to Parliament. But that didn't happen. British merchants hardly peeped, and without noisy protests, the British authorities became more determined than ever to bring Americans to heel. Figuring that, when pressed, Americans would not fight,[56] Britain geared up to force its policies on Americans, even if that meant war.

***

The spring of 1775 approached with no resolution to the crisis. The king barely glanced at the petition Congress had so laboriously drafted. His highness did peruse the terms of the Association and concluded: "The New England governments are now in a state of rebellion; blows must decide whether they are to be subject to this country or Independent."[57] Parliament agreed. Galloway had been right—the work of the First Continental Congress helped matters not one bit.

Wheels turned for the Second Continental Congress, set to begin in May. Once again, meetings, conventions, and gatherings of various kinds up and down the colonies chose delegates and sent them off. Royal authorities ordered governors to "use your utmost endeavors" to prevent the appointment of delegates to Congress.[58]

In some cases, the established elected assemblies chose delegates right under the nose of the royal governor, as happened in New Jersey, where Governor William Franklin did nothing to stop it. When Franklin received instructions from his royal master to prevent the naming of delegates, he responded that it was already too late. He argued that if he had obstructed the assembly, Patriot groups would have made other arrangements and sent off delegates anyway.[59]

Some of these delegates were on their way to Philadelphia when the powder keg that was Massachusetts exploded. It had to happen. General Thomas Gage, in his role as both the royal governor of Massachusetts and the British military commander, could not sit in Boston forever and let the rebel provincial government rule the countryside and prepare for war. Gage had to do something to bring all of Massachusetts back under royal control, or at least block rebels from arming. Knowing that rebels were stockpiling weapons in Concord, a village 18 miles northwest of Boston, Gage planned a mission to seize and destroy that equipment. The task was meant to be quick and quiet. Gage assigned a force just large enough to discourage the few rebel militiamen who might appear.

In the dark, before midnight on April 18, troops set out from Boston. Despite Gage's efforts to keep the mission secret, word of the British action spread everywhere, thanks to observers and riders. Shouts in the night roused militiamen, including those in Lexington on the way to Concord. At about daybreak, the British column entered Lexington, where militiamen had gathered on the green. At a fork in the road, the column could have gone left on the unobstructed road to Concord. But, with rebel militiamen in view, the column veered right and deployed. A one-sided skirmish, lasting less than a minute, left eight Americans dead and nine wounded. A single British regular, a private, was wounded.[60]

Who fired first? In the propaganda duel that instantly followed, the Americans were quickest on the draw. They said that someone on the British side delivered the opening shot, and thus the British were the aggressors. Most Americans believed that. But even today, no one knows where the first bullet came from.

The British pushed on to Concord, 6 miles away, entering the village unmolested at about 9am.[61] The troops found and disabled a few cannons, torched carriage wheels, dropped confiscated cannonballs into a pond, and smashed some barrels of flour.[62] At about 11am, about a half mile from the village center, a force of Concord men, augmented by dozens of militiamen now streaming in from the countryside, advanced on Regulars securing a bridge. It was another one-sided skirmish. This time, though, the British took a beating. American bullets found 12 Regulars, three of whom died.[63]

With mounting numbers of armed and angry Americans around them, the British soon started back toward Boston. Along the way, American guns pecked at them from behind walls, trees, and barns. In Lexington, British reinforcements dispatched from Boston joined the Regulars returning from Concord. The combined force then marched toward Boston, swatting at skirmishers all the way, and finally reaching safety after dark, exhausted and battered. There was a grim tally of dead: 65 British, 50 American.[64]

News of the battle reached Philadelphia in five days;[65] the Second Continental Congress would commence amid the thunder of war. Ready or not, Congress was now an improvisational government for a people not ready to be a nation.

With reports condemning the British as the aggressors at Lexington and Concord, opinion on the bloody events in Massachusetts came down solidly on the side of the Patriots. Massachusetts delegates to the First Congress had been welcomed as friends; this time they were cheered as heroes.

One of these heroes was John Hancock. As a key rebel leader in restive Massachusetts, he had been absent from the First Congress. Now he would be needed in Philadelphia to help rally support from Congress for the embattled province.

Hancock was the most popular Patriot leader in Massachusetts. More than Samuel Adams, John Adams, or anyone else in the colony, Hancock was the figure people looked to as their captain in this crisis. During the battle of Lexington and Concord, British troops heard Americans shouting "King Hancock forever."[66]

The son of a minister in Braintree, Hancock was destined for a modest and obscure life until the death of his father when young John was just seven. His mother, facing a future with no breadwinner and two other children to feed, agreed to let a rich and childless aunt and uncle raise the boy, and off he went to Boston to enjoy the finest upbringing that money could buy. Twenty years later, upon his uncle's death, Hancock was suddenly one of the wealthiest merchants in New England, and like other American

John Hancock, wealthy and popular in Massachusetts, was president of Congress when it declared independence. He was later governor of Massachusetts: This 1770–72 portrait of John Hancock by John Singleton Copley is in the collection of the Massachusetts Historical Society. (Image via Wikimedia Commons)

merchants, he bristled at the regulations from London that cut into his profits.[67] Likeable and generous, he soon stepped up as a key figure in the Patriot movement, bankrolling patriotic projects and winning elections.

By the time of Lexington and Concord, Hancock and Samuel Adams were the yin and yang of the rebel movement in Massachusetts. Hancock was the rich merchant with no qualms about displaying his wealth, the face of the movement, the man at center stage. Adams was the failed businessman, the frugal Puritan in the frayed suit, the organizer of the movement, the man behind the scenes. They were bedfellows politically and, the night before the battle of Lexington and Concord, literally. That night, they, along with Hancock's aunt, Lydia Hancock, and fiancée, Dolly Quincy, sheltered in the crowded house of a minister and his family just steps away from Lexington Green. Adams and Hancock had just attended the provincial Congress meeting in Concord and were reluctant to return to Boston, fearing that the British might now try to take them into custody.

Awakened just before dawn, Hancock and Adams fled before the battle, finding shelter a few miles away, and then moved about in tandem in the following days, finally winding up in Worcester. They prepared to depart for Philadelphia, with Hancock in a sour mood. The other delegates—John Adams, Thomas Cushing, and Robert Treat Paine—were nowhere to be seen. Hancock wanted them all to depart together as part of a dignified sendoff: "Where is Mr. Cushing? Are Mr. Paine and Mr. John Adams to be with us? What are we to depend on? We travel rather as deserters, which I will not submit to."[68]

Cushing, John Adams, and Paine were already on the road. But a military escort was eventually gathered up to give Hancock and Samuel Adams, along with Aunt Lydia and Dolly, a proper sendoff. In Connecticut, the ladies were left with friends, and Hancock and Samuel Adams continued on, joining John Adams, Cushing, and Paine just north of New York City.[69]

Their entry in New York was a celebration. Hancock wrote to his Dolly: "When we Arriv'd within three Miles of the City we were met by the Grenadier Company and Regiment of the City Militia under Arms, Gentlemen in Carriages and on Horseback, and many Thousands of Persons on Foot, the Roads fill'd with People, and the greatest Cloud of Dust I ever saw."[70] Admirers detached the horses from Hancock's carriage and pulled the vehicle with their own muscle-power through the city.

A few days later, a teeming crowd accompanied the delegates to the ferry. The triumphal march for the eight delegates—five from Massachusetts, three from Connecticut—continued across New Jersey. In Newark, four infantry companies greeted them. On the way to Trenton, relays of militiamen escorted delegates from town to town.[71]

About 6 miles from Philadelphia, the New England delegates, now joined by the New Jersey delegation, met up with about 200 of the city's "principal Gentlemen on

Horseback with their Swords Drawn," according to Deane. The parade continued on, until, about 2 miles from the city, a pair of militia companies joined in: "Thus rolling & gathering like a Snowball, we approached the City which was full of people, & the Crowd, as great as at New York, the Bells all ringing, and the air rent with Shouts & huzza's."[72]

Meanwhile, delegates from Southern colonies enjoyed similar courtesies and attention as they made their way north. Delegate Richard Caswell of North Carolina wrote that along the Potomac, militiamen "under Arms & in the uniform of hunting shirts" directed them to boats on the riverside "with all the Military honors due to General Officers."[73]

On approaching Baltimore, four militia companies greeted Caswell and his band of delegates and led the way to a tavern "with their Colours Flying, drums Beating & Fifes playing."[74]

Delegates found Philadelphia thrumming with martial sounds. Caswell wrote that "near 2000 Men who March out to the Common & go thro their Exercises twice a Day regularly. Scarce any thing But Warlike Musick is to be heard in the Streets."[75] Deane complained: "[T]he Drum, & Fife are hourly sounding in every Street, & my brainpan, is this moment echoing, to the beat, parading under my Window."[76]

Possibly delegates glimpsed the so-called silk-stocking company, young Quaker men who had "swerved from their tenets" to "learn the duty of soldiers." It was the custom of this force of about 70, supported by a wealthy commander, to gather in the afternoon at the house of their captain, where "capacious demijohns of Madeira" were set for the men's refreshment before drills.[77]

People who dared speak up against Congress or the Patriot cause risked public scolding. A Philadelphian reported in his journal about one "Thomas Loosly, shoemaker," who was brought to a coffee house and confronted by a "great number of reputable citizens." Thus encouraged, the shoemaker "very humbly and submissively entreated their pardon and forgiveness for his illiberally and wickedly villifying the measures of Congress ... and the people of New England." He was let go after promising to be "just, true and equitable."[78]

***

For this Congress, the delegates bypassed Carpenters' Hall, where they had met before, in favor of the Pennsylvania State House, the place they had previously snubbed, to the chagrin of Galloway. The State House was fashioned to celebrate the triumph of British power and culture in the wilderness of America. Now it stands in the heart of the city; then it stood on the outskirts of town.

It rose in the 1730s from the Pennsylvania landscape like an elegant English country manor. Its immaculate symmetry and straightforward Georgian style proclaimed reason and order on the edge of a wild and largely unknown continent. On

48 • NOBLE UNDERTAKING

The structure we know as Independence Hall was the Pennsylvania State House at the time of the American Revolution. The building today looks much as it did during the Revolutionary War, except for the clock in the tower, an 1828 addition. Pennsylvania's lawmakers, who normally met on the ground floor, moved upstairs to accommodate the Continental Congress and, after the war, the convention that drafted the United States Constitution. The building served as the nation's capitol from 1790–1800, when the federal government moved to Washington, DC. State lawmakers abandoned Philadelphia and Independence Hall for Lancaster in 1799, and then chose Harrisburg as the capital in 1812. (Image courtesy of the Library of Congress, Carol M. Highsmith, photographer)

The Assembly Room in Independence Hall, the former Pennsylvania State House, is where Congress usually met while in Philadelphia. The Declaration of Independence was formally adopted in this room, which is on the east side of the ground floor. It is also the room where, after the war, the convention took place to draw up the Constitution. In normal times, the room was occupied by the Pennsylvania Assembly. On the west side of the ground floor is a courtroom. (Image courtesy of the National Park Service)

the ground floor, a central hall nearly 20 feet wide, separated two great rooms—one for the Pennsylvania Assembly, one for the provincial Supreme Court—each 40 feet square with ceilings rising 20 feet.[79]

In the floor above was the "long room" facing Chestnut and rooms for the Provincial Council and committees of the Assembly.[80]

Around 1750, builders added a "wide and noble" staircase brightened by light cascading through a great window.[81] About the same time, the cupola that topped the original building gave way to a tower and steeple,[82] giving the building we call Independence Hall more or less the appearance it has today. The block occupied by the State House became a public square enclosed by a 7-foot-high brick wall.[83]

For passersby, the impressive view of the building came with volleys of insults hollered from the windows of the nearby jail.[84] On special occasions, the tower's bell would sound. Many years later, this bell would be transformed into a hallowed national symbol as the Liberty Bell. But back then, the only thing special about it was that its ring seemed a bit "off." The bell's "unusual Sound" was so unsettling that "incommoded and distressed" neighbors once petitioned that it be rung less often lest its irritating noise "prove fatal" to those "afflicted with Sickness."[85]

The bell cracked[86] in 1752, soon after its arrival from England. It may have been damaged during shipping, or it may have been flawed to begin with.[87] Local craftsmen recast the bell, but in doing so introduced metal that resulted in an unpleasant clang. The bell was recast again with a result that was passable, if not perfect. So, at the time of the Second Continental Congress, the bell—which once had a crack, and would crack again—was sound. The motto on the bell—"Proclaim LIBERTY throughout all the land unto all the Inhabitants thereof"—comes from Leviticus. That Bible verse begins with "And ye shall hallow the fiftieth year." This has led to speculation that the choice of motto was related to Penn's charter for the colony; 1751 was the 50th anniversary of the date the charter was granted.[88]

***

This Congress included delegates from all 13 colonies. Georgia was represented for the first time, though only by a single delegate sent by the Parish of St. John's. A full delegation representing the whole colony would not appear until July.

Newcomers to the Congress included, besides Hancock, the illustrious Benjamin Franklin. The great Dr. Franklin had clung long and tenaciously to the hope that Britain and America would settle this quarrel peacefully. But by this time, the spring of 1775, his feelings toward Britain had soured. He had only recently arrived back in America from many years in Britain, a land he loved, but where his dignity had been sorely battered by the British press and politicians.

CHAPTER 6

Too Saucy & Provoking

Franklin's story is an amazing tale of how a clever boy with a little luck and a lot of pluck could go far. But it is more than that—it is also the story of how the king and Parliament broke the heart of a devoted British subject. Born in Boston in 1706,[1] Franklin was the 15th child and youngest son of a maker of candles and soap, a trade near the bottom in the pecking order of craftsmen. Early on, a notion that Benjamin should be educated for the ministry dissolved. The cost of such schooling was well beyond the means of a candlemaker with so many mouths to feed. The boy's formal education ended after two years.[2]

Eventually, the boy apprenticed for an older brother, James, a printer. Benjamin, a sturdy 12-year-old and a keen reader, was ideal for the tasks of the trade. He liked the work and in his spare time copied essays he admired, rewriting them as poetry, then reconstructing them as essays.[3] As a 16-year-old, he submitted satirical essays to his brother's newspaper under the name Silence Dogood. The essays took potshots at established local institutions such as Harvard, where, according to one essay, the students learned not much more than "how to carry themselves handsomely, and enter a Room genteely."[4] The essays were a hit and no one, not even Franklin's brother, suspected that Silence, supposedly a middle-aged woman, was Benjamin's invention.[5]

But James grew annoyed at his little brother, nine years younger, apparently finding him a bit "too saucy & provoking." After James started beating Benjamin, which masters were entitled to do to apprentices, 17-year-old Benjamin ran away, winding up in Philadelphia with only "a Dutch Dollar and a Shilling in Copper"[6] in his pocket. He lived in the house of a carpenter and soon found a printer to take him on.[7]

Before long, Franklin's talents won the admiration of a potential patron, none other than the governor of Pennsylvania, who promised Franklin financial help to set up a print shop and establish a new newspaper in Philadelphia. Counting on the governor's promised letters to obtain credit, Franklin was soon off to London to buy printing equipment.

In London, Franklin discovered the value of the governor's word. No letters arrived; there was no credit. The betrayal stunned him.[8] Yet Franklin, ever nimble, quickly found work in his trade and took in the pleasures of London, enjoying "Plays & other Places of Amusement" and indulging in "Intrigues with low Women."[9]

Eventually returning to Philadelphia, Franklin landed back in the same printing shop where he worked before. Impatient and enterprising, Franklin and a fellow worker at the shop soon opened their own shop. After the partner lost interest, Franklin borrowed money and bought him out. At 23, Franklin owned his own business.[10]

At 24, Franklin had a common-law wife, Deborah Read, the daughter of the carpenter in whose house Franklin lived when he first arrived in the city. The couple had once been engaged, but that plan fizzled after Franklin went off to London, from where he wrote to Read just once, to tell her he would probably not return.[11] Taking a hint, she gave up on Franklin and soon married a potter, who turned out to be a spendthrift and possibly a bigamist. She left him and he went off to the West Indies, where, people said, he died. But no one knew for sure, and the law did not permit Read to divorce. She and Franklin found each other again and set up a household. This worked out nicely for Franklin, who promptly presented Read with a baby boy, his child by another woman (even today, we don't know who). Franklin would one day become bitterly estranged from his illegitimate son, William. But at this time and for many years he doted on him. Read never did, however, and by the time William was 24, she considered him "the greatest Villain upon Earth."[12]

Family life did not slow Franklin down one bit. Eager to improve himself, he and a group of other artisans—including a cabinetmaker, a shoemaker, and a glazier—came together each week for conversation. The talk might be literary or intellectual, or it might be about how to make more money.[13] By way of this loose organization, called the Junto, Franklin helped launch a lending library. He also joined the Masons, which multiplied his business contacts and suited his passion for cultivating a more virtuous society.

Brimming with ideas, he applied his energies to civic projects, such as organizing fire companies, and in inventing useful things, including a more efficient wood-burning stove.[14] Seeing the danger and cost of fire, he developed guidelines for the organization of fire companies.

He had a knack for making money—as a printer, shop owner, property owner, and agent for sales of indentured servants and even slaves. He snared the job of clerk for the Pennsylvania Assembly, which conveniently led to business as the official printer for the Assembly, which in turn put him on the path to winning similar work for Delaware, New Jersey, and Maryland.[15] He also launched a newspaper, the *Pennsylvania Gazette*, and produced a popular and profitable almanac, which featured his famous proverbs and his witty "Poor Richard" essays. He landed the job of postmaster of Philadelphia, which didn't pay much but was useful, Franklin wrote, for how it "facilitated the Correspondence that improv'd my Newspaper."[16] He formed partnerships with young journeymen printers, supplying printing equipment for a share of the profits. He invested in paper manufacturing, eventually having a hand in no fewer than 18 mills. His income soared; some say he made double what the Pennsylvania governor earned.[17]

Meanwhile, his family remained small. A boy, Franky, died at the age of only four. A girl, Sarah—known as Sally—survived.[18]

Wealth meant that at age 42, Franklin, the tradesman, could become Franklin, the gentleman. He left his shop. He and his family moved to a roomier house in a better part of town, acquired slaves, and he had his portrait done. His letters were now sealed with the Franklin coat of arms.[19] He left the day-to-day money-making grind to others, immersing himself in the mysteries of electricity and the rough and tumble of civic affairs.

Fascinated with the sparks produced by performing "electricians," Franklin acquired scientific equipment and spent months, then years, experimenting and having fun with the strange and little-understood force seemingly more akin to magic than science. He amused himself and friends with ingenious electric gizmos, like an electrified metal spider that jumped as if alive.[20] It was all entertaining, but also disappointing to Franklin, who valued usefulness above almost everything. After years of experiments, he was "Chagrin'd a little that We have hitherto been able to discover Nothing in this Way of Use to Mankind."[21]

But he also came up with ideas about how electricity worked and with terms, such as "conductor" and "charge," that would become the vocabulary of electricity we use today.[22] Probably his single most important contribution to scientific theory was his idea that electricity was made up of positive and negative charges created at the same time and in equal proportions.[23]

In his observations, he discovered that a pointed piece of metal could draw away a charge from an electrified metal ball. He surmised that electricity had something to do with lightning and wrote about it, suggesting the idea of lightning rods to protect steeples and other tall structures. The French edition of Franklin's book on the subject caught the eye of France's King Louis XV, who ordered that Franklin's theory be tested. The French scientists proved Franklin was right even before Franklin conducted his own famous test with a kite in a lightning storm.[24] Instantly, Franklin became an international celebrity and honors showered down upon him. Harvard, Yale, and William & Mary bestowed honorary degrees, while London's Royal Society gave him a medal.[25] King Louis commanded that Franklin be sent a message of thanks.[26] Lightning rods sprouted from churches, towers, and houses across Europe and America.

Franklin, now a distinguished scientist, could have spent the rest of his days experimenting, tinkering, and inventing. But for Franklin, the work of science was not as satisfying, as noble, or as useful as that of public service. When asked to serve, as wealthy gentlemen often were, Franklin did: first as city councilor, followed by justice of the peace, then city alderman.[27]

Meanwhile, he found time to propose and found an academy, America's first nonsectarian college, which became the University of Pennsylvania. He also lobbied for and won the job of running the postal service for North America. This was self-serving—many friends and relatives wound up with jobs in the system[28]—but he also made delivery faster and more reliable.[29]

In 1751, Franklin took a seat as an elected assemblyman, turning over his job as clerk of the provincial assembly to his son, William. Soon Franklin was promoting other civic improvements for Philadelphia, such as paved streets and streetlamps.[30]

Looking beyond Pennsylvania, Franklin recognized the weakness of the individual colonies in dealing with the French and the indigenous people. The French, building forts along the Ohio River, made a powerful impression on the indigenous tribes, who saw them as more reliable partners in trade and alliances than the quarrelsome colonies. Franklin insisted that the colonies must unite to better withstand the threat from the two groups. His vision emerged as the Albany Plan in 1754, a blueprint for a union within the British Empire. Franklin campaigned for it, but it was too far ahead of its time. Parliament shuddered at the thought of a united American "government." Leaders in the several colonies could not fathom sharing any bit of authority with their American neighbors within some sort of federal system. The plan was ignored.

In the realm of Pennsylvania politics, Franklin emerged as the leader of the faction opposing the Penn family, which retained enormous power over the colony. The family was led by Thomas Penn, son of the colony's founder. He lived in England, was not a Quaker, and was resented in Pennsylvania because he paid no taxes on his vast holdings in the province. This resentment soared during the French and Indian War when the governor, beholden to the Penn family, nixed a bill that would have taxed the Penn lands just like everyone else's to pay for defending the province. Referring to Thomas Penn, Franklin wrote: "[O]ur Lord Proprietary, though a Subject like ourselves, would *send* us out to fight *for* him, while he keeps himself a thousand Leagues remote from Danger! Vassals fight at their Lords Expence, but our Lord would have us defend his Estate at our own Expence!"[31]

The tiff with the Penns led the Assembly to ask Franklin to sail to England to talk with the Penn family and maybe to Parliament about the unhappy state of affairs in Pennsylvania. Franklin thus found himself at the age of 51 back in London. He brought with him son William, who was about 26, and two household slaves. Deborah, horrified at the thought of an ocean voyage,[32] stayed behind.

Meetings with Thomas Penn and his brother, Richard, started off friendly enough, but became nasty, and went downhill from there. The quarrel somehow required legal rulings, which pleased the Penns. They were in no hurry, and months passed.[33]

Franklin was a patient, good-humored, reasonable man, at ease with almost everyone. That didn't include Thomas Penn. After one meeting, Franklin "conceived ... a more cordial and thorough Contempt for him than I ever before felt for any Man living."[34] Penn, meanwhile, was determined never again to talk to Franklin about anything.[35]

Despite the lack of progress, Franklin stayed. He wanted to see a bit of England, and he adored the attention he was getting as an accomplished scientist. Meanwhile, he grew fond of the 18-year-old Polly Stevenson, the daughter of his landlady. Polly was one of a number of women, young and old, whom he befriended during his married life. He flirted with older women, charmed younger women, and corresponded with both in letters that were playful and flattering. Whether any of these relationships went beyond banter to something physical, we don't know.[36] With Polly, Franklin's affection was especially strong and lasting. She seemed to be more of a daughter to him than the one he left behind in America. He would later write long letters to Polly touching on many topics, including science, explaining to her, for example, how barometers work and how the moon affects tides. Polly would eventually marry, have three children, and become widowed. But she and Franklin never lost touch. Thirty-three years after meeting Franklin, she would be at his bedside when he died.[37]

Eventually, as Franklin stayed on in England, the Penns budged ever so slightly about taxes. They vaguely conceded that they might, after all, pay a little. However, in settling this matter they would not deal with Franklin. Again, it seemed time was up for Franklin in England. But with the consent of his allies in the Pennsylvania Assembly, he stayed on and continued to battle the Penns. His aim was to have Parliament strip control of Pennsylvania from the Penns and bring the colony under closer royal control. Thus, Franklin was at this time an ardent Loyalist toiling to bring Pennsylvania snugly under Parliament's authority. In the end, some compromises were found and Parliament did not take Pennsylvania away from the Penns. Franklin's mission was over.

But still he lingered. He hobnobbed with David Hume, the great philosopher. On a visit to Scotland, he received an honorary doctorate from the University of St. Andrews, and from then on was often called "Dr. Franklin." He also visited Holland and Flanders. He attended the coronation of King George III;[38] he was fully and loyally British in spirit, passionately supportive of a completely British North America, and as unlikely a revolutionary as could be imagined. In answer to the argument that the American colonies, if allowed to grow, would become a danger to Britain, Franklin responded that such an event could never happen:

> If they could not agree to unite for their defence against the French and Indians, who were perpetually harassing their settlements, burning their villages, and murdering their people; can it reasonably be supposed there is any danger of their uniting against their own nation, which protects and encourages them, with which they have so many connections and ties of blood, interest and affection, and which 'tis well known they all love much more than they love one another? In short, there are so many causes that must operate to prevent it, that I will venture to say, an union amongst them for such a purpose is not merely improbable, it is impossible.[39]

Finally, reluctantly, Franklin, in his mid-fifties, sailed back to America in 1762, fully expecting to return again to England to live out his life if he could "prevail with Mrs. F."[40] As it happened, Franklin sailed off to America just days before two momentous events in England in the life of his son—his wedding and a visit to St. James's Palace to receive his royal commission as royal governor of New Jersey.[41] Oddly, Franklin missed both events.

Back in America, he traveled. Inspecting postal operations was part of his job.[42] But it was also fun for the ever-curious wanderer. He also became re-engaged in Pennsylvania politics. He took a key role in rallying opposition to frontiersmen who were slaughtering peaceful indigenous people and threatening white people who sheltered them. The squabble with the Penn family resumed and once again Franklin geared up to get Parliament to snatch the colony from them and take direct control. However, others were not sure this was the right approach. Even Franklin's allies, on both sides of the ocean, were cool to the idea.

Franklin forged ahead. He had enough muscle in the Pennsylvania Assembly to push through resolutions asking that the Penn family be stripped of power over the colony. About this time, Franklin began to lock horns with John Dickinson. Dickinson was not happy with the Penns, but he saw, as others did, that governors and officials sent over by the king and Parliament might be worse than those under the Penns. In a vicious election battle, Franklin lost his seat in the Assembly. Nevertheless, his allies still had enough power to pass a petition against the Penns. Someone was needed to take this petition to England and present it to ministers. Why not Franklin? A terrible choice, said Dickinson and others. But Franklin was delighted. Alas, Deborah refused again to go with him, and neither would she allow their daughter to go.[43] So off he sailed. Franklin thought he would be gone for a few months, but it would be years, and he would never see his wife again.

Back in London in his familiar lodgings, with his friendly landlady and her charming daughter, Franklin was as convinced as ever that what was best for Pennsylvania was tighter royal control. While other Americans were starting to doubt the wisdom of royal authority, Franklin sought to strengthen it. He was also out of touch with American attitudes on taxation. He couldn't fathom at first the anger in America during the Stamp Act crisis. Franklin's reputation in America took a beating as he was suspected of profiting from the act. In Philadelphia, mobs threatened the new Franklin house. There was even talk Franklin might be hanged in effigy.[44]

Meanwhile, Franklin, as the most eminent American in London, was the man Britons turned to for answers about the Stamp Act fuss. In testimony before the House of Commons, Franklin shored up his tattered reputation among Americans by stoutly defending American opposition. His performance was so brilliant that some Americans later gave Franklin credit for the act's repeal.[45]

By this time, in the mid-1760s, Franklin was convinced that Parliament had no business meddling in American affairs. But he was still a half-step behind public opinion in America. Franklin still believed America's place was firmly in the British Empire.[46]

But even as Franklin failed to keep pace with the rapid changes in American public opinion, he remained in England as effectively the voice of America. Dozens of articles from his pen appeared in the British press. He tried to see all issues from both the British and American sides, which helped make him appear too American to the English and too English to Americans.[47]

Meanwhile, he kept putting off his return to America, despite pleas from his wife and lack of any progress on his original mission to change the status of the Pennsylvania colony. He loved England and his comfortable life in London. He confessed in 1773: "I begin to fear, that when I return, I shall find myself a Stranger in my own Country; and leaving so many Friends here, it will seem leaving Home to go there."[48]

While staying on in England, he served as agent—essentially a lobbyist—for not only Pennsylvania, but also Massachusetts, New Jersey, and Georgia.[49] As time went on, and as relations between America and Britain turned frigid, Franklin found himself less and less effective. British officials didn't want to hear from him. Changes in the British government gave him hope that his voice would once again be heard, but Franklin himself destroyed those hopes with a stupendous blunder.

It all began with a scandal that blew up in Boston in 1773 with the publication of various letters written years before. These included letters of Thomas Hutchinson, the royal governor of Massachusetts, when he was lieutenant governor. In the letters, Hutchinson seemed to recommend an "abridgement" of "English liberties" in America.[50] Hutchinson, once revered in Massachusetts, had seen his popularity plummet as one crisis led to another. With the publication of these letters, what popularity was left vanished. The letters confirmed to Bostonians, touchy about their liberties and suspicious of their governor, that Hutchinson had long been plotting with British officials to strip Americans of their cherished rights. The outraged Massachusetts House of Representatives sent off a demand to London that Hutchinson and the lieutenant governor be yanked from office.[51]

When news of the letters reached London, attention focused not on Hutchinson's behavior, but on the question of how these private letters became public. People pointed fingers; rumors flew. Who would be so dishonorable as to circulate such letters? Accusations even led to a duel in December 1773 and the wounding of one of the duelists. To prevent another duel, Franklin stepped up to publicly confess that he had obtained the letters and sent them to America. Londoners gasped.

Franklin's standing in London plunged lower than Hutchinson's in Boston. How could Franklin commit such a despicable act? According to Franklin, he had received the letters from a "Gentleman of Character and Distinction"[52] to this day, no one knows for sure who it was. Franklin knew that by sending off the letters to America he was putting his reputation at risk. But he thought it was worth it for the sake of repairing the British–American relationship. He hoped that the letters might only be circulated in Boston among leading radicals to convince them that their troubles were chiefly the fault of such people as Hutchinson, working in America, and not of officials in London, who were actually reasonable and well-meaning, but misinformed. He thought the letters would calm the Boston radicals.

Franklin was as wrong as a man could be. The Boston radicals were never going to keep these letters secret, nor were they inclined to suddenly believe, because of the letters, that decision-makers in London were not actually blockheads.

Then news of the Boston Tea Party reached England, and anger at America and Franklin boiled over. The Privy Council scheduled a meeting for January 29, 1774, ostensibly to review the request from Massachusetts to remove Hutchinson and the lieutenant governor. But this meeting, in Whitehall's "Cockpit"—a large hall with a gallery crammed with spectators—had little to do with Hutchinson and everything to do with Franklin. For almost an hour, Franklin stood in silence, his face expressionless, as Britain's solicitor general, amid cheers and laughter, raked over the American in words too shocking for contemporary newspapers to print. He charged that Franklin, not Hutchinson, was the man most responsible for the troubles in Massachusetts. Franklin was also said to be a thief and unworthy of respect. Of course, the Privy Council kicked aside the impertinent petition from Massachusetts, and just as obviously, the British government soon fired Franklin from his post as deputy postmaster general for North America.[53]

This humiliation was surely the tipping point that turned Franklin from a Loyalist to a rebel. He must have been ready now to return to America and cast his lot with the emerging Patriot cause. But he lingered on in England, groping for a way to turn back time and cultivate the old harmony between America and Britain. He offered to reach into his pocket and pay for the tea dumped in Boston Harbor, and pleaded for Parliament to refrain from punishing Boston and Massachusetts. He was hopeful that the measures from the First Continental Congress, especially those stopping the imports of British goods into America, would bring Parliament around. And indeed, on the first anniversary of his public shellacking in the Cockpit, he was deep into secret talks on a plan for reconciliation between America and Britain. But then the plan was read in the House of Lords, where the lords received it, according to Franklin, "with as much Contempt as they could have shown a Ballad offered by a drunken Porter."[54]

This may have been the final straw. The lords, these "Hereditary Legislators!," were not qualified "to govern a Herd of Swine." Angry, and maybe "a little out of his senses," according to a friend, he would no longer in his heart be both American and English. He was choosing sides—the American one. He sailed for America in March 1775, about a month before Lexington and Concord. He knew that Deborah would not be waiting in Philadelphia to welcome him, having by this time received word that she was dead. Did he feel guilt, heartbreak, loss, or anything when he learned that news? We don't know. Historians find no mention of her in Franklin's letters of this time. Curiously, there are no letters from friends or relatives that extend sympathy or even mention Deborah's death.[55]

Franklin arrived in Philadelphia in early May, a few weeks after Lexington and Concord. Accompanying him was William Temple Franklin, the 15-year-old illegitimate son of his own illegitimate son.[56] The family called him Temple. Franklin barely had time to move into his Market Street home when the Pennsylvania Assembly picked him as a delegate to the Second Continental Congress.

So the famous Dr. Franklin joined the Congress. Not everyone was impressed. There were lingering doubts that Franklin, with all his years in England, with his inclination toward compromise and getting along, with his tepid patriotism over the years, was truly willing to take a firm stand against British authorities; and everyone knew that Franklin's son, William, was the royal governor of New Jersey.

Franklin invited suspicions when, soon after his arrival, he visited Joseph Galloway, his old ally. That spring, he, William Franklin, and Galloway dined together at Galloway's estate in Bucks County. Franklin brought along his grandson, Temple, who was seeing his father, William, for the first time since William had left Temple as an infant in foster care in London. Franklin and son William, meanwhile, were meeting for the first time in 10 years.[57]

Galloway later recalled that there at Galloway's estate, "as the glass had gone about freely," the senior Franklin had "at a late hour, opened himself, and declared himself in favor of measures attaining to independence."[58]

Benjamin Franklin had changed, but it would take a while for delegates in Philadelphia to recognize just how much. Perhaps to convince them, Franklin later composed a letter to an old London friend, William Strahan, and then showed it around:[59]

> Mr. Strahan,
> You are a Member of Parliament, and one of that Majority which has doomed my Country to Destruction. You have begun to burn our Towns, and murder our People. Look upon your Hands! They are stained with the blood of your Relations! You and I were long Friends: You are now my Enemy, and I am, Yours,
> B. Franklin.[60]

But the wily Franklin never sent the letter, and he and Strahan remained fast friends. Upon Franklin's arrival in Paris the following year, Strahan shipped over from London a gift of Stilton cheese.[61]

We suspect that many of Franklin's American contemporaries assumed the old man had little to offer Congress. His efforts in England—regarding the problems between Pennsylvania and the Penns, and those of the American colonies as a whole and Britain—had produced nothing but failure. Did he now have the energy to contribute in a meaningful way? John Adams, for one, doubted it. Years later, Adams recalled Franklin "day to day sitting in silence, a great part of his time fast asleep in his chair."[62]

Franklin would remain more of a dozing listener than a speechmaker, but he was awake enough to know very well what was going on. Adams later drew a fuller portrait of the venerable printer and scientist:

> His Conduct has been composed and grave and in the Opinion of many Gentlemen very reserved. He has not assumed any Thing, nor affected to take the lead; but has seemed to choose that the Congress should pursue their own Principles and sentiments and adopt their own Plans: Yet he has not been backward: has been very usefull, on many occasions, and discovered a Disposition entirely American. He does not hesitate at our boldest Measures, but rather seems to think us, too irresolute, and backward.[63]

CHAPTER 7

The Great Jehovah and the Continental Congress

The Second Continental Congress looked much like the First. Of the 65 delegates to the Second Congress, 50 had been part of the earlier gathering. Among those missing from the Second Continental Congress was Galloway,[1] the moderate who had tried so hard to steer the First Congress off its collision course with Britain. The Pennsylvania Assembly picked Galloway to serve in the Second Congress, but he begged to be excused.[2] He would eventually cast his lot as a Loyalist, leaving fewer voices of caution at the Second Congress. Still, however, independence was for the moment not on the table. Delegates were faced with an awkward contradiction: fighting a war with Britain while groping for some kind of reconciliation.

As with the First Congress, most delegates arrived in Philadelphia with instructions from their respective colonies. Those guidelines were by and large less detailed than those for the First Congress. Indeed, Virginia sent no instructions at all. Instructions to New Hampshire delegates, meanwhile, were succinct: "to consent and Agree to all Measures, which said Congress shall deem necessary to Obtain redress of American Grievances."[3]

There was nothing about independence, not even from Massachusetts, whose delegates were advised to work toward measures "calculated for the recovery and establishment of American rights and liberties, and for restoring harmony between Great Britain and the colonies."[4] Rhode Island, besides calling for the placement of American rights "on a just and solid foundation,"[5] looked ahead to making the Congress a permanent fixture. The colony told its delegates to work toward an annual meeting of colonial representatives "for the Promotion and Establishment of the Peace Welfare and Security" of the colonies.[6]

Connecticut's Deane, staggered by the scope of Congress's tasks, wrote to his wife: "The scenes before us are so vast, That I can give no kind of Judgement as to the Term We Shall be detained here, and I tremble when I think of their vast importance."[7]

New York's James Duane was no less awestruck: "The eyes of Europe and America are fixed on this Assembly, and the fate of one of the greatest empires on earth, in no small degree depends on the issue of their deliberations."[8]

The Congress came together on May 10, and as in the First Congress, Peyton Randolph was chosen as president, with Charles Thomson again named secretary. This Congress would also have the services of an assigned doorkeeper, a messenger, and a clerk.[9]

It might have been prudent at this moment for delegates to take a long look at their procedures and possibly limit debate or streamline decision-making. After all, the situation for the Second Continental Congress, as it began its work, was much more complicated than that of the First. The First Congress had one job—to come up with a unified response to the crisis in Boston. The Second Congress, as everyone could see from day one, would have myriad issues to deal with, starting with conducting a war, organizing an army, designating military leadership, and financing the conflict while still searching for a path toward reconciliation with Britain. The issues would come at delegates like an avalanche.

However, fearful of any procedures that might limit debate, and thus possibly produce friction and dissent, delegates adopted the same rules for discussion, thereby permitting talk to run on and on. Voting procedures likewise would be the same—with each colony, no matter its population or the number of delegates, casting one vote.[10]

As in the First Congress, its proceedings were to be secret. Once again, Rev. Jacob Duché, who so moved delegates to the First Congress, "made a most pathetic, & pertinent prayer."[11]

Congress soon dug into a bundle of depositions documenting events at Lexington and Concord sent by the revolutionary Provincial Congress of Massachusetts, the rebel assembly that had emerged before Lexington and Concord from the turmoil between the royally appointed governor and the popularly elected House of Representatives. The Representatives, meeting in defiance of the governor's orders, had recast their body as the Provincial Congress and easily assumed command of the countryside.

These documents were first-hand accounts from militiamen and witnesses on the American side, but also from some British soldiers, such as one wounded at Concord Bridge and now "treated with the greatest Humanity ... by the provincials at Medford." Others deposed included terrorized civilians in the path of the Redcoats, such as Hannah Bradish, of Cambridge, who, "being in her bed-chamber, with her infant child, about eight days old, ... was surprised by the firing of the king's troops and our people, on their return from Concord."[12] At least 70 bullets were fired into the front of the family's house. She and the family had cowered in the kitchen while British soldiers rampaged through the residence. The troops took with them "one rich brocade gown, called a negligée, one lutestring gown, one white quilt, one pair of brocade shoes, three shifts, eight white aprons, three caps, one case of ivory knives and forks, and several other small articles."[13]

The Provincial Congress sent with the depositions a plea for an American army and a request for the "direction and assistance of your respectable Assembly."[14]

The rebel leaders at the Provincial Congress meeting in Watertown near Boston walked a tightrope. Now, the Provincial Congress effectively ruled Massachusetts, except for Boston. However, it was hardly a government. There was no functioning court system, no governor, and no second legislative house.

The Massachusetts Provincial Congress could have taken the initiative and put in place a full-fledged government on its own. But such bold action, besides further enraging British authorities, would have horrified the Continental Congress, still looking to mend ties with Britain. Patriot leaders in Massachusetts knew, as did their delegates at the Continental Congress, that Massachusetts could not be alone in this quarrel. It had to have the support of the other colonies, and therefore the support of the Continental Congress.

Delegates in Philadelphia delved into the challenge of raising an army,[15] but soon bumped up against the obvious question: what, exactly, was their goal? John Rutledge of South Carolina asked: "[D]o we aim at independency? or do We only ask for a Restoration of Rights & putting of Us on Our old footing?"[16]

As delegates talked, new issues intruded. From New York, for example, came a request for guidance. According to rumors, shiploads of Redcoats would land any day. How should colonists respond?[17]

Congress answered with detailed advice. British troops, if they arrived, could remain in their barracks "so long as they behave peaceably and quietly, but that they be not suffered to erect fortifications or take any steps for cutting off communication between town and country." If troops misbehaved, "the inhabitants should defend themselves and their property and repel force by force." Meanwhile, all "warlike stores" should be carted out of town, women and children should be provided "places of retreat in case of necessity," and local men should be "kept in constant readiness for protecting the inhabitants from insult and injury."[18]

Later, on May 17, Congress called a halt to all exports to Quebec, Nova Scotia, "the Island of St. John's" (Prince Edward Island), Newfoundland, East and West Florida, and Georgia, except for the parish represented in Congress.[19]

The same day, despite the press of business, delegates took time to attend commencement exercises at the College of Philadelphia. Delegates proceeded "as a body" from the State House to the college, where they were "received at the gate by the Provost."[20] Newspaper accounts reported that the speaker received especially enthusiastic applause, his topic being "The Fall of Empires."[21] Eight scholars graduated.[22]

Congress still had taken no action regarding the bloody events in Massachusetts when, on May 18—eight days after first coming together—it received the astonishing news that New England militiamen had taken Ticonderoga, the British outpost in northern New York on Lake Champlain. Some 83 New England militiamen overwhelmed the sleepy troops stationed at the crumbling fort. Not a shot was fired; not a man was lost.[23] Militia leader Ethan Allen, in writing later about the assault, added a dramatic flourish. In Allen's telling, when he and his men rushed into the structure, a British lieutenant shouted a challenge, asking by what authority Allen and his men had entered the fort. Allen gave a stirring reply: "In the name of the Great Jehovah and the Continental Congress."[24]

It seems Allen said no such thing. Other men who were there heard nothing about Jehovah or Congress, but instead something more prosaic as the Patriot leader was flushing out the fort's commander: "Come out of there you goddam old rat."[25]

Presumably, God Almighty knew well in advance about plans to attack Ticonderoga, but Congress certainly did not. Indeed, delegates in Philadelphia would have scotched the assault. Despite the blood at Lexington and Concord, Congress abhorred any military action that looked like Patriot aggression. That made an unprovoked attack on a British outpost the worst possible course of action.

However, the deed had been done, so Congress made the best of it. The capture of Ticonderoga and, as Congress soon learned, two other nearby posts was, after all, a dazzling coup. Lake Champlain was part of the watery inland route linking the American colonies with Canada. If the British chose to invade the American colonies from the north, their path would take them past Fort Ticonderoga. Thus, at a stroke, a possible invasion along this route was made much more difficult. Furthermore, the capture of Ticonderoga wonderfully multiplied American military options. Ticonderoga could be a stepping-off point for an American invasion of Canada, although Congress denied contemplating any such thing. In a letter to Canadians approved in late May, Congress tried to be reassuring: "[T]hese colonies will pursue no measures whatever, but such as friendship and a regard for our mutual safety and interest may suggest."[26] Congress also passed a resolution asking that "no expedition or incursion ought to be undertaken or made, by any colony, or body of colonists, against or into Canada."[27]

Congress immediately made excuses for the attack on Ticonderoga, pointing to "indubitable evidence" that the British were planning a "cruel invasion" from Quebec. This was not entirely laughable. Months before, British authorities had ordered troops to be sent from the north to calm a dispute—unrelated to Lexington and Concord—in the region east of Lake Champlain. The orders were later rescinded, but could be reissued. Still, an imminent attack from the north was difficult to imagine. British Regulars in all of Canada numbered fewer than 700.[28] The fib was the best that Congress could do to justify the attack. Congress then ordered that the cannons and military stores at the fort be inventoried and kept safely, "in order that they may be safely returned when the restoration of the former harmony between Great Britain and these colonies so ardently wished for by the latter shall render it prudent and consistent with the overruling law of self preservation."[29]

Before the month was over, Congress would ask the governor of Connecticut (popularly elected and sympathetic to the Patriot cause) to send reinforcements to Ticonderoga and Crown Point, an outpost farther north, and to put in place a trusted commander. Why didn't Congress ask New York to reinforce the posts? After all, they were in New York, not Connecticut. The answer seems to be that Connecticut was reliably patriotic, whereas New York was not.

The victory at Ticonderoga created another niggling problem for Congress. Ethan Allen, the hero, was actually an outlaw, at least as far as New York was concerned. The story of Allen is intertwined with the story of the so-called New Hampshire Grants, lands directly to the west of New Hampshire, including the Green Mountains. We know this area as Vermont, but then it was part of New York, and still would be today but for a certain Benning Wentworth, New Hampshire's royal governor from 1741–66. New York's claim to the area stemmed from its 1664 charter.[30] New Hampshire had no charter until 1679, and that charter gave New Hampshire no authority over the region. But Wentworth ignored such details. With plenty of highly placed relatives, of whom one was the British prime minister, Wentworth figured he could make up his own rules in America. Starting in 1741, he serenely grabbed 70,000 acres of the best timberland in the region while carving up the land into townships. Over 15 years, Wentworth amassed a fortune in fees related to grants for almost three million acres—about one-third of what would become the state of Vermont.[31]

The people paying these fees were mainly from New England. They flooded into the region, which many New York investors claimed as theirs. Those investors were largely speculators, who leased land in the region to tenant farmers.[32] To those speculators, the New Englanders settling on grants authorized by New Hampshire were squatters. Authorities in New York squawked, and London was called upon to sort out the dispute. In 1750, New York and New Hampshire agreed to stop granting land until the question was sorted out. New York kept its word; New Hampshire did not, and still more New Englanders grabbed up land, despite the dubious titles.[33] A 1764 decision from London came down on the side of New York, but that didn't settle the issue because New Hampshire kept litigating. As British authorities studied the problem, and as New York attempted to assert its authority in the area, the settlers holding land with New Hampshire titles organized themselves, for they had everything at stake. If New York prevailed, the New Hampshire titles would be worthless, and they would lose their land and be ruined. They thus defied New York magistrates and drove off settlers who appeared with New York titles.[34]

The chief of the rebels defying New York was Allen. Born in Connecticut, Allen was past 30 when he, with four brothers,[35] arrived in the New Hampshire Grants around 1769, when the dispute between New Hampshire and New York was already hot.[36] Brash, impulsive, boastful, and bold, with a spotty résumé that included fierce quarrels and a trial for blasphemy, Allen had a commanding presence and soon became leader of the Green Mountain Boys, a band dedicated to defending the settlers against New York authorities and rival land claims. Allen and the Green Mountain Boys killed no one—or so Allen claimed—but they destroyed crops, burned houses, and intimidated through shows of force, showers of curses, and threats of hanging.[37]

Thus, as far as New York authorities were concerned, Allen and his Boys deserved to be hanged. But now Allen and his band, mostly on their own, had seized Ticonderoga for Congress. How should Congress deal with these outlaw Patriots? Congress conjured a transformation: the outlaws became a recognized militia force, and under the authority of New York, no less.

Allen and his followers agreed to this arrangement. They wanted to prove they were Patriots, but they also wanted to squelch rumors that they were plotting to hold Ticonderoga hostage and trade it for a deal favorable to settlers defying New York.[38] Allen embraced the new relationship with "fond hopes for reconciliation"[39] between New York and the settlers.

***

Amid the crush of work, some delegates toyed with the idea of packing up Congress and resuming work in Connecticut, thinking they might be better informed and quicker to act if they were closer to the scene of the crisis.[40] This idea never gained traction. Perhaps a May letter from a Connecticut lawmaker to Deane killed the notion: "[Y]ou would have too many questions referred to you and too much business cast upon you by the New England colonies, to leave you the leisure you ought to have to digest and perfect matters of greater importance."[41]

On May 24, Congress paused to choose a new president to take the place of Randolph, called back to Virginia to attend the House of Burgesses, where he was speaker. Delegates chose Middleton of South Carolina, the same man who filled in for Randolph at the previous Congress. But he declined, citing poor health. Delegates then turned to Hancock of Massachusetts, who would remain in that post for more than two years.

By late May, more than a month after Lexington and Concord, Congress had been at work for several weeks but had yet to offer specific guidance for Massachusetts. What were delegates doing? Debates were secret, and letters from delegates reveal little except that they felt overwhelmed, weary, and sometimes ill. William Hooper of North Carolina wrote: "As we meet at 9 oClock in the morning and set till 4 in the Afternoon you will readily conceive that the little leisure we have is not sufficient for the common functions of life & exercise to keep us in health."[42] Delaware's George Read likewise lamented: "[T]here is but little entertaining at this Congress compared to the last."[43]

John Adams, who wrote so lovingly about feasts at the First Congress, didn't feel much like gorging at the Second. "I came from home Sick and have been so ever Since," wrote Adams. "My Eyes are So weak and dim, that I can neither read, write, or see without great Pain." Congress had too much to do, and Adams said everything took too much time: "Our unweildy Body moves very Slow ... Such a vast Multitude of Objects, civil, political, commercial and military press and croud upon Us So fast that We know not what to do first."[44]

Through these weeks, between interruptions, delegates continued debating about "the state of America." Dickinson, the esteemed Pennsylvania "Farmer," seized the floor with pleas for moderation, caution, humility, and a new petition to the king. Yes, he said, they should "procure Arms and Ammunition," take measures for the "Defence & Preservation of ourselves from the utter Destruction of our Lives and Liberties." But they should also "present an humble & dutiful petition to his Majesty." Dickinson, with such expressions as "beseeching his Majesty," "supplicate," and "Wisdom & Goodness of His Majesty and Parliament," proposed a message that seemed to be begging Britain's pardon.[45] Dickinson also wanted Congress to send a committee to Britain to negotiate.

Some delegates, such as John Adams, scoffed. A petition had been tried after the First Congress and the king brushed it aside. But Dickinson's petition would be different. It would take a softer approach. Instead of harping about American rights, it would emphasize "our Loyalty to the King—our Attachment to his person, Family and Government—our Love to our Parent State—our Desire to Preserve our usual Connection with her."[46]

Further, he proposed to wrap the petition in concessions, to give ground a little as an opening for negotiations. He suggested, for example, that Congress agree that Parliament had an unchallenged right to regulate American trade.[47] He or someone in the course of debates even brought up the possibility of paying for the tea steeping in Boston Harbor.[48]

Dickinson wanted to be certain that, before Congress led Americans off a cliff, it at least reached out one last time: "Let Us try every Method of avoiding Extremities, that when the Wheels of War shall begin to grind a little harder upon Us, People may not upbraid Us with having omitted proper applications for obtaining Peace."

A petition might work. And if it didn't, America would be no worse off: "If it produces no favourable Effect; the same Events must happen as if We had openly prepared for War."[49]

Deane described Dickinson's approach as "very timid."[50] But Dickinson's opinion carried weight. His was, after all, a long-respected voice of American discontent.

In the end, Congress agreed to petition the king and to allow negotiations of some kind. Congress, however, could not swallow Dickinson's idea of offering concessions. Congress put Dickinson on the committee to draw up the petition, but that would mainly rehash the demands of the petition drawn up the previous year.[51]

On the same day that Congress passed the resolutions on preparing "an humble and dutiful"[52] petition to the king, and for "opening a Negotiation"[53] with Great Britain, it also called for the colonies in general to make defensive preparations.

June began, and still the Continental Congress had yet to address the crisis in Massachusetts, where bands of New England militiamen, loosely overseen by the Provincial Congress in Watertown, bottled up British Redcoats in Boston. Now, in early June, came more communications from the Massachusetts Provincial Congress.

Of course, Patriot leaders in Massachusetts were fearful of British troops crowding Boston. But they were just as afraid of their own motley American force defending the countryside, a force that, without proper supply and control, could quickly mutate into roving gangs of armed and hungry thieves. No firm legitimate civilian government was in place to properly keep the military in line and to ensure order and security. In his letter to the Continental Congress, the president of the Massachusetts Provincial Congress, Joseph Warren, wrote: "[W]e tremble at having an army (although composed of our own countrymen) established here, without civil power to provide for and controul them."[54]

The Massachusetts Congress asked for guidance about setting up a civilian government: "We … humbly hope you will favor us with your most explicit advice, respecting the taking up and exercising the powers of civil government … and we shall readily submit to a general plan as you may direct for the colonies."[55]

The Massachusetts Congress also pleaded for the Continental Congress to take over the ragtag soldiers: "As the army, collecting from different colonies, is for the general defence of the rights of America, we wd. beg leave to suggest to yr. consideration, the propriety of yr. taking the regulation and general direction of it."[56]

Both issues put delegates in Philadelphia on the spot. In the vacuum left by the collapse of British authority, Massachusetts Patriot leaders needed to establish a responsible civilian government, and they needed a reliable and strong army—not a Massachusetts or a New England army, but an American army—to keep the British at bay. How could the Continental Congress give the Massachusetts Patriots the answers they wanted without dashing forever chances of reconciliation with Britain?

Congress was still tongue-tied, unable to agree on a response. Delegates seemed to be marching off one minute toward war and the next toward reconciliation. Delegates set up a committee to figure out how to borrow money to buy gunpowder for the "Continental Army," an army that had yet to be formally established. That same day, Congress named the committee to draft the petition to the king.[57]

Outside the Pennsylvania State House, the martial mood was evident. Connecticut's Eliphalet Dyer witnessed a "grand review of the Militia in this City." The 2,000 or so militiamen included "one Compleat Quaker Company their Uniform light blue lapelled &c with white who were exceeded by none in dress or exactness of discipline." He continued: "Military spirit runs full as high in this Country as in New England & all seem determined to stand or fall with us."[58]

On June 9, Congress gave Massachusetts guidance about governing: pretend the governor is absent. Congress advised Massachusetts to hold an election to choose representatives. Those elected representatives would then appoint councilors who would work with them to govern—without a governor—"until a Governor, of his Majesty's appointment will consent to govern the colony according to its charter."[59] Thus, Congress clung to the notion that the rebellion in Massachusetts was not against the king at all, but against his appointed governor, who was acting illegally.

On the heels of that response, Congress sent a plea to New York to send 5,000 barrels of flour to the hungry Patriot army encamped around Boston.[60] In the following days, Congress generated resolutions to address the critical shortage of gunpowder: New England colonies and towns were "earnestly recommended" to send as much powder as they could spare to "the American army before Boston." Americans elsewhere were called upon to collect "salt petre and brimstone"—ingredients of gunpowder—and put powder mills in working order.[61]

Those resolutions were soon followed by a call for a day in July of "public humiliation, fasting and prayer," to give Americans the opportunity to "offer up our joint supplications to the all-wise, omnipotent and merciful Disposer of all events" in order to, among other things, "bless our rightful sovereign, King George the third, and [to] inspire him with wisdom to discern and pursue the true interests of all his subjects."[62]

On June 14, Congress took a crucial step in making New England's war an American war: delegates resolved that companies of "expert riflemen" be raised in Pennsylvania, Virginia, and Maryland and dispatched to the Patriot army outside Boston. Pay was specified, ranging from $20 per month for captains to $6⅔ per month for privates. Volunteers were required to "find their own arms and cloaths."[63] Everyone understood the term "dollars" to mean Spanish dollars, silver coins minted by the Spanish government. These silver coins were the accepted international currency of the day. No mention was made of how exactly Congress was going to come up with those dollars—Congress had no money and no authority to collect it through taxes.

The next day, delegates finally answered Massachusetts's plea to take command of the army around Boston. The choice of commander went surprisingly quickly. Candidates included Charles Lee, a former British officer who had settled in Virginia in 1773. With military experience going back to his boyhood, he had fought in the French and Indian War in America and in various conflicts on battlefields in Europe. He had also been an outspoken supporter of the Patriot cause. He fearlessly insulted the king in pamphlets he wrote back in England. British observers in London, speculating on who would lead the rebel forces, guessed that Lee would be Congress's choice.[64] Meanwhile, Lee wasn't shy about promoting himself for the job. He had worked hard at convincing anyone who would listen that he was an ardent Patriot with ample military skills.

He was also, however, an oddball. He was indifferent to cleanliness, preferred dogs to people, tended toward slovenly dress, and habitually cursed and bragged. While amusing and fascinating to some,[65] to many others his behavior and habits were irksome.

Another even more obvious candidate was Artemis Ward, a storekeeper in civilian life who was the current commander of Patriot forces near Boston. To Lee, with his battlefield credentials, Ward was just an "old church-warden"[66] and laughably in over his head. Ward, nonetheless, was managing well enough, and it was just common sense to have a New Englander in charge of a force made up mainly of New England men.

However, delegates bypassed these two men and chose one of their own as commander of "all American forces, raised, or to be raised, for defense of American liberty."[67]

He was George Washington, age 42, a delegate from Virginia. He had, according to Deane, a "very young look and an easy soldierlike air and gesture." When Washington spoke, wrote Deane, it was "very modestly and in cool but determined style and accent."[68]

CHAPTER 8

No Harum Starum Ranting Swearing Fellow

Washington was famous in both America and Europe well before he arrived as a delegate from Virginia to the First Continental Congress the previous fall. He had a starring role some 20 years before in starting what some have described as the first ever world war[1]—the sprawling conflict comprising the French and Indian War in North America and the Seven Years' War in Europe. To many French back in 1754, Washington was a war criminal. To one British politician, the young man had merely fired the volley that "set the world on fire."[2]

Born into wealth in the Chesapeake region of Virginia, Washington was on track for a comfortable career as a planter until a fever took his father's life when George was only 11.[3] With that death, George's prospects seemed to melt away. As the third son, he inherited just a small farm. With a solid formal education out of reach, it appeared he would never be wealthy or important.

He remained, however, determined to rise into the world of his half brother Lawrence, who had married into a powerful Virginia family, was elected to the colonial assembly, and mingled with the rich, influential, genteel cream of Virginia society. George took dancing lessons,

This portrait by Charles Willson Peale shows George Washington as a colonel in the Virginia Regiment in 1772. Because of his noteworthy but controversial action fighting for the British in the French and Indian War, Washington was already famous on both sides of the Atlantic before he appeared as a delegate to the First Continental Congress. He returned to Philadelphia as a delegate to the Second Continental Congress, where he was appointed commander in chief of the new Continental Army. (Image courtesy of the Museums at Washington and Lee University) practiced fencing, studied etiquette, and resolved to model his conduct on that of the refined men and women he observed. As a teenager, he learned surveying, a skill that paid well. For five years,[4] he tramped the hills and forests of western Virginia with his instruments. He developed a sturdy body toughened by life in the outdoors. He grew tall, rising to 6 feet 4 inches, about 9 inches taller than the average American man at this time.[5]

Seeking adventure, craving respect, and envisioning a career as a soldier, 21-year-old Washington eagerly agreed in 1753 to lead a party of six into the western Pennsylvania wilderness in a region claimed by both Britain and France. His mission, as Major Washington, was to deliver a message to the French commander in the disputed Ohio Country. The message was from the British royal governor of Virginia, who was aggressively defending both British interests on the frontier and his own interests as a land speculator.[6]

The mission was a harrowing one. Washington was shot at and nearly drowned. But he delivered the message and returned with an answer. The message to the French was: get out. The answer was: *non*. With that reply, the governor—without orders from his superiors in London[7]—geared up for war.

Washington then won a spot as second in command of a regiment of Virginians. Its mission was to march into the Pennsylvania wilderness and establish a fort on the Ohio River. If the French interfered, or were there first, Washington, now a lieutenant colonel,[8] had orders to "kill & destroy them."[9] Virginia would take on the French virtually alone, with no authorization from London, and little help from the other colonies. Washington's superior on this mission was a former mathematics professor in his mid-fifties.[10] The men below Washington were mainly "loose, Idle Persons that are quite destitute of House, and Home and I may truly say many of them of Cloaths."[11] The expedition did not go well.

After leading some 150 men to within about 40 miles of the site of the planned fort, and with his commander well to the rear, Washington learned that some French soldiers were nearby. Washington and 47 men set out to find the French. Joining the mission was a band of 13 Mingo tribesmen led by Tanaghrisson (known as the Half King), who fiercely hated the French. No wonder: they had killed, cooked, and eaten his father, so he claimed.[12]

Washington's force moved quietly through the woods and found the French encampment, with about the same number of men, in a low-lying glen. The French were caught off guard. After a few volleys, they pleaded for a ceasefire. The lopsided skirmish was over in 15 minutes.[13]

Exactly what happened next has long been disputed. According to one version, the French commander attempted to read out a message to the British demanding they clear out of this disputed territory. But as he was reading, Tanaghrisson stepped up, drove a hatchet into the Frenchman's skull, and then "took out his Brains and washed his Hands with them."[14] A massacre followed as the Mingos fell on the wounded French, while Washington, apparently, stood by. By the time Washington asserted control, 13 or so Frenchmen were dead.[15]

Later, after his superior fell off his horse and died, Washington found himself in sole command. Washington had his men cobble together a fort, Fort Necessity, and waited for reinforcements. Some fresh supplies and more men did arrive, but the supplies didn't last and some of the new arrivals came with a captain who, unlike Washington, had a royal commission and scoffed at the notion of taking orders from the young Virginian. Meanwhile, Tanaghrisson and most of his followers vanished.

This left a poorly supplied, ragged, and ill-trained band of Americans, uncertain of who was in charge, occupying a flimsy fort, in the pouring rain, fighting on behalf of the British, and now facing a much larger French force.

The French attacked, firing down from hillsides and protected by trees. The American muskets, soaked in the downpour, couldn't shoot back. As order evaporated, men abandoned their posts and looted the fort's rum supply. As darkness fell, half the Americans were drunk.[16] A slaughter seemed inevitable.

However, the French unexpectedly offered an honorable surrender. Washington signed the terms of capitulation. This spared his men, but it was also a diplomatic blunder, for the terms—in French—blamed Washington for the earlier "assassination" of the surrendering French commander. Washington, who could not read French, later blamed his interpreter,[17] a Dutchman whose command of both French and English may have been spotty. Whatever the truth, the deed was done. Washington's signature was on the paper and the French would exploit it to blame Britain, by this act of murder, for starting the French and Indian War.[18]

With the surrender, the French allowed Washington and his men to go, and the remnants of his force stumbled back east, the mission a military failure and a diplomatic disaster.

Back in Williamsburg, Washington faced criticism at first for both the battlefield defeat and the shameful capitulation. But that initial slap soon gave way to praise after the full story of the events in the Pennsylvania wilderness became known. The Virginia House of Burgesses honored him for his bravery.[19]

Washington said farewell to the military. The terror; the gore; the wretched cold, damp, and smoky camps: these were reasons enough to quit. But those were not his. Rather, he was offended that, under the proposed command structure, he would be demoted. That, he could not abide. He still ached for a military career, ordering from London a fine uniform with a crimson sash, gilt buttons, gold lace, and embroidered loops.[20]

Perhaps spurred by his sartorial splendor, Washington was back in the military within a year after the disaster at Fort Necessity. He was now an aide to the British Major General Edward Braddock, assigned to clear the French out of the Ohio Valley. But Braddock, having gone to the trouble of putting the young Virginian by his side, ignored Washington's advice and warnings. Travel light, Washington had suggested, for the terrain was hilly and roads were awful, if they existed at all. He also advised to be wary of how the French and indigenous people had shrewdly adapted to the conditions of the frontier. But the general was hard-headed and condescending to colonials.[21] Braddock and his wagons of artillery and barrels of grain lumbered confidently along, thinking that superior numbers and brute force would scatter the indigenous people and humiliate the French.

The journey west was torment for Washington. His usually sturdy constitution surrendered to a vicious bout of dysentery, with diarrhea and hemorrhoids.[22] Riding was too painful, and he had to be carried in a wagon.

As Washington feared, the first real encounter with the French and their indigenous allies proved catastrophic. The indigenous fighters, shooting from behind trees, picked off officers and produced panic and confusion.[23] Weak, but well enough, Washington was in the thick of the fighting in Braddock's disastrous battle with the French and indigenous fighters. Washington performed boldly and courageously—two horses were shot from under him, and four bullets ripped through his hat and uniform.[24]

The bloodshed was appalling: about 1,000 casualties, many by British soldiers firing on their comrades in the confusion. The fallen included Braddock himself. By comparison, French and indigenous casualties came to just 23 dead and 16 wounded.[25]

Washington emerged from this misadventure with his reputation intact, indeed enhanced. A minister lauded the courage and conduct of this "heroic youth," whom "I cannot but hope Providence has hitherto preserved in so signal a manner, for some important service to his country."[26] In August 1755, the 23-year-old found himself chief of all of Virginia's military forces. To look the part, he accessorized—an order went to London for suitable ruffles, stockings, and gold and scarlet trim for his uniform.[27]

As commander, he applied harsh discipline. He decreed a punishment of 25 lashes for swearing.[28] For other infractions, a penalty of 600 lashes was common.[29] For desertion, he might order 1,000 or 1,500 lashes, or hanging. Meanwhile, he also dabbled in politics, running for a seat in the House of Burgesses. But in a field of three candidates, he finished a distant third.[30]

The chief military crisis that Washington faced was the destruction of settlements by indigenous people on the frontier. The problem was widespread, and Washington did not have the manpower to deal with it. His longed for "a union to the colonys in this time of eminent danger."[31]

Meanwhile, even as Washington admired and emulated British military customs and manners, he was becoming infuriated at how he and his Virginians were condemned to inferior status in perpetuity because they were colonials. His men, he felt, deserved to be part of the British Army: "We cant conceive, that being Americans shoud deprive us of the benefits of British Subjects; nor lessen our claim to preferment."[32]

Discouraged by his military prospects and then alarmed and weakened by a new bout of dysentery, Washington retreated to Mount Vernon, his estate on the Potomac, and contemplated a more settled life. He courted the wealthy 26-year-old widow, Martha Dandridge Custis, who was eight months older than he was and had two small children. Washington knew well that by marrying Martha Custis, he would gain control over more land. With the addition of her 85 slaves, the size of his workforce would double. He would vault to the crest of Virginia society.

Alas, Martha was not his first choice. He had had an infatuation with another woman, Sally Fairfax, but she was another man's wife and the man was his friend. For Washington, honor eclipsed passion, and so as he wooed Martha, he snipped the ardent—but apparently chaste—liaison with Sally, who remained friends with George and became a dear friend to Martha.[33]

In 1758, Washington tried again for a seat in the House of Burgesses. To persuade voters, his campaigners served 34 gallons of wine and 13 gallons of beer, as well as brandy, cider, and rum punch. This time, of 397 votes cast, Washington received 309.[34]

Washington was not done with soldiering. The newly elected—but still unmarried—lawmaker joined yet another military expedition in the western wilderness. This time, as an officer in charge of a brigade, he and his men—at twilight, in the woods, enveloped by a fog of musket smoke—were fired on inadvertently by fellow Virginians. The expedition in the end was a success, but there was little glory. The French, abandoned by their indigenous allies, chose to cut and run. They destroyed their own fort and fled before the British arrived. The British captured a smoldering ruin and on it built Fort Pitt, on the site of modern-day Pittsburgh.[35]

With the end of the campaign, and yet another setback to his health—probably dysentery—Washington resigned. But before letting him return to Martha, Mount Vernon, and civilian life, 27 officers honored him with a stirring farewell message extolling his "steady adherence to impartial Justice" and his "quick Discernment and invariable Regard to Merit." The officers lamented "the loss of such an excellent Commander, such a sincere Friend, and so affable a Companion. How rare is it to find those amiable Qualifications blended together in one Man?"[36]

In early 1759,[37] Martha Custis and George Washington married, and Washington, not yet 27, thus glided into the role of a rich tobacco planter. That meant a lavish lifestyle. Washington, like other wealthy planters with plenty of land but little cash, went into debt to merchants in London. This weighed on Washington, who frequently complained about being overcharged for shoddy goods, and rankled as yet another gripe against the mother country.

Owning enslaved people troubled Washington—he rarely used the term "slaves," preferring "servants," "Negroes," "my people," or "my family." He would never break up a slave family. He also showed sincere respect for certain slaves. He put them in charge of three of his five farms and allowed some to have firearms for hunting.[38] Still, whatever his humane instincts, Washington remained a slave owner to the end of his life. As a later visitor said of Mount Vernon: "The negroes are not treated as blacks in general are in this Country, they are clothed and fed as well as any labouring people whatever and are not subject to the lash of a dominating overseer—but still they are slaves."[39]

Washington ran again for the House of Burgesses, this time using a bit of trickery to get a competitive edge. At that time and place, there were no secret ballots—voters announced their preferred candidate. Washington knew he could create a bandwagon effect by getting his supporters first to the polls. The strategy paid off and he won.[40]

Into the 1760s, Washington's frustration with Britain grew. Like most other Americans, he damned the Stamp Act. Meanwhile, he continued to groan under his debts. Low tobacco prices didn't help, and he finally abandoned the crop altogether by 1766, shifting to such alternatives as wheat and corn, and making Mount Vernon less dependent on trade with London. He fostered an array of money-making schemes. For example, he developed a plan to harvest fish from the Potomac, salt them, stuff them in barrels, and sell them for shipment to the West Indies. But this plan, like others, bumped up against stifling government regulations. The best salt for this purpose came from Lisbon, but the rules dictated from London said he had to obtain inferior salt from Liverpool.[41] Here was yet another annoyance dictated from above.

Until 1769, Washington did little in Virginia's House of Burgesses except occupy a seat, and that he did infrequently. When he did attend he said little. But that year, he stepped out from the political shadows onto center stage. Fed up with British taxing policies, he and other burgesses, in defiance of the royal governor, met in a tavern, where Washington put forward a scheme to boycott British goods.[42]

As time went on, his attitude toward British policies continued to sour as he ran up against obstacles imposed by London on his plans to acquire lands to the west. Meanwhile, he clung to his fame as a military man from the French and Indian War. People addressed him as "Colonel," and when he sat for his first portrait, aged 40, he posed with a musket and in uniform—scarlet waistcoat under a blue coat with scarlet trim—as if contemplating a battle ahead.[43]

In 1771, Washington won re-election after encouraging voters with free suppers, cakes, and lively fiddle music.[44] In January 1774, when news of the Boston Tea Party reached Williamsburg, Washington did not cheer. The destruction of property and lawlessness disturbed his sense of order and propriety. But with the British response to the Tea Party—the closing of the port of Boston and the military occupation of the town—Washington boiled over. The conduct of the British commander in Boston, he wrote, was "unexampled Testimony of the most despotick System of Tyranny that ever was practiced in a free Government."[45] The cause of Boston "is and ever will be considerd as the cause of America."[46]

In the next election campaign, Washington won over voters with punch, chocolate, and coffee, but no tea.[47] He collaborated in drawing up statements protesting British highhandedness and asserting American rights. The statements also declared a "most earnest" desire to stop the "wicked, cruel, and unnatural" trade in the enslaved.[48]

When the Virginia burgesses met in defiance of the royal governor to form a rebel government, Washington was a leading figure. When it came time to elect delegates to represent Virginia at the First Continental Congress, Washington was named one of the seven.[49]

As a delegate at both the First and Second Congress, he was silent. His name rarely appears in the *Journals* of Congress or in letters and documents connected to each Congress. Reserved by nature, conscious of his limited education, and unsure of his rhetorical skills amid this collection of lawyers and facile speakers, he preferred to listen. Despite his reticence—or maybe because of it—he made a powerful impression. He seemed like a military leader.

Washington had clearly been a leading candidate for the job of commander since arriving in Philadelphia to the Second Congress in military uniform. In Washington's favor, in addition to his battlefield experience, was his birthplace. He was a native Virginian. John Adams and many of the other New England delegates were desperate to ensure that all the colonies were united in this military undertaking. The wholehearted commitment of Virginia, the largest and richest colony, was vital. Furthermore, the appointment of a Southerner would ease some anxieties from delegates from outside New England who, presuming the inbred belligerence of New Englanders, worried that a large New England army led by a New Englander might pose a threat to other colonies.[50] Connecticut delegate Eliphalet Dyer said the appointment of Washington "removes all jealousies, more firmly Cements the Southern to the Northern, and takes away the fear of the former lest an Enterprising eastern New England Genll proving Successfull, might with his Victorious Army give law to the Southern & Western Gentry."[51]

Washington accepted and promptly impressed delegates by promising to serve without pay. He asked only to be reimbursed for expenses. In agreeing to take the job, he offered no reassurance of his fitness for it. He spoke like a man duty-bound to try, but doomed to failure and dishonor: "I beg it may be remembered, by every Gentleman in this room, that I, this day, declare with the utmost sincerity, I do not think myself equal to the Command I am honored with."[52]

It took a few days for the new commander to find the words and the courage to inform "Patcy," his pet name for Martha. In his letter to her of June 18, he apologizes for taking on the task and leaving her to watch over Mount Vernon. As in his statement to Congress, he is full of anxiety and doubt, but says it was a duty he could not honorably turn down, and Washington valued his honor above all else:

> You may beleive me my dear Patcy, when I assure you, in the most solemn manner, that, so far from seeking this appointment I have used every endeavour in my power to avoid it, not only from my unwillingness to part with you and the Family, but from a consciousness of its being a trust too great for my Capacity and that I should enjoy more real happiness and felicity in one month with you, at home, than I have the most distant prospect of reaping abroad, if my stay was to be Seven times Seven years. ... [I]t was utterly out of my power to refuse this appointment without exposing my Character to such censures as would have reflected dishonour upon myself, and given pain to my friends.[53]

Apparently confident that somehow this dispute with Britain would last not years but a few months, he promised to return "safe" to Martha by fall—a pledge he hedged by enclosing his will, "as Life is always uncertain."[54]

Washington's self-doubts seemed not to bother delegates to Congress. Silas Deane, for one, was ready to cast his profile in bronze: "Let Our youth look up to This Man as a pattern to form themselves by, who Unites the bravery of the Soldier, with the most consummate Modesty & Virtue."[55]

Connecticut's Eliphalet Dyer had a more measured assessment. He surmised that Connecticut had men with as much or more military knowledge and experience. Even so, Washington was "Clever, & if any thing too modest. He seems discrete & Virtuous, no harum Starum ranting Swearing fellow but Sober, steady, & Calm."[56]

Following Washington's appointment, Congress quickly authorized the appointment of various top officers: major generals, brigadier generals, a paymaster general and his deputy, a chief engineer and two assistants, three aides-de-camp, and others.[57] John Adams thought the promised salaries created too wide a pay gap between the highest officers and the lowest privates. He wrote that he and other Massachusetts delegates fought in vain to set the salaries lower: "Those ideas of equality, which are so agreeable to us natives of New England, are very disagreeable to many gentlemen in the other colonies. They had a great opinion of the high importance of the continental general, and were determined to place him in an elevated point of light."[58]

Where was the money to pay these officers going to come from? The question had yet to be answered.

Delegates soon appointed Washington's senior generals. One was Artemis Ward, the Massachusetts man on the scene outside of Boston holding the ragtag New England force together. His appointment as second in command would quiet the grumbling among some New England delegates about a Southerner as the commander of an army of mostly Northerners. Two other top appointees were Charles Lee, as major general, and Horatio Gates, as adjutant general. Both were Virginians and former British officers. Lee, in accepting the position, insisted that Congress first promise to pay him back for any loss of property he might suffer as a result of his service. Congress complied.[59]

This would have completed the list of top commanders if not for the complaints from the New York and Connecticut delegates. To appease New York, Congress made Philip Schuyler, a New Yorker, major general. Though his résumé included some service in the French and Indian War, he had no business receiving such a high rank. But he was rich and had plenty of influence in New York political circles, and he also happened to be a delegate to Congress.[60] Congress was well aware, too, that New York's support for the Patriot cause was wobbly. As Dyer wrote, the naming of Schuyler was essential "to Sweeten, Add to, & keep up the spirit in that Province."[61]

Connecticut was likewise appeased with the appointment of Israel Putnam as a major general. Putnam was more qualified than Schuyler, but still unfit for the position. "Old Put" was a semi-literate bulldog of a man who, aged 57, was the oldest of the major generals. Tales of his exploits were legendary; some were even true. During the earlier war with France, he had been a member of the famous Rogers's Rangers, was captured and nearly burned at the stake by indigenous people before being exchanged.[62] The most famous tale about him had nothing to do with the military; it had to do with a female wolf that was killing livestock near his farm in Connecticut. He and his neighbors tracked the wolf to her den, which he entered, crawling in with musket and torch, a rope tied to his ankles. The second time in, he blasted the wolf with a shot. The third time in, after a few minutes, he tugged at the rope and was soon dragged out feet first, bringing with him the dead wolf by the ears.[63]

During the months of tension before Lexington and Concord, Putnam burnished his reputation for heroics by driving a herd of 125 sheep from Connecticut to Boston to feed the city suffering from the British blockade of its port in the wake of the Tea Party.[64]

Putnam's candidacy for major general got a further boost when exaggerated reports reached Philadelphia of yet more feats, this time at the "battle" of Noddle's Island near Boston. That battle, it turned out, was more like a skirmish. As American foragers were taking cattle from the island, about 40 British troops attacked. Putnam, with 1,000 Connecticut men, came to the rescue and drove off the British. Putnam was the toast of Philadelphia.[65]

***

On June 21, a lanky redhead from Virginia made his appearance in Congress to take the place of the departed Peyton Randolph. Samuel Ward of Rhode Island took note of "the famous Mr. Jefferson": he "looks like a very sensible spirited fine fellow."[66] Thomas Jefferson's fame stemmed from a pamphlet he wrote the previous summer, *A Summary View of the Rights of British America*. Written at Monticello, Jefferson's hilltop residence, the *Summary* was conceived as instructions for Virginia's delegates to the First Continental Congress. But Jefferson went on at length—some 6,700 words—to fling legal arguments about myriad British injustices and wag his finger at the king.

Some statements in the *Summary* are overblown or curious. For example, Jefferson claimed the law forbidding Americans from making their own hats was an "instance of despotism to which no parallel can be produced in the most arbitrary ages of British history." In another example, Jefferson scolded the king for repeatedly blocking American measures to restrict or stop the import of enslaved people to America. This, reasoned Jefferson—who typically owned about 200 slaves—somehow made it impossible to abolish slavery, "the great object of desire"[67] in the colonies.

Readers found the pamphlet's tone inspiring and bolder than much that had been written up to that time. Jefferson tallied act after act of injustice and concluded that Britain had "a deliberate, systematical plan of reducing us to slavery."[68]

Jefferson summoned history—the "Glorious revolution," "William the Norman," and "Saxon laws of possession"—to challenge the king, going so far as to assert that "his majesty has no right to land a single armed man on our shores." He picked at British motives about everything related to America. Even setting up a postal system, he claimed, had little to do with convenience for Americans, but was aimed to provide easy jobs and money for "his majesty's ministers and favorites." To the king, Jefferson advised: "Open your breast Sire, to liberal and expanded thought. Let not the name of George the third be a blot on the page of history."[69]

Thomas Jefferson, when he appeared in Congress as a delegate from Virginia in June 1775, was already highly regarded for *A Summary View of the Rights of British America*, a critique of British rule. This 1791 portrait by Charles Willson Peale is in the Independence National Historical Park collection. (Image via Wikimedia Commons)

Jupiter, a slave of Jefferson's, carried two copies of the document to Williamsburg, where it was read aloud in the home of Peyton Randolph. A copy came into the hands of a printer, who published it without Jefferson's knowledge. Washington bought several copies, calling the document "Mr. Jefferson's Bill of Rights." Copies circulated around the colonies and in London. In Britain, according to rumors, Jefferson's name was added to a legal document listing possible traitors.[70] In America, Jefferson found himself exalted as a fresh and powerful voice in the Patriot choir.

Consequently, as Jefferson entered Pennsylvania's State House for the first time, he was already widely known. Still, he was a relative latecomer to the Patriot leadership, and his sudden rise as a public figure in a time of rebellion was astonishing for such a reserved man who shrank from face-to-face confrontation, relished quiet intellectual pursuits, and abhorred public speaking.

He was born to privilege and modest wealth at Shadwell, his father's plantation near Charlottesville, Virginia. One of his earliest memories was the sensation of being lifted up to a slave on horseback and plopped on a pillow in advance of a long journey. His father, a likeable planter and surveyor, was locally famous for his impressive acts of courage, feats of strength, and hunting and riding skills. He died when Thomas was 14, but the admiring son never tired of recalling his father's noble character. Meanwhile, in all of Jefferson's immense collection of writings, his mother is rarely mentioned.[71] We learn from a granddaughter that the woman was "agreeable," "intelligent," and "a notable housekeeper."[72] She also proved resilient and determined, managing 66 enslaved people and 2,750 acres after her husband's death, while also shepherding her eldest son and seven other surviving offspring.[73] Also, we know she was from a prominent Virginia family, the Randolphs (Peyton Randolph was a cousin), which enabled her to endow her son with status and connections.

The household where Jefferson grew up was a place of gracious entertainment, where tables were set with silver, guests danced to fine music, and young Thomas could peruse Shakespeare and Swift in his father's library. But Thomas spent much of his young life away from home. Starting at the age of nine, he was sent off to live for most of the year with a rector who introduced him to French and a classical education. Later, he boarded with a minister for more classical enlightenment. At 17, Jefferson applied to enter the College of William & Mary in Williamsburg. Jefferson easily met the modest requirements: that a prospective student must know a little Latin, a little Greek, and not be "a blockhead or lazy fellow."[74]

Jefferson's two years at William & Mary were bliss. The young man was in his element among books and learned teachers, finding a professor whom he revered like a father.[75]

The college town was also the colony's capital, and Jefferson was a regular with the professor and George Wyeth, one of Virginia's leading lawyers, at the palace of the royal governor of Virginia, where the foursome would enjoy dinner, conversation, and music. From time to time, Jefferson was invited to play the violin. Thus, Jefferson absorbed a taste for elegance and good manners, and acquired a lifelong love of refined conversation. Meanwhile, the acquaintance with Wyeth paved the way for Jefferson's legal career, which took up most of his time and energy from 1767–74, when revolutionary events pulled him toward politics.[76]

His life seemed charmed, but not everything worked out well. An early attempt at romance was a disaster. He set his heart on a certain Rebecca Burwell, and had his chance on the dance floor of Williamsburg's Raleigh Tavern. But when he opened his mouth, out came "a few broken sentences, uttered in great disorder, and interrupted with pauses of uncommon length."[77] Jefferson retreated, regrouped, and tried over subsequent days and weeks to woo the entrancing Burwell, only to be rejected. Jefferson gave up and slumped under the pain of a vicious headache, a symptom of stress throughout his adult life. Less than a year later, Burwell married someone else.

Jefferson next pursued Betsy Walker, the new wife of an old friend. He persisted, even after she made it clear she had no interest in an adulterous affair. At a party, after the ladies had left to go to bed, Jefferson complained of a headache, exited the room, and made his way to Betsy's chamber, where "[h]e was repulsed with indignation and menaces of alarm and ran off."[78]

Jefferson found distraction from his thwarted love life by attending plays in Williamsburg.[79] Once he started to practice law, he lived at his mother's house, Shadwell, but traveled much, and his practice thrived.

He also immersed himself in a building project, a home for himself on a hilltop about 2 miles from Shadwell. He gave it an Italian name, Monticello ("little mountain").[80] He did have his setbacks, though. The death of a beloved sister was an especially wrenching loss, and he mourned the destruction of many books and papers after a fire destroyed Shadwell. But mostly, life was good to him.

His first meaningful activity on behalf of society was in raising money to remove rocks from a river to make it navigable. Then, in 1768, aged 25, he entered politics in the usual way—by purchasing drinks and cakes for landowners who could vote. They helpfully responded by electing him to Virginia's House of Burgesses.[81] He was well suited for the politics of the time. He was likeable, charming, and a wonderful listener, making everyone he met feel that he was sincerely interested in them, which in fact he often was, for he was endlessly curious.

In the House of Burgesses, Jefferson did little of notice except for an effort to allow slaveholders to unilaterally free a slave, an act that normally needed a judge's approval. The proposal failed.[82]

His private life brightened. He met an attractive widow, the daughter of a client. She was Martha Wayles Skelton—everyone called her Patty. He wooed her with music. They sang together, and he would play the violin or pianoforte. The 28-year-old groom and 23-year-old bride married on New Year's Day, 1772. Just over nine months later, their first child, a girl, was born: Patsy. Less than two years later, another daughter arrived: Jane.[83] This was about the time of the Boston Port Act in the wake of the Tea Party.

Virginians were as enraged as Bostonians, and Jefferson along with many other burgesses took a stand. Jefferson, called upon to craft instructions for Virginia's delegates to the First Continental Congress, produced his *Summary* and was suddenly famous.

Jefferson, aboard a coach and four and accompanied by two enslaved people, took a leisurely 10 days to make his way from Virginia, pausing along the way to buy a horse and harness and tour the Maryland State House in Annapolis.[84] In Philadelphia, Jefferson settled into the house of a cabinetmaker on Chestnut Street, about a block from the State House. Jefferson was so intrigued by the handsome fireplace in the parlor that he carefully took and recorded measurements. Ever bookish and inquisitive, Jefferson would devote some of his spare time in Philadelphia studying German.[85]

CHAPTER 9

Perfidious Double-Faced Congress

Soon after Jefferson's arrival in Philadelphia, Congress took its first stab at answering the nagging question: how would Congress pay for the American army and other costs? The delegates decided to pluck money out of thin air, or something like that. Congress authorized the printing of bills with face values totaling two million Spanish dollars "for the defense of America."[1] These, in denominations ranging from $1 through to $8 and also $20,[2] would be produced and then used mainly to pay soldiers.

Money was a topic of dizzying complexity in colonial America. The money of choice—the preferred medium of exchange—was precious metal, usually silver or gold, most often in the form of coins.[3] But coins were always in short supply. There were no gold or silver mines in colonial North America, and very few coins were minted in the colonies. Most gold or silver coins in America were minted by Spain or Portugal and arrived by way of trade for such goods as tobacco or wheat. Those gold and silver coins generally didn't stay in America long. They were sent back overseas to pay for the luxury goods Americans coveted from Britain and elsewhere, for merchants overseas would usually accept nothing else as payment. Americans always seemed to be buying more than they sold, so the flow of these coins tended toward the eastern side of the Atlantic.[4] Meanwhile, of those gold and silver coins that remained in America, many were hoarded. Some were melted down and cast into bowls, teapots, sugar bowls, and other beautiful and useful objects. This was how rich people stored and displayed their wealth, and the practice further depleted the supply of gold and silver coins.

Americans found creative ways to deal with the chronic shortage of hard currency. Sometimes they bartered. In some places, laws declared tobacco, wheat, rice, sugar, and even deerskins or beaver pelts the accepted medium of exchange.[5] Often, transactions occurred with no money at all changing hands, but instead accounts were set up and goods offered with the promise of payment later in the form of, for example, a portion of a farmer's crop.[6]

Buyer and seller would agree upon a price and the seller would make a note of it in a ledger. The buyer would pay it back, maybe more than a year later, in goods or services. To clear the debt, the buyer might perform a service, such as fixing a fence, for a third party to whom the seller was indebted.[7]

Up and down the colonies, prices everywhere were generally expressed in familiar British terms—pounds, shillings, and pence—and everywhere 20 shillings equaled a pound, and 12 pence equaled a shilling, just as in England. But the value of these units varied from colony to colony, and had nothing to do with the value of the pound sterling, the hard currency in Britain. About the time of the American Revolution, the value of the same silver Spanish coin was pegged at 6 shillings in New England, 8 shillings in New York, 7 shillings and 6 pence in Philadelphia, and 32 shillings and 6 pence in Charleston. Meanwhile, in Britain, the coin had a value of 4 shillings, 6 pence in sterling.[8] These differences didn't matter much for trade within each colony, but they baffled travelers and complicated accounting for intercolonial exchanges and overseas trade.

Americans craved mechanisms to simplify transactions. Paper currency was an obvious solution. Thus, colonies from time to time produced various kinds of paper bills. Land bank currency schemes were especially popular and sometimes quite successful. Normally, under such a scheme, a colonial government would issue paper money as loans to farmers and other property owners with houses or land as security. The money circulated until the indebted property owner paid back the loan, plus interest, to the colonial government, at which time whoever held the note could redeem it for hard currency from the colonial government. If the landowner defaulted, the colony could seize the land or building, sell it, and give hard currency from the sale to the holder of the note. Such schemes were especially successful in Pennsylvania, where at times the interest on the loans provided the government all it needed to function. However, British authorities opposed these land banks. Though sometimes slow in shutting them down, shut them down they did.

By the time of the Continental Congress, America had never had a single paper currency intended to circulate throughout the colonies. But Americans were acquainted with paper money and eager to put away their ledgers, so it is not surprising that they would welcome and accept the Continental dollar, the paper money issued by Congress.

Historians over the years have generally characterized the Continental dollar as "fiat" currency: paper money deriving its value only from faith in whoever issued it and designed to be exchanged at face value, like modern dollar bills.

But the notion that the Continental dollar was similar to the modern dollar might be a misunderstanding of what Congress had in mind when it generated Continental dollars. One economics professor who has examined this topic says that the Continental dollar was less like today's currency and more like the modern savings bond. That is, it was meant to be saved, not spent, and then cashed in at a later date for its face value.

This meant that a soldier with a $20 note understood that, at the time he received it, it was not actually worth $20, but something less. Its purchasing power might be in the range of $13 to $19 in 1775, but less than $20.[9] However, if he kept it, the note would be worth $20 in four to six years. That's when Congress determined that the bills could be redeemed. Delegates hoped that by then the war would be over.[10]

This idea is supported by the characteristics of the notes. Congress, between 1775 and 1779, ordered the printing of new notes 11 times.[11] In each instance, Congress determined the number of notes and specified the denominations. Over that time, the smallest denomination ever printed was one-sixth dollar. The value of that sixth of a Continental dollar was the equivalent of about $5 in 2012 money. Most of the bills printed were in much higher denominations. (Continental dollars came in many denominations, including $7, $8, $35, $65, up to $80, but curiously, never $10.)[12] Nearly 70 percent of the bills issued were in denominations with purchasing power of $100 or more in 2012 dollars.[13] The Continental dollars thus were, by and large, not useful for small everyday transactions, but they were practical for saving.

While the Continental dollars promised to be worth so much in gold, delegates didn't actually expect Congress to be doling out gold coins in exchange for notes. They did expect the notes to come back to Congress from the colonies, which would collect the notes in the form of taxes.

Thus, the soldier with his $20 note would never expect to redeem it for actual gold, but he would understand that the bill would be worth $20 that could be used to pay taxes.

Congress had no tax-collection system and no authority to tax. But the individual colonies did, or would soon after seizing it from the retreating royal authorities.

Just after authorizing the printing of bills, Congress resolved that the "confederated colonies be pledged for the redemption of the bills."[14] Congress was counting on the individual colonies to collect the old bills, through taxes, and clear the way for the printing of new bills.

In July 1775, Congress determined the amount in Continental dollars that each colony was expected to collect and send to Congress. These quotas were based on the approximate population of each colony. The method of collecting that money was left up to each colony. The old dollars were to be sent to Congress in four equal installments over four years, beginning in 1779.[15] Colonies that could not meet their quotas in dollars could make up the difference with specie—gold coins—of the same value. Congress would hold this specie and advertise its availability to be exchanged for paper dollars still held by individuals or by colonies still holding dollars after remitting their quotas.[16]

The currency scheme was entrancing. Supporters saw the plan not only as a practical and seemingly painless way to pay for the war, but also a clever mechanism for bringing the colonies closer together—they would be linked by a common

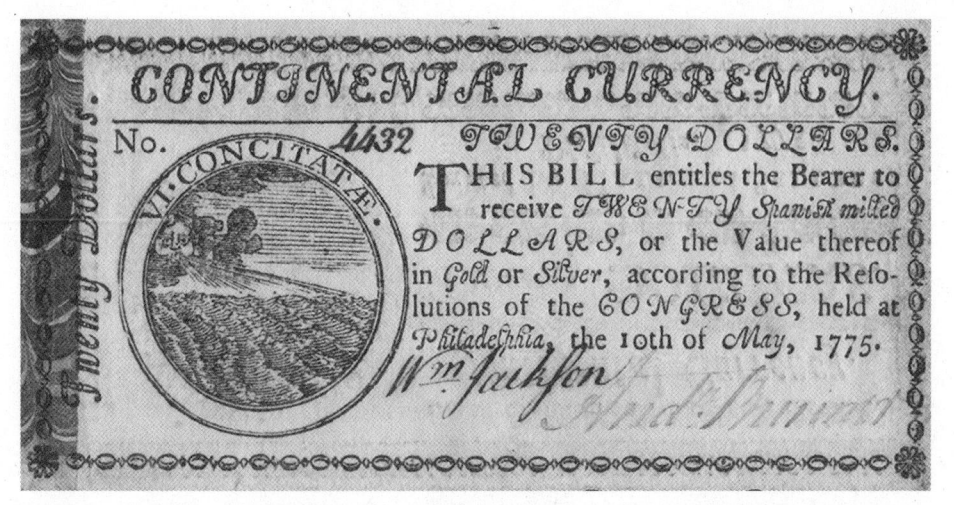

Congress issued Continental dollars to finance the war. This note is from the first batch, or emission, in May 1775. Ten more emissions would eventually follow, the last in 1779. The appearance of the bills from each emission would be distinctly different from those of other emissions. The motto on this $20 note, *VI CONCITATÆ*, means "Driven by Force." The image, devised by Benjamin Franklin, shows the wind, personified as a face, creating waves on the surface of a body of water. (Image courtesy of the Eric P. Newman Numismatic Education Society)

currency and a shared obligation to ensure its stability.[17] So the Continental dollar was launched, and Congress stepped out on what would prove to be a slippery slope.

As paper currency flowed out, delegates were aware of the potential economic catastrophe ahead for their "countries"—that is, their respective colonies. North Carolina's Joseph Hawes wrote in June: "I fear we shall be obliged to promise for our Colony much more than it will perform and perhaps more than it is able to bear."[18]

Meanwhile, however, the Continental dollar served wonderfully well as a tool for financing the war. While some soldiers may have saved the notes, many exchanged them for goods or more convenient state currency. Thus, the notes circulated and, as the public understood the nature of the notes, they traded below face value—as would be expected with any comparable money with a defined maturity date. But they were widely accepted.[19]

***

The men in Philadelphia had no time to ruminate about long-term implications of these decisions. Events moved too swiftly. The very day Congress blessed the plan to print the first American dollars, rumors reached Congress of some new fighting around Boston. "We have just a Report of a Battle," wrote John Hancock to Ward, the general still in charge of the Patriot forces in Massachusetts. "We are anxious ... God send us a good account."[20]

Aware that a battle had taken place, but unaware of the details, Washington and two of his generals left Philadelphia the next day. They had an escort for part of the way. To Abigail, John Adams wrote that all Massachusetts delegates took part, as well as many other delegates, "a large Troop of Light Horse, in their Uniforms [and] Many Officers of Militia besides in theirs, Musick playing, &c. &c. Such is the Pride and Pomp of war."[21]

Adams longed to join Washington as a soldier: "I, poor Creature, worn out with scribbling, for my Bread and my Liberty, low in Spirits and weak in Health, must leave others to wear the Lawrells which I have sown; others, to eat the Bread which I have earned."[22]

The country was now lurching toward a full-scale war of rebellion while somehow clinging to the trappings of loyalty to British authority. In a bizarre coincidence, Washington and his entourage, on their way to Massachusetts to take charge of the rebel army, approached New York City by land at the same time a new royal governor was arriving by sea from Britain. That was William Tryon, who in a stint as governor of North Carolina hanged a half-dozen rebels who dared challenge royal authority.[23]

Hedging their bets, New Yorkers prepared a grand welcome for both—for Washington on one side of town and for Tryon on the other. One militia company was dispatched to greet Washington, another sent off to welcome Tryon, and another eight companies stood ready to go one way or the other, depending on who arrived first.[24]

As it turned out, that was General Washington. Tryon, becoming aware of Washington's approach, prudently delayed his arrival, biding his time aboard ship in the harbor. Washington had a grand parade, ending at the best hotel in town. At about the time Washington disappeared into his room, a dignified crowd at the foot of Broad Street just a few blocks away welcomed ashore the new royal governor.[25]

The next day, Washington met with members of New York's provincial congress. They had a message for Washington that awkwardly straddled the line between loyalty and rebellion: they were loyal subjects of the king, but were also pleased with Washington's appointment. The general duly made an appropriate response and was soon again on the road to Massachusetts.[26]

Back in Philadelphia, definitive news about the battle of Bunker Hill finally flooded in. Itching for a fight, brash American militiamen had used the cover of night to plant themselves on the Charlestown Peninsula close enough to Boston to threaten the British. In response, the British sent out a massive force to scatter the Americans. The British, after burning Charlestown, succeeded, but at a ghastly cost. The Americans proved resilient, courageous, and determined, but hasty planning, poor organization, and lack of powder cost them dearly. The ferocity of the battle shook both sides, but left the situation unchanged. The British remained bottled up in Boston, while the Americans still ruled the countryside.

The news stunned delegates. But it also hardened them, which may explain why Congress about this time gave cautious permission to launch an operation that sounds, in retrospect, like madness—the invasion of Quebec. At the time, the conquest of Quebec seemed well within reach and essential if the English-speaking colonies expected to win a war with Britain. A glance at a map told delegates that British troops could easily storm down from Montreal via rivers and lakes into the Hudson Valley. It was not hard to imagine that a war with Britain would be impossible to win without taking Quebec.

Quebec seemed to be easy pickings for an American invasion from the south. Quebec was immense, thinly populated, and not well defended. All of Canada had a population of about 110,000. By comparison, Connecticut alone had population of nearly 200,000. The overwhelming majority of Quebec's population—about 99 percent—were French-speaking Catholics. Almost all lived within 2 miles of the three major waterways—the St. Lawrence, the Chaudière, and the Richelieu. Only about 10 percent of the population could read and write,[27] and very few were likely to come to the aid of the British in defending the province. As for the few English speakers in Quebec, chiefly in Montreal and Quebec City, many were offended at how they, living in Canada, did not enjoy the same rights as Englishmen in England. They too would not rally to support the British and would welcome an American invasion, or so the Americans assumed.[28]

By the spring of 1775, Quebeckers were well aware of the friendly invitation to join the Continental Congress. English and French versions of that letter had circulated. Unfortunately for Congress, so had a French translation of Congress's letter to the people of Great Britain, the letter that cast Catholicism as a religion of bigotry, murder, and persecution. The response of at least one Canadian was: "Oh! the perfidious double-faced Congress."[29]

In early 1775, Massachusetts Patriots sent off to Montreal an energetic Yale-educated lawyer, John Brown, to gather information, contact potential allies, and urge the Canadians to dispatch delegates to the Continental Congress. After a journey of "inconceivable hardships" by boat on icy Lake Champlain and then on foot along its flooded shores, he arrived in March, and met in a coffee house with a group of sympathetic merchants. Though "kindly received," Brown made no progress. The merchants were put off by the likelihood that membership of Congress might cost them trade with Britain. Brown concluded: "There is no prospect of *Canada* sending delegates to the Continental Congress." Regarding the French in Canada, Brown found no evidence that they were eager to throw off their British rulers. Quite the contrary: "The French in Canada are a set of people who know no other way of procuring wealth and honour but by becoming Court sycophants." At the same time, Brown saw little to suggest they would fight alongside British troops to help defend Quebec. "They appeared to have no disposition unfriendly toward the Colonies, but chose rather to stand neuter."[30]

A subsequent letter to Patriots in Massachusetts from English merchants in Montreal confirmed many of Brown's observations. The English there were sympathetic to the Patriot cause, but their numbers were too small to offer much help. Most people in the province—both the French and English speakers—"wish well to your cause, but dare not stir a finger to help you."[31]

In May, a representative of sympathetic merchants in Montreal showed up in Philadelphia. He was not a delegate but rather a kind of ambassador.[32] He informed Congress that, while the French "nobles" would be "bitter enemies," the ordinary people, the "plebians," would not resist an invasion from the American colonies.[33]

He was right. Ordinary French Canadians were not going to help the British resist the Americans. When, in the summer of 1775, British authorities tried to organize militias in rural areas around Montreal, they faced small-scale revolts. In one village, denizens swore not to take up arms on behalf of the government, promising to kill the cattle and burn the house and barn of any among them who did.[34]

In the wake of the capture of Fort Ticonderoga, Congress had explicitly ruled out an invasion. It would ruin overtures for peace. Too little was known about conditions in Canada, and there were too many other concerns to deal with.

As it turned out, however, without Congress's knowledge or approval, American militiamen crossed into Canada in May. It was not exactly an invasion; it was a raid. Thirty-five Patriot militiamen forced the surrender of 14 men holding dilapidated Fort St. Jean, just across the Quebec border from New York and only about 20 miles from Montreal. The Americans soon abandoned the fort and retreated south. Still, the event demonstrated how vulnerable Quebec was to an attack.

In the wake of the raid, militia leaders bombarded Congress and revolutionary allies in several colonies with letters urging an invasion.[35] The colonies and Congress remained lukewarm about the idea. But the notion ripened, fully maturing when Congress received a report that an indigenous tribe in the region had "taken up the hatchet"[36] at the urging of the British. Delegates in Philadelphia now began to imagine British-inspired indigenous attacks on the American frontier.

Thus, in late June, Congress gave its blessing for an invasion, but only if it was "practicable" and "not disagreeable to the Canadians,"[37] according to instructions given by Congress to Major General Schuyler, now commander of the Northern Army, the American military operations in the Northern Department, a region that included Lake Champlain. Schuyler had his cautious instructions, and he would prove cautious indeed.

CHAPTER 10

Spirited Manifesto

In other business, delegates in Philadelphia put the finishing touches to the rules and regulations for the Continental Army—69 articles of war. Article II "earnestly recommended" that "all officers and soldiers, [were] diligently to attend Divine Service." Article III said a commissioned officer guilty of "profane cursing or swearing" should forfeit "pay for each and every offence, the sum of Four Shillings, lawful money."[1] Under Article XX, any commissioned officer found drunk "on his guard, party, or other duty, under arms, shall be cashiered for it." Article LI ruled that court-martial punishments could include death, demotion, cashiering, "drumming out of the army, whipping not exceeding *thirty-nine* lashes, fine not exceeding two months pay," and "imprisonment not exceeding one month." Article LXIV stated: "No suttler shall be permitted to sell any kind of liquors or victuals, or to keep their houses or shops open, for the entertainment of soldiers, after nine at night, or before the beating of the reveilles, or upon Sundays, during Divine service or sermon, on the penalty of being dismissed from all future suttling."[2]

With their attention still fixed on the American army dug in around Boston, delegates approved a "Declaration on Taking Arms" to clarify what, exactly, they were fighting for. This "Spirited Manifesto," as John Adams called it,[3] was to be sent on to Washington to be published and distributed to the troops, but was also intended for Americans in general, and for readers across the sea. Jefferson produced a draft, which Dickinson found "too strong," as Jefferson later wrote. Jefferson explained that Dickinson "still retained the hope of reconciliation with the mother country, and was unwilling it should be lessened by offensive statements. He was so honest a man, & so able a one that he was greatly indulged even by those who could not feel his scruples."[4]

The final softened draft was largely the work of Dickinson, but it still packed a punch. It charged, for example, that British troops have "butchered our countrymen," that the British governor of Canada encouraged indigenous peoples to attack Americans, and that Parliament worked to "extort from us, at the point of a bayonet" with the aim of gratifying "ministerial rapacity": "We are reduced to the alternative of chusing an unconditional submission to the tyranny of irritated ministers, or resistance by force.—The latter is our choice."[5]

The document incorporated many of the complaints and ideas later echoed in the Declaration of Independence. But in contrast to the Declaration of Independence, this document was explicit in denying any plan to separate from Britain: "[W]e mean not to dissolve that Union which has so long and so happily subsisted between us, and which we sincerely wish to see restored."[6]

On July 8, still grasping for some peaceful solution, delegates put their signatures on a groveling petition to the king. For Adams and probably most delegates, Bunker Hill signaled that such gestures were a waste of time. But many delegates still insisted that Congress needed to go through the motions of reaching out. Chief among them was Dickinson, who was the main author of this document to the king asking—"with all humility submitting to your Majesty's wise consideration"—for the repeal of offending laws and for some process leading to "a happy and permanent reconciliation."[7] The tone was deferential to a fault.

No one in Philadelphia held much hope that the plea to the king would make any difference. John Adams detested it as a "measure of Imbecility."[8] Franklin wrote: "[F]or tho' this may afford Britain one chance more of recovering our Affection and retaining the Connection, I think she has neither Temper nor Wisdom enough to seize the Golden Opportunity."[9]

Even Dickinson was not optimistic, but felt that the effort was essential to assure Americans—who might be asked to make huge sacrifices in the months and years ahead—that every attempt was made to find a peaceful resolution. "If [the British] reject this application with Contempt," wrote Dickinson, "the more humble it is, [the more] such Treatment will confirm the Minds of [our] Countrymen, to endure all the Misfortunes [that] may attend the Contest."[10]

The exercise cost Dickinson the respect of some colleagues, but not Charles Thomson, the congressional secretary. He appreciated what Dickinson had accomplished. Dickinson, in Thomson's view, was being true to his constituents in Pennsylvania: "[H]e maintained his ground among the generality of the people in his own Province, and particularly among those who wished to see a Reconciliation take place; and it must be allowed that if his judgment had not quite approved the measure, yet on account of the people of Pennsylvania, it was both prudent and politic to adopt it."[11]

Dickinson, by pushing through the "Olive Branch" petition, may have kept lukewarm Pennsylvania from abandoning the Revolution, according to Thomson. The petition "obviated objections that would have been raised and had a powerful effect on suppressing opposition, preserving unanimity and bringing the province in a united body into the contest."[12]

Congress next approved a letter to the "Inhabitants of Great Britain." It spelled out American grievances, justified American actions, and warned Britons that "[s]oldiers who have sheathed their Swords in the Bowels of their American Brethren"[13] may one day do likewise to them. The language was tougher than the appeal to the king, but to John Adams, this collection of "Prettynesses," "Juvenilities," and "Peurilities" was unbecoming to "a great assembly like this the Representative of a Great People."[14]

On July 12, Congress turned its attention to the indigenous peoples. With memories fresh of the French and Indian War, when the French cultivated alliances with the indigenous tribes to raise havoc on the frontiers, delegates shuddered at the possibility that the British "will spare no pains to excite the several Nations of Indians to take up arms against these colonies." To prevent such trouble, Congress appointed three groups of commissioners to approach the indigenous people: one for the Six Nations—the Iroquois Confederation—and other indigenous peoples to the north and northwest; one for the Cherokees and other tribes in the southern frontier; and one for tribes between the Cherokees and Iroquois. Money was authorized for the cost of "treaties and presents." Delegates also approved the spending of $500 to support "nine or ten Indian youth" from Quebec then living in a seminary on the Connecticut River. Without the money for their support, "there is danger that these youth may be sent back to their friends, which will probably excite jealousy and distrust, and be attended with bad consequences."[15]

Delegates followed that up with a message for the indigenous "Brothers, Sachems and Warriors." The main point of the long-winded "talk" was not to win an alliance with them, but to keep them out of the conflict:

> What is it we have asked of you? Nothing but peace, notwithstanding our present disturbed situation—and if application should be made to you by any of the king's unwise and wicked ministers to join on their side, we only advise you to deliberate, with great caution, and in your wisdom look forward to the consequences of a compliance. For, if the king's troops take away our property, and destroy us who are of the same blood with themselves, what can you, who are Indians, expect from them afterwards?[16]

By this time, mid-July 1775, Congress had had plenty of time to learn about the battle of Bunker Hill and absorb its lessons. One was the critical shortage of gunpowder, muskets, cannons, and just about everything else an army needs. The Massachusetts delegates were so shocked by the lack of gunpowder, that three of them—John Adams, Samuel Adams, and John Hancock—spent an evening poking around Philadelphia "to beg some Powder." They scrounged "Ninety Quarter Casks" from a committee with "great Politeness and Sympathy for their brave Brethren in the Mass."[17] But obviously the army could not rely on the initiative of delegates going door to door.

So much more of everything was needed, and soon. America produced little gunpowder or weaponry, so delegates pushed through a resolution to permit American merchants to trade produce—"the non-exportation agreement notwithstanding"—for gunpowder, muskets, cannons, and other military goods and bring those into the colonies.[18]

With so much urgent business, Congress had no time to deal collectively with the larger question of making this union of colonies permanent. But delegates had been pondering the question and chatting about it. Franklin jotted down his own "Articles of Confederation and Perpetual Union"—a constitution—which he privately showed to Jefferson, who liked it, and to others. Jefferson later explained: "Some thought as I did. Others were revolted at it." Just bringing it to a vote would "startle many members so much that they would suspect we had lost sight of reconciliation with Great Britain."[19]

Despite the risk of igniting uproar among moderate delegates, Franklin quietly circulated his plan. This document was a blueprint for a "League of Friendship" called the "United Colonies of North America." It would make Congress a permanent fixture in America and establish its roles. Colonies would choose and send delegates annually, and Congress would meet in a different colony each year "in perpetual Rotation."

According to the document, Congress would have power to declare war, send and receive ambassadors, settle border disputes and other disagreements among colonies, and manage the formation of new colonies. However, Congress would have no power to touch the "Laws, Customs, Rights, and Privileges" of any colony. Congress would have a treasury for paying the costs of wars. Money for that treasury would come from taxes paid by each colony according to the "number of male polls" between the ages of 16 and 60. The number of male polls would also determine the number of delegates from each colony, and each delegate would have a vote. Thus, larger colonies by population would have more votes in Congress. There would be no single chief executive, like a president. Instead, executive functions would be in the hands of a council of 12 delegates appointed by Congress.[20]

Two of the document's 13 articles dealt with the indigenous people. One stated that no colony could make war on them without the consent of Congress or its executive council. The other called for, among other things, alliances with the various tribes, the determination of boundaries of indigenous-occupied land, and the appointment of officials to live among the tribes to stop "injustice in the Trade with them."[21]

The document set out a welcome mat for other North American colonies, such as Quebec, Nova Scotia, Bermuda, the islands of the West Indies, and the Florida colonies, to join "our Association."[22]

According to Franklin's plan, once approved by the various colonies and ratified by Congress, the proposed union would stay in place at least until the king agreed to various terms, including compensation for Boston's "Injury" from the shutting of its port, for the burning of Charlestown, and "for the Expense of this unjust War." Also, British troops would have to leave the colonies. The document concluded: "On the Arrival of these Events the Colonies [shall] return to their former Connection and Friendship with Britain: But on Failure thereof this Confederation is to be perpetual."[23]

Franklin's plan was duly presented and promptly ignored, as Franklin may have expected. But he had accomplished something—he had planted a seed. Months would pass before Congress would seriously contemplate a formal union.

The same day Franklin brought forth his plan, another controversial proposal came forward. This one called for the opening of all American ports to the world. But this, like Franklin's plan, was too provocative for moderates. It would be a bold repudiation of British authority over American trade, not a good approach if Congress was sincere in extending an olive branch. The topic was debated, discussed again at a later date, and then set aside.[24]

Congress again turned to the question of money, more of which was needed. Delegates authorized the printing of another million dollars in $30 bills. Deciding to do so was easy—the hard part was actually producing the bills. In the first authorization alone, more than 403,000 bills had to be printed, and each had to be signed. The congressional *Journal* groans: "[T]he signing of so great a number of bills as has been directed to be issued by this Congress, will take more time than the members can possibly devote to that business."[25] So Congress approved a list of 28 authorized signers—none of them delegates—to be paid $1⅓ for every 1,000 bills signed.[26]

At about that time Congress took on another core function of government. Before the end of July, Congress blessed the creation of a postal system. Its first postmaster general was Franklin, at an annual salary of $1,000.[27]

In other business, delegates plunged a dagger into a deceptive proposal from the British government to mend the breech between Britain and her American colonies. Under the British plan, cooked up in February, any colony that agreed to pay London its share for defending the Empire would not be required to pay any taxes to British authorities, except those necessary to regulate trade.[28] The plan was a lure to draw the lukewarm colonies away from rebellious New England. No colony had taken the bait, but Virginia, New Jersey, and Pennsylvania had each looked to Congress for its perspective. Congress complied, shredding the plan as "unreasonable and insidious" for many reasons. For example, the proposal seemed to suggest that the mode of taxation was America's only gripe and ignored the myriad insults to Americans—the treatment of Boston, the burning of Charlestown—and the British claims that Parliament has the right "to alter our charters and established laws, and leave us without security for our lives or liberties."[29]

Over those busy days in July and into August, delegates checked off one by one a long list of tasks: ordering $500,000 to be forwarded to the paymaster general for Washington's use; setting the pay of various military ranks, from fifer to colonel and deputy muster master general; approving a letter to the people of Ireland; encouraging the making of "Salt Petre," the collection of sulfur, and the manufacture of gunpowder; authorizing the establishment of a military hospital; issuing an address to the assembly of Jamaica;[30] and on and on.

Delegates also assigned to each colony its share of the tax burden for the first $3 million Congress had authorized, and set up a timetable when each colony was expected to turn in the Continental bills they collected "taking care to cut, by a circular punch, of an Inch diameter, an hole in each bill, and to cross the same, thereby to render them unpassable, though the sum or value is to remain fairly legible."[31]

Weary, frazzled, and eager to escape "Very hott"[32] Philadelphia, delegates called a halt to work on August 2,[33] adjourning with the promise of returning to business on September 5.[34]

***

John Adams, before going home, first went to see for himself the army encamped near Boston.[35] He accompanied General Lee and a cluster of his beloved dogs on a tour of an American outpost. Adams then traveled to Braintree to spend time with his family. On the way, he encountered a former client bursting with gratitude for the efforts of Adams and other Patriot leaders. This might have pleased Adams, except that the man then said he was in debt and that, with the closing of courts in Massachusetts, he now might well escape his creditors. The conversation made Adams miserable: "Is this the Object for which I have been contending? ... Are these the Sentiments of such People? ... If the power of the country should get into such hands, and there is great danger that it will, to what purpose have we sacrificed our time, health, and everything else?"[36]

In early September, delegates made their way back to Philadelphia, but by the 5th there were too few to start working. Finally, on September 12, there was a quorum, but an attack of gout kept President Hancock away.[37] He finally appeared on September 13, and business began. The first task was formal acceptance of credentials from the Georgia delegation. For the first time, all 13 colonies were fully represented in Congress.

Among the five Georgians was the "Rev'd Doctor"[38] John J. Zubly, a Presbyterian minister from Savannah who was known to preach in English in the morning, French in the afternoon, and German in the evening.[39] Born Hans Joachim Zublin in Switzerland, Zubly was the only member of the Continental Congress born outside the British Empire.[40] He had written boldly in defense of the colonies since the days of the Stamp Act and had remained steadfast in support of America's cause. But in the current crisis he was equally steadfast in opposing separation from Britain. That very July, he had preached: "[O]ur interest lies with perpetual connection with our mother country."[41] He had barely arrived in Philadelphia when he scribbled in his diary: "I made a point of it in every Company to contradict & oppose every hint of a desire of Independency or of breaking our Conexion with Great Britain."[42]

Meanwhile, another Georgian, Archibald Bulloch, turned heads with his patriotic fashion statement—his entire outfit was made in America.[43] This was astonishing, for most of the clothes Americans wore were imported.

Among the other delegates, there were few changes. Among the absent was Patrick Henry, who had taken a post as colonel in the Virginia militia.[44]

The reunion of delegates was chillier than it might have been thanks to a blunder by John Adams. Back in July, in a letter to James Warren, a Patriot colleague in Massachusetts, Adams indulged in a rant:

> A certain great Fortune and piddling Genius, whose Fame has been trumpeted so loudly, has given a silly Cast to our whole Doings. We are between Hawk and Buzzard … We ought to have had in our Hands a Month ago, the whole Legislative, Executive and Judicial of the whole Continent, and have compleatly moddelled a Constitution, to have raised a Naval Power and opened all our Ports wide, to have arrested every Friend to Government on the Continent and held them as Hostages for the poor Victims in Boston.[45]

Adams then entrusted the letter to one Benjamin Hichborn, a Boston man who happened to be in Philadelphia. Hichborn, whose loyalties were suspect, begged Adams to allow him to carry the letter to Massachusetts to prove he could be trusted.[46] Adams might have suggested that the young single man demonstrate his loyalties by simply joining the Patriot army around Boston. But that apparently did not occur to Adams. Hichborn was soon on his way with the volatile letter, along with a missive from Adams to his wife and a third letter—from Benjamin Harrison to George Washington. Traveling by way of Newport, Rhode Island, Hichborn boarded a ferry near where British ships patrolled. A British boat, sent from a ship, approached the ferry. Hichborn had ample time to toss the letters overboard, but instead he clung to them. Hichborn was duly snared and the letters confiscated.

The British and their Loyalist allies gleefully read the letters and copied them. Adams's private tirade became public. The letters to Abigail Adams and Washington got little attention, but the unsigned letter to Warren was a sensation. Some on the Loyalist side wrongly guessed the author was Samuel Adams[47] and that the "piddling Genius" was Hancock. It didn't much matter. What was important was this proof that, despite Congress's supine petitions, at least one delegate was hell bent on independence. Furthermore, the letter suggested that Congress, cloaked in secrecy, was not serenely harmonious, but churning with discord. The letter was published on both sides of the Atlantic.

By the time John Adams arrived back in Philadelphia, everyone knew that he was the author and that the "piddling Genius" was Dickinson. The scandal darkened the mood as delegates resumed work. Adams learned about Dickinson's reaction to the letter one Saturday morning in September when he came upon him on Chestnut Street: "We met, and passed near enough to touch Elbows. He passed without moving his Hat, or Head or Hand. I bowed and pulled off my Hat. He passed hautily by … We are not to be upon speaking Terms, nor bowing Terms, for the time to come."[48]

Meanwhile, Adams reassessed his colleagues: "[T]here appears to me a remarkable Want of Judgment in some of our Members." He drew more word portraits, most of which were not flattering. Eliphalet Dyer of Connecticut was "long winded and roundabout," while Edward Rutledge of South Carolina "Speaks thro his Nose, as the Yankees Sing," and Roger Sherman of Connecticut was "Aukward as a junior Batchelor."[49]

As delegates resumed work, they delved into the management of the war. Over the coming weeks, Congress formed more than a dozen committees to address issues connected with the military. They ruminated about military strategy, conjuring notions of strikes against British forces as far away as Detroit.[50] Nothing came of that idea, but Congress still dreamed about conquering Montreal and Quebec City. Permission for Schuyler to invade Quebec remained in effect.

On September 19, Congress established a committee—the Secret Committee—charged with buying and distributing arms and ammunition. This was "Secret" because of the utmost importance of ensuring that no details of its work be leaked to the British.[51] The Secret Committee would function as a sort of war department for this embryonic government.

Meanwhile, as Congress toiled in Philadelphia, so did Washington in Massachusetts. The general's letters to Congress complained of "a great want of powder,"[52] "Want of Engineers," "Want of Tools," and "Want of Tents,"[53] as well as the overriding problem, a want of money to keep the army intact.

In late September, delegates chose Franklin, along with Benjamin Harrison of Virginia and Thomas Lynch of South Carolina, to travel to Cambridge, meet face-to-face with America's military leader and top officials from the various revolutionary governments of New England, and report back to Congress.[54] At that meeting Washington made his case and then afterward dispatched a groan to Philadelphia: "[M]y Situation is inexpressibly distressing, to see the Winter, fast approaching upon a naked Army: The Time of their Service within a few Weeks of expiring, & no Provision, yet made for such important Events. Added to these, the Military Chest is totally exhausted."[55] Most troops "are in a State not far from Mutiny." Without more money soon, he added, "the Army must absolutely break up."[56]

In early November, Congress gave Washington much of what he asked—more troops, higher pay for officers and enlisted men, and new and tougher regulations for the army.[57]

Congress was reluctant to deny anything to its general, who already, without having accomplished anything on the battlefield, radiated an aura of greatness. About this time, a Philadelphian gushed: "He [Washington] seems to be one of those illustrious heroes whom providence raises up once in three or four hundred years to save a nation from ruin. ... There is not a king in Europe that would not look like a valet de chambre by his side."[58]

Many delegates to Congress likewise tended to bow before the commander, giving him ample respect and room to maneuver. However, behind the scenes, at least a few delegates were uneasy about the nature of the Continental Army and its growing strength. One such delegate was Samuel Adams. He of all people should have been pleased at how matters stood. Congress had come to the aide of Massachusetts and an American army was now poised to drive the British from Boston. That was just what he wanted—or was it? Adams well understood that the army created to rescue Massachusetts could become an oppressive, even terrifying, army of occupation—perhaps no better, and maybe even worse, than the despised Redcoats. Could the people of Massachusetts trust the Continental Congress, a dubious government if a government at all, to exert proper civilian control over the army? "It is always dangerous to the Liberties of the People to have an Army kept up among them over which they have no Controul," wrote Adams to a colleague in Massachusetts: "History affords us abundant Evidence of established Armies making themselves the Masters of those Countries which they were designd to protect."[59]

Adams imagined a time when all American military forces might be controlled by the Continental Congress. But for now, Massachusetts and all the colonies should also have their own militias:

> The Continental Army is at present very properly under the Direction of the Continental Congress. Possibly if ever such a Legislative should be formd, it may be proper that the whole Military Power of every Colony should be under its absolute Direction. Be that as it may, will it not, till then, be prudent, that the Militia of each Colony should be under the Direction of its own Legislative which is and ought to be the sovereign uncontroulable Power within its own Limits or Territory.[60]

As delegates wrestled with questions concerning the army, they found time to ponder the creation of a navy. The impetus for such a step came from the Rhode Island legislature, which had urged Congress to build a fleet big enough to "annoy our enemies" and help defend the colonies.[61] Maryland's Chase was aghast. The cost would be staggering—it was "the maddest idea in the World."[62]

Others, though, were willing to think about it. It was impossible to imagine a navy mighty enough to sweep the British from the coast, but a small navy might be useful if only to snipe at the British and add to their costs. "A naval Force might be created which would do something," wrote John Adams. "It would oblige our Enemies to sail in Fleets."[63]

Without actually authorizing a permanent navy, Congress took baby steps in that direction. Two ships—the *Andrea Doria* and the *Cabot*—would be bought, armed, and dispatched to go after British merchant ships.[64] Congress soon authorized two more vessels and handed responsibility for fitting the four-vessel fleet to a committee that included John Adams, Deane, Rhode Island's Stephen Hopkins, and four others. They would meet each evening at 6pm at the Tun Tavern, on the waterfront, where their chatter went beyond the business of ships and seamen. Late in life, Adams recalled the evenings at the tavern where Hopkins, aged 68, "kept us in Conversation" sometimes until midnight: "Hopkins never drank to excess, but all he drank was immediately not only converted into Wit, Sense, Knowledge and good humour, but inspired Us all with similar qualities."[65]

Eventually, that committee gave way to a larger one, the Marine Committee, with a delegate from each colony and the task of creating a comprehensive plan for a navy.[66]

CHAPTER 11

Their Rights as Dear as Our Own

In early October, promising news from General Schuyler brightened the mood in Congress. New Hampshire's John Langdon wrote: "We are likely soon to be in possession of St. John's [Fort St. Jean] and Canada, as the former is held Besieged by our Troops, and the Canadians join us, the Indians are also Friendly."[1] The Continental Army had at last invaded Quebec.

Through the summer, as Schuyler gathered military strength, he also collected promising intelligence indicating that at least some Canadians and even some British soldiers were hoping for an invasion. According to one report, "The Canadians have waited with the utmost impatience your coming, and begin to despair of seeing you. ... The soldiers are much harassed and would be glad of your arrival, and I make no doubt numbers will desert upon the sight of your army."[2] Schuyler received another report promising 3,000 men to fight alongside the Americans.[3]

Meanwhile, over those summer weeks, Congress gave Schuyler no further direction. The only word Schuyler received was a single letter from a single delegate in August. That letter, from Samuel Chase of Maryland, warned, "a *sine qua non*, of Marching into Quebec, is the Friendship of the Canadians: without their Consent and Approbation, it is not [to] be undertaken, so I understand the Resolution of the Congress."[4]

Thus, without a firm push from Congress, Schuyler hesitated, even after Washington gave him a nudge, letting Schuyler know that, if there was going to be an invasion in 1775, it better happen soon before winter closed in. Locked in a siege around Boston, Washington had a lot of men with not much to do. He was prepared to send off more than 1,000 from Massachusetts up the Kennebec River in Maine toward Quebec City. According to this plan, the Americans would mount a coordinated attack on that city and on Montreal. Washington would send men marching through the Maine wilderness toward Quebec City only if he was certain Schuyler was moving against Montreal.[5]

As it turned out, Schuyler never did pull the trigger on the invasion of Canada. Instead, a subordinate pulled it for him. In August, Schuyler left Ticonderoga to attend a conference in Albany. With Schuyler away, Brigadier-General Richard Montgomery was in charge, and he learned the British were building two ships for service on Lake Champlain. These would soon be joined by three galleys. Montgomery felt he had to strike before those ships were finished and the British moved to seize full control of the lake.[6]

Montgomery thus set the invasion in motion. In early September, about the time Congress reassembled in Philadelphia, Continental troops—mainly men from New York and Connecticut—entered Canada. Schuyler caught up with his men, but soon became ill with "a bilious fever" and "violent rheumatick pains"[7] and had to be evacuated to Ticonderoga, leaving Montgomery once again in charge.[8] Schuyler's letters to Congress, dated late September and written at Ticonderoga,[9] expressed confidence: "[T]he glorious end which we have in view ... will be attained." He also noted trouble on account of a "scandalous want of subordination and inattention to my orders" and a "vast variety of disagreable and vexatious incidents that almost every hour arise in some department or other."[10] Schuyler peppered Congress with questions:

> If we succeed, what Troops are to remain in *Canada*? ... The weather already begins to be cold. The Troops in three weeks more will with great difficulty be able to stand it, poorly and thinly as they are clad. How are they to be supplied? ... What kind of conduct am I to pursue with the Canadians respecting civil matters? ... Where shall I get gold or silver to pay for necessaries for the Army? paper of any kind not having the least currency in *Canada*.[11]

Congress would only learn snippets of the full story: Canadians indeed had responded to the invasion with encouraging support to the *Bastonnais* (Bostonians), as the Canadians called the Americans. Even so, the invasion force bogged down. The Americans were their own worst enemies. False reports spooked them; poor discipline hampered them; internal rivalries divided them; pilfering distracted them. Illness struck hundreds of soldiers as well. As for Montgomery, a former British officer, he became so disgusted with the Continentals he commanded that he looked for a chance to resign.[12] In a letter to Congress, Montgomery wrote: "Could I depend on the troops, I might venture to promise success."[13]

Still, Montgomery, like Schuyler, anticipated victory and begged Congress to dispatch three delegates to Canada to guide him on the occupation "lest I should make any *faux pas*."[14]

Hancock, on behalf of Congress, replied. For the moment, it would not be sending any delegation northward. Instead, Congress asked Schuyler to induce the Canadians to "accede to an Union with these Colonies" and to send delegates to Congress: "You may assure them that we shall hold their Rights as dear as our own." Congress would do its best to ensure a free government and provide security to people and property derived "from the British Constitution." Congress, even as it challenged British authority, revered the British foundation for laws and justice. Meanwhile, Hancock promised, Catholics in Canada could be confident that their religious practices would not be touched: "[Y]ou may further declare that we hold sacred the Rights of Conscience, and shall never molest them in the free Enjoyment of their Religion."[15]

As for the demand for hard money, Congress had none, so it turned to the Pennsylvania treasury and obtained, for Continental currency, gold and silver coins valued at about $17,000. These coins were sent along to Schuyler with "an escort of 4 of the light horse of this city."[16] Congress understood, as did Schuyler and Montgomery, the importance of this money.

As Schuyler suggested, Continental currency, while accepted by Americans, was worthless to Canadians. Of course, the Continental Army could simply steal what it needed. The Canadians couldn't stop them, but that would be a rude way to treat the people they wanted as friends. The Americans had to have gold and silver to pay for their supplies.

***

While military affairs consumed much attention that fall in Philadelphia, other matters intruded. One was the death of Peyton Randolph. The former president of Congress had returned to Philadelphia as a delegate. At a dinner at a country house near Philadelphia, he collapsed and died, felled by a stroke.[17]

Another distraction had to do with Benjamin Church, a respected Boston physician who had been at the center of the Patriot cause since early on. In July, Congress made Church surgeon general, the top medical man for the Continental Army. He was, everyone thought, a Patriot through and through.

As it turned out, however, about the time of Church's appointment, a young woman in New England gave a letter to a Rhode Island man and asked him to deliver it to an officer on a British vessel. The man happened to be a Patriot sympathizer and suspected something fishy. He took the letter and went on his way, but instead of delivering it, he opened it. Finding it was written in code, he passed it on to one of Washington's generals, who in turn gave it to Washington. When the code was broken, it was discovered that the letter contained information about American military strength. An investigation found that the woman was Church's mistress, and that Church was the letter's author. Church was arrested and confessed to the letter, but "made many protestations as to the purity of his intentions." Washington asked Congress "for their special advice and direction."[18]

Word of Church's arrest, arriving in Philadelphia in early October, stunned delegates, especially the New Englanders. Rhode Island's Samuel Ward wrote:

> Dr. Church, Who could have thought or even suspected it, a Man who seemed to be all Animation in the Cause of his Country, highly caressed, employed in several very honorable & lucrative Departments, & in full Possession of the Confidence of his Country, what a Complication of Madness & Wickedness must a Soul be filled with to be capable of such Perfidy, what Punishment can equal such horrid Crimes. I communicated the Affair to the Massachusetts Delegates. They could hardly conceive it possible.[19]

Indeed, John Adams was dumbfounded: "At the Story of the Surgeon General I stand astonished. ... Good God! What shall We say of human Nature? What shall We say of American Patriots? Or rather what will the World say?"[20]

After a few weeks, Congress responded: Church should be held in jail in Connecticut "without the use of pen, ink, and paper, and that no person be allowed to converse with him"[21] without a town official or sheriff present.

While the Church affair was a shock, it didn't take up much precious time. But there were a multitude of other issues that gobbled hours to no purpose. One was the matter of John McPherson. The "captain," wounded nine or 10 times at sea, so he said, came to Congress with a secret plan to destroy every British vessel in North America. Was McPherson a lunatic or a fraud? John Adams thought neither: "He is a Genius—an old Sea Warriour."[22] A three-member committee assigned to talk with McPherson returned with a report that McPherson's fantastic plan "appeared practicable." Congress doled out $300 to McPherson and sent him off to Massachusetts with a letter for Washington, suggesting to the general that McPherson's plan was "well worth attempting" on the British fleet at Boston.[23]

What, exactly, was his plan? It was all very hush-hush. Even John Adams, who was frequently indiscreet, revealed nothing in his correspondence: "Of Mr. McPhersons Errand to the Camp ask no Questions and I will tell you no false News. It will make a Noise, in Time—but for the present for Gods sake let not a Word be said."[24]

Washington, in Cambridge, gave McPherson's scheme "all that care and attention which the Importance of it deserved." However, Washington was skeptical and had McPherson talk to some of the army's artillery experts, who convinced McPherson that the idea, whatever it was, was based "upon wrong principles" and would "proove abortive."[25] Nothing came of it.

Back in Philadelphia, delegates managed matters large and small requiring attention, time, and patience. Congress churned out dozens of resolutions authorizing payment to individuals for services or goods: to Andrew McNair for serving as doorkeeper; to James Milligan for "sail cloth, Russia sheeting, oznabrigs, &c." for the army; to William Shad for services as messenger; to George Frank, John Powell, and James Alexander for "riding express"; to Frederick Bicking for 56 reams of paper for the currency;[26] and on and on.

Until this time, Congress's role was solely to handle matters related to the crisis with Britain. But in early October, delegates found themselves for the first time drawn into other matters—specifically a conflict between colonies. Most borders between colonies were well established, but there were still some places where more than one colony claimed the same land. One such overlapping claim was in the Wyoming Valley of what is now Pennsylvania. Both Pennsylvania and Connecticut had charters and treaties supporting their respective claims.[27] On October 7, Congress received a resolution from the Pennsylvania legislature concerning the "intrusion" of settlers into the colony "under the pretended claim of the colony of Connecticut, to the great annoyance of the good people"[28] of Pennsylvania. The lawmakers of Pennsylvania wanted Congress's help "to quiet the minds" of Pennsylvanians and prevent further settlements under Connecticut's claim.

The squabble on the frontier had erupted after a 1768 treaty with the indigenous people cleared the way for settlers in that region. Geography favored Pennsylvania: the disputed area was plainly contiguous with the rest of the province, but was separated from Connecticut by a portion of New York. However, Connecticut had the advantage of numbers. The Yankees, as those who recognized Connecticut's claims were called, outnumbered the so-called Pennamites, those who recognized Pennsylvania's claims. The failure to resolve the conflicting claims left a trail of injuries, confiscations, the taking of prisoners, and at least one death[29] as the Yankees tussled with the Pennamites over disputed land.

Officially, the task of sorting out quarrels among colonies was still the job of the king, despite the ongoing crisis. Pennsylvania did not dispute this. It was not asking Congress to seize authority from the king in this matter, just to suggest a resolution "until the matter shall be determined by King and Council."[30] Congress, with no interest in investing time in the matter, turned the matter over to the delegates from Pennsylvania and Connecticut to sort out and report back.

The committee made no headway and tossed it back into the lap of Congress. As disputes on the Susquehanna River "had proceeded to bloodshed," the Connecticut delegates urged Congress to form a new committee "out of the other colonies" to untangle the knot.[31] In the end, Congress put the knot on the shelf. Overwhelmed with other matters and afraid to suggest a resolution that might annoy either Connecticut or Pennsylvania, or both, and possibly shatter colonial unity, Congress let the matter fester, which it did until a settlement was eventually reached in 1782.[32]

While Congress dodged the squabble between Pennsylvania and Connecticut, it could not sidestep all the other troubling questions that came tumbling over the threshold. In November 1775, Congress declared itself an appeals court for spats over ships and cargoes seized from the British.[33] Thus Congress began to take on judicial, as well as executive and legislative, duties.

With no bureaucracy to rely on for research or handling small matters, Congressional committees were overwhelmed. These were by and large ad hoc committees, established only for a specific task. Then, as months went by, Congress attempted to streamline work by establishing standing committees, fixed committees specialized for handling major and continuing areas of importance. Periodically, Congress would form itself into a Committee of the Whole. Because no formal record of committee proceedings was kept, this maneuver gave delegates freedom to speak more freely than they might in regular sessions.

But everything, no matter how trivial, had to be voted on by the entire Congress. We see in the *Journal*, for example, scores of resolutions duly recorded for the payment for all kinds of bills: $35.80 to Christopher Hayne for kettles and canteens; $10.40

to Henry Valentine for "transcribing writings for the Congress"; $20.00 to Francis Lee for "horse hire."[34]

Meanwhile, there were more than enough crises elsewhere to fret about. One big one was in Virginia. A resolution on October 6 seemed to sanction the seizure of anyone opposed to the Patriot movement: "Resolved, That it be recommended to the several provincial Assemblies or Conventions, and councils or committees of safety, to arrest and secure every person in their respective colonies, whose going at large may, in their opinion, endanger the safety of the colony, or the liberties of America."[35]

The resolution stemmed from concern over one man in particular, John Murray, the Earl of Dunmore, who happened to be the royal governor of Virginia. Chase of Maryland said: "I dont think the Resolution goes far enough. ... Ld. Dunmore has been many Months committing Hostilities vs. Virginia, and has extended his Piracies to Maryland. I wish he had been seized, by the Colony, Months ago. They would have received the Thanks of all North America."[36]

Delegates in Philadelphia cast Dunmore as an arch-villain: arrogant, prickly, avaricious, unpredictable, and quick to make enemies, but also crafty. For the moment, delegates, especially those from the South, obsessed over how best to defang this snake.

Royal governor first of New York and then of Virginia, Dunmore, from the moment he came to America, had used the opportunity to amass vast tracts of land in the western wilderness. His claims included no fewer than 3.7 million acres in what is now Indiana. Later, determined to advance western expansion, Dunmore defied his royal superiors and plunged into a war with Ohio's indigenous tribes, defeated them, and forced them to surrender claims to what is now Kentucky and western Pennsylvania.[37]

With revolutionary fervor heating up in 1775, Dunmore had to focus on preserving his crumbling authority in Virginia, where he felt so threatened that in June he abandoned Williamsburg for the safety of a British warship docked at Yorktown.[38] Delegates' hand wringing about Dunmore in October likely had to do in part with raids by small British vessels on Patriot property along such rivers as the York and the James. Marauders dispatched by Dunmore pounced on plantations, looted them, and grabbed enslaved people. Thomas Jefferson was alarmed enough to send a warning to his wife, on a visit to relatives near the James River, to keep "at a distance from the alarms of Ld. Dunmore."[39] Washington had a similar notion that Dunmore might send a vessel up the Potomac to attack Mount Vernon and take Martha Washington hostage.

Plantation raids were just part of the problem with Dunmore. Delegates in Philadelphia were also likely stirred up by Dunmore's unofficial policy of inviting enslaved men to flee their owners and join his small force of soldiers, seamen, and Loyalist recruits. The move to incorporate escaped slaves was, in military terms, ingenious, as it would bolster his forces while also weakening the Patriots by compelling militiamen to return to their plantations and farms to keep their slaves in line.

For delegates in Philadelphia, Dunmore represented a dilemma—how could Congress sanction the capture of a royal governor and still hope for reconciliation with Britain? Richard Henry Lee of Virginia had no qualms and called for stronger measures: "I wish Congress would advise Virginia and Maryland to raise a Force by Sea to destroy Ld. Dunmores Power."[40]

But Georgia's Zubly was horrified. Grabbing Dunmore, he feared, would inflame Britain and cripple fading chances of a peaceful resolution to the crisis: "Seizing the K's Representatives will make a great Impression in England, and probably Things will be carried on afterwards with greater Rage."[41]

Many Americans, especially Virginians, were furious and fearful that Dunmore might set alight a slave rebellion. One angry Virginian was Washington. From Cambridge, Massachusetts, he found time to rant: "If the Virginians are wise, that Arch Traitor to the Rights of Humanity, Lord Dunmore, should be instantly crushd, if it takes the force of the whole Colony to do it."[42]

Dunmore's policy, though a wily military move, was a fatal political blunder. In luring enslaved people, Dunmore threatened the prevailing social and economic order, thus uniting Southerners—at least white Southerners—against British authority as never before.

As Dunmore offended Southern delegates in Congress, a British admiral similarly agitated New England delegates. In November, Congress received news from Washington of "an Outrage exceeding in Barbarity & Cruelty every hostile Act practised among civilized Nations."[43] This was the bombardment of Falmouth (now Portland) on the Maine coast. Under orders by Admiral Samuel Graves, a British naval squadron destroyed most of the town in retaliation for it firing on a British vessel. New England delegates, already dubious about chances of reconciliation, were now hardened against it.

Offsetting the shocking news about Falmouth was more promising news from Canada that the invading Continentals and their Canadian allies had taken Fort Chambly, an outpost north of Fort St. Jean. The fort was not significant—defended by just 83 soldiers[44]—but its capture provide the Continentals with 124 barrels[45] of precious powder. In addition to the gunpowder, the British also surrendered regimental colors, which were duly sent on to Philadelphia, presented to Congress, and promptly hung "with great Splendor and Elegance"[46] in the chamber of Hancock's bride (John had married Dolly Quincy that August[47]).

What about Fort St. Jean? Delegates in Philadelphia had no way of knowing this, but about the time the 7th Regiment's colors were going up in Dolly Hancock's room, Montgomery's Continental force entered Fort St. Jean after a 45-day siege. Before the end of the month, Montreal—less than 30 miles away—would be in American hands.

Meanwhile, as delegates well knew, another American force was making its way through the Maine wilderness to Quebec City. Those soldiers had sailed in September from Newburyport, Massachusetts, landed on the Maine coast, and paddled up the Kennebec River. With luck, Americans would soon control Quebec City. Congress dispatched a trio of delegates to meet with General Schuyler at Ticonderoga about plans in Canada. Delegates dared to think that their association of 13 colonies would soon have a 14th. "We wait in a State of most anxious suspense for Accounts of the total reduction of Canada and their accession to our League," wrote South Carolina's Thomas Lynch.[48]

Congress's focus when delegates looked north was on Quebec province and the vital St. Lawrence River. But in November, Nova Scotia also came into view with a petition from the people of Passamaquoddy and their application "to be admitted into the association of the North Americans, for the preservation of their rights and liberties."[49]

If delegates could imagine Quebec joining the Congress and standing arm in arm with the American colonies in this conflict, why not Nova Scotia as well? Indeed, in some ways, Nova Scotia seemed more promising—the population was largely Protestant and English-speaking, and three-quarters of the population was made up of transplanted New Englanders who had many of the same complaints about British authority as the people in the colonies to the south.[50] Of the remaining population, many were French-speaking Acadians who had evaded forced expulsion by the British back in the 1750s or had migrated back to Nova Scotia after being expelled. They too had little good to say about British authority. The colony had been mostly quiet in the run-up to the Revolution, but there had been some mild protests, such as the torching in Halifax of hay bound for Boston to feed British military horses.[51]

Congress needed more information. Before the end of the month, Congress dispatched two men to Nova Scotia "to inquire into the state of that Colony, the disposition of the Inhabitants towards the American cause," and to gather information about British forts, arms, ships, soldiers, and sailors.[52]

CHAPTER 12

The Child Was Not Yet Weaned

Over those crowded weeks in the fall of 1775, still other issues demanded attention. From New Hampshire, for example, came a plea to Congress for permission to form a provincial government independent of royal control.

By this time, the royal governor of New Hampshire, American-born John Wentworth—nephew of Benning Wentworth[1]—had fled.[2] For months he had been powerless as governor, his orders being increasingly ignored. Then mobs chased him out of his mansion. He stayed on for a few months in a British fort in Portsmouth before finally sailing off to England.

Now, no one could say just who was in charge. A firm authority of some kind needed to be established to maintain order, collect taxes, and gather, train, and supply troops to the war effort in Massachusetts. The colony's two delegates, dispatched by the colony's revolutionary provincial congress, wanted Congress's "advice & Direction" concerning "a Method for our Administering Justice and regulating our civil Police."[3]

This request was similar to the earlier one from Massachusetts. In that case, Congress gave its approval. But Massachusetts was at war and there was an urgent need to establish authority. Was there such urgency in New Hampshire? After all, to grant such permission would further provoke Britain and reduce chances of reconciliation.

In October 1775, as delegates debated how to respond, John Adams seized the moment. Not only should New Hampshire establish its own independent government, he said, but so should each of the other 12 "states." Adams was ready now to set off a scramble of conventions, elections, and constitution-making up and down America; not a single declaration of independence, but 12 independence movements in the new "states," as each of the former colonies joined Massachusetts in establishing governments free of British authority. Adams's use of the word "states" was deliberate and provocative.

Yet Congress was not about to follow Adams's suggestion and set off political upheaval. Nor were delegates ready to embrace the term "states." The resolution that emerged in November applied only to New Hampshire and preserved the term "province." But it gave Patriot leaders in New Hampshire a free hand: Congress recommended that the people's representatives in New Hampshire should, while the dispute with Britain continued, establish a government that "will best produce the happiness of the people, and most effectually secure peace and good order in the province."[4] Nothing was said about the royal charter.

As far as John Adams was concerned, Congress fell short. But this step was actually a big one. In advising Massachusetts, delegates had asked revolutionary leaders to follow the old charter as much as possible. The familiar old forms of government were to be maintained where it was practical. To New Hampshire, Congress offered no such advice. The people there could do as they pleased. New Hampshire was free to be independent, and that was fine with Congress.

Just as Congress finished with New Hampshire, a similar request came from South Carolina. As in New Hampshire, the royal governor had by this time been chased from his home. Though he remained in America, he was powerless.[5]

Power was in the hands of the Council of Safety established by South Carolina's revolutionary provincial congress. That Council had ordered measures to deal with possible slave uprisings and attacks by indigenous warriors.[6] It also took steps against surging Loyalism in the backcountry. There was plenty of anger in the remote areas far from the coast, but it wasn't about British taxes or oppression. Settlers resented the provincial congress and bristled when asked to obey the guidelines of Congress's Association. With the encouragement of the royal governor, they even organized their own Loyalist "Counter-Association."[7] In September, bloody fighting flared up as Patriot military groups skirmished with Loyalist Americans. Meanwhile, tension between the governor and the provincial government boiled over, leading the governor to scramble with a cluster of royal officials to the safety of a warship.[8]

The time seemed ripe for a new government in South Carolina formally unconnected with British authority. In early November, the four delegates from South Carolina in Philadelphia brought forward a petition from their province asking permission to craft a new government.[9]

In the ensuing debate, once again John Adams lobbied to set off an independence parade: give all colonies permission to set up new governments free of British control. He further advised once again to dispense with the term "colony" and use "state" instead, and also discard the pallid "dispute" for the more honest "war." Once again, those notions had yet to mature, or as Adams later noted, "the Child was not yet weaned."[10]

But Congress nonetheless granted South Carolina, as with New Hampshire, a free hand in crafting a new government.[11] Congress took pains to note that the new governments would exist only "during the continuance of the present dispute between Great Britain and the colonies."[12] Congress clung to the fantasy that, once Britain came to its senses, the new governments would give way to something like the old ones. The measures dealing with New Hampshire and South Carolina appear to have been the last straws for Georgia's Zubly, plainly uneasy about anything hinting of independence. In October, he wrote in his journal: "A Separation from the Parent State I wd dread as one of the greatest evils & should it ever be proposed will pray & fight against it. Some good men may desire it but good men do not always know what they are about."[13] In November, he said his goodbyes: "I am Setting off to Georgia greatly indisposed."[14]

Pennsylvania's Dickinson did not quit but was likewise disturbed at the way matters were heading. He tried to ensure that Pennsylvania delegates stood their ground against independence. His instructions for newly selected Pennsylvania delegates to Congress "strictly" ordered that delegates reject any proposals "that may cause or lead to a Separation from our Mother Country, a Change of the Form of Government, or the Establishment of a Commonwealth."[15]

However, when given a chance in December to challenge a measure nudging the colonies toward independence, Pennsylvania delegates ignored those instructions and joined the majority in supporting it.

The impetus for this move came from Virginia and the further mischief of Lord Dunmore. Congress learned that Dunmore declared martial law in Virginia and made official his scheme of promising freedom to any enslaved man able and willing to join British forces.[16]

Furthermore, Dunmore's regular troops with some Loyalist volunteers had attacked and defeated a Patriot force. Delegates seethed. Virginia's Francis Lightfoot Lee (brother of Richard Henry Lee) wrote: "Fatal consequences may follow if an immediate stop is not put to that Devil's career."[17] Without a formal request from Patriots in Virginia, Congress quickly gave the colony virtually the same instructions it provided to South Carolina and New Hampshire—establish an independent government. Congress also authorized three companies of troops from Pennsylvania to march off to Virginia to defend "against the enemies of America."[18]

The press of business left delegates little time for pleasure, or even sleep. Silas Deane confessed to his Elizabeth:

> I rise at Six, write untill Seven dress & breakfast by Eight go to the Committee of Claims untill Ten, then in Congress untill half past Three or perhaps four—Dine by five, & then go either to the Committee of Secrecy, or of Trade untill Nine, then Sup & go to Bed by Eleven. This leaves little Room for diversion, or any thing else, and to Tell You the Truth I expect this kind of Life must be my Lot for some time.[19]

John Adams told a similar story to his Abigail:

> The whole Congress is taken up, almost in different Committees from seven to Ten in the Morning—from Ten to four or sometimes five, we are in Congress and from six to Ten in Committees again. ... If I could visit the Coffee Houses, in the Evening and the Coffee Tables of the Ladies in the Afternoon, I could entertain you with many smart Remarks upon Dress and Air, &c. and give you many sprightly Conversations, but my Fate you know is to be moping over Books and Papers, all the Leisure Time I have when I have any.[20]

Committee work swallowed time, and there were committees for everything: supplying the army; buying woolens for the army; answering correspondence from Washington; instructing a committee meeting with Washington. Some committees returned with reports, such as one recommending that delegates wear more leather as an example to the people for reducing use of precious woolen cloth, normally imported from Britain.[21]

Meanwhile, the hoard of Continental dollars—$2 million authorized in June and another $1 million in July[22]—was quickly disappearing. John Adams was alarmed: "The Expense already accrued will astonish Us all, I fear."[23] But Franklin was not concerned:

> I am not terrified by the Expence of this War, should it continue ever so long. A little more Frugality, or a little more Industry in Individuals will with Ease defray it. ... Forbearing to drink Tea saves three fourths of the Money; and 500,000 Women doing each threepence Worth of Spinning or Knitting in a Week will pay the rest.[24]

Before 1775 came to an end, Congress authorized the printing of yet another $3 million.[25]

***

As for that war, the outlook appeared bright indeed, especially when news arrived in late November that Continental troops had taken Montreal.[26] As military victories go, it was not especially glorious. By the time the Americans approached the town, few defenders were there to stop them. Following that easy conquest, it was easy for delegates in Philadelphia to assume Quebec City would be in American hands. Some were ready to rearrange the chairs and desks at the State House to make room for more colleagues. "No doubt is entertained here, but that this Congress will be shortly joined by Delegates from Canada, which will then complete the union of 14 provinces," wrote Virginia's Richard Henry Lee.[27]

The news about Montreal came with a plea from General Schuyler: he had had enough of being a general and wanted to quit. Congress assigned some of its best writers to shower the general with rhetorical kisses: "You have hitherto risen superior to a Thousand Difficulties in giving Freedom to a great and an oppressed People. You have already reaped many Laurels, but a plentiful Harvest still invites you. Proceed therefore, and let the Footsteps of Victory open a Way for Blessings of Liberty, and the Happiness of well ordered Government to visit that extensive Dominion."[28] Schuyler stayed on.[29]

***

On November 21, 1775, many Philadelphians and the town's Second Battalion[30] gathered on Chestnut Street at the Schuylkill River to attend the arrival of Martha

Washington.[31] Proving false the rumors ginned up by the British that she had abandoned her husband,[32] the general's wife was on her way north from Virginia to join him in Massachusetts. She did not travel light. With her went all sorts of baggage—from hams and blankets to knitting wool—in addition to leather trunks studded with brass nails and stuffed with belongings. She had with her her son, Jack, his wife, and a nephew of George, plus five household slaves.[33] Along the way she picked up the wife of General Horatio Gates.[34] In Philadelphia, "Lady Washington" was greeted like royalty with an escort into town by infantry and troops on horseback.[35] A special celebration ball was hastily planned for the elegant City Tavern. Who could find fault with a festive event to honor the wife of America's first soldier?

In fact, many did. On the day of the planned ball, Christopher Marshall, a townsman well acquainted with many of the delegates, went to the State House and asked to see John Hancock. With Hancock nowhere to be found, he talked instead to Samuel Adams, advising him "to give my respects to Col. Hancock, desire him to wait on Lady Washington to request her not to attend or go this evening" to the ball in her honor. Marshall had heard alarming threats suggesting that, if the ball took place, the tavern "would cut but a poor figure to morrow morning."[36] That is, the business would be ripped apart—windows broken and doors smashed, at the very least. Such destruction of property was common enough in these tense times. Earlier that fall, a mob had smashed the windows, doors, and furniture of a targeted house. In that case, the house belonged to a man believed to oppose the Patriot cause.[37]

But why would Patriot mobs be offended by this festive and Patriotic event? As Marshall explained to Adams, the proposed ball appeared to violate terms of the Association that Congress created, specifically the resolve that encouraged frugality and discouraged "expensive diversions and entertainments."[38] If Congress was not going to enforce its own rules, a Philadelphia mob would.

Word of the threats circulated. A committee called on Martha Washington and, after "expressing great regard and affection to her," asked her "not to grace"[39] the party in her honor.

The event was canceled. Martha Washington took the matter in stride, assuring the committee "that their sentiments on this occasion, were perfectly agreeable unto her own." Meanwhile, Virginia delegate Benjamin Harrison was livid. After he learned of the cancellation, he stormed over to Samuel Adams's lodgings and gave him a scolding for his role in calling off the affair, which Harrison defended as "legal, just and laudable."[40]

Marshall, who was there along with Connecticut's Dyer, reported: "Many arguments were used by all present to convince him [Harrison] of the impropriety at this time, but all to no effect."[41]

On November 27, Martha Washington, "attended by the troop of horse, two companies of light infantry,"[42] was escorted out of town. As she wrote to a friend days later: "I left [Philadelphia] in as great pomp as if I had been a great somebody." She pronounced her visit to Philadelphia a delight: "[W]e were so attended and the gentlemen so kind, that I am lade under obligations to them that I shall not for get soon."[43]

***

As delegates juggled their myriad tasks, they remained alert for news from Great Britain. How would the king and Parliament respond to Congress's last plea for a peaceful way to settle this conflict? The answer came that same busy November when a ship from England brought news that the king refused to even glance at the petition.[44] The same vessel carried a proclamation from the king declaring the colonies in rebellion.[45] News also trickled into Philadelphia about the possible use of European mercenaries against Americans.

"We are told our Petition will be disregarded; that we shall be declared rebels, and our estates confiscated; we are threatened with ships of war, troops, Russians, Hanoverians and Hessians," wrote Joseph Hewes of North Carolina. "God knows how it will end."[46]

Rumors about mercenaries were true—the British would hire European soldiers, especially German soldiers, to help quell the rebellion. Some 30,000 would fight against the Americans, who almost always identified the German soldiers as Hessians, although about one-third of the German-speaking mercenaries came from outside the Hesse region.[47]

The news further unified delegates and clarified the issues. "To Be or not to be is now the Question; every private View, Passion & Interest ought to be buried," wrote Samuel Ward. "We are embarked in one common Bottom. If She sinks We all perish; if She survives the Storm, Peace & Plenty (the offspring of Liberty) and every thing which will dignify & felicitate human Nature will be the Reward of our Virtue."[48]

William Hooper of North Carolina saw no prospect of peace: "From newspapers & private Letters we are assured that next Summer will be a bloody one. The Sovereign has declared (we hear) that he will pawn the Jewels of his Crown or humble America. Indians, Negroes, Russians, Hanoverians & Hessians are talked of as the Instruments to accomplish this blessed purpose."[49]

The official response from Congress to the king's Proclamation of Rebellion came on December 6, just as Congress was digesting the disturbing news about Dunmore in Virginia. Challenging the king's accusation that some Americans were "forgetting the allegiance which they owe to the power that has protected and supported them,"[50] Congress pointed out the difference between allegiance to the king and allegiance to Parliament, a distinction difficult for modern Americans to understand, but critical back in 1775: "What allegiance is it that we forget? Allegiance to Parliament? We never owed—we never owned it. Allegiance to our King? Our words have ever avowed it,—our conduct has ever been consistent with it." Furthermore,

> [W]e oppose the claim and exercise of unconstitutional powers, to which neither the Crown nor Parliament were ever entitled. ... We know of no laws binding upon us, but such as have been transmitted to us by our ancestors, and such as have been consented to by ourselves, or our representatives elected for that purpose. ... The cruel and illegal attacks, which we oppose, have no foundation in the royal authority.[51]

***

As Congress crafted its response to the king, it also gave a thought to diplomacy. A committee of five—including Franklin, Dickinson, and New York's John Jay—was formed "for the sole purpose of corresponding with our friends in Great Britain, Ireland, and other parts of the world."[52] This Committee of Correspondence was the embryo of what would become the State Department. Significantly, the committee was given a free hand: letters could be sent without specific approval from Congress. All Congress required was for the committee to show the correspondence to Congress when thus directed.[53] Congress later gave the committee $3,000 for expenses and for employing agents.[54]

The Committee of Correspondence was quickly renamed the Committee of Secret Correspondence. This led to some confusion, as there was already a committee called the Secret Committee, with the task of arranging for imports of gunpowder and weapons. Because of the similar names, because the two committees worked closely together, and because sometimes membership overlapped, delegates occasionally mixed them up, at least until the name of the Secret Committee was changed in 1777 to the Committee of Commerce.[55]

***

In the deepening crisis, it was easy to imagine one, two, or more colonies abandoning Congress and their sister colonies and working out a friendly separate peace with Britain. This was always a dreaded possibility. That's why delegates were alarmed when news came from New Jersey that that colony's assembly was sidestepping Congress and reaching out on its own to Britain.

The source of the mischief was Governor William Franklin—Benjamin Franklin's Loyalist son—who remained bravely at his post. In defiance of the established government, a revolutionary provincial congress had sprung up and had even started collecting taxes. Predictably, people grumbled, but they proved more willing to hand over money to the revolutionary government than to the disintegrating royal government, and no one was going to pay taxes to both. So William Franklin's government was going broke. Even the governor could not count on receiving a salary.[56]

Meanwhile, the militia under the governor's control was evaporating as officers one by one quit to take up service on the Patriot side. Franklin no longer felt safe. Mobs threatened his property and he became increasingly isolated both politically, as his government and influence waned, and personally, as contact with his father became less frequent and more strained. On a visit by Benjamin to William in Perth Amboy that summer, father and son had argued violently enough to disturb neighbors.[57] They stayed in touch to work out arrangements for the teenage Temple Franklin—Benjamin's grandson, William's son—now in school in Philadelphia. But otherwise, Benjamin and William were estranged.

By November, William Franklin was one of just four royal governors still nominally in place.[58] Like his nervous counterparts in New York, Virginia, and Georgia, Franklin had a bad hand and few cards to play. But Franklin played them well, awaiting opportunities to awaken Loyalist sentiment, which he believed was mighty, just dormant. Thousands, he said, would risk their lives to defend the "old Constitution" and would come forward once they saw "a Chance of it being of any Avail."[59]

Sensing a backlash against the revolutionary movement, Governor Franklin seized the moment. He called together the assembly—the legally established assembly, sullen and edgy, but still submissive to royal authority. There in Burlington, then the capital of New Jersey, lawmakers buoyed Franklin's spirits with measures to his liking. He returned the favor with news from Britain that the king had agreed to a bill that seemed to ease the province's financial troubles.[60]

Franklin and the lawmakers now sang in harmony, for lawmakers churned out several resolutions that delighted the governor: they issued instructions to their delegates to the Continental Congress "utterly to Reject any Propositions … that may separate this Colony from the Mother Country."[61] Thus, New Jersey would join Pennsylvania in standing firm against independence.

The lawmakers also authorized the drafting of a petition to the king "humbly beseeching him to use his Interposition to prevent the Effusion of Blood" and express the lawmakers' wish for "a Restoration of Peace and Harmony with the parent State on constitutional Principles."[62]

News of these events alarmed delegates in nearby Philadelphia. The problem was not opposition to independence. That was arguably consistent with the official sentiment of Congress, still married to the idea of reconciliation.

The problem was with the other measure—the plan for New Jersey to draft and send off its own olive branch petition. That threatened to undermine Congress's role as the one voice—the only voice—of the colonies. If New Jersey broke ranks, other colonies might follow, and thus would begin the disintegration of colonial unity as colonies competed to bow lower and lower to Britain in exchange for favors.

Thus came a resolution: that "it will be very dangerous to the liberties and welfare of America, if any Colony should separately petition the King or either house of Parliament."[63]

To rein in the New Jersey lawmakers, Congress dispatched Dickinson and two other delegates to Burlington.[64]

In urging New Jersey lawmakers against drafting a petition like the one he had drawn up for Congress, Dickinson underscored the importance of colonial unity. Britain, he said, now understood America's willingness to fight. He spoke of Lexington. He boasted—prematurely—that Canada was "conquered in a few months as it took Britain years." Continued American "Unity" with "Bravery" remained essential. Separate petitions from the various colonies would only signal that Americans were divided: "we would become a Rope of Sand" and could expect "neither Mercy nor Justice" from Britain.[65]

Whether frightened or impressed, New Jersey lawmakers stepped back. After lengthy debate, they set the olive branch petition aside—a victory for Congress, and a defeat for William Franklin. New Jersey would not fracture the fragile union.

***

As 1775 wound down, the military picture for the American forces in Massachusetts and Canada appeared at a glance to be promising. In Massachusetts, Washington and his army, entrenched around Boston, still kept in check the British packed in the town. Meanwhile, Montreal was securely in American hands and Quebec City, it seemed, would soon follow.

But the picture was an illusion. In fact, disaster loomed. The threat to the American army in Massachusetts and Canada was not so much the British, but time.

In Massachusetts, Washington faced the possibility that come January 1, the army would melt away as men returned to their homes and farms. The problem was short enlistments. In cobbling together an army out of militiamen and other men available, Washington determined that it was useless to try to sign men up for the duration of the war, however long that would be. Few men would make such a commitment. Short enlistments were the rule. Everyone knew that at the year's end, the enlistments for many men camped around Boston would expire. New soldiers were urgently needed to take the place of those expected to leave.

In Canada, the circumstances for American forces were similar, but the crisis was already at hand well before the close of the year. General Montgomery, desperate to hold the army together long enough to take Montreal, had promised the men that they could leave once the city had been taken. Many took the general up on the offer, hurrying to be off before ice made it impossible to travel south by boat. Some officers were glad to be rid of the "Lame ... the lazy and the ... home sick" who were on their way back "to their Mommies and Daddies and Wives and pumkin Pies."[66] But then, who would complete the conquest of Canada? From some 1,800 men at the start of the campaign, the force had dwindled to about 1,000.[67]

CHAPTER 13

To Begin the World Over Again

On the first day of 1776, Connecticut's Eliphalet Dyer wrote: "God Grant it may be a Year of American deliverance from the Tyrrany, Oppression, Lawless & Hostile power, of Great Britain."[1] The next day, Congress called on the colonies to lock up "the more dangerous" Loyalists or ensure that they are "bound with sufficient sureties to their good behavior."[2]

In Philadelphia, outside the Pennsylvania State House, concerns about the crisis with Britain mingled with other worries—such as the small-scale war among Americans in the Wyoming district north of the city. The diary of a Philadelphian records on January 3: "News brought to-day of a skirmish between the Pennsylvanians and the Connecticut people in which Jesse Lukens was killed."[3]

A few days later, Philadelphia glimpsed for the first time the text of the king's October speech: "The rebellious war … is manifestly carried on for the purpose of establishing an independent empire." King George intended, he said, "to put a speedy end to these disorders by the most decisive exertions,"[4] including, perhaps, the use of foreign troops.

Rhode Island's Samuel Ward shared his thoughts with his daughter: "Thus you see my Love your Daddy's Sentiments are confirmed that the savage ever meant to make himself an absolute despotic Tyrant. May the Reward of his Hands & wicked Heart be given him."[5]

The notion of independence was in the air. Four colonies—New Hampshire, Virginia, Massachusetts, and South Carolina—had requested and received permission from Congress to set up governments independent of royal control. However, some other colonies pushed in the other direction. Maryland's delegates now had orders forbidding support for anything with a whiff of independence without approval from back home.[6] Thus Maryland joined Pennsylvania and New Jersey in resisting the tide. The colonies seemed to be wandering off in different directions.

Just where did Congress stand—for independence or against it? Pennsylvania's James Wilson stepped forward to take a crack at an official statement. Wilson and the committee he led delivered a draft in mid-February. It was, according to New Jersey's

Richard Smith, "very long, badly written & full against Independency."[7] It was indeed long—about 6,000 words—and arguably clumsy. However, the statement did not altogether rule out independence. It ends with: "That the Colonies may continue connected, as they have been, with Britain, is our second Wish: Our first is—that America may be free."[8] But the statement satisfied no one. The draft was set aside and forgotten. On the subject of independence, Congress was tongue-tied, lacking the will and the words to make a forceful stand one way or the other.

Outside Congress, up stepped Thomas Paine. Not a delegate to Congress, not even an American, this British immigrant—in America barely more than a year[9]—sounded the fanfare for separation. Paine's bugle was *Common Sense*, a pamphlet that appeared anonymously in Philadelphia in early January with a message that reverberated up and down the colonies.

Paine was a product of failure, disappointment, frustration, and some quite good luck. Born in Thetford, England,

Thomas Paine, an English immigrant, galvanized American support for independence with his pamphlet *Common Sense*, which appeared in 1776. His later essays helped revive support for the faltering cause. Congress eventually hired him as secretary to the Committee for Foreign Affairs. In 1781, he joined a mission to France seeking money and supplies. This portrait, done about 1805, is by John Wesley Jarvis. (Image courtesy of the National Gallery of Art)

about 70 miles northeast of London,[10] he was the only child of an Anglican mother and a Quaker maker of corset stays, a fashion essential for ladies—generally of linen or leather, reinforced with steel or whalebone, engineered to tame the tummy and boost the bosom. Young Paine (Pain, actually; he adopted the spelling Paine after he became famous) followed his father into the craft and served seven years as an apprentice.[11] Seeking adventure, 18-year-old Paine signed on as a crewman on a privateer, a ship authorized by the British government to attack and seize merchant vessels of the enemy, France. The portents were ominous: The name of the vessel was *Terrible*; the name of the captain was William Death. At sea, the *Terrible*'s luck was indeed terrible. A French privateer pounced on the vessel in the English Channel. Death died along with most of the crew. The 26 survivors were taken prisoner.[12] Fortunately for Paine, he never actually sailed. At the last minute, his father found him and dragged him back home.[13]

Despite the *Terrible*'s fate, young Paine remained keen to go to sea. He later signed on as a crewman on another privateer, returning after two years with money in his pocket.[14]

Back on land, he tried stay-making, first in London, then Dover, then Sandwich, where he married. But he was inept in business, with debts piling up. The couple started over in Margate. Then his wife died, perhaps in childbirth or after a long illness—no one knows.[15] At 23, a widower without money or prospects, he returned to Thetford to live with his parents.[16]

Desperate for an income of some kind, he studied to become an exciseman—a tax collector who inspected such commodities as tea, chocolate, tobacco, and alcohol. People hated excisemen and the pay was paltry, but it was a job. After gaining the proper qualifications, Paine landed a position.[17] However, less than a year later, he was fired, accused of taking shortcuts—declaring inspections that were never performed.[18]

He tried stay-making again, and quit again. He tried teaching, but couldn't make enough money. He then pleaded for another chance as an exciseman, got his wish, and worked for six years in that role near Brighton. He married again. He also found his voice as a spokesman for his fellow excisemen, lobbying on their behalf for more pay. His written arguments were powerful, but his campaign sputtered. He subsequently lost his job again and found himself more deeply in debt. After separating from his wife (whom he never divorced[19]) and then selling everything he had, he set off for London.

He was by then quite familiar with the capital city, having lived there and visited from time to time, lounging at coffee houses and attending lectures. His intellectual inclination in those days was not politics, but Newtonian science.[20] He had made a good impression in London with an influential man in the excise department. That man's circle of friends included writer Samuel Johnson, historian Edward Gibbon, and—most significantly—Benjamin Franklin, then living in London. Paine had met all three.

Uprooted, jobless, and determined to start anew in America, Paine knocked on Franklin's door. Franklin obliged Paine with two letters of recommendation: one addressed to son William, the Loyalist governor of New Jersey, and the other to Franklin's son-in-law, Richard Bache, a Philadelphia merchant. The letter to Bache recommended Paine, now aged 37, as "an ingenious worthy young man"[21] and suitable for a job as a clerk, tutor, or customs official.[22]

Paine was soon off to America, carrying those letters with him. He nearly died on the journey. By the time he arrived in Philadelphia, he was so weak from typhus that he had to be carried ashore.[23] This was December 1774, about a year after the Boston Tea Party and a few months before the battle of Lexington and Concord.[24]

Rising after six weeks in bed, Paine—with Franklin's letter in hand—called upon Bache, who opened doors, leading to work for Paine as a children's tutor. Bache also brought Paine to the attention of Robert Aitken, an immigrant who happened to own a bookstore and print shop. The two found common ground, a friendship blossomed, and Aitken made Paine editor of *Pennsylvania Magazine*, a new periodical.[25]

The periodical, promising "utility and entertainment,"[26] took off, building up a subscribership of more than 1,500, becoming the most widely read publication in America. Paine was not only chief editor, but also a prolific writer for the magazine, crafting about 20 percent of the articles.[27] His contributions included such light fare as "New Anecdotes about Alexander the Great," as well as meatier pieces, such as "African Slavery in America," a powerful condemnation of the institution.[28]

But the relationship between Paine and Aitken fractured, and by the fall of 1775, Paine was spending much of his time on a writing project unconnected with the magazine.[29] It was a time when authors trying to reach a wide audience with a single message would produce a pamphlet, a loosely stitched, cheap booklet. In Paine's case, the pamphlet was 46 pages long[30] and was titled *Common Sense*.[31] The pamphlet emerged from a Third Street print shop in Philadelphia on January 10, 1776. By January 13, it was the talk of the town and of Congress. Josiah Bartlett of New Hampshire wrote that day that *Common Sense* was being "greedily bought up and read by all ranks of people."[32]

Its straightforward, easy-to-understand style was refreshing at a time when much that was written was wordy, showy, legalistic, and forbidding to those less educated or well read. Meanwhile, its message was stunning. Most delegates in Congress, and most Americans, accepted the long-hallowed dogma that the British form of government was close to perfect. The current crisis, so the thinking went, was merely a consequence of corruption, short-sightedness, and stupidity. All would be well if only British authorities adhered to the principles of its faultless—though unwritten—constitution.

The monarchy was likewise sacrosanct. Everyone groaned about Parliament, but the king was good at heart, and few questioned the idea of monarchy.

Common Sense set a bomb under such notions and blew them to bits. The vaunted British constitution, it stated, "is imperfect, subject to convulsions, and incapable of producing what it seems to promise." Meanwhile, monarchy "cannot be justified on the equal rights of nature, so neither can it be defended on the authority of scripture." As for hereditary monarchy: "For all men being originally equals, no *one* by *birth* could have a right to set up his own family in perpetual preference to all others for ever."[33] As for the English monarchy specifically: "[N]o man in his senses can say that their claim under William the Conqueror is a very honorable one. A French bastard landing with an armed banditti, and establishing himself king of England against the consent of the natives, is in plain terms a very paltry rascally original."[34]

But what about the widely accepted benefits of monarchy—the idea that passing the crown from one generation to the next unites a nation and reduces the likelihood of civil strife? Nonsense, answered Paine: since the Norman Conquest in 1066, England had suffered eight civil wars and 19 rebellions.

Common Sense called on Americans to turn the page: "[A] new æra for politics is struck; a new method of thinking hath arisen." The time for independence was now:

"Every thing that is right or natural pleads for separation. The blood of the slain, the weeping voice of nature cries, 'TIS TIME TO PART.'" *Common Sense* proclaimed that independence would happen sooner or later, if not by Congress, then by armies or mobs. Should Congress usher in independence, "we have every opportunity and every encouragement before us, to form the noblest purest constitution on the face of the earth. We have it in our power to begin the world over again."[35]

Paine, in *Common Sense*, envisioned a national government. Congress would comprise at least 30 representatives, and all laws would require a three-fifths majority to pass. But that government, or something like it, would have to be hammered out in a "CONTINENTAL CONFERENCE"—a constitutional convention—which would "frame a CONTINENTAL CHARTER"[36]—a constitution. Paine was thinking ahead.

By messengers and by mail, the pamphlet soon reached readers throughout the colonies. Among the dazzled was General Charles Lee, who wrote to Washington: "[H]ave You seen the pamphlet Common Sense? I never saw such a masterly irresistible performance—It will, if I mistake not, in concurrence with the transcendent folly and wickedness of the Ministry give the coup de grace to G. Britain—in short I own myself convinc'd by the arguments of the necessity of separation."[37]

Washington, by this time, did not need convincing. However, he was taken by the pamphlet's "sound Doctrine, and unanswerable reasoning."[38]

A month after *Common Sense* appeared, a third edition and a German translation were in the works. After three months, 120,000 copies had been sold. Paine bolstered sales and undercut his profits by keeping the price low and giving printers all over America permission to publish editions.[39] The profits he received he promptly gave away, with a suggestion the money be used to buy mittens for the American soldiers in Quebec.[40] As sales and circulation soared, more people became aware of Paine, although many for years were skeptical that an English "nobody" fresh off the boat could have such a keen understanding of the American scene. Paine's name did not appear on the first edition; it only said the pamphlet was "written by an Englishman."[41] John Adams, as a diplomat in Europe years later, found it necessary to deny that he was the author.[42]

By the end of 1776, the total copies sold came to 500,000.[43] That amounted to about one in every household, making it roughly as common on domestic bookshelves as the Bible. The Declaration of Independence is often considered the defining document of the period, but the writing that turned heads and galvanized opinion was *Common Sense*.

Common Sense mesmerized delegates. Many, however, weren't quite sure what to make of it. North Carolina's Joseph Hewes called it "a Curiosity."[44] John Adams found the pamphlet important enough to mail off to Abigail,[45] but he never had much good to say about it. Years later, he wrote: "It has been a general Opinion, that this Pamphlet was of great Importance in the Revolution. I doubted it at the time and have doubted it to this day. It probably converted some to the Doctrine of Independence, and gave others an Excuse for declaring in favour of it. But these would all have followed Congress, with Zeal."[46]

As for Abigail, she wrote to John: "I am charmed with the Sentiments of Common Sense; and wonder how an honest Heart, one who wishes the welfare of their country, and the happiness of posterity can hesitate one moment at adopting them."[47]

Samuel Adams, like John, thought the pamphlet worth sending to his wife. Then he wrote to a colleague, suggesting he read it, but with a kind of apology:

> I have Sent to Mrs Adams a Pamphlet which made its first Appearance a few days ago. It has fretted some folks here more than a little. I recommend it to your Perusal and wish you would borrow it of her. Dont be displeasd with me if you find the Spirit of it totally repugnant with your Ideas of Government.[48]

A few weeks later, Samuel Adams referred to *Common Sense* and echoed its message in a piece published under a pseudonym:

> By declaring independence we put ourselves on a footing for an equal negotiation. ... Now we are called a pack of villainous rebels who ... can expect nothing more than a pardon for our lives, and the sovereign favor respecting freedom, and property to be at the King's will. Grant, Almighty God, that I may be numbered with the dead before that sable day dawns on North America.[49]

Of course, the British interpreted Paine's message quite differently. One British military man called it a "most flatigious Performance, replete with Sophistry, Impudence & Falsehood; but unhappily calculated to work upon the Fury of the Times, and to induce the full avowal of the Spirit of Independence in the warm & inconsiderate."[50]

This might have been a time for John Dickinson to counter Paine with his own pamphlet urging caution, but he remained quiet, saying nothing either publicly or, as far as we know, privately against *Common Sense*.[51] When another man, a plantation owner in Maryland, came out with *Plain Truth*, a hostile response to *Common Sense*, and dedicated it to Dickinson, it led Dickinson to make clear that he did not agree with the author of *Plain Truth* and its message of opposition to independence.

Dickinson seemed to come down on the side of independence, at least as a last resort: "The first wish of my soul is for the Liberty of America. The next is for constitutional reconciliation with Great Britain. If we cannot obtain the first without the second, let us seek a new establishment."[52]

***

After the bugle call of *Common Sense* came a dirge from Canada. Expecting to hear that Quebec had been conquered, delegates instead learned on January 17, 1776, of disaster. Hancock scribbled off a letter: "We have this Day rec'd disagreeable Accotts from Canada, poor Montgomery & severall officers kill'd."[53]

So much had gone wrong. The expedition of American soldiers through the Maine wilderness had been a nightmare. Bad maps misled them and storms soaked them, then food ran out. About one-third of the men turned back. The remaining force of about 600[54] stumbled to the outskirts of Quebec City, sick and starving. Too weak to attack, they awaited help from Montgomery, who sauntered down the St. Lawrence from Montreal with a force that had also shrunk considerably. Meanwhile, reinforcements arrived for the British. Montgomery finally appeared on December 1, and the Americans launched an attack in a snowstorm on the last day of 1775. The Americans never had much of a chance—about 1,000 against 1,850 behind the city walls. The attack barely started when cannon fire killed Montgomery. The attack then sputtered and failed.

In Philadelphia, Montgomery was duly mourned and honored. "Never was any City so universally Struck with grief, as this was on hearing of the Loss of Montgomery," wrote South Carolina's Thomas Lynch. "Every lady's Eye was filled with Tears."[55]

Historians have ruminated over the debacle. If only the military plan had been set in motion two months, one month, or just a few weeks sooner, to take advantage of better weather; if only Montgomery had moved faster; if only Montgomery had survived; if only Congress had done more to better arm and supply the force in Canada. There was also the problem that caused Washington so much anxiety—short enlistments. The American commanders arguably lacked the manpower to overwhelm the defenders of Quebec City, but they had enough to shut off the city and starve it. They might have sat tight and waited for the hungry British to capitulate. But they couldn't wait, because enlistments for many of the New Englanders were expiring at the end of 1775. An attack had to be carried out before the soldiers headed home.

We now know that with the catastrophe at Quebec City, Canada was lost to America. But that was not so apparent at the time. Delegates in Philadelphia were convinced that Quebec province could still be won and welcomed as the 14th colony on the Patriot side. They shuddered at the possible consequences should Britain fully retake Canada. As one delegate put it: "Should it [Canada] fall into the Hands of the Enemy they will soon raise a Nest of Hornets on our backs that will Sting us to the quick."[56]

Congress scrambled to supply the American army in Canada with the money and the men that Montgomery never had. Montreal remained in American hands and the Continentals, those who hadn't surrendered, still held the outskirts of Quebec City. If sufficient men and supplies could be sent north in a hurry, before the British could respond with reinforcements, Quebec City could yet be taken. Congress resolved to reinforce the army in Canada "with all possible dispatch."[57]

Congress churned out relevant resolutions, along with letters, including one to "Friends and Countrymen" in Canada promising them that Americans would yet rescue them from the wicked British. This may have been the first time the term

"United States" appeared in an authorized document: "We will never abandon you to the unrelenting fury of your and our enemies. Two batallions have already received orders to march to Canada, a part of which are now on their route. Six additional batallions are raising in the United States for the same service and will receive orders to proceed to your province as soon as possible."[58]

Meanwhile, Congress, which had found it so difficult to supply warm clothing to its soldiers in Canada, instantly granted money for a monument—ordered from France—to glorify the fallen General Montgomery.[59]

***

In the wake of the grim reports from Canada came sobering news from London. In late February, Americans learned that Britain now considered all American ships and cargoes as prizes and their crews as prisoners of war. British authorities proclaimed that American trade with any country other than Britain was forbidden.[60] Britain was in effect declaring war on America at sea.[61]

For Americans leaning toward independence, this was, in a perverse way, good news. By declaring American merchants and sailors enemies, no matter their loyalties, Britain was casting them out. By this measure, so the reasoning went, Britain was declaring Americans—and America—independent.

Virginia's Francis Lightfoot Lee wrote:

> Our late King & his Parliament having declared us Rebels & Enemies, confiscated our property, as far as they were likely to lay hands on it; have effectually decided the question for us, whether or no we shou'd be independant. All we have now to do, is to endeavour to reconcile ourselves to the state, it has pleased Providence to put us into.[62]

John Adams had a similar view:

> It is a compleat Dismemberment of the British Empire. It throws thirteen Colonies out of Royal protection, levels all Distinctions and makes us independent in Spight of all our supplications and entreaties. It may be fortunate that the Act of Independency should come from the British Parliament, rather than the American Congress: But it is very odd that Americans should hesitate in accepting Such a Gift from them.[63]

Odd or not, America and Congress were not quite ready to proclaim independence. The Prohibitory Act, this "gift" from Britain, was crammed with monstrosities, but also contained one shimmering hopeful gem "to encourage all well affected" Americans "to exert themselves in suppressing the rebellion." Tucked in paragraph XLIV was the prospect of a peace commission with power to selectively dispense with some or all of the tough measures of the Prohibitory Act and declare any colony, "county, town, port, district or place" to be "at the peace of his Majesty."[64]

Who would be on this peace commission? What rules would guide them? Americans didn't know, because the British were still hashing that out, a labor that they would still be working on into May. This glimmering possibility of reconciliation was excuse enough for holdouts in Congress still grasping at straws to hesitate on the question of independence. Why rush over the precipice when this nebulous peace commission, if it appeared in America, might yet find a way to restore harmony? Among those fixated on the phantom peace commission was Dickinson, who found time to draft proposals for conducting negotiations with the commissioners if and when they appeared.[65] Consequently, independence was on hold.

The mysterious peace commission notwithstanding, Congress braced for a long war, especially after shocking rumors reached Philadelphia that the king planned to hire mercenaries[66] to do his bloody work. America desperately needed weapons, gunpowder, uniforms, and everything else armies require. Franklin, naturally, harnessed his imagination for the cause—designing a pike and suggesting the use of bows and arrows.[67] Congress, while not ready to formally split with Britain, nevertheless felt compelled to seek help overseas for the fight.

Asking for that help, however, was a daunting and delicate task. America had no ambassadors; it was not even a nation. How could America arrange to obtain arms? How could it be done quietly, without London's knowledge? And who would supply America with arms and risk war with the greatest power in Europe?

Winds of good fortune blew in from France. While currently at peace with Britain, France still smarted from the loss of Canada to the British following the Seven Years' War some dozen years before. France had no appetite for a new war with its rival across the English Channel, but this simmering imbroglio between the British mother country and her 13 daughters was intriguing. A little discreet meddling might keep Britain preoccupied and drain its wealth. Perhaps, if everything worked out, France in the end might regain Canada.

Back in December 1775, the Chevalier Julien-Alexandre Archard de Bonvouloir, a 26-year-old Frenchman,[68] arrived in Philadelphia and looked up Francis Daymon, another Frenchman, who also happened to be Benjamin Franklin's French tutor and a librarian at Carpenters' Hall. Bonvouloir assured everyone that he was just a curious traveler[69] and had no official connections. But no one, including Daymon, quite believed that. Indeed, Bonvouloir, who pretended to be a merchant from Antwerp,[70] was on a hush-hush mission to sound out the Americans about possible secret deals. Franklin soon learned that Bonvouloir would like to meet him.

Evening meetings were quietly arranged between Bonvouloir, Franklin, and Franklin's committee in charge of diplomatic matters. They gathered at the library in Carpenters' Hall. To maintain secrecy and avoid attention, each committee member came to meetings by a different route.[71] Other delegates to Congress were kept in the dark—no one at the meetings was permitted to takes notes. What we know comes mainly from a report Bonvouloir prepared later. They met three times over two weeks, Daymon joining these meetings as a translator.[72]

Bonvouloir suggested that France might be willing to trade arms for such products as tobacco. When the committee asked whether the Americans, to facilitate such deals, should send an agent to France, Bonvouloir said that it was too soon and dangerous to do so because London would certainly find out.[73]

Bonvouloir gave Franklin and his colleagues little to chew on—an impression that France was friendly to an arms deal, but scant guidance on how best to make it happen.

In January 1776, two other Frenchmen appeared in Philadelphia. They likewise protested that they had no official ties to the French government, and likewise commenced chatting with delegates about possible exchanges of arms for goods. Still other Frenchmen slipped into Philadelphia to talk about shipments of gunpowder.[74]

Franklin's committee followed up these promising hints by doing precisely what Bonvouloir had discouraged—dispatching an agent to France. It was all to be secret, done without the explicit approval or knowledge of Congress as a whole.[75] The assignment went to Silas Deane. The lawyer and merchant was no longer a delegate to Congress. The Connecticut Assembly had sent another man to Congress in Deane's place, making Deane "Confoundedly Chagrind,"[76] but available for this new task. To those who denied him the opportunity to return to Congress, Deane wished "the worst of them no other punishment, than a Consciousness of the low, envious, jealous, & sordid motives by which they are actuated."[77] Deane had a thin skin. However, during his time in Congress he had been "Very Usefull" and "much esteemd," according to a colleague.[78] He had earned the respect and confidence of many delegates, including Franklin.

Deane was to travel to France openly as a private merchant, but to work secretly as an agent for Congress. With introductory letters from Franklin in hand, he was to make his way to Paris and seek out contacts—"all Friends to the Americans"—and through them finagle a meeting with the French foreign minister, Charles Gravier, Count of Vergennes. That might happen quickly or take weeks. Would a busy Yankee merchant appear conspicuous dallying in the French capital? *Mais non*, according to his instructions: "It is scarce necessary to pretend any other business at Paris, than the gratifying of that curiosity, which draws numbers thither yearly, merely to see so famous a city."[79]

Deane was told to inform Vergennes "that you are in France upon business of the American Congress," and that business chiefly concerned clothing and weapons for 25,000 men, 100 field pieces, and ammunition.[80]

Deane was to woo Vergennes with hints that favors from France now would mean favors later in return, after independence, should that happen: "[I]f we should, and there is a great appearance we shall, come to a total separation from Great Britain, France would be looked upon as the power, whose friendship it would be fittest for us to obtain and cultivate."[81]

To provide more plausible cover for Deane's mission, another delegate, who also happened to be a wealthy merchant, made him an agent for his trading firm. It was a clever arrangement. Deane would work on authentic deals for Pennsylvania's Robert Morris and his firm of Willing and Morris, while also secretly dealing on behalf of Congress. No one at the time anticipated the potential conflicts of interest and headaches to come with this setup.

Deane was chosen in large part because Franklin thought him suitable, and in matters of diplomacy Congress tended to defer to Franklin, with his long experience in Europe. Deane, as a merchant, could also plausibly carry on as a private merchant while managing delicate negotiations with the French government. Furthermore, Deane was intimately familiar with the issues facing the Continental Congress and understood military requirements as well as the nuts and bolts of shipping and financing.[82] Deane was available too, and willing to accept this daunting mission.

Still, it is astounding that someone better qualified was not found for such a vital task. Deane had no experience overseas, no personal contacts in France, and could not speak French.

CHAPTER 14

Motives of Glory as Well as Interest

Looking northward, Congress mapped out another diplomatic mission, this one bound for Canada. While many Quebecois were neutral, some had welcomed the American army, and most of those who backed the British did so with little zeal. Congress was obsessed with the notion that Canadians might yet become enthusiastic partners in the Patriot cause and rally to support the ragtag American military.

Congress named Franklin to lead this effort. He had been to Canada and had many contacts there. He was famous, charming, and he knew French, although perhaps not as well as he claimed.[1] John Adams, who earlier had doubts about Franklin, now thought him perfect for this job: "His masterly Acquaintance with the French Language, his extensive Correspondence in France, his great Experience in Life, his Wisdom, Prudence, Caution, his engaging Address, united to his unshaken Firmness in the present American System of Politicks and War, point him out as the fittest Character for this momentous Undertaking."[2]

However, he was also an old man—now aged 70.

Joining Franklin would be Maryland's Samuel Chase. He was half Franklin's age and an enthusiastic Patriot; perhaps too much so. John Adams on one occasion called him "violent and boisterous" and, during debates, "tedious upon frivolous Points."[3] But for this mission, Adams found Chase "deeply impress'd with a sense of the Importance of securing Canada, very active, eloquent, spirited, and capable."[4] Chase indeed was passionate about Canada: "[T]he Success of the War will, in great Measure, depend on securing Canada to our Confederation."[5]

Two other Maryland men would accompany Franklin and Chase. Neither were delegates to Congress, and both, significantly, were of the same faith as most Quebecois—Catholic. One was Charles Carroll of Carrollton (he added "of Carrollton" to his name to distinguish him from his father, Charles Carroll of Annapolis). From a wealthy family, the teenage Carroll had studied in Flanders and France, and thus knew French. He had been involved in the Patriotic cause at least since 1773 and was so fascinated by the Continental Congress that he visited Philadelphia from time to time to chat with delegates.[6] In recommending Carroll for the mission, Chase noted "[h]is attachment and zeal to the Cause, his abilities, his Acquaintance with the Language, Manner & Customs of France and his Religion, with the circumstances of a very great Estate."[7]

The fourth member of the mission was not only Catholic, but a priest. Father John Carroll, Charles Carroll's cousin, was bewildered to be asked to join the mission. He felt unfit to contribute anything as a fellow negotiator, not that it mattered much to Congress, which only wanted an authentic Catholic cleric as window dressing. How better to show the French in Canada how tolerant Protestant America was toward Catholics? Presumably, the Americans, when they came to talk with the Canadians, would not point out that both Carrolls, because they were Catholic, were barred from public office.[8]

Congress armed the mission with laborious instructions crafted after long debate. The delegation was to advise the Canadians that "their interests and ours are inseparably united; that it is impossible we can be reduced to a servile submission to Great Britain without their sharing our fate." Franklin and his team were to convince the Canadians "of the impossibility of the war being concluded to the disadvantage of these colonies, if we wisely and vigorously co-operate with each other." Furthermore, they were told that "you are in the strongest terms to assure them, that it is our earnest desire to adopt them into our union, as a sister colony, and to secure the same general system of mild and equal laws for them and for ourselves, with only such local differences as may be agreeable to each colony respectively." The Canadians must be urged to "put themselves under the protection of the United Colonies." Also, the delegation was to teach the Canadians some lessons in freedom:

> Explain to them the nature and principles of government among freemen. ... Endeavor to stimulate them by motives of glory as well as interest, to assume a part in a contest by which they must be deeply affected; and to aspire to a portion of that power, by which they are ruled; and not to remain the mere spoils and prey of conquerors and lords.[9]

In late March, Franklin and his team left for Canada.[10] After sailing up the Hudson, they arrived in Albany on April 8. Finding half a foot of snow on the ground in Saratoga, they paused for a week at the home of General Schuyler, his wife, Molly,[11] and two daughters, Betsy and Peggy, described as "lively, agreeable, black-eyed girls."[12] There, Franklin calculated the rigors of the journey that remained and figured they just might kill him. He wrote: "I begin to apprehend that I have undertaken a Fatigue that at my Time of Life may prove too much for me, so I sit down to write to a few Friends by way of Farewell."[13] In a letter to Hancock, he confessed his doubts about the mission: "[B]y the Advices from Canada ... I am afraid we shall be able to effect but little there."[14]

***

Towards the end of March, news also arrived in Philadelphia about a miracle in Massachusetts: the British had vanished. Troops and Loyalists had packed up, crowded onto ships, and disappeared over the horizon. American Patriots again controlled Boston.

Contrary to the proverb, Washington had hesitated and won. In December, Congress had given the commander its blessing to attack the British in Boston, even if it should destroy the town.[15] But Washington was not ready. Then, in January, an attack was impossible to even contemplate. With enlistments running out, it was all Washington could do to hold the army together as many disgusted, weary soldiers simply went home. Ranks dwindled to about 9,000 soldiers[16] as Washington scrambled to build back his meager force before the British got wise to the Americans' sorry state. Washington wrote: "It is not in the pages of History perhaps, to furnish a case like ours; to maintain a post within Musket Shot of the Enemy for Six Months together without [powder] and at the same time to disband one Army and recruit another, within that distance, of Twenty odd British regiments."[17]

Gradually, new soldiers joined the ranks, and then artillery arrived, retrieved from Ticonderoga and dragged over winter roads to eastern Massachusetts. In an ingenious overnight operation in early March, Washington's men hauled those cannons to heights overlooking Boston from the south. Suddenly, the British in Boston and their ships in the harbor were vulnerable. As the British prepared to attack the heights, Washington geared up to assault the town, but a violent storm disrupted everyone's plans. The attacks were canceled and the British chose to evacuate. On March 18, Washington and his men entered the town.[18]

Yet the triumph was not altogether satisfying. Although Boston was intact and under American control, all without a bloody battle, the British had escaped to fight again. They had sailed off to Halifax, Nova Scotia, but everyone knew they would be back. The war was not over; it had only just begun.

***

Back in Philadelphia, nerves were frayed: "We do not treat each other with that decency and respect that was observed heretofore," wrote North Carolina's Joseph Hewes: "Jealousies, ill natured observations and recriminations take [the] place of reason and Argument."[19]

They were also tired of waiting for the "Phantom of Commissioners"[20] from Britain to somehow pave a path to peace. "Where the plague are these commissioners?" wrote Pennsylvania's Robert Morris: "[I]t is time we shoud be on a Certainty & know positively whether the Libertys of America can be established & Secured by reconciliation, or whether we must totally renounce Connection with Great Britain & fight our way to a total Independence."[21]

On March 23, fed up with waiting and eager to strike back against the Prohibitory Act, Congress authorized Americans "to fit out armed vessels to cruize on the enemies of these United Colonies." This was privateering—legalized piracy. It was tit for tat: if the British could attack American shipping, Americans would do likewise against British merchants. The American navy was negligible, but many American merchants had enough ships and crewmen that, when armed, could threaten British cargoes. Those merchants were eager to turn their ships loose on lumbering and unprotected British vessels. Congress declared that American privateers who captured British merchant vessels were entitled to one third of the prize, with the balance "to the use of the United Colonies."[22]

A few weeks later, on April 6, Congress struck again with the declaration that all of America's ports were open to merchants everywhere in the world—except those from countries "under the Dominion of Great Britain." All goods were welcome, with the exception of "East India Tea" and enslaved people, an echo of the terms of the Continental Association.[23]

***

Sometime during these busy weeks, two delegates from North Carolina—John Penn and William Hooper—prepared to return home, hoping to play a role in framing the new North Carolina government that would soon spring up. They had been asked to bring with them from Philadelphia "every Hint, they could Collect concerning Government." John Adams couldn't resist, despite myriad responsibilities. He took up pen and paper, "borrowed a little Time"[24] from sleep, and scribbled out ideas for Penn and Hooper to ponder.

Adams wrote out his thoughts twice—with one copy for Hooper and another for Penn. Seeing Hooper's copy, George Wyeth of Virginia wanted one for himself. So Adams made another draft, and then a fourth for Jonathan Sergeant of New Jersey. After Virginia's Richard Henry Lee asked for a copy, Adams arranged to have Wythe's copy printed. Thus emerged the pamphlet *Thoughts on Government, Applicable to the Present State of the American Colonies.*

In this booklet, Adams addressed the "task of forming a plan for the government of a colony."[25] Everyone knew that the process of making America independent was more than just declaring independence in Philadelphia. It also meant that each colony—each new state—had to establish a government free of royal control and all signs of royal authority. By this time, New Hampshire already had a preliminary constitution; South Carolina had one by March 26.[26] The other colonies, one by one, would take up the task. Each colony, in remaking itself into a state, could recast a new kind of government. Here was a rare opportunity. In concluding his pamphlet, Adams rejoiced at being alive "at a time when the greatest law-givers of antiquity would have wished to have lived. ... When! Before the present epocha, had three millions of people full power and a fair opportunity to form and establish the wisest and happiest government that human wisdom can contrive?"[27]

***

North of Albany, the congressional mission to Canada continued north in open flatboats, dodging chunks of ice on Lake George and Lake Champlain. At night, they camped in the woods or slept on their boats under canvas. On their first night in Canada, they slept in a ruined house with smashed shutters and doors, "hinges stolen," and "scarcely a whole pane of glass" in any window.[28]

Carriages were needed to carry the illustrious foursome the rest of the way to Montreal. But there was a snag—the man dispatched to fetch carriages had only Continental dollars, which no one was willing to accept. He made a deal for the carriages only after a friendly Canadian came by who agreed to take the dollars for some silver.[29] This, in microcosm, was the core of the American dilemma in Canada: they had no money that Canadians would accept.

The quality of the carriages matched that of the roads. "I never traveled through worse roads, or in worse carriages,"[30] wrote Charles Carroll in his journal, but at last, on April 29, they arrived in Montreal, where they were greeted with a cannon salute and "other military honors." Once settled in a house, the commissioners sipped wine, received visitors, and "unexpectedly," as Father Carroll wrote in a letter to his mother, met with "a large assembly of ladies, Most of them French." Then there was tea, "an elegant supper," followed by "the singing of the ladies, which proved very agreeable."[31]

Later on, Father Carroll made the acquaintance of a fellow priest, who treated Carroll with courtesy. For his kindness, the Canadian priest was later censured by his bishop. The Catholic hierarchy in the province was firmly dug in against the Americans. Father Carroll would make no headway in softening that attitude.[32]

Meanwhile, after the warm welcome, the commissioners found themselves chilled by cold facts pointing to one conclusion: the critical shortage of hard money was far worse than they expected. Continental dollars were useless, and credit was exhausted. In reports to Congress, the commissioners made urgent pleas for hard money. "Not the most trifling service can be procured without an assurance of instant pay in silver or gold," they said, and those precious coins were scarce:

> It seems it had been expected, and given out by our Friends, that We should bring Money with Us. The Disappointment has discouraged every Body, and established an Opinion that none is to be had, or that the Congress has not Credit enough in their own Colonies to procure it. Many of our friends are drained dry; others say they are so, fearing, perhaps, we shall never be able to reimburse him.

The Canadian friends of the Americans had by now exhausted their credit: "They show us long accounts ... of the supplies they have furnished to our Army and declare that they have borrowed and taken up on credit so long for our service that they can now be trusted no longer, even for what they want themselves."[33]

The commissioners were seeing first-hand evidence that Canadian confidence in the Americans, always flimsy, had evaporated. The military failure at Quebec City was reason enough for Canadians to doubt the wisdom of linking arms with the Americans. The American army was plainly weak and unreliable. By now, Canadians had other reasons to wish Americans away and the British back. After the failure at Quebec City, portions of the American army had devolved from reasonably disciplined units to bands of armed thieves. Many of the new troops, those who arrived to shore up the force, could not be controlled and took to plundering.

Meanwhile, reports told of mistreatment of priests, which was no way to cultivate affection from the Catholic citizenry. Furthermore, many Canadian suppliers felt cheated by the American military, who sometimes forced the suppliers to accept receipts that were later not fully honored with hard currency.[34]

Canadians who were once friendly toward the Americans, or at least neutral, were signaling a possible uprising to throw off the occupiers. The commissioners reported: "[W]e have daily intimations of plots hatching and insurrections intended, for expelling us in the first news of the arrival of the *British* Army." The commissioners were, they reported, in a "critical and most irksome situation, pestered hourly with demands great and small"[35] that they couldn't answer.

Some sort of political union with the Canadians—with Canadian representation in Congress—was out of the question without first coming up with plenty of hard money to restore American credit and with more American forces to "secure the possession of the Country." Further, "if Money cannot be had to support your Army here with Honor, so as to be respected instead of being hated by the people, ... it is better immediately to withdraw it."[36]

Much of that army, besides being ill-fed, ill-kempt, and ill-disciplined, was just plain ill. Smallpox had struck the army. About one of every ten soldiers was sick, and of those who were healthy, about two-thirds had not had the disease and were thus vulnerable.[37] This sickly, hungry, unruly force would have little chance against the British once reinforcements of disciplined, healthy British troops arrived in Quebec City.

CHAPTER 15

We Cannot Make Events

In Philadelphia, delegates fretted about Canada when time allowed, but there were so many other pressing issues, not the least of which was the question of independence.

Delegates standing in the way of independence were becoming a rare breed. Among them was Virginia's Carter Braxton, a relative newcomer to Congress. Though his fellow Virginians in Philadelphia by now were ready for independence, Braxton sought delay. Independence, though tempting, was, he said, "a delusive Bait which Men inconsiderately catch at without knowing the hook to which it is affixed." There were many good reasons to wait. First, he argued, "our publick Honor" required that Americans first hear what peace commissioners had to offer. Second, with no navy to speak of and no alliances, the American colonies were "too defenseless." Third, the colonies were rife with unresolved disputes among themselves. The simmering conflict between Pennsylvania and Connecticut was just one. Virginia had claims on Pennsylvania, while Maryland had claims on Virginia. New York also had troubles with its neighbors. If independence was to be declared now, "the Continent would be torn in pieces by intestine Wars & Convulsions."[1]

Before independence, proper groundwork was needed. Disputes among the colonies "must be healed," Braxton maintained. Then, some sort of confederation—a "grand Continental League"—needed to be created along with "a superintending Power." He would favor independence only after a coalition was formed "sufficient to withstand the Power of Britain."[2] Braxton wanted the transition to independence to be tidy.

He was in the minority, but even with most delegates favoring independence, the time was not yet ripe for a declaration. Independence was too critical for anything less than the backing of all colonies. That meant the majority of delegates in each delegation had to approve, and no delegate would vote in favor of independence without instructions from his home colony explicitly to do so, or at least freedom to make that choice.

***

In these anxious days, Samuel Adams felt serene: "I have the Happiness of believing that what I most earnestly wish for will in due time be effected. We cannot make Events. Our Business is merely to improve them."[3] That's a good way to describe how he, and cousin John, "improved" events in Pennsylvania.

Generally, compared to the colonies of New England and the South, the so-called proprietary colonies—Pennsylvania, Delaware, and Maryland—along with the other Middle Atlantic colonies—New Jersey and New York—were laggards, or at least unreliable, on the question of independence. How could they be nudged forward?

Pennsylvania seemed to be the key. It was the largest of those five colonies. If it moved in the direction of independence, its four sisters in the region would likely follow. Now it was not moving at all, but standing in the way.

The problem in Pennsylvania, for those favoring independence, was not the governor. Grandson of the colony's founder, Governor John Penn had ample authority but chose to remain aloof and passive through the crisis.[4]

Thus, by default, the elected Pennsylvania Assembly, meeting in the State House in a room above where the Continental Congress gathered, held virtually all power in Pennsylvania. That Assembly's instructions to its delegates explicitly prohibited them from voting for independence. While Quaker influence was ebbing in the colony, the guiding Quaker principles of pacifism and respect for authority still carried ample weight in the colonial Assembly. With Pennsylvania's Assembly blocking the way, American independence seemed impossible.

Come May 1, that would all change. At least that's what the Adamses and others pushing for independence believed. They expected that day to mark the climax of two revolts in the colony: one against British authority and another against Pennsylvania's privileged classes.

For a long time, immigrants, settlers in western Pennsylvania, and many ordinary folks had grumbled that they were underrepresented in an assembly dominated by well-heeled Philadelphians, and that the Pennsylvania government thus did not fairly represent the colony's population. This simmering discontent had come to the boil back in June 1774, when an organization of Philadelphia shopkeepers, artisans, and craftsmen numbering about 1,200 marched to the State House, interrupted a meeting of established political leaders, and demanded representation.[5] It was a kind of working-class revolt.

The spirit that infused that action later seeped into Philadelphia's Committee of Inspection and Observation, the group that enforced the boycotts Congress called for against British imports. That committee, known as the City Committee, made it its business to not only poke into consumer habits, but also to jab at the elected Assembly. The City Committee petitioned the Assembly to revise laws the Committee thought unfair, asked for galleries in the Assembly room so people could watch lawmakers at work, and demanded published records of each member's votes.[6] It became a force for government reform, transparency, and wider suffrage.

In the wake of Lexington and Concord, as militia groups organized and drilled all over Pennsylvania, a leader of the City Committee, James Cannon, saw another opportunity to strengthen this movement to make government more responsive. In Pennsylvania, as in most places in America at this time, voting was restricted to white men with property. Scottish-born Cannon, a mathematics professor, had some astonishingly modern ideas. For example, he started an organization that put the unemployed to work in Philadelphia making cloth. The initiative helped the poor while also filling demand caused by the boycott of British goods.[7] Cannon recognized that many of the men in the militia units—known as associators—could not vote because they were too poor. Cannon helped create a political outlet for these voteless men, an organization that became known as the Committee of Privates. Each militia unit across the province could elect up to three[8] members of the committee,[9] which might include 100 or more members at any one time. They pushed radical ideas: they wanted the right to choose their brigadier generals and called for extending the right to vote to the poor and all militiamen.[10]

Thus emerged two feisty voices for reform in Pennsylvania—the City Committee and the Committee of Privates. The two groups were tightly linked and leaned in favor of American independence. Meanwhile, they were not shy about using threats and intimidation to get their point across. When a lawyer in Philadelphia tried to sue on behalf of a client whose British imports had been seized, the lawyer found himself yanked from his house, hoisted on a cart, paraded about the city, and forced here and there to publicly admit his error.[11] The City Committee's fingerprints were all over the threats that led to the cancellation of the ball to honor Martha Washington.

In February 1776, the City Committee called for a provincial convention to lay the foundation for a new Pennsylvania government.[12] If the Committee couldn't reform the government, it would overthrow it peacefully, or forcefully with the backing of sympathetic militia—through the Committee of Privates. The call for the convention came on the very same day the Assembly received petitions from five western counties asking for more representation in the lawmaking body.

The Assembly shrewdly responded to both developments by adding 17 new seats, some for Philadelphia and some for eight counties that had been created since 1700.[13] This, conservatives in the Assembly hoped, would calm the waters. Opponents outside the Assembly, meanwhile, were ecstatic and utterly convinced that the new seats, come the next election, would tip the balance of power in their favor—and in favor of independence. John Adams expected the next election would deliver a "finishing blow to Quaker interest" in Philadelphia and "strip it of all that unjust and unequal Power, which it formerly had over the Balance of this Province."[14]

With the promise of new seats in the Assembly, the City Committee backed off on its threat to have a convention. There now seemed to be no need for it. With those added seats, the Committee and other supporters of both wider suffrage and independence from Britain looked forward to prevailing at the next election.

On election day, Congress was watching: "This day is like to produce as warm if not the warmest Election that ever was held in this City,"[15] wrote Delaware's Cesar Rodney. Congress took the day off to free up its space in the Pennsylvania State House for balloting on that "Raw, Cold"[16] day.

Results demonstrated that voters were pleased with the Assembly more or less as it was,[17] with enough establishment lawmakers returned to their seats to offset inroads from reformers and those favoring independence. Voters in Pennsylvania seemed to be saying "no" to independence and "no" to extending the right to vote.

So Pennsylvania remained squarely where it was, blocking the path to independence. But for how long? Perhaps forever, for if the so-called peace commissioners arrived, attention would shift for weeks, months, maybe even years to their proposals, no doubt calculated to give hope to Loyalists and appeal to colonies still on the fence. The dream of an independent America might well slip away.

For many months, John and Samuel Adams had met and mingled with leaders and activists in Pennsylvania opposing the established Assembly and favoring independence and expanded suffrage. In the wake of the May 1 defeat at the ballot box, the Adamses and the activists came together again. The Pennsylvania Assembly had to be beaten one way or the other. If not with ballots, then another way: the Adams cousins and Congress would deftly pull the rug out from under the Pennsylvania government.

These secret meetings often took place in the rooms that the Adamses shared near the Delaware River waterfront. At the meeting on May 3 were Cannon, Marshall—the City Committee member instrumental in scotching the ball for Martha Washington—and Thomas Young, originally from rural New York, but until just recently from Boston. Young was a physician and a vigorous Patriot agitator with a history of shocking notions. In his twenties, he faced charges of blasphemy after being overheard spouting something about Jesus being a knave and a fool. Later, he had the radical notion of giving landless workers and indebted farmers land in the Green Mountains—between New Hampshire and New York—and supported Ethan Allen when he led the settlement of the region, in defiance of New York's claim. Young never settled there himself, but he coined the name for the region—Vermont. In Boston, his unorthodox methods and lack of formal medical training tainted him as a quack.[18] But he proved to be an effective and dedicated Patriot leader and an important ally for Samuel Adams as the crisis with British authorities came to a head in Boston.

Over the coming days, these sessions with the Adamses also included Thomas Paine, the author of *Common Sense*; Timothy Matlock, a clerk of the Congress with a dubious history—he was a chronic gambler who had spent time in a debtor's prison; and Benjamin Rush, a Philadelphia physician who burned with Presbyterian evangelical passion and opposed slavery.[19]

What little we know of these meetings did not come from the Adamses, well aware that what they were up to was arguably shady. The lack of documentation means we can't be sure what was being planned, but it likely had something to do with subsequent moves to undermine the status quo in Pennsylvania and to usher in a new government for the province.

While Congress had given four colonies—Massachusetts, New Hampshire, South Carolina, and Virginia—permission to set up governments free of royal authority, no blanket authorization had been issued for all other colonies to do likewise. For many months, the Adamses and others in Congress had pleaded for such a resolution, but delegates favoring reconciliation had always stood in the way.

Lobbying for such a resolution now intensified, coincidentally just as the war for the first time approached Philadelphia by way of the Delaware River. On May 5, a British man-of-war, the *Roebuck*, sailed from the Atlantic into Delaware Bay. It then inched its way against the current up the Delaware River toward Philadelphia, part of a small fleet assigned to blockade the city.[20]

Word of the *Roebuck*'s movements reached Philadelphia on May 6 along with rumors that the vessel had fired on New Castle, Delaware.[21] That was not true, but plausible considering that the British navy had already laid waste to Falmouth in Maine and Norfolk, Virginia. It was easy enough to imagine the *Roebuck* aimed to wreak havoc in Philadelphia.

In Philadelphia, alarm guns boomed and militiamen scrambled. Some townspeople, fearing the worst, began packing up their goods and moving them to the countryside.[22] Nine miles downstream from Philadelphia, brave rowers manned 13 galleys, each with at least one cannon. On the afternoon of May 8, that fleet, joined by a floating battery and a schooner, engaged the *Roebuck*. The galleys tormented the *Roebuck* like wasps on a bear, firing "scarcely within point blank Shot"[23] but at such angles—the *Roebuck* high in the water, the galleys low—that, over two hours of flailing, neither side inflicted much harm. At least one American died when a hot galley gun ignited a cartridge and "Blew him a way."[24]

Low on ammunition, the galleys retreated upstream. The hulking *Roebuck*, stuck in the mud, could not pursue. Its sister ship, the *Liverpool*, and three tenders arrived to protect the *Roebuck* until the rising tide overnight freed it. The next day, that fleet pushed upstream to confront the Americans again and the sparring resumed.[25] A diarist in Philadelphia recorded hearing the "Constant discharge of heavy Cannon."[26] In the end, the *Roebuck* got the worst of it. Sails torn and masts splintered, it and the other British vessels limped downstream and away. Philadelphia was jubilant.

Coinciding with the noisy drama on the Delaware was a fresh blast from the pen of Paine aimed at Pennsylvanian lawmakers. Paine had recently submitted letters to the *Pennsylvania Gazette* bashing Loyalists and defending arguments in *Common Sense*. But in a letter published on May 8, Paine took on the Pennsylvania government. He noted that newly elected assemblymen were required "to take an oath of allegiance to serve the same king against whom this province, with themselves at the head thereof, are at war." How could lawmakers be fighting a king they were pledged to? "Did ever national hypocrisy arise to such a pitch as this!" A new Pennsylvania government—independent of the king—was needed. He revived the idea of a convention to start the process of establishing a new government: "The House of Assembly in its present form is disqualified for such business, because it is a branch from that power against whom we are contending."[27]

Two days later, Congress stepped up to finally grant permission for all colonies to set up independent governments. Delegates "recommended" each of the colonies where royal authority had collapsed to put a government in place to promote "the happiness and safety of their constituents in particular, and America in general."[28] At first glance it seemed not controversial at all, but a reasonable step not only to avert chaos and lawlessness, but to provide stable support for the war effort. Delaware's Cesar Rodney wrote: "Nothing will tend more to Ensure Success in the prosecution of the war; because there is nothing so conducive to vigour, Expedition, secrecy, and every thing advantagious in War, as a well regulated Government." Besides, Rodney added: "The Continuing to Swear Allegience to the power that is Cutting our throats, and attesting Jurors to keep the Secrets and try offenders against the peace of our Sovereign Lord the King, &c is Certainly absurd."[29] John Adams hoped the resolution would also nudge colonies still uncommitted to independence to move in that direction.[30]

The resolution passed unanimously. Even the Pennsylvania delegation approved it. Those delegates took for granted that it did not really apply to Pennsylvania, where they saw no chaos or power vacuum. The government was fully functional. John Dickinson himself, the most respected voice against independence, voted for the resolution and promptly took a few days off from Congress to spend some time outside Philadelphia, as was his usual habit at that time of year.[31]

The delegates decided that the resolution needed a preamble, the conventional list of "whereas" this and "whereas" that, to provide context. A committee came together, John Adams took the lead, and soon that preamble made its appearance. It was no dreary, predictable, eye-glazing boilerplate statement. It was lightning. A sample stated:

> [I]t appears absolutely irreconcilable to reason and good Conscience, for the people of these colonies now to take the oaths and affirmations necessary for the support of any government under the crown of Great Britain, and it is necessary that the exercise of every kind of authority under the said crown should be totally suppressed, and all the powers of government exerted, under the authority of the people of the colonies.[32]

Since oaths to royal authority were still the practice in Pennsylvania, this part of the preamble seemed to be a dagger directed at the Pennsylvania Assembly—an invitation for Pennsylvanians to yank down the established government.

The proposed preamble ignited wrangling in Congress that went on for four days.[33] This was too much too soon, protested Wilson of Pennsylvania: "Before We are prepared to build the new House, why should We pull down the old one, and expose ourselves to all the Inclemencies of the Season?" He predicted chaos: "[T]here will be an immediate Dissolution of every Kind of Authority. The People will be instantly in a State of Nature." New York's Duane was likewise shaken by the blanket call for political disruption: "Why all this Haste? Why this Urging? Why this driving?"[34]

But many other delegates were only too happy to yank down the tottering remnants of British control. Samuel Adams said: "We can't go upon stronger reasons, than that the king has thrown us out of his protection. Why should we support governments under his authority?"[35]

The preamble passed on May 15, but narrowly, by six votes to four.[36] Delegates from Maryland, who had dissented, were so alarmed that they walked out. They would not come back to Congress without first getting new guidance from back home.[37]

Duane, writing to a colleague in New York, was not convinced any change was necessary back home: "There seems ... no Reason that our Colony shou'd be too precipitate in changing the present mode of Government. I woud wish first to be well assured of the Opinion of the Inhabitants at large. Let them be rather followed than driven on an Occasion of such momentous Concern."[38]

The dissent did not bother John Adams, who wrote: "This Day the Congress has passed the most important Resolution, that ever was taken in America."[39] To Adams, this was not just a step toward independence: "[I]t was independence itself." Some other delegates thought the same thing. Caesar Rodney wrote: "Most of those here who are Termed the Cool Considerate Men think it amounts to a declaration of Independance. It Certainly Savour's of it."[40]

All that was lacking was a formality—a declaration. But that was not yet on Congress's agenda or on the mind of Thomas Jefferson, who would soon draft it. Just the previous day, Jefferson had returned to Philadelphia from Virginia[41] after being absent since December.[42] That trip to Virginia, to look after his ailing wife, was extended after the death of his mother, then further extended because of his own crippling headaches.[43] Now he was back in Philadelphia and feeling better, but already hankering to turn around and head back. In Virginia, a blueprint of a new government—a constitution for an independent state government—would soon be worked out—exciting stuff for Jefferson's fertile mind. From our perspective more than two centuries later, the center of action was Philadelphia. But for many of the delegates, the more fascinating activities were in each of the home colonies. Jefferson, afraid of missing out on history being made in Virginia, hinted in a letter that his skills might be put to better use back home: "Should our [Virginia's] Convention propose to establish now a form of government perhaps it might be agreeable to recall for a short time their delegates. It is a work of the most interesting nature and such as every individual would wish to have his voice in."[44]

Jefferson remained in Philadelphia, but found spare time to scribble a draft constitution for Virginia, which Jefferson's colleagues carried to Virginia weeks later.[45]

CHAPTER 16

Knaves Imposing upon Fools

In Pennsylvania, the May 15 resolution, with its startling preamble, had an immediate effect, as delegates to Congress could see quite literally outside the windows of the Pennsylvania State House. There, on Monday, May 20, some 4,000 people gathered under a steady rain to hear orators call for a convention to establish a new provincial government in Pennsylvania.

John Adams reported that the moderator, with a "loud Stentorian voice that might be heard a Quarter of a Mile," read out the resolution just produced by Congress a few steps away. The "Multitude" responded with "three Cheers, Hatts Flying as Usual &c." The "entertaining Maneuvre" was carried out with "great Order, Decency and Propriety,"[1] according to Adams. Another witness had a different impression: "[P]eople behaved in such a tyrannical manner that the least opposition was dangerous."[2]

Within the State House, the momentous May 15 resolution—which seemed to many the equivalent of independence—was not enough to nudge Congress to make a formal declaration. The prospect of a peace commission continued to hold delegates back.

With momentum rising in favor of independence, time seemed to favor those clamoring for a final break with Britain. But those delegates feared the inertia would vanish if and when the nebulous peace commission arrived. It was easy to imagine laborious negotiations going nowhere as the British geared up their gargantuan land and sea forces while Patriot passion ebbed and courage faltered. Colonial unity might fracture, as individual colonies abandoned their sisters and begged for peace. Foreign powers, which might come to the aid of a united and independent America, would certainly not lend a hand to divided, timorous Americans unsure of themselves.

John Adams raged:

> America duped and bubbled with the Phantom of Commissioners, has been fast asleep and left that important Post undefended, unsupported. The Ministry have caught the Colonies, as I have often caught a Horse, by holding out an empty Hat, as if it was full of Corn. ... Nothing has ever put my Patience to the Tryal so much as to see Knaves imposing upon Fools, by such artifices.[3]

Some delegates dared to glance ahead to the issue of confederation—some sort of more formal and fixed arrangement linking the colonies. New Hampshire's William Whipple noted: "A confederation permanent and lasting, ought in my opinion to be the next thing and I hope is not far off."[4]

***

We imagine Congress fully focused on the question of independence, but the issue jostled with myriad others for delegates' time and attention. Among those, most had to do with fighting the war. But, as Hewes of North Carolina noted, all the hours dedicated to writing resolutions often failed to accomplish anything: "We resolve to raise regiments, resolve to make Cannon, resolve to make & import muskets, powder and Cloathing, but it is a melancholly truth that near half of our men, Cannon, muskets, powder, Clothe &c is to be found no where but on paper."[5]

One of the military issues that landed uninvited on Congress's doorstep involved the New Hampshire Grants. When handling this hot potato the year before, Congress deftly promoted Ethan Allen and his Green Mountain Boys from outlaws to Patriots, thus kicking down the road the core quarrel involving New York and the settlers in the area that eventually became Vermont. Since then, men from the New Hampshire Grants had served and suffered in the Canada campaign. Heman Allen, one of Ethan's brothers, was now in Philadelphia with a petition asking Congress to recognize the soldiers from the disputed region as men of the New Hampshire Grants, not of New York. "[W]e are entirely willing to do all in our Power in the General Cause, under the Continental Congress," stated the petition, "but are not willing to put ourselves under the honorable provincial Congress of New York in such manner as might in future be detrimental to our private property."[6]

This put Congress in a bind. Delegates wanted the services of Ethan Allen, the Green Mountain Boys, and anyone else from the New Hampshire Grants willing to fight. But to give in to the petitioners would amount to blessing the dismemberment of New York.[7] Congress tossed the problem to a committee, which came down in favor of New York. The petitioners should "submit to the government of New York." But as a morsel to appease the petitioners, the committee suggested that submission to New York now would not bear on the issue "when tranquility shall be restored" and "the final Determination of their Right" might be made.[8]

Heman Allen returned a few days later to ask that the petition be withdrawn. He said he needed to go back home to retrieve papers supporting the petition, But the real reason, apparently, was to discourage Congress from making any decision in New York's favor for the time being.[9] Congress happily allowed the petition to disappear.

***

On May 18, awful news reached Philadelphia from Canada.[10] Congress learned that, shortly after fresh British troops arrived at Quebec City on May 6,[11] Continental soldiers on the outskirts of the town scampered away "with the utmost precipitation and confusion,"[12] leaving a trail of discarded muskets, cartridges, and clothing.[13]

Delegates despaired, looked for a scapegoat, and found General David Wooster, who had taken command of American forces for a time after the death of Montgomery. "General Wooster has the credit of this misadventure and if he cannot give a better account of it than has yet been heard I hope he will be made an example of,"[14] wrote Jefferson. Described as dull, tactless, and quarrelsome, Wooster was over his head and—aged above 60—over the hill. But he had held a losing hand. Congress would one day vote to honor him, sort of—a monument was authorized but never built.[15]

Meanwhile, Congress reaffirmed its commitment to maintain a foothold in Canada. A resolution was passed on May 24 promising to "contest every foot of the ground with the enemies to these colonies."[16]

However, the depressing news from Canada had no effect on the momentum toward independence. "It appears to me that the eyes of every unbeliever are now open," wrote Elbridge Gerry of Massachusetts on May 20. "A final declaration is approaching with great rapidity."[17]

On the same day, John Adams crowed: "Every Post and every Day rolls in upon Us Independance like a Torrent. ... We cant be very remote from the most decisive Measures and the most critical Event."[18]

Now came news that Virginia, the largest and oldest colony, had formally called for independence. The Virginia Convention had instructed its delegates to Congress "to declare the United Colonies free and independent States."[19]

***

Dickinson, the most reluctant Patriot, was shifting closer to accepting independence, and so was the Pennsylvania Assembly. The authority of that Assembly was decaying fast. By this time the Pennsylvania military, on the side of the backers of a new government, was refusing to take orders from the old Assembly.[20] Thus, in effect, no civil authority held the colony's military in check—a dangerous situation.

Still, many Pennsylvania civilians continued to see the old Assembly in the State House as the colony's legitimate lawmakers. Among them were petitioners from Cumberland County, who begged the Assembly to give the colony's delegates to Congress permission to vote for independence. The Assembly gave in, and Dickinson himself led a committee to revise Pennsylvania's instructions. Those convoluted instructions, without using the word "independence," gave grudging permission for Pennsylvania's delegates in Congress to vote for separation.[21]

***

John Adams, even as he hungered for a formal declaration of independence, now admitted that the groundwork for such a declaration was not in place. On June 3, Adams wrote to Patrick Henry: "[T]he natural Course and order of things was this—for every Colony to institute a Government—for all the Colonies to confederate, and define the Limits of the Continental Constitution—then to declare the Colonies a sovereign State, or a Number of confederated Sovereign States; and last of all, to form Treaties with foreign Powers."[22]

But the Declaration could not wait:

> I fear We cannot proceed Systematically, and that We shall be obliged to declare ourselves independent States before We confederate, and indeed before all the Colonies have established their Governments. It is now pretty clear, that all these Measures will follow one another in a rapid Sucession, and it may not perhaps be of much Importance, which is done first.[23]

John Adams knew the question would soon come before Congress, and so did his cousin Samuel. On June 6, Samuel Adams wrote to James Warren: "[T]omorrow a Motion will be made, and a Question, I hope, decided, the most important that was ever agitated in America. I have no Doubt but it will be decided to your satisfaction. This being done, Things will go on in the right Channel and our Country will be saved."[24]

Indeed, on June 7 came the critical resolution. Virginia's Richard Henry Lee had the honor: "That these United Colonies are, and of right ought to be, free and independent States, that they are absolved from all allegiance to the British Crown, and that all political connection between them and the State of Great Britain is, and ought to be, totally dissolved."[25]

Two related resolutions followed, one calling for forming foreign alliances, another for a plan of confederation to be drawn up and sent out to the former colonies.[26]

That was on a Friday. The next day, delegates gathered for a long day of argument on the question. Work continued until seven in the evening.[27]

Dickinson and his few allies—including New York's Robert Livingston, James Wilson of Pennsylvania, and South Carolina's Edward Rutledge—attempted to hold back the flood. They made clear that they did not strictly oppose a declaration of independence; they just thought the timing was wrong. The people of the Middle Atlantic colonies—Maryland, Pennsylvania, New Jersey, New York, and Delaware—"were not yet ripe for bidding adieu to British connection."[28] If a declaration were made, one or more of those colonies might well secede, thus shattering the union. France and Spain, seeing the colonies fracture, might team up with Britain to reassert British authority over the colonies in exchange for a generous slice of the American continent—maybe Canada for France and Florida for Spain.[29]

They further argued that Congress might receive word any day from Deane, their man in France, about "the disposition of the French court."[30] It wouldn't hurt, and might help, to know the French attitude before taking such a momentous step.

Proponents of an immediate declaration—John Adams, Virginia's Richard Henry Lee, Virginia's George Wythe, and others—answered with their own volley of arguments. They noted that none of the delegates on the other side of the question had challenged the right of Americans to separate. No one even brought up the possibility that the connection with Britain would ever be restored.

John Adams and his allies further pointed out that the resolution changed nothing. It simply stated a fact: Americans always were independent of Parliament and the British people. As for the king, he effectively made Americans independent when he declared Americans out of his protection and waged war on America.[31]

People were waiting for Congress to act, said supporters of independence. The people in the Middle Atlantic colonies favored independence, even if the instructions to delegates said otherwise. Jefferson summarized in his notes: "[T]he voice of the representatives is not alwais consonant with the voice of the people, and that this is remarkeably the case in these middle colonies." In any case, if Congress waited for unanimity, independence would never be declared because it was "impossible that all men should ever become of one sentiment on any question."[32]

Further, a declaration was needed now "while our affairs wear a hopeful aspect" to help with the task of building alliances for, according to "European delicacy," no European country would deal with the Americans or receive an American ambassador without such a declaration.[33]

In the end, Dickinson and the voices of caution won a partial victory: by a vote of seven to five, Congress postponed for a few weeks—to July 1—further consideration of the resolution.[34] This would provide time for the delegates from the wavering colonies—the Middle Atlantic colonies and South Carolina—to gather definitive instructions from their respective home colonies.

***

At about this time, the delegates from the failed mission to Canada—the two Carrolls, Chase, and Franklin—arrived back in Philadelphia. Franklin, with Father Carroll, had left Montreal first, leaving behind Charles Carroll and Chase. Franklin's trip south was wretched. He was out of sorts and discouraged as he began the journey, and then annoyed along the way by two other traveling companions—a couple who had once been noisy supporters of the American invaders. For much of the way to Albany, the wife and then the husband (who joined her in Saratoga) whined about how Franklin and his fellow commissioners had bungled their mission. They parted in Albany "civilly tho' coldly," according to Franklin: "I think they both have excellent Talents at making themselves Enemies, and I believe, live where they will, they will never be long without them." By May 26, Franklin was in New York City, tormented by gout, and feeling his age: "I find I grow daily more feeble."[35]

While Chase and Charles Carroll remained for a time in Montreal, they churned out more despairing reports to Congress:

> We want words to describe the confusion which prevails thro' every department relating to the Army. Several of your Officers appear to us unfit for the Stations they fill, your troops live from hand to Mouth, they have of late been put to half allowance in several places and in some they have been without pork for 3 or 4 days past.[36]

In a report days later to Congress, they said they had authorized the military to force inhabitants to hand over flour, in exchange for receipts, to feed the troops:

> Nothing but the most urgent necessity can justify such harsh measures, but men with arms in their hands will not starve, where provisions can be obtained by force: to prevent a general plunder which might end in the Massacre of your Troops & of many of the Inhabitants we have been constrained to advise the General to take this Step.[37]

Exhausted and exasperated, the commissioners lashed out, without naming names, at those responsible for the catastrophe in Canada:

> We cannot conceal our concern that Six Thousand Men should be ordered to Canada without taking care to have Magazines formed for their Subsistance, cash to pay them, or to pay the Inhabitants for their Labour, in transporting the baggage, Stores, and provisions of the Army. We cannot find words strong enough to describe our Miserable Situation, you will have a faint Idea of it if you figure to yourself an Army broken and disheartned, half of it under innoculation or under other diseases, Soldiers without pay, without discipline and altogether reduced to live from hand to mouth, depending on the scanty & precarious Supplies of a few half Starved cattle & triffling quantities of flour which have hitherto been picked up in different parts of the Country.[38]

On June 1, the last two commissioners finally left Canada,[39] leaving American military leaders to somehow keep a foothold in Quebec. As the commissioners sailed south on the narrow lakes leading to Ticonderoga, they likely glimpsed coming the other way a great fleet of "about two Hundred Vessels," with cloth from tents as sails, carrying regiments from Pennsylvania. One Pennsylvanian recalled seeing those bateaux as "something like the Grecian Fleet going to the Seage of Troy."[40]

The American reinforcements produced a transformation. Habitants suddenly warmed to the invaders. Americans saw riverbanks crowded with "men Women & Children Leaping & Clapping their hands for Joy."[41] A local militia captain appeared with the promise of about 600 fighters, if they could be provided weapons and provisions.[42] "The Canadians are Flocking by the Hundreds to take part with us," wrote Major-General John Sullivan to Washington.[43]

Close behind the Pennsylvanians came American money—hard money—that Congress had scraped together and sent north, "the Sum of sixteen Hundred and sixty two Pounds one Shilling and three Pence … which was all that was in the Treasury."[44] The commissioners had left Canada, but their desperate pleas had been answered.

Canadians eagerly stepped up to supply the Americans in exchange for just IOUs. Commanders were amazed: "They [the Canadians] have come in with the greatest Chearfulness & what gives Still greater Evidence of their Friendship is that they have Voluntarily Offer'd to Supply us with what Wheat flour &c. we want & ask nothing in return but Certificates."[45]

However, the renewed hope of retaining Canada was soon dashed. The Americans marched to confront the British advance at Trois Rivières, along the St. Lawrence about halfway between Quebec City and Montreal. Plans went awry; the Americans got mired in a swamp and lost one key advantage—surprise.[46] The British were ready for them and sent them scattering.

With the rout at Trois Rivières, the sensible choice would have been to abandon Canada. The British had more men, and no more American reinforcements were coming.[47] The adventure into Canada was, in the end, a fiasco, defeated not so much by the British as by confusion and lack of supply—ultimately the fault of Congress. As an American colonel wrote:

> This Northern Army has been treated with most cruel neglect, or we might have been in possession of Quebeck. Sir, when I arrived there, I found Generals without men, and a small Artillery without supplies. And Commissaries without provisions, Paymasters without money, and Quartermasters without stores, and Physicians without Medicines, and the small-pox very brief in our Army: which has been our destruction.[48]

***

The delegates sent to Canada were back in Philadelphia as Congress laid the groundwork in June for the Declaration most expected to come on July 1. Franklin, laid up with gout, probably never actually stepped foot in the Pennsylvania State House during these weeks. Even so, as the presumed expert on foreign affairs, he was named to the committee to draw up terms for foreign alliances.[49]

Another committee was formed to come up with a plan for confederation,[50] a topic relegated to the back burner for many months because other issues were more pressing. John Dickinson, proving that he retained the esteem of delegates not named John Adams, found a place on both the foreign affairs and confederation committees despite his foot-dragging on independence.[51]

A third committee was named to draw up the Declaration itself. Had Dickinson come around to support a declaration at this time, he certainly would have been on the committee and likely would be honored today as its author. He would have been the perfect choice: for years, he had been the voice of resistance to British policies. He was famous and admired for his writing skills, and his record of prudence and caution would have made his ultimate call for independence that much more powerful and convincing. But Dickinson, dug in against a declaration, had no place on the committee writing it.

Instead, the five chosen for that task were John Adams, Franklin, Roger Sherman, Robert Livingston, and Jefferson. Adams, leading the charge for independence in Congress, was an obvious choice. Franklin also clearly belonged on the strength of his stature. Sherman, of Connecticut, was a less obvious choice. He made a poor impression, a Georgian describing him a few years later as "the oddest shaped character I ever met," and assessing his manner of speaking as "grotesque and laughable."[52] But he was a solid independence man and had been so at least from the time of Lexington and Concord.[53] Livingston, one could argue, didn't belong on the committee at all. He was a New York delegate and thus was under orders not to vote for independence. Furthermore, he had been slow to take up the Patriot cause—a few years before, he had lost an election at least in part because he was too fond of British policies.[54] However, while he remained a voice of caution on independence, he now indicated that he would go along if it was the will of the majority. Colleagues, assessing Livingston as a man of sound judgment, had named him to many committees and trusted Livingston with this key assignment.[55]

Jefferson seems to have been placed on the committee in large part because he was a Virginian. It seemed especially important that someone from the largest and most senior colony have a role in crafting such a key document. Arguably, Richard Henry Lee should have been the Virginian on the committee. Lee, after all, had introduced the critical resolution on June 7 calling for independence. But he didn't get the assignment, possibly because he was too chummy with Samuel Adams. Adams and Lee were so close that some Virginians grumbled that Lee was more interested in representing Massachusetts than his own home colony.[56] That made Lee a little too radical for the tastes of many delegates. Anyway, Lee seemed uninterested. He was eager to get back to Virginia as developments there threatened his speculative ventures in western land. Lee also wanted to lend a hand in shaping the new state constitution.[57]

Virginians Benjamin Harrison or Carter Braxton would also have fitted the bill. But it seemed they were not radical enough. On the question of independence, they were tepid at best.[58] Jefferson would suit: a Virginian who was firmly in favor of independence and who had not ruffled feathers.

Of the five on the committee, Franklin might have been the first choice to compose the document. After all, his writing had made him famous. But at that moment he was too ill, and even had he been well, he may have chosen to turn down the assignment. He knew Congress would mutilate whatever he wrote, and that he could not abide. As he later confessed to Jefferson, he avoided whenever possible "becoming the draughtsman of papers to be reviewed by a public body."[59]

John Adams was also suited for the role of writing the first draft. As anyone who has browsed his letters knows, his writing is electric and a pleasure to read. Adams, however, did not want the job. He preferred Jefferson, and indeed had lobbied to have him on the committee.[60] Adams recalled more than 40 years later that the committee asked the two of them to draw up the main points of the Declaration and "cloath them in a proper Dress."[61] Jefferson then asked Adams to work on the draft first. Adams declined, insisting that Jefferson have the honor. Jefferson had a different recollection. He remembered no discussion between the two; the committee simply and "unanimously pressed upon myself alone to undertake the draught. I consented; I drew it."[62]

So Jefferson won the high honor and weighty responsibility, even though he had been virtually invisible and nearly silent in Philadelphia. Indeed, he was not even in Philadelphia for the first four months of the year. When he was there, he had no leading role and rarely spoke on the floor of the State House. John Adams wrote about Jefferson: "[D]uring the whole Time I satt with him in Congress, I never heard him utter three Sentences together."[63]

While we don't know why others on the committee favored Jefferson, we do have Adams's reasons. In private conversations, Jefferson had caught Adams's attention. Adams found him "prompt, frank, explicit and decisive." Furthermore, Adams knew—from Jefferson's famous *Summary View of the Rights of British America*—that Jefferson had a "happy talent of composition": he could write well.[64]

Also, from Adams's point of view, Jefferson didn't have Adams's political and personal baggage. As a Massachusetts man, Adams was assumed to be on the radical fringe. Anything he wrote would likely be received as the predictable rantings of a Boston man. Another problem for John Adams was that he was John Adams. He rubbed people the wrong way. A declaration from Adams would be tainted just because it was from his pen. As he explained to Jefferson at the time, "I am obnoxious, suspected, and unpopular."[65]

So, in a parlor outside his rented room in a three-story bricklayer's house at Seventh and Market,[66] seated on a swiveling Windsor chair,[67] and using a custom-made mahogany "writing box"—a portable lap desk[68]—Jefferson put pen to paper. He later recalled: "Neither aiming at originality of principle or sentiment, nor yet copied from any particular and previous writing, it was intended to be an expression of the American mind, and to give to that expression the proper tone and spirit called for by the occasion."[69]

With the formal vote on independence put off at least to July 1, Congress officially set the subject aside. For weeks, the topic gets no mention in Congress's *Journal*.[70] Congress kept up a frantic pace on other matters curious, vital, and mundane. On June 11, Congress greeted several Iroquois chiefs, who accepted gifts, heard a message from Congress, and bestowed on President Hancock the name Karanduawn, the Great Tree; on June 14, Congress ordered a letter written to Thomas Mayberry, a manufacturer, to ship 5 tons of sheet iron to Thomas Bates, blacksmith, to make kettles for the troops; on June 19, Congress authorized payment of $12 to one Mary Thomas "for nursing and boarding two of Captain Benezet's men, in the small pox"; on June 24, Congress recommended that the various colonies pass laws against counterfeiting Continental currency; and on June 26, Congress approved payment of $2 to one John Osborne for "a coffin for one of Captain Vanzant's men."[71]

In this time of soaring tension, delegates were keenly aware that among the American population were many secret or open Tories dubious about the Patriot cause and opposed to independence. Among them were a few eager to spy for the British or otherwise undermine the push for independence. It is thus a credit to Congress, and even astonishing, that delegates resolved "that no man in these colonies, charged with being a tory, or unfriendly to the cause of American liberty be injured in his person or property" without an order from Congress or from some local authority.[72]

The catastrophe in Canada was a recurring theme. As if to address its own failures in managing the expedition, Congress created a five-member Board of War and Ordinance.[73] It could not undo the disaster, but it might reduce the likelihood of future military misadventures. Congress was recognizing that it needed specialized departments with delegates focused on a particular area, and even some staff to carry out the work. Authorized to hire a secretary and clerks, the board was assigned to keep military records, maintain accounts of weapons and other military equipment, oversee the raising of troops and the handling of prisoners of war, and generally watch over military matters.[74] John Adams, who seemed to be on just about every important committee, was on this one, too. The board quickly set to work churning out reports with recommendations by the dozens, such as one asking colonies

> forthwith to cause a suit of cloaths, of which the waistcoat and breeches may be made of deer leather, if to be had on reasonable terms, a blanket, felt hat, two shirts, two pair of hose, and two pair of shoes, to be manufactured, or otherwise procured at reasonable rates, in their respective colonies, for each soldier of the American Army, inlisted therein for the present campaign.[75]

CHAPTER 17

Comfort and Cheer the Spirits

In the weeks leading up to the critical vote on July 1, were Americans really yearning for independence? Some Patriot leaders didn't want to know. In Rhode Island, lawmakers scotched a plan to gather popular opinion about independence. They worried that a few towns would oppose it, and thus expose disunity in the colony.[1] In Massachusetts, where lawmakers did ask towns to chime in on the question, at least one—Barnstable—voted against it.[2]

Overall, however, a tide for independence was rising. Some 90 or so localities of one sort or another, such as towns and counties, produced between April and July "declarations of independence," statements urging representatives to work for independence.[3]

But what Congress needed from each colony—that is, from the assemblies or the revolutionary bodies that had seized authority and sent delegates to Congress—were unambiguous directions on how their delegates should vote. People such as John and Samuel Adams, of the pro-independence faction, hoped for clear orders from each of the colonies to vote in favor. Short of that, they wanted the colonies to at least unshackle the delegates—to remove the restrictions forbidding a vote in favor of independence and permit delegates to vote according to their best judgment or with the majority.

Before April, no delegation in Congress had explicit instructions to vote for independence. Even though the Adamses were beating the drums for exactly that, Massachusetts had given no such order. John Adams pleaded with colleagues in the assembly back home for direct orders, not so much for himself, but to inspire the other colonies to follow suit: "Vast Majorities in all the Colonies now see the Propriety and Necessity of taking the decisive Steps, and those who are averse to it are afraid to Say much against it. And therefore Such an Instruction at this Time would comfort and cheer the Spirits of your Friends, and would discourage and dishearten your Enemies."[4]

But his fellow Patriot back in the colony, James Warren, couldn't deliver, at least not in time to matter. Surprisingly, despite the reputation of Massachusetts as a leader in calling for separation, such explicit instructions came only after independence was declared. With no instructions barring them from voting for independence, the Massachusetts delegates considered themselves free to vote for separation.

While Massachusetts hesitated, other colonies boldly stepped forward. One was South Carolina. Given permission by Congress back in November to form a government free of royal authority, that colony's provincial Congress did just that, recasting itself in March under a new constitution that created a government exactly like the previous royal government, minus the royal part.[5] Almost at the same time, South Carolina issued new instructions for its delegates to Congress. They could now vote with the majority in Congress on measures "necessary for the defense, security, interest, or welfare" of South Carolina and America.[6] Independence was not mentioned. Even so, South Carolina delegates decided they were free to vote that way.[7]

Then in early April, the Provincial Congress of North Carolina produced instructions that, compared to South Carolina's, more plainly gave the delegates a free hand to vote for independence: "*Resolved*, That the Delegates for this Colony in the Continental Congress be impowered to concur with the delegates in the other Colonies in declaring Independency."[8]

Meanwhile, Rhode Island by this time had effectively declared independence. It was a simple matter there. With the governor elected by the people, Rhode Island was virtually independent anyway. In early May, the elected legislature simply passed the appropriate resolutions. Documents would no longer refer to royal authority but would instead be issued in the name of "the Governor and Company of the English Colony in Rhode Island and Providence Plantations."[9] Thus, curiously, the Rhode Island lawmakers, while rejecting royal authority, still identified their home as an English colony.

The transformation of Rhode Island to independence went hand in hand with new instructions to its delegates to Congress. In seven meandering paragraphs, those instructions somehow avoided the word "independence" but still nudged the colony's two delegates in that direction.[10] How curious, considering that Rhode Island was supposedly ablaze with Patriot passion. Why weren't lawmakers more explicit? It seems they didn't want to alarm anyone. The governor confided in a letter: "Dependency is a word of so equivocal a meaning, and hath been used for such ill purposes, and independency, with many honest and ignorant people carrying the idea of eternal warfare, the committee thought it best to avoid making use of either of them."[11] This was not so much a call for independence, as a nod and a wink.

Throughout June, word trickled in to Philadelphia about developments in other colonies. Connecticut's situation was similar to that of Rhode Island. With the governor elected by the people, the colony was virtually independent. The elected lawmakers could formally snip ties with Britain with a simple resolution, which it did on June 14. Inspired by Virginia's example,[12] Connecticut's lawmakers instructed its delegates to "propose" to Congress to declare the "United *American* Colonies free and independent States."[13] Meanwhile, reference to the king would vanish from official oaths, and documents would appear in the name of the governor, not the king.[14] Connecticut lawmakers, in supporting the work of Congress, also made clear that the union of colonies, in whatever form, shouldn't tread on the authority of the individual colonies.[15]

On the very next day, June 15, Delaware and New Hampshire joined the independence parade. Lawmakers in New Hampshire admitted they were following the "example of several of the most respectable of our Sister colonies before us" in instructing delegates to "join with the other Colonies in Declaring the thirteen united Colonies, a free & independent State." Note the singular "State," suggesting a vision of America as a single entity, rather than a confederation of 13 independent states. But despite that lofty wording, the New Hampshire lawmakers, like those in Connecticut, insisted on firm limits on a national authority: New Hampshire fully supported Congress and the united colonies, "[p]rovided the regulation of our internal police be under the direction of our own Assembly."[16]

Meanwhile, little Delaware, as if imitating little Rhode Island, was coy—agreeing to independence without uttering the word. The May 15 resolution from the Continental Congress worked in Delaware just as Congress intended. The resolution was presented to the Delaware Assembly, still functioning as usual under its royal charter. The Assembly unanimously approved it, thus signaling its intention to set in motion the process of creating a new provincial government stripped of royal references. As it turned out, Delaware was slow to get going on the transition: in late July, it finally called for a constitutional convention for late August.[17] But the Assembly wasted no time revising its instructions to delegates to Congress: the delegates were free to "concur" with those from other colonies in making agreements and in "adopting such other measures" needed to promote "the liberty, safety and interests of America."[18]

In New Jersey, a whirlwind of events transformed the colony in a matter of days. When representatives of the pro-Patriot Provincial Congress, newly elected in May, came together in Burlington for the first time on June 10, they were well aware of Virginia's bold call for independence, and they were inspired by the mid-May resolution in Congress giving license to colonies to snip their ties to Britain. The representatives also immediately recognized the rising threat from local Tories, whose hopes rose with expectations that British reinforcements would soon appear to restore British authority.[19]

By this time, New Jersey Governor William Franklin, staunchly Loyalist, was virtually powerless. He hung on in the Proprietary House, the governor's mansion in Perth Amboy some 50 miles from Burlington, and controlled a phantom government. The militia now answered to the Provincial Congress, not the governor. Patriot groups had seized at least three judges serving Franklin's government. Franklin's friends and associates abandoned him for the Patriot side. Meanwhile, the Provincial Congress was holding elections, managing the colony's military, replacing royal officials with their own, and naming delegates to the Continental Congress.[20] There was nothing for the governor to do and no reason for the old Assembly to meet. Still, to the Provincial Congress, Franklin posed a threat. It was easy to imagine the governor rallying Tories in a kind of counterrevolution against the Patriot tide.

But how exactly to depose the governor, who, as it happened, was now the last standing[21] royal governor in the colonies? This was tricky business, not least because he was the son of Benjamin Franklin, sitting in the Continental Congress. The Provincial Congress needed a pretext, however flimsy, to give the delicate task a legal veneer.

William Franklin obliged, issuing a call for the old Assembly to meet in Perth Amboy. Under normal circumstances, this was a routine matter. A royal governor was expected to call the Assembly into session from time to time to authorize spending and conduct other business. But these were abnormal times. This was two weeks after the May 15 resolution from the Continental Congress calling for colonies to unravel their royal connections. William Franklin, well aware of that resolution, was thumbing his nose at the men in Philadelphia. He was determined to carry on and prove that his government, however truncated, still functioned. He imagined it still might survive this crisis and assist in some sort of reconciliation with Britain or, short of that, at least pull New Jersey out of the orbit of the Continental Congress.[22]

The Provincial Congress pounced. On June 16, it determined that Franklin, in calling the old Assembly together, had acted in "direct contempt and violation" of the May 15 resolution of the Continental Congress. The New Jersey Provincial Congress further decided that Franklin, "an enemy to the liberties of this country," needed to be taken into custody. Orders went out to Colonel Nathaniel Heard of Middlesex County's First Battalion: "It is the desire of [the New Jersey] Congress that this necessary business be conducted with all the delicacy and tenderness which the nature of the business can possibly admit." Heard carried "a written parole" with blanks for Franklin to fill in depending on whether he preferred to spend his time under house arrest at Princeton, Bordentown, or on his farm at Rancocus: "[S]hould he refuse to sign the parole, you are desired to put him under strong guard, and keep him in close custody, until the further order of this [New Jersey] Congress."[23]

Heard did as ordered, but Franklin, as he later wrote, rejected the parole "with that contempt such an insult deserved from one who has the honor to represent His Majesty."[24] Heard placed a company of about 60 militiamen around Franklin's house and awaited further instructions.[25] The New Jersey Congress promptly ordered Heard to bring Franklin from Amboy to Burlington to face the lawmakers. They also sent off a report to the Continental Congress. Should New Jersey pack off Franklin to some other colony? Clearly, that's what the New Jersey Congress preferred: "Mr. Franklin, we presume, would be capable of doing less mischief in *Connecticut* or

Pennsylvania than in *New Jersey*." New Jersey also wanted the Continental Congress to give direction and maybe some reassurance that the New Jersey Congress had acted properly: "Whatever advice Congress may think proper to give us, we shall be glad to receive; and would further intimate, that the countenance and approbation of the Continental Congress would satisfy some persons, who might otherwise be disposed to blame us."[26]

Not surprisingly, about this time, the New Jersey Provincial Congress formally changed the instructions for the colony's delegates to the Continental Congress. Considering that the Provincial Congress had just grabbed the royal governor, one might have expected the new instructions to explicitly order its delegates to vote for independence. But the Provincial Congress, as if wishing for a miracle, let the delegates decide, keeping the door to reconciliation open a crack. Delegates were to vote for independence only if "necessary and expedient" for "supporting the just rights and liberties of America."[27] Delegates could also work with other delegates in establishing a confederacy.

As for William Franklin, he was brought before the New Jersey Congress and interrogated. Franklin said only that the revolutionary Congress had no authority and had "usurped the King's Government in this Province."[28] In Philadelphia, on June 24, the Continental Congress ordered Franklin packed off to Connecticut and placed under the custody of the Patriot governor there.[29] On June 26, a 23-man guard gathered up Franklin for the 200-mile journey to Hartford.[30]

How did Benjamin Franklin react to all this? The record is silent. We know that by this time, father and son were fully estranged. We don't know whether Benjamin Franklin was present in Congress when the subject of his son's fate was debated. Benjamin never lifted a finger on behalf of his only son or his daughter-in-law, Elizabeth, left alone in the governor's mansion in Perth Amboy, where her mail was intercepted and roaming soldiers cursed her from the street and plundered her apple trees.[31]

Meanwhile, in Pennsylvania, as the authority of the old Assembly, meeting in the State House, melted away, power was shifting into the hands of the upstart Provincial Conference, meeting in Carpenters' Hall.

The Provincial Conference announced its emphatic support for a declaration of independence, but took no steps to appoint new delegates to the Continental Congress or issue new instructions to delegates in place.[32]

For its part, the old Assembly failed to actually ratify the new instructions authorizing delegates to Congress to approve independence. That dwindling Assembly tried, but many members sympathetic to the new government—the Provincial Conference—simply stopped attending. The old Assembly could not get the quorum needed to pass the revised instructions.

That left Pennsylvania's delegates to Congress technically obliged to continue to follow the old instructions, which expressly prohibited them from voting in favor of independence. When Pennsylvania, some weeks hence, cast a vote in Congress in favor of independence, those delegates, strictly speaking, had no legal authority to do so.[33] But by then, events had progressed so far that such a fine point was never raised.

Maryland, like Pennsylvania, had no governor or any official appointed by royal authorities. Thus, there was no royal governor to blame for this or that, no royal official to be angry about. Possibly because they had no royal official to rally against, they sometimes reacted to events in unexpected ways. When Virginia's Governor Dunmore issued his shocking proclamation promising Virginia slaves freedom if they fought with the British—a proclamation that united Virginians against the British—some planters in Maryland stepped up reconciliation efforts.[34] John Adams, for one, was baffled by Maryland. He wrote on May 20 that Maryland was

> so excentric a Colony—some times so hot, sometimes so cold—now so high, then so low—that I do not know what to say about it or expect from it. ... When they get agoing I expect some wild extravagant Flight or other from it. To be sure they must go beyond every body else, when they begin to go.[35]

Indeed, the behavior of Maryland was hard to fathom. A few days before Adams wrote his letter, the Maryland Convention, meeting in Annapolis to craft a new government and instruct delegates to Congress,[36] did away for the time being with the usual oaths of office that supported "Government under the Crown of *Great Britain*." Soon after, the Convention decided that "every kind of authority under the said Crown should be now totally suppressed in this Province, and the powers of Government exerted under the authority of the people."[37]

Those actions seemed to point toward independence. Yet the Convention also voted to stick with its instructions denying delegates the freedom to vote for independence. A "reunion with Great Britain on constitutional principles" was the best way to "secure the rights and liberties ... of the whole empire."[38]

To prod the Maryland Convention to lift its restrictions, Maryland delegate to Congress Samuel Chase, fresh from his misadventure in Canada, dashed off in June to Annapolis, where he found that "a general Dissatisfaction prevails here with our Convention."[39] Maryland citizens were doing their own prodding. From Frederick County came a blast, demanding that Maryland join with the other colonies:

> That what may be recommended by a majority of the Congress, equally delegated by the people of the United Colonies, we will, at the hazard of our lives and fortunes, support and maintain; and that every resolution of Convention tending to separate this Province from a majority of the Colonies, without the consent of the people, is destructive to our internal safety, and big with publick ruin.[40]

Pressure from Frederick County and elsewhere did the trick. A letter from Chase to John Adams on June 28 reported "an Unanimous Vote of our Convention for *Independence* etc. etc. See the glorious Effects of County Instructions. Our people have fire if not smothered."[41]

Meanwhile, overshadowing the odd developments in Maryland were strange events in New York. New York's royal government was long gone. It had given way back in April 1775, about the time of Lexington and Concord. Assuming authority in the colony was the Provincial Congress, which was extra-legal—that is, outside the authority of the British government—but not exactly revolutionary. Various factions jostled for control of this Congress, ranging from ardent Patriots to outright Tories, who exerted more power in this colony than in any other. The faction in control, however, fell between these two extremes—conservatives unhappy with British rule but horrified at the thought of independence. Because of this conservative faction (largely merchants, urban professionals, and landlords), New York's delegates to the Continental Congress were among the most conservative.[42] They were the delegates most likely to welcome initiatives toward reconciliation and the least likely to join the chorus for independence.

When the Continental Congress came up with the May 15 resolution—crafted to upset the applecart wherever there were vestiges of British control—the conservatives in New York saw an opportunity, not a threat. They liked the prospect of shaping a new form of government to further secure their hold on power. Inspired by the May 15 resolution, the Provincial Congress set in motion a process for electing a new Provincial Congress empowered to create a new constitution and thus build the foundation of a new government for New York.[43]

But what was New York's position on independence? Its delegates to the Continental Congress had instructions over a year old requiring them to work on measures "for the restoration of harmony between Great Britain and the Colonies."[44] Were these instructions still valid? In early June, the four New York delegates in Philadelphia sent off a plea to New York asking for clarity.

The answer came back: delegates were not authorized to back independence. Further, the New York Congress was not likely to give such instructions because it lacked the authority, according to many of its own members, who doubted that "their constituents intended to vest them with a power to deliberate and determine on" the question of independence.[45]

Anyway, the timing was poor. With the province in the midst of "obtaining the consent and authority of the people for establishing a new and regular form of Government," it would be "imprudent to require the sentiments of the people relative to the question of Independence, lest it should create division, and have an unhappy influence on the other." But delegates to the Continental Congress were assured: "The earliest opportunity will, however, be embraced of ascertaining the sentiments of the inhabitants of this Colony on that important question."[46]

For the New York Congress, independence was a potato too hot to touch. Meanwhile, they expected at any moment that British forces would land in New York City.

CHAPTER 18

Boots and Spurs

Meanwhile, Jefferson worked on the Declaration as he found time, which was scarce. Like everyone in Congress, he served on various committees. As he ruminated over the Declaration, he was also drafting reports assigned to him about exchanging prisoners and the Canadian campaign.[1]

In those days, writers, especially those under a deadline, often adapted other texts for their own purposes. Indeed, a skillful reshaping of an honored document was a mark of erudition. Jefferson's model was the English Declaration of Rights of 1689. This document, virtually sacred to many Englishmen, marked the end of the reign of James II and the beginning of the reign of William (of Orange) and Mary. After James fled England to France, Parliament drew up and approved the Declaration of Rights, which was then presented to the new monarchs and later revised and re-enacted.[2] That Declaration stated that James, assisted by "diverse evil Councellors Judges and Ministers ... did endeavour to subvert and extirpate the Protestant Religion and the Lawes and Libertyes of this Kingdome." What followed were 13 clauses itemizing the faults of the king and, later on, "thirteen undoubted Rights and Liberties." Some of the clauses sound familiar to Americans because many were restated almost word for word in the American Bill of Rights, still years away. For example, the English Declaration stated that "excessive bail ought not to be required, nor excessive fines imposed, nor cruel and unusual punishments inflicted"[3]—virtually the same as the Eighth Amendment to the United States Constitution.[4]

The Continental Congress had drawn on the English Declaration back in 1774, before the war broke out, when it crafted its own Declaration of Rights in pleading at that time for justice. Jefferson himself had borrowed from the 1689 document when he drafted his own preamble to the Virginia constitution, which he had just completed and sent off to Virginia.[5] Now Jefferson was drawing again from that revered text, which made sense because Americans in 1776 were complaining about many of the same problems that the English railed about back in 1689. For example, the English Declaration scolded James for "raiseing and keeping a standing Army within this Kingdom in time of Peace without consent of Parliament and quartering

Souldiers contrary to Law."[6] The American Declaration, in its final form, reproved George for keeping "among us, in times of peace, standing armies without the consent of our legislatures."[7]

Jefferson also borrowed from a draft of the Virginia Declaration of Rights, a new document also inspired by the English Declaration of Rights.[8] The American Bill of Rights consists of amendments to the U.S. Constitution. That is, they were debated and added after the Constitution was written and ratified. In Virginia, however, the Declaration of Rights came first (approved June 12[9]), before the writing of the state's Constitution (approved June 29).[10] We can assume that Jefferson and many others in Philadelphia were acquainted with Virginia's Declaration of Rights because a version of it appeared in the *Pennsylvania Gazette*.[11]

The author of Virginia's Declaration of Rights was George Mason, an older man whom Jefferson knew. The parallels between Mason's Declaration and that of Jefferson are unmistakable. For example, Mason's Declaration states: "That all men are by nature equally free and independent, and have certain inherent rights, of which, when they enter into a state of society, they cannot, by any compact, deprive or divest their posterity; namely, the enjoyment of life and liberty, with the means of acquiring and possessing property and pursuing and obtaining happiness."[12] Jefferson's draft expressed similar ideas, but more elegantly: "that all men are created equal; that they are endowed by their Creator with certain inherent and inalienable Rights; that among these are life, liberty and the pursuit of happiness."[13]

The committee to oversee the draft liked what Jefferson wrote, for its members made few changes (Adams inserted two; Franklin made five[14]). The draft presented to Congress on Friday, June 28, was thus virtually all the work of Jefferson. Then it was read—probably by Secretary Charles Thomson.[15]

Delegates left no evidence of their first impression. There seems to have been little or no discussion or debate about the Declaration that day. Anyway, a more important question still had to be thrashed out: before considering the document, delegates had to decide on the question of independence itself. Everyone knew that debate about independence would resume after the weekend, on July 1.

On that day, to facilitate discussion, delegates reorganized as a committee of the whole. No minutes would be kept. With no formal record to be concerned about, delegates presumably would feel more inclined to speak freely. Congress picked Virginia's Benjamin Harrison to lead the discussion. He sat in Hancock's place at the table raised on the dais in the front of the room.[16]

Before the discussion began, everyone knew that the majority favored independence. That very morning, a rider had appeared with news that Maryland had blessed independence. Its delegates to Congress were now free to "concur" with other colonies on separation from Britain.[17] Thus, Maryland's delegates were on side with those from New Hampshire, Massachusetts, Rhode Island, Connecticut, Virginia, North Carolina, and Georgia—eight colonies clearly leaning toward independence.[18]

This painting by John Trumbull shows Thomas Jefferson (second from right of the five men standing before desk) presenting the draft of the Declaration of Independence on June 28, 1776, to John Hancock in the Pennsylvania State House (Independence Hall). With Jefferson are the other members of the committee that prepared the draft: John Adams, Roger Sherman, Robert Livingston, and Benjamin Franklin. The widely recognized image is historically inaccurate in many ways. The number and location of doors and windows in the room are wrong, the windows had no heavy draperies, and the captured British military flags were not displayed as shown. Trumbull also included witnessing delegates who were not actually there at that time. The painting is displayed in the Rotunda of the U.S. Capitol. A smaller identical painting by Trumbull is at the Yale University Art Gallery. (Image courtesy of the Architect of the Capitol)

To be approved, independence required a majority of nine. But rules or no rules, the question required more than nine votes to carry weight as a valid and united declaration of independence. The dissent of four colonies on such a vital issue would likely be fatal to the cause. If four colonies merely abstained, the nation—as yet hardly a nation at all—might well be stillborn.

Of the five delegations in doubt, New York's was the only one beyond influence by debate or discussion in Philadelphia. New York's delegates were still hamstrung by firm instructions to steer clear of independence.

But what of South Carolina, Pennsylvania, New Jersey, and Delaware? Delegates from each of those colonies were free to vote for independence. But uncertainty haunted the proceedings; delegations from South Carolina and Pennsylvania were divided, and the attitudes of the delegates from New Jersey and Delaware were unclear.[19]

Dickinson, the voice of caution, made the case against independence. By the time he rose to speak, it was early afternoon. To ensure secrecy, the doors and windows of the room were closed on a steamy day with temperatures in the 90s.[20] Dickinson knew his opinions were out of favor: "My Conduct, this Day, I expect will give the finishing Blow to my once too great, and ... now too diminish'd Popularity." But he was determined: "I must speak, tho I should lose my Life, tho I should lose the Affections of my Country."[21]

His message boiled down to one word: prudence. The time for independence might come, he said, but it was not now. He poked holes in the two chief arguments for independence—that it would inspire the people and help win allies. Nonsense, said Dickinson. People were plenty energized already, fighting to preserve their own lives, liberty, and property. As for the allies, they would not be impressed with words; they would be looking for victories on the battlefield. Indeed, potential allies might be offended that Congress declared independence without first consulting them. According to his own surviving notes from his speech, potential allies, such as France, might well conclude: "Yours is the most rash & at the same Time the most contemptible Senate that ever existed on Earth."[22]

Before declaring independence, Dickinson said, Americans needed more groundwork: a constitution and government in each former colony, and an agreement among the former colonies on confederation—how the states would work together and relate to one another. Such measures would show "Deliberation, Wisdom, Caution & Unanimity." To separate, to withdraw from British protection, before such preparations were in place would be like "Destroying a House before we have got another."[23]

Dickinson speculated that Britain, frustrated on the battlefield, might come forward after a season or two and address all American complaints. America, he said, might use the threat of independence and a potential alliance with France to bargain for such concessions.[24]

The chamber was full of men who both loved to make speeches and were raring to get on with independence. Thus, one might have expected a chorus of voices eager to answer Dickinson. Instead, the response to Dickinson was an awkward silence.

John Adams, in recalling the day, wrote that "after waiting some time, in hopes that someone less obnoxious than myself" would stand and state the case for independence, "I determined to speak."[25]

Unlike Dickinson, Adams had no notes, but he had spoken often on the topic. He launched into what was perhaps the most important speech of his life,[26] and for its historical importance, one that schoolchildren might be poring over today if anyone had taken it down—but no one did. We know Adams spoke over the rumbling of a storm that blew through the town that afternoon,[27] but we don't know exactly what he said on that pivotal day.

As Adams was winding up his speech, in walked two new delegates from New Jersey. One asked Adams to restate his argument. Adams balked: "I was ashamed to repeat what I had said twenty times before." But the New Jersey men insisted: "I summed up the Reasons, Objections, and Answers, in as concise a manner as I could."[28] Eventually others spoke as well, and debate dragged on for nine hours,[29] "an idle Mispence of Time," wrote Adams that evening, "for nothing was Said, but what had been repeated and hackneyed in that Room before an hundred Times, for Six Months past."[30]

Then delegates took a preliminary vote. The two new delegates from New Jersey who had just arrived were fully authorized, but not required, to vote for independence. That delegation joined eight colonies in favor. Meanwhile, Delaware was split, with one of its two delegates voting for and the other against. A third delegate was absent. South Carolina voted against, its delegation perhaps swayed by Edward Rutledge, who remained reluctant to commit to independence.

Likewise, Pennsylvania voted against, with four of its seven delegates, including Dickinson, resisting the tide.[31] As for New York, its delegation favored independence but had no authorization to vote that way. So those delegates abstained.[32] South Carolina's Rutledge was having second thoughts. He suggested the whole matter be postponed to the next day;[33] the weary Congress readily agreed.

That night, Virginia delegate Francis Lightfoot Lee added to a letter to his brother Richard Henry that he had started the previous day. Francis Lightfoot was annoyed: "The Pennsylvania delegates indulge their own wishes, tho they acknowledge, what indeed everybody knows, that they vote contrary to the earnest desires of the people." And he was troubled at the distraction: "[A]t the time when all our attention, every effort shou'd be to oppose the Enemy, we are disputing about Government & independence." But Francis Lightfoot Lee was confident that South Carolina would come around: "Tomorrow it [independence] will pass the house with the concurrence of S. Carolina."[34]

What happened in those late afternoon or evening hours to change South Carolina from "no" to "yes" on independence? No one will ever know for sure, but perhaps it had to do with Jefferson's draft of the Declaration. The draft included a catalogue of grievances against the king, including one final astonishing long-winded assertion that blamed the king for the slave trade. It said, in part:

> He [the king] has waged cruel war against human nature itself, violating its most sacred rights of life and liberty in the persons of a distant people who never offended him, captivating & carrying them into slavery in another hemisphere or to incur miserable death in their transportation thither. ... Determined to keep open a market where *Men* should be bought & sold, he has prostituted his negative for suppressing every legislative attempt to prohibit or restrain this execrable commerce.[35]

Historian John Ferling speculates that Rutledge, not keen on independence in the first place, was especially disturbed about such anti-slavery language in the Declaration, and that a deal may have been struck between the South Carolina delegation and pro-independence delegates: "yes" to independence in exchange for a promise to scratch out that part of the document.[36] If true, it was likely an easy compromise. The assertion, which might have been apt if the men in Philadelphia had fought to end slavery, was merely absurd considering that so many delegates, including Jefferson, prospered from their enslaved people's sweat, pain, and misery, and lifted not a finger to end the institution.

Whatever the reasoning, South Carolina came around, and Delaware would too. Delaware delegate Thomas McKean, at his own expense, had just sent out a messenger to Dover, Delaware, about 80 miles away, with a note for Cesar Rodney, another delegate from Delaware who had been absent. The note urged Rodney, who favored independence, to saddle up and get to Philadelphia post-haste.[37]

Rodney, 48 years old, had reason enough to be away from Philadelphia. As a militia officer, he was busy putting down a Loyalist rebellion in the colony.[38] Besides, he was ill, having skin cancer so advanced that he took to wearing a silk scarf to hide his disfigured nose and cheek.[39] Despite all that, Rodney responded to McKean's plea, arriving on the morning of July 2 as members began to gather at the State House, the weather a bit cooler after a hard rain. McKean met him at the door "in his boots and spurs."[40] Rodney, in a letter, distilled his heroics to a sentence: "I arrived in Congress (tho detained by thunder and Rain) time Enough to give my Voice in the matter of Independence."[41] With the addition of Rodney, Delaware's delegation could be counted on to support independence.

So, as July 2 dawned, it was apparent to everyone that the vote for independence would have the support of at least 11 colonies. Only the votes of New York and Pennsylvania were in doubt. After routine business involving "Sundry letters,"[42] Congress returned to the question of independence. Votes were once again counted, and sure enough South Carolina and Delaware favored independence.

Meanwhile, at the table where Pennsylvania's delegates sat, two chairs were empty. Records are murky, but we know Pennsylvania delegates Dickinson and Robert Morris did not vote that day. They may have stayed away entirely, or possibly they attended but, during the voting, simply slipped behind a rail that divided the room, thereby making themselves "absent" during the vote. Whatever the case, neither cast a vote, as both were unwilling to either endorse independence or obstruct the will of most delegates and most Pennsylvanians. That left five voting Pennsylvania delegates. Benjamin Franklin and John Morton favored independence, while Thomas Willing and Charles Humphries opposed. The fifth delegate, James Wilson, would illustrate the power of popular opinion to tip the balance in Pennsylvania.

Born in Scotland and educated at the University of St. Andrews, Wilson seemed destined for the ministry from an early age. But he abandoned his theological studies and, after dabbling as a tutor and bookkeeper, set off to America in 1765. Two years later, he found himself in Philadelphia, where he trained as a lawyer under Dickinson. He later moved around Pennsylvania, to Reading and then Carlisle, building up a successful practice and marrying an heiress. He had little interest in politics until about 1774, when he jumped in headfirst. His mentor Dickinson pushed to make Wilson a delegate to Congress, where the "young Gentleman" impressed John Adams, who found Wilson superior to Dickinson in "Fortitude, Rectitude, and Abilities too."[43]

For months, Wilson was lockstep with Dickinson in opposing independence. By January of 1776, he was a leader in resisting the split with Britain. In May, he opposed the pivotal resolution that encouraged colonies to establish independent governments. On June 8 and 10, he repeated his opposition to a declaration of independence.[44]

Then Wilson got wind of a backlash from people in his home county. They were outraged to learn that in the secret debates in Congress, Wilson opposed independence.[45] Some thought Wilson should be removed as a delegate, one man writing: "I will never trust a Scotchman again. They Cannot be honest when liberty is in question."[46]

Fearing the ruin of his political career, Wilson had an epiphany: he was really for independence and had been all along. To rescue his "Publick Character," Wilson asked colleagues in Congress around mid-June to sign a document attesting that he, in debates in Congress, had "declared it to be his opinion that the Colonies would stand justified before God and the World in declaring an absolute Separation from Great Britain forever," that he had felt until then restricted by instructions to vote against independence, but that now being "un-restrained" would vote for it.

The assertions in the long-winded document were fibs, but pro-independence colleagues were glad to attest to them if it meant getting Wilson on board the independence bandwagon. Twenty-two delegates signed, including both Adamses, Jefferson, and Hancock. So did Robert Morris, but not Dickinson.[47]

Sure enough, Wilson voted for independence on July 1 and again on July 2, putting Pennsylvania on the independence side of the ledger.

The vote for independence thus carried: 12 votes for; none against. New York abstained.

John Adams wrote to Abigail the next day: "The Second Day of July 1776, will be the most memorable Epocha, in the History of America.—I am apt to believe that it will be celebrated, by succeeding Generations, as the great anniversary Festival."[48] He had the right idea, but the wrong date.

CHAPTER 19

Singular and Delicate

So, what of New York? It was in limbo, neither for nor against independence. Was it part of the new nation or not? Was it an old colony or a new state? On the morning of July 2, New York's five delegates wrote a joint letter to the New York Provincial Congress promising to abstain, as per instructions ("We know the Line of our Conduct on this Occasion; we have your Instructions, and will faithfully pursue them"). Then they asked what to do next, assuming correctly that independence would pass: "What Part are we to act after this Event takes Place[?]... Our Situation is singular and delicate."[1]

New York's situation was indeed precarious, for by now word had reached Philadelphia that British soldiers had come ashore near New York City. "Part of General Howe's army is arrived at Sandy Hook," wrote Joseph Hewes of North Carolina on July 2. "We must expect warm work in that quarter in a few days."[2] The curtain was rising on the next act in the war for independence, and New York City would be center stage.

After the evacuation of Boston, British strategists decided that the easiest way to win the war was to isolate prickly New England.[3] By preventing communications and assistance from reaching Massachusetts and its restive siblings, the rebellion might be contained there and eventually crushed. The first step in that strategy was to take and hold New York City. New York Harbor would then be transformed into a British base for blocking shipping to and from New England.[4] Maritime trade in that region would slow to a trickle.

The British also saw New York City as a starting point for a military push up the Hudson River north to Albany and then beyond. Control of the waterway would block land communication between New England and the eight colonies to the south,[5] meaning New England would be cut off by land and sea.

The plan made sense, so much so that Washington anticipated it. Fully expecting a move on New York City, America's top general had been shifting men and weapons south from Massachusetts and focusing on building up the defenses on Manhattan Island and Long Island.[6]

In this context, the New York delegates at the Continental Congress pleaded for guidance from their lawmakers back home. But those lawmakers had their hands full. For one thing, Loyalists, anticipating the arrival of the British in force, were resisting with increasing audacity the authority of the Provincial Congress. Efforts to undermine the Patriot cause and return New York to British control led to the first execution for treason. This followed the discovery of a plot to kidnap Washington. The mayor of New York was caught up in the affair and was arrested. He was not hanged, but a guard assigned to protect Washington was.[7]

Amid this turmoil, New York's Provincial Congress agonized over its own claim to authority. To shore up its legitimacy, the New York Congress had called for new elections in June. That meant the old Provincial Congress would leave the question of independence to the new Provincial Congress. The old New York Congress met for the last time in New York City in late May, two days after British ships appeared in the city's outer harbor. The new Provincial Congress would not meet until July 9, and then in the relative safety of White Plains, about 30 miles to the north.[8] New York's delegates to Congress thus could not expect any new advice before then.

Meanwhile, the Continental Congress got back to work. Delegates turned their attention to Jefferson's draft declaration and poked at it over the next two days, to Jefferson's chagrin. Jefferson's censure of the king for the slave trade was "struck out" in deference to the wishes of South Carolina and Georgia, according to Jefferson, who noted that his Northern colleagues "also I believe felt a little tender" about the issue "for tho' their people have very few slaves themselves yet they had been pretty considerable carriers of them to others."[9]

Congress also deleted portions of the document that cast blame on the people of England for the quarrel with America. One troublesome section said:

> [T]hey [the English people] are permitting their chief magistrate to send over not only soldiers of our common blood, but Scotch & foreign mercenaries to invade & destroy us. These facts have given the last stab to agonizing affection, and manly spirit bids us to renounce for ever these unfeeling brethren. We must endeavor to forget our former love for them.[10]

This edit also irked Jefferson: "[T]he pusillanimous idea that we had friends in England worth keeping terms with, still haunted the minds of many."[11]

Congress made other changes here and there. For example, "endowed by their creator with inherent and inalienable rights" became "endowed by their creator with certain inalienable rights." Congress put a period after "to prove this let facts be submitted to a candid world," discarding Jefferson's "for the truth of which we pledge a faith yet unsullied by falsehood."[12] Congress left much untouched, including the famous beginning ("When, in the course of human events, …"). Still, by the time Congress was finished editing, about one-quarter of Jefferson's words were scratched out.[13]

Jefferson pouted. He later wrote to Richard Henry Lee: "I enclose you a copy of the declaration of independence as agreed to by the House, and also, as originally framed. You will judge whether it is the better or worse for the Critics."[14]

He had an ally in Abigail Adams, back in Massachusetts. Somehow she obtained a copy of the original draft—possibly from John, but maybe someone else (she had many correspondents)—and in mid-July compared the printed version with the draft. She wrote to John: "I cannot but feel sorry that some of the most Manly Sentiments in the Declaration are Expunged from the printed coppy. Perhaps wise reasons induced it."[15] But historians today tend to agree that Congress, with judicious editing, made the document more elegant and powerful.[16]

On July 4—maybe as early as 11am,[17] maybe late in the day[18] (historians are divided and the evidence isn't clear)—the debate about the Declaration wound up. Finally, Congress was satisfied, and another vote was taken on whether to approve the document. As on July 2, 12 former colonies—now states—approved. New York again abstained. Massachusetts delegate Robert Treat Paine wrote:

> Thus the issue is joined; and it is our comfortable reflection, that if by struggling we can avoid that servile subjection which Britain demanded, we remain a free and happy people; but if, through the frowns of Providence, we sink in the struggle, we do but remain the wretched people we should have been without this declaration. Our hearts are full, our hands are full; may God, in whom we trust, support us.[19]

The Declaration of Independence was thus approved on July 4 and, according to the official *Journal* of Congress, ordered "authenticated and printed."[20] Popular imagination has conjured a myth that the delegates one by one that day solemnly signed the Declaration by writing formally in script on parchment. Indeed, that very notion formed in the minds of people who should have known better, including Jefferson, John Adams, and Franklin, each of whom at some point years later recalled just such a July 4 event.[21]

But they were wrong. Historians have made a convincing case that no such collective signing took place that day. There was a collective signing, but that didn't happen until August 2.[22] How could Jefferson, Adams, and Franklin have been so wrong?

Historians puzzling over this question point to flaws in the official *Journal*. In the original manuscript of the *Journal*, a blank space was left for the text of the Declaration on the pages recording the events of July 4. That space was filled with a broadside of the Declaration printed on or sometime after July 4 and pasted in the space. That broadside included only the names of Hancock, president, and Thomson, secretary, below the text of the Declaration.[23] Nothing in the manuscript suggests a group signing.

However, when the official *Journal* was published in 1777, whoever submitted the material to the printer included the text and the signatures of those who signed on

August 2.[24] Thus, the published *Journal* gives the impression that 55 men signed the Declaration on July 4. We know Jefferson referred to the *Journal* years later. Possibly Franklin and Adams did too. Peeking at the *Journal* to refresh their memories, they may have conflated events of July 4 and August 2 in their hazy recollections.

In arguing that no collective signing took place on July 4, historians cite several pieces of evidence. For example, the 55 signatures on the Declaration include those of some men who weren't even delegates to Congress on July 4.[25] Also, in a July 21 letter, Gerry of Massachusetts asks John and Samuel Adams: "Pray subscribe for me the Declaration of Independence, if the same is to be signed as proposed."[26] Gerry was in Congress on July 4.[27] If he signed then, why would he say that a signing was "proposed"? We also have the words of John Adams that very July. In a letter dated July 9, he wrote about a planned signing: "As soon as an American Seal is prepared, I conjecture the Declaration will be Subscribed by all the Members."[28]

So no elaborate signing ceremony took place on July 4. Instead, Congress attended to other matters on that day, such as picking a committee to design a national seal. In retrospect, it seems odd that, with the press of so much urgent and critical business, Congress would fuss about a symbol that few Americans think about today. It seems odder still that it would appoint three delegates to the task who were already steeped in critical work. But evidently Congress believed in the importance and urgency of establishing emblems to give the infant nation the trappings of legitimacy, and—as John Adams's correspondence suggests—they likely wanted a seal for the Declaration to lend gravitas to the document, promote its legitimacy, and underscore its importance. Thus, Franklin, John Adams, and Jefferson, fresh from their work on the Declaration, now took on the task of coming up with an image or two to capture the new nation's spirit.

Congress, on July 4, also asked the five-member Declaration committee to see to it the Declaration was properly printed. They turned to John Dunlap of Philadelphia,[29] and he apparently handled it without much oversight. For example, the word "inalienable," which we associate with the Declaration, somehow became "unalienable." Capitalization, which in that century followed hazy rules, seemed to be left entirely up to Dunlap, without much guidance from the committee. Thus, the first Americans who read the Declaration saw this: "We hold these Truths to be self-evident, that all Men are created equal, that they are endowed by their Creator with certain unalienable Rights, that among these are Life, Liberty, and the Pursuit of Happiness."[30]

More importantly, the committee raised no objection to the date on the broadside—not July 2, when Congress declared America's independence, but July 4, thus helping to fix that date in the public mind.[31]

Another action on that July 4 was to order the broadside sent out across the country to lawmakers, assemblies, and military commanders, and to ask that it be proclaimed in each of the new states.[32] Congress made no mention of sending it off to France or to any other potential ally. This seems strange, because Congress all along had hoped that independence would trigger alliances from France and other rich and powerful European nations. But delegates were aware that the Declaration, with its assertion of the right to throw off royal authority, was not the kind of document to wave in face of the French king. The Declaration was meant first for Americans—to inspire them and to clarify their aims.[33] Delegates hoped that by announcing independence, America might gain allies. But the document—the Declaration itself—had nothing to do with that.

Of course, Congress could not keep the document from the French. They would see it, so it might as well come from official channels. Thus, like an afterthought, a committee of Congress on July 8 sent off the Declaration to Silas Deane, their man in France, to copy and distribute.[34]

Meanwhile, those 200 single-page broadsides[35] that Dunlap printed were dispatched to the various revolutionary authorities around the country. Hancock sent letters enclosing the Declaration to each of the new states "which you will please to have proclaimed in your Colony in such Way & Manner as you shall Judge best."[36] Note that Hancock, in this case, clung to the familiar term "colony," by then obsolete.

On July 6, the Declaration appeared in the *Pennsylvania Evening Post*, and this version as well as the broadside was soon circulating far and wide. Delegate William Whipple of New Hampshire folded a copy in a letter to his brother-in-law: "We are now free from those Cursed Shackles that has embaresed all our affairs ever since the Commensement of the war. I already feel myself Lighter."[37] Other copies went out in letters from Gerry ("I pray that we may never want the divine aid, or the spirit and the means to defend it")[38] and Samuel Adams ("The inclosd Catalogue of Crimes of the deepest Dye, which have been repeatedly perpetrated by the King will justify us in the Eyes of honest & good Men").[39]

John Adams enclosed a copy in a letter to "Miss Polly," a daughter of a friend ("It compleats a Revolution, which will make as good a Figure in the History of Mankind"[40]), another copy to Samuel Chase ("You will see by this Post that the River is past and the Bridge cutt away"),[41] and apparently one to Abigail, though curiously and uncharacteristically he didn't specifically remark about it ("I have this Moment folded up a Magazine, and an Evening Post and sent it off, by an Express").[42]

After Washington received it in New York City, he ordered on July 9 that the "several brigades" be drawn up "on their respective Parades, at six Oclock" and "the declaration of Congress ... read with an audible voice." The general hoped, according to the orders, that "this important Event will serve as a fresh incentive to every officer, and soldier, to act with Fidelity and Courage." To give the soldiers even more incentive, Washington also approved punishment of 39 lashes for two deserters.[43]

No public celebration took place that first July 4. The first ceremonies acknowledging independence came a few days later, in Philadelphia and Easton, Pennsylvania, and in Trenton, New Jersey, on July 8. In Philadelphia, before a "great concourse of people" in the State House Yard, the Declaration was read out not by Hancock, Jefferson, or anyone in Congress, but by one John Nixon, a merchant who had been active on revolutionary committees in the town. After the speech and "three repeated huzzas," nine designated men entered the building's courtroom and ripped down the king's coat of arms. Those went up in smoke atop one of the many bonfires on that starlit, "pleasant evening," in celebrations that also included ringing of bells and "other great demonstrations of joy."[44]

In Massachusetts, ministers were asked to read the Declaration to their congregations at the conclusion of services. In Savannah, Georgia, the Declaration was publicly read out four times in four places, including at the Liberty Pole, where the reading was followed by the firing of weapons. In Virginia, each sheriff was instructed to read the Declaration at the courthouse door in his jurisdiction.[45]

Nowadays, Americans find inspiration in the opening words of the Declaration of Independence. But there is little evidence that Americans in 1776 found those immortal thoughts especially moving. Nor did people dwell on the itemized grievances in the document. They had heard a lot of that before.

Purdie's *Virginia Gazette* of July 19, 1776, printed only the last part of the Declaration, and not on page 1 but on page 2, with a preface explaining that the first part was old news—a "recapitulation of injuries."[46]

Those who commented on specific parts of the Declaration tended to cite the end, where the document states that the colonies "are of right and ought to be free and independent states."[47]

Almost everywhere, the Declaration was celebrated, often with the firing of cannons and with bonfires. Celebrations seemed to follow the same script: events connected to the reading were always "conducted with greatest decorum" or the "greatest decency and good order." Meanwhile, people always responded with "huzzas," "loud acclamations," "general applause," or "utmost demonstrations of joy."[48] In Philadelphia, candles were placed in windows, a practice in former times to celebrate the king's birthday.[49] In Worcester, Massachusetts, celebrants repaired to a tavern where 24 toasts were drunk, number 14 being: "Perpetual itching without benefit of scratching to the enemies of America."[50]

Americans indulged in a frenzy of dismantling, smashing, and burning symbols of the king on tavern signs and the walls of public buildings. Churches weren't spared. The rector of Trinity Church in New York City received a message to have the king's coat of arms taken down, "or else a mob would do it." The rector "immediately complied."[51] That coat of arms, as it turned out, survived the war, was carried to Canada, and placed in a church in Saint John, New Brunswick.[52]

A crowd in New York City attacked a life-size equestrian statue of the king. Its lead carcass was later sent off to Connecticut to be melted down into 42,000[53] bullets for the American war effort.[54] In Dover, Delaware, an image of the king was cast into a fire in the public square with the words "thus we destroy even the shadow of that King who refused to reign over a free people."[55]

The exception was Connecticut. No evidence survives to indicate public readings or celebrations in the state, where the Declaration was duly received and passed along to the state's General Assembly, which approved it in October with little comment or fuss.[56]

The Declaration brought sudden clarity. Before the Declaration, the colonies were on the one hand fighting a war and on the other insisting they were, at heart, loyal and wished reconciliation. Now there was no confusion. A man in remote Sussex County, New Jersey, writing to his cousin, expressed what was likely a common feeling:

> Now we know what to depend on. For my part, I have been at a great stand: I could hardly own the King and fight against him at the same time; but now these matters are cleared up. Heart and hand shall move together.[57]

In Britain the Declaration was predictably attacked as a "wretched composition, very ill written."[58] One man who took pains to read the Declaration closely was Thomas Hutchinson, the American-born former royal governor of Massachusetts. Once revered in the home colony, he had fought a losing battle on the king's behalf in trying to apply the king's laws. In tearing apart the Declaration, he questioned the assertion about "unalienable" rights of "life, liberty, and the pursuit of happiness" in a land with slavery: "I could wish the delegates of Maryland, Virginia, and the Carolinas, how their Constituents justify the depriving more than an hundred thousand Africans of their rights to liberty, and the *pursuit of happiness*, and to some degree to their lives, if these rights are so absolutely unalienable."[59]

Hutchinson also pointed out that in listing the grievances against the king, the issue of taxes appeared far down a long list: the cause "of taxes seems to have been in danger of being forgot. It comes in late and in as slight a manner as possible."[60]

On the British side in America, the reaction to the Declaration of Independence was predictable. A British officer newly arrived in North America fulminated: "A more impudent, false and atrocious Proclamation was never fabricated by the Hands of Man. ... 'Tis impossible to read this Paper, without Horror at the daring Hypocrisy of these Men, who call GOD to witness the uprightness of their Proceedings, nor without Indignation at the low and scurrilous Pretenses by wch they attempt to justify themselves."[61]

Soon after the document appeared, it disappeared from public consciousness, and was ignored even at July 4 celebrations in the 1770s and 1780s. Modern Americans always associate the Declaration with Jefferson, but that was not so in those first years of independence. Few were even aware that he wrote it.[62] Only years later, well after the Revolution, was the document made sacred and Jefferson's genius acclaimed.

***

The new United States comprised 12, not 13, states at the time of the Declaration. But everyone expected New York to quickly join, and it did. On July 9, the day Washington ordered the Declaration read in New York City, and the day a mob in the city yanked down the statue of George III, revolutionary representatives of the province of New York decided officially, as expected, to join the other 12 colonies in declaring independence. The newly elected New York Convention resolved that the reasons for declaring independence were "cogent and conclusive" and that New York would join the other colonies in supporting it "at the risque of our lives and fortunes." New York's delegates were thus authorized "to concert and adopt all such measures as they may deem conducive to the happiness and welfare of the United States of America."[63]

On July 15, the Continental Congress received New York's resolution. One of New York's delegates greeted that decision with disgust. John Alsop, a merchant "of a good Heart,"[64] chose this moment to quit. He wrote to the New York Convention:

> As long as a door was left open for a reconciliation with Great Britain, upon honourable and just terms, I was willing and ready to render my country all the service in my power, and for which purpose I was appointed and sent to this Congress; but as you have, I presume, by that declaration closed the door of reconciliation, I must beg leave to resign my seat as a Delegate from New-York.[65]

No matter Alsop's dismay, New York declared for independence. On July 19, Congress authorized that the Declaration "be fairly engrossed on parchment, with the title and stile of 'The unanimous declaration of the 13 United States of America.'"[66]

CHAPTER 20

Perfidy & Tyranny

Congress had chosen a steep and stony path. Every delegate knew the obvious risks. Abraham Clark of New Jersey, a month or so after the Declaration, confided: "Perhaps our Congress will be Exalted on a high Gallows." He had faith in God, but little else: "Nothing short of the Almighty Power of God can Save us—it is not in our Numbers, our Union, or our Valour that I dare trust. I think an Interposing providence hath been evident in all the events that Necessarily led us to what we are."[1]

Delegates could imagine horrors other than mere ruin, disgrace, and the hangman's noose—such as assassination. They were easy and obvious targets for angry, hidden Loyalists. Delegates became aware of just such a possibility one day in July, just after the Declaration, when a note came to the State House "importing that some dark designs were forming for our destruction, and advising us to take care of ourselves." Some suggested they poke around the cellars for bombs. Joseph Hewes of North Carolina rejected even that prudent step: "I had almost as soon be blown up as to discover to the world that I thought my self in danger."[2] In the end, Congress did nothing about the threat and throughout the war made do with scant security.[3]

It is one thing to snub danger; it is another to chase it. In the wake of the Declaration, two delegates stepped away from the State House to take up arms. One was Thomas McKean of Delaware, an ardent supporter of independence;[4] the other was Dickinson, who had steadfastly opposed it. Both rushed off with the Pennsylvania militia to bolster Washington's forces around New York City. We can understand McKean's enthusiasm, but why would Dickinson march off to put his life on the line? In one way true to his Quaker mindset, he accepted his countrymen's decision and felt it his duty to support their will. In another way, by picking up a gun, he broke with his Quaker way of thinking. After the war, he explained his motivations: "[W]hen a determination was reached upon the question against my opinion, I regarded that determination as the voice of my country. That voice proclaimed her destiny, in which I was resolved by every impulse of my soul to share, and to stand or fall with her in that scheme of freedom which she had chosen."[5]

He never quit Congress; he was kicked out. In late July, the Pennsylvania Convention met to devise a new constitution, a framework for a new state government to take the place of the conservative, discredited, and now defunct Assembly. One of the tasks of the convention was to select delegates to the Continental Congress. That convention gave Dickinson's seat to someone else. Reflecting years later, Dickinson was still bitter: "While I was exposing my person to every hazard, and lodging every night within half a mile of the enemy, the members of the Convention at Philadelphia, resting in quiet and safety, ignominiously voted me, as unworthy of my seat, out of the National Senate."[6]

Curiously, the same Pennsylvania Convention that booted Dickinson from Congress decided Robert Morris should stay, even though Morris, like Dickinson, had opposed the Declaration. This inconsistency may have been a product of Morris's inoffensive style and reputation for sound judgment. It is telling that John Adams, who found Dickinson so hard to bear, was full of praise for Morris. Adams wrote in a letter:

> I think he [Morris] has a masterly Understanding, an open Temper and an honest Heart: and if he does not always vote for What you and I should think proper, it is because he thinks that a large Body of People remains, who are not yet of his Mind. He has vast designs in the mercantile Way. And no doubt pursues mercantile Ends, which are always gain; but he is an excellent Member of our Body.[7]

Morris was surprised but not pleased to remain as a delegate to Congress. He would have preferred to step away:

> I did expect my Conduct in this great Question woud have procured my dismission from the great Council but find myself disapointed for the Convention have thought proper to return me in the New Delegation, and altho my interest & inclination prompt me to decline the Service yet I cannot depart from one point that first induced me to enter in the Public Line. I mean an oppinion that it is the duty of every Individual to Act his part in whatever Station his Country may Call him to, in times of difficulty, danger & distress.[8]

With the Declaration, it seemed that a return to the old colonial relationship with Great Britain was most sincerely dead. But while the leaden King George on horseback was deposed and destined to be recast into Patriot musket balls,[9] the flesh-and-blood George still reigned. He was quite willing to continue bloodying his beloved American subjects if there was a chance of making them colonials again. As Congress hashed and rehashed the issue of independence, the king and his ministers in their ponderous way selected and dispatched a new military commander to smash the rebellion and turn the insurgent new American states back into submissive colonies.

That commander, Admiral Lord Richard Howe, was a sturdy man whose dark complexion and quiet courage earned him the nickname "Black Dick."[10] He would be Washington's chief military nemesis, but a reluctant one. He sincerely hoped to earn glory, not as a warrior, but as the man who peacefully brought America back into the British fold.

If any British military man could turn such a trick, it was Howe. Americans well knew that, besides being the older brother of General William Howe, the commander of the pyrrhic British victory at Bunker Hill and still chief of British Army operations in America, Richard Howe was the younger brother of George Augustus Howe, a brigadier general who had lost his life near Ticonderoga in the French and Indian War back in 1758.[11] The people of Massachusetts were so moved by the death of that promising and gallant 34-year-old[12] that their lawmakers paid to erect a monument to his memory at London's Westminster Abbey.

Richard Howe reciprocated the gesture for his late brother with sympathetic interest in American affairs. During the Stamp Act crisis back in the 1760s, he was one of only a few office holders in Britain willing to receive American pleas for relief.[13] As the later crisis between America and Britain came to a head, Howe stubbornly remained a friend to America and looked for a solution to the impasse. He became acquainted with Benjamin Franklin, who played chess from time to time with Howe's sister, Caroline. Howe and Franklin worked together on a plan to settle differences between America and Britain. The plan went nowhere, but Howe remained an ardent believer that the differences between the parent country and its colonies could be peacefully resolved. As trouble erupted in America, Howe's first wish was to sail to America as a peace commissioner.[14]

As it happened, he got his wish, but with the dual role of peace commissioner and chief of military operations. The peace commission, which had enticed hopeful delegates to Congress into delaying independence, was more than a rumor after all. Richard, with brother William, were the commissioners.

Richard Howe, as he sailed across the Atlantic, believed he might yet snatch peace and reconciliation out of the fires of the Revolution already begun. But to succeed he had daunting obstacles to overcome. First, Howe and his brother the general, while both peace commissioners, were also military men. That was not comforting to Americans who might otherwise be willing to talk about peace. Second, the admiral was a little too late. Independence, to most Americans, was a done deal. It was highly unlikely it could be peacefully undone.

Finally, Howe had virtually nothing to offer the Americans in exchange for peace and a return to the old relationship. Howe's masters back in Britain didn't want to give an inch to the defiant Americans. For that reason, and knowing Howe in his heart was a little too sympathetic with the Americans, the royal ministers tied Howe's hands. Sure, he could talk to the Americans about their complaints, but only in those places declared at peace; that is, only where Patriot assemblies dissolved and Patriot militias disbanded, where royal officials were allowed back to their posts, and where local representatives promised to obey Parliament.

Surrender was a prerequisite to any meaningful discussions. Even then, any concession Howe agreed to would have to be approved by London.[15]

Howe's only other authority as peace commissioner was to offer pardons to people who took an oath of allegiance to British authority.[16]

These restrictions did not discourage the admiral. Aboard his flagship, the 64-gun *Eagle*, Lord Howe prepared a declaration announcing that he and his brother, as peace commissioners, had authority to grant pardons and to treat favorably areas where Americans reinstalled the royal government.[17]

Dropping anchor on July 12 off Staten Island, a Loyalist stronghold, the admiral met up with his brother, the general, who—knowing better than Richard how much American attitudes had hardened—told him that the admiral's declaration would not win peace.[18] Richard sent it off the next day anyway, along with various letters, to Perth Amboy, fully expecting them to be intercepted and circulated among Patriot authorities.

The very next day, the admiral reached out to Washington. From his flagship, Howe dispatched a small boat with a lieutenant, Philip Brown, and a letter for Washington, whose Patriot forces controlled New York City.

Rebel boats intercepted Brown, and eventually got together with Washington's man, Joseph Reed. Brown attempted to deliver the letter addressed to "George Washington, Esq., etc., etc., etc.," but Reed said he knew of no such person. He was following precise instruction to accept the letter only if properly addressed to "General Washington." Brown protested that the letter was of a civil, not military, nature; that he had "great powers" to arrive at a peaceful resolution, and that he was sorry he had not arrived sooner.[19] Reed stood his ground. Brown and the letter returned to the *Eagle*.

Of course, both Reed and Brown understood the game. Howe was trying his best to avoid addressing Washington as "General" because to do so might be seen as an acknowledgement that Washington indeed had authority over a legitimate army of an independent nation. Washington, meanwhile, insisted on that title for the same reason. For Washington, the matter extended beyond etiquette to the treatment of his men who found themselves prisoners. While camped near Boston, he had been infuriated by reports of British abuse of American prisoners. Now, word reached him that American soldiers captured by the British in Canada had been killed—one roasted alive and two starved to death by indigenous allies holding the captive Americans.[20] The matter incensed Congress, which resolved to treat British prisoners likewise if more such acts come to light.

If Washington could force the British to acknowledge him as a general, they might be prodded into recognizing the American fighters as soldiers, not criminal rebels, and treat them in a more humane and dignified way.[21]

The issue regarding prisoners prompted Washington, just days after the meeting of Reed and Brown, to send off his own letter to Howe. Howe responded with another letter to "George Washington, Esq., etc., etc., etc.," which was again rejected.[22]

Howe persisted, coming up with a new formula. He soon sent off an officer not with a letter, but with a verbal message. At the right opportunity, the officer asked whether "General Washington" would agree to a meeting with an adjutant general of the British Army. Those were the magic words, and on July 20, with due pomp, the Americans welcomed British Lieutenant Colonel James Patterson in New York.[23]

The meeting touched at length on forms of address and treatment of prisoners, with Patterson assuring Washington that "no failure of respect was intended" and "Lord Howe utterly disapproved of every infringement of the rights of humanity." Finally, like an afterthought, Patterson plunged into the subject of possible reconciliation. The Howe brothers "had great powers, and would derive the greatest pleasure from effecting an accommodation." Washington cut that topic short. There was no point in discussing it; he had no authority in that regard, he said. Furthermore, he said that he understood the Howes' powers were only to grant pardons, and "that those who had committed no fault wanted no pardon, that we were only defending what we deemed our indisputable right."[24]

The meeting soon ended. Washington politely offered Patterson "to partake of a small collation."[25] Patterson politely declined, saying he had a late breakfast, and was soon on his way back to the *Eagle*.

As Washington made clear enough, the Howes would have to talk to Congress if they were sincere about "effecting an accommodation."

When Congress finally received the admiral's declaration about the peace commission and pardons, delegates were incredulous. This was the peace commission? Congress saw Lord Howe's declaration as so insulting that delegates authorized it to be printed and distributed just to reveal British insincerity.

In ordering Howe's letters published, Congress proclaimed "that the few, who still remain suspended by a hope founded either in the justice or moderation of their late King, may now, at length, be convinced, that the valour alone of their country is to save its liberties."[26]

Some delegates echoed this sentiment in letters. Maryland's Charles Carroll wrote: "I believe every man's eyes must now be open. The blindest & most infatuated must see, & I think, detest the perfidy & Tyranny of the British Court, Parlt. & Nation."[27]

Benjamin Franklin took the trouble to write a bristling note to Lord Howe himself: "It is impossible we should think of Submission to a Government, that has with the most wanton Barbarity and Cruelty, burnt our defenceless Towns in the midst of Winter, excited the Savages to massacre our Farmers, and our Slaves to murder their Masters, and is even now bringing foreign Mercenaries to deluge our Settlements with Blood."[28]

But not all delegates scoffed. Pennsylvania's Morris still believed that a conversation with the Howes might be worthwhile: "I am not for making any Sacrifice of Dignity, but still I woud hear them if possible, because if they can offer Peace on admissible terms I believe the great majority of America wou'd still be for accepting it."[29]

By August 2, the momentous Declaration was ready, hand-lettered on parchment probably by Timothy Matlack, a Philadelphia brewer, prominent Patriot, and master penman.[30] At least six of the signatures were added later. Matthew Thornton of New Hampshire, for example, could not have signed that day because he did not take his seat as a delegate until November 4.[31] In signing, they pledged "our Lives, our Fortunes, and our Sacred Honor," and the weight of that promise darkened the mood that August day. Years later, signer Benjamin Rush of Pennsylvania recalled "the silence and the gloom" of that morning as each approached, one by one, "the table of the President of Congress to subscribe what was believed by many at that time to be our own death warrants."

Virginia's Benjamin Harrison, a hefty man, offered a wisecrack to slender Elbridge Gerry of Massachusetts. When they were all hanged, he said, "I shall die in a few minutes, but from the lightness of your body you will dance in the air an hour or two before you are dead."[32]

Had the Revolution failed, hanging might well have been the fate of these men. As it turned out, none were hanged, but many suffered one way or another because they were signers, prominent Patriots, or unlucky. The homes of 15 signers were destroyed,[33] including that of New Jersey's John Hart, which was ransacked and burned by German mercenaries a few months after he signed. He was subsequently chased from one hiding place to another. He was never caught, but his health was ruined and in three years he was dead. The home of New York's Francis Lewis was burned, and his business property taken. He was never captured but his wife was, and her suffering shortened her life.[34]

The signers were brave that August day for stepping up and adding their names to the Declaration, but not so brave as to announce their signing to the world. Nervous about military prospects, they set the signed document aside. Not until the following January—after key victories on the battlefield—did Congress finally send to the states authorized copies of the Declaration with the names of the signers.[35]

***

The military situation brightened for Congress as the weeks passed. In the South at Charleston, rebellious Americans thwarted a British armada attempting to launch an invasion of the Carolinas. To the north, General Horatio Gates restored order at Crown Point, the key post on Lake Champlain, giving Congress hope that a British thrust from Canada might be blocked. The biggest worry was around New York City, where British land and sea forces were concentrating as they prepared to take the city and bring the hammer down on Washington and the ragtag Continental soldiers. Washington had an impossible task. Congress insisted that the city be held, but its geography—surrounded by water—made that impossible without a fleet of robust warships. The British had 52 warships at their disposal;[36] the Americans had no navy to speak of.

Congress had no miracle weapon for their general, but helpfully informed Washington "that Congress have such an entire confidence in his judgment, that they will give him no particular directions about the disposition of the troops."[37]

Meanwhile, delegates took another crack at a vital question that had yet to be resolved: how would the states relate to one another? The shift to independence went smoothly in most places as the states and various towns had in place reliable and tested procedures for holding elections, collecting taxes, enforcing laws, and settling disputes. Essential structures of local government generally held firm.

But uncertainty remained about the Continental Congress or whatever would take its place as a governing or advising council for the new states. This question had arisen when Congress first met in 1774. Delegates had fumbled along, making up rules as needed. But still no formal agreement had been approved by all of the colonies—now states—about their relationship to each other or whether to have a central government with some authority over the states. Delegates had understood this all along and from time to time someone, such as Franklin, offered ideas that were tossed around and then set aside in the press of other business.

Another blueprint for confederation was now available. This was from Dickinson, who completed a draft and left it behind when he went off to war. He never had the opportunity to defend or explain his ideas to the full Congress.

With some alterations, the Dickinson plan followed the framework of Franklin's 1775 plan. Both called for each colony to collect taxes to support a treasury for the confederation. In Franklin's plan, the process for changing the constitution was easy: approval by just a majority of the state assemblies. Dickinson's plan made amendments nearly impossible: approval by a convention ("an Assembly of the United States") followed by approval from every state legislature.[38]

Under the Dickinson plan, a 13-member council of state—with a member from each state—would perform executive functions limited mostly to responsibilities not easily done in the states, such as providing a common currency, dealing with trade issues, overseeing foreign relations, and coordinating defense.[39] Thus, the new government as Dickinson's plan envisioned wouldn't do much more than what the Continental Congress was already doing. At least, that is what it seemed at first glance. Anyone looking closely at the draft might find alarming what it didn't say—no power was specifically guaranteed to the states, while the powers of Congress were almost unlimited.[40] The Dickinson draft, while not explicitly taking power from the states and putting it in the hands of Congress, thus quietly left the door open for just that possibility.

Also, according to Dickinson's plan, the central government would have the job of sorting out disputes among the states over such matters as borders and land claims, including claims extending "to the South Sea."[41]

The reference to "the South Sea" might puzzle modern readers, but it was clear enough to delegates. That was the sea somewhere out west—to them the South

Sea,[42] to us the Pacific Ocean. Delegates knew it was out there, but didn't know how far. Under Dickinson's plan, the central government could deny land claims to the west of such states as Virginia, whose colonial charter gave the colony land as far as the South Sea—the Pacific.

Eight former colonies—Massachusetts, New Hampshire, Connecticut, New York, Virginia, North Carolina, South Carolina, and Georgia—had claims, based on their charters, to land beyond the Allegheny Mountains. Five states—Pennsylvania, Maryland, New Jersey, Delaware, and Rhode Island—had no such historic claims. However, some companies within those "landless" states claimed land in the west based on treaties with indigenous people or grants finagled from the British.[43] All that would eventually have to be fought over with guns or argument. It made sense that a central government had a role in sorting it out peacefully. But the notion that the central government would play this role raised the stakes for delegates formulating the structure of that government. The nature of the new constitution could determine the winners and losers in the bundle of issues related to borders and land disputes.

Delegates began debating this constitution—the Articles of Confederation—with some optimism that it could be quickly approved and put into place. On July 29, New Hampshire's Josiah Bartlett still believed confederation business could be wrapped up in another week to 10 days.[44] But other delegates realized that the challenge of agreeing on a constitution would be tricky indeed, and might never happen. Delegate Joseph Hewes moaned: "Much of our time is taken up in forming and debating a Confederation for the united States, what we shall make of it God only knows, I am inclined to think we shall never modell it so as to be agreed to by all the Colonies."[45]

So many details had to be picked over, and everyone had an opinion. In John Adams's notes, we catch a glimpse of delegates mired in debate about one of 20 articles in the proposed constitution:

> Chase moves for the Word deputies, instead of Delegates, because the Members of the Maryland Convention are called Delegates, and he would have a Distinction. Answer. In other Colonies the Reverse is true. The Members of the House are called deputies. Jefferson objects to the first of November. Dr. Hall moves for May, for the time to meet. Jefferson thinks that Congress will have a short Meeting in the Fall and another in the Spring. Hayward thinks the Spring the best Time. Wilson thinks the fall—and November better than October, because September is a busy Month, every where. Dr. Hall. Septr. and Octr. the most sickly and mortal Months in the Year. The Season is forwarder in Georgia in April, than here in May.[46]

Among the many points of contention, three stood out. One was an issue that arose the very first time Congress met back in 1774—how should power in Congress be determined? Should each state have an equal vote and therefore equal power, or should voting be determined in some other way, such as by population, with more populous states having more representation in Congress than less-populous ones? To larger states, this made sense. Obviously, however, the smaller states clung to the idea that they should have the same weight in Congress as the larger ones. Sherman of Connecticut offered a compromise:[47] devise a system that requires, for laws to be passed, both the approval of a majority of colonies and the majority of the population. Sherman's idea was ignored, but he planted a seed that would germinate years later when the later Constitution was being drafted. Sherman's compromise resulted in one house of Congress—the House of Representatives—based on popular vote alongside a second house—the Senate—with every state apportioned equal voting power.

The second question had to do with the support of the central government. Should contributions—that is, taxes—from each of the states be based on that state's population or wealth? If wealth, then according to land values or some other measure? If population, should the enslaved be counted? The discussion led to comparisons in the value of free people relative to enslaved people. One free man did the work of two slaves, Virginia's Harrison said, and therefore calculations of value should equate two enslaved people as no more than the value of one free man. Harrison's remark gained no traction at the time, but, like Sherman's remark on representation, the notion would reappear in a different formulation—equating five enslaved people to three free men—in yet another compromise when the current Constitution came to be written.[48]

The third great issue had to do with expansion west. Should Congress have the power to limit claims of the states that asserted authority over unsettled lands beyond the Alleghenies? Should those lands be left to those states to develop or should they be placed under the control of Congress for development and potential statehood?[49] This issue was in a way bound up with the first in that it, too, had to do with the power of small states relative to large states. For example, Virginia, already the largest state by population, had the potential to overwhelm the other states if allowed to maintain claims stretching hundreds of miles to the west. "The small Colonies have a right to happiness and security," said Chase of Maryland. "They would have no safety if the great Colonies were not limited." Harrison of Virginia, meanwhile, was firm that no colony—and certainly not Congress—had any business taking land away from Virginia: "How came Maryland by its Land? but by its Charter. By its Charter Virginia owns to the South Sea."[50]

By the end of July, Chase, for one, was thoroughly dismayed by the divisions in Congress over the terms of union:

> We do not all see the importance, nay, the necessity of a Confederacy. We shall remain weak, distracted, and divided in our councils; our strength will decrease; we shall be open to all the arts of the insidious Court of Britain, and no foreign court will attend to our applications for assistance before we are confederated. What contract will a foreign State make with us when we cannot agree among ourselves?[51]

On August 7, William Williams of Connecticut observed in a letter: "[E]very speck of ground is disputed. ... I almost despair of seeing it [ratification of the Articles] accomplished."[52]

After devoting all or part of 20 days to wrangling over the Articles,[53] delegates took a break. They were getting nowhere and there was too much other business to attend to.

Edward Rutledge, for one, was happy to stop talking about confederation—not that he was against it. But it was an issue too big, too important, too complex for Congress to deal with alongside everything else:

> We have done nothing with the Confederation for some Days, and it is of little Consequence if we never see it again, for we have made such a devil of it already that the Colonies can never agree to it. If my opinion was likely to be taken I would propose that the States should appoint a special Congress to be composed of new Members for this purpose—and that no Person should disclose any part of the present plan. If that was done we might then stand some Chance of a Confederation, at present we stand none at all.[54]

Thus, Rutledge wanted the task of drafting a constitution taken out of the hands of Congress and put in the hands of a special convention for that purpose—a constitutional convention. That is exactly what would come to pass, but years down the road.

Meanwhile, after a pause, Congress returned to the Articles on August 20,[55] and thus the debate resumed and continued through to the end of the month. Then, again stymied, delegates threw up their hands. Months would pass before Congress dared take on the issue again. Delegates would plod along for now without a constitution and with Congress muddling along as a kind of improvisational government with an army and currency, but with no power to tax and no formal authority over the states.

Congress had better luck on the diplomatic front—crafting a framework for its dealings with other nations, especially France. John Adams, on a committee to develop a "Plan of Treaties," came up with a draft using as a guide a volume of treaties lent to him by Franklin. That plan, modified by the committee, was presented to Congress on July 18.[56] It was not so much a plan as a proposed treaty between the United States and "the most serene and mighty Prince, Lewis the Sixteenth, the most Christian King, his Heirs and Successors"[57]—the king of France. The long document, containing 30 articles, was an amazing feat for Adams, with no diplomatic experience. It was debated but left nearly untouched by the time it was finally adopted in September. It became, with few changes, the treaty ultimately signed with France in 1778. It also served as the model for most treaties of the United States until 1800.[58]

Somehow, Adams also found time with Jefferson and Franklin to attend to the matter of the Great Seal of the United States. On August 20, they placed before Congress the fruits of their labors.

The trio, who had worked so amicably on the Declaration, came up with quite different ideas, none of which had much to do with America or even the New World. Franklin borrowed from the Old Testament—Moses, on the shore of the Red Sea, his hand extended, causing the waters to overwhelm the pharaoh in his chariot.

Franklin also suggested a motto: "Rebellion to Tyrants is Obedience to God." Jefferson likewise took from the Old Testament: the Israelites in the wilderness following a cloud by day and a pillar of light by night. Jefferson also proposed a second image, which would appear on the reverse of a coin or pendant incorporating the primary image on the front. For that, Jefferson mined misty English history: the image of Hengist and Horsa, brothers who, according to legend, led the first Anglo-Saxon settlers in Britain. Meanwhile, Adams imagined a seal that drew from Greek and Roman mythology. Adams was fascinated by an engraving in a book he owned picturing Hercules pausing at the junction of two paths, the flowery path of vice and self-indulgence and the rugged path of virtue and duty.[59]

Apparently dissatisfied and unable to agree, they sought the advice of one Pierre Eugène Du Simitière, a Swiss-born Philadelphian who painted portraits for a meager living.[60] Du Simitière was already working for Congress on a design for a medal honoring Washington and others for chasing the British out of Boston.[61]

Du Simitière came up with his own design, which hearkened back to the European roots of most white Americans. He proposed an image containing symbols of six European countries—England, Scotland, Ireland, France, Germany, and the Netherlands. These would be surrounded by small shields with initials representing each of the 13 new states, from NH for New Hampshire to G for Georgia. Also appearing on the seal would be figures of the Goddess Liberty and an American soldier in buckskin. For a motto, Du Simitière rejected Franklin's suggestion and proposed his own: *E Pluribus Unum*, "out of many, one," which he likely saw on a popular London publication that used the Latin phrase as its legend.[62]

This was, with slight modifications (the Goddess Justice replaced the soldier), the idea for the main image of the seal presented to Congress on August 20. For the reverse side, Adams, Jefferson, and Franklin offered up Franklin's idea of Moses at the Red Sea, with some modifications proposed by Jefferson.[63]

Congress gingerly placed it "on the table," a polite death sentence. Was it too convoluted? We don't know, for the records leave no remarks. With that idea dead, buried, unmourned, but not forgotten, the United States carried on without a seal. Years hence, when the idea of a seal was again taken up, several elements from Du Simitière's design were exhumed. Among those is the motto *E Pluribus Unum*, now incorporated in the Great Seal of the United States. Meanwhile, Franklin's motto impressed Jefferson so much that he incorporated it in his personal seal.[64]

Congress at this time had no interest in creating a national flag. Delegates waited nearly a year after declaring independence to resolve on June 14, 1777: "That the flag of the 'thirteen' United States be thirteen stripes, alternate red and white: that the union be thirteen stars, white in a blue field, representing a new constellation."[65]

***

Today's Congress makes laws, but the Continental Congress never did. Even after independence, it never crafted legislation or claimed authority to do so. It was understood that laws require a sanction[66]—some sort of penalty for violators—and Congress had no authority to impose penalties.

Instead of generating laws, the Continental Congress exerted what little power it had, even after independence, through resolutions and recommendations. When Congress wanted the states to take some action, it would produce a "recommendation" for states to, for example, pass laws for catching deserters or arranging the production of some military goods. Resolutions, meanwhile, dealt with any number of matters, such as the appointments of officers and the printing of money.[67]

CHAPTER 21

The Most Silent Man in France

Far from Philadelphia, American overtures to the French were getting a reaction. Silas Deane arrived in Paris early in July, after landing in Spain to avoid British warships and making his way over the Pyrenees.[1]

Unable to speak French and reluctant to speak English, lest he become known to British spies, he was in a quandary about how to even start his mission. A sympathetic Frenchman wrote: "M. Deane does not open his mouth before the English-speaking people he meets. He must be the most silent man in France, for I defy him to say six consecutive words in French."[2]

Deane eventually found the right contacts and, on July 17, met for the first time with Vergennes, the French foreign minister, whose chief secretary spoke good English. The two-hour meeting was cordial.[3]

Vergennes told Deane that France, so as not to irritate Britain, would not openly encourage arms deals. However, Vergennes assured the American that he was free to carry on commerce, and that France would not stand in the way of trade, even in military equipment.[4]

Deane soon learned that France had a surplus of old weaponry it was eager to unload. Recent reforms in the French Army had made up to 80,000 perfectly serviceable arms available for disposal or sale.[5]

Deane's job was to discreetly buy or somehow acquire these arms and other goods for the Continental Army, have them carted to a French port, and then arrange for vessels to carry the equipment across the sea. Then those ships had to evade British cruisers on the prowl, for the British were soon quite aware of Deane's activities, and they were not happy about it.

As Deane reported to Congress's Committee of Secret Correspondence:

> [M]y arrival here, my name, my lodgings, and many other particulars have been reported to the British Administration, on which they have sent orders to the British ambassador to remonstrate in high terms … [T]he city swarms with Englishmen, and as money purchases everything in this country, I have had, and still have, a most difficult task to avoid their machinations. Not a coffee-house or theatre or other place of public diversion but swarms with their emissaries.[6]

***

Throughout July and August, Congress kept an anxious eye on New York as the British prepared to pounce. Washington, facing the impossibility of holding a city on an island against a larger, better-trained foe supported by the largest navy in the world, made his long odds longer by ignoring conventional wisdom and dividing his forces,[7] placing part of his army on Manhattan and part on Long Island, across the mile-wide East River. As his army dug in over the summer weeks, Washington clung to the fantasy that the little army could stand up to the British, or at least give them a bloody nose, like at Bunker Hill.

Finally, in late August, the British made their move, landing a large force on Long Island. These soldiers met little resistance as they came ashore, gathered together, and marched west to within 3 miles of the American lines near Brooklyn. Washington, misinformed about the number of enemy troops, thought the landing was a ploy to draw his men away from Manhattan. He dithered, finally sending some help, but keeping back most of his troops in anticipation of an attack elsewhere.

The American commander on Long Island, a last-minute replacement for an officer who had fallen ill, had also been misinformed about everything—the terrain, the American plan, and even the positions of his own men. Washington wisely replaced him with a commander who at least knew the lay of the land. But like the man he replaced, this commander, the third in five days, had only vague notions of where his troops were.

Meanwhile, a last-minute attempt at reorganization confused everyone, leaving troops uncertain who was in charge and what needed defending.[8] Little wonder, then, that at the first whiff of battle, the American defenses around Brooklyn Heights collapsed. The little army soon appeared trapped, with the British arrayed in front of them and their backs to the East River.

Washington stopped the retreat, restored order, and got lucky. The British, haunted by the memory of Bunker Hill, called a halt to the advance so a siege could be planned and implemented. This would take longer than a direct assault, but promised fewer British casualties, and the cornered Americans would be bagged just the same, British commanders believed.[9] Meanwhile, winds blew in favor of the Americans, keeping British ships from sailing up the East River and blocking the Americans' last escape route.[10]

Thus, with that path open and the British assault slowed to a cautious crawl, Washington managed an evacuation that was brilliant and miraculous. At night, in fog and rain, most of the trapped American army slipped to the shore as a skeleton force manned the lines and fed campfires to fool the British into thinking their enemies remained dug in. Awaiting the army on the shore was a fleet of small boats. The men scrambled aboard and the boats slipped away into the darkness and across the river. Some 9,000–10,000 men, with their equipment, were thus saved from capture. Even the skeleton force escaped, withdrawing by 6am,[11] before the British realized that their quarry had vanished.

The maneuver was masterful, but it was no victory, merely saving Washington and his army from a worse catastrophe. During the fighting before the American troops slipped away, British casualties came to about 400. The Americans lost 1,000 men killed, wounded, or captured.[12]

Among those captured was General John Sullivan, who also happened to be a former delegate to Congress from New Hampshire. The British allowed him to carry a message to Congress from Admiral Howe:

> [T]hough he [Howe] could not at present Treat with Congress as such, yet he was very Desirous of having a Conference with some of the members, whom he would Consider for the present only as private Gentlemen, and meet them himself as such, at such place as they should appoint."[13]

In short, Howe wanted to talk.

Delegates were torn. Josiah Bartlett feared that just meeting with Howe when the admiral apparently had so little to offer would "lessen the Congress in the eye of the public" and alarm people "when they see us catching hold of so slender a thread to bring about a settlement." On the other hand, "if we should refuse the conference, I fear the Tories, and moderate men, so called, will try to represent the Congress as obstinate, and so desirous of war and bloodshed that we would not so much as hear the proposals Lord Howe had to make."[14]

John Adams, seeing no "Necessity, Propriety, or Utility" in it, opposed it "from first to last."[15] Even the presence of Sullivan disgusted Adams, who muttered that everyone would have been better off if Sullivan, instead of being captured, had been shot dead on the battlefield.[16] But, as Adams acknowledged in a letter, it was Howe, who through Sullivan's "most insidious, 'tho ridiculous Messages" had put Congress "rather in a delicate Situation, and gives Us much Trouble."[17]

As Congress hemmed and hawed about how to answer Howe, Philadelphia gave in to fear of a British attack. Adams was appalled: "The Panick, which is spread upon this occasion is weak and unmanly—it excites my shame, and Indignation."[18] He, for one, was not especially worried. While recognizing the power of the British Army and Royal Navy, he also understood their limits in the region:

> If they get Possession of New York, Long Island, and Staten Island, these are more Territory than their whole Army can defend, this year. They must keep their Force together. The instant they divide it they are ruined. They cannot march into the Country, for before they get Ten Miles into the Country they are surrounded or their Retreat cutt off.[19]

Congress sent off a desperate plea to nearby states to "send all the Aid in your Power to our Army at New York." Hancock, in a circular letter to seven states, wrote: "The State of our Affairs is so extremely critical, that Delay may be attended with fatal Consequences. ... Every Thing is at Stake—our Religion—our Liberty—the Peace & Happiness of Posterity—are the grand objects in Dispute."[20]

For the moment, Washington still held New York City, but for how long? And should he have to abandon it, should he first destroy it and leave no assets for the

British? Congress didn't give Washington a choice, insisting that the city, should Washington need to abandon it, be left to the British undamaged.[21]

After four days of talk,[22] Congress finally decided to send a committee to meet with the admiral. As if to ensure that "as little Evil might come of it, as possible,"[23] they named the skeptical John Adams to the committee, along with Franklin and Edward Rutledge.[24]

The three set off on September 9[25] on a two-day journey[26] to Staten Island. Along the way, they glimpsed the Continental Army, and the sight was not inspiring. Adams recalled: "We saw such Numbers of Officers and Soldiers, straggling and loytering, as gave me at least, but a poor Opinion of the Discipline of our forces and excited as much indignation as anxiety."[27]

They stopped at New Brunswick, New Jersey, where the inns and taverns were so packed that Franklin and Adams found themselves sharing a bed in a tiny room "little larger than the bed" with a single small open window, which Adams wanted shut. Franklin insisted it stay open. To explain why, the eminent doctor launched into a "harrangue, upon Air and cold and Respiration and Perspiration, with which I was so much amused that I soon fell asleep," as Adams later wrote.[28]

The three American delegates reached Perth Amboy on the morning of September 11, where they met a British officer dispatched by Howe from Staten Island on the admiral's red-and-gilt barge. The officer explained that he was a volunteer hostage. That is, he would remain at Perth Amboy until the Americans returned from Staten Island. He would thus guarantee that Franklin, Adams, and Rutledge would not be taken prisoner. Franklin and Adams agreed that such a precaution was nonsense, and the officer joined the American committee on Howe's barge for the ride to Staten Island.[29]

As the barge approached the island, Admiral Howe came down to the shore to greet the visitors. Noting that his "hostage" had been returned, Howe remarked: "Gentlemen, you make me a very high Compliment, and you may depend upon it, I will consider it as the most sacred of Things."[30]

Howe entertained the Americans "with the Utmost politeness," but also made sure they caught a glimpse of the military muscle on display. As they walked to the house where the conference would take place, they passed "between Lines of Guards of Grenadiers, looking as fierce as ten furies, and making all the Grimaces and Gestures and motions of their Musquets with Bayonets fixed."[31]

The house prepared for the meeting was "as dirty as a stable," according to Adams, but the conference room itself was made tolerable by a "Carpet of Moss and green Spriggs from Bushes and Shrubs in the Neighbourhood." They sat down to a feast of "good Claret, good Bread, cold Ham, Tongues and Mutton."[32]

The meeting was cordial, but produced nothing. A secretary for the admiral summed it up: "They met, they talked, they parted. And now nothing remains but to fight it out against a Set of the most determined Hypocrites & Demagogues, compiled of the Refuse of the Colonies, that ever were Permitted by Providence to be the Scourge of a Country."[33]

As the Americans later reported, the admiral had a single peace proposition: "That the Colonies should return to their Allegiance and Obedience to the Government of Great Britain." Beyond that, Howe made "Assurances" that troublesome acts of Parliament would be changed, that instructions to ministers would be altered, and that on the whole the British government would go easy on America.[34] The American trio reminded the admiral of the various "humble petitions" that Americans had submitted, and that those had been "treated with Contempt." There was no turning back: "We declared our Independence; that this declaration had been called for, by the People of the Colonies in general; that every colony had approved of it, when made, and all now considered themselves as independent States."[35]

During the meeting, lasting almost three hours,[36] Howe reminded Adams, Franklin, and Rutledge of his deep affection for America. "If America should fall," he said, he would lament it, "like the Loss of a Brother."[37]

Franklin pretended to be touched. His response, according to Adams, was: "My Lord, We will do our Utmost Endeavours, to save your Lordship that mortification."[38]

The delegation departed and the fighting resumed. Soon after the threesome returned to Philadelphia, Congress learned that the British had once again knocked Washington's army about. Thinned by mass desertions, the flimsy little army disintegrated at the first sight of British and German infantry landing on Manhattan.[39] Washington, brandishing a riding whip, tried but failed to stem the headlong panic of men shedding knapsacks, powder horns, and muskets and "flying in every direction and in the greatest confusion."[40] In the end, the exasperated general could only fling his hat to the ground and sputter: "Are these the men with whom I am to defend America?"[41] In the aftermath, an American colonel wrote: "I have often read and heard about instances of cowardice, but hitherto have had but a faint idea of it till now. ... Nothing appeared but fright, disgrace and confusion."[42]

New York was lost, but Washington managed to pull his army back together on Harlem Heights. That army had left behind plenty of precious weaponry and supplies in its frantic retreat, but few soldiers had been killed or wounded.[43] Now, somehow, the army found a backbone. Soldiers who earlier had scampered for their lives, now gathered up the gumption to perform "with bravery and Intrepidity"[44] in skirmishes with the British. Washington, in his report to Congress, offered a soupçon of optimism: "This Affair I am in hopes will be attended with many salutary consequences, as It seems to have greatly inspirited the whole of our Troops."[45]

Privately, though, Washington was ready to quit. In a letter to Lund Washington, a distant cousin and manager of Mount Vernon, he poured out his anguish. He did not dwell on his defeats, or the cowardly actions of his men, or the British forces looming nearby poised to shred his sorry band of warriors. Instead, he zeroed in on the old problem of short enlistments. Many soldiers served no more than 12 months and then went home, which made his job, difficult enough, impossible:

> [Y]ou have had great bodies of militia in pay that never were in camp; you have had immense quantities of provisions drawn by men that never rendered you one hour's service (at least usefully), and this in the most profuse and wasteful way. Your stores have been expended, and every kind of military [discipline?] destroyed by them; your numbers fluctuating, uncertain, and forever far short of report.

He had no chance of winning the war under the system in place. "I see the impossibility of serving with reputation, or doing any essential service to the cause by continuing in command," confided Washington to Lund. Yet he couldn't walk away because he was told that "if I quit the command inevitable ruin will follow from the distraction that will ensue." He longed to escape: "In confidence I tell you that I never was in such an unhappy, divided state since I was born."

Washington had not a moment to spare to think about anything other than his desperate military predicament. This was obviously not the moment to dwell on interior design, but astoundingly, that's what he did. In the same letter to Lund, as if escaping in his mind to his Virginia home, the general opined on home renovations:

> With respect to the chimney, I would not have you for the sake of a little work spoil the look of the fireplaces, tho' that in the parlor must, I should think, stand as it does; not so much on account of the wainscotting, which I think must be altered (on account of the door leading into the new building,) as on account of the chimney piece and the manner of its fronting into the room.[46]

CHAPTER 22

Too Many Members to Keep Secrets

Back in Philadelphia, the problem of short enlistments was no secret. One by one, delegates were letting go of the notion that the war could be won just with part-time soldiers—militiamen—and short-term enlistees fed on patriotism and little else. William Hooper, delegate from North Carolina, was nearly as despairing as Washington when he wrote at about the same time:

> The Enlistments have been so short that they were scarce on the field before it was time to disband them. They acquired no military knowledge from Experience. Their service was too short to establish subordination and discipline amongst them. Another great grievance has been the want of proper officers to command. The scantiness of pay or some other cause has drawn few Gentlemen into commands.[1]

Delegates wrangled over the sorry state of the army and took steps to add soldiers by authorizing a bounty of $20 for each man who enlisted. Men joining up for the duration were promised land—from 500 acres for colonels to 100 acres for noncommissioned officers and common soldiers.[2]

But it seemed unlikely that this would be enough. Men might happily join a local militia for adventure, glory, and to defend their own towns for a few weeks or months, but to go away, leaving their families, farms, and businesses for years to risk their lives to defend another state—to them a foreign country—was nonsense without ample compensation, and even that might not persuade them. John Adams put his finger on it. In his autobiography, he recalled that from New England, the only men interested in enlisting were the "meanest, idlest, most intemperate and worthless." Adams went on to ask: "Was it credible that Men who could get at home better living, more comfortable Lodgings, more than double the Wages, in Safety, not exposed to the Sicknesses of the Camp, would bind themselves during the War? I knew it to be impossible."[3]

To complicate the challenge of finding soldiers, the British were offering generous bounties to lure young American men to fight alongside the Redcoats.[4] The problems of recruiting, paying, and training men and then keeping them for the duration of the war would never go away.

Yet another headache for Congress in keeping an army in the field was the lure of privateering. For a young man, service on a privateering vessel, with the prospect of plunder, was far more appealing than the drudgery—and poverty—of a soldier's life. One observer noted the "excessive rage for privateering" among the young men of New England, who were so acquainted with seafaring: "Many of the continental troops now in our service pant for the expiration of their enlistments in order that they may partake of the Spoils of the West Indies."[5]

As time allowed, Congress set aside military questions and once again took up the issue of diplomacy. In late September, Congress signed off on specific instructions for working out an alliance with France and then named the three "commissioners" assigned to carry out those instructions:[6] Silas Deane, who was already in France, along with Franklin and Jefferson.

As it happened, Jefferson was absent. His wife, who had suffered a miscarriage earlier in the year, was in precarious health.[7] Throughout July, Jefferson was distracted with worry. He begged fellow Virginian Richard Henry Lee to take his place in Congress so he could leave Philadelphia and return to his wife's side: "For god's sake, for your country's sake, and for my sake, come. I receive by every post such accounts of the state of Mrs. Jefferson's health, that it will be impossible for me to disappoint her expectation of seeing me at the time I have promised."[8]

Thus, Jefferson was gone well before the appointment and unaware of it. A messenger was dispatched to Virginia with the news.

Meanwhile, Franklin, the oldest man in Congress, agreed to make another dangerous crossing of the Atlantic. He muttered to a colleague: "I have only a few years to live, and I am resolved to devote them to the work that my fellow citizens deem proper for me; or speaking as old-clothes dealers do of a remnant of goods, 'You shall have me for what you please.'"[9]

At this time, Franklin had little inkling of what, if any, success Deane was having in wooing the French. But then on October 1, Franklin received word that seemed to confirm that the novice diplomat had succeeded far beyond anyone's expectations. According to the message, Deane had arranged for the French to ship "£200,000 Sterling worth of Arms and Ammunition"[10] for the American cause. Delegates would have been delighted to know this spectacular news, but they were not told. Only Franklin and Morris, both members of the committee that handled such matters, knew of the shipments, and they would keep them secret from their colleagues while making arrangements for the goods to be brought from the Caribbean to America.

Why the secrecy from their fellow delegates? Knowing this decision might later raise questions, they prepared and set aside an explanation: Congress was a sieve. Franklin and Morris wrote: "We find by Fatal Experience the Congress Consists of too many Members to keep Secrets."[11] For example, when Congress appointed Franklin as a commissioner to France just days before, it also resolved that that appointment, as well as those of Deane and Jefferson, be kept secret for the time being. But that secret quickly found its way out onto the street, as Morris soon learned when a merchant, who was not a delegate, talked to him about Franklin's appointment.

The news of the arms shipments was far more sensitive. Should this information get "to the ears of our Enemies at New York they wou'd undoubtedly take measures to intercept the Supplies & thereby deprive us not only of these Succours but of Others expected by the same route."[12]

***

Franklin needn't have bothered keeping such secrets. The British knew everything thanks to Edward Bancroft, a man very much like Franklin: an enterprising American runaway apprentice from humble beginnings who became a successful writer and accomplished scientist. He was also a man whom Deane and Franklin both knew and trusted.

Born in Westfield, Massachusetts, Bancroft was two years old when his father died. His stepfather, a tavern proprietor, saw to the education of the boy, who found himself at age 14 in the Hartford, Connecticut, classroom of Silas Deane, a freshly minted graduate of Yale. At 18, unhappy with his apprenticeship to a physician, Bancroft ran away to Barbados and eventually found employment with a physician on a plantation in Surinam. There he happily acquired more education about medicine and science, focusing his attention especially on the study of the dyes and poisons that the natives used. He soon found his way to London for more formal medical studies, and, before he turned 25, published a worthy "Essay on the Natural History of Guiana." He also produced a three-volume novel, which got attention but little praise[13] (John Adams sneered at its "plentifull Abuse and vilification of Christianity"[14]).

Young Bancroft, a promising scientist, attracted the attention of Franklin, then in London, who gave him a step up, as he did so many people. A recommendation from Franklin earned Bancroft a job as a reviewer of publications related to America. Franklin also introduced him to an assortment of prominent scientists, leading to Bancroft's role as a founding member of the Medical Society of London in 1773.[15] On the strength of further research and discoveries related to ink and dyes, and with the recommendation of Franklin, among others, he was elected to the prestigious Royal Academy. By the time the American Revolution broke out, he was recognized on both sides of the English Channel as an authority on inks and dyes and held a patent related to dyed woolen fabrics and printed calicos.[16]

Franklin, in preparing his instructions for Deane, suggested that he contact Bancroft, who with his own acquaintances in France and England, and with current knowledge of events in London, might be useful. Because Bancroft was a former student of Deane's, the meeting between the two could be explained as an innocent reunion and thus should not arouse suspicions.[17] The two met in Paris two days before Deane's first meeting with Vergennes.

They soon arranged to work more closely. Bancroft was indeed useful—he knew French, was extremely knowledgeable, and had a manner that made him easy to get along with.[18] Bancroft quickly became Deane's confidante, translator, secretary, and sometimes partner in trade deals. Deane seems to have never doubted Bancroft's allegiance.

Deane was lucky to have such a capable, reliable, and useful assistant; but Britain was luckier. Bancroft was soon and eagerly betraying his old schoolmaster and his country by passing on troves of information to British spy handlers. Because of Bancroft, and because the British were so adept at intercepting communications to America, British ministers knew more about what Deane was doing than Franklin did, and Congress knew less than Franklin.[19]

Over time, Bancroft and his handlers streamlined their messaging system. Bancroft would compose innocent letters about "gallantry" using the name Dr. B. Edwards. Then, over the visible message, Bancroft would write a secret message in invisible ink. Bancroft then inserted the messages in a bottle that he would leave in a hole in a certain tree in Paris at a certain time every Tuesday. Bancroft would find messages from his British handlers in another designated tree. The system was almost too good. On one occasion, the British became aware of a planned communication between the Americans and the French and prepared a protest about it to the French. They then presented that protest to the French before the French minister had even received the communication in question from the Americans.[20]

Fortunately for the Americans, Bancroft was selective in the secrets he revealed. He invested and he speculated, and when it was in his financial interest to keep American secrets secret, that's what he did.[21] For example, he might have information that a certain ship was carrying weapons to America, but if he had a stake in some of the cargo, he might not disclose its precise destination. He might be aware of American privateers lurking in the waters around Britain, but if he had a stake in such ventures, might delay sending that information just long enough for the privateer to take prizes and bring them safely to a friendly port.

Had the British known all this, they likely would happily have hanged him and saved the Americans the trouble. Not fully trusting Bancroft, they ignored or mishandled some information he provided.

Another man positioned to help Deane in France was Thomas Morris, younger half brother of Pennsylvania's Robert Morris. Designated as a commercial agent for Congress—entrusted to handle all congressional business in Europe—he should have been invaluable to Deane, but he was less an asset than a liability.[22]

Thomas Morris was more like a son than a sibling to Robert Morris. After their father died when Robert was 16 and Thomas was an infant, Robert took responsibility for Thomas's upbringing and found a place for the boy in Morris's counting house about the time Thomas turned 16. To further Thomas's business skills, foster an acquaintance with Spanish and French, get him far away from his drinking companions, and thus wean him from a worrisome drinking habit, Robert sent Thomas to Spain to work for a trading company. After returning to America, Thomas was made junior partner in the Willing & Morris firm. In 1775, he returned to Europe, where he received instruction from Robert to meet up with Deane in Paris. Meanwhile, Robert advised Deane that, while Thomas understood French, had a sharp mind, and knew plenty about business, he had had a "wild youth" and needed oversight: "Keep him with you, advise him for his own sake to attend most constantly & steadily to the transactions you have in hand."[23]

As if Deane hadn't enough to do, he was to babysit the young man, who shortly after receiving his plum assignment, took off from Paris to London and then seemed to vanish. He failed to answer letters or properly cultivate business contacts. Word spread that he was drinking heavily.[24]

When Robert Morris learned his half brother was falling down on the job, he was embarrassed and angry, but not altogether surprised. He sent Thomas a scolding letter, advising him to turn over business to a trusted friend and return to America so "I may give you one chance more of retrieving your Character, & establishing yourself in the World. ... I look on you with Pitying Eyes for I was once your affectionate Friend &c."[25]

By the time Robert Morris sent the letter, Thomas had returned to the Continent and settled himself in Nantes, on the Loire in northwestern France. There, he at last accomplished something useful: he struck a deal involving tobacco with an organization that controlled most foreign imports into France.[26] It seemed that Thomas had cleaned up his act.

***

Astonishingly, despite the treachery and many other disadvantages, Deane within a year of stepping onto French soil succeeded in arranging at least eight cargoes of supplies for the American army.[27] Deane deserves much credit for that heroic accomplishment. But the real hero in engineering the initial trans-Atlantic deals between France and the new United States was a clever Frenchman, Pierre Augustin Caron de Beaumarchais. Today, he is remembered mainly as the playwright of two famous comedies that were recrafted into more famous operas—Rossini's *Barber of Seville* and Mozart's *Marriage of Figaro*. But Beaumarchais was also, among other things, a musician—he played the flute, harp, and violin—and a skilled watchmaker. He invented an escapement mechanism for timepieces[28] and once made a watch tiny enough to fit into a finger ring.[29] His résumé also included espionage.

The king of France found him useful for secret missions, such as one especially delicate task that sounds like the plot for a stage comedy. He was sent off to London to negotiate with one of the king's other spies, Chevalier D'Eon, who had fallen out with the French king and possessed papers that, if revealed to the British, could set off a war. As it happened, rumors flew that D'Eon was a woman, though he dressed as a man, and indeed had lived a thoroughly masculine life—as a soldier he earned a medal for valor.[30] Beaumarchais negotiated with D'Eon and, in a manner, wooed him. Beaumarchais later wrote: "[W]ho the devil would ever have imagined that Under the creative deal that to serve the king properly in this affair it would have been necessary for me to become the gallant knight of a captain of dragoons?"[31] Under the deal Beaumarchais worked out, the papers were returned safely to the king and Chevalier D'Eon was offered a comfortable pension and a chance to live out his life in France, as long as he dressed as a woman. Thus, Chevalier D'Eon proclaimed himself a woman and lived the remainder of his days—another three decades[32]—as Chevalière D'Eon. After the death of this soldier and spy, it was confirmed that all along D'Eon had the anatomy of a man.

Among Beaumarchais's myriad passions were assisting America in its struggle with Britain, promoting the interests of France, and amassing wealth. Thus, from Beaumarchais's fertile brain emerged a business scheme serving all three. Beaumarchais, working with Vergennes, pitched a plan to the king. With money from the French king and others, they would set up a company that would appear as a conventional, private business, but would actually be a conduit—a front—for secretly supporting the Americans. Gold and munitions would be shipped to America in exchange for such American products as tobacco and rice.[33] By so doing, the king, while pretending indifference to the squabble between Britain and its colonies, could secretly help the Americans and also make a tidy profit.[34]

Meanwhile, Beaumarchais would assume all risks, but if the company made money, so would he.[35] The king authorized a million *livres* to put the company, Roderigue Hortalès & Cie, in business. Soon, the Spanish king pitched in another million.[36] Beaumarchais would find French merchants to invest yet another million.[37] Thus, one month before the Declaration of Independence, Beaumarchais had set in motion a plan for providing French military support to the American rebels.[38]

By July, when Deane finally arrived in Paris, the foundation of this scheme was in place. Beaumarchais and Deane then worked together to arrange cargoes. However, obstacles and complications delayed every step. The shipments that Franklin learned about in October didn't reach American shores until the following April. Those first ships—the *Mercure* and *Amphitrite*—arrived in Portsmouth, New Hampshire, with 12,000 stands of arms and 60 cannons, as well as clothing, blankets, and gunpowder.[39] Eventually, about 40 ships would be involved in the trade, with Portsmouth the most common port of arrival. As for the tobacco and rice going the other way, Beaumarchais was left waiting. By September 1777, he had yet to receive a single American cargo.[40]

What if the British found out about his convoluted scheme? Robert Morris took a moment in September to ruminate:

> It appears clear to me that we may very soon Involve all Europe in a Warr by managing properly the apparent forwardness of the Court of France. Its a horrid consideration that our own Safety shou'd call on us to involve other Nations in the Calamities of warr. Can this be morally right or have morality & Policy nothing to do with each other? Perhaps it may not be good Policy to investigate the Question at this time.[41]

***

A messenger dispatched from Philadelphia to Virginia found Jefferson in Williamsburg. After reading the news of his appointment to Paris, Jefferson asked the rider to wait so he could return with a reply. The man waited three days as Jefferson agonized. He longed to accept this mission to France, but he knew his wife, because of her health, could not accompany him. Finally, he sent off the messenger with the answer: no.[42]

Jefferson thus declined an opportunity he craved. But what choice did he have? Fellow Virginian Richard Henry Lee, now back in Philadelphia as a delegate, was unsympathetic. He reminded Jefferson that the Revolution would fail if everyone took time away to tend to problems at home: "No Man feels more deeply than I do, the love of, private enjoyments; but let attention to these be universal, and we are gone, beyond redemption lost in the deep perdition of slavery."[43]

Congress got around to finding a replacement for Jefferson on October 22, when it named Arthur Lee to join Franklin and Deane in Paris. This seemed to be a perfect choice. Lee, brother of delegates Richard Henry and Francis Lightfoot, was already on the other side of the Atlantic—in London. He was clearly bright and energetic, as both a lawyer and a medical doctor, as well as a fellow in the Royal Society of London, the prestigious organization of scientists. He was also certainly an ardent Patriot. His political writing caught the attention of Samuel Adams, who was so impressed that, before the Revolution, he pushed to have the Virginian serve as a kind of lobbyist for Massachusetts in London.[44] Furthermore, Lee knew Franklin. They had become acquainted when Franklin was in London before his return to America.

Lee also had worthwhile connections overseas, one of whom was Beaumarchais. The two met up in London in the fall of 1774.[45] Lee told the Frenchman of Congress's interest in obtaining arms.[46] Beaumarchais in turn talked about his plan of setting up a phony trading company. Lee, in London, was thus acquainted with the plan to supply arms to America well before Deane arrived in France.

Finally, Lee, as a Virginian, was a Southerner, nicely balancing a team that included a New Englander (Deane) and a man from a Middle Atlantic state (Franklin).[47] Who better to team up with Deane and Franklin in Paris?

As it turned out, anyone or no one at all. Lee was cantankerous, prickly, and impossible to get along with, unless you were among the select few pure enough to bask in his spotless Patriot virtue. Among the long list of people he disliked, near the top was Franklin. While in London, Franklin had tried to befriend Lee. Indeed, it was Franklin who had sponsored Lee for admission to the Royal Society.[48] But Lee didn't trust Franklin. When Congress, early in 1776, asked Lee to be a special correspondent—to send confidential reports about the British political scene to Franklin's committee in charge of diplomacy for Congress—Lee huffed that he would not correspond with a committee that included Franklin or New York's John Jay. He would only correspond with the committee if it included John Adams, Samuel Adams, or one of Lee's brothers. Lee apparently set aside his distaste for Franklin, because Franklin and Jay stayed on the committee and Lee did send reports. As it turned out, these were worse than useless. Lee, despite his suspicious nature, trusted the wrong people. His "friends" in London, in cahoots with British authorities, fed Lee phony information about British military plans and capabilities, which Lee passed on to Congress.[49]

Franklin, as he got to know Lee better, would reach the conclusion that Lee was insane.[50] But at the time of the appointment, Franklin apparently had no misgivings about the Virginian. If he had, we presume he would have vetoed Lee's assignment to the Paris post.

On October 27, Franklin in Philadelphia boarded the *Reprisal*, which was loaded with a cargo of indigo, bound for France.[51] At least that was the plan, but the ship might be caught by the British or, considering the temper of the North Atlantic at that time of year, sink. Joining Franklin on the journey were his two grandsons, William Temple Franklin, 17, and Benny Bache, 7.[52]

The main assignment for the diplomatic trio—Franklin, Deane, and Lee—was clear: "It is the wish of Congress that the Treaty should be concluded; and you are hereby instructed to use every Means in your Power for concluding it, exactly conformable" to the plan laid out by Congress. Knowing the king of France would not go along with everything Congress wanted, it authorized its three commissioners "to relax the Demands of the United States" according to guidelines in the instructions. Congress well knew that, because of slow and uncertain communications, the commissioners required leeway to negotiate on their own. The best Congress could do was to indicate what terms to insist on and what could be waived.

Among the options Congress gave to the trio was to include in the treaty a clause promising that, if war broke out between Britain and France because of the treaty, then the United States would have to notify France six months in advance of the effective date of any agreement ending the war between Britain and the United States. Similarly, France would have to give the United States advanced notice of six months before the effective date of a treaty between Britain and France.[53] This complicated provision seemed prudent at the time, but would later become a troublesome issue.[54]

Beyond guidelines concerning a specific treaty, Congress also gave instructions about urgent needs: "You will solicit the Court of France for on immediate Supply of twenty or thirty thousand Muskets and Bayonets, and a large Supply of Ammunition and brass Field Pieces, to be sent under Convoy by France."[55] Of course, Franklin was well aware that this sort of help was already on the way.

Like an afterthought, Congress inserted into the instructions the following: "Engage a few good Engineers in the Service of the United States."[56] The point of this was to address the lack of expertise in the Continental Army. This sensible request would later create innumerable headaches for Washington and Congress.

CHAPTER 23

Excrement of Expiring Genius & Political Phrenzy

Well before the Declaration of Independence, the process of establishing state governments outside of royal authority was well underway. Seven months before July 1776, New Hampshire had a new constitution in place and a temporary government without a governor. A council of 12, selected by the elected House of Representatives, performed executive functions.[1]

Massachusetts likewise since 1775 had operated without a governor. Instead of making a new framework for government, the state dusted off a 1691 charter as its de facto constitution, but without the charter's problematic associations with royal authority. As in New Hampshire, a council, chosen by the popularly elected lower house, served as an executive.[2]

In May, Rhode Island, virtually independent anyway, simply scratched out all references to royal authority in the new state charter and discarded the trappings of royal authority. Meanwhile, South Carolina, Virginia, and New Jersey each had state constitutions in place before July 4.[3]

After independence, the other states one by one created new state constitutions or by other means cut all connections with royal authority. Delaware and Pennsylvania established governments under new constitutions in September. Maryland did likewise in November, as did North Carolina in December.[4]

Connecticut, virtually independent like Rhode Island, followed Rhode Island's lead in October, when it scrubbed royal references from its charter. The war interfered with constitution-making in Georgia and New York, but both states had constitutions in place by the spring of 1777.[5]

The new state governments tended to be much like the old colonial governments. However, one notable difference was the status of the chief executive, usually a governor. Remembering the tyranny of royally appointed governors, the states were determined to keep a tight rein on chief executives. Under most of the new state governments, the post of governor—where there was one—was stripped of much of its power. For example, in no state was the executive given exclusive power to appoint judges and government officials, and in North Carolina and New Jersey that authority was taken entirely away from the executive. In most states, lawmakers retained all that power to appoint, sometimes with and sometimes without the governor's concurrence. In most states, the governor had no power to veto legislation. Furthermore, constitutions called for frequent elections of the governor—annually in 10 of the states. The new constitutions also contained provisions for possible impeachment of the governor, as well as other officials, although curiously, in Delaware and Virginia, the new constitutions allowed impeachment of the governor only after he left office.[6] Georgia was so fearful that a governor would cling illegally to power that its constitution called for the incoming governor to swear to quit his office "peacefully and quietly"[7] at the end of his term.

All constitutions, except in Pennsylvania and Georgia, created two legislative houses. The upper houses, the senates, tended to be smaller than the houses of representatives and involved longer terms of office. The terms tended to be staggered, giving the senates more stability than the houses of representatives. In most states, senate candidates were required to have more property than candidates for the house.[8]

Remembering how governors once manipulated legislatures by controlling the frequency of elections, all states except South Carolina called for annual elections of the houses of representatives. Recalling as well how royal governors had obstructed the creation of new electoral districts, the states enlarged their houses of representatives, in some cases doubling or even tripling the number of representatives. Voting remained restricted to free men who owned an amount of property above a certain threshold, or who paid a minimum amount in taxes.[9] Revolutionary leaders liked democracy, but not too much of it. They likely agreed with British-born North Carolinian James Iredell, an influential essayist and lawyer, who wrote:

> Some think every man ought to have an individual vote for a representative. If every man was a good one, and had a tolerable understanding, this rule would be proper; but when poverty leads to temptation, and folly is ever capable of deceit, there must be some restriction as to the right of voting; otherwise the lowest and most ignorant of mankind must associate in this important business with those who it is to be presumed, from their property and other circumstances, are free from influence, and have some knowledge of the great consequences of their trust.[10]

Some constitutions addressed the problem of bribing voters or otherwise interfering in elections. Pennsylvania's constitution went furthest, explicitly barring candidates from giving, and voters from receiving, "meat, drink, monies,"[11] or anything else for a vote. Secret ballots, not common before independence, remained the exception, incorporated only in the constitutions of Pennsylvania, Georgia, and North Carolina.[12]

The most radical constitution was that of Pennsylvania, which had been among the last outposts of moderation in the days before the Revolution. This constitution placed most functions of government in the hands of a single elected house, the General Assembly, chosen annually. All free taxpayers, along with their sons aged

21 or older, could vote. All bills had to be printed and available to the public before final approval. Instead of a governor, the state had a Supreme Executive Council comprising 12 men elected by the people for three-year terms. The Council appointed high-ranking officials but had no role in making laws. Candidates for the Council needed no special qualifications. The Council's presiding officer—the state's president—was chosen by the Assembly and Council.[13]

Pennsylvania's constitution also included provisions allowing the militia to choose officers up to the rank of colonel, calling for the creation of free schools, and abolishing imprisonment for debt.[14] Also, all members of the Assembly had to swear they believed in God, with the oath: "I do believe in one God, the creator and governor of the universe, the rewarder of the good and the punisher of the wicked. And I do acknowledge the Scriptures of the Old and New Testament to be given by Divine inspiration."[15]

In Congress, at least a few delegates thought Pennsylvania had careened off the rails. Hooper of North Carolina called the new government "a Beast without a head":

> Taverns and dram shops are the councils to which the laws of this State are to be referred for approbation before they possess a binding Influence. ... It is truly the Excrement of expiring Genius & political Phrenzy. It has made more Tories than Lord North; deserves more Imprecations than the Devil and all his Angels. It will shake the very being of this once flourishing Country.[16]

John Adams chimed in: "Pensilvania will be divided and weakend, and rendered much less vigorous in the Cause, by the wretched Ideas of Government, which prevail, in the Minds of many People in it." He was especially incensed with a requirement in the state's constitution that each voter "swear that he will not add to, or diminish from or any Way alter that Constitution."[17]

The Pennsylvania constitution indeed proved troublesome. For 14 years, bitter factionalism distracted the state until a new constitution was finally adopted in 1790.

***

As state leaders worked on drafting constitutions and installing new governments, the war went on. In New York, in the fall of 1776, Washington and his little army still held much of the northern half of Manhattan Island, while the British controlled the waters around the island and occupied the city at the southern tip. One night, Washington looked south to see a glow on the horizon—New York in flames. The fire consumed nearly 500 houses, delayed British plans to attack the Americans, and complicated the challenge of sheltering the occupation force over the winter. Washington, ordered by Congress not to destroy the town,[18] was pleased: "Providence or some good honest fellow has done more for us than we were disposed to do for ourselves."[19]

Ample evidence suggests that the fire was deliberately set. For example, observers reported multiple fires breaking out in multiple locations at about the same time.[20] A British secretary for Admiral Howe wrote in his journal that rebel arsonists were to blame:

> One Man, detected in the Fact, was knocked down by a Grenadier & thrown into the Flames for his Reward: Another, who was found cutting off the Handles of the Water-Buckets to prevent their Use, was first hung up by the Neck till he was dead and afterwards by the Heels upon a Sign-Post by the Sailors. ... The New England People are maintained to be at the Bottom of this Plot, which they have long since threatened to put into Execution.[21]

For almost a month, Washington stayed put on Manhattan, with forces eventually concentrated on Harlem Heights, in the north,[22] and at Fort Washington, on the banks of the Hudson. That flimsy fort, in tandem with Fort Constitution on the opposite shore in New Jersey, guarded the Hudson to prevent British ships from sailing upriver.

On October 12, the British made a move, landing 11,000 men at a location that seemed well suited to trap the Americans on Harlem Heights. That might have happened but for marshes separating the landing place from the shore. Once the Americans tore apart a causeway, the British found themselves on a virtual island. Meanwhile, winds unfavorable to the British kept another wave of British troops from landing.[23]

Washington had caught a break. But he now saw how vulnerable he was on Harlem Heights. About this time, General Charles Lee appeared after his success in South Carolina, where he had led Americans in repulsing a British invasion at Charleston. That small victory in late June was a humiliation for the British and a morale boost for the Americans. While the outcome was more a result of British blundering than Lee's brilliance,[24] Washington chose to honor Lee by renaming the fort on the New Jersey side of the Hudson. Fort Constitution thus became Fort Lee. After a council of war, Washington ordered most of his men north, off Manhattan, and onward about 20 miles to White Plains. About 1,000[25] would remain on Manhattan holding Fort Washington.

About the time that news of these events reached Philadelphia, reports of other developments reached Congress from the north, where a brave makeshift little American navy was trying to hold Lake Champlain. The British, in the months after beating back the American invasion of Canada, had geared up to push down from the north and recapture Fort Ticonderoga. From there, it would be an easy matter to reach the Hudson River,[26] where the British could create more nightmares for Washington and his army and sever communications between New England and the rest of the United States.

By October, British commander Guy Carlton had 11,000 troops poised for this push,[27] more than enough to chase the Americans from Fort Ticonderoga. But these troops needed to travel by water, which meant the British first needed to sweep Lake Champlain clean of the American fleet of 15 leaky vessels, which had been hastily hammered together over the summer.

The British fleet sent south met up with the Patriot fleet on October 11 near Valcour Island, 5 miles south of modern-day Plattsburgh.[28] By October 13, the American flotilla was shattered: all but four craft were sunk, burned, or otherwise lost. Meanwhile, all of the 17 or so British gunboats remained afloat.[29] The heroic efforts to defend the lake had failed, and the door to a British invasion from Canada was wide open.

In Philadelphia, delegates hardly noticed the awful news from the north amid worse news from the east. British troops, bypassing Fort Washington, were soon on Washington's trail, pursuing him to White Plains. After a sharp battle with heavy losses on both sides,[30] the American general and his men had to pull back to higher ground 5 miles away.[31] It was yet another defeat for the Americans, but this time they fought tenaciously and the retreat was orderly.[32] At New Castle, New York, Washington braced for a major battle,[33] but the British, instead of fighting, packed up and marched away, back south toward Manhattan.

Washington consulted his generals. Were the British determined to pounce on Fort Washington or Fort Lee, or both? Or was this a feint south, with the real aim to drive east into New England? Or was there a plan to slip west to the Hudson, board ships, and head upriver? Another possibility was that the British would cross the Hudson, then cross to New Jersey and seize Philadelphia. Maybe, with the season being late, they were just going to curl up around New York City and wait until spring.[34]

Washington chose to split his army. He rushed south with 2,000 troops to support Forts Washington and Lee. Another 3,000 men were sent north to the Hudson Highlands at Peekskill, New York,[35] to guard the Hudson. The remaining force of 7,000 under General Lee remained nearby. They would be poised to either move west to support the men at Peekskill, east to protect against a possible invasion of New England, or south to help Washington.[36]

By the time Washington arrived at Fort Lee, he knew an attack on Fort Washington across the river was likely. Washington's general on the scene, Nathanael Greene, believed the fort impregnable.[37] Greene, however, like many of Washington's officers, was short on experience. This Rhode Island man with broad shoulders and powerful arms had made his living as an anchor smith and merchant before the war. His military knowledge came from books and experience on parade grounds. After the war started, he served as a brigadier general directing Rhode Island troops around Boston.[38] His adept management of those men caught the attention of Washington, who now put a little too much faith in a battlefield novice.

Washington should have known that an attempt to hold the fort was both hopeless and pointless. The fort had no barracks and no water supply. With winter approaching, it had no chance of withstanding a siege, even if it survived an attack. Even with improvements over weeks and more manpower in the fort, three British warships had slipped past it and up the Hudson. The fort thus proved unable to fulfill its main function—blocking British ships from sailing upriver. There was now no good reason to hold it. But Washington was swayed by Greene, who envisioned another Bunker Hill—staggering British losses after a frustrating effort to dislodge the Americans.[39] At the very least, the occupied fort would tie down many British troops, Greene argued.[40] Washington also heard assurances that, if necessary, the defenders could at the last moment slip across the Hudson to safety.[41]

The British attacked on November 16, and the fort fell in five hours.[42] There was no chance for an evacuation. Almost 3,000 Continental soldiers were captured, along with tools, tents, blankets, arms, and cannons.[43] Many of them, possibly 1,800, would die in ghastly British prisons in or near New York City.[44]

Washington, from the other side of the Hudson, saw through a telescope the catastrophe unfolding,[45] including perhaps the bayonetting of Americans begging for quarter. One biographer reported that men surrounding Washington saw him, as the scale of the defeat sank in, weep "with the tenderness of a child."[46]

Now the British zeroed in on Fort Lee. In this case, Washington ordered an evacuation soon enough for ammunition to be spirited away and for some 2,000 men to evade capture, but not soon enough to save precious food and equipment stockpiled in the fort. The British, upon entering the fort, found, besides 12 drunken soldiers, hundreds of tents, 1,000 barrels of flour, 50 cannons, and pots with water still boiling.[47]

Having narrowly escaped with his bedraggled army, Washington sent off an urgent request to General Lee: send help to stop or at least slow down the British, whom Washington expected would now push across the flat New Jersey countryside to Philadelphia. Soon, Washington and his men crossed the Passaic and approached Newark. They had no tents or tools, all left behind in Fort Lee. Of the perhaps 3,000 soldiers, many were shoeless, with rags wrapped around their feet.[48]

By November 29, Washington and his men had moved on to New Brunswick, New Jersey, where they were joined by more than 1,000 reinforcements, although some of them were without shoes or coats. These were not Lee's men. Indeed, Lee, in his initial reply to Washington, gave no hint that he intended to come to Washington's aid.[49]

The next day, Washington—exhausted, frazzled, and despairing after the train of defeats and so much retreating—felt another more personal blow. At last, another letter from Lee arrived. Maybe this was the precious news Washington was waiting for. However, the letter was addressed not to Washington, but to his assistant, Joseph Reed, who was off on a mission to plead for reinforcements.[50] Sensing that the contents were vital and could not wait for Reed's return, Washington tore open the letter, just as he had opened letters before from Lee addressed to Reed. The letter began:

My dear Reed,
I receiv'd your most obliging flattering letter—lament with you that fatal indecision of mind which in war is a much greater disqualification than stupidity or even want of personal courage—accident may put a decisive Blunderer in the right—but eternal defeat and miscarriage must attend the man of the best parts if curs'd with indecision.[51]

Presumably, Washington read this more than once before fully grasping that he was the man "curs'd with indecision." That was the judgment of his top general, with the concurrence, evidently, of his most trusted assistant.

Washington wrote out a note, enclosed it with the letter, and sent it on to Reed. In his note, Washington confessed to opening the letter, thinking it concerned "the business of your office" and "Having no Idea of its being a Private Letter, much less Suspecting the tendency of the Correspondence."[52] He made no further remark about the contents, but they must have wounded Washington deeply. Maybe, as he had suspected from the beginning, he really wasn't up to the job.

Could it get any worse for Washington? Well yes, it could. The very next day, December 1, with British columns two hours away and bearing down on Washington's army in New Brunswick, about 2,000 of his men simply packed up and walked away. Their enlistments had expired.[53]

Washington sent off yet another urgent message to Lee for help and ordered the destruction of the bridge over the Raritan River between his army and the British. That would slow the enemy, but would not stop them, for the river could be forded. By the next morning, the diminished American army was on the road again.[54]

On December 2, Washington led his dwindling army into Pennsylvania, crossing the Delaware at Trenton.[55] Washington soon confessed in a letter:

> I tremble for Philadelphia, nothing in my opinion but General Lee's speedy arrival ... can save it. We have brought over, and destroyed, all the Boats we could lay our hands on, upon the Jersey Shore for many Miles above and below this place; but it is next to impossible to guard a Shore for 60 Miles with less than half the Enemys numbers.[56]

CHAPTER 24

Our Little Handfull

In Philadelphia, 30 miles away, first alarm, then panic, seized the city as news of disaster after disaster trickled in. Reports confirmed that some units of the British Army were less than 20 miles away.[1] "Where shall we go; how shall we get out of town? was the universal cry," recalled one woman who was there as a girl. "Carriages of every description were few and all were anxiously sought. ... Happy was he who could press a market wagon or a milk-cart to bear off his little ones!"

To flee the city, she and her family crammed onto a small river craft "whose smoky cabin did not permit the ladies with infants in their arms, to sit quite upright."[2]

On December 8, martial law was declared. The next day, orders were issued to shutter all shops. Militiamen began street patrols.[3] "People have for some Days been removing their Familys and effects from this Place, which has occasioned a prodigious hurry amongst them," wrote Connecticut's Oliver Wolcott on December 11.[4] No one, it seemed, resolved to defend the town, just as no one had risen up to oppose the British Army as it swept across New Jersey. Samuel Adams scowled: "[N]othing can exceed the Lethargy that has seizd the People of this State & the Jerseys." He blamed Dickinson, who, Adams wrote, had urged accommodation with the British: "With this he has poisond the Minds of the People, the Effect of which is a total Stagnation of the Power of Resentment, the utter Loss of every manly Sentiment of Liberty & Virtue."[5]

Adams's condemnation of Dickinson was unfair. But for his part, Dickinson at this time was hardly a model of patriotism: he told his family not to accept Continental dollars. Meanwhile, one of Pennsylvania's leading families—the Allens—gave up on the cause, abandoning Philadelphia to go over to the British side.[6]

Congress called on the people of Pennsylvania, New Jersey, and nearby states to put up "an immediate and spirited exertion in opposition" to the British Army threatening Philadelphia. Painting the bleak scene in cheerful hues, Congress noted that to the north and south the war was going well, which was true enough. In New England and in the South, new state governments reigned, generally in peace. British soldiers were nowhere to be seen. Indeed, the little American navy on Lake Ticonderoga, though defeated, had slowed the enemy advance enough to force the

British to fall back to bases in Canada for the winter. Meanwhile, to the south, the British had made no new attempt to regain control of Southern states: "The enemy have been expelled from the Northern Provinces where they at first had possession, and have been repulsed in their attempt upon the Southern by the undaunted valour of the inhabitants."

Congress further explained that the American failure to stop British advances near Philadelphia stemmed from "a sudden diminution" in the size of the American army as enlistments expired: "Many have already joined the Army to supply the deficiency, and we call, in the most earnest manner, on all the friends of liberty to exert themselves without delay in this pressing emergency. In every other part your arms have been successful, and in other respects our sacred cause is in the most promising situation."

The statement concluded with a rousing call to defend Philadelphia:

> And though (blessed be God) even the loss of Philadelphia would not be the loss of the cause, yet while it can be saved, let us not, in the close of the campaign, afford them such ground of triumph, but give a check to their progress, and convince our friends in the distant parts that one spirit animates the whole.[7]

Congress also sought divine help. It called on the states to "to implore of Almighty God the forgiveness of the many sins prevailing among all ranks, and to beg the countenance and assistance of his Providence in the prosecution of the present just and necessary war." It also called for all officers, both military and civil, to strictly observe the articles of war, especially those forbidding "profane swearing, and all immorality."[8]

Delegates then turned to Washington for help in squelching rumors that they were about to flee the city:

> Whereas a false and malicious report hath been spread by the enemies of America that the Congress was about to disperse: Resolved, That General Washington be desired to contradict the said scandalous report in general orders, this Congress having a better opinion of the spirit and vigour of the army and the good people of these states than to suppose it can be necessary to disperse. Nor will they adjourn from the city of Philadelphia in the present state of affairs, unless the last necessity shall direct it.[9]

Washington, knowing too well the spirit and vigor of the army, politely but firmly refused to obey. In a response addressed to Hancock, Washington wrote: "As the publication of their [Congress's] Resolve in my opinion will not lead to any good end, but on the contrary may be attended with some bad consequences, I shall take the liberty to decline inserting it in this days Orders."

He coolly explained further:

> I doubt not but there are some who have propagated the report, but what if they have? Their [Congress's] remaining in or leaving Philadelphia must be governed by circumstances & events; If their departure should become necessary, it will be right; On the other hand, if there should

not be a necessity for it, they will remain & their continuance will shew the report to be the production of Calumny and Falsehood. In a word Sir, I conceive it a matter that may be as well disregarded, and that the removal or staying of Congress, depending entirely upon events should not have been the Subject of a Resolve.

Washington went on to admit that his little army could not stop the British from taking Philadelphia:

> Upon the whole there can be no doubt but that Philadelphia is their object, and that they will pass the Delaware as soon as possible. Happy should I be, if I could see the means of preventing them. At present I confess I do not. ... Our little handfull is daily decreasing by sickness and Other causes, and without aid, without considerable Succours and exertions on the part of the people, what can we reasonably look for or expect, but an event that will be severely felt by the Common Cause, and that will wound the Heart of every virtuous American, the loss of Philadelphia. The Subject is disagreable, but yet it is true.[10]

This was a brushoff that might have offended delegates in Philadelphia had they waited for it. But they were too busy doing just what the "false and malicious" reports suggested: abandoning the city.

On December 12, the very day Washington was writing his answer, Congress pushed through a raft of resolutions just before closing up shop and fleeing. Their destination was Baltimore, about 90 miles away, where they hoped to resume their work a week or so later. During this hiatus, Washington would have authority to do almost as he wished: Congress resolved that "until the Congress shall otherwise order, General Washington be possessed of full power to order and direct all things relative to the department, and to the operations of war."[11]

How curious that Washington's authority should be enhanced at a time when, arguably, he should have been fired. His leadership had produced, in recent months, only catastrophe. He failed to defend New York. He couldn't save Philadelphia. The time might have come to cast off the man who had earlier admitted that he was out of his depth, and to put in his place someone with more military skill, experience, and confidence—say, General Charles Lee, so recently victorious at Charleston.[12]

As it happened, Lee about this time was finally responding to Washington's pleas for help and was on his way across New Jersey with 7,000 men. His pace was leisurely, apparently in the hope that, while he was still at a distance, the British would smash Washington and his army, leaving Congress little choice but to find a new commander—for example, himself.[13] Also, as it happened, on that same December 12, Lee, still 40 miles from Washington's camp, made a fateful decision that no one has ever been able to explain—he chose to spend the evening not with his men but about 3 miles away, in White's Tavern[14] in Basking Ridge, New Jersey. He was not alone. He had a personal guard of 15 officers and men,[15] but he was vulnerable. The main body of the enemy was within 20 miles,[16] British scouting parties could be anywhere, and the countryside was full of Loyalists happy to help the British snag an American general.

The next morning, seated at a table and wearing a dressing gown, Lee took a moment from his paperwork to scribble out his frustrations in a letter to a fellow general, mainly about just how lousy Washington was at his job: "Entre nous, a certain great man is damnable deficient."[17]

As Lee was finishing the letter, a captain peering out of the tavern window said in amazement: "Here, Sir, are the British cavalry!"[18]

Sure enough, a British scouting party of about 25 men[19] pounced on Lee's guards. The skirmish lasted about 15 minutes.[20] Two of the guards were killed, and the rest fled.[21] Lee surrendered. Soon he was "hurried off in triumph, bareheaded, in his slippers and blanket coat, his collar open, and his shirt very much soiled from several days' use."[22]

***

Over in France, Silas Deane was a man in the dark. He knew nothing about what was happening across the ocean or whether Congress was honoring the transaction he was engineering. On December 3, in Paris, he scrawled a letter to John Jay back in America: "Without intelligence, without orders, and without remittances, yet boldly plunging into contracts, engagements, and negotiations, hourly hoping that something will arrive from America."[23]

As it happened, something arrived that very day: Franklin. He and his grandsons made good time on their voyage to France, but the trip was rough on the old man, who suffered along the way from boils and another skin condition, likely psoriasis. Franklin, being Franklin, distracted himself by tracking the temperature of the sea to learn more about the Gulf Stream. On December 3, the *Reprisal* approached Brittany, but winds prevented the ship from landing, so Franklin and his grandsons clambered aboard a fishing boat and were rowed ashore to the village of Auray.[24] Eventually they made their way farther inland by carriage. The driver amused the Americans with a tale of how just two weeks earlier some travelers had been murdered along the same route.[25]

Franklin's presence was soon widely known, and his movements reported. Franklin read about himself in the papers. He noticed seven paragraphs—one was actually true.[26]

By December 20, Franklin was in Paris. Two days later, Arthur Lee arrived.

Franklin took up elegant accommodations in the spacious wing of a grand house, the Hôtel de Valentinois,[27] in Passy, now a neighborhood of Paris, but then a village 2 miles from the center of the city. This residence, provided rent-free by a French entrepreneur eager to help the Americans,[28] became the unofficial embassy of the United States, with visitors coming and going. Many activities there were intended to be secret, but precautions were lax. Franklin was apparently unaware of the spying in his midst, and didn't much care anyway. He once scoffed that if he had a valet whom he discovered was a spy, he would keep him so long as he was a good valet.[29]

As for his grandsons, Franklin installed young Benny in a boarding school close enough to his grandfather that he could visit on Sundays. Teenager Temple became his grandfather's personal secretary.[30]

When he was in Paris in 1767, Franklin did as the French did. He wore a powdered wig in the French style, and he liked the look. But now, in Paris once again, he no longer bothered. To save time and trouble, and just to keep his balding head warm, he wore indoors and out a cap of marten fur pulled down low.[31] That hat on anyone else would have been a faux pas. But on Franklin it was a sensation. He also wore spectacles in public—very unstylish. The French king, despite being shortsighted, was never seen with his glasses.[32] For Franklin, the rules of fashion did not apply.

While his fur hat and eyewear set others talking, Franklin himself said little. Franklin could be very clever on paper, but he was never a confident speaker. In this city of chatter, bon mots, and witty repartee—with a population famous for talking much while saying little—this might normally signify a blockhead. Not so in Dr. Franklin's case. His reticence was "sublime." And what few words he uttered were reported instantly everywhere.[33]

His face was also everywhere. His portrait made a popular gift and many French families made room for his image on their mantel. The Franquelins of Picardy decided the great man must be related.[34]

Like Deane before him, Franklin was inundated with men eager for military glory in America. Most were French, but applicants also included Walloons, Russians, Poles, and amazingly, Peruvians. Résumés were skimpy or irrelevant. One applicant listed merely that he was well-born, tall, agile, and handsome.[35] A few diplomats came to Franklin's door. Franklin received them but conversed on scientific matters. His political role remained quiet.

Meanwhile, Deane continued to handle much of the work of acquiring and shipping war materiel, but also consumer goods—helping the struggling American war effort, but also helping himself. He energetically followed the script set forth by Robert Morris, his business partner and guide back in Philadelphia, who wrote: "[I]t seems to me the present opportunity of Improving our Fortunes ought not to be lost especially as the very means of doing it will Contribute to the Service of our Country at the same time."[36]

Morris promised Deane a third of the profits on private deals from Europe. For example, he rounded up linens and calicoes, which he knew would be especially dear in America because of the embargo of British products and the British naval blockade. He also promoted the shipment of silks, ribbons, brandy, and window glass.[37]

As for Lee, he was irked that Deane seemed to have full control of commercial matters. The French, meanwhile, didn't trust Lee. They believed that Lee, having just arrived from England, secretly maintained ties there and was anti-French. The French were mistaken—Lee was not pro-British, but he was not pro-French either.

He rigidly held to the view that America needed to be self-reliant. He was thus suspicious of any move that smacked of kowtowing to French aims. He bristled when Franklin and Deane seemed to subordinate America's interests to those of its European friends. To Lee, Franklin was far too congenial and submissive in dealing with the French, while Deane was wholly preoccupied with making money. Lee saw himself as the lone virtuous Patriot in Europe immersed heart and soul in the American cause.[38]

Deane, Franklin, and Lee met discreetly with Vergennes, the French foreign minister.[39] The French insisted on secrecy and urged the Americans to keep a low profile.[40] They knew the meeting would inflame the British, and the French, in the midst of rearming their navy, were in no position to provoke a war with Britain.[41]

The trio of American commissioners presented Vergennes with a shopping list: muskets, cannons, ammunition, plus eight ships of the line, the largest warships of the day. Vergennes took the Americans' request and later sent word that they would get nothing on that list, but the French government would offer a secret loan of 2 million *livres*. Early in 1777, the first million of that loan came through. The Americans promised to repay with tobacco.[42]

CHAPTER 25

Dismal & Melancoly

Back across the Atlantic, a top American general—Charles Lee—was in British custody, Congress was on the run, and Philadelphia's fate—maybe the fate of the whole country—depended on a failing commander with a pitiful and shrinking army. That army would presently be reinforced by Lee's army, minus Lee. But thanks to short enlistments, the enlarged army would still, bit by bit, melt away. Washington's flagging spirit found no comfort in the civilians around him in the land he was defending. When the British offered a pardon to anyone promising loyalty to the king,[1] thousands in New Jersey cheerfully stepped forward.[2] Washington feared the collapse of independent America: "Our only dependence now is upon the speedy enlistment of a new army. If this fails, I think the game will be pretty well up, as, from disaffection and want of spirit and fortitude, the inhabitants, instead of resistance, are offering submission."[3]

One who took the offered amnesty from the British—albeit under duress—was a delegate to Congress and signer of the Declaration of Independence, Richard Stockton. This lawyer[4] and "graceful speaker"[5] from the outskirts of Princeton had appeared in Congress for the first time in June. That fall, he happened to be in New Jersey when the British came through the state and in November was captured.[6] After being placed in irons and jailed, he fretted about his family and became ill.[7] Soon he signed the amnesty, but that didn't spare his handsome home near Princeton, which was ransacked, its library burned.[8]

Released from jail, he went home, resigned from Congress, and attempted to live quietly out of the public eye. Later, when British troops were not around to protect him, Patriot leaders threatened to force him from his home if he didn't take another pledge—this time promising allegiance to Congress. He agreed, changing sides once again.[9] His son-in-law summed up Stockton's character: he was "at all times sincerely devoted to the liberties of his country" but "timid where bold measures were required."[10]

***

The decision by Congress to leave Philadelphia was prudent, backed "by strong arguments"[11] from the two generals charged with defending the city. As Washington suggested, if circumstances dictated flight, then fleeing was the right thing to do. Connecticut's Oliver Wolcott noted: "[I]t was judged that the Council of America ought not to Sit in a Place liable to be interrupted by the rude Disorder of Arms."[12]

Still, for Congress, the sudden rush out of town was not a proud moment: the esteemed delegates who had declared independence less than six months before were now fleeing like refugees. Congress lost stature, even though delegates overall were a brave lot and willing to do their bit on the battlefield. Of the 342 men chosen to sit in the Continental Congress over its 15 years, 134 served in the Continental Army or in a militia unit. Of those, one lost his life in combat, 12 were severely wounded, and 23 were taken prisoner.[13] That's a commendable record considering that many delegates were well past the age of 40.

Absent from this flight to Baltimore was Pennsylvania's Robert Morris, who stayed behind in Philadelphia mainly to watch over his own business interests. War or no war, business went on and ships were due in port. Meanwhile, he sent his family—wife Mary, four children, and a domestic slave—away for safety to Mary's stepsister's place near Baltimore. He also prepared to follow if need be. Papers were shipped off for safekeeping; a wagon was packed with belongings.[14]

In Philadelphia, Morris worked and watched. He wrote on December 20: "This City was for ten Days the meerest Scene of Distress that you can Conceive. Everybody but Quakers were removing their Families & effects and now it Looks dismal & Melancoly. The Quakers & their families pretty generally Remain, the other Inhabitants are principally Sick Soldiers."[15]

Another witness to the chaos in Philadelphia was Thomas Paine, who entered the city about the time Congress was leaving. The famous author of *Common Sense* had left Philadelphia with a Pennsylvania unit in September to fight in the New York campaign and was part of the retreat across New Jersey.[16] Washington didn't want any soldier to walk away, but Paine was more useful at this moment pushing a pen than carrying a musket. At the American camp along the Delaware, Washington's officers asked him to return to Philadelphia and churn out essays to reignite Patriot enthusiasm. Paine was thinking the same thing. By that time, he had a draft essay more or less complete, having scribbled it out by the light of campfires as others slept.[17]

Composition in hand, he hiked 11 hours, fearing all the time that he might be captured. Entering the city, he found the people in a "deplorable and melancholy condition ... afraid to speak and almost to think, the public presses stopped, and nothing in circulation but fears and falsehoods."[18] He polished off the first of 13 articles "written in a rage when our affairs were at their lowest ebb and things in the most gloomy state."[19]

The move to Baltimore disrupted the routines of all delegates, but perhaps no one more so than Hancock, whose wife, Dolly, had just given birth:

My Scituation upon Leaving Philada. was really distressing, you well know the State of my Family at that time, a Wife but Nine Days in Bed, a little Infant just Breath'd in the World, a large Family & considerable Effects, all to take Charge of, in the Winter Season, cold Houses to put up at, & such a Number of passengers on the Road, doubtful whether I should even obtain Shelter, & among Strangers too.[20]

Baltimore Town, as Baltimore was known, had a population of about 6,000, not even one-sixth the size of Philadelphia. While in Philadelphia, delegates could peruse seven local newspapers. In Baltimore, they could find only two—both weeklies.[21]

Delegates groaned about the filth of the town, which had no paved streets, and the steep price of everything. Wolcott of Connecticut wrote: "[I]t is infinitely the most dirty Place I was ever in. No One can Walk about here but in Boots."[22] Hooper of North Carolina commented:

> This dirty, boggy hole beggars all description. We are obliged ... to go to Congress on Horseback, the way so miry that Carriages almost stall on the sides of them. When the Devil proffered our Saviour the Kingdoms of the World, he surely placed his thumb on this delectable spot & reserved it to himself for his own peculiar chosen seat and inheritance. As to the Inhabitants the congress can boast no acquaintance with them but what arises from their daily exorbitant claims upon our pockets.[23]

William Ellery of Rhode Island complained: "I thought that Philadelphia was the dearest Place that ever I knew. Baltimore exceeds it. On this Account, on Account of its Distance from the Scene of War, and on Account of its being the dirtiest Place I ever saw, I most sincerely wish myself back to Philadelphia."[24]

Basic supplies were expensive or hard to find. Hancock begged Morris back in Philadelphia "to send me by the next Express, Half a Ream of good Writing Paper, two Pounds of the best Sealing Wax, a Box of Wafers, and three Hundred of the best Quills. Excuse the Trouble I give you."[25]

Another problem was crime. The place Hancock eventually rented for his family—"the only one I could get"—was "in a Remote place among Whores & Theives." Within two days, robbers struck, taking "a Trunk with Linnen, Books, papers, some hard Money."[26]

James Smith of Pennsylvania was among the rare delegates with something pleasant to say about the emergency capital, finding Baltimore "much more sociable" than Philadelphia.[27] John Adams, for the moment in Massachusetts, had a mixed impression when he later arrived. Baltimore, he wrote to Abigail, is a "very pretty Town."[28] After attending church services, he described the view:

> The Presbyterian Meeting House in Baltimore stands upon an Hill just at the Back of the Town, from whence We have a very fair Prospect of the Town, and of the Water upon which it stands, and of the Country round it. Behind this Eminence, which is the Bacon [Beacon] Hill of Baltimore, lies a beautifull Meadow, which is entirely incircled by a Stream of Water. ... Beyond the Meadow and Canall, you have a charming View of the Country. Besides the Meeting House there is upon this Height, a large and elegant Court House, as yet unfinished within, and a small Church of England.[29]

216 • NOBLE UNDERTAKING

But like his colleagues, Adams was taken aback by the mud and prices: "The Streets are very dirty and miry, but every Thing else is agreable except the monstrous Prices of Things."[30]

The courthouse was spruced up and made available for the distinguished delegates, but Congress chose instead Henry Fite's spacious three-story brick home—originally built as a tavern[31]—on Market Street. Congress paid Fite rent for three months.[32] The room for Congress was a "long Chamber, with two fire Places, two large Closets, and two Doors."[33]

***

In Philadelphia, Morris had his hands full. While personal business was the motive for staying behind, he found most of his hours consumed with matters normally handled by Congress, such as directing shipments that came into port for the military and answering constant requests for money.[34] In a letter to Hancock a few days after

Congress fled Philadelphia for Baltimore in December 1776 and rented this building, a former tavern, as a meeting place. Congress returned to Philadelphia the following March. Built in 1770, this structure was known as the Henry Fite house and, after the war, as Old Congress Hall. It was on West Baltimore Street between South Sharp and North Liberty. A fire destroyed the building in 1904. This mural, by Allyn Cox, can be seen on the first floor of the U.S. Capitol's House wing. (Image courtesy of the Architect of the Capitol)

his colleagues left for Baltimore, Morris admitted he was likely overstepping his authority: "I hear so many complaints & see so much confusion from other quarters that I am obliged to advise in things not committed to me. Circumstanced as our affairs now are I conceive it better to take libertys & assume some powers than to let the general interest suffer."

Morris asked that Congress send back to Philadelphia a committee "with such powers as Congress may Judge proper" to "regulate the business" of Congress:

> There is the greatest Scene of confusion in the management of the Continental Horses, Wagons, & Expresses that ever was exhibited. It was bad enough before Congress departed but is ten times worse now. ... In short the Committee you send shoud have full powers to do whatever may be necessary to put every department on a Systematic footing. ... The Committee must have the Command of Money to answer Various purposes as the calls for it are loud, large & constant.[35]

***

It turned out that Congress could have safely stayed in Philadelphia that winter, as the British advance across New Jersey stopped on the east side of the icy Delaware River. Their plans did not include crossing into Pennsylvania that late in the season. The Howe brothers—Admiral Richard and General William—still believing they could prod Americans to walk back their claim of independence, had embarked on a strategy of restraint. The British, as they chased Washington's army out of New Jersey, had deliberately avoided combat, as if the final destruction of the rebel force was not worth the expenditure of men and gunpowder. A German mercenary observed that British forces, as they approached the Delaware River, seemed to move just slow enough to allow Washington to slip across the river unhindered.[36]

The Howes were focused not on squashing the remnants of the Continental Army, but on finding the best way to feed and house their own men for the winter and on securing territory so that Loyalists—assumed to be the true majority in America—could come out of hiding, assert themselves, and seize the reins of local authority.[37]

Meanwhile, in New England, Rhode Island was coming under British control thanks to the Royal Navy. As General Howe was sweeping Washington out of New Jersey, the British fleet was sailing from New York to Newport. There, British and German troops seized the city without a fight. Conveniently for the British, the harbor at Newport was superior to that of New York for winter anchoring thanks to the warm waters of the Gulf Stream, which flowed closer to New England than to New York, making the climate of Newport relatively mild and its harbor less likely to be clogged with ice.[38]

In New Jersey, after Washington was evicted from the state, the British scattered their forces in 17[39] small garrisons along a 77-mile line from Burlington to the Hackensack River,[40] the narrow central part of the state where most people lived.

Each garrison in turn set up further outposts and sent out patrols. The idea was to be visible so that Loyalists felt secure. The garrisons were to obtain most of their requirements—such as firewood, flour, grain, and forage—from nearby farms. Payment was supposed to be offered for everything. This occupation initially met little resistance. Indeed, as Washington had lamented, many Americans seemed all too eager to abandon the rebel cause.

Over the winter, the Howes hoped to demonstrate virtual British control over three states—New York, Rhode Island, and New Jersey. If by spring those three states were clearly outside rebel control, the Howes would have sufficient leverage to impose a peace deal to restore all of America to colonial status under the king's authority. Already the most vital parts of New York State—New York City and adjacent areas—were in British hands.

***

As delegates in Baltimore got back down to business on December 20, 1776, they had some catching up to do. They carried on briskly, according to Whipple of New Hampshire: "[Delegates] are now doing business with more spirit then they have for some time past. I hope the air of this place which is much purer then that of Phila. will brace up the weak nerves. I think it already has that affect."[41]

Early on, Congress gave Morris the help he wanted, dispatching two delegates, George Clymer of Pennsylvania and George Walton of Georgia, back to Philadelphia and giving the three of them "powers to execute such continental business as may be proper and necessary to be done at Philadelphia."[42] No one, apparently, complained that Morris was doing the work normally done by congressional committees. Perhaps, indeed, delegates were relieved to have Morris take over some of the tedium. Walton and Clymer proved useful to Morris, but Morris retained the lead role.[43]

We get a glimpse of Morris's frantic activities directing cargoes and ships from portions of just one report, from December 21, which he wrote to Hancock:

> I have determined to send 856 Blankets ... to Genl. Washington and have informed him they were imported for the use of the New Recruits. ... I have ordered the Fly, Capt Warner, down the Bay to watch the Enemies Ships & bring us word if they should quit that Station. I have sent an express across the Jerseys to Capt Baldwin of the Wasp to Cruize outward of them to give Notice to inward bound Ships, and have Stationed the Hornet, Capt Nicholson ... in Christeen Creeks Mouth to act in Conjunction with a large Galley of this State in defence of that Creek as there are many valuable Stores up it. I shall get the Sloop Independance hove down & some little damage she recd at Chincoteague repaired & then send her also to watch the Enemys Ships. ... I will order a good part of the Salt Provisions now in the Commissarys care to be carried up to Lancaster. ... I long to hear from you that I may judge whether Congress approve of these things which I have undertaken for the sake of serving my Country.[44]

The granting of authority to Morris and his committee—along with the handover of extraordinary power to Washington—reflected a shift in Congress. Wary of waste, corruption, and misuse of power, delegates before this time kept a stranglehold on everything under their control. Morris, for one, had recognized the problem and had chafed at the inefficiency of delegates trying to manage all and sundry, as well as set policies. In his view, delegates just didn't have the expertise or time to both craft policies and put them in motion:

> Long as that respectable body [Congress] persist in the attempt to execute as well as to deliberate on their business it never will be done as it ought & this has been urged many & many a time by myself & others but some of them dont Like to part with power or to pay others for doing what they cannot do themselves.[45]

Now, handing off responsibilities was in fashion. Congress soon appointed a committee, which included Morris, to "prepare a plan for the better conducting the executive business of Congress, by boards composed of persons, not members of Congress."[46] How Morris, in Philadelphia, was supposed to work with other members of this committee in Baltimore was not spelled out.

Also, early on in Baltimore, delegates took up Washington's polite but firm refusal to deny the "false and malicious report" about Congress leaving Philadelphia. Recognizing that the snub had likely saved delegates from acute embarrassment, they solemnly voted to approve Washington's "conduct in not publishing in general orders the resolve of Congress of the 11 instant."[47]

Having expanded Washington's authority, and now waving away the general's polite rebuff of Congress, delegates demonstrated their continued faith in their leading general, despite his failures. How far could they trust him?

Washington soon had the answer: as far as Washington wanted to go. A few days after settling in, Congress received a request from Washington to further expand his authority beyond those powers just granted a few weeks before. The needs were urgent, he explained, and the communications to and from Baltimore—about 140 miles away—too slow: "[T]he present exigency of our Affairs will not admit of delay either in Council or the Field." Washington knew this was a delicate subject:

> It may be said, that this is an application for powers, that are too dangerous to be intrusted. I can only add, that desperate diseases, require desperate remedies, and with truth declare, that I have no lust after power but wish with as much fervency as any man upon this wide extended Continent for an Opportunity of turning the Sword into a ploughshare.[48]

About the same time, Congress received a plea from General Greene, one of Washington's most trusted commanders. Greene argued that with enlistments expiring, a new army was needed, and Washington needed "full Power to take such measures as he may find necessary" to pull together that force: "Time will not admit nor Circumstances allow of a Reference to Congress. The Fate of War is so uncertain, dependent on so many Contingencies. A Day, nay an Hour is so important in the crisis of publick Affairs that it would be folly to wait for Relief from the deliberative Councils of Legislative Bodies."

Greene assured Congress that Washington would not violate the bounds of his expanded authority: "There never was a man that might be more safely trusted."[49]

Congress obeyed like a spaniel, putting in Washington's lap all that he wanted. Proclaiming "perfect reliance on the wisdom, vigour, and uprightness of General Washington," delegates bestowed on the general "full, ample, and complete powers to raise and collect together, in the most speedy and effectual manner, from any or all of these United States" a standing army of up to 76,000 men. The recruitment blueprint was a fantasy—the size of the army in 1777 would not reach 40,000. Furthermore, Washington had Congress's blessing to "take, wherever he may be, whatever he may want for the use of the army, if the inhabitants will not sell it." He could strip the countryside of whatever he needed provided he offered a "reasonable price." Also, he had carte blanche to arrest anyone "disaffected to the American cause."[50]

Delegates felt compelled to explain themselves with a circular letter to the states:

> Ever Attentive to the Security of Civil Liberty, Congress would not have Consented to the Vesting of such Powers ... to the Continental Commander in Chief, if the Scituation of Publick Affairs did not Require at this Crisis a Decision and Vigour, which Distance and Numbers Deny to Assemblies far Remov'd from each other, and from the immediate Seat of War.[51]

This expanded authority had a time limit: six months. Still, it was astonishing that no one in Congress seems to have stood up to oppose it. According to Whipple of New Hampshire, the measure "was thot absolutely necessary for the salvation of America."[52] Even Samuel Adams, the delegate most likely to be horrified at such a concentration of power, found the action necessary.[53] John Adams, another who might have been expected to oppose the measure, was away in Massachusetts at the time of the vote. But later he defended it and scoffed at critics: "Congress never thought of making him dictator, or of giving him a sovereignty."[54]

***

Congress bestowed these extraordinary powers on Washington before learning of his amazing feats in New Jersey as the year closed in. The size of his force for the moment had ballooned to about 6,000 men—thanks to the addition of some militiamen, Lee's troops, and another detachment.[55] But many of these men would likely head home after their enlistments expired come January 1. Washington knew his army might shrink to 1,400 men or fewer in the new year if not replenished with new recruits.[56] He had to do something with his army now or he might never have another opportunity, and he needed a morale-boosting victory to have a chance of attracting new men to replace the departing soldiers. Washington's military advisers had the same idea. In a letter, Joseph Reed—the same Joseph Reed who apparently earlier grumbled with Charles Lee about Washington's indecisiveness—told Washington that he had no choice but to seize the initiative: "[O]ur Cause is desperate & hopeless if we do not take the Oppy of the Collection of Troops at present to strike some Stroke. Our Affairs are hasting fast to Ruin if we do not retrieve them by some happy Event. Delay with us is now equal to a total Defeat."[57]

The notion of "some happy Event" seemed ludicrous, but perhaps not wholly far-fetched. Washington was heartened by the reports that the revolutionary cause, seemingly at its lowest ebb, was reviving. He knew a vigorous recruiting effort was paying dividends. These were not short-term recruits, but men who, lured with bounties and promises of land, signed up for three years or the duration of the war.[58] While most of these new recruits would not be available until the next year, recruiting success suggested that even in this dark moment, the wellspring of Patriot zeal still flowed.

Also, and more significantly, a Patriot uprising had at last caught fire in New Jersey. The British march across the state had met little opposition from ordinary people. Indeed, in some places, such as Hackensack, Loyalists came out to welcome the soldiers as liberators. But both British and German troops wore out their welcome quickly, with widespread looting, pillaging, and destruction everywhere they went. Even those Hackensack Loyalists found themselves plundered by soldiers who saw no distinction between rebellious and loyal Americans.[59] German women, who accompanied the German soldiers, also took part in the wholesale pilfering. A diarist told of a certain Mr. Cooke and his encounter with Germans in Crosswicks, New Jersey:

> The Hessians had taken every shirt he had except the one on his back; which had been their general practice wherever they have been. They have taken hogs, sheep, horses and cows, everywhere: even children have been stripped of their clothes—in which business the hessian women are the most active—in short the abuse of the inhabitants is beyond description.[60]

General Howe had men hanged for plundering, but even that didn't stop it. Washington likewise issued orders against marauding, and he too couldn't halt the theft of and destruction of civilian property. But the scale and severity on the American side paled by comparison with the misdeeds on the part of the British and German troops. In the wake of their looting and theft—and with the spread of many reports of rapes—this region, known for its lukewarm attitude toward independence, was now boiling with Patriotic fury. Civilians rose up and fought back. Armed bands roamed and ambushed isolated British messengers, attacked foraging soldiers, and fired at sentries. British troops were wary of traveling except in large groups.[61]

Near Trenton, now occupied by a German garrison of 1,500 men,[62] a band of New Jersey militiamen attacked enemy outposts and foraging parties. As a result, messengers carrying dispatches from Trenton went with escorts of 100 men. Meanwhile, another group of militiamen, these from Pennsylvania, crossed the Delaware again and again by boat to raid an outpost near Trenton and then dash back across the river.⁶³ These pesky militias were wearing on the German garrison at Trenton, where morale was slipping and anxiety rising.

Washington knew of these attacks and could guess that the weary and frazzled Germans at Trenton might be vulnerable. It was isolated from the other British posts, the nearest a half-day's march away. After so many weeks of retreat, Washington planned an attack, with Trenton as the target. The apt watchword for the operation: "Victory or Death."⁶⁴

CHAPTER 26

Violent, Seditious, Treasonable

Just before the plan was to be set in motion, a copy of Paine's first new series of pamphlets, *The American Crisis*, arrived in the American camp. Printers in Philadelphia would churn out 18,000 copies. Other printers in other colonies would eagerly reprint this and the other essays from the famous author. As with *Common Sense*, Paine took no profit from this work.[1] As with *Common Sense*, *The American Crisis* stoked patriotism. A Tory sympathizer in Philadelphia, after hearing an essay read to her, described it in her diary as "a most violent, seditious, treasonable paper, [written] purposely to inflame the minds of the people & spirit them on to rebellion, calling the King a sottish, stupid, stubborn, worthless, brutish man."[2]

Washington ordered this first essay read aloud to his men. It began:[3]

> THESE are the times that try men's souls. The summer soldier and the sunshine patriot will, in this crisis, shrink from the service of his country; but he that stands it now, deserves the love and thanks of man and woman. Tyranny, like hell, is not easily conquered; yet we have this consolation with us, that the harder the conflict, the more glorious the triumph. What we obtain too cheap, we esteem too lightly: it is dearness only that gives every thing its value. Heaven knows how to put a proper price upon its goods; and it would be strange indeed if so celestial an article as FREEDOM should not be highly rated.[4]

According to Washington's plan, the general would lead some 2,400 men 10 miles to a place where the men and 18 guns would be ferried across the Delaware River at sunset. They would then march in the dark 9 miles and attack the Germans from the west an hour before dawn.[5] Two other American forces—amounting to 2,600 men—were to cross the river as well, but at other locations. One of those units was supposed to approach Trenton from the south. The other was assigned to cut off roads, and thus block more distant British garrisons from rescuing the Germans.[6]

From the moment the operation began, on Christmas Day, it appeared doomed. Wicked weather—first rain, then sleet, then snow—lashed at Washington's men as they fumbled at the crossing place with flat-bottomed scows meant for carrying iron ore. As they stumbled in the snow, time slipped away. At almost four in the morning, they were across the river and ready to march. By then, on account of the storm, many of the muskets were too wet to be of use.[7] Meanwhile, the other Americans who were supposed to be part of the attack remained on the Pennsylvania side of the river, stymied by the weather. Washington and his men would have to manage alone.

As it happened, the fierce weather that wrecked Washington's plans proved an asset once he and his men were on the New Jersey side of the Delaware and marching toward Trenton. The storm made the Germans less wary and also muffled the clatter of the approaching rebel army.[8]

Washington got lucky too. Unbeknownst to him, German commanders had received a vague warning that the Americans were planning an attack. Then, also unbeknownst to Washington, a band of up to 50 New Jersey militiamen did just that—they raided a German outpost near Trenton at about sunset,[9] as Washington's operation was getting under way. The German garrison in Trenton responded to the alarm, but not before the Americans vanished back into the woods. German commanders assumed this was the attack they were warned about. Satisfied that there would be no more attacks that night, they told the men to put their weapons aside and return to quarters.[10]

Thus, that night, while the Germans were certainly not drunk on Christmas cheer, contrary to the mythology surrounding that day's events, they were caught off guard. Everyone was on duty, except for the sick, and the outposts were well guarded.[11] But because of the storm and the raid earlier in the evening, they were less alert than usual. When the Americans attacked, most Germans were nestled in their quarters, emerging in confusion to face American muskets on three sides. In less than an hour, the battle was over. The Americans captured a thousand men and much equipment. The American dead numbered just three, including one man who froze to death.[12]

Washington, according to his original plan, hoped to continue the offensive and march on to attack Princeton and New Brunswick. But without the support of the other American soldiers still on the Pennsylvania side of the Delaware, that plan was abandoned. He might have stayed in Trenton, but with the enemy nearby, it was safer to recross the river with his prisoners and exhausted men so that the Americans had the river between them and the aroused British. Getting back across the Delaware was almost as tricky as the original crossing, but Washington, his men, and prisoners finally were back in camp on the west side of the river by noon of December 27. Many of the men had been on the move for 50 hours with little or no sleep, marching 40 miles, mostly in miserable weather.[13]

In Baltimore, Congress got an inkling of the victory by December 30.[14] Official word from Washington followed the next day. The mood of Congress perked up. "[T]he agreable News from Genl Washington has given new life & Spirits to every body here,"[15] wrote James Smith, delegate from Pennsylvania. Soon, adorning the room where Congress met was a silken green Hessian battle standard featuring an image of a lion with a dagger in its right paw.[16]

In Philadelphia, delegates Clymer and Walton wrote cheerfully to Hancock: "We had yesterday the pleasure to see the Hessian Prisoners paraded in Front Street. They formed a line of two Deep up & down Front Street from Market to Walnut Street, and most people seemed very angry they shou'd ever think of running away from such a Set of Vagabonds."[17]

Now seemed to be the time for Washington to settle in for the winter, which is exactly what he planned to do until he learned of disorder among British troops at two New Jersey posts.[18] Washington seized the moment and led yet another crossing of the Delaware. On December 31, he and his men were back in Trenton. That was the day he received the resolutions from Congress giving him extraordinary powers.[19] It was also the day enlistments of many men were set to expire. Desperate to maintain his army, he offered a $10 bounty to men willing to serve another six weeks. Some 1,300 agreed,[20] but only if paid in hard money, not the dubious Continental notes. Washington had to dip into his own pocket, promising some of his personal fortune.[21]

With those 1,300 Continentals along with 3,500 Pennsylvania militiamen, Washington faced 8,000 British troops under Charles Cornwallis gathering 12 miles away at Princeton.[22] Not waiting for Washington to attack, Cornwallis advanced toward Trenton on January 2. Early in the march, American pickets sniped at the enemy from the roadside and then vanished into the woods. Farther along, other American fighters stood firm along the road, fired, and remained to fire again, despite being well outnumbered.[23]

The Americans failed to stop the British, but slowed them down enough that only an hour of daylight remained by the time Cornwallis and his men approached the main body of Washington's force. All that remained for the British was to cross a creek, but this proved to be a bloody fiasco. After several assaults with the Americans firing down on them, the British failed to complete the crossing, staining the creek red, and leaving the bank and a bridge strewn with bodies. By the time evening fell, the British had lost some 500 men killed or wounded.[24] Cornwallis, however, was confident of success in the morning. Washington, with the British in front of him and the icy Delaware to his rear, could not escape, or so the British commander thought.

Washington then conjured a disappearing act like the one back on Long Island. Orders went out to keep campfires ablaze in the bitter weather. Then, as the dozing British assumed the Americans were tucked in for the night, Washington's men slipped away, not back across the Delaware, but north along a back road unknown to Cornwallis, but familiar to Washington's assistant, Reed, who had lived in Trenton and studied at Princeton.[25] Having slipped the trap, Washington led his men around the sleeping British and then on toward Princeton. There, Washington's force pounced on 700 Regulars preparing to march to Trenton to reinforce Cornwallis. The brief, fierce battle on the edge of the village led to more fighting in the town and finally to another stunning American triumph: 450 Redcoats were killed, wounded, or taken prisoner.[26]

Finally, Washington closed the book on the campaign for the season, leading his men off to Morristown, about 40 miles away. With surrounding hills for protection,[27] Morristown was a safe winter refuge.[28] There were other advantages: it was in the middle of an agricultural region from which to draw food for his own army while denying it from the enemy. Morristown also made a good perch for watching and threatening the main British outposts around New York City.[29]

***

Thanks to Washington's daring and a lot of luck, the Continental Army had dodged obliteration, Philadelphia for the moment was secure, and swaths of New Jersey were back under rebel control. North Carolina's Hooper hailed Washington as "the Greatest Man on Earth."[30]

The British, for the moment, had been stymied, but a satisfying peace was still a misty dream. The challenges facing Congress seemed insoluble. Chief among them was the soaring cost of the war. A new army had to be raised and equipped to replace the many Continental soldiers whose extended enlistments would soon expire.

So far, through to about the end of 1776, the war had been financed in large part rather miraculously by the currency, the Continental dollar. The paper dollars had simply been printed, distributed to the military and others, and spent, first mainly for soldiers' wages and then increasingly for supplies. Generally, soldiers, merchants, farmers, and shopkeepers accepted the money. Congress, meanwhile, overwhelmed by the demands of the army, churned out three more batches of dollars that year, adding about $19 million to the $6 million issued in 1775.[31]

All these bills in theory would come back to Congress years down the road after the states collected them in the form of taxes and forwarded the bills to Philadelphia as their share of the war debt. But that process wouldn't begin for years—not before 1779. For the moment, few taxes were being collected, certainly none by Congress, and not much by the states. In many states, amid the confusion that went with the transition from royal to independent governments, the collection of taxes stopped. In some cases, the embryonic state governments, hoping to establish popular support and knowing that taxation would never win people's hearts, were reluctant to collect any taxes.[32] In some places, the war itself disrupted tax collection. The conflict also unsettled normal business. In New England, fisheries were disrupted. Middle Atlantic states could no longer trade readily with the West Indies, while Southern states were cut off from their usual markets for tobacco, lumber, and naval stores, such as tar, pitch, and turpentine.[33] The conflict interrupted exports and imports, so their related duties went unpaid. Men who might otherwise be paying property taxes set aside their occupations to go to war. And of course, no local taxes could be collected in areas controlled by the British. As a result, in 1775 and 1776, states collected almost no taxes at all.[34]

By the end of 1776, some $25 million in Continental dollars were circulating[35] and nothing yet was being done to tax those bills out of circulation.

Robert Morris, writing in December 1776, noted that the value of two Continental dollars had slipped to one silver dollar. Depreciation of the currency, Morris moaned, "threatens instant and total ruin to the American cause, unless some radical cure is applied, and that speedily."[36] He noted that part of the reason for the dollar's dip in value was "the success and near approach of the enemy,"[37] which, along with raising doubts about the future of Congress, undermined confidence in the dollar. But mostly, he blamed the "prodigious emissions of paper money."[38]

Delegates shared Morris's alarm. One observed: "Another emission of money will in my opinion be a public fraud which no State-necessity can justify. The loss of two or three provinces would not hurt our cause half so much as the news of our bankruptcy."[39]

The desperate delegates brainstormed: how about soliciting loans from Patriot investors? Thus, in October 1776, Congress authorized bills of credit. An investor could loan the government money for three years and get an annual return of 4 percent. The lender would give Congress Continental dollars and receive a loan office certificate with a blank space for the lender's name to be written in by hand. A blank was also provided for the signature of a witness.[40]

The reasons for borrowing in this way, rather than just printing more money, are not clear. Probably, delegates felt that it would not be inflationary—Congress could spend the borrowed dollars and leave the total supply of dollars in circulation unchanged.[41]

As investments, these bills of credit were not intended to compete with the Continental dollar as currency. For that reason, the lowest denomination of the bills was $300.[42] Congress hoped to draw in $5 million with this scheme.

In November 1776, there came another brainstorm: how about a lottery? Here, maybe, was a way to painlessly "tax" Americans. Patriotic citizens might be willing pay a little money for a chance to win a pile of money.

Congress thus authorized a lottery and crafted a plan of administering it. The dizzying structure of the proposed lottery started with sales of up to 100,000 tickets at $10 each in "ready money"—which could include currency issued by states—and the first drawing on March 1, 1777. If fully successful, the lottery could bring in nearly $7 million within a year.[43]

Some delegates themselves bought lottery tickets. We know Richard Henry Lee did for himself and some of his children. In a journal he carried in his vest pocket, he wrote the name of each of his daughters and the numbers of the lottery tickets he bought for each one.[44]

Eventually, the returns from the bills of credit and the lottery would prove disappointing. In the case of the bills of credit, an interest rate of 4 percent just wasn't alluring enough for investors.[45] As for the lottery, sales of tickets never lived up to expectations and the scheme's administration, while largely honest, was fraught with delays and complications. In the end, what Congress brought in through the lottery was mostly offset by costs—prize money, fees to managers, costs of rent and advertising, and losses from counterfeiting and cheating by subagents. The real profit—calculated in hard currency—amounted to less than $100,000.[46]

Meanwhile, Congress groped for other financial life rafts, such as France. Only a few days after delegates settled in Baltimore, they authorized their commissioners in Paris "to borrow on the faith of the thirteen United States a sum not exceeding two millions sterling, for a term not less than ten years." What were the chances that France would lend good money to such a wobbly enterprise as the Continental Congress? Congress hoped a return of up to 6 percent would pique the interest of the French government.[47]

Then in January 1777, delegates debated yet another strategy: price controls. Congress could ask states to stabilize prices by fixing them and punishing anyone who sold goods for more than allowed.

The idea was not new to Congress, which had at one time suggested maximum prices for coffee, tea, sugar, salt, and other imports.[48] Now New England revived the notion. In the fall of 1776, Massachusetts was sufficiently alarmed about soaring prices to call for a meeting of New England states in December to devise some joint action. The states' concern was not so much the Continental dollar but the soaring inflation overwhelming state currencies that also circulated. With Connecticut at first declining the invitation, the prospects for this "convention" were doubtful. Then, in early December, a British fleet with eight men-of-war and 80 transports appeared off New London, Connecticut.[49] With this threat just off the coast, and with the Continental Army too weak and far away to help, Connecticut was suddenly very interested in this convention, now recast as a meeting for coordinating military readiness in New England, with time set aside to also talk about how to rein in runaway prices.

On Christmas Day—the day of Washington's victory at Trenton—delegates from the four New England states—Massachusetts, New Hampshire, Rhode Island, and Connecticut—met in Providence. By that time, British warships were anchored nearby at Newport, with the British military in possession of the city, having expelled some 600 Rhode Island troops.[50]

This convention was organized much like the Continental Congress. Connecticut sent four delegates, while the other three states sent three each.[51] Its stated purpose was as follows:

> [T]he expediency of raising and appointing an army for the more immediate defense of the New England States against the threatened invasion as well as for the more general defense in the common cause, and of such regulations as may be necessary to support the credit of our currencies, to prevent the oppressing [of] the soldiers and inhabitants by extravagant prices, and in general of every measure to expedite the raising and appointing an army ... for common defense.

As if to close off suggestions that delegates were defying the Continental Congress, the convention noted that their activities would be pursued only "until the whole subject matter can be laid before the Hon'ble Continental Congress of the United States of America and measures taken and directions given by them thereon."[52]

This was like a mini-Continental Congress, though not intended as a challenge to Congress. Governor Jonathan Trumbull of Connecticut, a leader in pushing for the convention, wrote to Hancock to explain the gathering: "I presume that under these circumstances, when the least delay in preparation for defense might be attended with fatal consequences, immediate self-preservation will not only excuse the procedure, but obtain the approbation of Congress thereon."[53]

The talk in Providence focused first on military measures. It directed 6,000 troops, a mix of state militias and Continental troops scattered around New England, to march in defense of Rhode Island. Then delegates took on the currency problem and sensibly agreed to stop printing money, to beef up tax collection, and if necessary, to borrow. Delegates also agreed on a schedule of prices for goods ranging from stockings, shoes, and flannels, to rum, coffee, cheese, butter, molasses, salt, pork, and wheat. Tough penalties were established for sales above those prices. The schedule also fixed wages for summertime farm labor and ordered a ceiling on profits from imported goods. Despite the costs and risks to merchants of getting past British sea patrols, such imports as woolen goods should not be sold at a rate of more than "two hundred and seventy-five pounds sterling for what costs one hundred pounds sterling in Europe."[54]

Before adjourning in early January, the convention dealt with a raft of other issues, such as wages for troops, privateering, and the postal service, and even found time to designate the last Wednesday in January as a "Day of Fasting, Public Humiliation and Prayer."[55]

Following the convention, Trumbull sent Congress a report that triggered three weeks of chatter as time allowed over issues the convention brought to the fore, including the wisdom of price controls.

In Philadelphia, a motion was put forward to recommend that states follow New England's example and set prices. Some delegates felt a broad attempt to control prices was urgently needed. "The mines of Peru would not support a war at the present high price of the necessaries of life," said Samuel Chase of Maryland. "Your Soldiers cannot live on their pay. It must be raised unless we limit the price of the cloathing & other articles necessary for them."[56]

Others protested that controls would never work. Pennsylvania's Rush, according to his own notes, said the measure was a recipe for failure that would only diminish Congress's shrinking stature:

> Consider sir the danger of failing in this experiment. The Salvation of this continent depends upon the Authority of this congress being held as sacred as the cause of liberty itself. Suppose we should fail producing the effects we wish for by the resolution before you. Have we any

charecter to spare? Have we committed no mistakes in the management of the public Affairs of America? We have sir. It becomes us therefore to be careful of the remains of our Authority & charecter. ... The extortion we complain of arises only from the excessive quantity of our money.[57]

John Witherspoon of New Jersey similarly argued that controls were doomed to fail: "Remember laws are not almighty. It is beyond the power of despotic princes to regulate the price of goods." James Wilson of Pennsylvania agreed, adding that if controls actually succeeded, they would paralyze the war effort: "Foreign trade is absolutely necessary to enable us to carry on the war. This resolution will put an end to it, for it will hang as a dead weight upon all the operations of external commerce."[58]

In the end, Congress gave a tepid blessing to New England's plan for regulating prices and then recommended that other states "adopt such measures, as they shall think most expedient to remedy the evils occasioned by the present fluctuating and exorbitant prices of the articles aforesaid."[59]

Congress also called for regional meetings of state representatives for this purpose to take place in York, Pennsylvania, and Charleston, South Carolina. That meeting in York came off, but the plan it produced failed. The meeting in the South never happened.[60]

Meanwhile, in New England, those price controls were popular at first, at least in Massachusetts. But soon merchants started to prefer barter or a combination of cash and goods. A salt merchant, for example, openly advertised a preference for buyers who "stow a few turkeys or fowls in the corner of their bags." By summer, another New England convention recommended price controls be removed.[61] But the idea of price controls would come back to life again and again in New England, in Congress, and elsewhere in America as the problem of inflation worsened.

CHAPTER 27

Great and Interesting Consequences

Despite the efforts of Trumbull and others in Providence to demonstrate deference to Congress, some delegates in Baltimore harrumphed that the convention in New England had trod on Congress's toes. The convention had revived the issue of sovereignty: where did state authority end and congressional authority begin?

With a national union in its infancy, it was easy to imagine regional governments emerging and Congress withering away. In muddy, expensive Baltimore, Congress had already shriveled to 25 or fewer delegates, about half the number who had attended in Philadelphia.[1] When Congress abandoned Philadelphia and hit the road, some delegates simply headed for home, and states had been slow to send replacements. Letters of delegates from this period are peppered with pleas to states to send delegates as well as gripes about overwork and the failure of some states to be properly represented. North Carolina's Hooper wrote: "I lament ... the very small representation which America presents in Congress. The members will soon be reduced to the number of 22, how unequal to the importance of its councils!" The states with the poorest attendance were New York, Delaware, and—amazingly—Maryland. These states, Hooper wrote, "may almost as well desert the Cause as so lamely support it by their appearance in its publick Councils."[2]

On January 24, 1777, Congress authorized Hancock to send scolding letters to New York and Delaware "requesting them immediately to send to Congress representations of their respective states, and to provide, that for the future, applications of this kind may be rendered unnecessary."[3]

It appears that on at least one day that month, January 27, Congress did no business because it lacked a quorum.[4] Pennsylvania's Benjamin Rush worried that the New England gathering set an alarming precedent. He recorded in his notes what he said to his fellow delegates:

> I think the meeting is full of great and interesting consequences, and should be regarded with a serious & jealous eye. Their business was chiefly continental, and therefore they usurped the powers of congress as much as four counties would usurp the powers of legislation in a state shd. they attempt to tax themselves.[5]

Delegates debated about whether Congress needed to approve and thus validate the New England meeting. John Adams had no quarrel with what the New England convention did, and he acknowledged that they had a perfect right to meet. But because they touched on "continental" issues, congressional approval was needed. Samuel Adams, like his cousin, was untroubled by what happened at the convention. Indeed, he found the action admirable. But he disagreed with John about whether the meeting needed approval from Congress. As far as he was concerned, Congress had no business questioning the meeting: "That a right to assemble upon all occasions to consult measures for promoting liberty & happiness was the priviledge of freemen." Richard Henry Lee sided with Samuel; Congress had yet to agree on confederation, so "no law of the union infringed."[6]

Meanwhile, delegates dispatched other congressional business with astonishing efficiency. Samuel Adams remarked about how well Congress carried on away from the distractions of Philadelphia: "[W]e have done more important Business in three Weeks than we had done, and I believe, should have done, at Philadelphia, in six Months."[7]

It helped that Morris and his committee in Philadelphia was shouldering much of the work. "I believe we dispatch about ⅞ths of that damn'd trash that used to take up ¾ths of the debates in Congress; and give them no trouble about the matter,"[8] wrote Morris.

North Carolina's Hooper wrote to Morris about delegates' high regard for the financier: "Congress seems unanimously sensible of the obligations which they owe you. And you may boast of being the only man whom they all agree to speak & I really believe think well of."[9] Hancock was no less exuberant praising and thanking Morris: "I can assure you your whole Conduct since our Flight is highly approv'd, & happy I am that you Remain'd. Many agreeable Consequences have Resulted from it, and your continu'd Exertions will be productive of great good."[10]

While in Baltimore, Congress stabbed at the sticky problem of military promotions. The Continental Army established in the wake of Lexington and Concord was just a collection of colonial militias. Congress appointed Washington and other top generals, but the various colonial governments named all officers below the rank of general. Since independence, those governments were now state governments, but the structure of the army endured. Below the rank of general, neither Washington—in control of the main army—nor Schuyler—commander of the Northern Army—nor Congress had the authority to name officers or make promotions.[11] Each state government separately named and promoted officers.

Washington hated this system from the start, when he struggled to bring order to the motley collection of men attempting to drive the British from Boston back in 1775. He recognized that any volunteers who came from outside New England to fight alongside the New Englanders would never have a chance of promotion over local candidates. He wanted Congress to take on the job of granting all field-grade commissions, which would be doled out strictly on merit. When Congress took up the question in October that year, New England delegates dug in against any effort by Congress to grab the authority to appoint officers. Reasons varied. Connecticut's Dyer argued that New Englanders would not serve under anyone they did not know. Others were wary of a large military force established in one colony but independent of the control of that colony.[12]

In the end, Congress seized responsibility for naming all officers in the army above the rank of captain. However, in practice, Congress mostly simply rubber-stamped recommendations forwarded by the individual colonies.[13] In effect, the colonies, and later the states, thus still pulled the strings on who were named officers and who got promotions.

Of the various flaws in this plan, the most obvious was the lack of input from people who actually saw officers in action. By September 1776, Congress put in place a clumsy way to involve the top military man, Washington, in weeding out the nincompoops among the officers without stripping states of their say in making promotions. According to instructions from Congress, Washington was to forward to Congress his recommendations of officers "he is desirous of having again engaged in the Service." Congress would pass that list on to the appropriate delegates, who would in turn send that on to the appropriate state or states, along with encouragement for states to appoint "Gentlemen of Education to military offices as a Measure absolutely necessary for saving the Country."[14]

Now, in early 1777, the issue of military promotions landed again in the lap of Congress when Washington told delegates that they needed to appoint three major generals and 10 brigadiers.[15] Delegates went back and forth about principles Congress should apply. Should officers be appointed from each state according to the number of men each state contributed to the army? That was rejected. Should officers be promoted based on seniority? That was rejected too.[16]

Finally, Congress established a policy so malleable that it was no policy at all: "[I]n voting for general officers, a due regard shall be had to the line of succession, the merit of the persons proposed, and the quota of troops raised, and to be raised, by each State."[17] In other words, Congress could promote according to seniority, or merit, or a state's contribution, or whatever it pleased.

This fuzzy policy would mean trouble, as at least one delegate predicted. It was, he urged, better to have one rule adopted and followed: "Officers hold their honor the most dear of any thing. Setting them aside when they were entitled to promotion would wound that honor very sorely."[18]

He was right, and among the first so wounded was Benedict Arnold, a brigadier general and hero. He, along with Ethan Allen, had helped direct the daring assault on Ticonderoga early in the war. He had also led the bold mission through the Maine wilderness to the outskirts of Quebec City. On the last day of 1775, Arnold fought in the futile attack there, where he suffered a wound to his right knee.[19] As

American forces retreated from Canada, Arnold was the last American on the last boat heading south on June 18.[20] Among his last acts before boarding was shooting his own horse.[21] Then, in late 1776, he led the effort to cobble together a fleet on Lake Champlain. He and his brave little navy, by slowing the British advance south, prevented the enemy from retaking Ticonderoga that season, possibly thereby saving the infant nation.[22]

He had led and bled for his country with extraordinary courage, energy, and initiative. He was also often reckless, certainly thin skinned, and difficult to manage. But the men he commanded loved him. In late 1776, cannon salutes greeted him when he rode through the towns of Connecticut, his home state. Proud veterans of the march to Quebec wept as they came to embrace him.[23] He expected and deserved to be promoted to major general.

But Arnold was passed over in favor of men with a lower rank, less experience, and fewer accomplishments. He was embittered, doubly so because about this time the 16-year-old girl he was wooing (he was a 36-year-old widower) dumped him in favor of an apothecary's apprentice.[24]

Mystified and offended,[25] Arnold complained to Washington that Congress evidently wanted him to quit: "Their promoting Junior Officers to the Rank of Major Generals, I view as a very Civil way of requesting my resignation, as unqualified for the Office I hold."[26] Further, he asserted that "my being Superceeded must be View'd as an Implicit impeachment of my Character."[27]

Washington was no less puzzled by Congress's decision. "I confess I was surprized when I did not see your Name in the list of Major Generals," Washington wrote. He attempted to dissuade Arnold from demanding a review of his performance: "As no particular Charge is alledged agt you, I do not see upon what Ground you can demand a Court of Enquiry." Washington relayed his own information about why Congress passed over Arnold: "[A]s Connecticut had already two Majors General it was their full share. I confess this is a strange mode of reasoning, but it may serve to shew you, that the promotion which was due to your seniority was not overlooked for want of Merit in you."[28]

Indeed, it was strange. While Congress could have used merit or seniority in choosing its major generals, it fell back to the old practice of doling out promotions according to geography. Arnold was evidently passed over because his state already had its quota of major generals. At least that seemed to be the reason. Arnold suspected other factors, and he may have been right. While many of Arnold's men adored him, many officers and others found him despicable, some of them giving to Congress dubious reports about Arnold's alleged misdeeds. One especially sticky accusation was that, while in Canada, he illegally snatched army goods for his private use.[29] Nothing was proven, but the whiff of wrongdoing was in the air. Delegates may have been disinclined to promote a man so tainted. It also didn't help that, for all his heroics, Arnold failed at Quebec and most of the little navy was at the bottom of Lake Champlain. Delegates who only glanced at Arnold's record might not have appreciated his extraordinary abilities.

In a letter to Horatio Gates, Arnold grumbled about the injustice: "I cannot ... help thinking it extremely cruel to be judged and condemned without an opportunity of being heard or even knowing my crime or accuser. ... When I received a commission of brigadier I did not expect Congress had made me for their sport, or pastime, to displace, or disgrace whenever they thought proper."[30]

Many expected Arnold to resign, but he did not.

CHAPTER 28

Worst of All Possible Places

As weeks went on, delegates tested the limits of their imaginations to describe the awfulness of Baltimore. After some of their number fell ill, William Hooper, for one, thought being dead and buried might be better than being

> in this worst of all possible places. ... With one united voice we ascribe this Catalogue of Ills to this place. I declare to you the Congress presents such a scene of yellow death like faces, that you wou[ld] imagine Rhadamanthus [a judge of the dead in the Underworld, according to Greek mythology] had shifted his quarters & was holding Court in Baltimore. I believe were it the case he would soon be glad to get back to his friend Pluto's regions.[1]

Abraham Clark of New Jersey moaned about the prices for lodging, wine, rum, and maintaining a horse: "This is one of the most horrible places I have seen ... these people might be pictured with hooks on every finger sure to catch something if you come near them."[2] Meanwhile, William Whipple of New Hampshire groaned about the mud: "This place is so intolerable muddy there is no such thing as walking."[3]

Rush of Pennsylvania, for his part, complained about how isolated he felt: "We live here in a convent. We con[verse] only with One another. We are precluded from all opportunities of feeling the pulse of the public upon our measures. We rely upon the Committee of Philada. to feel it for us."[4]

As delegates grumbled, they also fretted about their personal affairs. Richard Henry Lee worried about his two sons being educated in England. He pleaded with his brother Arthur on the other side of the Atlantic: "I am exceedingly uneasy about my poor Boys & beg of you to get them to me in the quickest and safest manner."[5]

Facing financial ruin, New Jersey's Jonathan Dickinson Sergeant asked permission to quit Congress so as to "apply myself to some Business for the Support of my Family." He explained that

> my own private Circumstances have assumed rather a melancholy Complexion. ... The Loss of my House is the least part of my Misfortune, as my Attention to Politicks during these unhappy Times has at once superseded my Business & prevented the Collecting my Accounts 'till the greater part of my Debtors, it is to be feared, are either ruined or not to be found.[6]

Meanwhile, in distant homes, wives of delegates, relying on snippets of dated news, were left to wonder and worry about the fate of their husbands. Samuel Adams got a note from his wife about reports of British troops being so near Congress. His reply was stiff and patronizing:

> I have long known you to be possessd of much Fortitude of Mind. But you are a Woman, and one must expect you will now and then discover Timidity so natural to your Sex. I thank you, my dear, most cordially for the Warmth of Affection which you express on this Occasion, for your Anxiety for my Safety and your Prayers to God for my Protection.[7]

Connecticut's Oliver Wolcott, writing to his wife, Laura, was similarly formal but more tender:

> I feel the Warmest Wishes for your Welfare, and hope that it will please God to bestow upon you and our Children every Blessing. I am not able to give you the least Advice in the Conduct of any Business, your own Prudence in the Direction of it I have no doubt of. I can only Wish that the cares which must oppress you were less, but if the present Troubles shall terminate in the future Peace and Security of this Country (which I trust will be the Case) the present Evils and Inconveniences of Life ought to be borne with Cheerfullness.[8]

At last, Congress bid adieu to despised Baltimore. Delegates adjourned for the last time in the town on February 27, 1777, with instructions to gather again in Philadelphia at the State House on March 12.[9]

A shortage of wagons meant that some people had to be left behind in the scramble to get back to Philadelphia. Thus, Dolly Hancock, daughter Lydia, and other members of the Hancock household were still in Baltimore when she received a letter from John dated March 3, writing from "Mr. Godgraces" in Philadelphia, with details of his latest meal: "Dinner Serv'd up, Boil'd Beef, Roast Turkey, Ham, Roast Beef, Green Sallad, Goose Berry & Apple Tarts, Cheese, Apples &c. Baltime Punch, Wine &c."[10] The turkey, he noted, was so tough that he broke a tooth.

As the delegates returned to Philadelphia, they once again searched out accommodations. On Chestnut near Fourth, Hancock found a furnished house for himself and his family. At Fourth and Market, Samuel Adams took a room at "Mrs. Cheaseman's" place, operated by a widow who had buried four husbands.[11]

At Fifth and Market, delegates from Virginia and South Carolina returned to the establishment of Mary House and daughter Eliza Trist. At Third and Walnut, John Adams, as well as Connecticut's Wolcott and New Hampshire's Whipple, stayed in the home of the Duncans, a couple from Boston.[12]

The town the delegates returned to was not the one they had left. John Adams lamented to Abigail:

> This City is a dull Place, in Comparason of what it was. More than one half the Inhabitants have removed into the Country, as it was their Wisdom to do—the Remainder are chiefly Quakers as dull as Beetles. From these neither good is to be expected nor Evil to be apprehended. They are a kind of neutral Tribe, or the Race of the insipids.[13]

The assignment of getting back to Philadelphia in a timely way proved impossible for some members of Congress. Virginia's Mann Page found himself stuck in Baltimore on March 5, apparently with his wife, puzzling about how to get out: "I am left prettily in the lurch. Expecting that we were fixed at this place, I sent back our chariot and now do not know how to move my baggage. Wives are sometimes sad incumbrances."[14] But eventually, on March 12, enough delegates were present in Philadelphia to achieve a quorum, and Congress got back to work.[15]

Meanwhile, the military situation, in the wake of Washington's audacious feats in New Jersey, was hopeful indeed. The New Jersey militias that had so effectively pestered the British in late 1776 attacked over the winter months with greater ferocity and daring, capturing supply wagons and ambushing patrols.[16] Their successes inspired more men to join the militias and spawned more raids. John Adams was ecstatic: "The People of that Commonwealth, begin to raise their Spirits exceedingly, and to be firmer than ever. They are actuated by Resentment now, and Resentment coinciding with Principle is a very powerfull Motive."[17]

In Morristown, the arrival of new recruits couldn't offset the loss of men with enlistments expiring. The army at mid-March came to 2,500 men, fewer than Washington had in the doldrums of December. Washington used his little army to support the militia uprising. He understood that militias were unreliable, difficult to command, poorly trained, and often unwilling to fight except in their home regions. But he was also learning how to manage these farmers-turned-soldiers in the right circumstances. This was such a circumstance, and they proved their mettle. In a battle on January 20 near Somerset Courthouse, some 400 militiamen, along with 50 riflemen from Pennsylvania, took on 600 British troops and came away with 43 baggage wagons, 104 horses, 115 head of cattle, and several dozen sheep. The Americans lost no more than five men; the British at least 24.[18]

The British seemed paralyzed. Robert Morris summed up: "[T]he Enemy have since Christmass lost so many Horses, are in such want of Forage, and their remaining Cavalry so worn down, that the defects in this department alone wou'd render any Movement of their Main body impossible without strong reinforcements."

And the British difficulties in New Jersey would not end soon. With the spring thaw, the roads would turn to mud, making movement of food, fodder, and equipment nearly impossible. Morris wrote: "General Howe's situation somewhat resembles that of a strong Bull in Trammells, sensible of his own strength, he grows mad with rage & resentment when he finds himself deprived of the use of it."[19]

Thus, over the winter, the Americans gained in strength and confidence as the British vigor waned and morale plummeted. Richard Henry Lee was amazed, writing to Washington:

> I realy think that when the history of this winters Campaign comes to be understood, the world will wonder at its success on our part. With a force rather inferior to the enemy in point of numbers, and chiefly militia too, opposed to the best disciplined troops of Europe; to keep

these latter pent up, harrassed, and distressed—but more surprising still, to lessen their numbers some thousands by the sword and captivity! All this Sir must redound to your glory, and to the reputation of the few brave men under your command.[20]

By March, the British strategy of the previous year was in shreds. The British held New York and Rhode Island, but New Jersey, once arguably neutral or leaning Loyalist, was now mostly under Patriot control. John Adams stated:

> The Jersy Militia have done themselves the highest Honour, by turning out in such great Numbers, and with such Determined Resolution. This was altogether unexpected to the British and Hessian Gentry. They were persuaded that the People would be on their Side, or at least unactive but when they found Hundreds who had taken their Protections and their oaths of allegiance, in Arms against them, and with terrible Imprecations, vowing Vengeance, their Hearts sunck within them and they sneaked away in a Panic.[21]

The British failed in holding the state and protecting their Loyalist friends, and now their power was diminished. By the end of the winter, less than half of the men who had arrived in America to join Howe's army were still able to fight. Most were dead, wounded, missing, sick, or held by the Americans as prisoners.[22]

***

Arthur Lee in Paris, itching for a mission, set off for Madrid in early 1777. Since King Louis XVI had indicated that France would not enter the war on the side of the Americans without Spain entering as well, Lee reasoned it might be worth a try to go in person to Charles III of Spain to lobby for the American cause.[23]

This approach—pushing uninvited for diplomatic recognition and running roughshod over established protocols—came to be labelled "militia diplomacy." The term suggests that the American envoys in the European diplomatic world were like the American militia in the military realm—lacking experience and training, unfamiliar with conventions, flouting norms. The term stems from a comment from John Adams, who, during his turn as a diplomat later, defended unorthodox initiatives: "Your Veterans in Diplomaticks and in Affairs of State consider Us as a kind of Militia, and hold Us perhaps, as is natural, in some degree of Contempt, but wise Men know that Militia sometimes gain Victories over regular Troops, even by departing from the Rules."[24]

For its part, Congress seems never to have encouraged its diplomats to stray from the accepted diplomatic protocols.[25] As Pennsylvania's Wilson wrote: "In our Transactions with European States, it is certainly of Importance neither to transgress, nor to fall short of those Maxims, by which they regulate their Conduct toward one another."[26]

For his part, Franklin opposed any strategy that smacked of appearing like a boorish party-crasher. Better, he thought, to make like a shy damsel on a settee demurely awaiting an offer to dance. As he explained to Lee: "[A] Virgin State should preserve the Virgin Character, and not go about suitering for Alliances, but wait with decent Dignity for the applications of others."[27] Despite reservations, Franklin did not veto Lee's plan, and nor did Deane. Perhaps both were glad to get the annoying Arthur Lee out of their hair.[28]

Whatever the case, Lee in setting out for Spain had reason to think he would be welcomed. The Spanish ambassador in Paris had encouraged him to go.[29]

On his way to Spain, Lee detoured to Nantes to check in on Congress's commercial agent, Thomas Morris. Business affairs were a mess, Lee reported to Congress. To his brother Richard Henry, Arthur wrote that Thomas Morris was a drunk unworthy of employment at any European countinghouse.[30]

Arthur Lee went on from Nantes toward Spain and got as far as Burgos, 120 miles from Madrid. In Burgos, on March 4, he met with Spanish officials who advised him to turn around and return to France.[31] There was a new foreign minister in Spain, and he was determined not to annoy the British ambassador.[32]

Lee pleaded his case by pen. In a letter sent off to Madrid, he argued that, should Britain prevail in the contest with the Americans, it would use America against Spain and France. Now was a chance to chasten the British. The chance might not come again.[33]

The letter failed to win an invitation to Madrid. Spain would not openly recognize the rebel Americans. But Lee's efforts did win for Congress some secret aid. Permission was granted to direct munitions, blankets, and clothing to New Orleans and Havana, where the goods could be retrieved by American vessels. Lee also obtained an agreement on a joint American–Spanish expedition against the British at Pensacola in Florida.[34] An attack on Pensacola eventually took place on May 9, 1781. The Spanish captured the outpost from the British without American help.[35]

***

The Congress that returned to Philadelphia from Baltimore was not the one that left a few months before, and certainly not the one that boldly declared independence the previous July. In a letter to Washington in February, Robert Morris confessed his worries about the ebbing stature of Congress as so many capable men departed, replaced by less experienced men. In lamenting the loss of some of the best delegates, Morris listed 12 (including Franklin, Jay, Duane, Deane, Dickinson, but not Jefferson):

> [I]f great care is not taken, that Body, so respectable from the Nature of the appointment, the Importance of its objects, and the respectable Characters of its heretofore individual Members, will loose great part of its Weight & Consequences in the Eyes of our own People. ... [W]hat is to become of America & its cause if a constant fluctuation is to take place amongst its Counsellors?[36]

High turnover would continue to be a chronic problem for Congress as delegates periodically dashed back home to attend to personal affairs or, often enough, immerse themselves in state politics. Another problem was low representation, which meant more committee work for the remaining delegates. Congress became so frustrated at low attendance that in February, delegates toyed with several ideas to force states to send more delegates. A rule was proposed denying a state's vote if that state was represented by fewer than three delegates. The lone delegate from North Carolina bristled that such a requirement was unreasonable. He argued that it was up to each state to determine the adequacy of its representation. The majority agreed; the idea failed.

That lone North Carolina delegate was Thomas Burke, a newcomer to Congress who made up for his inexperience with vigor, imagination, and a keen suspicion of power. "Power," he wrote, "will one time or other be abused, unless men are well watched, & checked by something which they can not remove, when they please."[37] Among those men to be watched were his own colleagues in Congress.

New Hampshire's Whipple was impressed by the newcomer: "[He] is the Best man I have seen from that Country."[38]

Born in Galway, Ireland, Burke came to America at the age of 17,[39] trained as a physician, and treated patients for a time in Virginia. Eventually, he turned to law and managed to practice both medicine and law in Norfolk, while also making extra income as a bill collector.[40] He extolled liberty and condemned slavery in poetry, no less. Even so, records indicate that during his lifetime he owned at least two enslaved people.[41] He took up residence in North Carolina about the time the Revolution began.[42]

He came to Congress when it was still sitting in Baltimore, and as North Carolina's only voice in Congress, soon confessed that he "found his Experience and abilities far Inferior to his Duty."[43] But before long he showed his willingness to defy his colleagues even on issues that seemed, at first glance, unworthy of debate. On February 25, while still in Baltimore, Congress took up the issue of military deserters, a problem for both the British and the Americans. The original version of one resolution appeared to direct constables and others, on the authority of Congress, to arrest deserters from the American army in any of the various states.[44] Delegates quickly approved this measure with hardly a thought before Burke rose to insist that his objection be recorded. Here, he said, Congress was butting in where it had no right to be, "assuming a Power to give authority from themselves to persons within the States to seize and Imprison the persons of the Citizens, and thereby to endanger the personal Liberty of every man in America."

Wilson of Pennsylvania scoffed. Of course Congress had the authority to order the arrest of deserters: "Nothing could be more necessary to prevent Desertion than to take Effectual Measures for apprehending deserters, that this Power must necessarily be in the Congress, and that they certainly had Power to authorize any persons in the States to put them in Execution."

Burke countered: "[T]he subject of every state was entitled to the Protection of that particular state, and subject to the Laws of that alone, because to them alone did he give his Consent."[45]

In the end, Burke's argument prevailed. The final resolution "earnestly recommended to the committees of observation or inspection in these united States"[46] that they look for deserters and turn them in to the nearest Continental Army officer.

Burke again made himself conspicuous after Congress settled back in at the Pennsylvania State House and dusted off an old topic—confederation. In April, delegates agreed to devote at least two days each week to Dickinson's proposed Articles of Confederation.[47] They took up the task with renewed vigor and even confidence that the blueprint for government could quickly be settled and readied for ratification by each of the states.

Soon, Article III in the proposed articles came up for debate. It read: "Each Colony shall retain and enjoy as much of its present Laws, Rights and Customs, as it may think fit, and reserves to itself the sole and exclusive Regulation and Government of its internal police, in all matters that shall not interfere with the Articles of this Confederation."[48]

The article was straightforward enough for most delegates, who to a man were wary that an oppressive central government might arise to interfere in state affairs. After all, the Revolution was all about throwing off an overbearing authority. This article seemed an adequate enough barrier against a future Congress muscling into state affairs. But to Burke, this wall between Congress and the states was way too flimsy.

Burke seized on this article as a mortal threat to the right of the individual states to manage themselves: "[I]t left in the power of the future Congress or General Council to explain away every right belonging to the States and to make their own power as unlimited as they please."

Burke thus hoisted the flag of states' rights, proposing a stout barrier to protect the interests of the individual states from the intrusion of Congress. His amendment said "that all sovereign Power was in the States separately, and that particular acts of it, which should be expressly enumerated, would be exercised in conjunction, and not otherwise; but that in all things else each State would Exercise all the rights and powers of sovereignty, uncontrolled."[49]

In short, states retained all powers except those expressly delegated to Congress.[50] Burke's amendment caught delegates by surprise. It was, he wrote, "so little understood that it was some time before it was seconded."[51] The amendment was debated for two days before at last it was passed, with only Virginia voting against it.[52]

Burke's amendment eventually emerged as Article II of the Articles of Confederation: "Each State retains its sovereignty, freedom and independence, and every power, jurisdiction, and right, which is not by this confederation expressly delegated to the United States, in Congress assembled."[53]

Burke's idea lives on in the Bill of Rights, specifically the 10th Amendment to the United States Constitution. Significantly, that amendment does not use the word "expressly," suggesting that Congress might have implied powers to poke into state matters, making the amendment a weaker shield for states' rights than what Burke had in mind.[54] The 10th Amendment reads: "The powers not delegated to the United States by the Constitution, nor prohibited by it to the states, are reserved to the states respectively, or to the people."[55]

By May 1777, Burke was satisfied that he and other delegates were of one mind in restricting the power of Congress and ensuring the supremacy of the states: "I never had more hopes of Congress than I have now. All seem sensible that the honour and dignity of the Magistrates of the States ought to be preserved sacred and inviolable; whether for applying the force of the States, or restraining abuses, and suppressing ambition."[56]

Indeed, Burke was not opposing his colleagues so much as clarifying for them principles they shared—that the power of Congress should be limited to only what it absolutely needs.

CHAPTER 29

Laying the Foundation of Future Evils

Work on the Articles proceeded, but bogged down as weeks went by. The toughest issue was the allocation of power. Should each state have the same number of votes in Congress? Should states with larger populations have more votes? Or should votes be allocated some other way? Obviously, the less populous states, such as Delaware and Rhode Island, believed each state should have equal power, while the more populous states, such as Virginia and Massachusetts, favored representation in Congress based on population or some measure that reflected those states' greater size.

As work went on, Burke once again stepped up with an idea that might have led to a solution had delegates given it more thought. Burke proposed a Congress made up of two houses—a General Council and a Council of State.[1] All measures needed to be approved by both houses to go into effect. Burke's idea for a bicameral Congress would later be embraced and recast in the United States Constitution with the establishment of the House of Representatives—with representation based on population—and the Senate—with equal representation for each state.

But the Continental Congress of 1777 was not ready to consider a Congress with two houses. Burke's notion was rejected for reasons that are murky, but possibly in part because delegates believed a bicameral Congress would make the lawmaking process too cumbersome.[2]

Congress found no way to address the demand of large states to be represented in proportion to their size without also shrinking the influence of small states. Burke wrote in May: "So unequal as the States are, it will be nearly impossible to effect this: and after all it is far from improbable that the only Confederation will be a defensive alliance."[3]

Delegates soldiered on, working on the Articles as time permitted. Maryland's Charles Carroll of Carollton wrote in August:

> [A]lmost every member of Congress is anxious for a Confederacy, being sensible, that a Confederacy formed on a rational plan will certainly add much weight and consequence to the united States, collectively and give great security to each individually, and a credit also to our paper money.

If only, Carroll wrote, "little and partial interests could be laid aside."[4] But that didn't happen. There was more debate, but little progress. On September 2, a motion was made to dedicate part of each day's business to resolving the problem of confederation. The resolution failed.[5]

***

Over in France, frostiness enveloped the American diplomatic team. Finding Lee impossible to work with, Deane and Franklin arranged midnight meetings with their French contact just to avoid involving their colleague.[6]

For his part, Lee, by June, had someone nearby to commiserate with about the wily Franklin and loathsome Deane. That was William Lee, Arthur's older brother by one year (as well as younger brother of Richard Henry and Francis Lightfoot, signers of the Declaration). William was less cantankerous than Arthur, but equally zealous. He, like Arthur, would come to distrust Franklin and despise Deane. In a few months, William Lee would confide to Richard Henry Lee about Deane: "I never knew a man in my whole life that I would not sooner trust. … Weigh with caution, but trust not any thing that comes from him, whether it is on paper, or verbal, or by insinuations, or little hints, or private anecdotes."[7]

This Lee would also come to complain, as Arthur did, that Deane and Franklin were keeping him in the dark about important matters: "I am convinced from the mode of carrying on business here, that I shall not be informed of anything from hence until it has been in half the Gazettes of Europe."[8]

William Lee relocated from Virginia to London in the 1760s, where he lived for a time next door to Franklin. He became interested in politics, rubbed elbows with radical John Wilkes, and managed to get himself elected Sheriff of London—essentially a judicial post. In 1775, as Americans in his homeland rebelled, he became an alderman in the City of London. As a prominent and politically active American increasingly under attack in England, he slipped away to Paris in the summer of 1776.

In France, he hoped he could make money trading tobacco, but that dream crashed against the French government's monopoly in the business. William was not shy about sending off a plea to Richard Henry in Congress for some suitable employment.[9] By this time, Arthur had also helpfully suggested to Richard Henry that brother William would be the perfect candidate to replace the drunk and unreliable Thomas Morris in Nantes.[10]

Sure enough, Congress soon made William supervisor of commercial deals in Europe negotiated by American diplomats. However, Deane and Franklin appeared to undermine Congress's wishes when they placed Jonathan Williams Jr.—who just happened to be a grandnephew of Franklin—to take on Thomas Morris's job.[11]

This further annoyed the Lees, of course. It was about this time that Arthur Lee accused Deane of embezzlement and fraud, and the Lees—Arthur and William—put in motion their plot to shove Franklin and Deane aside: they suggested to Congress that their colleagues be sent off to set up other diplomatic posts, leaving the plum position in France to the Lees. They recommended that Congress dispatch Franklin to Vienna and Deane to Amsterdam.[12] Congress ignored the proposal.

As America's diplomats sniped, they also fumbled in the dark while getting their pockets picked. News or direction from Congress came sporadically. Six months could pass without a single message getting through, thanks to the British navy.[13] Messages going the other way were likewise intercepted or betrayed. On one occasion, the commissioners wrapped up eight months of confidential correspondence and entrusted it to Joseph Hynson, a Marylander traveling from Paris to the French coast. He was supposed to hand over the packet to an American captain in Le Havre sailing to America. The packet delivered to the captain eventually reached Congress, but it contained only blank pages. Hynson carried the real packet to his spymaster in England. The British rewarded Hynson with £200 and promised another £200 per year.[14] The British spy chief called him "an honest rascal."[15]

Besides Hynson and Bancroft, other Americans feeding intelligence by accident or on purpose to the British included William Carmichael, another Marylander, who happened to be in Europe in 1776 and became Deane's secretary. The British found him conveniently chatty after a few drinks.[16] He later returned to America and became a delegate to Congress.[17] Meanwhile, William Lee would correctly find Carmichael wholly untrustworthy: "I am irrevocably determined that no consideration in this world shall ever induce me to hold any kind of correspondence, or have any kind of intercourse with him."[18]

Another American helpful to the British was Paul Wentworth, a descendant of the prominent New Hampshire family. Back in 1774, he was trusted by Congress as a reliable correspondent in London, where, when offered a tidy salary and a whiff of such rewards as a baronetcy, a seat in Parliament, and an easy government job, he happily and enthusiastically spied for the British.[19]

Arthur Lee, suspicious of just about everyone, properly raised alarms about Hynson, Bancroft, and Carmichael. But no one paid much attention except for Bancroft, who apparently challenged both Arthur and brother William separately to duels, neither of which took place.[20]

Intelligence not lost to treachery was snatched by thieves. Arthur Lee, after his disappointing mission to Spain, went off to Vienna and Berlin to see if he could wangle commercial treaties from Austria and Prussia.[21] As with the Spanish adventure, this trip had no sanction from Congress—he was freelancing. Those missions east accomplished nothing except to prove American ineptitude. In Vienna, Lee found only "a Cold tranquillity ... that bodes us no good."[22] He did not meet with any officials; he may not have even tried.[23]

While in Berlin, a burglar snatched a diary and pile of letters from his hotel room. These soon found their way to the British embassy,[24] where they were duly copied and returned to Lee. The British representative in Berlin confessed his role in engineering the thefts. The British gave him a scolding, had him recalled, and then presented him with £1,000.[25]

All the larceny and teachery added up to heaps of intelligence for the British, almost more than they had time to sift through. Eventually, the British ambassador to France confronted Vergennes, the French foreign minister, with very accurate information about ships destined for America. The Frenchman feigned astonishment.[26]

In the meantime, Franklin worked 12-hour days dealing with correspondence—a postman came nine times daily!—meeting visitors, and performing myriad duties. He was diligent, except for tracking how, and how much, American money was being spent—those records remained in chaos. Despite the long hours, he never let pass an opportunity to play chess. Opponents learned not to leave the room during a game lest the great man attempt a time-honored stratagem—rearranging the pieces. Franklin also found time to sit for portraits, to soothe his skin condition at a bathhouse,[27] and to flirt. Grandson Temple wrote: "The air of Passy and the warm bath three times a week have made quite a young man out of him. His pleasing gaiety makes everyone in love with him, especially the ladies, who permit him always to kiss them."[28]

As for Deane, he now had his brother working with him. In 1777, Simeon Deane was in Europe working with Silas on tobacco deals. Silas arranged for a 36-gun frigate bought for the American government to escort a vessel stuffed with Simeon's merchandise.[29]

Relations with the French remained delicate. Secretly, the French government was eager to help the Americans; publicly, however, they remained rigidly neutral. This pretense became especially problematic as American privateers feasted on British shipping in waters nearby. With a wink and nudge, Franklin and his colleagues assured Vergennes that they were definitely not directing the privateers to bring their prizes to French ports for sale,[30] but everyone knew that's exactly what they were doing, and nothing was done to stop it.

Of course, the British raised a fuss and the French felt obliged to lock up in the Bastille an American who had been outfitting a privateer. Franklin protested, but the man remained jailed for six weeks. With the French in a chilly mood, the prospect of any sort of treaty or alliance seemed impossibly remote.[31]

***

Meanwhile, in Philadelphia over the spring and summer of 1777, myriad issues, new and old, demanded delegates' attention. There was, for example, the matter of Benedict Arnold and the decision by Congress to pass him over for promotion to major general. Now Congress learned that Arnold, instead of resigning as a matter of honor, had the audacity to perform yet more amazing battlefield heroics.

While at his home in New Haven, visiting his sister and his sons and sorting out the wreckage of his personal finances—drained by the war and his own extravagance—Arnold got word that the British were conducting a daring raid nearby. They had landed troops on the Connecticut coast near Fairfield and were marching inland to destroy an American military depot.[32]

Arnold sprang into action. Teaming with Major General Wooster—an old nemesis—and another general, he rounded up about 600 militiamen, including a regiment that Arnold had helped support out of his own pocket. They responded too late to stop the destruction of tents, shoes, hogsheads of rum and wine, and barrels of flour and beef, along with the Danbury town meeting house and about 40 houses.[33] But Arnold and his fellow generals did manage to harass the 2,000 raiders on their return march to the coast.

On the whole, the episode was an embarrassment for Connecticut and the Patriot cause. Connecticut Patriots failed to rally en masse to challenge the raiders and botched the responsibility of defending the depot. John Adams was disgusted: "[T]he stupid sordid cowardly torified Country People let them pass without Opposition."[34] It was a startling contrast to the battle of Lexington and Concord, where militiamen by the hundreds appeared overnight to ambush British troops attempting a similar raid.

Nevertheless, Arnold, in leading his outnumbered militia force against the raiders, was magnificent in directing his men and charging into danger. A day after one horse he was riding collapsed, struck by nine musket balls, another mount was shot from under him.[35] Though the Americans failed to trap and destroy the raiding party, and Wooster was killed, Arnold emerged as brilliant and brave.

News of all this reached Congress in early May, and within a week delegates decided that Arnold—despite the handicap of belonging to Connecticut—earned a promotion after all for his "Vigilance, Activity, and Bravery, in the late Affair at Connecticutt," in the words of John Adams.[36] While musing in a later letter about the inspirational value of medals in the Patriot cause, Adams envisioned one showing Arnold "on Horseback, His Horse falling dead under him."[37] With the death of Wooster, a Connecticut man, there now could be no objection to the appointment of another man from that state.

So Arnold at last won his promotion. But he wasn't satisfied—he wanted the promotion backdated to the day when the five recently promoted generals were made major generals. This would put him on equal footing in terms of seniority. Without this backdating, they would still be his superiors.

Arnold soon appeared in Philadelphia. Convinced that certain damning reports had swayed delegates against him, Arnold demanded that Congress investigate these allegations. Congress obliged and a committee quickly produced a report confirming "entire satisfaction ... concerning the general's character and conduct, so cruelly and groundlessly aspersed."[38] Delegates also ordered that the new major general be given a suitable "token of their approbation of his gallant conduct"[39]—a horse. However, on the matter of backdating, Congress would not budge. Arnold would have the lowest seniority of the major generals.

***

Another old problem troubled Congress like a pest. As the effervescent Burke of North Carolina reported: "The inhabitants of what is usually called the New Hampshire Grants, have attempted to set up a distinct State, and sent Delegates to Congress to claim a seat."[40] In January, a convention of settlers in the New Hampshire Grants[41] had, in defiance of New York, declared a new state—"New-Connecticut, alias Vermont."[42]

In their declaration of independence, the settlers borrowed the very words of the Continental Congress when it "recommended" back in May 1776 that governments be established where there was none "sufficient" to the task.[43] Claiming to be "at present without law or government," the settlers asserted that a "right remains to the people of the said Grants to form a government best suited to secure their property, well being and happiness." Furthermore, "the people on said Grants, have the sole and exclusive and inherent right of ruling and governing themselves in such manner and form as in their wisdom they shall think proper, not inconsistent or repugnant to any resolve of the Honorable Continental Congress."[44]

The delegation from the Grants arrived in Philadelphia in early April, along with a "deputation"[45] of Green Mountain Boys, to present their case. Burke wrote: "Congress laid the papers on the table, and I hope will be wise enough to decline any interposition."[46] Congress, indeed, had no intention of giving hope to the people of the New Hampshire Grants, or New Connecticut, or Vermont, or whatever the place was called. Delegates seem to have shared Burke's opinion:

> I am for my own part clearly against assuming a Judiciary power. Such certainly never was the purpose of our Delegation. As I consider all jealousies as injurious to our common cause and as laying the foundation of future evils, I use my best endeavours to discourage them; and I endeavour as much as possible to keep our attention to the main business, that of subduing our common enemy.[47]

According to Burke, the "affair which is something embarrassing" only heightened a "virulent jealousy" of New York toward its New England neighbors, whom New York delegates believed were sympathetic to the Grants settlers.[48] Indeed, letters to Congress from New York authorities bristled with indignation. The southern part of New York state and its most important city were firmly in the British grip. To the north, the British were poised to invade from Canada. Now the beleaguered state suspected its New England neighbors of meddling on behalf of the "deluted"[49] New Hampshire Grants settlers. "The various evidences and informations we have received, would lead us to believe, that persons of great influence in some of our sister states have fostered and fomented ... divisions, in order to dismember this state," harumphed Abraham Ten Broeck, president of the New York Convention to John Hancock. "[B]ut as these informations tend to accuse some members of your honorable body [Congress] of being concerned in this scheme, decency obliges us to suspend our belief."[50]

Contrary to "these informations," nobody in Congress openly encouraged the Vermonters in their quest to separate from New York. Indeed, New Hampshire's Whipple remarked about the "deputation" of Green Mountain Boys: "I sho'd not much care if the Devil had them all."[51]

Most wanted the issue to go away, which it did, only to reappear in June. Samuel Adams was bored with it, writing to Richard Henry Lee in June: "Yesterday and the day before was wholly spent in passing Resolutions to gratify N Y or as they say to prevent a civil war between that State and the Green Mountain Men, A matter which it is not worth your while to have explained to you."[52]

At New York's urging, delegates buried the issue for good, or so they thought. Their resolution was: "That the independent government attempted to be established by the people stiling themselves inhabitants of the New Hampshire Grants, can derive no countenance or justification from the act of Congress declaring the United Colonies to be independent of the crown of Great Britain, nor from any other act or resolution of Congress."[53]

But the people of the New Hampshire Grants weren't paying attention. About this time, they were drafting Vermont's first state constitution.[54] Adopted in July, this document was the first state constitution to ban the trading and ownership of enslaved people. The new government set up at the Catamount Tavern in Bennington.[55]

CHAPTER 30

A Great Expenditure of Liquor, Powder &c

In July 1777, delegates in Philadelphia rallied around diplomatic initiatives meant to foster links with potential European friends while also jamming the British war machine. Congress assigned William Lee to visit courts in Vienna and Berlin,[1] following the trail of brother Arthur, whose earlier visits to both capitals had been both fruitless and embarrassing.

Congress instructed William Lee to "proceed with all convenient expedition to those courts" and "lose no time" in announcing the Declaration of Independence: "The reasons of this act of Independence are so strongly adduced in the declaration itself, that further argument is unnecessary." Then, as it is "of the greatest importance ... that Great Britain be effectually obstructed in the plan of sending German and Prussian troops to North America, you will exert all possible address and vigour to cultivate the friendship and procure the interference" of Prussia and the Habsburg emperor in Vienna.[2]

At the same time, Congress assigned Ralph Izard to visit the court of the Duke of Tuscany on the Italian peninsula. His instructions were nearly identical: "[Y]ou will exert all possible address to prevail with the grand duke to use his influence with the emperor and the courts of France and Spain [to obstruct the plan] of sending German and Prussian troops to North America."[3]

Izard, a South Carolinian in Europe, was the son of a rich indigo and rice planter. He left America for London in 1771, and there he likely would have happily stayed if not for the Revolution. By nature and background, he was a Tory. Yet he bristled at British conventions. According to his daughter, Izard would not consent to being presented in court in England because he refused to bow to anyone. In 1776, life in London became intolerable for the American, so he and his family moved on to Paris.[4]

These diplomatic initiatives were shots in the dark. Delegates knew little about the dynastic politics of Europe or attitudes there toward the American cause. But they were encouraged by scraps of evidence suggesting that diplomatic overtures might be welcomed.

It seemed worth a try. Getting the court in Vienna to recognize the United States would be an especially significant prize. The Habsburg monarchy, centered at Vienna, was one of the most powerful dynasties in Europe. The vast territories under the family's control included Liège, in what is now Belgium, one of the largest centers for arms manufacturing in the world.[5] With friends in Vienna, the Americans would have a new, rich source of military supplies.

The monarch, Joseph II, besides being a Habsburg, happened also to be the Holy Roman Emperor. This made him the nominal head of all German princes, including the Duke Elector of Brunswick-Lüneburg, who happened to be George III, king of England. The Americans dreamed that Joseph would flex Habsburg muscle and threaten George's holdings in Germany, another distraction for the British monarch and another complication for Britain.[6]

Congress's hopes rested on flimsy evidence related to, of all places, the port of Livorno in Tuscany. Since well before the Revolution, merchants in Livorno had cultivated a robust trade with New England for cod. By 1775, those merchants were often also seen in New York, Baltimore, Charleston, Philadelphia, and other American ports. Hoping to keep that trade going even when hostilities began, the Duke of Tuscany declared in 1775 that Livorno, a Tuscan port, would remain open to all traders.[7] Though this was hardly an endorsement of the Revolution, Deane in France grasped the straw, reporting to Congress that the Grand Duke was "zealously in favor of America."[8]

Meanwhile, an agent from Tuscany, who came to Virginia in 1773 and whose contacts included Jefferson, prodded American leaders to send a mission to Tuscany. As it happened, the Grand Duke, Pietro Leopoldo, was the brother of Emperor Joseph, which explains why Congress ordered envoys to both Florence and Vienna. Congress thought the brothers might share similar views about the American struggle.[9]

Congress's determination to send an envoy to Berlin as well may be traced similarly to Deane, who reported to Jay that he received "overtures from the king of Prussia"[10] for some sort of commercial deal.

***

Distracted by these diplomatic initiatives and myriad other matters, delegates in Philadelphia nearly overlooked the first anniversary of independence.

Not until July 3 were plans set in motion, and that was "too late to have a sermon, as every one wished," according to John Adams. Delegates took the day off and dined together at the same tavern where they had met for the first time in 1774. They were "very agreeably entertained with excellent company, good cheer, fine music from the band of Germans taken at Trenton, and continual vollies between every toast"[11] from soldiers drawn up in front of the tavern.

Adams recorded his impressions: vessels on the river "beautifully dressed in the colours of all nations, displayed about upon the masts, yards, and rigging"; the people along the wharves and shores "shouting and huzzaing"; "the whole city lighting up their candles at the windows"; "the ringing of bells all day and evening, and the bonfires in the streets, and the fireworks played off." It was all delightful: "I was amazed at the universal joy and alacrity that was discovered, and at the brilliancy and splendour of every part of this joyful exhibition."[12]

His colleague, William Williams of Connecticut, had a different view. He wrote on July 5: "Yesterday was in my opinion poorly spent in celebrating the anniversary of the Declaration of Independence … A great Expenditure of Liquor, Powder &c took up the Day, & of Candles thro the City, good part of the night, I suppose. I conclude much Tory unilluminated Glass will want replacing &c."[13]

Indeed, much glass was broken: A Quaker woman with Tory sympathies noted in her diary:

> This being the anniversary of the declaration of independence, at 12 o'clock the vessles were all hauled up & fired, & about 4 the firing of cannon began which was terrible to hear, about 6 the troops paraded thro' the streets with great pomp, tho' many of them were barefoot & looked very unhealthy, & in the evening were illuminations, & those people's windows were broken who put no candles in.

She calculated that about 80 windows had been cracked or smashed, "& all this for joy of having gained our liberty."[14]

Celebrations over, delegates went back to work. Among their concerns was a national shortage of Bibles. On July 7, three Presbyterian ministers appeared and alerted delegates that "unless timely care be used to prevent it we shall not have bibles for our Schools, & families, & for the publick Worship of God in our Churches." Since the Pilgrims came to America, Bibles had been printed in German and even in Maumee, an indigenous language, but American printers had yet to produce a complete Bible in English.[15] Until the war there was no need, because English Bibles could be readily shipped in from Britain and Ireland. The Presbyterians proposed that Bibles be printed in America and cheaply sold under Congress's "care" and "encouragement."[16]

The matter was referred to a committee, which developed a 15-point plan for completing the project. One point stated: "That instead of the old Dedication to King James, a new Dedication to the Congress be drawn up & prefixed to the Bible."[17] The committee reported back months later that the project be put off: it required type and paper that needed to be imported, and that was difficult, risky, and costly. The committee recommended instead the importation of 20,000 Bibles from "Holland, Scotland, or elsewhere." A resolution to import them was approved, but in the end Congress never actually implemented even that decision.[18]

***

Henry Laurens, from South Carolina, built much of his wealth on the slave trade. He was elected president of Congress in 1777, succeeding John Hancock. Laurens resigned as president in December 1778. After the British captured him on his way to Europe on a diplomatic mission, he was held prisoner in the Tower of London for 15 months. His release came in December 1781. John Singleton Copley painted this portrait of Laurens in 1782 in London. Laurens later had a small role in the ongoing peace negotiations. (Image courtesy of the National Portrait Gallery, Smithsonian Institution)

In July, Congress welcomed two fresh delegates from South Carolina, one of whom would soon emerge as a leader. That was Henry Laurens, a swarthy man, a little smaller than average, with a look that seemed, according to a biographer, "aggressive and just a bit cock-sure." His ancestry was pure Huguenot. His mother and father were children of French Protestants who had migrated to America. Henry's parents moved to Charleston from New York shortly after their marriage. Henry's father learned the saddler's trade, bought and sold real estate, and prospered. Henry was his parents' third child and eldest son.[19]

Laurens had a sound, practical education. He learned no Latin or Greek, and while he may have understood French, it was not well enough to write in that language. He read widely and learned to write with elegance and vigor. He set out to become a merchant, and when a potential partnership with a leading merchant fell through,[20] he nimbly teamed up with another. His first key assignment, at the age of 24, was to cultivate business deals in England in Bristol and Liverpool, involving the shipment of rice and indigo from Charleston to Europe and the shipping of enslaved people from Africa to Charleston.[21] He would eventually deal in many kinds of goods: deer skins, wine, rum, beer, even coffee.[22] But much if not most of his eventual fortune came from importing slaves from Africa. Over an 18-year period, his firm shipped over some 7,600 enslaved Africans.[23] The slave trade later apparently tugged at his conscience—he quit it by 1773[24]—but surviving business letters from this time reveal a young man eagerly calculating fortunes to be made selling this human cargo.[25] While Laurens's brother and father disapproved of the slave trade, Henry pursued the business with vigor, in fact reviving commerce that had been neglected.[26] He knew the trade well enough to assess which Africans were best for captivity and which were not. For example, he wrote, apparently with cool callousness, that those from a certain area of what is now Nigeria were inferior because of their annoying tendency, once enslaved, to kill themselves.[27]

When aged 26, he married 19-year-old Eleanor Ball, a Charleston woman of English descent. It was a happy marriage, and Laurens prospered. Eleanor had many children, but as was sadly common in that day, many did not live long. At least 12, maybe more, were born, yet only four reached adulthood.[28]

It was also tragically common at the time that women died after childbirth. Thus, in 1770, Laurens lost Eleanor, leaving him "staggered ... almost to the gates of death."[29] By that time, he was wealthy enough to set aside much of his business affairs to devote more time to his surviving children.[30]

He was also then a war veteran, a planter with vast estates, and well established as a prominent politician. His military experience included a stint as lieutenant-colonel of a colonial regiment fighting alongside British Regulars against the Cherokee tribe. By 1768, he owned 20,000 acres, chiefly for growing rice and indigo.[31] By the early 1770s, he had acquired at least eight plantations in Georgia and South Carolina, and was one of the wealthiest men in America.[32] As for his political life, he was first elected in 1757 to the South Carolina Commons House of Assembly, the lower house of the colonial legislature. He was reliably re-elected, except for one occasion, until the time of the Revolution.[33]

When the Stamp Act crisis arose in the 1760s, Laurens was on the side of restraint. He opposed this attempt by the British authorities to tax colonists, but he also abhorred the violence associated with protests and even refused to vote in favor of sending delegates to the Stamp Act Congress. His respect for British authority diminished over time, especially after conflicts with high-handed customs officers and corrupt, royally appointed judges.[34]

As a lawmaker, one of his interests was education. Well aware of how backward schooling was in South Carolina, he pushed for the establishment of a college in the province. But that effort foundered, largely because of a long dispute between lawmakers and the royal authorities that all but paralyzed legislative activity for years.[35]

Education, however, was very much on his mind when, in 1771, he traveled to England with his two oldest surviving sons. He had sent a third son—just seven years old—ahead. He was determined to see that his sons got the best education—which he assumed could only be had in England—and he would be on hand to guide them.[36]

He lived abroad for three years, overseeing his sons, but also observing British politics and society up close. He found British society frivolous and immoral, the ruling class unworthy of respect, and the king undeserving of veneration.[37]

By December 1774, he was back in Charleston. A month later, he was elected to the revolutionary Provincial Congress of South Carolina. Within this body, he held the middle ground between those pushing for independence and others hoping to preserve British rule.[38]

Curiously, after war broke out in early 1775, Laurens did not call for his sons' return from abroad. Instead, he sent over his two remaining daughters, apparently to watch over one of their brothers, who was in poor health. So as Laurens was immersed in revolutionary activities, and with a war ongoing, all five of his surviving children were in Britain.[39]

When the new revolutionary government took shape in South Carolina, Laurens found himself president of the General Committee, making him in effect the province's chief executive. After leaving that post, he remained a key figure in the government and helped draft the state's constitution, even though he found the idea of independence painful.[40] Separation from Britain made him feel like a good son "thrust by the hand of violence out of his father's house."[41] When news arrived in South Carolina that Congress had declared the nation free, he wept.[42]

As Laurens was coming to grips with independence, he was also trying to face up to a personal and moral dilemma that threatened to shatter his tight relationship with his oldest son, John. Correspondence between father and son show how much they loved and respected each other, as one might expect, but in this case the powerful bond is noteworthy considering the yawning gap between them on a fundamental issue: slavery. John had dedicated himself to the cause of abolition.[43] Henry, in a letter to his son, seemed embarrassed by his own moral failure and afraid of losing his son's respect. "You know, my dear son, I abhor slavery," wrote Henry,[44] who in that period seems to have owned about 500 enslaved people.[45] He gave excuses: he was not the original enslaver of the people he owned; freeing them was complicated: "Great powers oppose me—the laws and customs of my country." Still, he said he hoped to free his slaves with John's "advice & assistance ... in good time."[46] He pointed out to his son that he treated them so well that none of his had ever been lured by British promises of freedom and protection if they escaped and fought on the side of the Redcoats. As it happened, the very day he wrote that letter—August 14, 1776—five of his enslaved people in Georgia ran away to the British side.[47] In the end, Henry never found the "good time" to free his slaves. He lived another 15 years, and in that time bothered to emancipate only one.[48]

About six months after independence, in January 1777, Henry Laurens's colleagues in South Carolina selected him, with Arthur Middleton and Thomas Heyward, to represent the state at the Continental Congress. He protested, saying he had personal matters that needed attention, but he took the assignment. Those personal matters may have been the reason for delaying his departure for several months.[49]

On the way north to Philadelphia, he noted the evident prosperity of the farms he passed—a reminder that in the midst of war, many Americans far away from the fighting were doing well: "The Landskapes are delightful, fine Farms & almost without exception abounding with Crops of Grain, Cotton, Flax & Sheep. The Spinning Wheel & Loom are seen on every farm & very few with less than Eight Children, that number seemed almost to be the Standard. What an increase will an Age or two of peace make."

The only shortage that the country people remarked about, Laurens wrote, was salt, an essential preservative in those days.[50]

By this time, son John was back in America. About the time Henry was settling in at Philadelphia, John became part of Washington's military entourage as an assistant.[51] Henry was oddly dismayed, calling this turn of events his "greatest disappointment":[52] "I am persuaded he has made an indiscreet choice for his outset in life. His Talents & his diligence would have enabled him to have been much more extensively & essentially useful to his Country in a different line."[53]

Soon after taking his seat in Congress, Henry Laurens was shocked to hear delegates kick around "vague and undigested plans"[54] for seizing from the British the colony of West Florida, a thinly populated area of about 5,000 people[55] along the Gulf Coast, including parts of present-day Florida, Mississippi, Alabama, and Louisiana. According to the scheme, 1,000 or more men would travel down the Ohio and Mississippi rivers to Spanish-held New Orleans. Meanwhile, three or four American frigates would meet up in Havana—under Spanish control—and eventually rendezvous at or near New Orleans with the Americans, who by this time were presumably to have acquired plenty of money and arms from the friendly Spanish. The operation was to be conducted in secret and accomplished before Christmas, five months away.

The plan's supporters figured that, because the colony was made up mainly of migrants from the other 13 colonies, the colonists would welcome the American force and pitch in to overthrow the British authorities. Also, the plan had the endorsement of Benedict Arnold,[56] considered a keen judge of such matters. If the plan worked, West Florida might be welcomed as the 14th state.[57]

Laurens attacked the plan: neither ships nor troops could be spared; no one knew the size of the British force in Florida; many men would "Sicken & die very fast" in the swamps that time of year; and the planned rendezvous of the soldiers and the frigates was "precarious to the highest degree." He scoffed at the idea that the Spanish would provide a safe and secret harbor in Cuba or provision American soldiers who appeared unannounced. Crucially, he asserted that the colonists there were Loyalists: "[T]hey would join with numerous tribes of Indians ... in order to repel our Troops as the most dangerous invaders whose design was to plunder their present Stock & cut off the means of future Supplies."[58]

Laurens was exaggerating about Loyalist sentiment in West Florida,[59] but no one in Philadelphia knew for sure. Laurens's logic, expressed with vigor and certainty, won over the delegates. For the time being, there would be no expedition to take West Florida. Laurens was relieved but still troubled that Congress took the plan seriously enough to even debate it. He recalled the episode, along with other impressions of Congress, weeks later: "I can hardly forebear concluding that a great Assembly is in its dotage."[60]

In other letters over the following weeks, he amplified his disgust and dismay. He griped about hours wasted in directionless debate: "At 5 oClock I returned from

Six hours Session without doing one hours business."[61] He harped about the empty seats in Congress: "[D]uring the important debates on the Subjects of borrowing money & removing Enemies from our bosoms we have Seldom seen more than 20 members upon the floor, & more than once, business has been interrupted by want of Members (9 States) to make a Congress."[62]

He regretted his decision to accept the post. In one letter he wrote: "Congress is not the respectable body which I expected to have found."[63] In another he complained: "I am wasting time to no good purpose."[64]

Having just arrived in Philadelphia, Laurens was already hankering to leave. Many others who had served much longer were just as unhappy. The work in Congress was tedious, living in Philadelphia was expensive, and they missed their families. John Adams wrote 13 letters to Abigail in July alone. In early July, as he awaited news of the birth of another child, he admitted:

> And now I think I feel as anxious as ever.—Oh that I could be near, to say a few kind Words, or shew a few Kind Looks, or do a few kind Actions. Oh that I could take from my dearest, a share of her Distress, or relieve her of the whole. Before this shall reach you I hope you will be happy in the Embraces of a Daughter, as fair, and good, and wise, and virtuous as the Mother.[65]

But John soon learned from Abigail that "the dear Infant is numberd with its ancestors"—the daughter was stillborn. She wrote: "[I]t appeard to be a very fine Babe, and as it never opened its Eyes in this world it lookd as tho they were only closed for sleep."[66] John grieved: "Is it not unaccountable, that one should feel so strong an Affection for an Infant, that one has never seen, nor shall see? Yet I must confess to you, the Loss of this sweet little Girl, has most tenderly and sensibly affected me."[67]

A few days later, John groaned to Abigail:

> Never was Wretch, more weary of Misery than I am of the Life I lead, condemned to the dullest servitude and Drudgery, seperated from all that I love, and wedded to all that I hate. Digging in a Potato Yard upon my own Garden and living in my own Family would be to me Paradise. The next Time I come home, shall be for a long Time.[68]

But Adams remained and got to know Laurens, writing that South Carolina had "sent Us a new Delegate, whom I greatly admire, Mr. Lawrence, ... a Gentleman of great Fortune, great Abilities, Modesty and Integrity—and great Experience too. If all the States would send Us such Men, it would be a Pleasure to be here."[69]

Adams and his fellow delegates found much to keep Laurens busy. Within three months, his colleagues appointed him to 14 different committees.[70]

CHAPTER 31

A Painful Dilemma

One of the many headaches for Congress that spring and summer was Phillippe Charles Jean Baptiste Tronson de Coudray.[1] This war, like all wars, was a magnet for men seeking adventure, glory, money, status, or the thrill of dodging death on the field of battle. Thus, soon after the war began, European warriors, mostly would-be officers, flocked to America to be a part of it.

Congress, despite a shortage of manpower, never resorted to hiring whole units of common soldiers, like the German formations that fought for the British. While Revolutionary leaders bandied about the idea of hiring companies of German, Swiss, French, or Irish soldiers, such mercenary units were never solicited because American leaders had qualms about them: how could the new states, fighting for freedom, tolerate the use of mercenary professional armies? These were the hammers that tyrants wielded to smash liberty. But Patriots had few reservations in principle about hiring individual mercenaries, especially skilled men who came on their own initiative. Of course, Americans preferred not to call these foreign warriors *mercenaries*. That was such an ugly word, applied only to the men—mostly Germans—that the British hired to do their fighting. Americans preferred to call them *volunteers*.[2]

This flood of eager military men should have been a boon to the American cause. After all, the army was desperate for skilled military people. But in the spring and summer of 1777, these foreigners, especially Coudray, were more trouble than they were worth.

The invasion of foreign military men was evident almost from the moment independence was declared. That month of July 1776, Jefferson advised a colleague in Virginia not to send any hopeful Frenchmen to Philadelphia: "We have so many of that country, and have been so much imposed on, that the Congress begins to be sore on that head."[3] A few months later, in October, New Hampshire's Josiah Bartlett reported: "A great number of foreigners Especially French officers are Daily almost arriving here & requesting to be employed in our Army, many of whom are well recommended."[4] By mid-February 1777, Robert Morris was begging a correspondent "to spare me all you can in the Introduction of French Officers to me." Morris didn't know French and he didn't have the time anyway to *parler*: "[T]he time they take from me in Visits & Applications can very ill be spared." French officers were "flocking over in such Numbers from every Port & by every Ship that I dont know what we shall do with them."[5]

By March 1777, Congress was sufficiently fed up to order its agents overseas "to discourage all gentlemen from coming to America with expectations of employment in the service, unless they are masters of our language, and have the best of recommendations."[6] That might dry up the stream of foreigners eager to sail off to America, but what should they do with those already arrived?

Coudray represented an especially ticklish problem for Congress. It was easy enough for delegates to turn away Europeans, with or without recommendations, who simply showed up on their own initiative and asked for employment. However, the rejection of a French officer with an agreement in hand from Deane, Congress's own representative in Paris, was bound to put relations between the United States and France out of joint, something Congress could not afford to do. Laurens summed up the problem:

> The late flood of French Men rushed in upon us under agreements with Mr. Deane has reduced Congress to a painful dilemma. If we employ with all his unwarranted Contracts, many of our best Generals will be grosly affronted; if we do not, the United States will be exposed to the reproach & probably resentment of Men who have been deceived & ill used.[7]

The difficulty with Coudray began with the instructions Congress gave Deane encouraging him to send back to America skilled military engineers. Deane thought he had found the perfect man in Coudray. As an advisor to several secretaries of war in France, Coudray seemed to have sterling military expertise. In helping Deane round up military equipment to be sent secretly to America, Coudray proved himself cooperative, enthusiastic, and competent. In September 1776, Deane signed a deal with Coudray. Under the agreement, Coudray would sail to America with other French officers and men, as well as military materiel, and would have the rank of major general with the title of General of Artillery and Ordnance.[8] In making the arrangement, Deane exceeded his authority, but still felt he made a prudent choice: to offer Coudray less would insult him and possibly wreck the relationship Deane was trying to nurture with the French government.[9]

By November 1776, Coudray was on his way and Deane was writing to Congress: "The extraordinary exertions of this Gentleman [Coudray] and his Character intitle him to much from the United States, and I hope the sum I have stipulated with him will not be considered as extravagant when you consider it is much less than is given in Europe."[10]

Coudray proved troublesome even before his arrival in America. Finding his quarters aboard the *Amphitrite* not to his liking, he demanded to return to France. The captain complied, and the *Amphitrite*, after 17 days at sea, was back in a French port, thus delaying the transport of not only Coudray, but the men who accompanied him and the cargo so desperately needed in America.[11] This did not set well with Coudray's superiors. Beaumarchais sent off a curt note that began: "As your conduct, sir, in this affair is inexplicable; I will not waste time in trying to comprehend it."[12] Permission for Coudray to go to America was revoked, whereupon he discovered his quarters on the *Amphitrite* were suitable after all, whereupon permission to go to America was once again granted.[13]

The *Amphitrite* resumed its journey, reaching Portsmouth, New Hampshire, in May 1777. Coudray promptly marched off to New Jersey to join Washington, who just as promptly sent him on to Philadelphia. Washington anticipated trouble: "Congress will undoubtedly make a genteel and honorable provision for him [Coudray]; but I hope it may be done, in such a manner, as not to give disgust to any of the general officers in our army."[14]

But disgust it duly gave. Word of Coudray's arrival—and his expected appointment as major general—swiftly reached the ears of the many American officers vying for high rank. Generals Nathanael Greene, John Sullivan, and Henry Knox promptly wrote to Congress vowing to resign if Coudray, a mere colonel brigadier in France, was given the rank of major general in America.[15] Some of Coudray's compatriots were also put off. These were other French officers who had arrived earlier and felt themselves more qualified.[16] Several French engineers who refused to serve under Coudray spent time with James Lovell—one of the few delegates to Congress who knew French—complaining about how Deane had been duped.[17]

Delegates in Philadelphia found themselves in a bind. John Adams at first was dead set against giving Coudray the rank he bargained for: "Mr Deane I fear has exceeded his Powers. Mr Du Coudray shall never have my Consent to be at the Head of the Artillery."[18] But later on, Adams retreated: "Coudray has cost Us dear. His Terms are very high, but he has done Us such essential Service in France, and his Interest is so great and so near the Throne, that it would be impolitick not to avail ourselves of him."[19]

Delegates fumed not only at Deane for engineering this deal, but also at Greene, Sullivan, and Knox for unseemly meddling. Eliphalet Dyer of Connecticut blasted the generals for making it impossible for Congress to reach a decision in the generals' favor, for such a decision, "instead of being Imputed" to the "Justice & prudence" of Congress,

> will be entirely attributed to their fear occasioned by the threats of those Gentn and the Consequence will be, in every matter for the future. ... We must be either Dictated to or threatned by the Army or if we do not do this, or that, or just what they please, they will give up the cause or goe over to the Enemie, Sacrifice their Country, &c.[20]

John Adams dashed off a hectoring letter to Greene: "I must be careful my Friend in Saying, that if you or the other Generals Sullivan and Knox, had seriously considered the Nature of a free Constitution, and the Necessity of preserving the Authority of the Civil Powers above the military, you never would have written such Letters."

Adams worried that such threats

> passing with Impunity establishes a Preceedent for all future officers, and one stride after another will be taken, one Breach of the Priviledge of Congress after another will be made, and one Contempt of its authority after another will be offered, untill the officers of the Army will do as most others have done, wrest all authority out of civil Hands and set up a Tyrant of their own.

Adams added that delegates were angry: "It was universally considered as betraying the Liberties of the People to pass them by unanswered. Some were more for dismissing all three of you instantly from the service, others for ordering you to Philadelphia, under arrest to answer for this offence."[21]

Congress did not order the generals arrested, but they did, in a resolution, call the letters "an attempt to influence" the decisions of Congress, "and an invasion of the liberties of the people, and indicating a want of confidence in the justice of Congress." Congress further expected each of the generals to "make proper acknowledgments for an interference of so dangerous a tendency." If they failed to do so, "they shall be at liberty to resign their commissions and retire."[22]

The problem for Congress was further complicated by promises made to some or all of the 28 other officers and 12 sergeants of artillery[23] who accompanied Coudray. They also expected appointments in the army.[24]

After wrestling with the issue for weeks, Congress seized upon a temporary solution. Coudray would be a major general "of the staff," which gave him no authority over major generals "of the line."[25] This, delegates thought, would somehow smooth the ruffled feathers of the American generals.

Then fate lent a hand. On September 16, about a mile from Philadelphia, Coudray, on horseback, approached the ferry to cross the Schuylkill River. Instead of sensibly dismounting, he remained in the saddle while boarding. At some point, his nervous young mare leaped into the water. The horse and Coudray both drowned.[26] In his diary, John Adams made a droll notation: "This Dispensation will save Us much Altercation."[27]

With Coudray thus dispensed, Congress settled the problem of the French officers who had come to America with the unlucky man. For all who wanted to return to France, Congress would pay the costs. Some decided to stay and serve in the ranks according to their own merits. Among these "volunteers" was Pierre-Charles L'Enfant, who years later would plan the capital city for the new nation.[28]

The Coudray affair, coupled with the parade of dubious military applicants drifting into Philadelphia, made delegates to Congress more than a little dubious of Deane's ability in France to choose competent military talent. It seemed that Deane, in the words of one delegate, "could not say nay to any Frenchmen who called himself Count or Chevalier."[29] But among the dross were some gems. One was Marie Joseph Paul Yves Roch Gilbert du Motier, the Marquis de Lafayette.

A member of an illustrious and well-connected family, Lafayette found himself orphaned but immensely rich soon after he entered his teens. Wealth brought the attention of alert families with daughters, and 16-year-old Lafayette quickly had a 14-year-old bride.[30] He could have settled into a life of idle luxury, but as the only son of a grenadier colonel who died a war hero at the battle of Minden in 1759, Lafayette was drawn to the military, rising to the rank of captain in the French Army as a mere 18-year-old.[31]

In the summer of 1776, Lafayette went to a dinner where guests included the Duke of Gloucester, brother of Britain's King George. The conversation turned to the rebels in America and British measures to stifle them. Lafayette was intrigued and soon resolved to help the Americans.[32] He made the acquaintance of "Baron" Johann de Kalb, a Bavarian peasant who invented his title after acquiring a very rich wife.[33] De Kalb had served in the French military and settled in Paris.[34] Well past 50, de Kalb had also traveled to America and knew English. With de Kalb as interpreter, he and Lafayette both approached Deane to ask about serving the American cause.[35]

In his memoirs years later, Lafayette recalled the meeting: "When I presented to Mr. Deane my boyish face (for I was scarcely nineteen years of age,) I spoke more of my ardour in the cause than of my experience; but I dwelt much upon the effect my departure would excite in France."[36]

Indeed it would, for Lafayette circulated with royalty—he had danced the quadrille with the French queen, Marie Antoinette. Deane quickly came to an agreement with both Lafayette and de Kalb, promising each the rank of major general.[37] What was Deane thinking? How did it make sense to promise the lofty rank to a teenager who spoke no English and had never set foot on a battlefield? In the agreement Deane and Lafayette signed, Deane explained that the high rank was proper for the young man because of his "high Birth, his Alliances, the great Dignities which his Family holds at this Court, his considerable Estates in this Realm, his personal merit, his Reputation, his disinterestedness, and above all his Zeal for the Liberty of our Provinces."[38] In short, Lafayette was rich, eager, well connected, and seemed like a good lad.

The challenge now for Lafayette and de Kalb was getting to America. Lafayette told Deane he would buy a ship, equip it, and take on the cost of sailing to America with himself, de Kalb, and like-minded companions.[39]

In April 1777,[40] leaving behind his son, his pregnant wife, and his furious father-in-law, Lafayette sailed off to America aboard the *Victoire* with de Kalb and other hopeful friends of the American cause.

After arriving safely on the South Carolina coast, Lafayette and the 44 other Frenchmen made their way to Charleston, and then set off for Philadelphia by horseback and carriage, until the carriages broke apart from the fierce jostling on the miserable roads. In North Carolina, they abandoned the carriages and discarded much of their baggage. Then, in the heat, the horses one by one collapsed, and the Frenchmen, one by one, came down with dysentery. In late July, the bedraggled Frenchmen stumbled into Philadelphia, where they showed up at the doorstep of John Hancock. Expecting an effusive welcome, they got instead the brushoff. Hancock had no interest in even saying "hello." They were directed to call upon Robert Morris. He, too, had no time for them, but at least offered to meet up the next morning outside the State House.[41] Morris appeared at the appointed time and place, along with Lovell, with his facility in French. Morris soon left Lovell alone to deal with the unwelcome visitors, who had arrived when the Coudray affair was still on boil and no one in Congress had any patience for Frenchmen.

The visitors were soon impressed by Lovell's French, but not so much by what he said—dismissing them as adventurers and advising them that, because America had all the Frenchmen it needed, they should turn around and go back home.[42] Plainly, Frenchmen were out of fashion in Philadelphia.

However, Lafayette's trampled hopes revived the very next morning when Lovell, along with New York's William Duer, who also spoke French, told Lafayette that Congress might after all find him useful. Since the previous day, delegates had taken the time to read the papers that Lafayette had thrust into someone's hands. Deane's explanation, so flimsy from a modern perspective, swayed delegates, who resolved "that, in consideration of his zeal, illustrious family and connexions, he have the rank and commission of major general in the army of the United States."[43]

Many delegates likely thought along the lines of Laurens: "This illustrious Stranger whose address & manner bespeak his birth will Serve a short Campaign & then probably return to France & Secure to us the powerful Interest of his high & extensive connexions."[44] That is, Congress had no expectation that the young man would contribute much to the army, but he might be influential enough to foster closer ties between France and the new nation.

Meanwhile, de Kalb and another man took posts in the American army. Most of the others were on their way back to France on the *Victoire* before the end of the year.[45]

Lafayette's first glimpse of the great Washington was a thrill for the young man, who later recalled how the general made him feel welcome and invited him immediately to inspect forts together and to share meals.[46] This was actually Washington's impeccable courtesy disguising his dismay at seeing yet another overeager and unqualified Frenchman. Just before meeting Lafayette, Washington summed up his impression of the men who came over from France—including those who, like Lafayette, offered to serve without pay:

> They embarrass me beyond measure, which would be the case, were their pretensions ever so moderate, from the difficulty of giving employment to so great a number of strangers, unacquainted with our genius, language and customs; but the inconvenience is very much increased by the immoderate expectations, which, almost every one of them, I have seen,

entertains, and which make it impossible to satisfy them. And I have found by experience, that however modest, they may seem at first to be, by proposing to serve as volunteers, they very soon extend their views, and become importunate for offices they have no right to look for.[47]

Indeed, Lafayette's relationship with Washington quickly got off on the wrong foot. It was Washington's impression that the young man's rank was merely honorary and that he would not actually command anyone. But within a month, Lafayette made clear that he fully expected to lead at least a division. Washington pleaded with Congress for guidance regarding "Marquis de, le, Fiatte." In a letter to Virginia's Benjamin Harrison, Washington all but burst into flames:

> What the designs of Congress respecting this Gentn were—& what line of Conduct I am to pursue, to comply with their design, & his expectations, I know no more than the Child unborn, & beg to be instructed. If Congress meant that this rank should be unaccompanied by Command I wish it had been sufficiently explain'd to him—If on the other hand it was intended to vest him with all the powers of a Major Genl why have I been led into a contrary belief, & left in the dark with respect to my own conduct towards him?[48]

Harrison quickly responded. It was never Congress's intent, he assured Washington, that Lafayette have a command.[49] So Washington, for the moment, denied his adoring and eager general a meaningful leadership role but soon gave the marquis his first taste of combat.

CHAPTER 32

The Wretched Spectator of a Ruin'd Army

Through the spring and early summer of 1777, the war was on hiatus as the British made plans and geared up for the next campaign. By mid-June, that campaign was ready. The master plan called for a giant British Army to glide south from Canada on Lake Champlain, overpower American resistance, and meet up with another British force, also originating in Canada, but moving south from a starting point farther west and then along the Mohawk Valley. These two forces would come together at Albany.

It was possible that a third British force, from New York, would also converge on Albany.[1] Indeed, that was what the British General John Burgoyne, in Canada, was told—to anticipate meeting up with General William Howe and his army coming up the Hudson.[2] But Howe never received such specific instructions; he only knew that the rendezvous with Burgoyne in Albany was an option, not an order—that he could move up the Hudson or make some other plans, depending on his best judgment.

On the American side, the task of stopping the British invasion was the job of the Northern Army, which was now holding the key fort of Ticonderoga. But that army had been embroiled in a leadership crisis for more than a year.

Despite knowing an invasion was likely, the Americans were unprepared to face it, in large part because Congress couldn't decide on a commander. A tug of war within Congress and a rivalry between Generals Philip Schuyler and Horatio Gates had needlessly hampered efforts to prepare the Northern Army for the British offensive.

Early in the war, to mollify the New York delegation, Congress had appointed New Yorker Schuyler to lead the Northern Army, which had invaded Canada and then fallen back into New York state. Schuyler always had solid support from New York's delegates in Congress. Those delegates came and went over the months, but they usually included allies of Schuyler and often they were his relatives. Through marriages over many generations, he was related to John Jay, James Duane, and Philip Livingston, who each at one time or another represented New York in Congress.[3]

However, Schuyler was unpopular with New England delegates in Congress, and over time their opinion of Schuyler sank. The New Englanders, who made up a large share of the Northern Army, saw Schuyler as a tyrannical and inflexible aristocrat.[4] New Englanders were further put off by Schuyler's robust support for New York's claims in Vermont.[5] As for Schuyler's skills as a commander, New Englanders and others noted how little time Schuyler spent with his men and how much time he was away at his fine estate near Albany.[6] Indeed, Schuyler would earn the peculiar distinction of being the only high-ranking officer in the American army during the Revolution never to be actually present at any battle. In his defense, poor health sometimes kept him from the front and he believed his time was better spent well behind the scene of action. However valid these excuses, Schuyler's absence did not inspire respect from the men doing the fighting. Then there was the 1775 calamity in Quebec, a failure some attributed to Schuyler's indecisiveness. Schuyler, in turn, blamed the men and officers from New England, which of course did nothing to endear him to New England delegates in Congress.[7]

Philip Schuyler was a wealthy and influential New York politician as well as a general. He commanded the Northern Department of the American army, but over time lost the confidence of Congress. Though removed from command before the battle of Saratoga, he deserves much of the credit for laying the groundwork for the American victory. This etching, from about 1841, is by Thomas Kelly and is based on a portrait by John Trumbull. (Image courtesy of the Library of Congress)

The wrangle over Schuyler's leadership—usually with New Englanders on one side and New Yorkers on the other—brought out plenty of rancor. New York's William Duer, firmly on Schuyler's side, despised Virginia's Richard Henry Lee, who like his political allies in New England opposed Schuyler. Duer couldn't contain his glee after learning that Lee was caught up in a scandal ignited by rumors back in Virginia: "The Chaste Colo. Lee will I am credibly informed be left out of the new Delegation for Virginia which is now in Agitation. The mere Contemplation of this Event gives me Pleasure."[8]

Lee rushed off to Virginia to save his reputation and political skin. The scandal had to do with Virginia's war currency. According to rumors, Lee undermined the stability of paper money in the state. As it turned out, all Lee did was give his hard-pressed tenants the option of paying rents in tobacco or wheat rather than cash. Lee was exonerated, received a formal apology, and returned to Congress with his reputation aglow and his influence intact.[9]

This left Duer in a sour mood as Lee returned to Congress "Crownd with Laurels ... I suppose he will return here more rivitted than ever to his Eastern [New England] Friends."[10]

Schuyler remained on thin ice as commander of the Northern Army, with Gates eager to take his place.

An English-born son of a housekeeper, Gates joined the British Army at an early age, rose rapidly, and served in America—including a role in Braddock's disastrous expedition.[11] Later, with the help of Washington, whom Gates met during the Braddock campaign,[12] Gates settled in Virginia and chose the Patriot side when the Revolution began.[13] In June 1775, Gates was named as Washington's adjutant general. He was older than most generals, and he looked it. Thanks to gray hair and spectacles that slipped to the end of his nose, he acquired the nickname "Granny."[14] But he was effective in handling such essential but unappreciated tasks as gathering and distributing supplies, directing sanitation measures, and getting the medical department in order.[15] He also proved effective in cozying up to delegates in Congress, especially John Adams. Through their shared endorsement of strong measures in the Patriot cause,[16] Adams became "the best Friend and the most efficacious Supporter he [Gates] ever had in America."[17] In April 1776, Adams confessed to Gates, "I wish you was a Major General,"[18] and helped make that wish come true. The next month, Congress promoted Gates to that rank.[19] Though Gates called Virginia home, he was New England's candidate to take Schuyler's place, which appeared to be what Congress had in mind when, in June 1776, with the Northern Army still in Canada, it directed Washington to send Gates into Canada "to take the command of the forces in that province."[20]

Off went Gates, thinking he was taking over from Schuyler as commander. But in Albany, Schuyler quickly corrected his fellow major general. Schuyler informed Gates that the Northern Army was no longer in Canada—and indeed by that time the army had retreated south of the border. Therefore, Schuyler explained, Gates had no army to command. Gates countered that Congress clearly intended for him—Gates—to take over command of the army, wherever it was. Seeking clarification, Schuyler wrote to Washington, who sent the letter on to Congress[21] along with his own opinion that two major generals for the Northern Army was one too many.

Congress cooked up a resolution that pleased no one and solved nothing. Gates and Schuyler were to "carry on the military operations with harmony, and in such manner as shall best promote the public service."[22] Thus, Congress effectively made the generals co-commanders of the Northern Army.[23] This puzzling decision only made sense if considered in context of the date: July 8, 1776. Congress had just approved the Declaration, so this was not the time for a rancorous debate pitting Schuyler's New York supporters against New England delegates favoring Gates.

Fortunately, the two generals, to their credit, accepted Congress's decision—or rather indecision—and worked as a team, although not quite in harness together. For most of the time, they were physically apart—Gates in Ticonderoga, Schuyler elsewhere.[24] Schuyler assured Washington that "the most perfect harmony exists between us [he and Gates], and that I shall, by every attention to General Gates, strictly cultivate it."[25] Gates tolerated the arrangement, but was bitter. He dashed off a letter to John Adams complaining of "how much I have been Deceived, and Disappointed in being removed from a place where I might have done the Publick Service, and Fix'd in a Scituation where it is exceeding Doubtfull, if it will be in my Power to be more than the wretched Spectator of a ruin'd Army."[26]

Over the weeks that followed, confidence in Schuyler slipped as questions arose about the management of supplies to the soldiers. New England delegates suspected dishonesty,[27] and delegates from outside New England were wondering what to think.

Then Schuyler gave New England delegates an apparent gift: he sent Congress a letter of resignation. He was angry for myriad reasons, but what triggered the letter was mainly a congressional report about the Canada fiasco. While the report did not single out Schuyler for blame—even though as top commander he deserved some of it—it failed to heap sufficient scorn—in Schuyler's opinion—on Wooster, the Connecticut general whom Schuyler despised.[28]

But Schuyler had no real intention of quitting. As Schuyler likely expected, and perhaps coordinated, his New York allies made certain that plenty of Schuyler's friends were appointed to the committee in Congress that considered the letter of resignation. That committee included New Yorkers but also South Carolina's Edward Rutledge, who thought Schuyler had been wronged in the tittle-tattle circulating in Congress: "[T]he Rascals who took much Liberty with the Character of that Gentleman would not venture to look him in the Face."[29]

Other delegates noted the wave of support for Schuyler. William Williams of Connecticut remarkd about his "many & fierce" friends leading "a Torrent in his Favr."[30]

The committee came through with a report favorable to Schuyler, whose timing was superb. This was a terrible time, October 1776, for America to lose a key commander. Washington's army was getting clobbered around Manhattan, and to the north the British were poised to reclaim Lake Champlain. Congress surrendered to Schuyler and his allies with a resolution refusing Schuyler's resignation and assuring him that delegates were "fully satisfied of his attachment to the cause of freedom."[31]

Consequently, Schuyler emerged from this drama more firmly in command. This should have satisfied him, but he soon petitioned Congress with whining letters and yet another threat to resign. Even Schuyler's friends in Congress were finding him tiresome.

Relations between Schuyler and Congress came to a boil after Congress fired the doctor in charge of military hospitals in Schuyler's Northern Department.[32]

Schuyler sent off a protest, saying he should have been consulted.[33] Congress then took umbrage, huffing that Schuyler's response was "highly derogatory to the honour of Congress."[34]

Meanwhile, Gates found time to lobby Congress on his own behalf. He was in Baltimore in early 1777 to meet with friendly delegates. Samuel Adams reported: "General Gates is here. How shall we make him the Head of that [the Northern] Army?"[35]

Sure enough, in March, Gates received a letter from Hancock on behalf of Congress ordering him to "repair to Ticonderoga immediately, and take the Command of the Army in that Department."[36] Gates cheerfully assumed once again that he was the new commander of the Northern Army as he headed north and had a pleasant breakfast near Albany with, of all people, Schuyler's wife, who invited him to stay at the Schuyler house, an offer Gates declined.[37]

Schuyler, as it happened, was in Kingston, New York, when he heard rumors that his job had been snatched away and given to Gates. The New York Convention, the state's lawmaking body meeting in Kingston, was squarely behind Schuyler in his tiff with Congress. The convention promptly made Schuyler a delegate to Congress from New York, and off he went to Philadelphia to lobby for his job as general.[38]

Schuyler took his seat in Congress and promptly asked delegates to investigate and report on his own behavior. His aim was to clear his name and thus erase any cause to remove him from command.

But had he been removed? Was Gates now the commander? The precise wording of the resolution from Congress provides little clarity. Apparently, it was the intent of Congress to separate the commands: Gates would control troops at Ticonderoga, while Schuyler would command the remaining troops elsewhere in the north.[39] But to friends of Schuyler, it appeared that Congress was intent on, if not removing Schuyler, then "paring away his authority to nothing."[40]

As a committee took on the task of examining Schuyler's record, he and his allies in Congress beat the drum for Schuyler. Shrewdly, they noted how New York had perhaps more Loyalists than any other state and thus was more likely than any other state to abandon the Patriot cause and seek reconciliation with Great Britain. It was only Schuyler, they argued, who kept the state from renouncing independence. Without his leadership, masses would rush to the British side, his allies contended.[41]

This argument was laughable, but Schuyler and his friends had another: that the creation of an apparently independent command at Ticonderoga left too many questions unanswered. Not all the troops in the north should be stationed at the fort, but how many should be there and who should make that decision?[42] The idea of a divided but equal leadership—with Gates in Ticonderoga and Schuyler commanding forces elsewhere—was plainly unworkable.

In the end, Congress favored Schuyler again. The resolution called for Gates to be informed "that Major General Schuyler is order'd to take upon him the Command in the Northern Department" and that Gates may either "continue in the Command in the Northern Department, under Major General Schuyler" or return to his old job of adjutant general with Washington.[43] Schuyler barely survived, thanks in part to absenteeism in Congress. At that moment, no one was in Congress to represent Rhode Island, which would have opposed Schuyler. Meanwhile, New Jersey's delegation was missing two key delegates who were likely opponents of Schuyler. In their absence, the vote from that state was split, producing an outcome neither in favor nor against.[44] Schuyler failed to get the support of the majority of states, but still kept his job.

By this time, May 1777, delegates were tired of it all. "No single debate has been more tedious with us; having lasted whole days,"[45] wrote Lovell of Massachusetts. But it was not over. Now it was Gates's turn to visit Congress, and he was furious. At about noon on June 19, he appeared at the door of the State House in Philadelphia and asked to "communicate Intelligence of Importance." According to New York's Duer, Gates was "usher'd in, and after some Awkward Ceremony sat himself in a very Easy Cavalier Posture in an Elbow Chair."[46] After reporting, according to Duer, that "the Indians were Extremely friendly, much delighted with seeing French Officers in our Service, and other common place Stuff which at present I cannot recollect," Gates launched a tirade. Citing Congress's resolution in May confirming Schuyler as his superior, Gates roared: "My Rank, my Station, my Services entitled me to more Regard than such unceremonious Treatment ... [I]t is impossible that so wise, so honorable and so just an Assembly can have treated one of the first Officers in the American Army with such unmerited Contempt."[47]

These remarks and "malicious Insinuations" against James Duane, a New York delegate and friend of Schuyler, prompted a motion that Gates "be ordered to withdraw," in turn prompting calls to allow him to continue, then a "General Clamour" with more calls that Gates "Withdraw." Duer summarized in a letter to Schuyler: "[Gates's] Manner was ungracious, and Totally void of all Dignity, his Delivery incoherent ... the Tenor of his Discourse a Compound of Vanity, Folly, and Rudeness ... I felt for him as a Man—and for the Honor of human Nature wishd him withdraw before he had plunged himself into utter Contempt."[48]

Gates did withdraw and the dust settled. Duane later noted that he and Gates patched up, or at least clarified, their differences under more congenial circumstances: "We have had an Exploration on this subject over a Bottle!"[49]

Gates had good reason to be upset, but Congress for the moment stuck with Schuyler and in July ordered Gates "to repair to head quarters, and follow the directions of General Washington."[50]

Gates did not immediately follow those orders, nor did he resign, as many expected. He bided his time and remained curiously quiet, believing the job he coveted might yet fall into his lap. About this time, an election campaign was heating up for governor of New York. Gates was aware of this and knew Schuyler was a candidate. As governor, Schuyler would presumably quit the military, conveniently making way for Gates to finally take sole command of the Northern Army.[51]

CHAPTER 33

Marks of Deliberation & Design

As Congress wrangled over who would control the Northern Army, the British closed in on Fort Ticonderoga. Burgoyne and a mighty force had set off from Canada in mid-June 1777,[1] launching the great plan to cut off New England from the rest of the United States. The British commander began his invasion with some 9,500 officers and men, a vast assemblage of carts, tents, and horses, 138 pieces of artillery, many civilian workers, hundreds of women, and even some children.[2]

The Americans long fretted that an invasion from the north was coming and knew about such plans. About the time that Burgoyne and his army began moving south, an American posted at Ticonderoga described the plan in his journal in quite accurate detail.[3]

But despite plenty of rumors and reports, some Americans were unconvinced that the British would try yet again the same invasion that had failed the year before. One of them was Washington. Believing that the enemy cooked up reports about an invasion to trick him, he was reluctant to reinforce remote Ticonderoga. Instead, he put precious men and supplies in places more convenient for defending Philadelphia and other key sites.[4]

The Americans thus failed to bar the door. Burgoyne expected to face a force of 12,000 at Ticonderoga. In fact, there were perhaps 2,500 or 4,000, and of those many were ill and some had no shoes, blankets, or even guns.[5]

As Burgoyne zeroed in on Ticonderoga, one might have thought that Schuyler would have placed himself there to direct its defenses. But Schuyler seldom spent time at the outpost in the wilderness, preferring instead Albany or Philadelphia.[6] Schuyler left General Arthur St. Clair to hold the fort, and he was in a bind. St. Clair might have pleaded for more men, but he was reluctant to ask because he was short of food. He barely had enough provisions for the men on hand. Those men made do with little food and not enough weapons—many had no firelocks, and when called out appeared armed with spears.[7]

As for the fort itself, St. Clair well understood that the structure assumed by all to be impregnable was quite pregnable indeed. The French had built the isolated outpost in the 1750s to stop the British from moving north to invade Canada. Positioned to stop an army coming from the south, it was poorly oriented to stop an invasion from the north.[8] Besides thus being situated badly, the fort was in ruins. After the British evicted the French from Canada in 1763, the fort had little military purpose and was allowed to decay. While some work had been done to restore the structure after the Americans took control, the stone and earthen walls were crumbling, and important wooden structures had been dismantled to provide firewood.[9]

St. Clair, who took command about the time Burgoyne launched his invasion, had no opportunity to make much headway on any of these problems. Still, his men might have been able to put up a credible defense if St. Clair had not made an astonishing blunder. Near the fort was Sugar Hill, with a small plateau on top. If guns could be positioned on the hill, they could easily fire down on the fort. The hill had cliffs on three sides and a slope on the fourth side that was steep, but not too steep for a crude road. Americans had scouted the hill and knew that if anyone took the trouble to build that road,[10] guns could be placed at the top of the hill. Presumably, St. Clair knew this as well, but took no steps to seize it.

Burgoyne and his floating army finally approached Ticonderoga in late June.[11] Scouts surveying the landscape quickly recognized the importance of the undefended hill. By noon on July 5, Americans could spot scarlet jackets amid the trees on the plateau.

St. Clair, promptly recognizing that his position was hopeless, ordered an evacuation, thus giving up the fort without a fight. He hoped his army might slip away at night and be far away by the time the British noticed. But the plan for a quiet evacuation evaporated when flames suddenly appeared from a building. An officer, disobeying orders to extinguish fires, had ignited his own quarters. The conflagration lit up the scene of American soldiers scrambling to get away.[12] The British pursued the Americans until the remnants of the American force stumbled into Fort Edward, about 40 miles south, on July 12.[13]

To some, the fall of Ticonderoga appeared to clinch the war for the British. That's certainly what King George thought. When he got the news in August, he clapped and shouted: "I have beat them! beat all the Americans."[14]

In Philadelphia, delegates hearing the awful reports wrung their hands. "The News we have recievd from Ticonderoga is truly Alarming," wrote Dyer of Connecticut. "Fear it will throw the New England States into the greatest Consternation."[15] Henry Marchant, a delegate from Rhode Island, tried to raise spirits: "We are not to dispond but rise with new Vigour and manly Fortitude. Let New England now shew Her Prowess, Her Vigilance and Her every Virtue."[16] Henry Laurens blamed Congress for the catastrophe: delegates "were lulled by misplaced confidence & that kind of timidity which makes Men too often neglect their most important duties through fear of offending popular Men."[17]

John Adams was disgusted. He wrote to Abigail: "Dont you pitty me to be wasting away my Life, in laborious Exertions, to procure Cannon, Ammunition, Stores, Baggage, Cloathing &c. &c. &c. &c., for Armies, who give them all away to the Enemy, without firing a Gun." Weeks later, the ignominious loss of the fort was still on his mind: "I think We shall never defend a Post, untill We shoot a General."[18]

Cousin Samuel Adams suspected treachery: "It appears to me difficult to account for the Evacuation of those Posts even upon the Principle of Cowardice. The whole Conduct seems to carry the evident Marks of Deliberation & Design."[19] In another letter, he couldn't resist a potshot at Schuyler and a call to make Gates the commander: "I confess it is no more than I expected, when he [Schuyler] was again intrusted with the Command there. ... Gates is the Man of my choice; He is honest and true, & has the Art of gaining the love of his Soldiers principally because he is always present and shares with them in Fatigue & Danger."[20] Samuel Adams would get his wish. But not right away.

The situation for the Americans after the loss of Ticonderoga seemed bleak indeed at first glance. With Burgoyne in possession of the fort and the Americans in disarray, it appeared the British could easily march and sail south via Lake George and the Hudson River clear to Albany, squashing American resistance along the way. Once established in Albany, Burgoyne could effectively control the Hudson and cut off New England from the other colonies. Possibly, Americans would then see that the tide of the war favored the British, that the rebellion was hopeless, and that the jig was up.

But the distance from Ticonderoga to Albany was more than 100 miles. It would take time for Burgoyne and his ponderous army to cover that distance, and in that time the Patriots' cause could yet be saved. What were needed most urgently were men. Washington, understanding this more than anyone, sent off Continental soldiers he could hardly spare. He knew these would have to be augmented by militiamen, and most of these would have to come from New England. He implored Congress to dispatch the one military man he could count on to rally men to turn out and "check Genl Burgoyne's progress." That man was Benedict Arnold: "He is active—judicious & brave, and an Officer in whom the Militia will repose great confidence. ... I am persuaded his presence & activity will animate the Militia greatly & spur them on to a becoming conduct."[21]

However, on the very day Congress received Washington's letter, Arnold delivered to Congress his resignation.[22] Disgusted at the failure of Congress to make him fully equal to the five major generals promoted before him—and also frustrated that Congress had not yet reimbursed him for expenses related to the Canada campaign—Arnold had had enough.

Nevertheless, Congress ignored Arnold's letter, instead soothing him with the relevant extract from Washington's letter and asking him to "repair to head quarters" and follow Washington's orders.[23] Arnold forgot his quarrel and obeyed. He visited

Washington, who sent him on to the scene of action north of Albany. Because Arnold was so popular with the men, his appearance could only help boost sagging morale.

The Northern Army would also get assistance from a sudden surge in patriotism thanks in part to an astonishing success by the Americans against the British to the east of Ticonderoga, at Bennington. The British, desperate for horses, cattle, and carriages to move and feed their massive force in and around Ticonderoga, planned a raid into areas presumed to be poorly defended. But the raiders—about 1,400 men, mostly German mercenaries[24]—ran headlong into the amazing John Stark and a brigade some 1,500 strong. Stark, a hero at Bunker Hill and a veteran of Trenton and Princeton,[25] had quit the Continental Army when, like Arnold, he was passed over for promotion.[26] But he was a stalwart Patriot nonetheless, and a valued New Hampshire militia commander. The New Hampshire government, alarmed by the British invasion, authorized Stark to raise a force. Stark and his men thrashed the raiding party, capturing equipment and denying the British the supplies they hoped to pilfer.[27] The American victory was inspiring proof that well-led and motivated militiamen defending their land could succeed against professional soldiers.

The American forces got another boost when Congress finally fired Schuyler. The writing was on the wall after Ticonderoga. In a letter to Washington, Schuyler himself reported how confidence in his leadership had collapsed:

> The people, especially in the Eastern [New England] States, are industriously propogating that the general officers that were at Ticonderoga, and myself, are all a pack of traitors. This doctrine has been preached in the army by many of the people that have come up from New England and by some from this state [New York], which greatly prejudices the service, as it tends to destroy that confidence which troops ought to have in their officers.[28]

On July 26, about the time Schuyler was writing that letter, a New Jersey delegate, Jonathan Sergeant, introduced a motion to recall Schuyler, as well as St. Clair.[29] Schuyler's backers in Congress raised a fuss. Virginia's Benjamin Harrison cautioned against removing a man who was popular in New York: "Remove him, you disoblige that whole country & risque the entire loss of it."[30]

But the mood against Schuyler was overwhelming. New York's Duer wrote to Schuyler: "Your enemies in this quarter are leaving no means unessayed to blast your character. ... The friends to truth find an extreme difficulty to stem the torrent of a calumny."[31] Those friends in fact were wavering. The New York delegates recognized that Schuyler's continued role as commander might further hinder vital militia support from New England.[32] Maybe his removal was for the best.

Finally, Congress acted, removing Schuyler from command once and for all. New York delegate Duane consoled Schuyler—the firing was not because of Ticonderoga, but was necessary to get militia help from New England:

> Your Enemies relentless and bent on your Destruction woud willingly involve you in the Odium of loosing Ticonderoga. The Change of Command was not however founded on this

principle but merely on the Representation of the Eastern States [New England] that their militia suspicious of your military Character woud not turn out in Defence of New York while you presided in the Northern Department.[33]

Delegates ordered an investigation into the evacuation of Ticonderoga and sent word to Schuyler, as well as St. Clair, to attend a court of inquiry at Washington's headquarters.[34]

Who would replace Schuyler? Gates was the obvious choice, but Congress hesitated. New York delegates persuaded Congress to throw the matter onto Washington's lap with a resolution asking him to decide.[35]

Both Adamses and five other New England delegates sent Washington a helpful letter: "[I]n our Opinion, no Man will be more likely to restore Harmony, order & Discipline, & retrieve our affairs in that Quarter, than Majr. Genl. Gates. He has on Experience acquired the Confidence, & stands high in the Esteem of the eastern States & Troops."[36]

But Washington, in his long-winded manner, demurred. He wrote to Hancock: "At the same time that I express my thanks for the high mark of confidence which Congress have been pleased to repose in me by their Resolve authorizing me to send an Officer to command the northern Army, I should wish to be excused from making the appointment."

Washington explained that Congress had always nominated the officers for the Northern Department and that "I have never interfered further than merely to advise and to give such aids as were in my power, on the requisitions of those Officers." This was true enough, but beside the point. Congress was in this case asking Washington to make the decision. Washington merely pointed out what was obvious to everybody—that the decision was momentous: "The present Situation of that department is delicate and critical, and the Choice of an Officer to the command may involve very interesting and important Consequences."[37]

So, without Washington's explicit endorsement, Congress finally, on August 4, voted in Gates as commander of the Northern Department, with the support of 11 of the 13 states.[38]

Laurens of South Carolina remarked: "I wish him Success; upon that I may Say almost depends the Cause of America. If he gives Burgoyne an effectual Check the British Campaign will be over & Gates will Stand next to Washington."[39]

John Adams was jubilant: "I hope every Part of New England will now exert itself, to its Utmost Efforts. Never was a more glorious Opportunity than Burgoine has given Us of destroying him, by marching down so far towards Albany. Let New England turn out and cutt off his Retreat."[40]

Adams's cockiness seems out of place considering the unceasing train of bleak news from the north. But by this time, other Americans in Congress and elsewhere were seeing what Adams saw: Burgoyne mired in the American wilderness with no easy way out.

But why was Washington shy about endorsing Gates? Likely he wanted to stay out of the bitter quarrel between New York and New England. Also, by this time, Washington may have had doubts about Gates's respect for Washington's authority. Earlier, Gates had sent a sniping letter to Washington about tents for his men, and had "in an extraordinary manner"[41] seized for his own men clothing intended for one of Washington's regiments. To avoid a head-on confrontation with Gates, Washington requested and received from Congress assurance that, should circumstances force him and Gates to bring their forces together, Washington, not Gates, would be the overall commander.[42]

CHAPTER 34

Calculated to Deceive

Washington had plenty more on his mind than Gates and the Northern Department. He had to contend with the British General Howe, a vexing matter because Washington had no idea in early August the whereabouts of the general and the bulk of the British Army. For many weeks, Washington had expected that Howe would push up the Hudson and attempt to link up with Burgoyne, who was moving south from Canada. Then, in late July, Washington learned that Howe and about 18,000 men, along with horses and supplies crammed aboard ships in New York, had sailed, not up the Hudson, but out into the Atlantic, leaving behind a force just large enough to keep the city in British hands.[1] Where were they going? Howe, figuring Burgoyne needed no help,[2] had no plans to meet up with the army from the north. But just what was Howe up to?

Washington, along with the Philadelphia delegates, was puzzled. As Laurens reported, Howe "may now be in the Moon for aught we know."[3]

About this time, Philadelphia was a sauna: "Numbers have dropd down dead in the Streets occasioned by the imprudence of drinking cold Water."[4] John Adams guessed that if it was scorching in Philadelphia, it was broiling in Howe's overstuffed ships at sea: "How many Men, and Horses, will he loose in this Sea Ramble, in the Heat of Dog days."[5]

Weeks passed with no certain news, but various reports of ships along the coast to the south. "Where can Howe be gone, we begin to be under great Apprehensions for South Carolina," wrote Benjamin Harrison.[6] "Where the Scourge of God, and the Plague of Mankind is gone, no one can guess,"[7] wrote John Adams. "Whether he is going to Virginia to steal Tobacco, to N. Carolina to pilfer Pitch and Tar, or to South to plunder Rice and Indigo, who can tell? He will seduce a few Negroes from their Masters .... But is this conquering America?"[8]

Washington guessed that Howe's target was Charleston. Many delegates thought likewise.[9] Congress took action of sorts, recommending to authorities in North Carolina that tar and other naval stores be removed or destroyed, "rather than be possessed by the enemy," and appointing a committee "to consider the state of South Carolina and Georgia."[10]

Washington, who by this time had settled most of his army about 20 miles north of Philadelphia, determined that an effort to save Charleston was pointless: "Genl Howe might accomplish every purpose he had in view, before we could possibly arrive to oppose him."[11] Washington sought Congress's permission to march back to the Hudson, where his army might be in a position to help the Northern Army fight Burgoyne.

Then, on August 22, in Philadelphia, "at ½ past 1 oClock PM," John Hancock dashed off a note to Washington: "This moment an Express is Arriv'd from Maryland with an Accott. Of near Two hundred Sail of Mr Howe's Fleet being at Anchor in Chesapeak Bay."[12] So, Howe wasn't bound for Charleston. Congress now guessed that "the enemy have the city of Philadelphia in contemplation." They were right: Howe planned to move up the Chesapeake as far as possible, offload the men, horses, and supplies, and march northeast about 50 miles to attack the capital. Delegates politely pleaded for Washington to save the city: "Congress wish the General, in consequence of this information, to proceed in such manner, as shall appear to him most conducive to the general interest."[13]

Washington, after receiving the report, wondered why the British were taking such a roundabout way to Philadelphia: "By Genl Howe's coming so far up Chesapeake, he must mean to reach Philadelphia by that rout, tho' to be sure it is a very strange one."[14] Howe could have sailed up the Delaware instead and shortened his journey considerably. That, in fact, is what Howe originally had in mind. Why he abandoned that plan remains a mystery. Possibly he believed that Patriot defenses along the Delaware were pricklier than those along the Chesapeake. But if so, his intelligence was wrong. He would have met little resistance up the Delaware.[15]

Howe's landing place near present-day Elkton, Maryland, was about 20 miles farther from Philadelphia than Wilmington, where his men would have stepped ashore had he chosen to sail up the Delaware.[16]

John Adams, bringing Abigail up to date, was astounded at the British strategy:

> If Congress had deliberated and debated a Month they could not have concerted a Plan for Mr. Howe more to our Advantage than that which he has adopted. He gives Us an Opportunity of exerting the Strength of all the middle States against him, while N.Y. and N.E. are destroying Burgoine. Now is the Time, never was so good an Opportunity, for my Countrymen to turn out and crush that vapouring, blustering Bully to Attoms.[17]

Delegate James Lovell was equally confident: "We have army enough to swallow Howe and all his troops including his Horses as well as their Riders."[18]

Washington was compelled to shift his army from north of Philadelphia to the south to defend the city. Well aware that many Philadelphians were closet Loyalists, Washington took the opportunity to parade his men through the town. The demonstration, he hoped, would "have some influence on the minds of the dissaffected [in the city] and those who are Dupes to their artifices and opinions."[19] He may also have wanted to make an impression on Congress.

Despite all the pressing demands on him, and the urgency to reposition the army, Washington crafted detailed instructions to ensure the Patriot force more closely resembled soldiers marching in step than a shambling mob. The army would move out at 4am, reaching the city by 7am or so. They would, per orders, march in one column down Front Street, turn west on Chestnut—and thus pass by the State House. Washington dictated the order of march and distances between various brigades, companies, regiments, and divisions. Woe betide any soldier who strayed: "[I]f any soldier shall dare to quit his ranks, he shall receive Thirty-nine lashes at the first halting place afterwards."

Drums and fifes were to play a "tune for a quick step ... but with such moderation, that the men should step to it with ease, and without *dancing* along, or totally disregarding the music, as too often has been the case."

Except for some ammunition wagons, all wagons as well as spare horses and baggage were to be routed around the city. Camp followers were also banned from the parade: "Not a woman belonging to the army is to be seen with the troops on their march thro' the city."[20]

The day of the march started with a downpour, but by 7am the weather had cleared. As the parade made its way through town, delegates took notice: "From the State House We had a fair View of Them as They passed in Their several Divisions," wrote Marchant. The troops, about 16,000 of them,[21] took two hours to march by "with a lively smart Step."[22]

John Adams penned a note to Abigail: "The Army, upon an accurate Inspection of it, I find to be extreamly well armed, pretty well cloathed, and tolerably disciplined." Still, the intended picture of order was a bit askew:

> Our soldiers have not yet, quite the Air of Soldiers. They dont step exactly in Time. They dont hold up their Heads, quite erect, nor turn out their Toes, so exactly as they ought. They dont all of them cock their Hats—and such as do, dont all wear them the same Way.[23]

Washington's army crossed the Schuylkill, camped at Darby, and continued southwest the next day.[24]

Meanwhile, after nearly seven weeks of cramped, steamy misery aboard ship, Howe's men stumbled ashore at Head of Elk, Maryland, some 57 miles from Philadelphia,[25] on August 25, and they were luckier than the horses. The brutal journey killed 170 of them; the remaining 150 were too weak to be much use for a while.[26]

The few American militiamen on the scene to oppose the landing didn't bother to fire even one shot before fleeing. That night, a thunderstorm soaked the British troops huddled in hovels made of fence rails and cornstalks.[27]

With the British Army again threatening Philadelphia, delegates chose to fret about treachery. On August 26, they approved a resolution urging authorities in Pennsylvania and Delaware to disarm and seize anyone "notoriously disaffected." They also asked authorities in Philadelphia to search the houses of anyone who had not "manifested their attachment to the American cause" and to confiscate weapons.[28]

Two days later, Congress took sterner steps targeting certain rich Quakers:

> [T]he uniform tenor of the conduct, and conversation of a number of persons of considerable wealth, who profess themselves to belong to the society of people commonly called Quakers, render it certain and notorious, that those persons are, with much rancour and bitterness, disaffected to the American cause: that, as these persons will have it in their power, so there is no doubt it will be their inclination, to communicate intelligence to the enemy, and, in various other ways, to injure the councils and arms of America especially, but also anyone else.[29]

From early on, Congress had found the Quakers infuriating. Because they were pacifist, many refused to support the military in any way. Most balked at becoming soldiers, while many refused to pay taxes to the new governments because the money might be used to support the war. Some Quakers would not sell grain to the American military or even grind it for them. Others refused to accept Continental currency because it was a tool for financing the war.[30] In 1776, delegate Edward Rutledge suggested that if the Quakers "make a point" of refusing the currency, then "we must make a point of hanging them."[31] Occasionally, spies for the British posed as Quakers,[32] which further undermined trust in anyone claiming to be a Quaker. Some Quakers, defying the majority in the Society of Friends to support the Patriot side and the new government, formed a group known as Free Quakers. Most Quakers, however, remained neutral or boldly pro-British.

By August 1777, therefore, anger at the Quakers was nothing new. But a letter and documents from an American general provoked a new spasm of outrage against the sect. The documents suggested that a group of Quakers in a remote part of New Jersey were passing on valuable information to the British. The documents were likely fake, but Congress didn't know and didn't bother to check.[33]

As delegates considered this evidence, they were reminded of a "sedicious Publication"[34] back in 1776 discouraging Quakers from taking part in the war[35] "when the enemy, in the month of December ... were bending their progress towards the city of Philadelphia."[36] The evidence of betrayal in New Jersey combined with a history of writing against the Patriot cause were more than enough to convince delegates that toleration of the Quakers was too risky in this time of peril.

Congress now called upon the states to arrest Quakers or anyone who "have, in their general conduct and conversation, evidenced a disposition inimical to the cause of America."[37] It was felt that such people should be "debar'd of all correspondence and connection with Persons of the same persuasion, and that they be confined in such places, and treated in such manner, as shall be consistent with their respective characters and security of their persons."

Furthermore, delegates named 14 Pennsylvanians who should be arrested.[38] They were to be taken into custody not for committing any particular crime, but because they might do something unlawful or obstructive.

Pennsylvania authorities duly complied and went further, identifying 40 for arrest and rounding up most of them in early September.[39] One was Thomas Fisher, a well-traveled, well-educated, firmly pacifist, and royalist Quaker. When war broke out, he had refused to pay war taxes, accept Continental money, or swear allegiance to Patriot authority.[40] For this, he and his family had already received unwelcome attention. His wife, Sarah Logan Fisher, kept a diary that included scattered comments about the Quakers' tormentors, such as the local Committee of Safety, the busybodies alert for signs of Toryism: "[T]hey are men of very little principle, under no discipline, & so intolerably dirty that even in the cleanest of their houses the stench of their dirt is great enough to cause an infectious sickness."[41]

In her diary, Sarah Fisher described her husband's arrest:

> Three men came for him & offered him his parole to confine himself prisoner to his own house, which he refused signing. They then told him he must go with them, and be confined to the Lodge [Masonic Hall]. He refused going till he had seen a warrant. Upon which they read over a paper which they called one, which was an order from the Congress.[42]

The wholesale confinement of so many wealthy and prominent men raised a stir. A petition signed by more than 100 supporters found its way to the Pennsylvania Supreme Executive Council. Petitioners demanded a hearing for the confined men. The Council passed the buck to Congress: the arrests, the Council argued, were made on the recommendation of Congress, so Congress should hold the hearing, if there were to be one.[43]

Congress tossed it back to the Pennsylvania Council, recommending that the Council "hear what the said remonstrants can allege, to remove the suspicions of their being disaffected or dangerous to the United States."[44]

The Council refused, claiming that there was no time for it in the "midst of the present load of important business." But the Council was willing to release any prisoner who swore allegiance to the independent state of Pennsylvania. Some did, but many refused. The Council tossed the problem back to Congress to "hear and dispose of the gentlemen prisoners in the Mason's Lodge."[45]

Some of the prisoners themselves sent a plea to Congress to be heard:

> Most of you are not personally known to us, nor are we to you; and few of you have had the opportunity of conversing with any of us, or of knowing any thing more of our conduct and conversation, than what you have received from others, and thus we are subjected to the unjust suspicions, you have entertained from the uncertain reports, of our adversaries, and are condemned unheard, to be deprived of our most endearing connections, and temporal enjoyments, when our personal care of them, is most immediately necessary.[46]

Congress responded that it would be "improper" for Congress to hold a hearing, because the men were "inhabitants of Pennsylvania"[47]—as if people who lived in the state lived outside the nation.

At least some delegates must have been troubled by the handling of the Quakers, for Congress in one session spent five hours talking about it. But that was five hours too long over the "Silly point," in the opinion of Laurens:

> They now profess themselves to be "real & true friends to America," but read their testimonials ... & answer, are they friends to the Independence of the 13 United States? Are they friends to the Laws & Constitution whose protection they claim in the State of Philadelphia? Can there be more dangerous Inmates than Men who are in close correspondence with & giving intelligence, to the open Enemies of those with whom they dwell & to whom they outwardly profess Love & friendship? Can there be an instance produced of more refined insulting hyprocrisy than an artful declaration of Specious truth calculated to deceive?[48]

Virginia's Richard Henry Lee likewise sniped at the imprisoned Quakers: "Altho nothing can be more certain than that Allegiance & protection are reciprocal duties, yet these Men have the assurance to call for the protection of those laws and that government, which they expressly disclaim and refuse to give any evidence of their Allegiance to."[49]

John Adams was similarly unsympathetic: "[W]e have been obliged to attempt to humble the Pride of some Jesuits who call themselves Quakers, but who love Money and Land better than Liberty or Religion. The Hypocrites are endeavouring to raise the Cry of Persecution, and to give this Matter a religious Turn, but they cant succeed."[50]

In the end, the remaining 20 prisoners, all men, were escorted into "exile." A troop of cavalry led them and several wagons out of the city on September 11, leaving some of the baggage behind to eventually catch up once wagons and horses were found to carry it. The prisoners were bound for Virginia, but because the British Army was directly in their way, they first went northwest to Reading, where townspeople lined the road to hurl abuse and stones at them. The men were shut up in a tavern to protect them from a surly mob. They continued far to the west, before finally heading south. After three days on the road, with some men still wearing the same clothes they had on when they left the city, the cavalry was persuaded to allow the exiles to linger in Pottsgrove long enough for the baggage to catch up.[51]

Their route led them through Carlisle, Shippensburg, and Chambersburg, eventually in and out of Maryland.[52] At Watkins Ferry, they crossed into Virginia. By September 29, they were in Winchester, where they occupied a large house, were treated well, and had freedom to take long walks under guard.[53]

***

As Congress battled the Quakers, Washington faced the British. From Philadelphia, the American army marched southwest to Wilmington, Delaware, where Washington established his headquarters. He soon placed his army near a ford on the east bank of Brandywine Creek, blocking the British path to Philadelphia. On September 11, the British bombarded the American position. It seemed a prelude to an attack, but was merely a distraction. As Washington's army braced for an assault from the other side of the creek, Howe directed a part of his army 17 miles upstream. American officers received accurate intelligence about these British movements, but they also heard reports that the British were not, after all, on the move. They believed the latter, false report, and British troops crossed the creek upstream unopposed and maneuvered to attack the rear of the American army.[54]

Washington, soon aware of the threat, ordered his right flank to oppose the British behind the American army. Meanwhile, the British directly across the creek attacked.[55] Many of the Americans were soon on the run. They had failed to stop the British, who resumed their march to Philadelphia.

Washington managed to extricate his army from the rout, but the army's losses—300 killed, 600 wounded, and 400 captured—were about double those of the British.[56] Among the wounded was young Lafayette. Now with a bloodied thigh, he won the respect he craved.[57]

Congress got a vivid and dispiriting impression of the battle from Burke of North Carolina, who witnessed the encounter firsthand: "[O]ur Troops and Inferior Officers are exceedingly good, but that our Major Generals (one only excepted) are totally inadequate."[58] Burke pointed at General John Sullivan, whose reputation had already been tainted by failure and dubious battlefield decisions:[59]

> [S]o uninformed was he of the Ground that he knew not even the roads by which the Enemy might march to attack his flank, and altho he was warned by the General [Washington] that the Enemy would in all likelihood make that movement, and was ordered to keep out reconnoitring parties in order to know certainly their force and motions, yet he relied on the Information of a Country man who passed along One road while the Enemy were marching on the other.

After itemizing Sullivan's other blunders, Burke concluded that Sullivan "by his Folly and misconduct ruined the Fortune of the Day."[60]

On September 14, acting on Burke's report, Congress demanded that Sullivan "be recalled from the Army, until an enquiry ... into his conduct, shall be duly made."[61] Washington, doing his best with his bruised army to slow the British advance on Philadelphia, pleaded with Congress to delay the recall:

> Our Situation at this time is delicate and critical, and nothing should be done to add to its embarrassments. We are now most probably on the point of another Action, and to derange the Army by withdrawing so many general Officers from it, may and must be attended with many disagreeable, if not ruinous, Consequences. Such a proceeding at another time, might not produce any bad effects, but How can the Army be possibly conducted with a prospect of Success, if the General Officers are taken off, in the moment of Battle?[62]

Congress, as usual, deferred to Washington. The timing of the recall was left to his discretion.[63]

This was indeed a delicate and critical time, and delegates could see the writing on the wall. Without another miracle, like the one Washington pulled off at Trenton the previous winter, Philadelphia would fall.

William Williams of Connecticut wrote in panic: "We are indeed at a most critical & tremendous Crisis, a powerful Army, flushed with victory & animated by the strongest motives, Riches & Glory before them, no hope of Escape from Shame & Death but by Conquest, pursuing & at the Gates of this great City."[64]

If this were New England, delegates might have expected flocks of local militiamen to appear—as at Lexington and Concord—to defend Philadelphia, harass the British, and give Washington and his army a helping hand. But this was not New England. Letters from military men expressed shock at local indifference to the cause. According to one: "We have mustered from the whole State, by exerting every Nerve about 4000 Men, who as soon as a Gun was fired within ¼ of a mile of them would throw down their arms & run away worse than a company of Jersey Women."[65]

Another stated: "How astonishing is it that not a man is roused to action when the enemy is in the heart of the country, and within 12 miles of their grand capital, of so much importance to them and the Continent!"[66]

Washington likewise thought it astonishing "that Pensylvania, the most opulent and populous of all the States, has but Twelve hundred Militia in the Field, at a time, when the Enemy are endeavouring to make themselves compleatly masters of, and to fix their winter Quarters in her Capital."[67]

As the British moved north toward Philadelphia, civilians watched from their homes. Some came out and, eager to obtain hard currency, sold provisions to the invaders. Others provided information eagerly. Still, while nobody resisted, few actually welcomed the British. The British military leaders were disappointed that they did not sense the support they had hoped for from the local populace.[68] The people were largely bystanders hoping that both armies—British and American—would just go away.

Preparing to flee Philadelphia, Congress directed that printing presses—with one exception—be removed from the town.[69] Congress also asked Pennsylvania authorities to take all the town's bells "to a place of security."[70] Those bells, including the State House bell (now known as the famous Liberty Bell), were carted off to Allentown and stored in a church basement.[71]

In his diary on September 16, John Adams wrote: "The Prospect is chilling, on every Side. Gloomy, dark, melancholly, and dispiriting. When and where will the light spring up?"[72]

CHAPTER 35

Women Running, Children Crying, Delegates Flying

The light would spring up soon in the north. As delegates prepared to flee Philadelphia, they found comfort in reports from north of Albany that the prospects for the American forces there, once so bleak, seemed on the verge of turning spectacularly in the Patriots' favor.

The appearance of Arnold, the victory at Bennington, and the removal of Schuyler had indeed reignited Patriot zeal, which was further inflamed by a terrible tale that swept across the frontier. Back in late July, a young woman named Jane McCrea was staying in a cabin near the American-held Fort Edward, about 50 miles north of Albany. Indigenous warriors allied with the British attacked the fort and subsequently fled into the woods, but not before seizing McCrea and another woman.[1] By the time the warriors appeared at British-held Fort Anne[2] a few miles away, all they had of McCrea was her scalp—identified as hers by her own fiancé,[3] an American Loyalist serving as an officer with the British. One of the warriors later claimed McCrea was killed by Americans who had fired on them as they attempted to take the women away. According to another story, an argument between the warriors led to McCrea's death.[4] An inquiry led to the identification of an indigenous man as the murderer, but Burgoyne, afraid of alienating his indigenous allies, pardoned him.[5]

As it happened, at least six others, both men and women, were reported killed and scalped in connection with the same attack at Fort Edward.[6] But it was the death of McCrea that Americans seized upon, blaming the British as much as the indigenous warriors for the atrocity. A Boston newspaper pointed out that the murder "was done by British hirelings. No reason can possibly be given for their cruelty, but this, the captive, was an American."[7] "Jenny" McCrea, though likely a Loyalist, became a martyr for the Patriot cause in lurid prose that invariably called attention to her hair—described as black, blonde, or something else (it was red), and so long that, when she stood and let it fall, it touched it floor.[8] The tale of her grisly death became a rallying cry. In his own piece of propaganda published in American newspapers, American General Gates heaped scorn on Burgoyne for sanctioning barbarism and canonized McCrea as "a young lady lovely to the sight, of virtuous character and amiable disposition."[9]

An assortment of factors—changes of leadership, the inspiration of Bennington, the awful fate of Jane McCrea—thus generated a tide of militiamen marching in from New York, Connecticut, Massachusetts, and elsewhere. These, combined with Continental troops, suddenly made the Northern Army a formidable force. In mid-July, the Patriots on hand to face Burgoyne came to fewer than 5,000 men; by mid-August, that force had swollen to 13,000.[10] Time would only add to those numbers as fall approached and more farmers, after completing their harvests, left their homes to join their brothers in arms in the Northern Department.

Meanwhile, on the British side, the great unstoppable army under Burgoyne was fast shrinking. The disaster of Bennington reduced Burgoyne's army by one-sixth.[11] The army lost more men as it moved south, leaving behind garrisons at Ticonderoga and other key places to secure the supply route from the north. Now his indigenous allies were walking away. In the wake of the McCrea incident, Burgoyne had tried to bring them under better control with firm rules for combat—no stealing, no killing of women or children. The indigenous warriors were annoyed and offended. This was not war as they understood it. Fed up, many vanished into the woods, never to return. Their departure did not cripple Burgoyne's army—their numbers had never been large—but left it blind. The tribesmen were superb at penetrating the wilderness and scouting. Besides being marvelous at terrifying the Americans, they had been Burgoyne's eyes and ears. Without these allies, Burgoyne was left in a fog.[12]

Burgoyne expected that losses might be offset at least somewhat by the appearance of American Loyalists eager to fight with the British. The expedition had from the start included Loyalists, such as John Peters, who had fled Vermont for Canada. He had signed on with Burgoyne and led a Loyalist band known as the Queen's Loyal Rangers. Burgoyne had expected many Americans would follow Peters's example and join the conquering army as it moved south. Loyalists did indeed appear, but fewer than Burgoyne had expected, and of those who did join the British, many had no weapons and proved unreliable.[13]

Burgoyne also counted on help from the second invasion force working its way from Lake Ontario to the Mohawk River. Yet that help never materialized because those troops, under Barry St. Leger, scampered back to Canada in retreat thanks to trickery concocted by Benedict Arnold. St. Leger, his men, and indigenous allies had marched to the Mohawk and laid siege to Fort Stanwix (present-day Rome, New York), an American outpost about one-third of the way from Lake Ontario to the Hudson River. Arnold and a brigade of Continental troops were dispatched to lift the siege. Nearing Fort Stanwix, Arnold knew he lacked the manpower to drive away the British.

About that time, his men seized some Loyalists and condemned them to death as spies. One of them, Hon Yost Schuyler (his father was a cousin of the general[14]), had been raised among the indigenous tribes and knew their ways, their superstitions, and their languages. White people considered Hon Yost mad because sometimes he spoke gibberish,[15] but the indigenous people, at least some of them, believed he had special powers. Hon Yost's mother appeared and begged for her son's life. Arnold made a deal—Hon Yost would be spared if he agreed to travel to the British lines and convince the British and their indigenous allies that Arnold's force was much larger than it really was. Hon Yost was willing. His brother remained with Arnold as a hostage to ensure Hon Yost kept his word.[16]

Hon Yost embraced the role with gusto. He made his way to the British camp and told his tale. That, along with testimony from several indigenous warriors also sent by Arnold, was enough to sway St. Leger's indigenous allies, who were already discontented. After looting clothing and liquor from officers, they disappeared into the woods. St. Leger, too weak to push on without help from the indigenous tribesmen, retreated back to Lake Ontario.[17]

On top of these various setbacks, Burgoyne faced a yawning crisis of supply. He had relied on a stream of boats from Canada to deliver vital food and equipment, but that supply line was impossibly long and his army too big. He was also counting on seizing grain, livestock, and other supplies from the countryside. But Schuyler, before he was fired, wisely stripped the region of anything useful to the enemy. As the British Army faced starvation, Burgoyne's confidence gave way to desperation. Too proud to retreat to Canada, he wagered everything on his push toward Albany, and he had to move quickly—supplies were dwindling and winter was approaching. In Albany, he believed he would find the shelter and food he needed to maintain his troops over the winter.

As Burgoyne pushed south, the Americans gave way, retreating and falling back. This strategy, instituted by Schuyler, was terrible for American morale, but proved wise as it gave the army precious time to gain strength before making a stand.

The Americans fell back as far as the Mohawk. Then, under Gates, the army turned around in early September and began marching north. The Americans stopped at Bemis Heights, a bluff above the Hudson and an ideal place to block an army attempting to move south. By September 15—four days after the battle of Brandywine about 300 miles to the south—the American network of defenses was in place.[18]

***

Delegates in Philadelphia, aware of Burgoyne's predicament and the rising Patriot response, had reasons to be hopeful even as the scene in Pennsylvania appeared grim. "I look, Sir, to the North with the utmost solicitude," wrote New York's Duane to his state's governor. "Pleasing as are the Prospects I await the important Event with the utmost Impatience. Good news from thence woud animate every Breast. Oh may it arrive, and arrive speedily! that my poor bleeding Countrymen, after all their severe Labours and sufferings, may enjoy Security and Repose."[19]

For delegates, there would be no "Security and Repose" over these tense weeks as the British Army closed in on Philadelphia. On September 17, Congress laid the groundwork for a quick exit. After noting that Philadelphia "may possibly, by the fortune of war, be, for a time, possessed by the enemy's army," and that Congress might have to "adjourn to some place more remote than this city from the scene of action," delegates gave Washington wide-ranging authority in the Philadelphia vicinity for 60 days, "unless sooner revoked by Congress."[20] Delegates voted to make Lancaster, about 60 miles to the west, their temporary meeting place, should they have to flee.[21]

By mid-September, some delegates had already left town.[22] Some of those who stayed tried to carry on as usual. Laurens noted in a letter dated September 18 that he was asked to meet with colleagues that evening and the next day to discuss, not the dire military situation, but rather confederation: "Fright sometimes works Lunacy. This does not imply that Congress is frighted or Lunatic but there may be some Men between this & Schuylkill who may be much one & a little of the other."[23]

Outside the State House, ordinary Philadelphians appeared a little too complacent, according to one delegate, who suspected that a good many citizens were closet Loyalists. "The People of the City seem to be a little stirred & but very little," wrote Williams of Connecticut. "They are amazingly stupid & seem to think no harm will come to them, tho there is little doubt but the murderers are promised the plunder of the Town. Indeed tis hard for me to say whether the greater part will be well pleased with Howe's success."[24]

As it turned out, Congress never formally voted to leave Philadelphia. Sometime after adjournment on Thursday, September 18, a letter reached Hancock from an aide to Washington. It advised that delegates should leave the city forthwith.[25]

On the 19th, at about 1am, Philadelphians heard the "first alarm" that the British had crossed the Schuylkill on their way to the city. Then came a "great knocking at people's doors." Thomas Paine wrote to Franklin: "[T]he Confusion, as you may suppose was very great. It was a beautiful Still Moonlight Morning and the Streets as full of Men women and Children as on a Market day."[26] A diary told of "wagons rattling, horses galloping, women running, children crying, delegates flying, & altogether the greatest consternation, fright & terror that can be imagined."[27]

Burke wrote that delegates took to the roads "by universal Consent, for every Member Consulted his own particular safety."[28] According to one report, New Hampshire's Nathaniel Folsom rode off in such a hurry that he didn't bother to saddle his horse.[29] Some departed in a leisurely way, as if going on holiday. Laurens, though awakened at 4am, took his time: "[A]fter many thousands had passed by me I made my breakfast, filled my Pipe & soberly entered my Carriage, drove gently on to Bristol."[30] He would have lingered a while longer, but for an assignment to attend to Lafayette, now recovering in Bristol, about 20 miles to the northeast. Laurens found the town "covered by fugitives," and the "Road choaked by Carriages, Horses & Waggons." Laurens carried Lafayette to Bethlehem, another 50 miles to the northwest, where he left the Frenchman "in Bed anxious for nothing but to be again in our Army as he always calls it."[31]

The alarm in Philadelphia turned out to be false, as Lovell of Massachusetts surmised. As most delegates were fleeing, he ventured back to Philadelphia and quite likely passed Laurens going the other way. Lovell was drawn back to the city by "a desire to ascertain the true state of affairs & a little unfinished business of my own."[32] That is, he "had left some linen" in the city "and expected some things by a waggon." He spent enough time in "this Sodom,"[33] as he called the city, to get his pocket picked of some papers, more than a dozen lottery tickets he was holding for another delegate, and $260.[34] "My Loss of that money effectually joins with the exorbitant Prices in Boston to starve my Family," wrote Lovell, whose wife in Boston was "at the Point of Confinement," managing seven children, and "unable to get one Loaf of Bread per Day."[35]

With the British in no hurry to take the undefended city, Lovell "tarried" for nearly a week. The delay in taking the city had little to do with Washington and the American army. The retreating American army attempted to at least harass the British, yet even this effort turned into a bloody fiasco. An American force of 1,500 assigned to pester the advancing British were themselves surprised. Many of the 450 American soldiers who died at Paoli, 19 miles from Philadelphia, were bayonetted in their beds.[36]

By the 25th, Howe and the British settled in at Germantown, about 7 miles north of Philadelphia, and dispatched troops back south to take the city. On that day, Lovell finally left town. He "Slipt" across the Delaware into New Jersey, apparently choosing that route because he was escorting a young woman to safety: "It was lucky that I had a young Lady to gallant thither; for 3 or 4 Officers who left Philada. before me were taken on the Franckfort Road."[37]

***

Sometime in these crowded days, Lovell took on the task of ensuring that the *Journals* of Congress were safely carried out of town. The British, had they stumbled on them, would have found them interesting and useful for propaganda purposes if nothing else. Arrangements were made for the *Journals* to be carried by wagon 10 miles outside Philadelphia, where they were buried on or near the farm of a miller, John Roberts.[38]

In the weeks that followed, Lovell learned that Roberts was a Loyalist. Lovell sent a frantic letter to Washington to ask that someone be sent to dig up the *Journals* before they landed in British hands. Washington assigned a trusted Pennsylvania officer familiar with the area to rescue the records, which were dug up and taken away by a Continental regiment. As it turned out, Roberts, though a Loyalist, was also a Quaker and felt bound by honor and faith not to betray the location of the papers.[39]

Meanwhile, other papers were spirited out of town by various means to various places; some were carried by sloop to Trenton. Some documents were stuffed into casks before being taken away.[40]

***

As many of the departing delegates suspected, the arrival of British troops into Philadelphia was a welcome sight to a good many Philadelphians, including Sarah Fisher, who wrote the following in her diary for the 25th: "People in very great confusion, some flying one way & some another as if not knowing where to go, or what to do. I was much favored not to be at all fluttered, tho' it was an event I had so long wished to take place."

The next day she added: "Rose very early this morning in hopes of seeing a most pleasing sight. About 10 the troops began to enter. The town was still, not a cart or any obstruction in the way."

A band, she noted, "played a solemn tune, & which I afterwards understod was called 'God save great George our King.'" Meanwhile, the soldiers "looked very clean & healthy & a remarkable solidity was on their countenances, no wanton levity, or indecent mirth, but a gravity well becoming the occasion seemed on all their faces." After the soldiers, "Baggage wagons, Hessian women, & horses, cows, goats & asses brought up the rear." In just a few hours, "you would not have thought so great a change had taken place. Everything appeared still & quiet. ... Thus was this large city surrendered to the English without the least opposition whatever, or even firing a single gun."[41]

CHAPTER 36

A Dead Weight on Us

After scattering from Philadelphia, delegates one by one straggled into Lancaster. Many took a roundabout way to get there. John Adams calculated that he traveled 180 miles. "[W]e were induced to take this circuit," he wrote, "to convey the Papers, with safety, which are of more Importance than all the Members."[1] Adams, like a tourist, recorded his impressions along the way. In Bethlehem, he attended a Moravian service: "There were about 200 Women and as many Men. The Women sat together in one Body and the Men in another. The Women dressed all alike. The Womens Heads resembled a Garden of white Cabbage Heads."[2]

Delegates found Lancaster "crowded and in other Respects exceptionable."[3] The Pennsylvania government, also in exile from Philadelphia, were using the courthouse and refugees were everywhere.[4] Yet Lancaster was a little too close to the British for comfort, so delegates conducted business in the courthouse in Lancaster for just one day, September 27.[5] With hearts "still fluttering in some bosoms,"[6] they adjourned to York, about 25 miles farther away and across the Susquehanna River.

York—or York Town, as it was called—was a community of 1,800 people and about 210 houses.[7] John Adams wrote: "The People of this Country, are chiefly Germans, who have Schools in their own Language, as well as Prayers, Psalms and Sermons, so that Multitudes are born, grow up and die here, without ever learning the English. In Politicks they are a breed of Mongrels or Neutrals, and benumbed with a general Torpor."[8]

The town had more than a dozen inns and taverns, but these were not enough to accommodate the usual business plus the delegates and various servants. The Adamses, Richard Henry Lee, Henry Laurens, and four other delegates found rooms in the largest mansion in town.[9]

The town also had a brick two-story courthouse. Its courtroom, with a wood stove and gallery, was ample enough for delegates to meet. Twenty were present for the first session, but this room and the room upstairs could not accommodate all congressional activities. A residence near the courthouse and the law office of James Smith, a Pennsylvania delegate, provided additional office and meeting space.[10]

The Continental Congress met for nine months in the courthouse in York, Pennsylvania. Here, Congress adopted the Articles of Confederation and received news of the victory at Saratoga. The original courthouse, built in 1754, was demolished in 1841. The building was reconstructed in the 1950s and is part of the York County History Center's Colonial Complex. (Photo courtesy of "smallbones," via Wikimedia Commons)

Among the delegates who found their way to York was John Hancock, still serving as president of Congress. But now his wife, Dolly, was no longer by his side. She was somewhere in New England—in the chaos, John had lost track of her. On October 1, he scrawled a letter to her and handed it to a man he trusted, with a request that he "forward it by special Messenger to whatever place Mrs. Hancock may be." John described his "constant hurry" since the alarm that drove him from Philadelphia and the "round about course" leading him to York: "After what I have mention'd of the Scenes I have pass'd thro' since your Departure, I know you will hold me excus'd that I have not oftner wrote."

Hancock's letter exemplified the personal and family concerns of the men normally so preoccupied with affairs of war and government. He noted letters he received from her, including one from New Haven, "which gave me much pleasure," and one from Worcester, "which Rejoic'd me exceedingly." He reported he had a "Touch of the Cholick" and was "sadly Afflicted with my old disorder"—perhaps gout. Weary, ill, and longing for her, he was clearly thinking about leaving Congress and returning to Boston. He asked her to arrange that a certain carriage be painted and repaired to bring her to York, if he should stay over the winter, or to meet him on the road to Boston, should he decide to return to Massachusetts: "I hope the Campaign will soon be over, & give me an Oppory of Returning home, at least for a time."

He asked if she could send along "a little Keg of pickled peppers." He also urged her to visit his mother. In closing, he wrote: "I long to See you, & hope for that pleasure soon. Adieu, My Dear Dolly. May a kind providence ever Guard you, & with my best wishes for every Good, Am, Yours most affectionately, John Hancock."[11]

About a week later, another letter went out to Dolly:

> I sat in the Chair yesterday & Conducted the Business Eight hours, which is too much, & after that had the Business of my office to attend to as usual. I cannot Stand it much longer in this way. I have been very unwell since you left me, but Thank God, I am much better, my appetite is return'd, & I do tolerably well. I am exceedingly happy in my Lodgings, I have the best in the place, & the Lady of the House very Agreeable, which makes my Scituation pleasant, she is vastly Obliging, & I am in hopes I shall prevail on her to Consent that I shall Dine at her Table (for I now only Breakfast with her) which will be more agreeable than dining every day at the Tavern. ... [I]f I should be oblig'd to Spend the winter here, I shall certainly Send for you, but of that I cannot with certainty Judge; this is a pleasant Town, & if I had you with me, I should be very easy & happy but my Intention is for Boston as soon as the Campaign is over.[12]

James Duane of New York was just as eager to get away from Congress. He pleaded to New York's governor to send a replacement:

> I depend on your Excellency's Attention to get me relievd. Since the first sitting of the second Congress, which is now upwards of two years & five months, I have not on the whole spent four months with my Family. My feelings as a husband and a Parent are hurt upon the Reflection and I hope I may without Presumption say that my past Services entitle me to some Indulgence: and that it is not unreasonable to ask a little time to repair the waste which, from my total neglect of every thing which related to myself, has been made in my private Affairs.[13]

Delegates, besides being exhausted, homesick, and frustrated, were also angry and disgusted. Their rage was directed mainly at the people of Pennsylvania, who meekly allowed their state to be invaded. Indeed, many Pennsylvanians treated the British like friends. Eliphalet Dyer wrote:

> [I]nstead of the Country rising for their defence & surrounding & harrassing the Enemy in every Movement the Militia which were Collected have principally run of[f] & left the Genll with his Continental forces to shurk for himself. ... How[e] seems to be among his friends favoured with every advantageous Intelligence & supplied with every Necessary & Conveniencie both of Provission & Carriage while Genll Washington being in the midst of his Enemies & those disaffected to the Cause was deficient in both.[14]

Charles Carroll likewise thought Pennsylvania more a hindrance than a help to the nation: "The State of Pena. is either disaffected, or its Governt. so weak that it is become rather a burthen than strength to the Union."[15]

Why was there so little resistance to the British invaders? Delegates had varying opinions. John Adams blamed the Quakers: Howe in his march to Philadelphia passed "thro the very Regions of Passive obedience."[16]

William Williams put his finger on frustration over the sluggish economy in a state normally brimming with prosperity. He wrote that many people of the state appeared "weary of the Stagnation of Business, by the shutting up the Ports whereby They have so much lost their Gain, which seems to be all the God they know. ... They despise Continental Money, & take it only thro fear, & most extravagant quantitys for Trifles."[17]

Others blamed the revolution within the Pennsylvania state government and the resulting government that many hated. New York's Duane wrote:

> It's new Constitution and laws are unfit for this tempestuous Season ... and no proper means are exerted as far as I can see, to reanimate the sluggish spirits of the people, oppose the successful Efforts of the disaffected, or to draw forth the vast Strength of this State, which of itself is able to crush General Howe's slender army, humanly speaking, into the Dust.[18]

Pennsylvania that fall of 1777 was indeed a topsy-turvy world. Its city of York was, for the moment, the nation's capital. But Pennsylvania appeared cool at best to being part of that nation. The British had seized the largest and most important city with no local resistance. The American army outside Philadelphia existed almost as if in enemy territory, with little support from the people it was supposedly defending.

Meanwhile, Congress despised the state government for being a little too egalitarian, too democratic, too revolutionary even for the most ardent revolutionaries in Congress. That state government now reacted to the British invasion by authorizing a reign of terror. It created a Council of Safety with authority to do anything without respecting such rights as free speech or bothering with such niceties as fair trials. It could make regulations it thought necessary and summarily "seize, detain, imprison, punish, either capitally or otherwise" anyone who disobeyed or anyone whose "general conduct or conversation may be deemed inimical to the common cause of liberty, and the United States of North America."[19] As it turned out, the reign of terror was brief and meek. The Council of Safety was too hesitant and weak in the chaotic times to use its powers to any significant extent.[20] Delegate John Harvie of Virginia was disgusted: "Pennsylvania is at present a dead weight on us. Their Councils and Executive are puerile weak and Inanimate."[21]

Congress was similarly moved in this time of crisis to cast aside rights the Revolution was being fought to protect. On October 8, Congress authorized Washington to arrest anyone within 30 miles of the British Army if found acting as a guide for the British, for giving them information, or for furnishing them "with supplies of provisions, money, cloathing, arms; forage, fuel, or any kind of stores." Those arrested would be "treated as an enemy and traitor to these United States" and could be court-martialed and sentenced to death.[22] Such civilians would not have access to civilian courts or juries.[23] The restrictions were to remain in force until January.[24]

***

Just as delegates were settling in at York, Congress received a packet from General Gates containing "very agreable intelligence."[25]

The news concerned events to the north. On the morning of September 19, in a cold, damp fog, Burgoyne's army was close enough to Gates's forces that the Americans could hear British drums. As the fog lifted, Americans could glimpse British activity. Gates's response was to do nothing. He was perfectly content to wait for Burgoyne to crash against the American defenses. Gates was a cautious man, with ample respect for the disciplined Redcoats. He thought his best bet was to be on the defensive and wait for Burgoyne to attack his superb position.[26]

Arnold, in command of part of the American army, had a different idea. He believed that if the British were allowed to maneuver at will, they could find a way to outflank the Americans. The Americans should seize the opportunity to attack the British where the Americans would have an advantage. Arnold had already annoyed Gates for openly disputing earlier orders. Gates was not about to give in to Arnold's arguments in this case. He authorized Arnold to lead just a small force out to observe what the British were up to. They might harass the British if the chance arose, but nothing more.[27]

But when the chance arose, at a clearing called Freeman's Farm, the Americans were not shy, and chaos ensued. Gates, behind the lines, dispatched reinforcements. This was not the battle he planned for, but he felt he had no choice. By noon, under a baking sun, the field was strewn with Redcoats and Americans bleeding and dead. The fighting resumed in the afternoon and raged past sunset. By dark, the British commanded the bloody field and thus, arguably, won the day's glory, but their army was so crippled by the heavy losses that doubts arose about whether it was strong enough to continue.[28]

***

Uncertain but hopeful that events to the north would soon turn definitively the Americans' way, delegates at York got back to work. To Charles Carroll of Carrollton, little had changed: "The Congress still continues the same noisy, empty & talkative assembly it always was since I have known it."[29]

But very soon, and with astonishing determination, delegates resumed the long-postponed task of creating a confederation: drawing up a constitution that defined the national government and the nature of the union.

The loss of Philadelphia provided a sense of urgency to the task by reminding delegates of America's weakness. If the American army could not stop the British from taking the nation's capital, how likely was it that it would ever be able to drive the British out of the country? Americans needed help. That is, allies. To attract an ally, such as France, Congress needed to show the Europeans that the United States had a stable, sound, and reliable government. A confederation would be a step in that direction. Confederation—combined with a hoped-for victory up north—would impress France.

Confederation was also taking on more importance as doubts about the reliability of the Continental dollar gained traction. Confederation could boost public confidence in the national government and strengthen trust that tax measures would be put in place to ensure the dollar's viability.[30]

On October 7, delegates dusted off Dickinson's plan for confederation and launched into debate on a core issue that had haunted Congress from the first weeks delegates came together back in 1774: how votes in Congress should be determined. Would it be by population, by state, or by some other means? A motion was offered to have one representative for every 50,000 inhabitants. That was defeated, with only two states—Virginia and Pennsylvania—voting in favor. A similar motion—proposing one representative for every 30,000—also lost, with Virginia the lone state in favor. Another motion called for representation based on taxes from each state. That also lost. Again, Virginia was alone.[31]

Inevitably, a motion was brought forward for one vote for each state. This passed, with Virginia the lone state opposing, though Delaware was absent, and North Carolina divided.[32]

Then, over five days, delegates chewed over how to determine each state's financial contribution to the national government. According to population? According to land values? According to some other way?[33] Would the value of the enslaved be considered? After a few days of talk, Laurens observed: "[S]ome sensible things have been said, & as much nonsense as ever I heard in so short a space."[34] A bare majority finally settled on land values plus improvements as the basis. The four New England states—Massachusetts, New Hampshire, Connecticut, and Rhode Island—opposed. Those states were densely settled with more improvement than in other states. Southern states favored the formula, which did not consider the value of enslaved people. Delegates from New York and Pennsylvania could not agree on the issue. New Jersey cast the key vote for the majority.[35]

On October 15, Congress took up the question of western land claims. What if any power should the national government have over claims by some states of lands to the west, even as far as the Pacific Ocean? The early draft of the Articles of Confederation by Dickinson proposed that the national government have the power to deny western claims and determine boundaries of new states.[36] Delegates rejected that notion. Congress, under the revised draft, would have no say about western boundaries. On this question, Virginia, with audacious claims to the west, was the winner. With these big issues out of the way, the path to completing the Articles seemed clear.

Meanwhile, the war went on. Washington, embarrassed at Brandywine and unable to stop the British from taking Philadelphia, grabbed a fleeting opportunity to snatch a victory. Admiral Lord Howe had maneuvered vital supply ships bound for Philadelphia up the Delaware River, but he couldn't get those ships past river fortifications still held by Americans. The admiral's brother, General Howe, dispatched troops from Germantown to attack and seize those American posts.[37]

That left Germantown with about 9,000 British soldiers. Washington had some 11,000.[38] With this small advantage, Washington planned to pounce. On the misty dawn of October 4, the Americans charged into the village, little more than a main street with scattered stone houses. The British were surprised and fell back, abandoning kettles with breakfast cooking. The Americans appeared to be on the winning side of a rout. But momentum was lost when American troops paused to surround and bombard a stone mansion, barricaded and transformed into a fort by British troops.[39]

With the delay, coordination among the various American companies fell apart. Meanwhile, dense fog led to confusion, disorientation, and Americans firing on Americans. The British recovered, and with reinforcements from Philadelphia, compelled an American retreat.[40]

Again, Washington had failed, yet Congress gave him a pat on the back, thanking him "for his wise and well concerted attack upon the enemy's army near Germantown. … Congress being well satisfied that the best designs and boldest efforts may sometimes fail by unforeseen incidents, trusting that, on future occasions, the valour and virtue of the army will, by the blessing of Heaven, be crowned with complete and deserved success."[41]

Richard Henry Lee was convinced that the battle revived morale: "Our Army is now upon the ground they left before the battle, in the high spirits, and satisfied they can beat the enemy."[42]

***

From the north, delegates heard nothing new about fighting between the British and Americans. The only conflict they heard about was that between the commander and one of his generals: "Gates & Arnold are not on speaking terms."[43] That put it mildly, as the simmering feud between the two was now at full boil. Gates set Arnold off by first leaving Arnold's name out of a report to Congress about the battle on September 19, and then by taking away Arnold's command of a key corps of riflemen. Arnold, vain and touchy, stormed into Gates's quarters and the two exchanged volleys of curses. Arnold left, drew up a list of grievances, and sent it to Gates. Gates responded with written permission for Arnold to leave the camp—effectively telling Arnold to get lost. But Arnold had support: every general officer except Gates and one other signed a petition asking that Arnold stay. Arnold remained, but apparently with no one to command.[44]

CHAPTER 37

Very Curious and Extraordinary

On October 20, 1777, a letter "of a very curious and extraordinary nature" came to the attention of Congress. Washington, after receiving it, "thought proper" to send it on to Congress.[1] It was a plea for Washington to talk Congress into "rescinding the hasty & ill-advised declaration of Independency."

The author was none other than Rev. Jacob Duché, the Philadelphia cleric who had led Congress in prayers. In this lengthy letter, Duché explained that he never truly supported independence in the first place. He explained that he had "rashly accepted the appointment" as chaplain for Congress because he feared that otherwise the Anglican churches might be forced to close. Since resigning as chaplain in October 1776, he had opposed everything Congress did.

Of particular interest to delegates were Duché's remarks about Congress: "Take an impartial View of the present congress. What can you expect from them?" Regarding the Virginia delegates he wrote: "Your feelings must be greatly hurt by the representation from your native province." And he had the following to say about the Pennsylvania delegates: "[S]ome of them are so obscure, that their very names have never met my ears before, & others have only been distinguished for the Weakness of their understandings, and the violence of their tempers."

As for the New England men, he added: "[C]an you find one, that as a gentleman, you could wish to associate with? unless the soft & mild address of Mr Hancock, can atone for his want of every other qualification necessary for the Station he fills. Bankrupts, Attorneys & men of desperate fortunes are his Colleagues."

Duché summed up:

> Are the Dregs of a Congress, then, still to influence a mind like yours? These are not the Men you engaged to serve. These are not the Men that America has chosen to represent her. Most of them elected by a little low Faction, and the few gentlemen, that are among them, now well known to be upon the Balance, & looking up to your hand alone to move the beam. ... The most respectable characters have withdrawn themselves, and are succeeded by a great majority of illiberal & violent men.

After ripping into Congress, Duché likewise castigated the army: "Have they not frequently abandoned even yourself in the hour of extremity? Have you, can you have the least Confidence in a Sett of undisciplined Men, & Officers, many of whom have been taken from the lowest of the People, without Principle, without Courage."

He went on. Most of the tiny navy, he said, comprised vessels that were either unmanned, unrigged, or soon to be captured. Regarding resources he stated: "Your Army must perish for want of common necessaries; or thousands of innocent families must perish to support them. Whereever they encamp, the country must be impoverished."[2]

Washington, in his note to Congress, called Duché's letter a "ridiculous—illiberal performance."[3] He said he replied to the letter with a message for Duché that he would have returned it unopened had he known the contents.

Delegates themselves were, as might be expected, furious. The letter was condemned as "very long, apologetic, expostulatory, Censorious, Rascally,"[4] while Duché was said to be a "Wretch,"[5] "the first of Villains,"[6] an "Invidious Hypocrite,"[7] "an Apostate and a Traytor,"[8] and "a Judas."[9]

The letter was remarkable not least for its timing. As Congress was considering the letter, they were also getting unofficial news of a great victory at Saratoga. "We learn that Burgoyne was totally defeated ... that General Gates's Army was in full pursuit of [enemy troops not] killed or Captured & we expect every hour an Account of particulars from the General,"[10] wrote Laurens on October 17.

The reports "lifted us up to the Stars," according to John Adams.[11] Some even glimpsed the war's conclusion. Gerry of Massachusetts wrote: "If the States are vigorous, they may destroy the Residue of the British Army in America before Reinforcements can be sent from Britain, & thus put an End to a most unnatural & inhuman War."[12]

But this news was as yet unconfirmed. Congress heard nothing from the commander, Gates. Delegates were mystified. Some speculated that Gates was just too busy with "his necessary attention to the great business of disposing properly of so many prisoners &c., &c."[13]

Finally, on October 31, the "official" report arrived. Colonel James Wilkinson rode in with a packet of dispatches from Gates along with an official message from the general, not written down but apparently carried in Wilkinson's head. Wilkinson begged for time to put the papers in order and properly write out Gates's message. Eventually, on November 3, Congress heard the official confirmation and details of the great victory.[14]

Delegates also learned why it took so long for them to hear from Gates. It turned out that Gates had not been tardy in broadcasting his success; Wilkinson had simply tarried on his way to York. Wilkinson explained that he fell ill,[15] but a story circulated that the 20-year-old stopped in Reading to woo a young lady.[16] A delegate mockingly suggested that as a reward for taking 15 days to reach York from

Saratoga, a distance he should have covered in much less time, Wilkinson should be awarded a set of spurs.[17]

***

Although the delay in informing Congress about the victory at Saratoga was thus not wholly Gates's fault, why did he neglect to send the official news promptly to his commander, Washington? Early unofficial reports had found their way to Washington as early as October 18. But 10 days later, he was still awaiting an official confirmation from Gates. It was not just a matter of courtesy. The information was vital in the calculations for deploying men and supplies, as Washington explained: "I ... cannot help complaining, most bitterly, of Genl Gates's neglect in not giving me the earliest authentic advice of it; as an Affair of that magnitude might, and indeed did, give an important turn to our Operations in this Quarter."[18]

Gates finally sent off a letter to Washington dated November 2, more than two weeks after the surrender. Gates cheerfully explained that he assumed Congress would pass along the news: "Congress having been requested, immediately to transmit copies of all my Dispatches to them, I am Confident Your Excellency has received all the Good News from this Quarter."[19] (Congress indeed sent out an official letter, dated October 31, informing Washington of the great triumph.)[20]

The victory at Saratoga was nearly as satisfying as delegates imagined from earlier reports, and further spiced with drama involving Arnold and Gates.

In the wake of the inconclusive battle at Freeman's Farm back on September 19, the Americans had braced for fighting the next day. But the British paused to recover, and on the following day, Burgoyne called off a planned attack after receiving a message from the south.

Communication between Burgoyne and his fellow generals, Clinton and Howe, was always difficult and spotty. For correspondence to get through, messengers risked their lives moving secretly over miles of Patriot-held territory that separated Burgoyne from the British commanders to the south. If caught, the messengers were treated as spies and executed. Despite the tenuous nature of communications, one message did reach Burgoyne on September 21. That message, from Clinton, contained a hint—not a promise—that 2,000 men might be dispatched to help.

It was a feeble lifeline, but a lifeline nonetheless, and Burgoyne grabbed it. From Clinton's information, Burgoyne figured that the relief force might appear in a week or two. He waited and hoped. Meanwhile, the Americans—so close that the British sometimes confused the rebel drums as their own—bolstered their defenses.

Burgoyne waited one week, then another. Clinton never arrived; nor did a message. Clinton had sent one, but the messenger was caught. Had the message arrived, it would have made no difference. Clinton and his army had moved up the Hudson and captured two American forts, but he acted too late and was too far away from Albany to be of any use to Burgoyne.

Finally, Burgoyne concluded that no army from the south would come in time. Too proud to consider a humiliating retreat to Canada, he concocted a desperate plan. With 1,500 Regulars, along with about 100 Canadians, 50 indigenous warriors, and 450 Loyalists, he planned to approach the American right wing and probe for a weak point, and then attack the next day.

The operation began on October 7. After a difficult march, the British reached a clearing containing a cabin. Burgoyne and key officers climbed onto the roof and peered into the nearby woods with spyglasses, but saw only trees. Burgoyne still had no clue of where the Americans might be vulnerable. He hardly knew where they were at all.[21] Burgoyne had failed to achieve even the first goal of the mission—to discern the American positions and find a soft spot.

Meanwhile, the hidden Americans watched. Soon, American sharpshooters were picking off British officers, and the battle began.[22]

Some distance away, Gates, at his mess dining on ox heart,[23] could hear the shooting. Arnold appeared and asked permission to observe the fighting. Gates reluctantly granted the request, and off went Arnold, accompanied by another general, Benjamin Lincoln. The two soon returned with a report that the American left flank was threatened. Reinforcements were needed. Gates, unconvinced and wary, ordered a maneuver but not reinforcements. Arnold sputtered: a strong force should be sent, he insisted. Gates snapped: "General Arnold, I have nothing for you to do. You have no business here."[24]

General Lincoln, with more tact, convinced Gates that, indeed, more men were needed. Gates relented and ordered in reinforcements. He had plenty to spare. The Americans had by now about 12,000 men. Burgoyne had fewer than 2,000 at hand, and his entire army—including the wounded and those back at camp—came to little more than 7,000.

At the battlefield, before American reinforcements arrived, the British drove back the American shooters. All was quiet for a while. The British concluded that the Americans were waiting for them to attack, but the Patriots took the initiative and emerged from the woods with a ferocious charge. Here and there, the British troops were soon on the run, but they also held on at several strongholds.

Meanwhile, Arnold, with amazing audacity, seized command of three regiments. He rode off toward the battlefield and hollered at the units to follow him. They did, charging into German mercenaries holding a position. The Germans stood firm for a while until, nearly surrounded, they fell back.

Arnold later made wild, reckless dashes near the remaining British redoubts, sometimes riding like a madman between British and American lines, as if determined to die. He didn't, although a bullet found the same leg that was wounded at Quebec. Then Arnold's horse was shot and toppled to the ground, breaking that same cursed limb.

By the time Arnold was carried from the field, the battle was over. The British had failed to dislodge the Americans and open the way to Albany, and had lost more than half of their force. The Americans counted just 30 dead and 100 wounded. It was a complete victory for the Patriots.

But who was the hero? Gates? Arnold? Both? Neither? Gates failed to get within 2 miles of the fighting and issued just two orders of any consequence on the day of the battle.[25] But ultimately, even if he wasn't at the front lines, he was in charge, and his caution and prudent plans for battle arguably put the Americans in the best position to win. Burgoyne later gave Arnold the main credit for the American victory.[26] Indeed, even Gates took pains to remark about Arnold's gallantry.[27] But one historian suggests that Arnold merely "stole the glory of a battle already won," and that the real heroes were the American riflemen who so effectively picked off British officers.[28]

The Americans and the unforgiving American wilderness had crushed Burgoyne's dreams. But Burgoyne could have still saved the remnants of his army. If they moved fast enough, and stayed ahead of the pursuing Americans, they might slip back to Ticonderoga, 60 miles to the north.[29] From there, with good luck and fair weather, they might yet escape back to Canada by boat before starving or freezing.

Knowing that a retreat in daylight would invite an American attack, Burgoyne arranged a nighttime withdrawal. The battered army crawled north. Most of the few indigenous allies who had stayed with the British Army now disappeared into the forests, while rain turned the trail to mud. From behind, American rifles pecked at the rearguard. Over 24 hours, the miserable line of soldiers, supplies, women, children, and servants covered just 8 miles.[30] They might have moved faster had they abandoned the remaining 29 pieces of artillery, but exhausted horses and oxen continued to drag cannons mile after muddy mile, a senseless burden for an army trying to get away fast.[31]

On October 9, the soaked and forlorn British force reached the village of Saratoga (now Schuylerville). Burgoyne settled into an elegant and vacant house, Philip Schuyler's country estate. The British general might have pushed on, knowing that at any moment he could be surrounded and blocked from further retreat. But he seemed to have lost his will.

In the following days, discipline wavered. The liquor was gone. Drinkable water was almost impossible to obtain. Men were starving. Dozens deserted, and many dozens of others were taken prisoner by the Americans skulking nearby.[32] With the Americans closing in, Burgoyne and his staff abandoned Schuyler's house and moved into tents. He gave orders to burn the house, the mill, and all buildings on the property. Only the privy was spared. Now, in the village, everyone was exposed to American fire. A cannonball sailed past Burgoyne and became wedged in a tree.[33]

On the evening of October 12, the Americans finally cut the last thin escape route north.[34] On the 13th, after a council of war, Burgoyne dispatched a cadet,

General Horatio Gates posed for this portrait around 1792, well after the battle of Saratoga, which made him a hero. He is shown with the medal that Congress struck to honor him. In his right hand he holds the Convention of Saratoga, the controversial surrender document that was so problematic for Congress. (Image of the Gilbert Stuart work courtesy of the Metropolitan Museum of Art)

just 12 years old,[35] and a drummer with a message for Gates about a "matter of high moment."[36]

Soon the guns fell silent and testy surrender negotiations followed. These sputtered and nearly broke down. Then finally, under an elm on October 17, Burgoyne signed the surrender.[37] Gates agreed to Burgoyne's request to call the document the "Treaty of Convention," a face-saving gesture to paint the capitulation as something less humiliating than a surrender.[38] But no one was fooled. Nearby fluttered the new American flag, with 13 stars and 13 stripes, pieced together from scraps of clothing. British and German troops piled their arms near the ruins of an old fort at the edge of the village.[39] That evening, Gates drafted a letter to his wife: "If Old England is not by this lesson taught humility, then she is an obstinate old slut, bent upon her ruin."[40]

Thumbnail histories of the Revolution cast Saratoga as the great turning point of the war, and indeed it was. But there was far more fighting ahead. The period between Saratoga and the last battle would be twice as long as the period of conflict leading to Saratoga, and twice as many soldiers would die in the next four years.[41]

CHAPTER 38

Essential to Our Very Existence

In York, the response to the "official" news from Saratoga was muted. Congress duly set aside December 18 for "solemn thanksgiving and praise," with a recommendation that on that day "servile labour" and "unbecoming" recreation be avoided.[1] Delegates also studied the terms of the surrender and discovered that the great victory was not as total as early reports seemed to promise. Under the deal Gates negotiated with Burgoyne, British soldiers, once they laid down their arms, would be permitted to march east to Boston, board British ships, and return to the British Isles. They could resume their military service with the promise that they would never fight again for Britain in the American war.[2]

To Gates, the agreement was the best he could manage under the circumstances. The American commander thought he had to be generous to seal the deal quickly. He knew that, as he was negotiating with Burgoyne, British troops under Clinton were approaching from the south. Had negotiations dragged on, those forces might have gotten close enough to embolden Burgoyne to resume fighting.[3]

Colonel Wilkinson, speaking for Gates to Congress, underscored Gates's predicament:

> Lieutenant General Burgoyne, at the time he capitulated, was strongly entrenched on a formidable post, with twelve days' provision; that ... the enemy's consequent progress up the Hudson's river, endangered our arsenal at Albany, a reflection which left General Gates no time to contest the capitulation. ... [T]his delicate situation abridged our conquests, and procured Lieutenant General Burgoyne the terms he enjoys.[4]

Congress duly thanked Gates, along with Lincoln, Arnold, and the troops under their command, and authorized that a gold medal be struck to commemorate the event.[5] Laurens, in a letter to Gates, wrote: "Your Name Sir will be written in the breasts of the grateful Americans of the present Age & sent down to Posterity in Characters which will remain indelible."[6]

Eliphalet Dyer assured Gates that Congress was delighted not only with the victory on the battlefield, but also with the surrender terms: "The preventing [of] a further Effusion of the blood & especially of your own Troops was Humane and discreet."[7]

In fact, Congress was not delighted at all. Delegates recognized that this arrangement allowed the British to swap soldiers on one side of the Atlantic for soldiers on the other side: the soldiers from Saratoga could take the place of those in England, who could be shipped to America to fight. The British would thus not have to recruit and train a new force.[8] Gates, it appeared, had let the British off the hook. Delegates soon appointed a committee to scrutinize the deal for an honorable way to weasel out of it.[9]

Meanwhile, Washington, when he heard about the convention, resisted the temptation to second-guess Gates: "I am perfectly well satisfied that the critical situation ... would not allow him to insist upon a more perfect Surrender." Even so, he hated the deal even more than did the delegates in York. Washington anticipated that the British, once they had their soldiers under their control, would find an excuse to repudiate the terms. The ships carrying the soldiers would not go to England, but would be rerouted to New York or another port controlled by the British: "[W]ithout great precaution, & very delicate management, we shall have all these Men—if not the Officers—opposed to us in the spring." He feared the British would somehow justify "a breach of the Covenant on their part—do they not declare (many of them) that no faith is to be held with Rebels?"[10]

***

By coincidence, on the same day delegates received definitive news about Saratoga, they also heard John Hancock's farewell. He was quitting Congress—and the presidency—to return to Massachusetts: "My health being much impaired, I find some relaxation absolutely necessary."[11]

Hancock, never robust, had a recurrence of his familiar tormenter, gout.[12] Furthermore, he was simply weary from 29 months at the helm in Congress, and he missed his family. It seemed to be a good time for a break. The work of cobbling together a blueprint for the young confederation seemed nearly done.

Hancock may have by this time worn out his popularity. We get that impression from Laurens. When Hancock first hinted that he might be taking his leave from Congress, Laurens brought forth a motion to "intreat & solicit his continuance." The motion got a shrug: "[T]o my surprise I was seconded and no more."[13]

Before Hancock's departure, another resolution was duly brought forth to thank him "for the unremitted attention and steady impartiality which he has manifested in discharge of the various duties of his office."[14] It seemed a proper, benign resolution suitable for quick and unanimous approval. But Congress labored over it for an entire afternoon.[15] It finally passed, but over the opposition of four states, including Hancock's home state of Massachusetts.

Samuel Adams likely had the leading hand in this. He opposed thanking Hancock on principle: "We have had two Presidents before, Neither of whom made a parting

Speech or receivd the Thanks of Congress."[16] Possibly, Adams also wanted to bring Hancock down a peg. Adams and Hancock had long been political allies, but they were, in important ways, opposites: Hancock, rich and happy to let the world know it; Adams, puritanical, poor, and proud of his poverty as a sign of virtue. They had an uneasy friendship. Adams, we can imagine, was irked at the thought of Congress further stroking Hancock's ego.

As it turned out, Hancock's ego got plenty of loving attention upon his return to Boston. A newspaper there described the celebration:

> [L]ast Wednesday arrived here, under the escort of light dragoons, His Excellency John Hancock, Esq. ... His arrival was made known by the ringing of bells, the discharge of thirteen cannon ... on the Common, the cannon from the fortress on the hill, and the ships in the harbor. The independent and light infantry companies paid him their military salutes. He received the compliments of gentlemen of all orders.[17]

Soon after Hancock left York, others followed, including both Adamses.[18] When they reappeared in Massachusetts, few took notice. The newspaper that trumpeted Hancock's return devoted one sentence each to note the return of Samuel and John Adams.[19] Meanwhile, the Massachusetts delegation in Philadelphia missed the Adamses: "The Absence of these Gentlemen occasions a Chasm in Congress."[20]

Laurens predicted that the departures of Hancock, the Adamses, and others would leave Congress with just 20 or 21 delegates until replacements arrived.[21] Those left behind in York groaned. Cornelius Harnett of North Carolina wrote often, like an inmate pleading for parole:

> I am fatigued to death attending Congress Night & Day & can hardly find time to write to any of my friends.[22]
> I have a great inclination to return home & wish to be in future excused from this kind of Service. Between you and I we shall be ruined in it, & I wish to make way for some Gentm who values his honor in this way, at a much higher rate than I do.[23]
> I heartily desire to be at home. & whenever I get there I shall with pleasure give up this disagreeable & troublesom Office.[24]
> For Gods sake endeavor to get some Gent. appointed in my stead. I cannot stay here any longer with any pleasure.[25]

Those who remained chose a new president. They picked Laurens, evidence of how quickly the "worthy, sensible, indefatigable Gentleman"[26] from South Carolina—who joined the Congress only a few months before—had won the respect of his fellow delegates. Lovell of Massachusetts described him as "a very good man both for order and dispatch."[27] The vote was unanimous, except for a dissent cast by Laurens himself.[28] Laurens accepted the post with a sigh. He wrote to his son John: "[U]pon my inmost honour I am weary & long to be at rest. The World have determined I shall find none till I arrive at the place where the Wicked cease from troubleing."[29]

Work on the Articles of Confederation resumed, with touches added here and there. Whole articles were drafted, submitted, and quickly approved.[30] That work was done by November 15, when Congress authorized 300 copies of the Articles to be printed.[31] With no suitable printer available in York, they went to Lancaster. But the printer there would take his own good time. The delegate who dealt with him complained: "[T]he printer, on this as on all other Occasions, is tedious beyond all possibility of being hurried. ... What can I do? I had rather be a Hogg driver than attend his press; but will do what I can to forward the Work."[32]

By November 28,[33] the work was done. Copies were dispatched to the state legislatures, which would each have to approve the Articles for them to become the law of the land. Congress sent out with the Articles a long-winded plea, crafted by Richard Henry Lee,[34] for lawmakers in the states to put aside possible misgivings about the document and quickly approve it:

> [I]t will confound our foreign enemies, defeat the flagitious practices of the disaffected, strengthen and confirm our friends, support our public credit, restore the value of our money, enable us to maintain our fleets and armies, and add weight and respect to our councils at home, and to our treaties abroad. In short, this salutary measure can no longer be deferred. It seems essential to our very existence as a free people, and without it we may soon be constrained to bid adieu to independence, to liberty and safety.[35]

Delegates were relieved to have finished the job. New York's Duane called the Articles "liberal and salutary & probably will meet with pretty general Ratification."[36] North Carolina's Harnett was less hopeful. In a letter to Burke, who was no longer in Congress, Harnett wrote: "The Child Congress has been big with these two years past, is at last brought forth (Confederation). I fear it will by several Legislatures be thought a little deformed, you will think it a Monster."[37]

It was deformed indeed, historians agree. The Articles are now dead, buried, and mostly forgotten. This first constitution of the United States lies unmourned in the shadow of the towering Constitution, the nation's second constitution and the current blueprint of the federal government. The Articles are damned. The Constitution, crafted in 1787, is scripture.

The two documents and the circumstances of their creation will forever be compared. The Constitution was composed in a time of peace. The Articles emerged amid war. The men who drafted the Constitution came together in a convention for that purpose only, accomplishing the job in less than five months. The Articles were drawn up over 17 months by men who came and went and who were pestered by interruptions and charged with myriad other duties.[38] Issues wrestled to the ground once were revived by newcomers to be grappled with again. Men who made important contributions when the work began—such as Dickinson, Deane, and Franklin—weren't in Congress to see it through.

Also, with the crush of business in all those hectic, confusing months, some of the best, most capable men in Congress were simply too preoccupied with other work to invest their energy in the Articles. John Adams, for example, never asked to be on the committee that drafted them, even though delegates recognized him as the best authority in Congress on the theory of government.[39] Adams had plenty of other work to do that to him was more important and more urgent.

The finished Articles sent to the states formed a plan for a government quite similar to the ad hoc government already in place. At its core would be Congress, whose delegates would be appointed by each of the state legislatures. Each state would be represented by two to seven delegates, but each state would have only one vote in Congress.[40] The states would be responsible for levying taxes to pay for the costs of war and other expenses of Congress. Each state's proportion of the costs would be based on the value of the land in each state. Congress would be the last resort to settle differences among states.

The Articles made no provision for a separate executive—a president of the United States—with authority over a separate branch of government. Congress could authorize a "Committee of the States"—made up of one delegate from each state—to manage the affairs of the nation, but only while Congress was in recess. There would be no permanent executive branch outside the authority of Congress.[41]

The Articles reflected widespread misgivings about letting anyone hold a government office for very long. No member of Congress could serve for more than three years out of any six-year period, and the president of Congress could serve no more than one year out of any three.[42]

The lingering obsession with Canada found its way into the Articles. Canada could join the United States merely by "aceding to this confederation, and joining in the measures of the United States."[43] Any other colony wishing to join would need the approval of at least nine states.

Congress was not powerless. The Articles conferred on it the authority to oversee diplomacy, manage war, operate a postal service, handle affairs with the indigenous peoples, borrow money, establish the value of coinage, and issue bills of credit. However, Congress had no way to compel states to supply troops or money,[44] and the states were free to print their own paper money.[45]

The Articles, as historians have suggested, created exactly the kind of government called for in the Declaration of Independence.[46] The Articles confirmed what the Declaration had announced: a separation from a powerful and distant central government, and the establishment of 13 free and independent states. The new United States government would have almost nothing to say about what the state governments did within their own borders. It was the only kind of constitution the various states might accept. But approval was no sure thing. In fact, the path to ratification would be long and tortuous.

With the Articles dispatched, delegates turned again to the tricky problem of the Saratoga Convention: how to repudiate the document without repudiating Gates, the hero of Saratoga.

CHAPTER 39

Men Cursing, Women Shrieking, Children Squalling

Consistent with the genteel manners of the time, Burgoyne and other top British generals were, following the surrender, treated like royalty at Philip Schuyler's mansion in Albany. The British commander's serenity was disturbed only by Schuyler's 4-year-old son one morning when little Rensselaer charged into Burgoyne's room and announced, "Surrender! You are all my prisoners."[1]

As Burgoyne lounged, his shattered and bedraggled army, the so-called Army of the Convention, marched east through Massachusetts with American escorts[2] toward Boston. The number of officers and soldiers came to about 5,900. Of those, about 2,500 were German and the rest British. Along with the men were about 1,000 women and children, the camp followers.[3] They trudged for 13 days in cold, stormy weather.[4] According to one account, when caught in a snowstorm while crossing the Green Mountains, confusion reigned, "carts breaking down, others sticking fast, some oversetting, horses tumbling with their loads of baggage, men cursing, women shrieking, children squalling!" In the midst of it all, a soldier's wife, lying on a baggage cart, sheltered from the snow by a "bit of an old oil-cloth," delivered a baby.[5] Sometimes denied shelter, they were often forced to bed down in barns and in the open. One grenadier froze to death.[6] Some horses were stolen.[7]

It was not all misery. Among the women and children making the trek across Massachusetts was Baroness Friederike von Riedesel, the wife of a German general, and their three daughters, ages 6, 3, and 19 months.[8] The baroness found that the people along the way were intensely curious but friendly, "and were particularly pleased that I could speak their native language, English."[9]

Another German reported similarly about one village where the people put the men up in their houses. They were, he wrote, "tolerably kind, but damned inquisitive. ... [W]hole families of women with their daughters came to visit us, going from house to house to gaze upon the prisoners. From the general down to the common soldier, all had to stand inspection.[10]

The Americans along the 200-mile route noted the pets that soldiers had adopted. Those included foxes, racoons, deer, and even a chained bear.[11]

The prisoners discovered quickly along their route that Americans "received our guineas with much cordiality," gladly trading the flimsy Continental dollars for British coins at about twice the standard rate, thereby showing "how considerable the distinction still is, notwithstanding their great veneration for Independency and Congress, between gold and paper." A story was told of a British officer who, along the way, complained that his boots had been lost with his baggage and he needed a pair. An American brigadier general, hearing this, promptly struck a bargain, pulling off his own boots and giving them to the officer for a precious gold guinea.[12]

There were other surprises that amazed the British prisoners. Near Williamstown, Massachusetts, an officer asked for shelter for the night at a "small log-hut" occupied by a man, his wife, and their black-eyed daughter, Jemima, about 16 or 17. Only two beds were available. The officer asked where he should sleep. The man's wife replied that, obviously, he should sleep with Jemima. The officer offered to sit up all night. The father protested: "Oh, la! Mr. Ensign, you won't be the first man our Jemima has bundled with."[13] Bundling was the practice of people of the opposite sex sleeping chastely together fully clothed. It was allowed in New England, normally during courtship.

A German soldier gaped at the American girls and young women, with their "sparkling, laughing eyes … open frank countenances, and much native assurance." While wearing "stylish sun-bonnets" and a silk or woolen wrap,

> a girl will walk, run, or dance about you, and bid you a friendly good-morning or give you a saucy answer according to what you may have said to her. At all the places through which we passed dozens of girls were met with on the road, who either laughed at us mockingly, or now and then roguishly offered us an apple.[14]

The charms of the Yankee girls, as well as the prospect of a good life in a bountiful country, prompted some of the German soldiers to desert along the route east.[15]

On November 6,[16] residents of Cambridge, a few miles from Boston, got their first peek at this once proud force. It was, wrote one Patriot woman, a "sordid set of human creatures—poor dirty emaciated men, great numbers of women, who seemed to be beasts of burthen," all guarded by "fine noble looking guard of American brawny victorious yeomanry."[17]

At Cambridge, the soldiers were assigned to flimsy barracks built by Americans during the siege of Boston more than a year before. The Germans were sent to Winter Hill, part of what is now Somerville; the British settled in on Prospect Hill, part of present-day Waltham. Officers were allowed to find quarters in Cambridge and nearby towns, but not Boston.[18]

The barracks were wretched—open holes in the walls passed for windows. Under such miserable conditions, many soldiers died from scurvy and many others deserted.[19] Quarters for at least some officers and their families were spartan and cramped, but for others pleasant enough. Baroness von Riedesel wrote that she and her family "lived in Cambridge quite happily"[20] and would have been glad to stay as long as the Americans held the British and German soldiers. Burgoyne, having finally torn himself away from the comforts of Schuyler's home, settled into accommodations he called "dirty, small, miserable"[21] in a tavern off Harvard Square. After eight days, he decamped to a mansion offered to him.[22]

This huge influx of people to feed and house strained communities already beset by wartime shortages and bitter toward the invaders. The baroness encountered a Mr. Carter, whom she learned had suggested that the Americans should "behead our generals, put the heads in small barrels, salt them, and send one of these barrels to the English for each village or town which they had set on fire."[23]

Congress made certain the nation would not lose money on arrangements to supply the prisoners. Indeed, it connived to make a profit. Congress paid for housing and supplies with the flimsy Continental dollar, but demanded payment from Burgoyne in hard money, which normally had about three times the purchasing power.[24]

Meanwhile, Burgoyne's soldiers found themselves in "continual broils"[25] with the American militiamen guarding them. In the first month that the prisoners were in Cambridge, American sentries shot two British soldiers. Another 40 were arrested.[26]

To clarify and sort out friction between the Americans and their captives, letters went back and forth between Burgoyne and various American officers. On November 14, Burgoyne sent Gates a letter pronouncing his satisfaction with the way his army was treated during the march from Saratoga. But then he complained that housing for his officers in and around Cambridge was inadequate—six or seven officers were crowded in a room about 10 feet square "without distinction of Rank"; "Gentlemen of our suite" were forced to "lodge upon the Floor in a Chamber adjacent, a good deal worse than their Servants have been used to." Summing up, Burgoyne wrote: "[T]he public Faith is broke."[27] Better housing for Burgoyne and his officers was eventually found, but those five words from the general would later prove very interesting and useful for Congress.

By November, Burgoyne was aware that ships from England had arrived off the coast of Rhode Island, supposedly to carry the prisoners back to England.[28] But the Americans could not be sure. Congress soon received a request from the general to allow the prisoners to march to a port under British control, such as Newport. This would have saved time. Congress refused, insisting that the British abide precisely by the terms of the convention,[29] which meant the prisoners had to leave via Boston. Congress was plainly stalling—delegates were in no hurry to let the prisoners slip out of American control.

***

Following the battle of Germantown—a lost opportunity for Washington to score a stunning rout—the British General Howe pulled all his nearby forces into

Philadelphia. This gave him short-term security, but made his long-term situation precarious. The Americans still held the Delaware River, thus blocking the British from supplying the city by sea, and Washington dispatched troops to hamper British foraging parties gathering firewood, fodder, and food.[30] How would Howe keep his men fed? For that matter, how would Philadelphians survive the winter?

Howe moved to open the Delaware. That meant seizing two American forts, Mifflin and Mercer, on opposite shores downstream. Built to prevent ships from moving upriver, the forts were poorly designed to withstand attacks from Philadelphia itself. The British shifted some artillery to an island at the mouth of the Schuylkill upstream from the forts, and on October 10 began bombarding Fort Mifflin against its weakest side.[31] The fort, hardly more than parallel rows of timber with gaps filled with dirt, had few defenders and little ammunition. But those defenders had rum, and an officer promised a pint for every enemy cannonball collected from the bombardment that fitted the fort's lone heavy cannon.[32]

The British also attacked Fort Mercer. The stubborn Americans in both forts, outnumbered and outgunned, hung on for weeks, but by late November the Delaware was in British hands.[33] Howe could then be certain of supply by sea from New York, or even Britain.

***

In late November, John Adams arrived in Massachusetts on horseback. He had been in Congress for four years, and all his pay for that service was less, he figured, than the pay of a farm laborer. He wanted to return to his law practice, get his family's finances back in order, and watch his children grow.[34] At least that's what he thought he wanted, and probably what he told Abigail. That's certainly what she wanted. She had been managing the household, farm, and offspring without her husband for those four years.

Then in mid-December, while John was away in New Hampshire representing a client, a package arrived at the house. Thinking it urgent, Abigail opened it and found various letters and documents, including a formal notification that Congress had named John to replace Deane as one of the American commissioners in Paris.[35] She, quite understandably, ignited. A smoldering letter was soon on its way to John Lovell in York. How dare he—and Congress—"contrive to rob me of all my happiness … And can I, sir, consent to be separated from him whom my heart esteems above all earthly things, and for an unlimited time? My life will be one continued scene of anxiety and apprehension, and must I cheerfully comply with the demand of my country?"[36]

When John Adams heard the news, he could not have been surprised, for the matter was discussed with him before he left York. What words he used to mollify Abigail, we'll never know. But within 24 hours of returning to Braintree, he sent off a letter accepting the post. Despite her terror of the sea, Abigail wanted to go with him. But they decided, probably because of the cost and the need to have someone watch the farm, that she would remain at home. He sailed for Europe in February aboard the *Boston*, taking with him 10-year-old John Quincy.[37]

The decision by Congress to replace Deane was no surprise. Delegates' confidence in him had plunged ever since the parade of overzealous, underqualified French officers, carrying papers signed by Deane, began arriving on America's shores. Delegates worried that Deane's questionable judgment might prove a liability as the Americans in Paris worked through the critical negotiations in the wake of Saratoga.[38]

As for Congress's decision to send over John Adams as Deane's replacement, one might well ask, what were delegates thinking? Adams had many fine qualities, but few of those had anything to do with European diplomacy. As a long-time friend observed, "He cannot dance, drink, game, flatter, promise, dress, swear with the gentlemen, and small talk and flirt with the ladies."[39]

***

In late November or early December 1777, an American merchant landed in Nantes, France, with dispatches from Boston. By December 4, he was in Versailles, where he gawked for an hour before riding on to Passy, where Franklin, excited by rumors and anticipating the merchant's arrival, interrogated him before the man could even dismount.[40]

"Is Philadelphia taken?" Franklin asked. The merchant said yes. Franklin, downcast, turned away. "But sir," the merchant said. "I have greater news than that. General Burgoyne and his whole army are prisoners of war!"[41]

Franklin was soon the debutante everyone wanted to take to the ball. William Lee noticed a sea change in French attitudes: "[S]ince B[urgoy]ne's fate was known, everything wears a different face—we are Smiled on and Caressed everywhere."[42]

On December 12, French government officials and the American envoys started discussing a formal alliance.[43] On January 3, 1778, Franklin huddled for hours with a British envoy authorized to give the Americans everything they wanted short of independence.[44] That only heightened French ardor, and in February treaties were signed. Franklin, Deane, and Arthur Lee, representing the United States, and Conrad Alexandre Gérard, representing France, each signed three documents. The first was the Treaty of Amity and Commerce, by which France became the first state in the world to recognize the United States as an independent nation. The second was the Treaty of Alliance, which committed the United States to become an ally of France if, as a result of the Treaty of Amity and Commerce, war should result between France and Great Britain. This military treaty prohibited both France and the United States from agreeing to a peace treaty with Britain until the independence of the United States was established. Meanwhile, France agreed to reject any claim to Canada, and the United States agreed keep its hands off the French islands in the West Indies.[45] The third document was the Act Separate and Secret, which allowed Spain to join the Franco-American alliance at a later time.[46] The Americans and especially the French had hoped Spain would join the alliance. But for now, Madrid was aloof.[47]

The French, afraid of embarrassment in the unlikely chance that Congress rejected the treaties, wanted to keep the documents secret until Congress approved them. They put them on board the *Belle Poule* in Bordeaux without telling the captain what they were or even where they were to be taken. He thought he was heading to another French port, Brest. At sea, he was finally told he was heading to America. But the ship was not equipped for a transoceanic voyage. After six weeks at sea, he was back in a French port. Another vessel was given the assignment.[48]

Newspaper readers in France would have seen nothing about the treaties with America. Instead, they would have perused myriad reports about the great Voltaire, the prolific writer, philosopher, and wit, who had just returned to Paris after decades in exile. At the end of April, Franklin and Voltaire, two giants of their age, came together at the Académie des Sciences, where the assembly insisted they embrace. The rotund 71-year-old American and the skeletal 84-year-old Frenchman awkwardly complied.[49] This meeting and any appearance of either of the two men anywhere, rather than the treaty with America or the likely war with Britain, were the talk of the town.

Without waiting for word from Congress, Vergennes arranged for Franklin, his fellow commissioners, and assorted Americans—about 20 of them—to be formally presented to King Louis XVI in the Hall of Mirrors at Versailles. Franklin wore a plain brown suit and carried no ceremonial sword. He held a white hat under his arm. No wig covered his balding head. One observer said that, compared to other diplomats sporting wigs and ribbons, Franklin looked like a farmer. Deane was included in the delegation, even though he had already received news of his recall.[50]

Deane, with a gold snuffbox presented to him by the French monarch, was soon on his way back to America in style. Signaling to Congress their high opinion of Deane, the French put him on board the flagship of French Admiral Charles Hector Théodat Compte d'Estaing.[51]

Arthur Lee learned of Deane's departure after he had sailed. Word came not from fellow commissioner Franklin, but from a Frenchman.[52] Lee was properly apoplectic about once again being kept in the dark. To Franklin he wrote: "If you have anything to accuse me of, avow it; and I will answer you. If you have not, why do you act so inconsistent with your duty to the public, and injurious to me? ... Is this the example you in your superior wisdom think proper to set of order, decorum, confidence, and justice?"[53]

Franklin wrote at least three long letters in response. Historians believe none were actually sent.[54] In one, he wrote:

> It is true I have omitted answering some of your Letters. I do not like to answer angry Letters. I hate Disputes. I am old, cannot have long to live, have much to do and no time for Altercation. If I have often receiv'd and borne your Magisterial Snubbings and Rebukes without Reply, ascribe it to the right Causes, my Concern for the Honour and Success of our Mission, which would be hurt by our Quarrelling, my Love of Peace, my Respect for your good Qualities, and my Pity of your Sick Mind, which is forever Tormenting itself, with its Jealousies, Suspicions and Fancies that others mean you ill, wrong you, or fail in Respect for you. If you do not cure your self of this Temper it will end in Insanity, of which it is the Symptomatick Forerunner, as I have seen in several Instances.[55]

In another letter, Franklin explained that he was asked by Deane not to tell anyone about his leave-taking.

In April, John Adams arrived on the scene. On Franklin's advice, Adams moved into the rooms that Deane had occupied, and John Quincy was enrolled in the same boarding school that Franklin's grandson, Benny Bache, attended.[56] Soon joining Benny and John Quincy at the school was 13-year-old Jesse Deane, the only child of Silas Deane. After the recent death of the boy's mother in America, he had been sent to France to join his father, whom he hadn't seen in years. But just days before the son's arrival, his father had sailed. Franklin took responsibility for the boy's care.[57]

Adams was soon inundated with gripes, rumors, and tittle-tattle from various members of the American circle about the distrust, dysfunction, and intrigue plaguing the diplomatic efforts. One member of that circle was Ralph Izard, the South Carolinian tapped by Congress to cultivate diplomatic relations with the Duke of Tuscany. As it turned out, Izard would never go to Italy, despite an official invitation to live in Florence. Told that he could only come as a private individual, not as an official envoy,[58] Izard chose to stay in Paris, where he remained with too much time on his hands.

An ally of Arthur and William Lee, Izard told Adams that Franklin was "one of the most unprincipled Men upon Earth: that he was a Man of no Veracity, no honor, no Integrity, as great a Villain as ever breathed."[59] Adams knew better, although he also saw Franklin's various shortcomings and soon discovered that the accounts Franklin kept—or rather failed to keep—were a mess.[60] Adams further noted a "Priviledge" that Franklin enjoyed that is "much to be envyd: [T]he Ladies not only allow him to embrace them as often as he pleases, but they are perpetually embracing him."[61]

CHAPTER 40

We Must Change Our Mode of Conduct

In late 1777, Congress at York chose to revamp its Board of War, the committee that managed military matters. The board needed an overhaul, and now with the departure of John Adams, who had presided over the committee, it seemed a good time.

When the Congress first gathered, delegates handled military questions one by one as they came up by creating committees of five or so delegates for each particular issue: a committee to figure out how to obtain cannons; another for promoting the manufacture of firearms; another for handling prisoners of war; still others for hospitals, saltpeter, clothing, beef, salt, cavalry, and on and on. These committees were generally assigned only to investigate and report.[1] Rarely did they have authority.

In 1776, Congress determined that a standing committee was necessary, and thus in June of that year created a Board of War and Ordnance made up of five delegates. The board's tasks included almost anything related to the army. It was expected, for example, to maintain records of officers and troops, keep track of ammunition, artillery, and various war materiel, and supervise the recruitment of soldiers and care of prisoners. Its power was constrained, as any matter of importance had to be brought to the full Congress for approval, and Congress still appointed special committees to handle particular tasks related to the military, such as revising the articles of war.[2]

The problems of the Board of War were twofold. First, it was overwhelmed with the tasks of handling and responding to correspondence about men and equipment from commanders, assessing what was needed, and reporting to the full Congress. The routine when Congress was in Philadelphia was for the board to meet from 6am to 10am at an office on Market Street, then board members would come together with other delegates for the regular sessions at the State House, which could continue into the evening. Sometimes the board would meet again until very late.[3] Members of the board were overworked and exhausted.

Second, the board included no one with military expertise. The delegates on the board tried to educate themselves. Adams was keen about posting lots of maps on office walls to make the board more familiar with geography,[4] an idea not without some merit, but a pitiful substitute for military experience. By the fall of 1776, several delegates were eager for some reform, especially the inclusion of people with that vital military knowledge. Samuel Chase of Maryland wrote: "If we expect to succeed in the present war, we must change our mode of conduct. The business of Congress must be placed in different hands. Distinct and precise departments ought to be established. A gentleman of the military must be of the Board of War."[5]

Washington, for his part, fully supported a restructuring of the board,[6] and the plan was consistent with the direction Congress had envisioned since meeting in Baltimore—to turn over more of the work of Congress to boards made up of men who were not delegates.[7] A step in this direction was the creation in April 1777[8] of the Committee for Foreign Affairs, to take the place of the Committee of Secret Correspondence. This embryonic Department of State had as its first paid employee Thomas Paine as secretary.[9]

After deciding that the new Board of War would be made up of three members who were not delegates to Congress, delegates sought out suitable candidates with military credentials. Richard Henry Lee identified a perfect choice—his friend, Thomas Mifflin. Indeed, Mifflin seemed ideal. A former merchant from a prominent and wealthy Philadelphia family,[10] Mifflin was in Congress at the time Washington was appointed commander in chief back in 1775. Mifflin won much applause when, in a theatrical touch, he held the stirrup for Washington as the newly minted commander in chief mounted up to leave Philadelphia to take control of the American forces in New England.[11]

Despite his pacifist Quaker upbringing, Mifflin had no qualms about accompanying Washington as his aide-de-camp, and was soon made quartermaster general. It was a daunting job. As he was the first quartermaster general, he had no precedents to guide him; yet he managed with competence, honesty, and efficiency. Longing to lead men into battle, he quit as quartermaster general and commanded a small unit during the retreat to Manhattan in the New York campaign.[12]

Without Mifflin in charge, the quartermaster department slipped into dysfunction, and in October 1776 Congress persuaded him to take it over again. He did so, but reluctantly.[13] He was, it seemed, essential in that role, an unheralded but vital job.

Mifflin had other useful skills. He was a virtuoso recruiter. With a gift for speechmaking, he had a magic touch for rallying men to the cause, especially in Pennsylvania, where he was popular. He was instrumental, during the campaigns of Trenton and Princeton in late 1776 and early 1777, in bringing out local militiamen in support of the Continental Army.[14] In February 1777, Congress rewarded Mifflin with the rank of major general.[15]

Mifflin was thus well qualified to serve on the Board of War, which would be overseeing the task of supplying the army. He was also available. Citing ill health, he had just informed Congress that he was resigning as both major general and quartermaster general. Congress answered with the offer of this new role on the Board of War, where he could retain his rank of major general. Suddenly, Mifflin felt better and accepted the position.[16]

Mifflin, leveraging his influence in Congress, then set about expanding the role of the new Board of War. Its responsibilities would extend beyond matters of supply to almost everything having to do with the military. It would also be independent of the commander in chief,[17] which pleased Mifflin, who by this time was thoroughly fed up with Washington.

Mifflin resented how Washington had denied him a significant combat role; he also resented how Washington ignored his military advice. He especially resented how Washington favored the counsel of Nathanael Greene, whom Mifflin disliked.[18] He was also disappointed by Washington's failure to defend Philadelphia, his city.[19] Mifflin still admired much about Washington, and is said to have remarked that Washington was the best friend he had. But he wished the general would place more trust in his own—that is, Washington's—good judgment and instincts and rely less on the advice of others not named Thomas Mifflin.[20] His resignation as quartermaster general almost certainly had less to do with ill health than with his disappointments and frustrations, and perhaps—coming in the gloomy days just before news of Saratoga—a touch of defeatism.

To join him on the new board, Mifflin lobbied for the appointment of none other than Gates, the hero of Saratoga. Congress soon made Gates president of the board. To fill out the board, Congress named Timothy Pickering, who was serving on Washington's staff as adjutant general, and Richard Peters, who had been the Board of War's secretary but would now be a full member.[21]

The new board seemed to be just what the war effort needed: a group of men experienced in the needs of the military and dedicated to ensuring better order and economies. But at its birth, it faced a sticky complication, as the relationships between Washington and the two chief members of the board were decidedly cool. For Washington, the departure of Mifflin as quartermaster general was a cruel blow. In the absence of a quartermaster general for an extended period, Washington had to add that to his myriad responsibilities.[22] It must have rankled. Also, it was apparently Washington's opinion that Mifflin had neglected his job for months before his resignation. In a December letter, Washington, without naming Mifflin, clearly castigated him by saying "we have had no assistance from the Quarter Master Genl"[23] since July. Mifflin had resigned in October.

Meanwhile, whatever rapport Washington and Gates may have once had, it was now tainted by suspicion in the wake of the odd communication delay after Saratoga.

How would the board and Washington work together, and how would Congress supervise them both? Difficulties weren't hard to predict, especially as the board soon became entangled in a web of rumors and insinuations suggesting a plot to remove Washington from the top military job.

***

Thomas Conway, born in Ireland, was taken to France at the age of 6 by his Catholic family.[24] Aged 14,[25] he enrolled in the French military and embraced military life. He was in his forties when he approached Silas Deane in France for a letter of introduction to open doors in America, where he sought action as an officer.[26] When Conway, carrying Deane's letter, met Washington in May 1777, the general promptly sent him off to Congress with his own letter, describing Conway as "from Mr Dean's recommendation, ... an Officer of merit." Conway, wrote Washington, "appears to be a Man of candor," adding that "I should suppose him infinitely better qualified to serve us, than Many who have been promoted, as he speaks our language."[27]

Congress duly made Conway a brigadier general,[28] and the Irishman soon demonstrated competent leadership at Brandywine. Washington rewarded him with the honor of leading the attack at Germantown.[29] This time Washington was not so pleased, observing that Conway had been separated from his men for too long and had misdirected an attack. Washington for a time pondered a court martial for Conway.[30]

Meanwhile, as people discovered, Conway had a knack for rubbing people the wrong way. He seemed to have contempt for the Americans he commanded, and he won no allies among his fellow officers with his rigorous drilling to make his men more like soldiers. The American officers regarded such activity as subtle criticism of their own training methods.[31]

More significantly, he sometimes disobeyed orders and annoyed Washington in particular by saying nothing in councils and then later whining about the decisions made there. Soon, it was no secret that Washington and Conway despised each other.[32]

Congress, meanwhile, ignorant of Conway's troublesome nature, but well aware of his apparent brilliance on the battlefield, recommended a promotion for him to major general. Conway was all for it—it was a matter of honor. He insisted that he must outrank Johann de Kalb, the Bavarian soldier of fortune who had accompanied Lafayette to America. Conway argued that he was de Kalb's superior in France, and therefore must likewise be his superior in America.[33]

Washington opposed the promotion with unusual fervor. In a letter to Richard Henry Lee, he wrote that making Conway a major general would be "as unfortunate a measure, as ever was adopted—I may add (& I think with truth) that it will give a fatal blow to the existence of this army."

First, Washington pointed out, Conway was not as talented as he led people to believe: "General Conways' merit then, as an officer, and his importance in this Army, exists more in his own imagination than in reallity."

Second, and more importantly, Washington felt such a promotion would trigger wholesale disgust among officers more senior and more deserving. Many would refuse to serve under him and more than a few would quit: "These Gentn have feelings a[s] officers; & tho they do not dispute the authority of Congress to make appointments, they will judge of the propriety of acting under them—In a word the service is so dificult, & every necessary so expensive, that almost all your officers are tired out; do not therefor afford them good pretexts for retiring."

Washington reassured Lee dubiously that "I have no prejudice against Genl Conway." But, he hinted, if defied on this issue, he might quit: "To sum up the whole, I have been a Slave to the service: I have undergone more than most men are aware of, to harmonize so many discordant parts but it will be impossible for me to be of any further survice if such insuperable difficulties are thrown in my way."[34]

In his response, Lee assured Washington that Congress was unlikely to make the appointment: "I am very sure Congress would not take any step that might injure the Army, or even have a tendency that way; and I verily believe they wish to lessen your difficulties by every means in their power."[35]

Meanwhile, de Kalb challenged Conway's assertion that Conway was his superior in France. Who was to be believed: de Kalb or Conway? Congress wasted time on the issue and considered asking Washington to look into "the priority of rank between the Baron de Kalb and General Conway in France, and report the same to Congress."[36] Thankfully, the resolution failed.

Many delegates believed Conway would indeed resign if he was not promoted. Others thought the opposite—that he would resign if he was promoted, because then he could return to France; that his aim in coming to America was only to achieve a rank that would benefit him in France. Eventually, Congress decided not to decide: for the moment, the promotion was put off.[37]

Amid this skirmishing over ranks and promotions, Washington received a letter from Conway's immediate superior with a note: "In a letter from General Conway to General Gates he says, 'Heaven has been determined to Save your Country; Or a Weak General or bad Councellors would have ruined it.'"[38] The "Weak General," of course, was Washington.

The note concerning Conway formed the seed for what became known as the Conway cabal, a movement to replace Washington with Gates as commander in chief. The term "cabal"—which Washington himself used[39]—suggests that there really was an organized effort to push Washington aside. It also hints that Conway was its leader. In fact, the supposed cabal that ripened was leaderless, disorganized, and hardly a movement at all. It amounted mostly to scattered grumbling about deficiencies in leadership and what to do about them. Over the coming months, it would rattle Washington's position as commander in chief, which is hardly surprising considering his many failures and disappointments and the presence of a military hero—Gates—available to take his place.

Washington's first response to the note was to send a brief letter to Conway repeating word for word the offending missive without comment, closing politely with "I am Sir Yr Hble Servt."[40]

In his reply, Conway said he did not have a copy of the letter in question, but he doubted he was guilty of what was said in the note: "I Believe i can attest that the expression *Weak General* has not slipped from my penn."

However, Conway admitted that when he wrote to Gates "i Spoke my mind freely" and had been critical of several measures taken by Washington. He also groveled:

> [M]y opinion of you sir without flattery or envy is as follows: you are a Brave man, an honest Man, a patriot, and a Man of great sense. [Y]our modesty is such, that although your advice in council is commonly sound and proper, you have often been influenc'd by men who Were not equal to you in point of experience, Knowledge or judgment.[41]

Conway indeed was innocent of writing the nasty remark. Gates, the recipient of the letter in question, later confirmed that the original letter did not contain the words reported to Washington: "[T]he Paragraph, conveyed to Your Excellency, as a genuine Part of it, was in Words, as well as in Substance, a wicked Forgery."[42] What Conway actually wrote was "ten times" nastier, according to Henry Laurens, who later got a peek at it.[43] But Laurens exaggerated. A copy of an extract eventually reached Washington: "What a pity there is but one Gates! but the more I see of this Army the less I think it fit for general Action under its actual Chiefs & actual discipline—I speak [to] you sincerely & freely & wish I could serve under you."[44]

Even if it had been 10 times worse, what of it? Washington didn't know it, but other officers had put to paper more damning assessments of their commander in chief. De Kalb, a favorite of Washington's, was one. His remarks, written in French a few weeks before Washington received the note about Conway, translate to: "[H]e is too slow, even lazy, much too weak, and not without a dose of vanity and presumption. My opinion is that if he does anything sensational he will owe it more to his good luck or his adversary's mistakes than to his own ability."[45] However, Washington never learned of de Kalb's remarks.

In his next communication with Washington, Conway wrote that he wanted to return to France to be part of the war he anticipated would soon break out between Britain and France. He intended to submit to Congress his resignation from the American army.[46]

Washington, likely delighted to see the irksome Conway on his way, responded cordially with a wish for "a favourable passage and a happy meeting with your Family & Friends."[47]

The little tempest might have ended there, but Conway did not resign. Congress, considering him an especially valuable officer, soon did what Washington had counseled against—it promoted Conway to major general. In the same resolution, Congress named Conway one of two inspectors general, new positions under the new Board of War to ensure better order and discipline by, for example, reviewing "from time to time, the troops," and seeing "that every officer and soldier be instructed in the exercise and manoevres which may be established."[48]

The promotion seemed at first glance a crafty way to please both Conway and Washington. Conway got the promotion he wanted, but as inspector general, he would be a staff officer, not a line officer. Washington would not have to worry about touchy officers resigning rather than serving under Conway. Also, Conway was just the kind of man Washington had wanted for that post—an experienced foreign officer. Conway seemed an ideal choice, except that Washington loathed him, and now, as inspector general, Conway had authority much broader than that suggested by Washington. Conway would answer to the Board of War, not to Washington. If Conway decided reforms were needed, he could order Washington to implement them. The Board of War—at the moment led by Mifflin, with Gates still in Albany, not York—then failed to notify Washington of all this.[49]

Meanwhile, Gates got wind that a letter addressed to him had, without his permission, somehow found its way to Washington. He sent off a letter to Washington asking him to divulge the name of the person who betrayed the contents of his private correspondence. Washington duly informed Gates that the source was a man on Gates's staff, Colonel Wilkinson, the aide to Gates who belatedly delivered to Congress the news about Saratoga. On the way to Congress, Wilkinson, stopping in Reading, had tattled to one officer, who gossiped to another, who blabbed to Washington.[50]

CHAPTER 41

Too Important to Be Trifled With

In the meantime, a war was going on. In December, about a dozen miles separated the British in Philadelphia from the American army to the north.[1] Congress, wanting action, dispatched a committee to meet with Washington about "carrying on a winter's campaign with vigour and success, an object which Congress have much at heart."[2]

The pressure was on Washington to produce some results soon by mounting an attack on Philadelphia. The commander in chief was sorely tempted. How satisfying it would be to conjure a triumph as stunning as Saratoga. But he took the advice of one of his most trusted generals, Greene, who recognized that an attack would be a disaster: "The Cause is too important to be trifled with to shew our Courage, & your Character too deeply interested, to sport away upon unmilitary Principles."[3]

Washington met the committee and they returned to Congress with the news that no winter attack would be attempted. The winter months would be used instead for recruiting and training so the army could emerge stronger in the spring.[4]

On the British side, Howe likewise contemplated an attack late in the season. On December 10—which as it happened was the very day Martha Washington arrived at the American camp via sleigh to join her husband—British troops slipped out of Philadelphia to pounce. Then, strangely, they scampered back. Howe later explained that Washington's position was too well fortified. In fact, as a temporary camp, it was barely fortified at all.[5]

Howe and the British would curl up in Philadelphia for the winter. But where would Washington's army go? Washington had favored scattering the army in small camps, much as Howe had done the previous winter in New Jersey, to enable foraging over a wider area. But that had its risks: Washington's army thus dispersed would be vulnerable and in a poor position to stop Howe should the British emerge from the city to strike anywhere. Washington heard the anxious pleas of delegates from Pennsylvania, New Jersey, and Delaware that the army must remain together, poised for action and near Philadelphia, to keep Howe in check.[6]

Washington chose Valley Forge, a village about 20 miles northwest of Philadelphia where the Valley Creek ran into the Schuylkill River.[7] This seemed to be a sensible choice. It was in the midst of rich farming communities, so provisions should have been close at hand. Furthermore, many furnaces, gristmills, and forges were nearby to serve the army's needs, and the Schuylkill made it relatively secure against an enemy attack.[8]

Over a week, the soldiers trudged, under an onslaught of rain, sleet, and snow, toward their winter camp.[9] They were hungry, cold, and ragged. A military surgeon wrote in his diary:

> There comes a Soldier, his bare feet are seen thro' his worn out Shoes, his legs nearly naked from the tattere'd remains of an only pair of stockings, his Breeches not sufficient to cover his nakedness, his Shirt hanging in Strings, his hair dishevell'd, his face meagre; his whole appearance pictures a person forsaken & discouraged. He comes, and crys with an air of wretchedness & despair, I am Sick, my feet lame, my legs are sore, my body cover'd with this tormenting Itch—my Cloaths are worn out, my Constitution is broken ... I fail fast and I shall soon be no more![10]

As the army shuffled into the campground, Washington ordered that the men be organized in squads of 12, with each squad receiving tools to build its own hut. Washington's instructions were precise: each hut was to be

> fourteen by sixteen [feet] each—sides, ends and roofs made with logs, and the roof made tight with split slabs—or in some other way—the sides made tight with clay—fire-place made of wood and secured with clay on the inside eighteen inches thick, this fire-place to be in the rear of the hut—the door to be in the end next the street—the doors to be made of split oak-slabs, unless boards can be procured—Side-walls to be six-and-a-half-feet high.[11]

These were dismal log cabins, built without nails by laying logs in notches.[12] A reward of $12 was offered for the squad "which finishes their hut in the quickest, and most workmanlike manner."[13] The soldiers labored "like a family of Beavers"[14] in bad weather with too few axes and not enough wood to erect some 900 ramshackle shelters for an army of about 11,000.[15]

Those huts were just part of a military town cobbled together on a meadow. It would include shops for blacksmiths, makeshift hospitals, pens for cattle, slaughterhouses, privies, barns, granaries, stables, and parade grounds. The inhabitants were mostly men—the soldiers were generally young (in their teens or early twenties) and unmarried. In some units, nearly half the men were Irish. Possibly 20 percent of the troops were German immigrants or of German extraction. Almost every regiment included Black soldiers. Some were enslaved, serving for a drafted owner with the promise of freedom. In one brigade, 13 percent of the soldiers were Black.[16] About 400 women also marched in with the men to Valley Forge.[17] Some had husbands among the soldiers. One was Anna Maria Lane, who had posed as a man, wore a uniform, and with her husband fought at Germantown, where she was wounded and then discovered to be female. After that she wore female attire but stayed with her husband as they together entered Valley Forge. Most of the women at Valley Forge earned their rations by cooking, washing, or sewing. Some traded other services for food or money. One diary mentioned a woman being drummed out of camp for spreading venereal disease.[18]

***

It is often stated that the winter of Valley Forge, with Washington's little army shivering and starving, was perhaps the most desperate months of the war for the Americans. If the army disintegrated, the war would be lost, or so we sometimes are led to believe. But on this subject, history has exaggerated and embellished. The British may have held Philadelphia, New York City, and Newport, Rhode Island, but they controlled little else.[19] For all the blood and treasure the British had spent, almost all of the United States remained independent and free of British control. Although the Americans were in no position at the moment to drive the British out, it was unimaginable that the British would ever be able to reconquer all the states and all their militias and reinstate royal control.

Still, the winter of Valley Forge was a critical time for the army's survival, not least because the commissary system for providing soldiers with food, clothing, and equipment was in a shambles. Delegates in Congress had themselves to blame. In a well-meaning attempt to come up with an honest, streamlined commissary system, Congress had instead created a nightmare—a complex, clumsy bureaucratic monstrosity that was impossible to manage.

At the beginning of the war, when Congress established its commissary system, it used the British structure as a model. Commissaries, the buyers of provisions for the troops, were reimbursed for what they paid for food and then given an additional amount, based on the cost of the food, as payment for their service.[20] The system invited corruption. Commissaries had no incentive to drive a bargain; indeed, they were rewarded for overpaying. Some appeared to collude with the people who sold them the food.[21]

After two years, Congress had endured enough of this wasteful, corrupt system and set about crafting a new one. Delegates split the commissary department. One commissary would be in charge of obtaining supplies, while the other would handle distribution of those supplies. In theory, these two would each serve as a check on the other to detect possible corruption. Congress then took on responsibility for hiring the deputies for the commissaries. Thus, commissaries could not directly hire, fire, or very well control the people under them.[22]

In another attempt to end corruption, Congress did away with the practice of paying commissaries a percentage of what they spent. They would each now receive a salary.[23]

To make sure that all transactions were accounted for, Congress drew up a variety of forms and myriad instructions for the commissary department, which filled

15 pages in Congress's *Journal*.[24] The size, quantity, and quality of everything had to be documented. Congress further demanded that all the deputy commissaries post $5,000 bonds to ensure their honesty.[25]

The reforms produced widespread resignations. Many of the men Congress found as replacements had no clue about what they were doing. Complaints were heard in late 1777 that the commissary general assigned to help Washington's army was hopelessly incompetent.[26]

In the months just before Washington's army marched into winter camp, the system of supply had been adrift for months. Hospitals caring for soldiers had no wood to keep the ill and wounded warm. Hundreds of barrels of flour intended for the military were inexplicably left along a riverbank, according to one diary. Congress compounded the problem with its meddling; for example, it set the cost for hiring a wagon to haul military goods at one-third the charge normally demanded on the open market.[27]

All this might have been tolerable if the normally flourishing region of Valley Forge had been well stocked with grain and other supplies. But the British and American armies, marching and camping in the area for weeks, had already consumed much of what was available nearby. The Americans had wisely warehoused some supplies, but several caches of food had been raided by the British, including one that had contained 4,000 barrels of flour.[28]

Problems handicapped the haphazard efforts to get supplies to the army: shortages of wagons and horses; lack of civilians to drive the wagons, as such drivers often could make more money moving goods for private business than for the army; unscrupulous drivers who would, for example, put rocks in casks meant to contain flour or drain the brine from the barrels of salt pork to lighten the load, thus causing the meat to spoil. Meanwhile, some wagons stuffed with goods and sent over long distances would be seized by armed bands of one sort or another.[29]

Obtaining goods directly from farmers was not always easy, even when the farmers had surplus to sell. Some Quakers, as pacifists, refused to sell to the army. Some farmers willing to sell to the army did not because they found other buyers who could offer more. Many were happy instead to sell to the British Army, when the opportunity arose, because the British offered good hard money, not the dubious Continental dollars[30]

Congress knew of the supply crisis. Delegates advised Washington to do what armies usually did in such circumstances—strip the food, fodder, and whatever else was needed from farms and communities within reach. If anyone refused to sell, the army was to just take it.[31]

Washington was hesitant. Military confiscation would turn the people against the army, as he knew from experience. Back in the French and Indian War, while about to seize some grain, a furious farmer had nearly shot him.[32] He wrote to Congress: "I confess, I have felt myself greatly embarrassed with respect to a rigorous exercise of Military power. An Ill placed humanity perhaps and a reluctance to give distress may have restrained me too far."[33]

As the army fashioned its crude winter village and the problem of supply remained unresolved, Washington foresaw the horrors to come. In a letter to Laurens on December 23, he laid out to Congress the dire conditions as winter closed in. He also raged at the naive expectations of civilian "Gentlemen"—men in Congress and lawmakers in Pennsylvania and New Jersey—who prodded the general to defend those states with his shadow of an army:

> [W]e have by a Field return this day made, no less than 2898 Men now in Camp unfit for duty, because they are barefoot and otherwise naked ... I can assure those Gentlemen, that it is a much easier and less distressing thing, to draw Remonstrances in a comfortable room by a good fire side, than to occupy a cold, bleak hill, and sleep under frost & snow without Cloaths or Blankets: However, although they seem to have little feeling for the naked and distressed Soldier, I feel superabundantly for them, and from my soul pity those miseries, which it is neither in my power to releive or prevent.[34]

Meanwhile, Washington and other high-ranking officers frequently enjoyed quite satisfying meals: meat, vegetables, bread, desserts, and wine. On Christmas Day, two days after writing about "superabundantly" feeling for his suffering men, Washington dined on mutton, veal, potatoes, and cabbage.[35]

***

Soon after Washington settled in at Valley Forge, Thomas Conway made his appearance to announce his duties as inspector general. Washington's reception was icy, as he later admitted: "[M]y feelings will not permit me to make professions of friendship to the man I deem my Enemy." Even so, Conway "was received & treated with proper respect to his Official character."[36] Washington reminded Conway that he was supposed to have instructions from the Board of War about maneuvering troops—did Conway have such instructions? Conway could only answer "no." So Conway left, and later sent a letter to Washington offering to resign and return to France if his new role was at all "productive of inconvenience or in any ways disagreeable."[37]

Washington's answer was stiff but polite. The appointment to inspector general, he wrote, was not problematic. The problem was with the promotion to major general: "[Y]ou may judge what must be the Sensations of those Brigadiers, who by your promotion are Superceded." The old, intractable hostility among officers over their promotions (or lack thereof) had reappeared. Washington assured Conway that all he wanted was that "no Extraordinary promotion take place, but where the Merit of the Officer is so generally acknowledged as to Obviate every reasonable cause of Dissatisfaction thereat."[38]

Conway responded with a sneer and sarcasm:

> What you are pleased to call an extraordinary promotion is a very plain one. There is nothing extraordinary in it, only that such a place was not thought of sooner. The general and universal merit, which you wish every promoted officer might be endowed with, is a rare gift. We see but few men of merit so generally acknowledged. We know but the great Frederick in Europe, and the great Washington in this continent. I certainly was never so rash as to pretend to such a prodigious height.

He then offered to quit:

> I perceive that I have not the happiness of being agreeable to your excellency, and that I can expect no support in fulfilling the Laborious Duty of an inspector general. I Do not Mean to give you or any officer in the army the Least uneasiness therefore I am very readdy to return to france and to the army where I hope I will Meet with no frowns.[39]

Washington didn't respond to him, at least not by letter. In another dispatch, however, he cast Conway as "a secret enemy" and a "dangerous incendiary."[40]

CHAPTER 42

My Heart Is Full, My Eyes Overflow

With the final weeks of 1777 and the uncertain dawn of 1778, the dreary work of Congress continued. Possibly because of the presence of Congress, the townspeople in York discovered more reasons to entertain. The diary of a local minister recorded: "Balls have been given so often, as to call forth remonstrances from all the clergymen of the town."[1] The minister also noted a hanging in May "in the presence of a large crowd of people. Many school children who witnessed the execution from a distance, were warned to shun all evil doing."[2]

Delegates were overworked and overwrought. A scare in March didn't help. That month, Laurens gasped in a letter: "We have this very Evening received an intimation of a most horrid & dangerous conspiracy." After referring to "Sir William" (British commander Howe), Laurens disclosed little else: "the tale is yet mysterious."[3]

Surviving letters from other delegates shed no light on this puzzle. But the diary of a local minister from March 19 appears to offer a clue: "Throughout the entire night the soldiers kept guard, since a plot on the part of the Tories and Howe's light cavalry to capture Congress, had been discovered." The diary reported the arrest of one man.[4] We know nothing more. Possibly, the "plot" was no more than the product of noises in the night and a little imagination.

No one had a good thing to say about York. Many delegates were homesick, although at least one had the companionship of a spouse. We know because Francis Lightfoot Lee wrote at the end of a letter to Samuel Adams: "Tis late, Mrs. Lee in bed & asleep but she left her commands with me to present her best respects to Mrs. Adams & Yourself, in which I beg to be joined."[5]

Most if not all of the other delegates in York had no family with them. Harnett of North Carolina advised a colleague planning to come to York to leave his wife behind. "I beg you will not think of it. Be assured it is Impossible, you will hardly be able to get a bed to Sleep in. ... I never Lived in so wretched a manner in my life."[6]

Misery was a running theme in Harnett's letters: "Beleive me it is the most Inhospitable Scandalous place I ever was in. ... If I once more can return to my family all the Devils in Hell shall not Seperate us." He asked to be sent "2 or three

Gallons of Pickled Oysters ... I have not tasted One since I left home, also a few dryed fish of any kind, a dozen or two, if they even Stank, they would be pleasing."[7]

If anyone was more wretched than Harnett, it was Henry Laurens. From his perch as president of Congress, he oversaw "the deplorable Situation of our affairs in general." He agonized over the squalor and suffering at Valley Forge: "[M]y heart is full, my Eyes overflow, when I reflect upon a camp ¼th & more of Invalids for want of necessary covering—an Army on the very verge of bankruptcy, for want of food—that we are Starving in the midst of plenty—perishing by Cold, & surrounded by Clothing Sufficient for two Armies, but uncollected."[8]

His old persecutor, gout, returned, ushered in by Laurens's habit of consuming a bottle of Madeira each day.[9] Foreseeing "a continuance of pain & Crippleism for many Weeks,"[10] he offered to resign as president of Congress. But the delegates would not have it. Congress soldiered on in his absence, awaiting his return to health. As it turned out, they couldn't wait. An issue came up that was so pressing that they had to fetch him—not because he was president, but because he was the lone delegate from South Carolina. In that, the state was hardly unique. At this time, Rhode Island and Connecticut were also each represented by just one delegate. At that moment, the whole of Congress comprised just 20 men.[11] Often enough, the number of delegates in York dipped to 13, and on occasion even to nine.[12] Patriots willing to leave homes and business to toil in miserable York were scarce. Laurens, in too much pain to walk, had to be carried to the meeting place.

There, days later, at a desk during a pause, and still suffering as he sat with "both feet & Legs bound up in a basket," he lamented in a letter to a colleague in his home state about South Carolina's failure to find someone to send to York to share the toil: "O Carolina! O My Country, shame to you!—that in this great, this momentous Cause, so few among your many worthy Sons are found Zealous Advocates. ... [F]ill your Delegacy in Congress with able Men—able Men I say—no frolickers—no Jolly fellows—or you will be despised & you will have cause to rue your neglect."[13]

So, what was the issue of "highest importance"[14] that required Laurens to be carried from his sickbed? Congress was engrossed in questions concerning the convention troops, the British prisoners from Saratoga who were still lodged on the outskirts of Boston. The day was fast approaching when British transports to carry them away would be ready to receive them in Boston Harbor. Would the Americans just let the prisoners go? The matter couldn't wait.

The significance of this now-forgotten problem is difficult to appreciate. To delegates then, the fate of the nation might well turn on how this issue was handled. To abide by the terms of the convention and return the prisoners to British control would give the enemy another army to quickly put in the field. But to tear up the convention and retain control of the prisoners would be dishonorable—no small matter in that age. That too could cost America. Potential allies, such as France, might well consequently turn their backs, enabling Britain over time to throttle the young nation fighting alone.

Connecticut's Dyer summed up the dilemma:

> [O]n the one hand there is every thing to fear if he [Burgoyne] is suffered to embark that he will join the Enemy in America instead of going to Great Britain, on the other hand it concerns us inviolably to keep our faith, & maintain our honor, pledged for the punctual fullfillment on our part of all treaties, Contracts or Conventions made even with our Enemies. ... In the beginning of this infant Empire the greater care is to be taken to establish a fair & reputable Carracter, which if once lost is hardly to be regained.[15]

Congress concocted excuses for more delays. Laurens ordered the commander in Massachusetts overseeing the British prisoners to inspect the transports intended to carry the troops and check whether provisions were indeed sufficient for a voyage across the ocean. These and other duties deemed by Congress to be "indispensibly necessary" would "employ some days" and buy time without "subjecting the honour" of Congress "to any unfavourable imputation from the World."[16]

But Congress could not stall forever. It needed to come up with a plausible reason to block the handover of prisoners. Up stepped John Witherspoon, a delegate from New Jersey, to rescue Congress from this predicament. For weeks, Witherspoon led a committee that pored over the problem.

Born in Scotland and trained as a Presbyterian minister, Witherspoon emigrated to America in 1768 with his wife and five surviving children to take over the presidency of the College of New Jersey (now Princeton University).[17] He found time to travel around America to preach and recruit students—among them, James Madison[18]—but showed little interest in the conflict between America and the mother country until 1774. He was chosen as a delegate to the Continental Congress in June 1776, just in time for immortality as a signer of the Declaration.[19]

Witherspoon and his committee came up with an elegant—and devious—way to keep the Convention Army in America under American control without seeming to violate the Saratoga Convention. In the surviving text of a speech, Witherspoon shows how he, like Washington and Laurens, expected the British to violate the convention. Witherspoon noted that the British had already fudged on certain terms. For example, they had failed to hand over cartouche boxes—containers for ammunition—as required. The Americans suspected—and documents have long confirmed—that the British and Germans still retained some military flags[20]—another violation. But to Witherspoon, these transgressions were hardly worthy of a fuss.

More serious was what Burgoyne had written to Gates back in November—the letter complaining of cramped quarters—and Burgoyne's phrase "the public faith is broke." Witherspoon explained:

> [W]e have here the declared opinion of one of the parties, that the public faith is broken by the other. Now, the simplest man in the world knows, that a mutual onerous contract is always conditional; and that if the condition fails on one side, whether from necessity or fraud, the other is free. Therefore we have reason to conclude, that if Mr Burgoyne is of opinion that the convention is broken on our part, he will not hold to it on his. He would act the part of

a fool if he did. ... If he has conceived the convention to be broken on so frivolous a pretense as that his lodging is not quite commodious ... what are we to expect from him as soon as he shall recover his liberty, and the power of doing mischief?[21]

The resolution Witherspoon's committee brought forth rehashed some of these same points and added another—that Burgoyne had prevented the Americans from recording detailed information about the prisoners, such as the name and rank of every officer and the name and description of every soldier. This was indeed suspicious. The Americans would need this information if they later suspected that former prisoners from Saratoga were again fighting in America on the side of the British. To Witherspoon, this suggested that Burgoyne aimed to ignore the terms of the convention. His acts and words demonstrated his intention to "disengage himself, and the army under him, of the obligation they are under to these United States."[22]

The resolution concluded not with a repudiation of the Saratoga Convention, but with something else—a demand that Parliament endorse the convention and properly notify Congress of that action: "That the embarkation of Lieutenant General Burgoyne, and the troops under his command, be suspended till a distinct and explicit ratification of the convention of Saratoga shall be properly notified by the court of Great Britain to Congress."[23]

This seemed, at a casual glance, not altogether unreasonable. But delegates knew the measure would keep the prisoners under American control for the duration of the war. The resolution in effect called for Parliament to recognize Congress, and that Parliament would never do.[24] The resolution seemed to allow Congress to escape the terms of the convention without explicitly tearing it up.

Congress approved the resolution, but of the 19 delegates present, four "timerous dunces,"[25] as Laurens called them, voted against. One was Rhode Island's William Ellery, who trembled for his state and New England. Would the British, now occupying Newport and enraged by this perfidy, pounce on Providence and strike north?: "I am suspicious that the enemy will consider the suspension of the embarkation of General Burgoyne and his troops as an infraction of the convention, attempt to rescue those troops, and at the same time pour their resentment on our State."[26]

***

Witherspoon did not know for certain whether the British really intended to wriggle out of the terms of the convention; neither did Washington or anyone else on the American side. But we do. In 1932, scholars got their first glimpse of the secret letters of certain British commanders in 1777. Among the letters was one dated November 16, 1777, from General Howe in Philadelphia. In the correspondence, Howe ordered Henry Clinton, the British commander in New York, to pass on "secret Directions" to redirect the British troops from the Convention Army to New York. Howe urged strictest secrecy of the plan: "I conceive it to use every possible

Precaution to keep the Enemy ignorant of my Intentions, as on the least Suscpicion the Troops wd. be infallibly stoppt."[27]

***

Back in October 1777, before John Adams left Congress, he wrote to Abigail about the nation's good fortune that the victory at Saratoga was "not immediately due" to Washington: "If it had been, Idolatry, and Adulation would have been unbounded, so excessive as to endanger our Liberties for what I know. Now We can allow a certain Citizen to be wise, virtuous, and good, without thinking him a Deity or a saviour."[28]

Adams was not alone in recoiling at the widespread adulation of the general, and he was correct in assuming that much of the reverence for Washington vanished that fall. With Saratoga, Gates was the new national hero. Washington, with the catastrophe of Brandywine and the fall of Philadelphia, had slid off Mount Olympus.

After Adams's departure from York, the chatter against Washington grew louder, both inside and outside Congress. Some were even saying that Washington, besides being human, was a losing bet, that there was no reason to maintain this failure as commander in chief when there was a winner—Gates—waiting in the wings.

One of the most persistent chatterers outside Congress was Benjamin Rush, energetic Philadelphia physician and something of a busybody—inquisitive, talkative, and inclined to speak his mind a little too freely. Fully committed to the cause of the Revolution, he had friends in Congress and was for a time a delegate himself. He signed the Declaration and was married to the daughter of another signer. He championed Paine's *Common Sense*, came up with the title (Paine had wanted to call it *Plain Truth*), and found a daring publisher.[29]

Rush had initially adored Washington. He was with Washington's men when they crossed the Delaware on that pivotal icy December night of 1776, and he cared for the wounded at Trenton and Princeton. He once proposed that the general be given dictatorial powers to save the cause.[30]

But by late 1777, his attitude toward Washington had changed. In a series of letters to John Adams, he railed about the miserable state of the army and Washington's ineffective leadership.

During this period, while serving as a physician for Washington's army, he witnessed the bloody chaos at Brandywine and in its aftermath went behind enemy lines to attend the American wounded.[31] Rush told Adams how astonished he was by the contrast between Howe's army and that of Washington. In the British camp, he noted, besides attention to vigilance and secrecy, the "supreme regard to the cleanliness and health of their men." He was amazed at the efforts to obtain vegetables for the men and impressed with the medical care. He was struck by the overall regard for "discipline, order, economy and cleanliness."

When he made his way to the American camp, no sentry challenged him. Soldiers were "straggling from our lines at every quarter without an officer." Furthermore, when officers did appear, they failed to keep track of their men: "General Washington never knew within 3,000 men what his real numbers were."[32] As for the medical facilities for the Americans—"waste," "peculation," "unnecessary officers." While not calling specifically for Washington's removal, that seemed to be what he had in mind: "New measures and new men alone can save us."[33]

Following the battle of Germantown, Rush rehashed many of the same complaints in another letter: "We lost a city, a victory, a campaign by that want of discipline and system which pervades every part of the army."

He also identified "the idol of the whole army," none other than Thomas Conway:

Benjamin Rush, a Philadelphia physician, was a delegate to Congress, a signer of the Declaration, and much involved over the years with the politics of Congress. His support for Washington wavered after the battle of Brandywine. This painting, by Charles Willson Peale and dated 1783 and 1786, is in the Winterthur Museum, Winterthur, Delaware. (Image via Wikimedia Commons)

> He is entitled to most of the glory our arms acquired in the late battle. ... He is exact in his discipline and understands every part of the detail of an army. ... Some people blame him calling some of *our generals* fools, cowards, and drunkards in public company. But these things are proofs of his integrity and should raise him in the opinion of every friend to America.

Conway, it appears, gave Rush his assessment of Washington's performance in the battle. Rush wrote:

> General Conway wept for joy when he saw the ardor with which our troops pushed the enemy from hill to hill, and pronounced our country free from that auspicious sight. But when he saw an officer low in command give counterorders to the Commander in Chief, and the Commander and Chief passive under that circumstance, his distress and resentment exceeded all bounds.[34]

In yet another letter to Adams, Rush noted the contrast between Gates and Washington. Of Gates, he commented that he was "at the pinnacle of military glory, exulting in the success of schemes planned with wisdom and executed with vigor and bravery, and above all the country saved by their exertions." But he added that Washington was "outgeneraled and twice beaten, obliged to witness the march of a body of men only half their number through 140 miles of a thick-settled country, forced to give up a city the capital of a state, and after all outwitted by the same army in a retreat."[35]

In January 1778, frustrated and determined to press his point, Rush wrote a further letter on the topic, this one to Patrick Henry, who was now governor of Virginia. In this letter, Rush summarized the dismal state of affairs, then hinted at a remedy: "But is our case desperate? By no means. We have wisdom, virtue, and strength *enough* to save us if they could be called into action. The northern army [Gates's army] has shown us what Americans are capable of doing with a GENERAL at their head."

He named three generals who could turn Washington's army into "an irresistible body of men": Gates, Charles Lee—who was still in British custody but was expected to be swapped for a captured British general—and Conway.[36]

Rush was uneasy about what he wrote, as if he were dabbling in treason. He did not sign the letter. He told Henry that if he recognized the handwriting, to tell no one and to destroy the letter. Henry did not recognize the handwriting, and neither did he burn it. Rather, he sent it to Washington.

Another former delegate especially critical of Washington was Jonathan Dickinson Sergeant of New Jersey. He wrote in the wake of Brandywine and Germantown:

> We want a General; thousands of Lives & Millions of Property are yearly sacrificed to the Insufficiency of our Commander in Chief. Two Battles he has lost for us by two such Blunders as might have disgraced a Soldier of three Months Standing: and yet we are so attached to this Man that I fear we shall rather sink with him than throw him off our Shoulders. And sink we must under his Management.[37]

***

Within Congress, the delegate most scornful of Washington was James Lovell of Massachusetts. In a letter to Gates (unsigned but attributed to Lovell[38]), he heaped disdain on Washington and enticed Gates with the possibility of becoming the new senior general:

> We have had a noble army melted down by ill judged marches—marches that disgrace their authors & directors—& which have occasioned the severest & most just sarcasm & contempt of our enemies. ... In short, this army is to be totally lost unless you come down & collect the virtuous band, who wish to fight under your banner. ... Prepare yourself for a jaunt to this place—Congress must send for you—I have ten thousand things to tell.[39]

Lovell, like many Americans then, was well acquainted with tales of famous Romans, and like other Americans he recognized that Washington's military strategy echoed that of Fabius, the Roman general. Fabius, in waging war against Hannibal's superior Carthaginian army, avoided direct combat and attempted to wear down the enemy through harassment and slow attrition. The strategy seemed sensible for Washington, with a motley, hastily trained army facing a larger, more-disciplined, and better-equipped force. But to Lovell, the strategy was hugely wasteful and ineffective. In another letter to Gates, he wrote:

> Good God! what a Situation we are in! how different from what we might have expected! You will be astonished when you come to know accurately what numbers have at one time and another been collected near Philada. to wear out stockings, shoes and breeches. Depend upon it for every ten Soldiers placed under the Command of our Fabius 5 Recruits will be wanted annually during the war. … [I]f it was not for the defeat of Burgoyne and the strong Appearances of an European war, our Affairs are fabiused into a very disagreeable posture.[40]

Others in Congress losing patience with Washington included Joseph Reed of Pennsylvania and Abraham Clark of New Jersey.[41]

Some of uneasiness in Congress about Washington may have stemmed from phony letters, attributed to Washington, that appeared almost simultaneously in newspapers in Philadelphia, held by the British, and in Boston. The letters, apparently drafted by Loyalists trying to undermine Washington, insinuated that he and delegate Richard Henry Lee despised each other and that Lee coveted Washington's post as commander in chief.[42]

Lee's name has been connected with the so-called Conway cabal. Lee was certainly a friend of Mifflin, a man known to have differences with Washington. And Lee had allied politically with New England delegates who had been on the Gates side of the Gates–Schuyler hullabaloo. Certainly Lee, like others, may have had doubts about Washington's skills as a commander. But we see no hard evidence that Lee was working behind the scenes to push Washington out. Historians find the notion far-fetched.[43]

Lee wrote to Washington about a pamphlet containing the fake letters: "The design of the Forger is evident, and no doubt it gained him a good Beef Steak from his Masters."[44] Washington asked for a copy.

Washington learned enough from allies and friends to suspect that he was on thin ice. One was Patrick Henry, who passed along the unsigned damning missive from Rush (Washington recognized the handwriting). Another was Lafayette, who had been visiting York. In a letter to the general, the Frenchman wrote:

> There are open dissensions in Congress … parties who hate one another as much as the common enemy, stupid men who without knowing a single word about war undertake to judge you, to make ridiculous comparisons; they are infatuated with Gates without thinking of the different circumstances, and believe that attacking is the only thing necessary to conquer. Those ideas are entertained in their minds by some jealous men and perhaps secret friends to the British government who want to push you in a moment of ill humor to some rash enterprise.[45]

However, while there was much smoke, there was little fire. No movement in Congress to remove Washington—or provoke him to quit—ever gained traction. With the exception perhaps of Lovell, no one in Congress was at all interested in putting anyone else in charge of the army.[46]

In March, delegate Dyer wrote: "Be assured there is not the most distant thought of removing Genll Washington, nor ever an expression in Congress looking that way."[47]

If such a movement against Washington existed, Henry Laurens, as president of Congress, likely would have known. He wrote to Lafayette in January:

> I think the friends of our brave & virtuous General, may rest assured that he is out of the reach of his Enemies, if he has an Enemy, a fact which I am in doubt of. I beleive I hear most that is said & know the outlines of almost all that has been attempted, but the whole amounts to little more than tittle tattle.[48]

It helped that Washington maintained the stout support all along of Laurens. That support received a lift from Laurens's son John, who, at Washington's elbow as aide de camp and secretary, was fiercely devoted to the commander. Henry Laurens, who had a higher regard for the general than for many of his fellow delegates,[49] took pains to hide criticism of "[t]his great and virtuous man" from Congress. On January 25, a delegate handed Laurens an anonymous document of nearly a thousand words "that had been picked up on the Stairs." With the title "Thoughts of a Freeman," it hammered at America's military leadership. Laurens later wrote: "I passed my Eye cursorily over the pages, put them in my pocket and intimated to the House, that it was an anonymous production containing stuff which I must be content with, as perquisites of Office—that the hearth was the proper depository for such Records."[50]

Laurens did not show the document to delegates, nor did he toss it in the hearth. Instead, he sent it to Washington. Washington, to his credit, advised Laurens to let delegates read it:

> As I have no other view than to promote the public good, & am unambitious of honours not founded in the approbation of my Country, I would not desire in the least degree to suppress a free spirit of enquiry into any part of my conduct …. The anonymous paper handed you exhibits many serious charges, and it is my wish that it be submitted to Congress; this I am more inclined to, as the suppression, or concealment, may possibly involve you in embarrassments hereafter; since it is uncertain how many, or who may be privy to the contents.[51]

We find no evidence that Laurens followed Washington's advice. It appears the document was never presented to Congress, and its author remains unknown.[52]

The document itself, which Washington copied for his own records, accused the general, without naming him, of costing American lives by failing to attack the British in Pennsylvania:

> That the proper methods of atacking beating and conquering the Enemy has never as yet been adapted by the Commander in C—f. That More men will dye this winter then it would have cost lives to have conquered the Enemy last Summer and fall. That it is better to dye honourably in the field then in a stinking Hospital. That the many Fruitless and unacountable marches has had a great tendancy to fill the Hospitals with Sick.

The letter also pointed out the lackluster performance of America's professional army in comparison with its militias and urged Congress to rein in the influence of "Military men," presumably meaning Washington in particular:

> That in every victory as yet obtained by the Americans the Militia has had the principal share. That the Liberties of America are safe only in the hands of the Militia. That the Honourable Congress in many cases has been too much led by Military men. That such presidents [precedents] may in time become dangerous. That it is High time for the Honble Congress as the supream power of America to exercise their Othority with strict justice & impartiality.

The letter further insinuated that the army's woes, or many of them, had to be attributed to Washington's ineptness and that the general had been treated with way too much unwarranted veneration: "That the Head cant posobly be sound when the whole body is disordered. That the people of America have been guilty of Idolatry by making a man their god—and that the God of Heaven and Earth will convince them by wofull experience that he is only a man."[53]

Silence was often Washington's response to the cacophony of criticism and the inevitable comparison with Gates. But sometimes he let loose, as he did in a letter to Patrick Henry:

> I was left to fight two battles, in Order, if possible, to save Philadelphia, with less numbers than composed the Army of my Antagonist. ... How different the case in the Northern department! There the States of New York and New England, resolving to crush Mr Burgoyne, continued pouring in their Troops, 'till the surrender of that Army; at which time not less than 14,000 Militia were actually (as I have been informed) in Genl Gates's Camp, and these composed, for the most part, of the best Yeomanry in the Country well armed, and, in many instances supplied with provisions of their own carrying. Had the same spirit pervaded the People of this and the neighbouring States, we might before this, have had General Howe nearly in the situation of General Burgoyne.[54]

CHAPTER 43

A Most Shameful Deficiency

For everyone who found General Washington inadequate, there were at least as many who thought likewise about Congress. Many such critics were delegates themselves. Congress, observers complained, was not what it used to be; the states weren't sending enough delegates—indeed some states during some periods weren't represented at all in Congress—and many of those men who were sent were not up to the job.

Laurens wrote:

> A most shameful deficiency in this branch is the greatest Evil & is indeed the source of almost all our Evils. ... Is it not ... incumbent upon every Man of Influence throughout our Union to exert his powers at this Crisis, to exhort each State to fill up its Representation in Congress with the best, that is the most sensible, vigilant & faithful Citizens? At present it seems as if every such Man had bought his yoke of Oxen & prayed to be excused. ... If there be not Speedily a Resurrection of able Men & of that Virtue which I thought had been genuine in 1775, We are gone—we shall undo ourselves—we must flee to the Mountains.[1]

Joining Laurens in Philadelphia in the spring of 1778 was fellow South Carolinian John Mathews. This may have heartened Laurens, for here was an energetic man with sound experience, a man who should be quite useful in Congress. Mathews, a fifth-generation South Carolinian, had studied law in London before returning to Charleston in 1765 to begin his legal career. Before coming to Congress in the spring of 1778, he had served in various assemblies and had been speaker of the South Carolina House of Representatives. He was thus not naive about the ways of lawmaking bodies. But Mathews was also impatient, and he was soon as disgruntled and disillusioned as Laurens with the men around him.[2] Mathews found Congress exasperating with its slow pace, endless talk, and pointless frittering away of time. In July, he pleaded to a friend back home: "I have wrote to you for leave to come home in December; for God's sake procure it for me, & I'll be dam'd if ever you catch me here again. Those who have dispositions for Jangling, & are fond of displaying their Rhetorical abilities, let them come. I never was so sick of any thing in my life."[3]

In September, he sent another letter to the same man:

> Oh! my Worthy friend, never was Child more sick of a school, than I am, of this same business, I am sent here upon. ... I fully intended when I came into Congress, to have accustomed my self to deliver my sentiments upon every important Question, but I have found the thirst for Chattering so extremely prevalent, that it absolutely disgusts me, & frequently seals my lips.[4]

***

Congress had changed, and so had the army. Many of the first soldiers had been farmers and artisans who owned property. Most were motivated by genuine devotion to the cause. Over time, they left the military to return to their farms and shops. In their place appeared a mix of immigrants from Germany and the British Isles, indentured servants, and poor men with no land, as well as some indigenous and Black people.[5] While a good number were devoted Patriots, many were men with few options, lured by the prospect of pay and adventure. Washington and his officers had all they could handle in managing this diverse band of soldiers.

In late 1777, Washington and Congress agreed that the army urgently needed many reforms. To that end, Washington proposed that Congress send to his camp at Valley Forge a delegation from the Board of War and Congress with a broad mandate to prepare a plan "for correcting all abuses."[6]

Congress thought it a capital idea and sensibly planned to send Gates, Mifflin, and Pickering, from the Board of War, along with a few delegates. But Gates, who had arrived in York on January 19, begged permission of Congress to stay put.[7] His request was strange. Who was better suited to meet with the commander in chief than the president of the Board of War? And wouldn't Gates want the opportunity to personally resolve the misunderstandings between himself and Washington?

But Gates felt his place was in York. By this time, people in and out of Congress were aware of a falling out between Gates and Washington. Benjamin Rush certainly knew of it, referring in mid-January to a "rupture"[8] between the two generals.

Laurens, too, wrote about the "unhappy dispute" between Washington and Gates. Laurens confided to his son that Gates would have been happy to mend the relationship: "In conversation with General Gates without seeking on my side, I discovered an inclination in him to be upon friendly terms with our great & good General, it cannot be doubted but that there is the same disposition on the other side. What would I not give to see a perfect & happy reconciliation."[9]

Congress, apparently to sidestep an awkward and possibly disastrous confrontation between the generals, respected Gates's wishes. Gates was excused, and Mifflin and Pickering likewise bowed out. Congress, in the end, sent out five delegates and no one from the Board of War.

One of the delegates was Gouverneur Morris of New York, a newcomer to Congress and just 11 days shy of his 26th birthday when he arrived at York only the day before. Morris was a fast-rising attorney from a wealthy and well-connected family—an American aristocrat if there ever was one. His distinctive first name was the maiden name of his mother, who descended from Huguenots. She abhorred independence and remained a Loyalist throughout the war. He likewise detested the idea of independence at first, but came over to the Patriot side before the Declaration. In early 1776, he volunteered to be a colonel of a new militia regiment. A shoemaker was made colonel instead, and Morris, miffed, would not serve under him.[10]

Morris immersed himself in politics and was elected and then reelected to New York's provincial legislature. In April 1776, Morris was on a committee that dealt with Washington on his arrival in New York City with 8,000 men to defend the city.[11]

"The Tall Boy," someone called him, and indeed, at over 6 feet tall, Morris matched Washington in stature. His right arm and side were disfigured from terrible burns suffered when, aged 14, he accidentally upset a kettle of boiling water. The injury didn't seem to handicap his appeal with the ladies,[12] as he acquired a reputation for being never at a loss for enthusiastic lovers, and potential lovers seemed to be a preoccupation. He wrote on February 5, having spent maybe one night in York before going on to Valley Forge: "I would that I were quit of my congressional Capacity which is in every Respect irksome ... There are no fine Women at York Town."[13] Morris's famous wit both amused and annoyed his political colleagues. Fellow New Yorker Duer admired his "Coolness of Temper, and happy Vein of Irony."[14] Laurens would call him "guardless and incautious,"[15] and another colleague found him "a little too whimsical."[16]

In late January 1778, Morris and the other delegates arrived at Valley Forge and settled in about 3 miles west of the encampment in a large stone house called Moore Hall.[17] Morris left his first impression of the American soldiers he saw: "Our Troops. *Heu miseros*! The Skeleton of an Army presents itself to our Eyes in a naked starving Condition out of Health out of Spirits."[18]

These delegates, known as the Committee at Camp, would stay at Valley Forge until about late March. Washington cooperated with the committee as best he could, attending meetings when it was possible.

The committee members arriving at Valley Forge were on balance skeptics of Washington. Francis Dana of Massachusetts and Nathaniel Folsom of New Hampshire were New Englanders, who tended to have a jaundiced view of the commander. Joseph Reed of Pennsylvania, as Washington well knew, had been critical of the general's leadership while serving as his aide. Young Morris's opinion of Washington was likely yet unformed. John Harvie of Virginia may have been the only member of the committee firmly sympathetic with the general.[19]

But the weeks at Moore Hall transformed the committee. They saw firsthand the state of the army, heard from Washington about its many problems, and learned from their own interviews and examination of books and equipment that the fraud they expected to find as the basis for shortages was not taking place. Records were well kept. The immense quantities of food and clothing desperately needed were not being stolen; they were nowhere, never having been acquired and transported.[20] The committee learned that the myriad difficulties did not stem from a want of leadership on the part of Washington, but rather from many failures of organization, supply, and training beyond his control. The committee, seeing the problems as Washington did, became his ally and partner.

Washington helped himself by being well prepared. He soon presented to the committee a lengthy report—more than 16,000 words[21]—about the army's problems. The heavy lifting in preparing the report was done by Washington's staff, the final draft being in the handwriting of Alexander Hamilton, an aide on whom, along with John Laurens, Washington relied heavily.

Hamilton, just 23 or even younger (his year of birth is uncertain), was born in the West Indies to the daughter of a Huguenot physician and planter.[22] Hamilton's father, James Hamilton, a Scot, never married Alexander's mother,[23] drifting away from the family when Hamilton was about 8.[24] Hamilton's mother died when the boy was about 11, leaving him and his brother virtual orphans.[25]

Hamilton then worked diligently, capably, but unhappily as a merchant's clerk on the island of St. Croix.[26] Some merchants and other people of means recognized young Hamilton's potential and collected money to send the boy to New York City to further his education in the hope that he might return one day to the island as a physician or minister. Hamilton seized the opportunity; he would never set foot on St. Croix again. He attended a preparatory school in New Jersey for nine months and then went to King's College (now Columbia) in New York City just as tensions between Patriots and Loyalists were coming to a head in advance of the Revolution.[27]

Passionate about everything, young Hamilton was fiercely pro-British in his first months in America. Then, amid the turmoil in New York City during his days at King's College, his attitude changed, and he emerged an ardent and convincing speaker and writer, asserting the Patriot point of view. When the war began, Hamilton and his college cohorts immersed themselves in military training.[28] Possessing narrow shoulders, a slight build, and, according to portraits, quite rosy lips, he appeared frail and delicate. He lacked the look of an officer, but that's what he aspired to be. As an artillery captain, he was involved in the battles on Long Island[29] and joined in Washington's humiliating retreat across New Jersey. Hamilton was also part of the demoralized American army that crossed the Delaware to attack Trenton.[30]

Later that desperate winter, Washington, seeking talented men he might add to his staff, learned about Hamilton and his reputation as a deft writer. A position as Washington's aide would mean a big promotion.[31] It would also give him the privilege of being at the commander in chief's side and privy to the goings-on at the top of the American military structure. Craving combat, Hamilton had turned down similar opportunities from other generals,[32] but this offer he accepted.

Hamilton thus joined Washington's military "family," assuming increasingly important responsibilities in addition to handling much of the work in drafting reports and responding to correspondence. He became, for example, the principal negotiator in working out prisoner exchanges.[33]

After Saratoga, he was entrusted with a sensitive mission to cajole Gates into sending spare troops to Washington. Near the conclusion of that exhausting trip to the north and back, Hamilton fell ill. After a slow recovery, he arrived at Valley Forge in late January and was soon back to work, which included compiling Washington's long report for the Committee at Camp.[34]

Washington's report, which also relied on input from various generals, including Nathanael Greene, sounded the alarm in the first paragraph: "Something must be done—important alterations must be made; necessity requires, that our resources should be enlarged and our system improved: for without it, if the dissolution of the army should not be the consequence, at least, its operations must infallibly be feeble, languid and ineffectual."

The report identified key shortcomings and possible solutions. The first problem listed was the discontent of the officers. Washington cited "frequent resignations, dayly happening, and the more frequent importunities for permission to resign, and from some officers of the greatest merit."[35]

One way to make officers happier was to promise them a pension. While they fought for a republic, the officers in the American army saw themselves as equal to those fighting for the king, and those officers were promised pensions of half pay when they left the military at the end of the war. British officers were also allowed to sell their commissions. Many of the American officers had been serving since 1776 or before.[36] When they joined the American military, no one had promised them pensions, and there was no custom of allowing commissions to be sold. By 1778, these officers were frustrated about serving in an undermanned and poorly supplied army, angry at civil mismanagement, and disillusioned. They were still Patriots, but wanted what they felt they deserved; they wanted what their British counterparts got. Washington proposed that officers receive half pay for life after the war.[37]

Next, the report discussed the shortage of manpower. So far the army had relied on men who voluntarily enlisted. By this time, the country was "pretty well drained"[38] of men so inclined. The report proposed to draft men from each state's militia and require them to serve for one year.[39]

Further on, the report noted the disorder in the quartermaster, commissary, and hospital departments. Other problems identified included poor and inconsistent training of soldiers, the "lavish distribution of rank," irregular promotions, failure to pay soldiers on time, and wild inconsistency in the sizes of regiments.

Before concluding, Washington also tossed in some fresh ideas for the committee to digest. One had to do with indigenous warriors. Since the British were using them against the Americans, perhaps the Americans should do likewise: "[W]ould it not be well to employ two or three hundred indians against General Howe's army the ensuing campaign?" Washington said Cherokees and members of "Northern tribes" might be willing: "Such a body of indians, joined by some of our woodsmen would probably strike no small terror into the British and foreign troops, particularly the new comers."[40]

CHAPTER 44

I Schall Be Laughed At

With the Committee at Camp brainstorming about reforming the army, what would keep the new Board of War busy? Congress had an idea: "Resolved, That an irruption be made into Canada, and the Board of War be authorized to take every necessary measure for the execution of the business."[1]

The idea of trying once again to invade Canada seemed almost sensible. With Burgoyne's army captured, the path north, by way of Ticonderoga and Lake Champlain, was clear, and the British now had few troops in Canada to defend the vast land. Some delegates from New England and New York found the notion alluring.[2] It dovetailed with Gates's thinking too—he had been contemplating such an assault since November.[3] Indeed, he likely planted the notion in the minds of delegates.[4] Laurens, in opposition, called the plan an "indigested romantic Scheme."[5] But this "wild plan," as Eliphalet Dyer called it, won the support of all but three of the other delegates.[6]

Who would lead this invasion? Congress knew the perfect man for the job: Lafayette. Delegates assumed French Canadians would welcome an American army with this gallant young Frenchman at its head. As for the second in command, Congress found another perfect candidate: Washington's nemesis, Conway.[7] Lafayette would benefit from having the older, more experienced Conway by his side. As Conway spoke French, he would be useful in dealing with the *habitants*. An additional benefit was that he and Washington would be far apart. By this time, the idea of forcing Conway on Washington as inspector general had been abandoned.

Washington thought the plan a "child of folly," but did not voice his objections: "[A]s it is the first fruit of our new board of War I did not incline to say anything against it."[8]

The plan had two huge flaws. Firstly, Lafayette was just 20 years old, with almost no experience as a commander.[9] Additionally, the task of supplying yet another army would draw scant resources away from the hungry and shivering force at Valley Forge.

Other complications soon became apparent, some related to the appointment of Conway. Gouverneur Morris, learning of the plan, suggested to Laurens that it perhaps was not "prudent to trust a Person whose object it is to push his Fortunes in France with an opportunity to imbue the Minds of the Canadians with a Love of the Grand Monarque who may as probably like Canada as any of his Predecessors."[10] Morris thus feared that Conway, to win the favor of the French king, might conspire to make Canada not an American state but once again a French colony.

Lafayette likewise raised objections to Conway, but for different reasons. Lafayette, like many others, had initially cheered Conway's rise. However, by this time, Lafayette—fiercely loyal to Washington—was aware of how the commander in chief detested the Irishman. Lafayette wrote to Laurens: "Amongs All the men who could be sent under me Mr Connway is the most disagreeable to me and the most prejudiciable to the cause."[11]

Instead of heading off to northern New York to begin the task of gathering forces and supplies for the invasion, Lafayette rushed to York to lobby Congress and the Board of War to have Conway replaced as the deputy commander of the mission.[12] Lafayette, according to his own account, told the board that if Conway were not dropped in favor of one of the men he preferred, he would immediately return to France and take all the foreign officers with him.[13]

Congress squirmed. "A good deal of struggle was made to elude the Marquis's demands," wrote Laurens. But in the end, Congress caved in to avoid the embarrassing fallout had Lafayette carried out his threat: "Had an Irruption of this nature taken place, the World at large must have been informed of the unmeritted insult offered the General & Commander in Chief, & Censure must have followed both on Congress & the Board of War."[14] Conway was duly dumped in favor of the man Conway had insisted was his military inferior, de Kalb.[15]

So Lafayette got his command and his preferred subordinate. But the lobbying in York had taken time, and Lafayette then dawdled in Valley Forge to confer with Washington. It wasn't until February 17 that he finally arrived in Albany, the starting place for the expedition. This was very late for a project that called for setting off on frozen Lake Champlain that very month.[16]

Lafayette was greeted in Albany by none other than Conway, who had arrived three days earlier.[17] Conway promptly announced that the mission was "quite impossible."[18] Lafayette made his own assessment and found himself agreeing with the subordinate he despised. Conway also had letters from Schuyler, Arnold, and Lincoln advising against the expedition.[19] Only a few troops had been assembled, and those were "reluctant to the utmost degree" to attempt the invasion. Lafayette had expected a bustling scene, the product of groundwork set in motion by the Board of War. But almost nothing had been done, and it was already too late to gather up the men and supplies. The expedition was thus a fiasco before it began. Lafayette, who had boasted in letters to France about his role in the grand enterprise, felt humiliated and betrayed. He poured out his anger and frustration to Washington:

> I have consulted every body, and every body answers me that I schould be mad to untertake this operation. I have been schamefully deceived by the board of war. ... [T]he want of men, cloathes, money and the want of time deprives me of all hopes about this expedition. ... I am affraïd it will reflect on my reputation and I schall be laughed at.[20]

Lafayette soon reported to Congress, and on March 13 Congress quietly canceled the scheme.[21] There would be no new attempt to invade Canada.

Congress's romance with Conway was now over. Delegates were widely aware that the he was distrusted and disliked, but what should they do with him? In March, he was given a new assignment far away from Washington and Lafayette. Conway didn't like it. He wrote to Laurens, complaining that his talents were being wasted and calling upon Laurens to "Make my resignation acceptable to Congress."[22] Congress leaped at the opportunity: his resignation was accepted.[23] The vote was eight states to one. Curiously, the lone dissent came from Washington's home state.[24]

Conway protested that he had not actually intended to resign. Nevertheless, the door was shut. Congress had had enough of him. Laurens wrote: "I desire never again to converse or correspond with him."[25] When it came time for Congress to issue an honorable discharge to Conway, which was customary and normally routine, delegates refused. Even Lafayette found this unfair and cold. He wrote to Laurens: "[Y]ou know my sentiments of some parts of his life, which remain fixed in my mind—but gnl connway is an officer in the french service, a gentleman of bravery and talents, and I ca'nt refuse to my own feelings to beg you would mention to Congress that I have wrote to you on his behalf."[26] Both Lafayette and Gates repeatedly asked Congress to give Conway the recommendation, but to no avail.[27]

Thus ended Conway's career in America, but he stayed on the western side of the Atlantic long enough to get himself shot by an American general.[28] "Having been informed of some disrespectful words spoken of him"[29] by General John Cadwalader, Conway challenged the general to a duel. In that July 4, 1778, confrontation, Cadwalader's aim at 12 paces[30] was true, as reported by Henry Laurens: "General Conway received on the anniversary of Independence a Pistol Ball on one side of his Nose which passed to the back part of the Neck where it was extracted by a very light scission."[31] Conway, assuming he would die, penned a farewell note to Washington:

> I find myself just able to hold the pen during a few minutes, and take this opportunity of expressing my sincere grief for having done, written, or said any thing disagreeable to your Excellency. My career will soon be over; therefore justice and truth prompt me to declare my last sentiments. You are in my eyes the great and good man. May you long enjoy the love, veneration, and esteem of thos States, whose liberties you have asserted by your virtues.[32]

**

By March 1778, Washington's position as commander in chief seemed once again to be on solid ground. His critics had, for the most part, fallen silent. The so-called cabal, if it ever existed, had evaporated. In a kind of surrender to Washington, Gates protested that he had "no personal Connection" to Conway: "I Solemnly declare that I am of no Faction; & if any of my Letters taken aggregately, or by paragraphs, convey any meaning, which under any construction, is Offensive to Your Excellency; that was by no means the intention of the Writer."[33]

Washington, writing to an aide, was smug: "Matters have, & will, turn out very different to what that party expected. ... I have good reason to believe that the machinations of this junto [faction] will recoil upon their own heads."[34]

The Board of War, which with Gates at its head seemed likely to push against Washington's clout, lost the confidence of Congress. Laurens wrote in March: "The New Board of War has hitherto wrought nothing beneficial."[35]

Over the weeks, Gates and Washington mended fences. Gates often rode out to Valley Forge to take part in meetings with Washington and his council.[36] Whatever differences the two generals may have had seemed to have been smoothed over.

Then, itching to get back into action, and perhaps embarrassed by the board's role in the aborted Canadian adventure, Gates asked Washington to recommend him for another command. Washington gladly complied, and on April 15 Congress directed Gates to Fishkill, New York, to take charge of the Northern Department with the important jobs of holding the Hudson River and maintaining communications between New England and the Middle Atlantic states.[37]

Thomas Mifflin also quit the Board of War and, with approval from Congress, rejoined Washington's army. General Greene, Mifflin's nemesis, was furious. Washington gritted his teeth and assigned Mifflin a division.[38] Washington, revealing in a letter to Gouverneur Morris his low opinion of Mifflin, focused not on Mifflin's role in the suspected cabal, but on how Mifflin had earlier left the quartermaster department at a critical moment:

> I was not a little surprized to find that a Gentn who, sometime ago (when a cloud of darkness hung heavy over us & our affairs looked gloomy) was desirous of resigning, now stepping forward in the line of the Army—But, if he can reconcile such conduct to his feeling as an Officer & Man of honor ... I have nothing personally to oppose to it. Yet, I must think, that Gentlemens stepping in, and out, as the Sun happens to beam forth, or obscures, is not quite the thing, nor quite just with respect to those Officers who take the bitter with the sweet.[39]

Mifflin's return to the army was awkward and brief. Talk about possible mismanagement of the quartermaster department caught up with him. In June, delegates in Congress, after four hours of wrangling and over "violent opposition"[40] from Mifflin's allies, called for an inquiry into the conduct of Mifflin and his officers in the quartermaster department.[41] Henry Laurens found it suspicious that Mifflin would have his friends in Congress resist such an investigation: "[A]s a Man of honor, the

General must wish for an investigation in order to satisfy the public who at present clamor exceedingly upon the subjects of neglect, mis-application, peculation &c."[42]

Mifflin asked for leave from the army to defend himself. Before the inquiry got far, Congress gave Mifflin $1 million to settle various outstanding claims in his accounts. Even with that, some accounts remained unresolved. He eventually quit the army altogether to focus on politics.[43]

Meanwhile, the Board of War, with new members, limped along, its role and influence now diminished.

***

Starting about this time, people spoke of Washington as the "Father of his Country." Books were dedicated to him. One anointed him "Saviour of his Country, the Supporter of Freedom, And the Benefactor of Mankind." Almanacs appeared noting his birthday.[44]

It was apparent that, unless Washington made an unspeakable blunder, Congress would never replace him. Win or lose, the war was in his hands. Robert Morris wrote: "[Washington's] Country & his Country's Cause will inevitably suffer more or less with him. His private Character has been too long & too amiably & well supported to suffer by the Combined Force & Arts of Malice, Envy, Hatred & detraction."[45]

Now, even his boss—Congress—cringed at the faintest criticism of Washington, as revealed by an episode involving the uncompromising and prickly Thomas Burke of North Carolina, now back in Congress.

The context of the drama was a resolution of Congress from December. The resolution said any Americans who took up arms for the British and were captured should be turned over to the state they were from to be prosecuted.[46] In other words, Americans caught fighting on the British side would be treated as traitors, not prisoners of war.

Over the weeks that followed, Washington negotiated with General Howe in Philadelphia over various issues, including the exchange of prisoners. In the course of the talks, Washington, through designated commissioners, agreed to Howe's request that captured Loyalists bearing arms for the British would be treated as prisoners of war and not turned over for prosecution as traitors. Washington was thus allowing Howe to dictate terms that contradicted the will of Congress.

When Congress learned of this, Laurens, on its behalf, informed Washington that the deal with Howe must not contravene the December 30 resolution: there should be no agreement to treat captured Loyalists fighting for Britain as prisoners of war.[47]

Washington responded: "[M]y sensibility is not a little wounded. ... The Views of Congress seem to be very different from what I supposed them, when I entered into my late engagements with General Howe." Not wishing to derail the complex negotiations, which were nearly concluded, or to be embarrassed by having to backpedal on terms already agreed to, Washington asked that the issues be "suffered to sleep."[48] That is, he wanted Congress to give way, to concede Howe's request that Loyalists in custody be treated as prisoners of war.

Delegates bristled. Burke wrote:

> It appears to most of us that giving up a matter of this kind is betraying our independence and in effect giving licence to the enemy to recruit in our country. If we suffer our citizens who adhere to our enemies, and actually take arms against us to be considered prisoners of war, and subject to no municipal laws, I see not where our independence remains ... These are the sentiments, I believe of a great majority in Congress as well as mine.[49]

Burke was right. Delegates agreed that Congress needed to stand firm. All that needed to be done was to draft a response to tell Washington, in no uncertain terms, who was boss. It should have been easy; it was not.

At 4pm on April 10, delegates began debating the draft letter, mostly about prisoners but also concerning other issues related to the negotiations. Hour after hour, speakers droned on. Burke, feeling ill, was losing patience with his long-winded colleagues.

At last, at 10pm, a motion was made to adjourn. Burke voted "Aye" and then "declared the states might vote as they pleased, he would upon his honour adjourn himself."[50] He walked out without waiting for the vote to be completed. He feared the vote to adjourn would be defeated, for it seemed the majority were determined to finish the work that night.[51] As he later explained: "[T]he noise of loud, incessant Declamation, occasioned so violent pain in my head that I was totally unable to attend any longer."[52] He also later confessed another motivation—he didn't like the letter as drafted. It was too insulting to Washington, he thought. By removing himself, he left Congress without a quorum, effectively delaying a vote on the letter at least for a day.[53]

Another delegate, Georgia's Edward Langworthy, also left. Everyone else stayed behind. This behavior would not do. A messenger was dispatched to retrieve the two delegates. Langworthy returned,[54] but Burke refused. Burke's message, as reported in the congressional *Journal*, was: "Devil take him if he would come; it was too late and too unreasonable."[55]

The next morning, Congress set aside the letter long enough to focus on Burke. When delegates charged him with violating the order of Congress, Burke protested that he would not bow to "a tyranny of the majority of this Congress, who would keep me here at unreasonable hours."[56] In any case, Congress had no power to discipline any delegate. If one misbehaved, it was up to his state to castigate him.[57]

He admitted that the offensive term "Devil" slipped into his response. However, he would not apologize for being rude to Congress, for by the time he made the remark, Congress had adjourned and thus "ceased to be a body,"[58] and therefore could not be offended.

Burke's colleagues, now inflamed by the charge of tyranny, thought about expelling the North Carolinian. But to do so required a quorum, which required Burke's presence. And if Burke cooperated in his own expulsion, Congress would be left paralyzed without a quorum to function. Burke thus remained undisciplined. He would later win a victory of a sort when Congress took a symbolic step to reduce the hot air emanating from the illustrious body: a pledge that members speak no more than 10 minutes at a time. Burke won another victory when the North Carolina legislature endorsed his conduct and returned him to Congress.[59]

Returning to the letter to Washington, Congress finally approved a draft that, in its opening paragraph, set a high standard for verbal contortions to cushion the general's dignity:

> Congress with great Concern perceive that your Sensibility is wounded by their Resolutions. Placing the firmest Confidence in your Prudence, Abilities and Integrity, they wish to preserve that Harmony with you, which is essential to the general Weal: You may rest assured that far from any intention to give you Pain, their Resolutions have no other Motives or End, but the public Good; they therefore hope that you will not in future be distresst by Apprehensions, as injurious to their Honor, as they are to your own Feelings.[60]

Nevertheless, in the end, Congress insisted that the resolution about Loyalist prisoners be followed.[61]

Congress agonized over other portions of the letter. Parts were extensively rewritten, with forceful, stern instructions stricken in favor of limp sentences with squishy advice. Congress had no taste for admonishing the great general.

Washington accepted the letter in his stride, offering thanks for the "fresh assurances ... of [Congress's] confidence."[62] It didn't matter much now anyway. By this time, the negotiations between Washington and Howe had broken down on account of other issues. For the moment, there would be no exchange of prisoners.[63]

CHAPTER 45

Fire Cake & Water

Questions about prisoner exchange mingled with those regarding treatment of prisoners. According to the accepted practice, the British were obliged to pay for the care of prisoners held by the Americans, and vice versa. Thus, if the Americans failed to pay the British for the cost of feeding and housing the American prisoners in custody, the British could let them starve and freeze.[1]

That's what happened, thanks in part to congressional quibbling. About the time Washington's men were trudging into Valley Forge, Congress in York determined that the British must pay the Americans in hard money—gold or silver coins—for maintaining the British soldiers held by the Patriots. Congress simultaneously declared that the money it sent into Philadelphia to pay for the Americans held by the British would be strictly in Continental dollars.[2]

With this policy, Congress was trying to attack two problems. One was counterfeiting. The British had already sent out from Philadelphia a wagonload of Continental dollars to pay for prisoner upkeep. It was likely a show of mockery to demonstrate how worthless the dollar was. But it was just as likely an effort to further weaken the currency by dumping fake Continental bills into the economy. The wagon and the suspect bills were ordered sent back to Philadelphia.[3] By demanding gold and silver, the Americans could fend off British attempts to further exacerbate the inflation of the Continental currency.

The second problem Congress was trying to address was the trouble the British were causing in Philadelphia by prohibiting the circulation of Continental bills. If the Americans sent in Continental dollars to pay for the care of American soldiers, the British presumably would be forced to spend that money.

But Congress only made conditions worse for the American prisoners in Philadelphia, as the British would rather let the Americans starve than accept rebel dollars.

While these issues were being thrashed out, the normal practice for maintaining prisoners broke down. The Americans continued to feed the British captives, but the British let the American prisoners go hungry.[4] In a letter to General Howe,

Washington pointed out the contrast: "[I]f you are determined to make Captivity as distressing as possible to those whose lot it is to fall into it, let me know it that we may be upon equal terms For your Conduct must and shall mark mine."[5]

About 60 American officers were held in the Pennsylvania State House, while about 500 American enlisted men were stuffed into the New Jail, a stone building on Walnut Street just a block away. The enlisted men had it the worst, some going for five days straight with no food.[6] Many died.

***

In our collective historical lexicon, Valley Forge is a synonym for brutal, penetrating, excruciating cold. In fact, the winter of Valley Forge was mild.[7] Soldiers counted six snowstorms, but some frequently described the weather as pleasant.[8]

We also tend to assume that the soldiers at Valley Forge experienced unrelenting hunger. However, the food supply, though erratic, was often quite sufficient. The shortage of food was at its worst that very first week.[9] A private recalled a two-day period when all he had to eat was half a pumpkin cooked on a hot rock. More typical fare was fire cake: flour and water mixed, formed into patties, and baked on hot stones.[10] A weary surgeon in camp, scribbling in his diary on December 22, called on the Lord to make the commissary live on "Fire Cake & Water, till their Glutted Gutts are turned to Pasteboard."[11] Then for about a month, supplies came in. Then they stopped, and for two weeks in February came another crisis and the hunger returned. Supplies later arrived, but soldiers suffered through another week or so of scant food at the end of February.[12]

Meanwhile, the shortage of clothing, shoes, blankets, and other supplies persisted throughout the winter. The lack of kettles amplified the problem of disease because, without a sufficient number of them, soldiers could not make enough soap.[13] Typhus, typhoid, dysentery, influenza, and smallpox smoldered, spread, sickened, and killed.[14] Scabies, which soldiers called the itch, didn't kill, but inflicted constant torment. To relieve the agony, one man tried an ointment made with mercury, while another tried swilling a pint and a half of rum. Both subsequently died.[15] The terrible shortages might have been alleviated somewhat with an appeal for civilians to collect and bring supplies to the camp, but Washington feared that such an effort would tip off the enemy and invite the British to attack. More than 2,500 men—about one in seven—perished at Valley Forge.[16] About a thousand others deserted.[17]

Congress, aware of the desperate situation, quietly dispatched pleas for supplies to the various states. Of all the states, New York and New Jersey were especially responsive with shipments of meat.[18]

Some of the men at Valley Forge that winter found amusing distractions. Plays were performed, probably at the camp's bakehouse. Whoever distributed tickets flubbed his job. A soldier complained to his diary that he and other ticket holders tried to attend and found no seats available. In May, players performed in an improvised open-air theater along the banks of the Schuylkill.[19]

***

In the talks about exchanging prisoners, Washington and Congress were both obsessed about Charles Lee, the eccentric general who blundered into captivity back in December 1776. At first, Lee, because he had once been a British officer, faced the possibility of being shipped back to England, charged with desertion, and executed.[20] The evidence against him was thin: Lee, after all, before accepting his American commission, had properly and publicly resigned from the British military.[21] Even so, just the remote chance of that dire outcome may have led Lee to quickly become chatty with his captors. He offered, for example, helpful hints on how best to squash the American revolt.[22] He also worked with General Howe and other British officers on a peace plan, which he sent off to Washington and Congress in early 1777 with the request that Congress send representatives to New York to begin talks.[23]

Congress rejected that idea. Delegates felt that no such conference should be held except with ambassadors properly authorized by London.[24] But delegates took seriously the potential threat to Lee, stepping in to save him with its own threat, which Washington relayed to General Howe: "[A]ny Violence which you may commit upon his [Lee's] Life or Liberty will be severely retaliated upon the Lives or Liberties of the British Officers or those of their Foreign Allies at present in our hands."[25]

Washington actually opposed this approach. The British held six Patriot prisoners to every prisoner held by the Americans. In Washington's view, the Americans would likely come out on the losing end if a tit-for-tat game of reprisals gained momentum.[26] Nevertheless, Congress's threat seemed to work; the British backed off.

Curiously, Lee persisted in offering information and advice about the American army, even after the risk of being tried passed.[27] Was Lee on the side of the British, of the Americans, or just on the side of Charles Lee? Lee later explained that he was only trying to fool the enemy. That seems to be what the British thought, too, as they generally ignored his counsel.[28]

Lee spent much of his first months of captivity in quarters prepared for him in the council chamber of New York's city hall. He had two small chambers and a large living room. The British paid for his candles, firewood, wine, and ample meals. He was comfortable but under guard, and had little freedom. The British later put Lee aboard a ship in New York Harbor. Congress, figuring again that the British intended to ship him to England, issued another threatening resolution: however American prisoners were handled, that's how British in American hands would be treated.[29]

Again, any ideas of shipping Lee off to England seemed to be discarded. Lee appeared safe, but was still in British custody. The question arose of how to arrange an exchange. According to the usual protocol, because Lee was a major general, the British would demand another major general in return. However, the Americans had no major generals locked up to offer. That problem was solved when a Connecticut officer with 38 men slipped behind British lines in Rhode Island, yanked British Major General Richard Prescott out of bed, and took him away—all with surprisingly little resistance from Prescott's men. Congress thanked the Connecticut officer, gave him a sword, and promoted him.[30]

Now the Americans had Prescott as trade bait. They also had someone new to condemn just in case something should befall Lee while in British custody. Henry Laurens, writing in the context of reports about "repeated Instances of British cruelty exercised upon American Prisoners," said that he would "have no Objection" to hanging Prescott "for Injuries done to Lee."[31]

The British held out on a trade—Prescott had been captured and exchanged once before.[32] Maybe Howe wanted Prescott to stew awhile over this irksome habit. A secretary to Admiral Howe noted in his journal: "News came, that Prescot was taken Prisoner at Rhode Island in a very idle Way; He is not much regretted."[33]

For the moment, there would be no exchange. But the British did make life for Lee much more pleasant. He was brought ashore and put on parole, which meant living in a house with old friends who also happened to be British officers.[34] Lee had the freedom to roam Manhattan, was attended by a servant, and enjoyed the companionship of one of his beloved dogs.[35] British generals provided horses for Lee. The Americans gave Prescott comparable privileges in Connecticut.[36]

In March, the Americans allowed a British officer to escort Lee overland across New Jersey to Philadelphia. There, Howe, who seemed eager a few months earlier to ship off Lee for execution, now prattled on with Lee like they were old acquaintances, according to Lee. Howe all but confessed that he regretted taking on the job of commanding British forces in America.[37] It was common knowledge in Philadelphia that Howe had a mistress, the wife of a Loyalist employed by the British. The general, not troubling himself to hide the affair, would take her to the theater.[38] Lee would later famously sum up Howe's career in America as just three activities repeated again and again: he "shut his eyes, fought his battles, had his little whore."[39]

On April 5, Howe allowed Lee to leave Philadelphia and go to Valley Forge. He had still not been formally exchanged, being bound by a pledge not to take the field with the Americans.[40] However, he could now join Washington.

Washington, knowing Lee was on his way, galloped 4 miles toward Philadelphia, dismounted, and waited. When Lee appeared, Washington greeted him "as if he had been his brother." At the camp, the two reviewed the troops assembled as part of a grand reception for Lee. In the evening, Lee was Washington's special guest at a dinner with chamber music and song. In the same building where Martha Washington was staying with her husband, a room was prepared for Lee to sleep in. It happened to be adjacent to Martha Washington's sitting room. Somehow he arranged for his "miserable dirty hussy ... from Philadelphia"[41] to slip into the room.

***

Compared to the hungry, squalid, and cold existence for American soldiers at Valley Forge, life that winter for British troops in Philadelphia was infinitely more pleasant. But it was not easy at first. The American Patriots made sure, as they fled the city, to strip it of everything useful. That included arms, ammunition, vessels, horses, and carts, along with almost everything made of metal, including lead pipes in homes. Much food was also taken, although some was deliberately left for the remaining 20,000 or so civilians, and some provisions remained that were well hidden.[42]

The Americans also initially made it difficult for the British to supply Philadelphia by water, and they stripped the surrounding countryside of food, fodder, and anything useful to the British. American militia patrols were assigned to hamper foraging parties, along with civilian farmers and merchants who attempted to bring supplies to the city.[43]

But fears of starvation evaporated once the British opened up the Delaware to shipping, and by December many stealthy traders were finding gaping holes in the leaky militia cordon around the city. One Philadelphia woman recorded that she found ample quantities of honey and butter from one source and goose, pork, and beef from another. A German reported in January that trade in the city was flourishing. Women found it especially easy to come and go as militia blithely let them pass. In at least one case, Patriot soldiers on horseback, in a gesture of gallantry, helped carry some of a woman's goods to town.[44]

Men were more likely to be stopped. Some were just turned back. In one case, a man carrying eggs and butter was stopped, tied to a tree, and pelted with his merchandise. For those apprehended for supplying the enemy, the common punishment was to be whipped with up to 250 lashes.[45]

Often enough, however, the Pennsylvania militia was nowhere to be seen.[46] With many roads unguarded, wagons of goods rolled in. In January 1778, Washington received the following report:

> I can Assure your Excellency not less Flour than is Sufficient to maintain Eight or Ten Thousand men goes daily to Philadelphia, Carried in by Single Persons, Waggons, Horses &ca, the Quantitys of other Provisions are great, last Wednesday Night Col. Miller of the Malitia Informs me Twelve Head of Cattle, Cover'd by a Small Party of Arm'd Country men were carried in one drove.[47]

On at least one occasion, when the militia got up the gumption to actually interfere with trade, civilians became so annoyed that they reported details to the British, who sent out a column to smash the rebel militia camp.[48]

On other occasions, militiamen would abuse what little power they had. A militia colonel reported: "[T]he length of time they have been on the Station has made them too well Acquainted with the Girls, and People from Town, who I fear Seduce, and make them Commit many things highly Improper, such as Seizing flour &ca from one person, and delivering it to their favorites."[49]

In late winter, the Americans initiated a brutal campaign to both stop commerce to the city and ensure a flow of supplies to Valley Forge. Washington assigned General Nathanael Greene to sweep the farmlands around Philadelphia for anything not already stripped or sold. He soon reported: "The inhabitants cry out and beset me from all quarters—but like the Pharoh I harden my heart."[50] There was not much to take: "[T]he face of the Country is strongly markt with poverty and distress—All the Cattle and most of the best Horses have been carried into the City. ... We take all the Horses and Cattle, Hogs and Sheep fit for our use—but the Country has been so gleand that there is but little left in it."[51]

Meanwhile, as people learned of this foraging expedition, they rushed with what goods they had to the city.[52] The whole effort backfired. It gained few supplies for the Americans, increased the flow of goods to the British, and destroyed what little goodwill the Continental Army might have had in the region.

Washington sent off another general, Anthony Wayne, to New Jersey with much the same mission. What Wayne found, he either took or burned. But much was hidden. The British sent out a force to surround Wayne and his men far away from Valley Forge. Yet before they could corral Wayne and his men, the Americans slipped back into Pennsylvania. Wayne reported to Washington: "I doubt not that they [the British] are now Employed in Collecting the Cattle &ca which the Inhabitants in that Quarter took great pains to hide from us."[53] Thus the main result of this expedition, like Greene's, was to drive local opinion against the Patriot cause.

The militia, meanwhile, also employed harsher measures as time went on. They were given authorization to summarily shoot people carrying goods to market in the city. People heard reports of farmers bound to tails of horses and dragged to death.[54]

***

For civilians in Philadelphia not connected with the rebels, the arrival of the British brought at first relative calm, order, and a refreshing feeling of stability. Joseph Galloway, the former delegate to Congress and now with the British, managed interactions between the locals and the occupying army.[55] At first his role was informal, but in December Howe put him in charge of the city's civil government.[56] He built a network of spies, put in place a town watch, and saw to it that arms were taken away from any likely supporter of independence.[57] He also set prices on certain goods, formulated regulations, and otherwise did what he could to ensure that life and business in town resumed their normal pace.[58] Galloway found time to cook up a wild scheme to seize the Congress.[59] It was never attempted.

Galloway's wife, Grace, was outside Philadelphia. Galloway sent Washington a request that she be allowed to come into the city from their country house and bring in furniture. Washington gave Grace a pass to travel, but demanded that the furniture be left behind.[60]

Meanwhile, British military authorities applied harsh justice to maintain discipline among the soldiers and instill fear and respect among civilians. Anyone passing by the back of the State House before sunset on November 1, 1777, would have seen the swaying body of Corporal William McSkimming, hanged for assaulting an officer. Two waggoners convicted of raping two servant girls were given 1,000 lashes, forced to march through town with a noose around their necks, and banished from the city.[61]

Despite such measures, Howe was unable to keep his soldiers fully in control. The town was now cursed with opportunistic looting and plundering. Galloway managed to put in place a civil police force, but it did a poor job of protecting citizens from illicit acts of wayward troops or larcenous civilians. Lists of stolen items often appeared in the newspapers.[62]

With about 600 houses left vacant by fleeing Patriots, the city at first accommodated the occupying British soldiers better than might be expected. But then with the influx of men who had been stationed at Germantown, more civilians found themselves sharing lodgings with military men. One woman found herself forbidden from coming and going through her front door. Her "guest" officer, who brought in his mistress, demanded the home's owner access her own home through a back street. When another woman agreed to allow a major into her large house (she may have had no choice), she also allowed in three or four German soldiers, who came and went as orderlies and messengers, and the major's three servants—two white, one Black. Meanwhile, out in the yard in stables were the major's three horses, three cows, and two sheep. He also had several birds.[63]

For the most part, soldiers felt welcome in the city and the locals got along with them. A Quaker woman recorded in her diary: "I went this morning to H. Pemberton's; found her smoking her pipe, with two officers—one of whom is quartered there."[64]

Clubs sprang up to offer the men entertainment. They could attend concerts, go to church, pass the time in taverns, and visit theaters. Cock fights were organized. At least one footrace was held: one soldier from each battalion, running 3 miles in full uniform and equipment![65] Officers staged their own plays and even organized parades,[66] including a St. Patrick's Day procession of Irish soldiers passing in front of General Howe's door.[67]

The soldiers also had a plentiful assortment of Philadelphia ladies to gaze upon. Because so many American men had fled the city to avoid arrest, local women outnumbered civilian men by 30 percent, according to a British census.[68] The young women were not shy. For some, the winter in Philadelphia was a swirl of dances and entertainment, with plenty of handsome single men about. In February, 18-year-old Rebecca Franks[69] sent out from Philadelphia, with the permission of General Howe, a package containing some handkerchiefs and ribbons for her friend, Anne Harrison Paca, who happened to be the wife of William Paca, delegate to Congress from Maryland. The package also contained a letter for Mrs. Paca bursting with excitement:

> You have no idea of the life of continued amusement I live in. I can scarse have a moment to myself. ... I am but just come from under Mr. J. Black's hands and most elegantly am I dressed for a ball this evening at Smith's where we have one every Thursday. ... No loss for partners, even I am engaged to seven different gentlemen for you must know 'tis a fix'd rule never to dance but two dances at a time with the same person.[70]

The reassurance felt at first by Philadelphians toward the occupiers gave way to disillusionment and a sense of betrayal over matters concerning money. In the days before the Declaration of Independence, Pennsylvania had its own currency. With the appearance of the Continental dollar, those old colonial bills created under royal sanction were increasingly rejected by Patriots and then suppressed altogether.[71] The notes became worthless. Even so, Loyalists and some others held them in the belief that, when British rule was restored, that old currency would come back into use and be supported by royal authorities. With the arrival of Howe and his troops, the old currency that Loyalists had saved reappeared in Philadelphia, displacing Continental bills. For some weeks, Howe tolerated this old currency.

But then, when the Delaware opened for shipping, outside merchants flooded into Philadelphia and insisted on completing transactions using hard currency—gold and silver. Howe gave in—those merchants could reject the old Pennsylvania currency. Soldiers followed suit, and soon the value of the old money plunged.[72] Spies from Philadelphia reported to Washington: "Money is very ill to be got. Numbers of people in town will take no paper money of any currency."[73] Only hard currency had value, and that was scarce. For Loyalists, it was a kind of betrayal, an ominous demonstration that they could not count on the British authorities to reward them for their loyalty. With paper money useless, and firewood and food scant and costly even with hard money, the winter outlook for many civilians in the city, according to one diary, was "inevitable Beggary and Ruin."[74]

The occupying military provided no support for civilians. Loyalist or not, they had to fend for themselves. As might be expected, the poorest fared the worst. The British commandeered the Alms House, forcing managers to find emergency housing for the poor. Some were relocated to Carpenters' Hall. Unable to find enough food for these destitute souls, the manager overseeing them forced 40 of them from the town. They became refugees, told to wander and find work, shelter, and food in winter somewhere in the ransacked countryside.[75]

Most supplies that came in by water were reserved for the military, who lived well once the Delaware was opened. A high-ranking officer wrote home that the men were in great health. His only worry seemed to be that his bored junior officers might go broke from drinking and gambling.[76]

Conditions for the poor improved somewhat over time, thanks largely to Galloway, who scoured the city for donations. For other civilians, access to provisions improved as the American efforts to block supplies from the country collapsed and more provisions brought by ship became available.[77]

For some Quaker families, April brought joy: the return of the exiles who had been sent away the previous September for showing insufficient devotion to the Patriot cause. In Lancaster in March, the rebel Pennsylvania state government, responding to loud complaints, asked Congress to allow the Quaker men taken to Virginia to return to Philadelphia.[78] Congress agreed, and the prisoners were duly brought back as far as Pottsgrove, about 35 miles northwest of Philadelphia, where they were released to make their way home. None were offered a pardon, apology, or reimbursement for the costs for their food and lodging during their time away.[79]

CHAPTER 46

Most Wicked, Diabolical Baseness

In France in early 1778, William Lee prepared to head off on his diplomatic mission to Austria and Germany. He also spared some time to finally tender his official resignation as alderman to the City of London.[1]

Knowing little French, less German, and nothing about diplomacy, Lee realized he was out of his depth:

> I doubt my abilities, for however anxious and zealous, it must require both much time and more capacity than is common for a man not versed in the crooked paths of court to get into the mysteries of the most subtle cabinet of Europe, and besides, above 40 years old, it is somewhat awkward to go to school to learn languages.[2]

There was another problem—his credentials were amiss. The documents from Congress authorized him to deal with Emperor Joseph II, but made no mention of the emperor's formidable mother. Lee quickly sent off a message to Congress for revised documents that properly acknowledged "The Most Serene and Most Potent Princess Maria Theresa, Queen of Hungary and Bohemia, Arch Duchess of Austria." She, Lee informed Congress, "is extremely jealous of her power and authority, not permitting her son to interfere in any manner in the government of her dominions."[3] The revised credentials didn't arrive in time. Lee thus appeared in Vienna without them.[4]

Another difficulty was that Lee was strapped for cash. He wrote to Congress for money, but in the meantime, he borrowed. He finally set off from Paris on March 24, 1778, uncertain about whether he would visit Berlin or Vienna first, and at a loss about how exactly he would achieve anything. In Frankfurt, he stopped to weigh intelligence about political developments and sort out his options.[5]

On May 13, Lee slipped into Vienna like a spy, quietly at night. He quickly came to rely on the French ambassador, who was soon introducing Lee as "a gentleman traveller." The Frenchman reckoned that Lee would have better luck reaching the people he wanted to see as a private individual rather than as an emissary of an unrecognized nation. But the ploy fooled no one; everyone knew Lee had a diplomatic purpose. That included the British ambassador, who did all he could to ensure Lee met no one of importance.[6] So while the French ambassador was trying to open doors for Lee, the British ambassador pushed from the other side. The doors remained bolted. In this tussle, Lee never had his audience with either Emperor Joseph or Maria Theresa. It didn't help that Lee was inept and that the Habsburg rulers had other things on their minds, like a possible war with Prussia. Nor did it help that despite close ties between France and Austria—the French queen, Marie Antoinette, was Maria Theresa's youngest daughter—the friendship was at the moment fraying.[7] Yet all that probably didn't matter anyway. The Habsburgs had cemented themselves into a posture of neutrality, and they were never going to let the American push them in any direction.[8] With long experience in putting down rebellions of their own restive subjects, the Habsburgs were unlikely to support a revolution of any kind anywhere.[9]

While Lee made no headway with the Habsburgs, he caused a sensation in Vienna. He was a star guest at many dinners, where he was something of a laughingstock. At one table, he was peppered with questions about America. He gamely did his best in his miserable French, sometimes making no sense. Asked if there were any serfs in America, Lee said indeed, there were many "cherries" and "strawberries."[10]

Despite the blundering, Lee seems to have succeeded in making the American Revolution a keen topic of interest in the Habsburg realm. We know that one Viennese had his son baptized Benjamin Silas Arthur in honor of the American trio of envoys in Paris.[11]

On July 2, Lee was on his way out of town.[12] He returned to Frankfurt, where he waited for an invitation to Berlin from Frederick the Great, the Prussian ruler. Frederick, like Maria Theresa, was not inclined to talk to revolutionaries. The invitation never came, but he obtained from the Prussian a token concession for the United States: Frederick promised that no German mercenaries recruited by the British would be allowed to cross his Rhineland territories.[13]

Restless, frustrated, and trying to make himself useful, Lee embarked on some freelance diplomacy. Word of his presence in Frankfurt reached Amsterdam, leading to a connection with Jean de Neufville, a merchant who acted as a kind of foreign secretary for the United Provinces.[14] Lee and de Neufville agreed to meet. In Aix-la-Chapelle (today's Aachen, Germany), they came together and hatched something like a treaty between the United States and the seven provinces of Holland. It was only a draft, a brainstorm of dilettantes. Neither Lee nor de Neufville had any authority from anyone to craft or even outline such a document.[15]

Lee sent it off, unsigned, to Congress.[16] There it should have been buried and forgotten, but it was not. It would, by and by, ignite a war.[17]

Lee stayed on unhappily in Frankfurt with his family, traveling to Paris from time to time, mainly to consult with brother Arthur.[18] Sickness struck William and two of his children. Lee's wife gave birth after a difficult pregnancy to a third child, Brutus, who survived about eight months. Lee lamented about his time in Frankfurt: "We breath[e] indeed, and that is all."[19]

***

In late April, Washington sent to Congress what appeared to be a draft of a bill from the British Parliament. The document had been brought to his headquarters by a "Gentleman" sent out from Philadelphia.[20] It mentioned a peace commission to be sent to America, as well as various proposals that amounted to some concessions to the Americans.[21] What was to be made of this? Washington, in his note to Congress, suspected a fabrication cooked up in Philadelphia: "[I]t is certainly founded in principles of the most wicked, diabolical baseness, meant to poison the minds of the people and detach the wavering, at least, from our cause."[22]

Henry Laurens in York was equally skeptical, calling it a "spurious draught of a Bill insinuated to be Parliamentary." He reckoned that General Howe and his "Emissaries" were behind it. "I believe it to be of Philadelphia manufacture probably under hints from the other side of the water." He supposed Congress would "return it decently tarred and feathered."[23]

Then a few days later, Washington sent on to Congress something more: a copy of a speech introducing the measures in Parliament. Now Washington was convinced that the bill and speech must be authentic. In a private letter, he speculated about what was behind these surprising gestures from London. Something had happened in Paris, he concluded: "I think France must have ratified our independance." The British, it appeared, were now scrambling to cut a quick deal with the Americans before a French treaty could cross the Atlantic and be formalized.[24]

Washington had no clue about what was going on in Paris, and neither did Congress. Delegates had not received even a note from their men in France for nearly a year. But Washington was mostly correct. Government leaders in London, who knew more about negotiations in Paris than Congress did, were aware that progress was being made toward a treaty between the United States and France. Over seven weeks of consultations in London, Lord North, the prime minister, devised a plan to change course—to woo Americans with a package chock full of many but not all of the concessions Americans had asked for before the war. In early reports reaching America, the specifics of the plan were unclear. But at the very least, Parliament was willing to concede that it did not have unlimited authority over the Americans. Parliament was prepared to cast aside the core principle that was the basis for the war—the power to tax the Americans.[25] If only the Americans would break off their romance with the French, the British would offer nearly every bauble they desired, except independence.

Congress now assumed that the documents were not the product of Howe's imagination but really did originate in London. John Henry, a delegate from Maryland, feared the British initiative might sap Patriotic resolve: "I dread the impressions it will make upon the minds of many of our people. If it should ... make its appearance in the form of a Law, it will prove more dangerous to our cause than ten thousand of their best troops."[26]

Delegates, needing to stamp out the spark before it set the house on fire, got to work on a response. A committee—comprising Gouverneur Morris of New York, William Henry Drayton of South Carolina, and Francis Dana of Massachusetts[27]—prepared a report. It concluded:

> [A]ny men, or body of men, who should presume to make any separate or partial convention or agreement with commissioners under the crown of Great Britain, or any of them, ought to be considered and treated as open and avowed enemies of these United States. ... [T]hese United States cannot, with propriety, hold any conference or treaty with any commissioners on the part of Great Britain, unless they shall, as a preliminary thereto, either withdraw their fleets and armies or, in positive and express terms, acknowledge the independence of the said States.[28]

Congress unanimously approved the report and ordered it published.[29] Delaware's Thomas McKean soon wrote to Cesar Rodney to let the state's assembly know that "I am determined never to give up the Independence of the United States, after so much expense of blood and treasure, whilst I have a breath to draw; that I shall neither be allured nor intimidated into it; and that, if this resolution should not meet with their fullest approbation, they would be pleased to remove me immediately."[30]

***

Of all the issues Washington reported to the Committee at Camp and Congress, the most contentious was that of pensions for officers—half pay for life. When word of this reached Congress, delegates quickly chose sides and dug in their heels. Those in favor, a slim majority, argued that officers were unable to support themselves on their pay and thus left the military for lucrative opportunities that were abundant elsewhere in wartime. A possible solution would be to raise their pay, but that would further flood the economy with paper money and probably accelerate the collapse of the Continental dollar.[31] The promise of pensions and the ability to sell commissions seemed to be the best way to give officers the incentive to stay in the army and serve for the duration of the war.

One argument on the opposite side was that Congress had no authority to offer such pensions, or, in Burke's words, that "the Congress being instituted only for the purposes of War have no power without particular instructions, to make any peace establishment."[32]

Another line of reasoning pointed to the danger that might follow from this scheme: that it would promote the creation of a permanent standing army, a peacetime monster threatening civil liberties.[33]

Laurens was among the most vigorous in opposing the pensions. In the interest of the cause, he had "already lost a great Estate & am in a fair way to part with the present small remainder." Patriotism should be motivation enough for the officers, he said, as it was to "many Thousands ... who have not bowed the Knee to Luxury nor to Mammon."[34]

Another opponent was Lovell of Massachusetts. He feared the pension scheme would undermine American society by introducing among industrious citizens "a set of haughty, idle, imperious Scandalizers."[35]

The debate over officers' pensions raged nearly every day for over a month, even as common soldiers shivered and starved at Valley Forge.[36] From that camp, Washington added his two cents' worth in favor of the proposal: "I do most religiously believe the salvation of the cause depends upon it—& without it, your Officers will moulder to nothing, or be composed of low and illiterate Men void of capacity for this, or any other business."[37]

In a separate private letter, Washington confided irritation at what he saw as Congress's "jealousy" of the army. To Washington, the opposition to half pay was part of an ingrained and unwarranted fear and suspicion of the military. "You may be assured, there is nothing more injurious—or more unjustly founded," Washington wrote. This distrust stemmed largely from examples in other countries of abuses by standing armies. But those, in many cases, were peacetime armies employing mercenaries, added Washington. The American army was at war and made up of its own citizens. "[W]e should all be considered, Congress—Army &c., as one people, embarked in one cause—in one interest; acting on the same principle, and to the same end." Congress seemed to be casting the army as if it were the adversary and a threat to civil authority. Washington felt that was unfair and wrongheaded:

> [I]t may be said, that no history, now extant, can furnish an instance of an army's suffering such uncommon hardships as ours have done, and bearing them with the same patience and Fortitude—To see men without Cloat[hes] to cover their nakedness—without Blankets to lay on—without Shoes, by which their Marches might be traced by the Blood from their feet—and almost as often without Provisions as with; Marching through frost & Snow, and at Christmas taking up their Winter Quarters within a days March of the enemy, without a House or Hutt to cover them till they could be built & submitting to it without a murmur, is a Mark of patience & obedience which in my opinion can scarce be parallel'd.[38]

But to some opponents of half pay, suspicion of the army was only prudent. The opposition was centered among New England delegates[39] with fresh memories of the Boston Massacre, the killing in Boston of civilians by British soldiers back in 1770. Opponents in Congress to the half-pay measure offered a motion to refer the matter to the states, where the idea would likely die. The motion narrowly lost. After some weeks, and with the departure of some delegates and the arrival of others, opponents tried again. Once more, the motion lost.[40]

Finally, in May, a compromise was found. Congress agreed to offer a half-pay pension for seven years, starting when the war ended. Congress also added a provision to encourage the long-suffering common soldiers to remain in the army:

an immediate bounty of $80 if they committed to remain in service for the duration of the conflict.[41]

Two days later, Laurens wrote to a leader in South Carolina: "After two Months labor on a scheme for half-pay to officers ... ridden by amendments and new Resolves, the original project by the Grace of God, was the day before yesterday rid to Death, and from the Ashes, the inclosed Act of Congress of the 15th May produced."[42]

Delegates from Connecticut dispatched a similar note to their governor: "The inclosed Resolution of Congress is the result of the most painful and disagreeable question that hath ever been agitated in Congress. ... If the Inclosd Resolve is not the best measure the nature & Circumstances of the Case would admit, it is certainly the best that could be obtaind."[43]

Meanwhile, in the course of fighting for half-pay pensions for officers, Washington never raised the possibility of increased pay or pensions for common soldiers.[44]

***

To bring more order into the quartermaster department, Congress needed to appoint someone fast. Washington suggested Phillip Schuyler, the New Yorker despised by New England delegates. Congress quietly set Washington's recommendation aside.[45]

Later, Washington nominated another candidate: Nathanael Greene. Greene was unenthused.[46] He explained to Washington that it was a step down for him and offered no prospect of glory:

> There is a great difference between being raisd to an Office and decending to one; which is my case. There is also a great difference betwext serving where you have a fair prospect of honor and laurels, and where you have no prospect of either let you discharge your duty ever so well. No body ever heard of a quarter Master in History.[47]

However, with Washington's urging, and the support of the congressional committee, Greene accepted the post. Meanwhile, Congress ratified reforms that permitted the department to return to the old practice of paying commissions. Instead of salaries, the quartermaster and his top assistants would receive 1 percent of the money spent on purchases. At the urging of the congressional committee, Congress agreed to put in place similar reforms for the commissary department. To head that department, Congress appointed Jeremiah Wadsworth, a friend of Greene's.[48]

Despite his earlier misgivings, Greene threw himself into the work. Within a week, he had found forgotten in warehouses and barns thousands of shovels and other tools and bolts of tent cloth. He also quickly arranged emergency shipments of food, forage, and clothing to the camp. Coordinating with Wadsworth, he put in place a system to ensure that arms, uniforms, and tools shipped from France were properly met at ports in New England, unloaded, and moved to where they were needed.[49] Thanks to Greene, Wadsworth, and the reforms, the army gradually got a handle on the supply crisis.[50]

Before April 1778 was out, Congress received more hints that something noteworthy had occurred on the other side of the Atlantic. A letter sent to Pennsylvania's Robert Morris was read. That communication, dated "February 5, House of Commons," was from George Johnstone, a stout defender of American rights in Parliament,[51] an "old Friend"[52] of Morris, and an acquaintance of several of the men sitting in York.[53] The letter dropped some enticing clues concerning a "treaty" and "France."[54] Johnstone warned that Congress should not be too hasty in making decisions involving a foreign power. A later letter from Johnstone suggested that a treaty between the United States and France was a done deal and on its way to America.[55]

By this time, about 11 months had passed since Congress received its last report from its diplomats in France. The British had been masters at intercepting every scrap of news coming west. James Lovell, on behalf of Congress, dispatched a letter he hoped would eventually reach Paris:

> By the Gazettes which accompany this letter you will see that the Enemy are entering upon a plan which must shortly perplex us much, unless we receive dispatches from you to enlighten us as to your Situation & Transactions of which we have had no information since the latter end of May. ... [W]e cannot charge our present want of letters to negligence in you; but we think you should not rest satisfied without sending triplicates of your dispatches.[56]

Assuming the men in Paris received Lovell's letter, that they immediately replied, and that the replies in triplicate weren't all snared by the British, the answer had no hope of reaching York for another three months or so.[57] That was the current pace that information traveled.

As it turned out, Congress didn't have to wait three months, but only a few days. On Saturday, May 2, after delegates had adjourned for the day, they were suddenly called to meet again at the courthouse. Simeon Deane, brother of Silas Deane, had arrived with news to tell and treaties in hand.[58] Simeon had sailed on March 8 in a French frigate that landed in Casco Bay, Maine, from where he came overland to Boston and then Philadelphia.[59]

The treaties—a treaty of alliance and one of amity and commerce—were duly read. Delegates objected to two articles; France would be asked to strike them.[60] But otherwise Congress was delighted. Both treaties were unanimously approved. Little York celebrated with candles in the windows. Letters streamed out of York with cautious praise for the treaties and expressions of hope that the war soon would be over. With the Americans now arm in arm with the French, the British would surely see the light and give up trying to squash the rebellion. The Virginia delegation wrote to Governor Patrick Henry: "[W]ith a strong Army, we shall, under God, be perfectly secure, and it will probably compel G.B. [Great Britain] to a speedy recognition of our Independence, and thus secure the peace of Europe, with the peace, happiness, and glory of America."[61]

At Valley Forge there was, reported a witness, "unfeigned and perfect joy."[62] Washington whooped and hollered in his own manner: the agreements with France, he wrote, "afford me the most sensible pleasure."[63] The next day, May 4, the general joined soldiers in a game of wicket,[64] a sport akin to cricket.

To properly celebrate, a ceremony on the parade ground was staged on May 6, a suitably warm, sunny day. The men marched out, portions of the treaties were read, and chaplains honored each brigade with an hour-long sermon. Following a cannon blast, the companies each marched past Washington on his gray horse. Then cannons and muskets fired 13 rounds, one by one, right to left, and left to right. Between rounds, the men shouted, "Long live the king of France," followed by "God save the friendly powers of Europe," and then "To the American States."[65] Among Washington's actions that day were orders that two prisoners sentenced to death for desertion be pardoned.[66]

As the men marched off to their dismal huts, the officers strolled to the shade of nearby festive canopies. They were joined there by other officers and some young women who lived nearby. They enjoyed cold meats and various liquors and wines into the evening.[67]

That same day in York, Congress, giddy in securing an ally in its fight against one oppressive monarch, cheerfully linked arms with another, King Louis XVI of France, now cast as "the protector of the rights of mankind." Americans, Congress suggested, should "consider the subjects of his most Christian Majesty as their brethren and allies, and that they behave towards them with all the friendship and attention due to the subjects of a great prince."[68]

Still, Congress worried that, with the prospects of peace dangled before them, the American people might yet falter and want to bargain away independence. Within a few days, Congress sent off an address, written by Gouverneur Morris, with the recommendation that it be read in churches following Sunday services, where it promised to make a bracing contrast to lessons of peace, forgiveness, and loving thy neighbor. The address raged against the fresh overtures coming from Britain and trumpeted a fresh call to arms:

> You have still to expect one severe conflict. Your foreign alliances, though they secure your independence, cannot secure your country from desolation, your habitations from plunder, your wives from insult or violation, nor your children from butchery. ... Arise then! to your tents, and gird you for the battle! It is time to turn the headlong current of vengeance upon the head of the destroyer.[69]

***

Meanwhile the task of getting the Continental Army in shape for another campaign went on. We know Washington detested Conway and was glad to be rid of him, but what the commander in chief objected to was Conway's haughtiness and duplicity, not his skills. Washington very much wanted and needed a qualified man to help instill greater order and discipline in the Continental troops. He needed a drillmaster quickly to fill Conway's shoes as inspector general.

As if on cue—and right out of Central Casting—came one Lieutenant General Frederick William Augustus Henry Ferdinand Baron von Steuben.[70] Steuben had never been a lieutenant general anywhere, and he concocted the title "Baron" out of thin air. No matter; he knew his business. He had grown up in a Prussian military family and was at home on parade grounds. He understood guns and fortifications, had led a regiment in the Seven Years' War, and had been on the staff of Frederick the Great.[71]

On a visit to France in 1777, Steuben met up with military men who recognized that the Prussian might be useful in America. Soon, he was introduced to Deane and then Franklin. By September, the pretend baron was on his way to America aboard a French warship posing as a commercial vessel pretending to be bound for Martinique. The ship reached Portsmouth, New Hampshire, on December 1. Steuben went on to Boston—where he visited Hancock—and then set off to York to introduce himself to Congress.[72]

Congress quickly agreed to give him a chance. How could they refuse? He offered to work for nothing, and he didn't want a rank, at least until he proved himself. Thus, it would cost nothing and would ignite none of the bitter squabbles about rank that perpetually roiled the American military.[73]

Off went Steuben to Valley Forge, where he arrived in February. Washington rode out miles from his headquarters to welcome the phony baron, who brought with him several aides and Azor, his greyhound.[74] The next day, Steuben reviewed the troops.[75]

Washington soon learned that Steuben's résumé was partly fiction. But the commander in chief had no second thoughts about the German, because Steuben got the job done. He made slumping privates into ramrods. Years later, one of those privates would recall: "Never before or since, have I had such an impression of the ancient fabled God of War as when I looked on the baron; he seemed to me a perfect personification of Mars. The trappings of his horse, the enormous holsters of his pistols, his large size, and his strikingly martial aspect, all seemed to favor the idea."[76]

Steuben spoke German and French, but no English. He memorized English commands, but then would forget them as the men were marching, causing him to swear in German, then French as the men continued obediently marching into walls or other obstacles. Then he would call upon aides to swear for him in English.[77]

Steuben's drills brought uniformity to the way the army marched and maneuvered; efficiency in the manner soldiers carried, loaded, and fired their weapons; precision in techniques of forming columns and deploying; and deadly effectiveness in firing volleys.[78] He also imbued a spirit of pride as troops competed to respond quickly and flawlessly to commands.

Meanwhile, Steuben came to understand a marked difference between the American soldiers and those he had commanded in Europe. In Europe, when he gave an order, the soldier simply followed it. In America, when he gave an order, soldiers tended to ask why: "I am obliged to say, 'This is the reason why you ought to do that,' and then he does it."[79]

Washington was delighted with Steuben, and so was Congress. Henry Laurens, after receiving a reassuring report from his son, wrote: "[H]e has hit the taste of the Officers, gives universal satisfaction & I am assured has made an amazing improvement in discipline."[80] On May 5, delegates officially made Steuben inspector general and gave him the rank of major general.[81]

CHAPTER 47

Ridiculous, Undeserved and Unmerited

Civilians in Philadelphia took for granted that it would serve as a base for the British military for a good long time. Galloway looked forward to a vigorous campaign launched from the city to rout Washington at Valley Forge. Military men on both sides found it impossible to believe that the British, after the monumental effort and cost of taking Philadelphia, would give it up without a fight.[1] But that's what they did.

The American alliance with France upended everything for the British. British decision makers across the Atlantic had to recalculate their equations. Britain would now have to fight not just the Americans, but also France, a more formidable foe, and maybe Spain as well.[2] The British had to think about defending their sugar islands in the Caribbean, which France coveted. British interests in India and the sea route around Africa had to be protected too. Canada might also be threatened.[3] Measures even had to be taken to prepare for a possible invasion of the British Isles, where garrisons had been stripped of much of their manpower on account of the American war.[4]

The government came up with a new plan for America. That plan called for most British warships patrolling America's coast to be sent to the West Indies and about 10,000 soldiers in America to be redeployed, some south to the West Indies and Florida, others north to Halifax and Newfoundland. The dream of taming all 13 states by military force was discarded.[5]

But the war in America would continue. The British would focus on the South. They hoped to pry the Southern states loose from the infant nation and make them colonies again. These were to Britain the most valuable of all the former colonies because they produced exports that Britain especially wanted—tobacco, indigo, rice, and materials for building and equipping ships. Meanwhile, Southerners had always been eager—at least before the war—to sell to Britain. Leaders also figured that Southerners—especially white Southerners fearing slave rebellions—would welcome once again strong, stable British authority. Furthermore, the South—unlike, say, Puritan New England, Quaker Pennsylvania, and Catholic Maryland—was chiefly

Anglican. Trade, security, and religion were the factors that made authorities in England assume the South teemed with latent Loyalism that would rise up with the appearance of a dazzling army of Redcoats.[6]

If all went according to plan, the South would fall back into British hands, and the Middle Atlantic states, with their lukewarm attitude toward independence, might follow suit. The United States would be chopped to a stump—only incorrigible New England. Britain would again control the rest of the United States—the other nine states—along with virtually all the rest of North America west to the Mississippi.[7]

The initial phase of the plan did not hinge on British control of Philadelphia. But the decision to hold the city would be up to the top general in America, who would no longer be Howe. Howe had endured enough. He submitted his resignation back in October, and in early 1778 got his wish. At the same time William Howe's resignation was accepted, the British government asked his brother, Admiral Richard Howe, to resign and return to England once a successor was named.[8] For both Howes, the war was over.

General Howe's successor was Henry Clinton, the British commander in New York. To Clinton, it made sense to pull out of Philadelphia—especially vulnerable to a shipping blockade[9]—and use New York, still occupied by the British, as the base for launching the new strategy. Operating with fewer soldiers than his predecessors,[10] who after all had failed, he saw no reason to hold and defend Philadelphia when the main objective now was to conquer the South.

Clinton arrived in Philadelphia on May 8 and immediately told his top officers that Philadelphia would be abandoned.[11] Even as word leaked out and preparations to evacuate were started, many were perplexed because work went on through May and into June on defensive works around the city. That activity was a ploy to keep Washington guessing about Clinton's true intentions.[12] It worked, keeping Congress guessing too. Lovell of Massachusetts wrote: "Here we are still the Sport of Lyars. One day we are told the Enemy are filling their Ditches and preparing to leave Phila. ... [I]n the next we are informed of new Works & freshly arrived Troops."[13]

***

The British would desert Philadelphia without a fight, but not without a ridiculous pageant that was wasteful and offensive, especially to Loyalist civilians who had suffered through the winter and now could see only misery on the horizon.

William Howe, for all his faults, was much beloved by his officers and men. After they learned that Howe would be replaced, 22 officers prepared a grand event for May 25 to honor the general. This *meschianza*—Italian for "medley"—began with a floating parade on the Delaware, with decorated flatboats and galleys carrying hundreds of men and women in costume. Three flatboats each carried a band to provide musical accompaniment. Ships crowded with spectators assembled north of the city and drifted down, landing southward. Two warships each roared a 17-gun salute when Howe's barge touched the shore. At the landing place, a Doric arch, a carousel, and two small amphitheaters had been prepared. The amphitheaters were used to stage mock medieval tournaments, with men pretending to be Black Knights of the Burning Mountain pretending to joust other men pretending to be White Knights of the Blended Rose, all proclaiming that their respective ladies excelled all other ladies everywhere. Each of the esteemed damsels wore a white silk robe with a spangled pink sash, spangled shoes and stockings, and a spangled and lace-trimmed veil. Pearls and jewels adorned their towering headdresses.[14]

Fireworks followed, and then began a banquet. As Howe, the honored guest, made his appearance, "twenty-four black slaves, in Oriental dresses, with silver collars and bracelets, ranged in two lines" and bowed to the ground.[15] The dancing carried on until four in the morning.[16]

A bitter Loyalist later assessed the festivities as "one of the most ridiculous, undeserved and unmerited triumphs ever yet performed. Had the General been properly rewarded for his conduct while Commander-in-Chief in America, an execution and not a Mischianza would have been the consequence."[17]

Howe's own secretary found the "strange" festivities an embarrassment: "It cost a great Sum of money. Our Enemies dwell upon the Folly & Extravagance of it with Pleasure. Every man of Sense, among ourselves, tho' not unwilling to pay due Respect, was ashamed of this mode of doing it."[18]

***

On June 6, the promised peace commission from England arrived in Philadelphia. Hopes of Loyalists rose as orders went out to reverse evacuation preparations. Provisions and munitions that had been made ready to ship were returned to storage.[19] Would the British actually stay? Might there yet be a way to restore happy royal rule in America? Howe's secretary noted: "Spirits of the Town seem revived upon the Occasion. People conceiving a Hope that they will not now be abandoned."[20] It was a cruel mirage.

King George III, when he named the commissioners in April, thought it unlikely they would succeed in their mission.[21] Indeed, he seemed to have wanted them to fail. He and his ministers sent off men who were ill-suited and ill-prepared, who were dispatched too late, and who had too little to offer.

Leading the commission was Frederick Howard, fifth Earl of Carlisle, known as a fop with a gambling habit and vast wardrobe.[22] He was also a poet and a friend of a prominent politician sympathetic to the Americans.[23] The second commissioner was William Eden. As the brother of the last royal governor of Maryland,[24] he presumably had a passing knowledge of American affairs. He also happened to be a close friend of the British prime minister.[25] The third was Johnstone, the old acquaintance of Robert Morris.[26]

The Howe brothers—the admiral and general—were also named as commissioners, but played no role. General Clinton would replace General Howe as commissioner, but likewise was passive.[27]

On the eve of the commission's departure from England, Eden was stunned by how casually the mission was being treated. He later recalled his final meeting with Lord North and the impression of the farewell "in the style of a common acquaintance who is stepping from your room to the water closet and means to return in five minutes."[28]

Still, the government heaped money on the enterprise, doling out enough cash for the commissioners to cover expenses for carriages, clothes, servants, wine, and furniture. They brought along several private secretaries and 20 footmen.[29]

By the time the civilian commissioners sailed from England, 69 days had already passed since the American commissioners in Paris signed the treaties with France.[30] The peace commissioners had an entourage that included no one particularly useful in finding the path to peace: Eden's wife, four months pregnant; a certain Anthony Morris Storer, acclaimed in London as a fine ice skater and dancer; and one Adam Ferguson, a friend of Johnstone and a professor of moral philosophy at Edinburgh.[31] They also had in hand an impressive supply of diplomatic goodies—authority to give the Americans virtually everything they had asked for before independence. But they lacked permission to recognize independence itself.

They were instructed to treat Congress as if the United States was for the moment independent, but that independence would be rescinded once the peace treaty came into effect. If Congress proved stubborn, the commissioners could cut a deal with any state that wished to revert to its old status as a colony under a governor appointed by the commission. To encourage prominent rebels to regain their senses, the commissioners could also grant pardons.[32]

As they glided up the Delaware River toward Philadelphia, commissioners heard shots. The bullets from distant riflemen fell way short, but the gesture let the commissioners know that, while the British controlled the river, the rebels held the shore.[33] Upon their arrival in the city—31 days after Congress ratified the treaties with France—the commissioners were embarrassed and angry to learn not only that General Howe had been replaced, but that Philadelphia was to be abandoned and that thousands of soldiers were being redeployed.[34] These changes had been kept secret from them even though they were ordered or at least contemplated while the commissioners were still in London.[35] For the peace mission to succeed, the threat of British force was essential. Diminishing that threat rendered the mission "both ineffectual and ridiculous."[36]

As Carlisle later wrote, the position of the commissioners was irreparably undermined: "[O]ur offers of peace wore too much the appearances of supplications for mercy from a vanquished and exhausted State."[37]

The mission, a long shot to begin with, now seemed guaranteed to fail. But the commissioners still went through the motions. Peace talks were initiated with a joint letter to Congress from Generals Howe and Clinton. The letter arrived in York, with the conciliatory acts of Parliament, the same day the commissioners arrived in Philadelphia.[38]

Congress glanced at the letter from the generals and answered it by repeating the firm rebuff issued when delegates first saw unofficial copies of the acts: no peace treaty until Britain withdrew all its forces and fully acknowledged American independence.[39]

The civilian commissioners then dispatched Ferguson, acting as their secretary, to carry messages from the commissioners to Washington at Valley Forge. Ferguson was subsequently sent on to Congress at York under a flag of truce.[40]

Eventually, a packet of documents arrived at York with an impressive seal showing "a fond Mother embracing returning Children."[41] Laurens dutifully read out the first page, then the second until the words "insidious interposition of a power, which has, from the first settlement of these colonies, been actuated with enmity to us both; and notwithstanding the pretended date or present form of French offers."[42] At that point, Gouverneur Morris stood and made a motion to stop the reading "because of the offensive language against his most Christian majesty";[43] that is, the French king. A debate followed, the motion was approved, and the documents resealed.[44]

In the next several sessions, delegates talked more about whether to even hear the documents read to them. Morris wanted the "insolent letter" to be returned "with contempt,"[45] but the majority disagreed. Finally, on June 16, they decided to unseal the papers and fully learn what the commissioners had to say. In sum, the commissioners offered an immediate end to hostilities, free trade, the end of any military presence in America without American consent, cooperation in measures dealing with debts and a restoration in the value of the currency, and representation of Americans in Parliament and corresponding representation by British agents in American assemblies.[46]

Richard Henry Lee summed up the commissioners' letter as "a combination of fraud, falsehood, insidious offers, and abuse of France, concluding with a denial of Independence."[47]

Delegates initially considered making no new response, and letting the response from April stand as their answer. There was debate and even fleeting thoughts among a few that reconciliation without independence might be possible.[48] Eventually, delegates agreed that a reply was needed. That answer repeated familiar arguments and concluded with what Congress had plainly stated before: no peace treaty with the king without "an explicit acknowledgment of the independence of these states, or the withdrawing [of] his fleets and armies."[49]

Then, instead of dispatching this response immediately, Congress held on to it, just to see what was happening in Philadelphia.[50] Were the British really evacuating?

Meanwhile, lobbying to give up independence for peace was ongoing behind the scenes. Washington received letters from Johnstone and Eden, as well as from Eden's brother, the former governor of Maryland, who knew the general.[51] Laurens was bombarded with missives—a personal note from Johnstone "much too polite to be sincere" and letters from his "old & best friends in London all tending to the same point to wheedle us into resubjection."[52] Other delegates, including Francis Dana, Robert Morris, and Joseph Reed,[53] received letters from the commissioners crafted to sway the opinion of Congress in favor of the peace plan. A letter from Johnstone to Robert Morris hinted at personal enticements: "[H]onour and emoluments should naturally follow the fortune of those who have steered the vessel in the storm and brought her into port." He also suggested that rewards be heaped on Washington and Laurens if they played their cards right: "I think that Washington and the president [of Congress] have a right to every favour that grateful nations can bestow if they could once more unite our interest and spare the miseries and devastation of war."[54]

Reed said he was offered a bribe of £10,000. Thomas McKean found this torrent of earnest appeals delicious: "I have lived to see the day when, instead of 'Americans licking the dust from the feet of a British Minister,' the tables are turned." But he warned: "Be upon your guard with regards to letters from the Enemy; they intend to seduce, corrupt, and bribe by every method possible."[55]

Delegates were alarmed enough to consider a motion to require colleagues to "lay before Congress" any correspondence of a political nature from the commissioners or anyone from Great Britain.[56] The motion failed. Delegates were not ready yet to give Congress the authority to peek at their personal correspondence.[57] Laurens called it "a dangerous attempt to stretch the power of Congress."[58]

Lobbying was also taking place outside Congress. A Loyalist newspaper in British-held New York reminded Americans what a good deal they could be getting: freedom from British taxation forever, restoration of the status quo of 1763—when there was harmony, more or less, between Britain and its American colonies—and of course, peace. The alternative was said to be the waste of more "Blood and Treasure," and inevitably far more taxes than Britain ever would have imposed: "[T]he hopes of every Family shall be dragged into the Field, there to Perish by War, Pestilence, or insupportable distresses."[59]

CHAPTER 48

You Damned Poltroon

As it turned out, the business of the peace commissioners prompted only a brief pause in British plans to leave Philadelphia. Evacuation activities soon resumed, and the certainty of the move sank in. Soldiers were mystified and humiliated—many deserted. Loyalists were horrified. Many had hidden their Loyalist sympathies before the British arrival, but now they were exposed. Some others were Loyalist refugees who had fled to Philadelphia from Delaware, Maryland, or New Jersey.[1] What would they do? How would they be treated when the rebels took back control of the city? "Now a Rope was (as it were) about their necks," wrote a British civilian with the military.[2] Bitter civilians unloaded on departing soldiers. One German soldier recalled: "They told us to our faces that the army had come only to make us miserable."[3]

As a British man recorded in his diary, the evacuation effectively put an end to any dream of a return of America to British rule, at least in the North: "No man can be expected to declare for us, when he cannot be assured of a Fortnight's Protection. Every man, on the contrary, whatever might have been his primary Inclinations, will find it his Interest to oppose & drive us out of the Country."[4]

Loyalist Galloway was up to the last minute urging an assault on Valley Forge and claiming that a substantial Loyalist body of troops could be raised in Pennsylvania once Washington was swept away.[5] But he was ignored.

As Clinton prepared to evacuate Philadelphia, the Continental Army at Valley Forge coiled to strike. Washington had 13,000 men, a few more than Clinton had,[6] and those men were now rested and rigorously trained for a new fighting season. By this time, the creaky supply system was in good repair.[7] Richard Henry Lee at York remarked: "The Continental Army is now on a much more respectable footing, both for numbers & discipline, and supplies of every kind, than it has been since the War began."[8]

Delegate Joseph Reed, who once disparaged Washington, now dispensed praise. In a letter to Henry Laurens, he wrote:

> I cannot but congratulate you, Sir, on the respectable Appearance of our Army & their Improvement in Discipline & every soldierly Quality—On the Extinction of every Spark

of Discontent & Faction against the best of Men & the Regularity with which the several Departments seem now to be conducted. To the latter I ascribe very much of the former, as the Attention & Care of the General being no longer called off from his Command to exercise the Duties of the Staff, his Time & Talents are devoted more directly to the military Duty of his Troops, the happy Consequences of which are more & more conspicious every Day.[9]

Meanwhile, Charles Lee was back in place as Washington's number two. Lee, while on parole, had made a sojourn to York, to ladle advice on Congress. Stay on the defensive, he said; the next target for the British will be the Baltimore area and the lower Susquehanna, he predicted; make the cavalry the core element of a reorganized army, he recommended. Congress paid no attention. Lee was helpful, however, in smoothing out issues related to exchanging prisoners. From York, Lee went on to Virginia to check on his estate, Prato Verde.[10] The long-anticipated exchange involving Lee had finally been completed. Lee, back at Valley Forge, could again take the field.

Lee heaped counsel on Washington, as he had on Congress, and Washington likewise disregarded most of what he had to say. While Congress and Washington were pleased to have Lee back in the fold, niggling doubts about his judgment and motives were creeping in, and Lee's brilliance was no longer assumed.

Lee, meanwhile, was positive that he was brilliant and just as sure that Washington, who had invested so much in getting him back, was not. Lee was said to have remarked that "Washington was not fit to command a Sergeant's Guard."[11]

Finally, on June 18, Clinton made his move. The British evacuation back to New York was in motion. Some of the army would go by sea down the Delaware and up the Atlantic coast. Most would go by land across New Jersey. In taking the overland route, Clinton was defying specific orders. The plan from London was for the British to evacuate the entire force by sea.[12]

Clinton, touched by the anguished voices of the many Loyalists fearful of reprisals, offered to transport civilians by sea to New York. It was a humanitarian gesture. It was also smart. Had he abandoned the Philadelphia Loyalists, he would have wrecked his Southern strategy, which relied on Southerners to trust British protection.[13]

However, following that gallant offer, Clinton found himself swamped with civilians desperate to get out of town. There just wasn't enough room on the vessels for civilians plus soldiers, horses, equipment, weapons, and supplies.[14] A suggestion was made to make more room on the transports by leaving behind 5,000 horses—with their throats slashed. This idea was discarded as making an already mortifying retreat more humiliating.[15] In the end, Clinton found room for some 3,000 Loyalists and their belongings on the water transports, along with two regiments of Germans and most of the cavalry and artillery.

Meanwhile, some 20,800 people—85 percent of them soldiers[16]—with baggage carried by 1,500 wagons, would go overland.[17] The long, slow, 100-mile[18] march northeast toward New York began. The procession of soldiers, wagons, and camp followers crept just 35 miles during the first six days.[19]

Washington followed. While a small force entered Philadelphia, most of the army set off for New Jersey. Should the Continental Army simply harass the British as they lumbered across New Jersey, or should a more aggressive and riskier scheme be tried? Washington, seeming uncertain, gathered around him a council of war. Then, after ruminating for two days, Washington settled on an aggressive plan. Lee promptly threw a wrench into it. When he learned he was assigned a force of 1,500, he sputtered that the number was too trifling for an officer of his rank. The force was duly reassigned to Lafayette. Then the plans were modified, and that force was quadrupled. Lee then decided he did after all want the assignment. Washington put Lee in charge again and reassigned Lafayette in a convoluted way so as not to bruise the Frenchman's feelings.[20]

New Jersey was an oven, and the oppressive heat was harder on the Redcoats than on the Americans. The British, with their heavy backpacks and wool uniforms, melted. Some fell from heat stroke.[21] But Clinton was not shrinking from a battle. After three days of maneuvering, his rearguard of about 6,000 men[22] planted themselves near Monmouth Court House, a village of few houses where three roads came together near a wooden courthouse.[23] This was about 60 miles from Philadelphia and still 40 miles from New York.

Lee and his men closed in, and Lee ordered an attack, followed by a succession of orders that seemed to follow no plan—march, countermarch; attack, fall back. Some orders were ignored; some officers took actions without orders.[24] Lafayette, operating nearby, repositioned his men. Another general observed this and assumed Lafayette was retreating and withdrew his own men. Lee's men saw what was happening and began falling back too. Exactly what happened is anybody's guess, as surviving reports are complicated and contradictory. But eventually, out of this mayhem, this hellish fog of steamy dust and smoke, some of Lee's men stumbled off and ran away.[25]

Lee, knowing his situation was precarious and fearful of a wild flight, now ordered a withdrawal.[26] The retreat was prudent, timely, and well executed, but some of his men had already bolted the battlefield.

Washington, leading a column and moving up to help, came upon one, then another, then many dozen of these fleeing soldiers.[27] The commander in chief was shocked. No sounds of battle could be heard, so how could there be a retreat? He then came upon Lee.

According to Lafayette, Washington demanded: "What is the meaning of this, sir? I desire to know the meaning of this disorder and confusion!" Lee replied: "The American troops would not stand the British bayonets." Washington countered: "You damned poltroon. You never tried them."[28]

This encounter seems plausible enough. The problem is, Lafayette wasn't actually there.[29] But Lee was and later confirmed a tongue lashing of some kind: "I confess I was disconcerted, astonished, and confounded by the words and manner in which His Excellency accosted me."[30]

Whatever happened, it lasted only seconds for there was no time to waste. Just moments before, Washington believed the British, after swatting at the Americans, were continuing their march toward New York. Now, with disorder all about, Washington learned that the enemy was coming after him and his army. They would be upon him in 15 minutes.[31] A misstep now and the British might at last achieve what had long eluded them—a general engagement ending with the annihilation of the Continental Army.

Washington scanned the terrain, noting woods, roads, swampy areas, slopes, and hedgerows. He ordered the wreckage of Lee's force, as they stumbled past, to move to the rear and pull themselves together.[32]

Now he heard the sound of men marching toward him. Were they the British? No, it was a Pennsylvania regiment under General Anthony Wayne, retreating, but in good order. He told Wayne to have his men make a stand there with three regiments and two pieces of artillery.[33]

With British artillery now lobbing cannonballs all about, Washington rode among the men, rounding up soldiers and positioning them along a fence. Washington's calm, courage, and decisiveness restored order and confidence. It also helped that Washington found himself on terrain that worked to his advantage. Furthermore, reinforcements came up that suddenly put the Americans in a more favorable position.[34]

In the relentless, scorching heat, the British came on. One assault was followed by another, then another. The Americans, behind hedgerows, remained firm as they blasted volley after volley. Around 6pm, the battle settled down to an artillery duel. One of those American cannons, so goes a legend, was operated by a Mary Ludwig Hays of Carlisle, Pennsylvania, known to history as Molly Pitcher. This woman, whose assignment before then was to bring water to the men, took over a field gun after her husband was mortally wounded, so the story goes.[35]

That night, the Continental Army slept on the open ground, expecting another battle the next day. But by morning, the British had gone, resuming their march. Washington's army gave up the chase.

Monmouth proved to be the longest one-day battle of the whole war. It also turned out to be the last important battle outside the South.[36] But it was not decisive. The Continental Army survived, and Clinton's army reached New York.

The battle is remembered chiefly for the story of Molly Pitcher, which might only be a fable, and for the clash between Lee and Washington, which likely took but a few seconds. Lee, shocked by the incident and feeling his skills and courage were now in question, acted quickly to shore up his reputation. He sent off a letter to Richard Henry Lee complaining of his mistreatment and asserting that his wise and timely actions in the battle preserved the army.[37]

He also asked for a court martial to clear his name. Just six days after the battle, the trial began. Scholars who have picked over the trial record conclude that Lee indeed did nothing to warrant conviction on the most serious charges—not following orders and leading a needless and chaotic retreat. But the deck was stacked against him. Any verdict in his favor put Washington in the wrong. Such a verdict was not to be expected from men who found Lee annoying and who, no matter the result, would have Washington as their senior commander. Lee was convicted of the main charges and of disrespecting Washington. He was suspended from command for one year.[38]

Congress approved the sentence, despite resistance from Samuel Adams, now back in Congress, and James Lovell, the usual Washington skeptics. Richard Henry Lee was absent for the vote. But his brother, Francis Lightfoot Lee, backed the sentence.[39]

Charles Lee didn't accept the verdict quietly. He pleaded his case in newspapers, tossing in insults here and there. That only earned him within a 30-day span no fewer than three challenges to duels—from Steuben, John Laurens, and Anthony Wayne.[40] Only one took place, the shots that Lee and Laurens exchanged leaving Lee with a slight wound to his side.[41]

CHAPTER 49

The Sluttish Manner of Washing Our Linnen

Back in Philadelphia, meanwhile, Philadelphia light horse troops and Massachusetts Continentals paraded into the city following the departure of the British. Trailing the soldiers was Benedict Arnold aboard a coach with liveried servants.[1]

Arnold, the appointed military governor of the city and surrounding countryside, would be in charge until a civilian authority was restored. It was a job Arnold had wanted. In May at Valley Forge, the general suggested to Washington that he be given the assignment once the British evacuated the region.[2] The commander quickly agreed. It seemed an honorable and appropriate duty for the lame hero—Arnold still needed a crutch to stand[3]—until he could return to active duty. Arnold seemed amply qualified. Back at Lake Champlain in 1775, after the capture of Fort Ticonderoga, civilians had commended Arnold for how well he kept order and for his humane treatment of enemy prisoners.[4] He had the experience and stature needed to revive the city, apply justice fairly, and prevent excessive mistreatment of Loyalists.

Arnold moved into the elegant townhouse near Market and Sixth that General Howe had just vacated.[5] He delayed the opening of markets so that an inventory could be taken of all merchandise in the city.[6] He was obeying Congress and following the advice of local politicians. However, most townspeople strongly opposed this move, making Arnold unpopular in Philadelphia from the outset.[7]

The British left behind a battered and filthy town—pews had vanished, stripped from churches for firewood; nearly all fences, some deserted houses, many shutters,[8] and much woodwork had likewise disappeared in the scramble for fuel over the winter. Valuable objects disappeared with the British. People returning to private houses found fine tables, beds, and chairs missing. A minister reported the loss of a thousand books.[9] Many sanctuaries had been used for stables.[10] In some of those churches, holes were cut in the floors so that manure could be shoveled into cellars.[11] In many public buildings, windows had been broken for months, allowing rain to soak interior floors. Toppled gravestones littered cemeteries where horses had been exercised.[12] The officer who occupied Benjamin Franklin's house took a portrait of the sage and scientist with him.[13] Charles Thomson's summer place and John Dickinson's grand country estate were both left in ruins.[14]

Many thousands of Loyalists and others remained in the city following the evacuation, choosing to stay with their property and take their chances with the returning rebel rulers. Among those who stayed was Grace Galloway, wife of Joseph Galloway. Galloway himself toyed with the idea of approaching Washington and pleading for some sort of amnesty so he might have a future in the new republic.[15] Indeed, Howe encouraged Galloway and other Loyalists to negotiate with the Patriots. However, Clinton, Howe's replacement in the city, forbade any such deal-making, fearing it might lead to wholesale desertions to the Patriot side from Loyalists not only in Philadelphia, but in New York as well, which was defended in large part by Americans favoring British rule.[16] In the end, Joseph Galloway rode off to New York and exile, taking with him the Galloways' only surviving child, Elizabeth.[17] Grace stayed behind.

***

Over these weeks, as delegates contemplated moving from York back to Philadelphia, letters show how much thoughts of home distracted them from the business of Congress. Josiah Bartlett of New Hampshire asked his wife for a full report about the farm: "I want to Know how hay is likely to be with us; how the English Corn is like to be; whither the worms Destroy the Indian Corn; how the flax is like to turn out &c &c."[18]

Pennsylvania's Joseph Reed longed for a return to the bustle of family life. He wrote to Esther, his wife:

> I am very impatient to see you & the dear Children, their diverting Prattle & Company makes them every Day more dear. I was very near buying a Poney for Joe the other Day but had Resolution enough to get over the Temptation; I do not know whether I should do as well if it fell in my Way again. Kiss them all for me & endeavour to keep up your Spirits. I would not have you a dull, moping, dejected Wife for the World.[19]

Meanwhile, John Hancock, back in York as a delegate from Massachusetts, was thoroughly distracted with worries about his wife, Dolly, and their newborn son, John George Washington Hancock. On June 23, he wrote to Dolly:

> I embrace the oppor'y of writing you, altho' I wrote you Two Letters the Day before yesterday, & this is my Seventh Letter, & not one word have I heard from you. ... This moment the Post arriv'd, and to my very great Surprise & Disappointment not a single line from Boston; I am not much dispos'd to Resent, but it feels exceedingly hard to be slighted and neglect'd by those from whom I have a degree of Right to expect different Conduct. ... Devote a little time to write me, it will please me much to hear of you. ... I wish to know every Occurrence since my departure, pray be particular as to your health in your Letters & give me an exact state of little John.[20]

Hancock, for the moment, had no thought of resuming his old post as president of Congress, and we see no evidence that anyone in Congress wanted him to displace Laurens.

After Congress learned that the British were gone from Philadelphia, delegates set June 27 as the last day of work in York, and scheduled July 2 as the day to reconvene in the city.[21]

***

Before exiting York, delegates returned to unfinished business—the Articles of Confederation. Congress had been waiting for responses from each of the states to the draft constitution sent out the previous November. Only Virginia responded on time—before the March deadline—and with no demands or requests for amendments.[22] New York missed the deadline, but its answer, like Virginia's, supported the Articles with no conditions. Some others responded, but none accepted the Articles entirely as drafted.

Now, in late June, the goal of ratifying the Articles of Confederation seemed especially urgent because a minister from France was expected to arrive in America any day. In negotiating with France, Congress was acting as if it represented a nation, but arguably that was a sham. There was yet no agreement among the states. Congress still had no constitution it could point to, duly approved by each state, to support its claim to head any union of states. Delegates hoped to address that problem quickly by getting ratification behind them, to prove to France and the world that Congress led a legitimate government.

As new reports from the states came in, delegates from New Hampshire could say that their state could join with New York and Virginia in accepting the Articles of Confederation with no conditions or amendments.[23] Congress then, one by one, took up the amendments and conditions brought forward from the various states. Over two days, delegates debated a particular amendment proposed by Maryland reviving an issue raised long before. Maryland wanted Congress to have the power to restrict the western boundaries of states claiming land west to the Mississippi River or to "the South Sea"[24]—the Pacific Ocean. Predictably, when the amendment was voted on, delegates from the so-called landless states—those without western claims—voted in favor. These were Maryland, Delaware, New Jersey, Rhode Island, and Pennsylvania.[25] But the majority voted against it, and the amendment lost.

In a flurry of activity, Congress then took up each of the other amendments. Some proposed giving Congress more power. Others wanted power taken away. New Jersey suggested Congress be given the authority to regulate commerce between the states. Connecticut and New Jersey wanted to prevent Congress from maintaining a peacetime army. All were rejected, usually by an overwhelming vote. Over a week, delegates took up and discarded 36 amendments.[26] Some of the states with proposed amendments had instructions to their delegates to go ahead and ratify the Articles even if the proposed changes were rejected. Confidence that the Articles would be ratified as drafted was so firm that delegates arranged for a formal document to be prepared for signing,[27] even without the signatures of the Maryland and New Jersey delegates, who were still awaiting authorization from their respective states.[28] Richard Henry Lee wrote on June 20: "The friends to the future happiness and glory of America are now urging the Confederation to a close, and I hope it will be signed in a few days."[29]

But then the preliminary copy came back with errors.[30] Delegates set aside the Articles once again, expecting to pick up where they left off after returning to Philadelphia.

Delegates planned no special event to mark Congress's departure from York, long derided as inhospitable and severely lacking in taverns and inns. Josiah Bartlett, grumbling to Mary, his wife, summed up the predominant attitude of most delegates:

> This Town is not large Enough to accomodate the multitude of people that have constantly Business with Congress. This lays us under great Difficulties and raises the price of Every thing to an Enormous heigth. Beside the Disagreable Manner in which these people Cook their victuals, and the sluttish manner of washing our linnen in Cold water only, which has already almost ruined mine, makes me willing to quit this place.[31]

Samuel Holten, just arrived as a delegate from Massachusetts, wrote that on the last evening in the village he "walked out with a number of gentlemen of Congress about a mile to a farmhouse. The people was kind, we eat Cherries and drank whiskey."[32]

CHAPTER 50

Preventing Every Wish of My Heart

Congress had agreed to resume work in Philadelphia on July 2, but that day came and went, and delegates had not yet reassembled. There were two problems. One was a shortage of delegates. Some had taken advantage of the hiatus to ramble home or elsewhere before eventually winding their way to Philadelphia. The other was the lack of a proper place to meet. The British left the State House a stinking mess. The building had served as a prison and hospital for wounded American soldiers.[1] It had also been a barracks, and some soldiers had found it convenient during the night to urinate in the stairways.[2] The building's condition was, according to Laurens, a disgrace "to the Character of civility."[3] Meanwhile, bodies of dead men and horses had been tossed into a pit nearby.[4]

Before Congress got back down to business, Philadelphians and delegates in town celebrated the second anniversary of independence. In the morning, a parade, organized by Arnold, gave townspeople a glimpse of the new American flag.[5] In the afternoon, delegates gathered for a "very elegant diner"[6] at the City Tavern attended by about 80 gentlemen and enlivened by an orchestra of clarinets, oboes, French horns, violins, and bass viols. The meal featured a giant baked pudding which had, planted in its center, a flag. It was not the Stars and Stripes but a crimson banner with various illustrations, including one depicting an eye, symbolizing Providence, and another showing a man holding a sword in one hand and the Declaration of Independence in the other.[7]

The dinner concluded with the requisite 13 toasts:[8] the first to the United States of America; the second to "The Protector of the Rights of Mankind"—the title Congress had bestowed upon the French king.[9] The day's events included plenty of noise: "The firing of a vast number of cannon proved that there was no want of powder."[10] In the afternoon,[11] Patriots—"Whigs"—mocked the Loyalist—"Tory"—women and their extravagant hairstyles with an impromptu parade, as reported by Richard Henry Lee:

> The Whigs of the City dressed up a Woman of the Town with the Monstrous head dress of the Tory Ladies and escorted her thro the Town with a great concourse of people. Her head was elegantly & expensively dressed. I suppose about three feet high and of proportionable width, with a profusion of curls &c. &c. &c. The figure was droll and occasioned much mirth.[12]

The next day, a Sunday, the delegates collectively attended morning and afternoon religious services.[13] Delegates finally resumed work on July 7,[14] but not in the State House, which was still being cleaned up and repaired. Laurens refers to the Congress "shuffling from Meeting House to College Hall,"[15] a two-story building on Fourth Street that housed the College of Philadelphia.[16]

***

On July 9, the Articles in newly corrected form were ready, and delegates from eight states approached and signed. Delegates from two states, North Carolina and Georgia, were still absent, but when they appeared they signed as well. Delaware, New Jersey, and Maryland remained yet unwilling to commit themselves to the terms of confederation.

New Jersey delegate Nathaniel Scudder pleaded with lawmakers in his state to get on board, as the French minister would soon be in Philadelphia: "How must he be astonished and confounded and what may be the fatal Consequences to America when he discovers (which he will immediately do) that we are ipso facto unconfederated, and consequently, what our Enemies have called us, 'a Rope of Sand'?"[17]

Mathews of South Carolina used the same metaphor as he contemplated the likely disintegration of the feeble union once the threat from Britain was beyond the horizon. Without confederation, "we shall be literally a rope of sand, & I shall tremble for the consequences that will follow, at the end of this War."[18]

In this state of evident disunion, with three states yet unwilling to confederate, delegates in the Congress of the purported United States now had to welcome for the first time a minister of its new ally, France. Delegates bustled and scurried, primped and prepared.

Congress learned that a French fleet, under Vice Admiral Count d'Estaing, had arrived at Delaware Bay. While most of the fleet sailed up the coast to cooperate with General Washington on operations against the British, the French minister plenipotentiary was sent up the Delaware aboard *La Chimière*, a frigate.[19]

A barge with 12 oarsmen dressed in scarlet with silver trim carried a congressional delegation of four, led by Hancock,[20] to formally greet the Sieur Conrade Alexandre Gérard at Chester. Fifteen guns bellowed as the delegates boarded. After exchanging pleasantries, the delegates and the minister were rowed ashore, where four coaches awaited to carry them to Philadelphia. Another 15 guns boomed as the minister was carried through the streets to Benedict Arnold's townhouse. Thirteen cannons roared as the minister stepped down from his carriage.[21] Gérard would be a guest in Arnold's home until a suitable residence was ready. One of Gérard's first demands was to arrange for a "goodliving priest, who should reside at the legation of the King."[22]

As the State House was freshened for Gérard's public audience, delegates conferred about ceremonies and protocols. Samuel Adams, to his own surprise, found himself on a committee—with Richard Henry Lee and Gouverneur Morris[23]—to sort out what was proper: "Would you think that one so little of the Man of the World as I am should be joynd in a Committee to settle Ceremonials. It is however of some Importance that we agree upon Forms that are adapted to the true republican Principles; for this Instance may be recurrd to as a Precedent in Futurity."[24]

Delegates wrestled with myriad other questions that appear trivial and pointless from the distance of time, but were critical and delicate then and there. For instance, how many delegates should travel with Gérard to the State House, and how should they be seated in the coach? At first, three seemed a good number. But then seating might prove awkward. They settled on two, one in the back to the left of the minister, and one in the front seat.[25]

The questions seemed endless. At what level should President Laurens's chair be? What about the minister's chair? Delegates decided to place the president's chair on a podium 2 feet above the floor of the hall. The chair for Gérard would be set 18 inches above the floor.[26]

And what titles were to be used? How should introductions be made and who should make them? When should people sit, and when should they stand? Who should bow to whom, and when? Much of a week was consumed ironing out these wrinkles.[27] Several Southern delegates tut-tutted that the ceremonies as planned lacked the dignity that Europeans expected. Gérard, who insisted on approving the plans, initially raised an objection—the president's chair was a little too high, he thought. But he gave way when the Americans stood their ground.[28]

A more important matter was the response President Laurens would give to the minister's speech. Delegates spent two weeks chewing over a draft.[29]

Meanwhile, delegates of at least one state, Massachusetts, took the trouble of collectively calling on Gérard as if the minister, in the absence of confederation, was establishing ties with each of the states individually.[30] Samuel Adams wrote: "We were receivd with Politeness and heard some handsome Things said of the State we have the Honor to represent."[31]

By early August, the State House was ready and so were delegates, almost. One evening was taken up reviewing the many fine points of etiquette and procedures.[32] On the appointed day, August 6, Samuel Adams and Richard Henry Lee rode with the minister in a coach to the State House, with an escort of Pennsylvania officers. At noon, the audience began. For the first time, Congress let the public in to observe delegates in action. The members of the public, in this case, were not the hoi polloi. The two hundred or so spectators in the back were military officers, Pennsylvania officials, and selected gentlemen.[33]

The ceremony deftly mixed age-old European traditions geared to monarchies and new-fashioned notions of republicanism. The practice of bowing at certain points and of standing and being seated at designated moments would have been familiar in Versailles. But Gérard would have appreciated the novelty of bowing to the entire hall of delegates, not just to President Laurens. Gérard may have been astonished at the simplicity in the manner of addressing the Congress. He was not required to call them "excellencies" or some other exalted term; they were just "Gentlemen of the Congress."[34]

The event was completed with no grievous faux pas. A banquet followed.

Delegates for the most part were pleased, even euphoric, with the new alliance. But some were troubled. Andrew Adams of Connecticut was one:

> I was fully of the Oppinion that the War was drawing to a speedy issue ... [U]pon this View of the Case I would quere whither the arrival of this [French] fleet will not be a Means of lengthening out the War, and also ley us under an Obligation of affording France an arm'd force in Case they Need it ... [B]esides would it not be much to our Advantage had we settled the present Controversy in our favour without a foreign Aid? Under such Ideas I have never been fond of the Assistance of any foreign power.[35]

Soon after his arrival, Gérard began sending off long dispatches about his impressions of America and Congress. In one, he explained the attitude of the people toward Congress and that of Congress toward the states:

> It [Congress] has succeeded in securing the entire confidence of the State governments as well as of the citizens. Whatever emanates from it is received with a sort of veneration. This happy disposition is essentially due to the constant care it takes not to decide any important question before preparing the minds of the people for it, and having assured itself of their sentiments. This is also due to the unanimity with which important affairs are considered and to its extreme deference to the special (State) governments. The rights of State sovereignty are so carefully respected by it that the resolutions passed by some of the legislative bodies, often contrary to the measure recommended by Congress, do not affect the consideration in which it is held.[36]

***

Once the rebel state government reclaimed Philadelphia, it sought vengeance on collaborators with the British. Joseph Reed, as prosecutor, persuaded a grand jury to indict 87 men for assisting the British in some way. But Philadelphia judges wouldn't cooperate and threw out all but 30 of the cases. Trials of those 30 led to only two convictions. One was Abraham Carlisle, a Quaker carpenter who never bore arms against anyone. His main task during the occupation had been to supervise a gate into the city, where he issued passports and possibly allowed spies to pass through. Another was John Roberts, a Quaker miller—on whose property the *Journals of Congress* were briefly stashed. Charges against him included recruiting Loyalists, warning people about raids on cattle, and saying nasty things about the Pennsylvania state government. Both were sentenced to death and hanged. Witnesses included Roberts's sobbing wife and their nine children.[37]

The state government also forced residents to swallow a bitter pill, the Test Act, which required all adult males to take an oath renouncing the king, promising allegiance to the independent state of Pennsylvania, and promising to expose any evidence of treason against Pennsylvania or any state. Pennsylvania lawmakers had imposed this before, back in 1777, but many had refused to take the oath, and the state then was too weak to enforce it. Now lawmakers felt empowered, and put in place harsh penalties. Anyone who failed to take the oath could be denied his rights to vote, hold public office, serve on juries, transfer property, sue for unpaid debts, and bear arms. In addition, their taxes could be doubled. If they made a habit of snubbing the oath, they might be banished and lose all their property to the state.[38]

One of the first to suffer retribution from the angry state was Grace Galloway, the Loyalist abandoned by her husband when the British left the city. The daughter of one of Pennsylvania's richest men and wife of the man who was once second only to Franklin as a political force in Pennsylvania, she had known only pampered privilege.[39] Now, expecting eviction from her house at Sixth and Market, she faced hardship. Her diary records: "I find I am a beggar indeed I expect every hour to be turn'd out of doors & where to go I know not[. N]o one will take me in. ... I am fled from as a Pestilence."[40] In fact, she turned down a pair of offers,[41] but her circumstances were indeed diminished. Despair crushed her: "[A]m very low and Unwell[;] every thing oppressive & dark—"[42]; "My hopes & spirits are quite gone"[43]; "very low & unwell: all dark & gloomy."[44] Meanwhile, though, as her diary shows, she seemed always able to find company for tea.

Arnold dispatched a guard to block the eviction,[45] and for months Galloway fought the seizure of her house in the courts.[46] She declared that she would never leave her home "Unless by ye force of a Bayonet."[47] But in the end she indeed was turned out. Charles Willson Peale, remembered today as an artist of the period, was also an agent of the state. On August 20, he was authorized with a group of other men to break into Galloway's house and remove her.[48] She described in her diary the scene where Peale and his men forced their way in and coaxed her out of her home:

> [A]s the Chariot drew up Peel [Peale] fetched My Bonnets & gave one to me ... then with greates[t] air said come Mr[s] Galloway give me your hand[.] I answer'd indeed I will not nor will I go out of my house but by force. [H]e then took hold of my arm & I rose & he took me to the door[.] I then Took hold on on[e] side & Look[ed] round & said pray take Notice I do not leave my house of My own accord or with my own inclination but by force & Nothing but force shou'd have Made Me give up possession[.] Peel said with a sneer very well Madam & when he led me down ye step[.] I said now Mr Peel let go My Arm I want not your Assistance[. H]e said he cou'd help me to ye Carriage[.] I told him I cou'd go without & you Mr Peel are the last Man on earth I wou'd wish to be Obliged to.[49]

She was not entirely abandoned by friends. She stayed with one for a few days and then "removed to Deborah Morris": "Glad I am to have a room I can call My own."[50] With "Debby," her outlook rose a little, but then crashed one evening when a rainstorm caught her as she was walking back to her room: "I was so wett in My feet & pettycoats as if I had been dipp'd in water." As she walked on, she noticed a carriage passing by. It had been hers, but was now owned by someone else: "My dear child came into My Mind & what she wou'd say to see her Momma walking 5 squares in the rain at Night like a common Woman & go to rooms in an Alley for her home."[51]

Her mood, documented almost daily, was often bleak. But occasionally her spirits soared. In late November, she seemed almost cheerful when she described herself as "happy & yᵉ Liberty of doing as I please Makes even poverty more agreeable than any time I ever spent since I married." She ached for her daughter; not so much for her husband. By this time, they were on their way to England or already there:

> My child is dearer to me than all Nature & if she is not happy or any thing shou'd happen to her I am lost[. I]ndeed I have no other wish in life than her wellfare & indeed I am concern'd for her father but his Unkind treatment makes me easey Nay hapy not to be with him & if he be safe I want not to be kept so like a slave as he always Made Me in preventing every wish of my heart.[52]

***

In Paris, on July 17, the ratified treaties were formally exchanged. Franklin and John Adams drew up a letter asking for a portrait of the French king to be sent to America and displayed where Congress gathered. Arthur Lee found the notion disgusting. He refused to sign the letter.[53]

Meanwhile, Adams applied himself to study. Like Deane before him, Adams arrived in France with almost no French. He crammed, but progress was slow. It would be a year before he could hold his own with a shopkeeper.[54]

When he wasn't poring over conjunctions and verb forms, Adams was valiantly trying to instill more efficient practices among the three commissioners. He urged Lee, for example, to move to the same house where he and Franklin lived. This would make meetings easier to arrange and streamline communications. Lee found excuses to remain apart. Franklin soldiered on, finding time to woo his neighbor's wife, who would often perch on Franklin's lap. Madam Brillon agreed to marry him, but only in the afterlife and provided he promised that in heaven he would not gawk at virgins.[55]

***

So Congress was back in Philadelphia and the United States had an ally. The British had failed so far to pry away a single state from the infant republic fighting alone. What chance was there of succeeding now that America had France on its side? It was high time for Great Britain to turn the page, accept American independence, and make peace.

But this war, like most wars, chugged along on inertia fed by pride, obstinance, and unwillingness to see the obvious. The conflict would carry on for another six years.

After 1778, the situation for Congress shifted. It was almost unimaginable that Britain could subdue all 13 colonies. Independence of some kind seemed assured. While the British might yet lure or compel some states, such as Georgia and the Carolinas, to return to the British nest, New England was certainly lost, and a miracle would be needed to regain Virginia and the Middle Atlantic states.

Congress could feel more secure, but many old challenges remained, and new ones would arise, even as the nation gained the confidence that indeed it could outlast the British in this bloody quarrel. The story of Congress and the war continues in the second and concluding volume of this series, *Noble Undertaking: Volume 2: The Continental Congress and the American Revolution, 1778–84.*

Endnotes

Chapter 1: Eyes of Millions Are Upon Us

1. John Ferling, *A Leap in the Dark: The Struggle to Create the American Republic* (Oxford, UK: Oxford University Press, 2003), 115; Richard R. Beeman, *Our Lives, Our Fortunes, and Our Sacred Honor: The Forging of American Independence, 1774–1776* (New York: Basic, 2013), 79.
2. Silas Deane to Elizabeth Deane, August 31, 1774, in Paul H. Smith, *et al.*, eds., *Letters of Delegates to Congress, 1774–1789.* 25 volumes (Washington, DC: Library of Congress, 1976–2000), 1:19.
3. Diary of John Adams, August 29, 1774, in L. H. Butterfield, ed., *The Adams Papers. Diary and Autobiography of John Adams*. Vol. 2 (Cambridge, MA: The Belknap Press of Harvard University Press, 1962), 108–9.
4. George W. Boudreau, *Independence: A Guide to Historic Philadelphia* (Yardley, PA: Westholme, 2016), 130.
5. *Pennsylvania Packet*, February 14, 16; March 2, 23, 1774, in John David Ronalds Platt, *Independence City Tavern* (Denver, CO: Denver Service Center, National Park Service, 1973), 7.
6. *Ibid.*, 63–66.
7. Boudreau, *Independence*, 130–31.
8. Beeman, *Lives*, 79.
9. Ferling, *Leap*, 115.
10. Charles E. Peterson, "Carpenters' Hall," *Transactions of the American Philosophical Society* 43, no. 1 (1953): 97, 100, 127; Boudreau, *Independence*, 146.
11. Carpenters' Company of Philadelphia. *Carpenters' Hall: Meeting Place of History* (Philadelphia: Carpenters' Company of Philadelphia, 2006), 2.
12. Diary of John Adams, August 29, 1774, in Butterfield, *Adams Papers*, Diary and Autobiography, 2:122–24.
13. Worthington Chauncey Ford, ed., *Journals of the Continental Congress: 1774–1789*. 34 vols. (Washington, DC: Government Printing Office, 1904–1937), 1:13, September 5, 1774.
14. James Duane's Notes of Debates, September 5, 1774, in Smith, *Letters*, 1:25.
15. Joseph Galloway to William Franklin, September 5, 1774, in *ibid.*, 1:27.
16. Ferling, *Leap*, 112.
17. Beeman, *Lives*, 57.
18. David Ammerman, *In the Common Cause: American Response to the Coercive Acts of 1774* (Charlottesville, VA: University Press of Virginia, 1974), 4.
19. Mark Mayo Boatner III, *Encyclopedia of the American Revolution* (New York: David McKay Company, 1974), 99.
20. Ammerman, *Common Cause*, 9.
21. *Ibid.*, 10–11.
22. *Ibid.*, 11.
23. Jack P. Greene, ed., *The Diary of Colonel Landon Carter of Sabine Hall*. Vol. 2, 1752–78 (Charlottesville, VA: The University Press of Virginia, 1965), 817–18.
24. Anne M. Ousterhout, "Frontier Vengeance: Connecticut Yankees vs. Pennamites in the Wyoming Valley," *Pennsylvania History: A Journal of Mid-Atlantic Studies* 62, no. 3 (1995): 330.
25. Ferling, *Leap*, 109–10.
26. *Ibid.*
27. Ammerman, *Common Cause*, 20.
28. Lynn Montross, *The Reluctant Rebels: The Story of the Continental Congress, 1774–1789* (New York: Harper & Brothers Publishers, 1950), 26.
29. *Ibid.*
30. *Ibid.*
31. Henry Flanders, *The Lives and Times of the Chief Justices of the Supreme Court*. Vol. 1 (New York: James Cockcroft & Company, 1875), 474–75.

32. Brian Deming, *Boston and the Dawn of American Independence* (Yardley, PA: Westholme, 2013), 273.
33. Ammerman, *Common Cause*, 36.
34. Beeman, *Lives*, 123.
35. Ferling, *Leap*, 111–12.
36. Joseph Galloway, *The Examination of Joseph Galloway, Esq; Late Speaker of the House of Assembly of Pennsylvania. Before the House of Commons, in a Committee on the American Papers* (London: J. Wilkie, 1779), 11.
37. Ammerman, *Common Cause*, 46.
38. Montross, *Reluctant Rebels*, 36.
39. Ford, *Journals*, 1:30, September 14, 1774.
40. Joseph Galloway to William Franklin, September 3, 1774, in Smith, *Letters*, 1:24.

Chapter 2: Excited No Terror

1. Thomas Bradbury Chandler, *What Think Ye of the Congress Now? Or, An Enquiry, How Far the Americans are Bound to Abide by, and Execute the Decisions of, the Late Congress?* (New York: James Rivington, 1775), 48.
2. Joseph Galloway, *Reflections on the Rise and Progress of the American Rebellion* (London: J. Paralmore, 1780), 47.
3. William Franklin to Benjamin Franklin, New York, July 3, 1774, in William B. Willcox, ed., *The Papers of Benjamin Franklin*. Vol. 21, January 1, 1774, through March 22, 1775 (New Haven, CT: Yale University Press, 1978), 237–39.
4. William Franklin to Earl of Dartmouth, June 28, 1774, in Frederick W. Ricord and William Nelson, eds., *Documents Related to the Colonial History of the State of New Jersey*. Vol. 10 (Newark, NJ: Daily Advertiser Printing House, 1886), 465.
5. Ammerman, *Common Cause*, 50.
6. Ford, *Journals*, 1:16, September 5, 1774.
7. Beeman, *Lives*, 44.
8. Page Smith, *John Adams*. Vols. 1–2 (Garden City, NY: Doubleday & Company, Inc., 1962), 1:163–64.
9. George L. Clark, *Silas Deane: A Connecticut Leader in the American Revolution* (New York: G. P. Putnam's Sons, 1913), 3, 17–18.
10. Diary of John Adams, August 23, 1774, in Butterfield, *Adams Papers*, Diary and Autobiography, 2:108–9.
11. Silas Deane to Elizabeth Deane, undated, in Silas Deane, "The Deane Papers. Vol. 1. 1774–1777," *Collections of the New-York Historical Society for the Year 1886* (New York: New-York Historical Society, 1887): 7.
12. Silas Deane to Elizabeth Deane, September 8, 1774, in Deane, "Deane Papers," 1:10.
13. Silas Deane to Elizabeth Deane, September 8, 1774, in *ibid.*, 1:10–11.
14. Montross, *Reluctant Rebels*, 32.
15. Smith, *Adams*, 1:168.
16. Diary of John Adams, August 29, 1774, in Butterfield, *Adams Papers*, Diary and Autobiography, 2:114–15.
17. Montross, *Reluctant Rebels*, 28.
18. *Ibid.*, 29.
19. *Ibid.*
20. National Archives, "The Founding Fathers—Connecticut."
21. Beeman, *Lives*, 158–59.
22. Harry M. Tinkcom, "The Revolutionary City, 1765–1783," *Philadelphia: A 300-Year History* (New York: W. W. Norton & Company, 1982), 121.
23. Beeman, *Lives*, 44, 47, 54; Montross, *Reluctant Rebels*, 32, 39.
24. Diary of John Adams, August 29, 1774; Butterfield, *Adams Papers*, Diary and Autobiography, 2:114–15, note 4.
25. Silas Deane to Elizabeth Deane, September 19, 1774, in Deane, "Deane Papers," 1:26.
26. Aaron Sullivan, *The Disaffected: Britain's Occupation of Philadelphia during the American Revolution* (Philadelphia: University of Pennsylvania Press, 2009), 13.
27. Harold E. Selesky, ed., *Encyclopedia of the American Revolution: Library of Military History* (Detroit, MI: Charles Scribner's Sons, 2006), "Populations of Great Britain and America."
28. Peter Furtado, *Quakers* (Oxford, UK: Shire Publications, 2013), 13.
29. William Penn to William Crispin, John Bezar, and Nathaniel Allen, September 30, 1681, in Samuel M. Janney, *The Life of William Penn* (Philadelphia: Hogan, Perkins & Co., 1852), 169.
30. Charlene Mires, *Independence Hall in American Memory* (Philadelphia: University of Pennsylvania Press, 2002), 5.
31. William C. Kashatus III, *Historic Philadelphia: The City, Symbols & Patriots, 1681–1800* (Lanham, MD: University Press of America, 1992), 4–5.
32. Mires, *Independence*, 5.
33. Montross, *Reluctant Rebels*, 33.
34. William Murchison, *The Cost of Liberty: The Life of John Dickinson* (Wilmington, DE: ISI Books, 2013), 21.

35 Silas Deane to Elizabeth Deane, August 31, 1774, in Smith, *Letters*, 1:16.
36 Diary of John Adams, August 30, 1774, in Butterfield, *Adams Papers*, Diary and Autobiography, 2:115–17.
37 Ammerman, *Common Cause*, 45.
38 Ferling, *Leap*, 68–69; Beeman, *Lives*, 75.
39 Murchison, *Cost of Liberty*, 33; Jane E. Calvert, *Quaker Constitutionalism and the Political Thought of John Dickinson* (Cambridge, UK: Cambridge University Press, 2009), 203; Beeman, *Lives*, 77.
40 John Dickinson, *The Late Regulations, Respecting the British Colonies on the Continent of America Considered* (London: J. Almon, 1765), 54–56. Emphasis in original.
41 Murchison, *Cost of Liberty*, 44.
42 Ferling, *Leap*, 70
43 John Dickinson, "Letters from a Farmer in Pennsylvania to the Inhabitants of the British Colonies," Letter ii, in Forrest McDonald, *Empire and Nation* (Englewood Cliffs, NJ: Prentice-Hall, Inc., 1999), 15.
44 John Dickinson, "Letters from a Farmer in Pennsylvania to the Inhabitants of the British Colonies," Letter iii, in *ibid.*, 17.
45 Calvert, *Quaker*, 212.
46 John Dickinson, "The Liberty Song"; Frank Moore, *Songs and Ballads of the American Revolution* (New York: D. Appleton and Company, 1856), 37.
47 John Dickinson, "The Liberty Song," in *ibid.*, 39.
48 Account of Deborah Logan, quoted in Charles J. Stillé, *The Life and Times of John Dickinson, 1732–1808* (Philadelphia: The Historical Society of Philadelphia, 1891), 313.
49 Quoted in David McCullough, *John Adams* (New York: Simon & Schuster, 2001), 94.
50 John Dickinson draft to Samuel Miller, August 10, 1807, in R. R. Logan Collection, Historical Society of Pennsylvania, based on letter image provided by Jane E. Calvert, ed., *The John Dickinson Writings Project*, University of Kentucky, 2015; Murchison, *Cost of Liberty*, 105; David L. Jacobson, "John Dickinson's Fight against Royal Government, 1764," *The William and Mary Quarterly* 19, no. 1 (1962): 2.
51 Calvert, *Quaker*, 190.
52 *Ibid.*, 193.
53 Diary of John Adams, August 31, 1774, in Butterfield, *Adams Papers*, Diary and Autobiography, 2:117–18.
54 Murchison, *Cost of Liberty*, 24.
55 Diary of John Adams, September 12, 1774, in Butterfield, *Adams Papers*, Diary and Autobiography, 2:132–33.
56 Ferling, *Leap*, 112.

Chapter 3: Eats Little, Drinks Little, Sleeps Little, Thinks Much

1 Montross, *Reluctant Rebels*, 29.
2 Galloway, *Reflections*, 49.
3 J. Kent McGaughy, *Richard Henry Lee of Virginia: A Portrait of an American Revolutionary* (London: Rowman & Littlefield Publishers, Inc., 2004), 102.
4 Edmund Jennings Lee, *Lee of Virginia, 1642–1892* (Philadelphia: Franklin Printing Company, 1895), 125.
5 McGaughy, *Lee*, 17–18, 23.
6 *Ibid.*, 24.
7 *Ibid.*, 24–26.
8 *Ibid.*, 173.
9 *Ibid.*, 41–42.
10 *Ibid.*, 47.
11 *Ibid.*, 51.
12 *Ibid.*, 52, 55.
13 *Ibid.*, 61–62.
14 *Ibid.*, 59, 77–78.
15 *Ibid.*, 85.
16 *Ibid.*, 89–90.
17 *Ibid.*, 56, 104.
18 *Ibid.*, 105.
19 *Ibid.*, 108.
20 Jack N. Rakove, *The Beginnings of National Politics: An Interpretive History of the Continental Congress* (New York: Alfred A. Knopf, 1979), 43.
21 Beeman, *Lives*, 137.
22 Silas Deane to Elizabeth Deane, September 10, 1774, in Smith, *Letters*, 1:61.
23 Montross, *Reluctant Rebels*, 36.
24 Beeman, *Lives*, 81–82.
25 Diary of John Adams, August 30, 1774, in Butterfield, *Adams Papers*, Diary and Autobiography, 2:115–17.
26 Edmund Cody Burnett, *The Continental Congress* (New York: W. W. Norton & Company, Inc., 1964), 34.
27 Silas Deane to Elizabeth Deane, August 31 to September 5, 1774, in Smith, *Letters*, 1:20.
28 Joseph Galloway to William Franklin, September 5, 1774, in *ibid.*, 1:27.
29 Lewis R. Harley, *Life of Charles Thomson* (Philadelphia: George W. Jacobs & Co., 1900), 18.

30. Montross, *Reluctant Rebels*, 37.
31. James Duane's Notes of Debates, September 5, 1774, in Smith, *Letters*, 1:25.

Chapter 4: A State of Nature

1. Thomas S. Kidd, *Patrick Henry: First among Patriots* (New York: Basic Books, 2011), 1, 15, 19, 22.
2. Ibid., 37, 48, 51–52, 81.
3. Patrick Henry to Robert Pleasants, January 18, 1773, in Robert Douthat Meade, *Patrick Henry: Patriot in the Making* (Philadelphia: J. B. Lippincott Co., 1957), 299–300.
4. Kidd, *Henry*, 90.
5. Silas Deane to Elizabeth Deane, September 19, 1774, in Deane, "Deane Papers," 1:27.
6. James Duane's Notes of Debates, September 6, 1774, in Smith, *Letters*, 1:30.
7. John Adams' Notes of Debates, September 6, 1774, in *ibid.*, 1:27–28.
8. Silas Deane to Elizabeth Deane, September 10, 1774, in *ibid.*, 1:61.
9. James Duane's Notes of Debates, September 6, 1774, in *ibid.*, 1:31.
10. John Adams' Notes of Debates, September 6, 1774, in *ibid.*, 1:28.
11. Smith, *Adams*, 1:171.
12. Boatner, *Encyclopedia*, 883.
13. Ford, *Journals*, 1:25, September 6, 1774.
14. *Ibid.*, 1:26–27, September 6, 1774.
15. Samuel Ward's diary, September 7, 1774, in Smith, *Letters*, 1:33.
16. Diary of John Adams, September 6, 1774, in Butterfield, *Adams Papers*, Diary and Autobiography, 2:124.
17. Robert Treat Paine's Diary, September 6, 1774, in Smith, *Letters*, 1:31.
18. Montross, *Reluctant Rebels*, 47.
19. John Adams to Abigail Adams, September 16, 1774, in Lyman H. Butterfield, ed., *The Adams Papers*, Adams Family Correspondence, Vol. 1, December 1761–May 1776 (Cambridge, MA: Harvard University Press, 1963), 156–57.
20. Caesar Rodney to Thomas Rodney, September 9, 1774, in Smith, *Letters*, 1:58.
21. John Adams to Abigail Adams, September 8, 1774, in Butterfield, *Adams Papers*, Family Correspondence, 1:150–51.
22. Silas Deane to Elizabeth Deane, September 7, 1774, in Deane, "Deane Papers," 1:20.
23. Silas Deane to Elizabeth Deane, September 7, 1774, in *ibid.*
24. Burnett, *Continental Congress*, 41.
25. Silas Deane to Elizabeth Deane, September 8, 1774, in Deane, "Deane Papers," 1:23.
26. Diary of John Adams, September 8, 1774, in Butterfield, *Adams Papers*, Diary and Autobiography, 2:127.
27. Silas Deane to Elizabeth Deane, September 10, 1774, in Deane, "Deane Papers," 1:26.
28. Caesar Rodney to Thomas Rodney, September 19, 1774, in Smith, *Letters*, 1:86.
29. Richard Henry Lee to William Lee, September 20, 1774, in *ibid.*, 1:88.
30. Ford, *Journals*, 1:32–33, September 17, 1774.
31. *Ibid.*, 1:36, September 17, 1774.
32. *Ibid.*, 1:34, September 17, 1774.
33. *Ibid.*, 1:39, September 17, 1774.
34. Galloway, *Reflections*, 49.
35. Diary of John Adams, September 17, 1774, in Butterfield, *Adams Papers*, Diary and Autobiography, 2:118–46.
36. Solomon Drowne to Honour'd Sir, October 5, 1774, in Harrold E. Gillingham and Solomon Drowne, "Dr. Solomon Drowne," *The Pennsylvania Magazine of History and Biography* 48, no. 3 (1924): 232.
37. Solomon Drowne to Hon'd. Parents, October 3, 1774, in *ibid.*, 231.
38. Ferling, *Leap*, 116.
39. Silas Deane to Elizabeth Deane, September 19, 1774, in Smith, *Letters*, 84.
40. Diary of John Adams, September 3, 1774, in Butterfield, *Adams Papers*, Diary and Autobiography, 2:120–22.
41. Diary of John Adams, September 1, 1774, in *ibid.*, 2:118–19.
42. Silas Deane to Elizabeth Deane, September 7, 1774, in Smith, *Letters*, 1:35.
43. John Adams' Notes of Debates, September 26–27, 1774, in Butterfield, *Adams Papers*, Diary and Autobiography, 2:137–40.
44. Ferling, *Leap*, 116.
45. Samuel Eliot Morison, *Oxford History of the American People* (New York: Oxford University Press, 1965), 208.
46. Boatner, *Encyclopedia*, 337.
47. Willard Sterne Randall, *Ethan Allen: His Life and Times* (New York: W. W. Norton & Company, 2011), 200–1.
48. *Ibid.*, 201.
49. Beeman, *Lives*, 128–29.
50. Diary of John Adams, August 28, 1774, in Butterfield, *Adams Papers*, Diary and Autobiography, 2:113–14.

51 Walter Stahr, *John Jay: Founding Father* (New York: Hambledon and London, 2005), xiii, 2–4, 6.
52 Quoted in William Jay, *The Life of John Jay: With Selections from His Correspondence*. Vol. 1 (New York: J. & J. Harper, 1833), 11.
53 *Ibid.*, 1:13.
54 Quoted in *ibid.*, 1:15.
55 *Ibid.*
56 Stahr, *Jay*, 25, 29, 31, 34.
57 *Ibid.*, 35.
58 *Ibid.*
59 John C. Miller, *Sam Adams: Pioneer in Propaganda* (Stanford, CA: Stanford University Press, 1964), 322.
60 Ammerman, *Common Cause*, 57.
61 John Ferling, "Compromise or Conflict: The Rejection of the Galloway Alternative to Rebellion," *Pennsylvania History: A Journal of Mid-Atlantic Studies* 43, no. 1 (January 1976): 9.
62 Ammerman, *Common Cause*, 58.
63 John Adams' Notes of Debates, September 28, 1774, in Butterfield, *Adams Papers*, Diary and Autobiography, 2:141–44.
64 Burnett, *Continental Congress*, 50.
65 Ammerman, *Common Cause*, 59.
66 Ford, *Journals*, 1:56, October 6, 1774.
67 *Ibid.*, 1:59, October 10, 1774.
68 *Ibid.*, 1:58, October 8, 1774.
69 Thomas Balch, ed., *The Examination of Joseph Galloway, Esq., by a Committee of the House of Commons* (Philadelphia: The Seventy-Six Society, 1855), 58–59.
70 Montross, *Reluctant Rebels*, 51.
71 Ford, *Journals*, 1:67, October 14, 1774.
72 *Ibid.*, 1:71, October 14, 1774.
73 *Ibid.*, 1:73, October 14, 1774.
74 Rakove, *Beginnings*, 54.
75 Robert M. Calhoon, "'I Have Deduced Your Rights': Joseph Galloway's Concept of His Role, 1774–1775," *Pennsylvania History: A Journal of Mid-Atlantic Studies* 35, no. 4 (1968): 358.
76 James H. Hutson, ed., *A Decent Respect to the Opinions of Mankind: Congressional State Papers, 1774–1776* (Washington, DC: Library of Congress, 1975), 50–52.
77 Edwin Wolf, "The Authorship of the 1774 Address to the King Restudied," *The William and Mary Quarterly* 22, no. 2 (1965): 199.

Chapter 5: We Will Never Submit

1 Diary of John Adams, October 24, 1774, in Butterfield, *Adams Papers*, Diary and Autobiography, 2:156–57.
2 Samuel Ward to Mary Ward?, October 10, 1774, in Smith, *Letters*, 1:172.
3 Ford, *Journals*, 1:78, October 20, 1774.
4 Diary of John Adams, October 24, 1774, in Butterfield, *Adams Papers*, Diary and Autobiography, 2:156–57.
5 Ford, *Journals*, 1:76–77, October 20, 1774.
6 *Ibid.*, 1:77, October 20, 1774.
7 T. H. Breen, *American Insurgents, American Patriots: The Revolution of the People* (New York: Hill and Wang, 2010), 71.
8 Ford, *Journals*, 1:79, October 20, 1774.
9 Burnett, *Continental Congress*, 55.
10 Silas Deane to Elizabeth Deane, September 7, 1774, in Smith, *Letters*, 1:35.
11 Diary of John Adams, August 30, 1774, in Butterfield, *Adams Papers*, Diary and Autobiography, 2:115–17.
12 Ferling, *Leap*, 122.
13 Ford, *Journals*, 1:102, October 22, 1774.
14 *Ibid.*, 1:118, October 26, 1774.
15 *Ibid.*, 1:120–21, October 26, 1774.
16 *Ibid.*, 1:89, October 21, 1774.
17 *Ibid.*, 1:88, October 21, 1774.
18 *Ibid.*, 1:108, October 26, 1774.
19 *Ibid.*, 1:109, October 26, 1774. Emphasis in original.
20 *Ibid.* Emphasis in original.
21 *Ibid.*, 1:112, October 26, 1774.
22 *Ibid.*, 1:100–1, October 21, 1774.
23 Diary of John Adams, October 28, 1774, in Butterfield, *Adams Papers*, Diary and Autobiography, 2:157–58.
24 Joseph Reed to Charles Pettit, January 14, 1775, in William B. Reed, ed., *Life and Correspondence of Joseph Reed*. Vol. 1 (Philadelphia: Lindsay and Blakiston, 1847), 91.
25 Diary of John Adams, October 28, 1774, in Butterfield, *Adams Papers*, Diary and Autobiography, 2:157–58.
26 John Dickinson to Arthur Lee, October 27, 1774, in Smith, *Letters*, 1:250.
27 Joseph Galloway to Thomas Nickleson, November 1, 1774, in *ibid.*, 1:255.
28 William Hooper to James Duane, November 22, 1774, in *ibid.*, 1:262.
29 Silas Deane to Sam Adams, November 13, 1774, in *ibid.*, 1:258.
30 Samuel Ward to John Dickinson, December 14, 1774, in *ibid.*, 1:269–70.
31 Chandler, *What Think Ye*, 40.
32 *Connecticut Gazette and the Universal Intelligencer* [New London], February 17, 1775, in Breen, *Insurgents*, 169. Emphasis in original.

33 Burnett, *Continental Congress*, 61.
34 Ammerman, *Common Cause*, 103.
35 *Ibid.*, 106–7.
36 Breen, *Insurgents*, 251.
37 Ammerman, *Common Cause*, 107.
38 *Ibid.*, 105.
39 Isaac Mansfield, *A Sermon, Preached in the Camp at Roxbury, November 23, 1775* (Boston: S. Hall, 1776), 21.
40 William A. Benedict, *History of the Town of Sutton, Massachusetts* (Worcester, MA: Sanford & Company, 1878), 92–93.
41 *Ibid.*, 94.
42 *Ibid.*, 93.
43 *Ibid.*, 94.
44 Thomas Bradbury Chandler, *A Friendly Address to All Reasonable Americans on the Subject of Our Political Confusions* (New York, 1774), 37.
45 Samuel Seabury, *Thoughts on the Proceedings of the Continental Congress* (New York: Richardson and Urquhart, 1775), 2, 36.
46 Peter Force, ed., *American Archives, Fourth Series*. Vol. 2 (Washington, DC: M. St. Clair Clarke and Peter Force, 1839), 115.
47 Nicholas Cresswell, "'I Am Now in an Enemy's Country': Travel Journal of Nicholas Cresswell, November 1, 1774," *Making the Revolution: America, 1763–1791* (Research Triangle Park, NC: National Humanities Center).
48 Ammerman, *Common Cause*, 116–17.
49 William L. Saunders, *The Colonial Records of North Carolina*. Vol. 9 (Raleigh, NC: Josephus Daniels, 1890), 1091.
50 Quoted in Breen, *Insurgents*, 192.
51 Janet Schaw, *Journal of a Lady of Quality* (New Haven, CT: Yale University Press, 1923), 194.
52 Purdies' *Virginia Gazette* (Williamsburg), February 17, 1775, supplement, in Ammerman, *Common Cause*, 115.
53 John Wentworth to Lord Dartmouth, December 2, 1774, in Rakove, *Beginnings*, 66.
54 Earl of Dunmore to Lord Dartmouth, December 24, 1774, in *ibid.*
55 Joseph Galloway to Samuel Verplanck?, December 30, 1774, in Smith, *Letters*, 1:283.
56 Ammerman, *Common Cause*, 126, 132.
57 King George III to Frederick, Lord North, November 18, 1774, in J. Fortescu, ed., *Correspondence of King George the Third, From 1760 to December 1783*. Vol. 3, July 1773–December 1777 (London: MacMillan and Co., Limited, 1928), 153.
58 Earl of Dartmouth to the Governors of North America, January 4, 1775, in Ricord, *New Jersey*, 10:534.
59 William Franklin to Earl of Dartmouth, April 3, 1775, in *ibid.*, 10:571.
60 Ferling, *Leap*, 133.
61 *Ibid.*
62 Deming, *Boston*, 339–40.
63 Ferling, *Leap*, 134.
64 *Ibid.*
65 Pauline Maier, *American Scripture: Making the Declaration of Independence* (New York: Alfred A. Knopf, 1998), 5.
66 Frederick Mackenzie, *A British Fusilier in Revolutionary Boston* (Cambridge, MA: Harvard University Press, 1926), 57.
67 Deming, *Boston*, 8, 55.
68 John Hancock to Committee of Safety, April 24, 1775, in Abram English Brown, *John Hancock His Book* (Boston: Lee and Shepard, 1898), 197.
69 Deming, *Boston*, 263.
70 John Hancock to Dolly Quincy, May 7, 1775, in Brown, *Hancock*, 198.
71 Montross, *Reluctant Rebels*, 66.
72 Silas Deane to Elizabeth Deane, May 12, 1775, in Smith, *Letters*, 1:346.
73 Richard Caswell to William Caswell, May 11, 1775, in *ibid.*, 1:339.
74 Richard Caswell to William Caswell, May 11, 1775, in *ibid.*, 1:340.
75 Richard Caswell to William Caswell, May 11, 1775, in *ibid.*
76 Silas Deane to Elizabeth Deane, May 12, 1775, in *ibid.*, 1:347.
77 Alexander Graydon, *Memoirs of His Own Time: With Reminiscences of the Men and Events of the Revolution* (Philadelphia: Lindsay & Blakiston, 1846), 122–23.
78 Diary of Christopher Marshall, May 2, 1775, in Christopher Marshall, *Extracts from the Diary of Christopher Marshall: Kept at Philadelphia and Lancaster During the American Revolution, 1774–1781* (Albany, NY: Joel Munsell, 1877), 22.
79 Mires, *Independence*, 6–7.
80 *Ibid.*, 8.
81 Quote from French General François Jean de Beauvoir, Marquis de Chastellux, in National Park Service, "Interior Architecture of Independence Hall."
82 *Ibid.*
83 Mires, *Independence*, 10.
84 Beeman, *Lives*, 53.

85 "Petition from Divers Inhabitants of the City of Philadelphia," September 12, 1772, in Boudreau, *Independence*, 350–51; Charles F. Hoban, ed., *Pennsylvania Archives, Eighth Series*. Vol. 8. January 7, 1771–September 26, 1776 (Harrisburg, PA: Pennsylvania Archives, 1935): 6856.
86 National Park Service, "The Liberty Bell."
87 Boudreau, *Independence*, 349.
88 *Ibid.*, 347, 349.

Chapter 6: Too Saucy & Provoking

1 Edmund S. Morgan, *Benjamin Franklin* (New Haven, CT: Yale University Press, 2002), 315.
2 Gordon S. Wood, *The Americanization of Benjamin Franklin* (New York: The Penguin Press, 2004), 17–18.
3 *Ibid.*, 19–20.
4 "Silence Dogood, No. 4, May 14, 1722," in Leonard W. Labaree, ed., *The Papers of Benjamin Franklin*. Vol 1, January 6, 1706 through December 31, 1734 (New Haven, CT: Yale University Press, 1959), 14–18.
5 Wood, *Americanization*, 21.
6 Benjamin Franklin, *The Autobiography of Benjamin Franklin* (New Haven, CT: Yale University Press, 2003), 70, 75.
7 Wood, *Americanization*, 24
8 *Ibid.*, 28–29.
9 Franklin, *Autobiography*, 128.
10 Wood, *Americanization*, 31–32.
11 *Ibid.*, 30–31.
12 Diary of Daniel Fisher, July 28, 1755, in Daniel Fisher and Mrs. Conway Robinson Howard, "Extracts from the Diary of Daniel Fisher, 1755," *The Pennsylvania Magazine of History and Biography* 17, no. 3 (1893): 276.
13 Wood, *Americanization*, 41.
14 *Ibid.*, 45.
15 *Ibid.*, 52.
16 Franklin, *Autobiography*, 172.
17 Wood, *Americanization*, 52–54.
18 *Ibid.*, 52.
19 *Ibid.*, 56–57.
20 Walter Isaacson, *Benjamin Franklin: An American Life* (New York: Simon & Schuster, 2004), 136.
21 Benjamin Franklin to Peter Collinson, April 29, 1749, in Leonard W. Labaree, ed., *The Papers of Benjamin Franklin*. Vol. 3, January 1, 1745, through June 30, 1750 (New Haven, CT: Yale University Press, 1961), 352–65.
22 Wood, *Americanization*, 62.
23 Isaacson, *Franklin*, 135.
24 Isaacson, *Franklin*, 139; Wood, *Americanization*, 64.
25 Wood, *Americanization*, 65.
26 Benjamin Franklin to Jared Eliot, April 12, 1753, in Leonard W. Labaree, ed., *The Papers of Benjamin Franklin*. Vol. 4, July 1, 1750, through June 30, 1753 (New Haven, CT: Yale University Press, 1961), 465–67.
27 Wood, *Americanization*, 67–68
28 Isaacson, *Franklin*, 147, 157.
29 Wood, *Americanization*, 37.
30 Isaacson, *Franklin*, 153–54.
31 Pennsylvania Assembly: Reply to the Governor, August 19, 1755, in Leonard W. Labaree, ed., *The Papers of Benjamin Franklin*. Vol. 6, April 1, 1755, through September 30, 1756 (New Haven, CT: Yale University Press, 1963), 140–63. Emphasis in original.
32 Isaacson, *Franklin*, 176, 179.
33 *Ibid.*, 184.
34 Benjamin Franklin to [Isaac Norris], January 14, 1758, in Leonard W. Labaree, ed., *The Papers of Benjamin Franklin*. Vol. 7, October 1, 1756, through March 31, 1758 (New Haven, CT: Yale University Press, 1963), 360–64.
35 Isaacson, *Franklin*, 186.
36 *Ibid.*, 165.
37 *Ibid.*, 177–78.
38 *Ibid.*, 198, 200.
39 *The Interest of Great Britain Considered*, [April 17, 1760], in Leonard W. Labaree, ed., *The Papers of Benjamin Franklin*. Vol. 9, January 1, 1760, through December 31, 1761 (New Haven, CT: Yale University Press, 1966), 47–100.
40 Benjamin Franklin to William Strahan, August 23, 1762, in Leonard W. Labaree, ed., *The Papers of Benjamin Franklin*. Vol. 10, January 1, 1762, through December 31, 1763 (New Haven, CT: Yale University Press, 1959), 149–50.
41 Isaacson, *Franklin*, 204.
42 *Ibid.*, 207.
43 *Ibid.*, 217.
44 Wood, *Americanization*, 103, 108, 112.
45 *Ibid.*, 120
46 *Ibid.*, 122–23.
47 *Ibid.*, 125.
48 Benjamin Franklin to Deborah Franklin, September 1, 1773, in William B. Willcox, ed., *The Papers of Benjamin Franklin*. Vol. 20, January 1 through December 31, 1773 (New Haven, CT: Yale University Press, 1976), 383–84.

49 Wood, *Americanization*, 136.
50 Thomas Hutchinson to Thomas Whately, January 20, 1769, in Thomas Hutchinson and Andrew Oliver, "Copy of Letters Sent to Great-Britain by His Excellency Thomas Hutchinson, the Hon. Andrew Oliver, and Several Other Persons" (Boston: Edes and Gill, 1773).
51 Deming, *Boston*, 212.
52 "Tract Relative to the Affair of Hutchinson's Letters, [1774]," in Willcox, *Franklin*, 21:414–35.
53 Wood, *Americanization*, 146–47.
54 Ibid., 148, 150.
55 Ibid., 150, 154.
56 Ibid., 153.
57 Sheila L. Skemp, *William Franklin: Son of a Patriot, Servant of a King* (New York: Oxford University Press, 1990), 38, 175.
58 Diary of Thomas Hutchinson, January 6, 1779, in Peter Orlando Hutchinson, *The Diary and Letters of His Excellency Thomas Hutchinson, Esq.* Vol. 2 (Boston: Houghton, Mifflin, & Co., 1886), 237–38.
59 Isaacson, *Franklin*, 296.
60 Benjamin Franklin to William Strahan, July 5, 1775, in William B. Willcox, ed., *The Papers of Benjamin Franklin*. Vol. 22, March 23, 1775, through October 27, 1776 (New Haven, CT: Yale University Press, 1982), 85.
61 Isaacson, *Franklin*, 297.
62 John Adams to Mercy Otis Warren, August 8, 1807, in *Massachusetts Historical Society Collections, Fifth Series*. Vol. 4 (Boston: Massachusetts Historical Society, 1878), 431.
63 John Adams to Abigail Adams, July 23, 1775, in Butterfield, *Adams Papers*, Family Correspondence, 1:252–54.

Chapter 7: The Great Jehovah and the Continental Congress

1 Ferling, *Leap*, 135.
2 Ford, *Journals*, 2:17, May 11, 1775, footnote.
3 Ibid., 2:13, May 11, 1775.
4 Ibid., May 11, 1775.
5 Ibid., 2:50, May 15, 1775.
6 Ibid., 2:51, May 15, 1775, footnote.
7 Silas Deane to Elizabeth Deane, May 12, 1775, in Smith, *Letters*, 1:347.
8 James Duane's Notes for a Speech in Congress, May 23–25, 1775, in *ibid.*, 1:391.
9 Ford, *Journals*, 2:12, 2:49, May 10, 15, 1775.
10 Burnett, *Continental Congress*, 66–67.
11 Silas Deane to Elizabeth Deane, May 12, 1775, in Smith, *Letters*, 1:347.
12 Ford, *Journals*, 2:40–41, May 11, 1775.
13 Ibid., 2:40, May 11, 1775.
14 Ibid., 2:24, May 11, 1775.
15 Rakove, *Beginnings*, 71.
16 Silas Deane's Diary, May 16, 1775, in Smith, *Letters*, 1:351.
17 Ford, *Journals*, 2:49, May 15, 1775.
18 Ibid., 2:52, May 15, 1775.
19 Ibid., 2:54, May 15, 1775.
20 *Pennsylvania Packet*, May 29, 1775, in *ibid.*, 2:54–55, May 17, 1775, footnote.
21 Dunlap's *Pennsylvania Packet or, the General Advertiser*, May 22, 1775, in Smith, *Letters*, 1:355, footnote.
22 Robert Treat Paine's Diary, May 17, 1775, in Smith, *Letters*, 1:355.
23 Randall, *Allen*, 315.
24 Ethan Allen, *A Narrative of Col. Ethan Allen's Captivity* (Burlington, VT: C. Goodrich, 1846), 14–15.
25 According to Israel Harris, who was present and reported Allen's words to his grandson, James D. Butler, in B. A. Botkin, *A Treasury of New England Folklore* (New York: Bonanza Books, 1947), 297.
26 Ford, *Journals*, 2:70, May 29, 1775.
27 Ibid., 2:75, June 1, 1775.
28 Jonathan Gregory Rossie, *The Politics of Command in the American Revolution* (Syracuse, NY: Syracuse University Press, 1975), 5.
29 Ford, *Journals*, 2:56, May 18, 1775.
30 Jerrilyn Greene Marston, *King and Congress: The Transfer of Political Legitimacy, 1774–1776* (Princeton, NJ: Princeton University Press, 1987), 244.
31 Randall, *Allen*, 189, 191.
32 Ibid., 202.
33 Marston, *King*, 244.
34 Clarence W. Rife, "Ethan Allen, An Interpretation," *The New England Quarterly* 2, no. 4 (1929): 564.
35 Rowland Evans Robinson, *Vermont: A Study of Independence* (Boston: Houghton, Mifflin and Company, 1892), 69.
36 Rife, "Allen," 563.
37 John McWilliams, "The Faces of Ethan Allen," *The New England Quarterly* 49, no. 2 (1976): 259, 261.
38 Marston, *King*, 246.
39 Ethan Allen to New York Congress, July 30, 1773, in Force, *American Archives, Fourth Series*, 2:1695.
40 Silas Deane to Samuel Webb, May 14, 1775, in Smith, *Letters*, 1:348.

41 Titus Hosmer to Silas Deane, May 28, 1775, in *Collections of the Connecticut Historical Society*. Vol. 2 (Hartford, CT: Connecticut Historical Society, 1870), 241.
42 William Hooper to Samuel Johnston, May 23, 1775, in Smith, *Letters*, 1:398.
43 George Read to Gertrude Read, May 23, 1775, in *ibid.*, 1:400.
44 John Adams to James Warren, May 21, 1775, in *ibid.*, 1:364.
45 John Dickinson's Proposed Resolutions, May 23–25?, 1775, in *ibid.*, 1:384.
46 John Dickinson's Proposed Resolutions, May 23–25?, 1775, in *ibid.*
47 John Dickinson's Notes for a Speech to Congress, May 23–25, 1775, in *ibid.*, 1:378.
48 Silas Deane's Diary, May 23, 1775, in *ibid.*, 1:371.
49 John Dickinson's Notes for a Speech in Congress, May 23–25, 1775, in *ibid.*, 1:376, 1:380.
50 Silas Deane's Diary, May 16, 1775, in *ibid.*, 1:352.
51 Rakove, *Beginnings*, 74
52 Ford, *Journals*, 2:65, May 26, 1775.
53 *Ibid.*, 2:66, May 26, 1775.
54 *Ibid.*, June 2, 1775.
55 *Ibid.*, June 2, 1775.
56 *Ibid.*, June 2, 1775.
57 *Ibid.*, June 3, 1775.
58 Eliphalet Dyer to Joseph Trumbull, June 8, 1775, in Smith, *Letters*, 2:459.
59 Ford, *Journals*, 2:84, June 9, 1775.
60 *Ibid.*, June 9, 1775.
61 *Ibid.*, 2:85–86, June 10, 1775.
62 *Ibid.*, 2:87, June 12, 1775.
63 *Ibid.*, 2:89–90, June 14, 1775.
64 James Thomas Flexner, *George Washington in the American Revolution (1775–1783)* (Boston: Little, Brown and Company, 1968), 17–18.
65 *Ibid.*, 18.
66 Charles Lee to "My Dear Friend," July 19, 1776, in Charles Lee, *Life and Memoirs of Major General Lee* (New York: Richard Scott, 1813), 319.
67 Ford, *Journals*, 2:91, June 15, 1775.
68 Silas Deane to Elizabeth Deane, [September 10–11, 1774], in Smith, *Letters*, 1:61.

Chapter 8: No Harum Starum Ranting Swearing Fellow

1 Lauries Collier Hillstrom, Lawrence W. Baker, and Kevin Hillstrom, eds., "Events Leading to the French and Indian War," *French and Indian War*. Vol. 1 (Detroit: UXL, 2003): 3.
2 A. G. Bradley, *The Fight with France for North America* (New York: E. P. Dutton and Company, 1900), 68–69.
3 Ferling, *Leap*, 3.
4 *Ibid.*, 3–4.
5 John Ferling, *Winning Independence: The Decisive Years of the Revolutionary War, 1778–1781* (New York: Bloomsbury Publishing, 2021), 14.
6 Ron Chernow, *Washington: A Life* (New York: The Penguin Press, 2010), 31.
7 Fred Anderson, *Crucible of War: The Seven Years' War and the Fate of Empire in British North America* (New York: Alfred A. Knopf, 2000), 51.
8 *Ibid.*, 50.
9 Robert Dinwiddie to George Washington, January 1754, in W. W. Abbot, *The Papers of George Washington*, Colonial Series. Vol. 1, 7 July 1748–14 August 1755 (Charlottesville, VA: University Press of Virginia, 1983), 63–67.
10 Chernow, *Washington*, 39.
11 George Washington to Robert Dinwiddie, March 9, 1754, in Abbot, *Washington*, 1:73–75.
12 Anderson, *Crucible*, 53; John Shaw, "Affidavit of John Shaw," *Colonial Records of South Carolina: Documents Relating to Indian Affairs, Series 2, 1754–1765* (Columbia, SC: South Carolina Department of Archives & History, 1970): 4–5. Chernow, *Washington*, 34.
13 *Ibid.*, 42.
14 Shaw, "Affidavit," 4.
15 *Ibid.*; Chernow, *Washington*, 42.
16 Anderson, *Crucible*, 63.
17 *Ibid.*, 48, 64.
18 Chernow, *Washington*, 49.
19 *Ibid.*, 50.
20 *Ibid.*, 51.
21 *Ibid.*, 53–55.
22 *Ibid.*, 57.
23 Anderson, *Crucible*, 99.
24 Chernow, *Washington*, 59.
25 *Ibid.*, 60.
26 Samuel Davies and Publishing Committee, *Memoir of the Rev. Samuel Davies* (Boston: Massachusetts Sabbath School Union, 1832), 73–74.
27 Chernow, *Washington*, 64.
28 *Ibid.*, 66.
29 Fred W. Anderson, "The Hinge of the Revolution: George Washington Confronts a People's Army," *Massachusetts Historical Review* 1 (1999): 43.
30 Chernow, *Washington*, 65, 67, 73.

31. George Washington to Robert Hunter Morris, April 9, 1756, in W. W. Abbot, *The Papers of George Washington*, Colonial Series. Vol. 2, 14 August 1755–15 April 1756 (Charlottesville, VA: University Press of Virginia, 1983), 345–47.
32. George Washington to Robert Dinwiddie, March 10, 1757, in W. W. Abbot, *The Papers of George Washington*, Colonial Series. Vol. 4, 9 November 1756–24 October 1757 (Charlottesville, VA: University Press of Virginia, 1984), 112–15.
33. Chernow, *Washington*, 79, 81, 98, 126.
34. *Ibid.*, 88.
35. *Ibid.*, 90–91.
36. Address from the Officers of the Virginia Regiment, December 31, 1758, in W. W. Abbot, *The Papers of George Washington*, Colonial Series. Vol. 6, 4 September 1758–26 December 1760 (Charlottesville, VA: University Press of Virginia, 1988), 178–81.
37. Chernow, *Washington*, 99.
38. *Ibid.*, 110, 112, 114, 116.
39. Tobias Lear to George Long, in Stephen Decatur, Jr., *Private Affairs of George Washington, from the Records and Accounts of Tobias Lear, Esquire, His Secretary* (Boston: The Riverside Press, 1933), 315.
40. Chernow, *Washington*, 128–29.
41. *Ibid.*, 141–42.
42. *Ibid.*, 145–46.
43. *Ibid.*, 149, 159.
44. *Ibid.*, 165.
45. George Washington to Bryan Fairfax, July 20, 1774, in W. W. Abbot and Dorothy Twohig, *The Papers of George Washington*, Colonial Series. Vol. 10, 21 March 1774–15 June 1775 (Charlottesville, VA: University Press of Virginia, 1995), 128–31.
46. George Washington to George William Fairfax, June 10–15, 1774, in Abbot, *Washington*, 10:94–101.
47. Chernow, *Washington*, 167.
48. Fairfax County Resolves, July 18, 1774, in Abbot, *Washington*, 10:119–28.
49. Chernow, *Washington*, 171.
50. *Ibid.*, 185.
51. Eliphalet Dyer to Joseph Trumbull, June 17, 1775, in Smith, *Letters*, 1:499.
52. Ford, *Journals*, 2:92, June 16, 1775.
53. George Washington to Martha Washington, June 18, 1775, in Philander Chase, ed., *The Papers of George Washington*, Revolutionary War Series. Vol. 1, June 1775–15 September 1775 (Charlottesville, VA: University Press of Virginia, 1985), 3–6.
54. George Washington to Martha Washington, June 18, 1775, in *ibid.*, 1:3–6.
55. Silas Deane to Elizabeth Deane, June 16, 1775, in Smith, *Letters*, 1:494.
56. Eliphalet Dyer to Joseph Trumbull, June 17, 1775, in *ibid.*, 1:499–500.
57. Ford, *Journals*, 2:94, June 16, 1775.
58. John Adams to Elbridge Gerry, June 18, 1775, in Smith, *Letters*, 1:504.
59. Ford, *Journals*, 2:98, June 19, 1775.
60. Rossie, *Politics*, 14.
61. Eliphalet Dyer to Joseph Trumbull, June 20, 1775, in Smith, *Letters*, 1:521.
62. Boatner, *Encyclopedia*, 902.
63. David Humphreys, *The Life and Heroic Exploits of Israel Putnam* (New York: E. Strong, 1834), 10–12. Tourists can still visit the den, the most famous feature of Mashamoquet Brook State Park in Pomfret, Connecticut.
64. Boatner, *Encyclopedia*, 903.
65. Silas Deane to Elizabeth Deane, July 20, 1775, in Smith, *Letters*, 1:638–39.
66. Samuel Ward to Henry Ward, June 22, 1775, in Smith, *Letters*, 1:535.
67. Jack Rakove, ed., *Founding America: Documents from the Revolution to the Bill of Rights* (New York: Barnes & Noble Classics, 2006), 24, 29.
68. *Ibid.*, 25.
69. *Ibid.*, 25, 32–34.
70. Jon Meacham, *Thomas Jefferson: The Art of Power* (New York: Random House, 2012), 74–75.
71. *Ibid.*, 3, 6, 9, 12.
72. Quoted in *ibid.*, 11–12.
73. *Ibid.*, 11.
74. Quoted in *ibid.*, 15.
75. *Ibid.*, 18.
76. *Ibid.*, 20, 22.
77. *Ibid.*, 25.
78. Version of John Walker, Betsy's husband. Quoted in *ibid.*, 42.
79. *Ibid.*, 43.
80. *Ibid.*, 44.
81. *Ibid.*, 35, 44.
82. Kevin J. Hayes, *The Road to Monticello: The Life and Mind of Thomas Jefferson* (Oxford, UK: Oxford University Press, 2008), 166–67.
83. Meacham, *Jefferson*, 57–58, 67.
84. Hayes, *Monticello*, 167.
85. *Ibid.*, 167–68.

Chapter 9: Perfidious Double-Faced Congress

1. Ford, *Journals*, 2:103, June 22, 1775.
2. *Ibid.*, 2:105, June 22, 1775.
3. Ron Michener, "Money in the American Colonies," Economic History Association.
4. E. James Ferguson, *The Power of the Purse: A History of American Public Finance, 1776–1790* (Chapel Hill, NC: University of North Carolina Press, 1961), 4.
5. *Ibid.*; Michener, "Money."
6. Ferguson, *Power*, 4.
7. Michener, "Money."
8. *Ibid.*
9. E-mail communication with Farley Grubb, June 17, 2024.
10. Farley Grubb, *The Continental Dollar: How the American Revolution Was Financed with Paper Money* (Chicago: University of Chicago Press, 2023), 19.
11. *Ibid.*, 35.
12. *Ibid.*, 266–67, Table B1.
13. *Ibid.*, 39.
14. Ford, *Journals*, 2:103, June 22, 1775.
15. Grubb, *Dollar*, 18.
16. *Ibid.*
17. Jared Sparks, *Life of Gouverneur Morris*. Vol. 1 (Boston: Gray & Bowen, 1832), 39.
18. Joseph Hawes to Samuel Johnston, June 5, 1775, in Smith, *Letters*, 1:446.
19. Grubb, *Dollar*, 48.
20. John Hancock to Artemas Ward, June 22, 1775, in Smith, *Letters*, 1:534, footnote.
21. John Adams to Abigail Adams, June 23, 1775, in *ibid.*, 1:537.
22. John Adams to Abigail Adams, June 23, 1775, in *ibid.*
23. Boatner, *Encyclopedia*, 928.
24. Richard M. Ketchum, *Divided Loyalties: How the American Revolution Came to New York* (New York: Henry Holt and Company, 2002), 348.
25. *Ibid.*, 348–49.
26. *Ibid.*, 350–51.
27. Mark R. Anderson, *The Battle for the Fourteenth Colony: America's War of Liberation in Canada, 1774–1776* (London: University Press of New England, 2013), 17–18, 27.
28. William Renwick Riddell, *Benjamin Franklin and Canada: Benjamin Franklin's Mission to Canada and the Causes of Its Failure* (Toronto: [no publisher indicated], 1923), 33.
29. "Extract of a Letter from Canada, Dated Montreal, March 24, 1775," in Force, *American Archives, Fourth Series*, 2:231.
30. J. Brown to the Committee of Correspondence in Boston, March 29, 1775, in *ibid.*, 2:243–44. Emphasis in original.
31. Committee of Montreal to the Committee of Safety of Massachusetts, April 8, 1775, in *ibid.*, 2:305.
32. Silas Deane's Diary, May 27, 1775, in Smith, *Letters*, 1:412.
33. Nathaniel Wales, Jun., and Others to the Speaker of the Assembly of Connecticut, May 23, 1775, in Force, *American Archives, Fourth Series*, 2:685.
34. Anderson, *Fourteenth*, 80–81.
35. *Ibid.*, 88.
36. Albany (New York) Committee to the Continental Congress, June 21, 1775, in Force, *American Archives, Fourth Series*, 2:1048.
37. Ford, *Journals*, 2:109–10, June 27, 1775.

Chapter 10: Spirited Manifesto

1. Ford, *Journals*, 2:112, June 30, 1775.
2. *Ibid.*, 2:121, June 30, 1775. Emphasis in original.
3. John Adams to James Warren, July 6, 1775, in Robert J. Taylor, ed., *The Adams Papers*, Papers of John Adams. Vol. 3, May 1775–January 1776 (Cambridge, MA: Harvard University Press, 1979), 60–63.
4. Thomas Jefferson, *Autobiography of Thomas Jefferson: 1743–1790* (New York: G. P. Putnam's Sons, 1914), 18–19.
5. Ford, *Journals*, 2:153, July 6, 1775.
6. *Ibid.*, 2:155, July 6, 1775.
7. *Ibid.*, 2:161, July 8, 1775.
8. L. H. Butterfield, ed., *The Adams Papers*, Diary and Autobiography of John Adams. Vol. 3, Diary, 1782–1804; Autobiography, Part One to October 1776 (Cambridge, MA: The Belknap Press of Harvard University Press, 1961), 321–40.
9. Benjamin Franklin to Jonathan Shipley, July 7, 1775, in Smith, *Letters*, 1:605.
10. John Dickinson to Arthur Lee, July ?, [1775], in *ibid.*, 1:687.
11. Charles Thomson to William Henry Drayton, in *Collections of the New-York Historical Society for the Year 1878* (New York: New-York Historical Society, 1879), 284.
12. Charles Thomson to William Henry Drayton, in *ibid.*, 285.
13. Ford, *Journals*, 2:169, July 8, 1775.
14. John Adams to James Warren, July 11, 1775, in Taylor, *Adams Papers*, Papers of John Adams, 3:71–72.

15 Ford, *Journals*, 2:174–75, 177, July 12, 1775.
16 *Ibid.*, 2:182, July 13, 1775.
17 John Adams to James Warren, June 27, 1775, in Taylor, *Adams Papers*, Papers of John Adams, 3:49–51.
18 Ford, *Journals*, 2:185, July 15, 1775.
19 Comments on Soulés's *Histoire*, August 3, 1786, in Julian P. Boyd, ed., *The Papers of Thomas Jefferson*. Vol. 10, 22 June–31 December 1786 (Princeton, NJ: Princeton University Press, 1954), 368–77.
20 Ford, *Journals*, 2:195–99, July 21, 1775.
21 *Ibid.*, 2:198, July 21, 1775.
22 *Ibid.*, July 21, 1775.
23 *Ibid.*, 2:199, July 21, 1775.
24 Burnett, *Continental Congress*, 93–94.
25 Ford, *Journals*, 2:207, July 25, 1775.
26 *Ibid.*, July 25, 1775.
27 *Ibid.*, 2:209, July 26, 1775.
28 W. Baring Pemberton, *Lord North* (London: Longmans, Green and Co., 1938), 239–40.
29 Ford, *Journals*, 2:227, 2:232, July 31, 1775.
30 *Ibid.*, 2:204, 2:219, 2:235, July 25, 28, August 1, 1775.
31 *Ibid.*, 2:222, July 29, 1775.
32 Robert Treat Paine's Diary, August 2, 1775, in Smith, *Letters*, 1:695.
33 Possibly August 1. *Journal* indicates August 1. Letters from Francis Lewis and Benjamin Franklin indicate August 2 (Francis Lewis to Philip Schuyler, Benjamin Franklin to Jane Mecom, both August 2, 1775, in *ibid.*, 1:694).
34 Montross, *Reluctant Rebels*, 86.
35 *Ibid.*, 89.
36 Diary of John Adams, August 1775, in Butterfield, *Adams Papers*, Diary and Autobiography, 3:324–27.
37 Burnett, *Continental Congress*, 103.
38 Ford, *Journals*, 2:240, September 5, 1775.
39 Jim Schmidt, "John J. Zubly," *New Georgia Encyclopedia*.
40 Montross, *Reluctant Rebels*, 94.
41 Lilla Mills Hawes, ed., *The Journal of the Reverend John Joachim Zubly, A.M., D.D., March 5, 1770, through June 22, 1781* (Savannah, GA: Georgia Historical Society, 1989), xii.
42 John Zubly's Diary, September 16, 1775, in Smith, *Letters*, 2:21.
43 Burnett, *Continental Congress*, 104.
44 Beeman, *Lives*, 260.
45 John Adams to James Warren, July 24, 1775, in Taylor, *Adams Papers*, Papers of John Adams, 3:89–93.

46 Allen French, "November Meeting. The First George Washington Scandal," *Proceedings of the Massachusetts Historical Society* 65 (1932): 461–62.
47 *Ibid.*, 467.
48 Diary of John Adams, September 16, 1775, in Butterfield, *Adams Papers*, Diary and Autobiography, 2:173–75.
49 Diary of John Adams, September 15, 1775, in *ibid.*, 2:172–88.
50 Montross, *Reluctant Rebels*, 96.
51 Beeman, *Lives*, 264.
52 George Washington to John Hancock, June 25, 1775, in Chase, *Washington*, 1:34–36.
53 George Washington, letter sent July 10–11, 1775, in *ibid.*, 1:85–97.
54 Ford, *Journals*, 3:265–66, September 29, 30, 1775.
55 George Washington to John Hancock, September 21, 1775, in Philander Chase, ed., *The Papers of George Washington*, Revolutionary War Series. Vol. 2, 16 September 1775–31 December 1775 (Charlottesville, VA: University Press of Virginia, 1987), 24–30.
56 George Washington to John Hancock, September 21, 1775, in *ibid.*, 2:24–30.
57 Beeman, *Lives*, 266.
58 Benjamin Rush, *Letters of Benjamin Rush*. Vol. 1. 1761–1792 (Princeton, NJ: Princeton University Press, 1951), 92.
59 Samuel Adams to Elbridge Gerry, October 29, 1775, in Smith, *Letters*, 2:277–78.
60 *Ibid.*
61 Ford, *Journals*, 3:274, Oct. 3, 1775.
62 John Adams' Notes of Debates, October 7, 1775, in Butterfield, *Adams Papers*, Biography and Autobiography, 2:198–202.
63 John Adams to James Warren, October 19, 1775, in Taylor, *Adams Papers*, Papers of John Adams, 3:214–15.
64 Beeman, *Lives*, 268.
65 Autobiography of John Adams, In Congress, November and December 1775, in Butterfield, *Adams Papers*, Diary and Autobiography, 3:349–51.
66 Burnett, *Continental Congress*, 120.

Chapter 11: Their Rights as Dear as Our Own

1 Josiah Bartlett and John Langdon to Matthew Thornton, October 7, 1775, in Smith, *Letters*, 2:140.
2 James Livingston to Philip Schuyler, August 1775, in Peter Force, ed., *American Archives, Fourth Series*. Vol. 3 (Washington, DC: M. St. Clair Clarke and Peter Force, 1840), 468–69.

3   Anderson, *Fourteenth*, 97.
4   Samuel Chase to Philip Schuyler, August 10, 1775, in Smith, *Letters*, 1:700.
5   Anderson, *Fourteenth*, 100.
6   Ibid.
7   Philip Schuyler to Continental Congress, September 19, 1775, in Force, *American Archives, Fourth Series*, 3:738.
8   Anderson, *Fourteenth*, 113.
9   Ford, *Journals*, 3:279, October 6, 1775.
10 Philip Schuyler to Congress, September 20, 1775, in Bayard Tuckerman, *Life of General Philip Schuyler, 1733–1804* (New York: Dodd, Mead and Company, 1903), 113–14.
11 Philip Schuyler to Congress, September 19, 1775, in Force, *American Archives, Fourth Series*, 3:739. Emphasis in original.
12 Anderson, *Fourteenth*, 133.
13 Richard Montgomery to Philip Schuyler, September 24, 1775, in Force, *American Archives, Fourth Series*, 3:840.
14 Ibid.
15 John Hancock to Philip Schuyler, October 11, 1775, in Smith, *Letters*, 2:161.
16 Ford, *Journals*, 3:287, October 10, 1775.
17 Meacham, *Jefferson*, 94.
18 George Washington to John Hancock, October 5, 1775, in Chase, *Washington*, 2:98–103.
19 Samuel Ward to Henry Ward, October 11, 1775, in Smith, *Letters*, 2:163–64.
20 John Adams to Charles Lee, October 13, 1775, in Taylor, *Adams Papers*, Papers of John Adams, 3:201–4.
21 Ford, *Journals*, 3:334, November 7, 1775.
22 John Adams to James Warren, October 20, 1775, in Taylor, *Adams Papers*, Papers of John Adams, 3:217.
23 Ford, *Journals*, 3:301, October 20, 1775.
24 John Adams to James Warren, October 20, 1775, in Taylor, *Adams Papers*, Papers of John Adams, 3:217.
25 George Washington to John Hancock, November 8, 1775, in Chase, *Washington*, 2:330–33.
26 Ford, *Journals*, 3:258–60, 3:264–65, September 21–22, 27, 29, 1775.
27 Ousterhout, "Frontier Vengeance," 333.
28 Ford, *Journals*, 3:283, October 7, 1775.
29 Ousterhout, "Frontier Vengeance," 345.
30 Ford, *Journals*, 3:283, October 7, 1775.
31 Ibid., 3:295, October 14, 1775.
32 Ousterhout, "Frontier Vengeance," 338.
33 Ford, *Journals*, 3:374, November 25, 1775.
34 Ibid., 3:337, 3:356, 3:370, November 8, 16, 25, 1775.
35 Ibid., 3:280, October 6, 1775.
36 John Adams' Notes of Debates, October 6, 1775, in Smith, *Letters*, 2:124.
37 Kevin Phillips, *1775: A Good Year for Revolution* (New York: Viking, 2012), 478, 480.
38 Benjamin Quarles, "Lord Dunmore as Liberator," *The William and Mary Quarterly* 15, no. 4 (1958): 497.
39 Thomas Jefferson to Francis Eppes, November 21, 1775, in Smith, *Letters*, 2:366–67.
40 John Adams' Notes of Debates, October 6, 1775, in Butterfield, *Adams Papers*, Diary and Autobiography, 2:194–98.
41 Ibid.
42 George Washington to Joseph Reed, December 15, 1775, in Chase, *Washington*, 2:551–54.
43 George Washington to John Hancock, October 24, 1775, in *ibid.*, 2:227–28.
44 Anderson, *Fourteenth*, 130.
45 Samuel Adams to Elbridge Gerry, November 4, 1775, in Smith, *Letters*, 2:297.
46 John Adams to Abigail Adams, November 4, 1775, in Butterfield, *Adams Papers*, Family Correspondence, 1:319–20.
47 Deming, *Boston*, 393.
48 Thomas Lynch to Philip Schuyler, November 11, 1775, in Smith, *Letters*, 2:330.
49 Ford, *Journals*, 3:316, November 2, 1775.
50 Eric Jay Dolin, *Rebels at Sea: Privateering in the American Revolution* (New York: Liveright Publishing Corporation, 2022), 177.
51 Emily P. Weaver, "Nova Scotia and New England during the Revolution," *The American Historical Review* 10, no. 1 (1904): 52, 63.
52 Instructions to Aaron Willard and Moses Child, November 24, 1775, in Chase, *Washington*, 2:424–45.

Chapter 12: *The Child Was Not Yet Weaned*

1   Randall, *Allen*, 206.
2   Beeman, *Lives*, 283.
3   Ford, *Journals*, 3:298, October 18, 1775.
4   Ibid., 3:319, November 3, 1775.
5   Beeman, *Lives*, 286.
6   James Haw, "The Rutledges, the Continental Congress, and Independence," *The South Carolina Historical Magazine* 94, no. 4 (1993): 242.
7   Gary D. Olson, "Loyalists and the American Revolution: Thomas Brown and the South Carolina Backcountry, 1775–1776

ENDNOTES • 407

8. (Continued)," *The South Carolina Historical Magazine* 68, no. 4 (1967): 203–6.
8. Beeman, *Lives*, 285–86.
9. Ford, *Journals*, 3:326–37, November 4, 1775.
10. Diary of John Adams, November 4, 1775, in Butterfield, *Adams Papers*, Diary and Autobiography, 3:357–59.
11. Ford, *Journals*, 3:326–37, November 4, 1775.
12. Ibid., 3:319, 3:327, November 3, 4, 1775.
13. Hawes, *Zubly*, 43.
14. John Zubly to John Houstoun and Archibald Bulloch, [November 10, 1775], in Smith, *Letters*, 2:328.
15. John Dickinson's Proposed Instructions, November 9, 1775, in ibid., 2:320.
16. Proclamation by the Governor of Virginia, November 7, 1775, in Force, *American Archives, Fourth Series*, 3:1385.
17. Francis Lightfoot Lee to Robert W. Carter, December 2, 1775, in Smith, *Letters*, 2:425.
18. Ford, *Journals*, 3:403–4, December 4, 1775.
19. Silas Deane to Elizabeth Deane, October 7, 1775, in Smith, *Letters*, 2:138.
20. John Adams to Abigail Adams, December 3, 1775, in ibid., 2:430.
21. Ford, *Journals*, 3:257, 3:260, 3:266, 3:269, September 21, 23, 30, 1775.
22. Ferguson, *Power*, 26.
23. John Adams to James Warren, October 19, 1775, in Smith, *Letters*, 2:204.
24. Benjamin Franklin to Richard Bache, October 19, 1775, in ibid., 2:209.
25. Ford, *Journals*, 3:390, November 29, 1775.
26. Ibid., 3:389, November 29, 1775.
27. Richard Henry Lee to Catherine Macaulay, November 29, 1775, in Smith, *Letters*, 2:405.
28. John Hancock to Philip Schuyler, November 30, 1775, in ibid., 2:415.
29. Montross, *Reluctant Rebels*, 107.
30. Benjamin Irvin, *Clothed in the Robes of Sovereignty: The Continental Congress and the People Out of Doors* (Oxford, UK: Oxford University Press, 2011), 48.
31. Diary of Christopher Marshall, November 21, 1775, in Marshall, *Extracts*, 51.
32. Benjamin H. Irvin, "The Streets of Philadelphia: Crowds, Congress, and the Political Culture of Revolution, 1774–1783," *The Pennsylvania Magazine of History and Biography* 129, no. 1 (2005): 13.
33. Chernow, *Washington*, 216.
34. Patricia Brady, *Martha Washington, An American Life* (New York: Viking, 2005), 101.
35. Irvin, *Sovereignty*, 48.
36. Diary of Christopher Marshall, November 24, 1775, in Marshall, *Extracts*, 52.
37. Irvin, *Sovereignty*, 49.
38. Ford, *Journals*, 1:78, October 20, 1774.
39. Diary of Christopher Marshall, November 24, 1775, in Marshall, *Extracts*, 52.
40. Diary of Christopher Marshall, November 24, 25, 1775, in ibid., 53.
41. Diary of Christopher Marshall, November 24, 1775, in ibid.
42. Diary of Christopher Marshall, November 27, 1775, in ibid.
43. Martha Washington to Elizabeth Ramsay, December 30, 1775, in Joseph E. Fields, compiler, *"Worthy Partner": The Papers of Martha Washington* (Westport, CT: Greenwood Press, 1994), 164.
44. Beeman, *Lives*, 277.
45. King George III, "Proclamation of Rebellion," in William MacDonald, ed., *Documentary Source Book of American History* (New York: The MacMillan Company, 1916), 189–90; Montross, *Reluctant Rebels*, 110.
46. Joseph Hewes to James Iredell, November 9, 1775, in Smith, *Letters*, 3:322.
47. Boatner, *Encyclopedia*, 426.
48. Samuel Ward to Henry Ward, November 11, 1775, in Smith, *Letters*, 2:331.
49. William Hooper to Samuel Johnston, December 2, 1775, in ibid., 2:425.
50. King George III, "Proclamation of Rebellion," in MacDonald, *Source*, 189–90.
51. Ford, *Journals*, 3:410–11, December 6, 1775.
52. Ibid., 3:392, November 29, 1775.
53. Burnett, *Continental Congress*, 118.
54. Ford, *Journals*, 3:423, December 11, 1775.
55. Burnett, *Continental Congress*, 118–19.
56. Skemp, *Franklin*, 184.
57. Ibid., 179–81.
58. Ibid., 186.
59. William Franklin to the Earl of Dartmouth, August 2, 1775, in William Nelson and Frederick William Ricord, eds., *Documents Relating to the Colonial History of the State of New Jersey, 1631–1776*. Vol. 10 (Newark, NJ: New Jersey Council, 1890), 653.
60. Skemp, *Franklin*, 188.
61. Votes and Proceeding of the General Assembly of the Province of New Jersey, November 15 to December 6, 1775, in New Jersey, *Votes and Proceedings of the General Assembly of the Province of New Jersey. 1772–76* (Philadelphia: Andrew Bradford, 1772–1776), 20.

62 Votes and Proceeding of the General Assembly of the Province of New Jersey, November 15 to December 6, 1775, *Votes and Proceedings*, 19.
63 Ford, *Journals*, 3:404, December 4, 1775.
64 Burnett, *Continental Congress*, 126.
65 "Notes of What Mr. Dickinson said before the House of Assembly of New Jersey," Nelson, *New Jersey*, 10:691.
66 Rudolphus Ritzema to Alexander McDougall, November 19, 1775, in Anderson, *Fourteenth*, 160.
67 Ford, *Journals*, 3:447, December 23, 1775.

Chapter 13: To Begin the World Over Again

1 Eliphalet Dyer to Joseph Trumbull, January 1, 1776, in Smith, *Letters*, 3:4.
2 Ford, *Journals*, 4:20, January 2, 1776.
3 Diary of Christopher Marshall, January 3, 1776, in Marshall, *Extracts*, 54.
4 King George III, "His Majesty's Most Gracious Speech," October 27, 1775 (Washington, DC: Library of Congress).
5 Samuel Ward to His Daughter, January 8, 1776, in Smith, *Letters*, 3:61.
6 Burnett, *Continental Congress*, 128.
7 Richard Smith's Diary, February 13, 1776, in Smith, *Letters*, 3:252.
8 Ford, *Journals*, 4:146, February 13, 1776.
9 Craig Nelson, *Thomas Paine: Enlightenment, Revolution, and the Birth of Modern Nations* (New York: Viking, 2006), 12.
10 Scott Liell, *46 Pages: Thomas Paine, Common Sense, and the Turning Point to American Independence* (Philadelphia: Running Press, 2003), 24.
11 Nelson, *Paine*, 19
12 Mark Benson, "The Unfortunate Captain Death of the Terrible Privateer," *Royal Museums Greenwich*.
13 Liell, *46 Pages*, 31.
14 Ibid., 32.
15 Ibid., 33.
16 Nelson, *Paine*, 38.
17 Ibid.
18 Liell, *46 Pages*, 34.
19 Nelson, *Paine*, 45–46.
20 Robert A. Ferguson, "The Commonalities of *Common Sense*," *The William and Mary Quarterly* 57, no. 3 (July 2000): 474.
21 Nelson, *Paine*, 49.
22 Benjamin Franklin to Richard Bache, September 30, 1774, in Willcox, *Franklin*, 21:325–26.
23 Liell, *46 Pages*, 49.
24 Nelson, *Paine*, 48.
25 Ibid., 48, 60.
26 "Publisher's Preface," *Pennsylvania Magazine* 1 (Philadelphia: R. Aitken, 1775).
27 Liell, *46 Pages*, 51.
28 Nelson, *Paine*, 61, 64–65.
29 Ibid., 78.
30 Liell, *46 Pages*, 58.
31 Nelson, *Paine*, 81.
32 Josiah Bartlett to John Langdon, January 13, 1776, in Smith, *Letters*, 3:88.
33 Thomas Paine, *Rights of Man; Common Sense* (New York: Alfred A. Knopf, 1994), 253, 257, 260. Emphasis in original.
34 Ibid., 262.
35 Ibid., 266, 269–70, 299.
36 Ibid., 277–78.
37 Charles Lee to George Washington, January 24, 1776, in Philander Chase, ed., *The Papers of George Washington*, Revolutionary War Series. Vol. 3, 1 January 1776–31 March 1776 (Charlottesville, VA: University Press of Virginia, 1988), 182–84.
38 George Washington to Joseph Reed, January 31, 1776, in *ibid.*, 3:225–29.
39 Liell, *46 Pages*, 92.
40 Nelson, *Paine*, 91.
41 Ibid., 89.
42 Liell, *46 Pages*, 93.
43 Ibid., 95.
44 Joseph Hewes to Samuel Johnston, February 13, 1776, in Smith, *Letters*, 3:247.
45 John Adams to Abigail Adams, February 18, 1776, in *ibid.*, 3:272.
46 Diary of John Adams [In Congress, Spring 1776, and Thomas Paine], in Butterfield, *Adams Papers*, Diary and Autobiography, 3:330–35.
47 Abigail Adams to John Adams, March 2, 1776, in Butterfield, *Adams Papers*, Family Correspondence, 1:352–56.
48 Samuel Adams to James Warren, January 13, 1776, in Smith, *Letters*, 3:87.
49 Adams, Samuel, "An Earnest Appeal to the People," February 3, 1776, in Harry Alonzo Cushing, ed., *The Writings of Samuel Adams*. Vol. 3, 1773–1777 (New York: G. P. Putnam's Sons, 1907), 264.
50 Ambrose Serle, Edward H. Tatum Jr., ed., *The American Journal of Ambrose Serle, Secretary to Lord Howe, 1776–1778* (San Marino, CA: The Huntington Library, 1940), 39, July 20, 1776.
51 Beeman, *Lives*, 324.
52 Quoted in *ibid.*, 326.

53 John Hancock to Thomas Cushing, January 17, 1776, in Smith, *Letters*, 3:105.
54 Phillips, *1775*, 292.
55 Thomas Lynch to Philip Schuyler, January 20, 1776, in Smith, *Letters*, 3:125.
56 Robert Morris to Horatio Gates, April 6, 1776, in *ibid.*, 3:495.
57 Ford, *Journals*, 4:70, January 19, 1776.
58 *Ibid.*, 4:86, January 24, 1776.
59 *Ibid.*, 4:90, January 25, 1776. Monument was installed in 1789 on Broadway side of St. Paul's Chapel in New York (Trinity Church Wall Street, "The General and the Monument").
60 Marston, *King*, 60–61.
61 Beeman, *Lives*, 330.
62 Francis Lightfoot Lee to Landon Carter, March 19, 1776, in Smith, *Letters*, 3:407.
63 John Adams to Horatio Gates, March 23, 1776, in *ibid.*, 3:431.
64 Great Britain, *A Collection of All the Statutes Now in Force Relating to the Revenue and Officers of the Customs in Great Britain and the Plantations*. Vol. 2 (London: C. Eyre and W. Strahan, 1780), 1473–74.
65 Beeman, *Lives*, 332.
66 Montross, *Reluctant Rebels*, 121.
67 Jonathan R. Dull, *Benjamin Franklin and the American Revolution* (Lincoln, NE: University of Nebraska Press, 2010), 47.
68 Joel Richard Paul, *Unlikely Allies: How a Merchant, a Playwright, and a Spy Saved the American Revolution* (New York: Riverhead Press, 2009), 123.
69 Burnett, *Continental Congress*, 141.
70 Helen Augur, *The Secret War of Independence* (New York: Dull, Sloan and Pearce, 1955), 77.
71 Francis Wharton, ed., *The Revolutionary Diplomatic Correspondence of the United States*. Vol 1 (Washington, DC: Government Printing Office, 1889), 334.
72 Paul, *Unlikely Allies*, 120, 122–23.
73 *Ibid.*, 123.
74 Burnett, *Continental Congress*, 142.
75 Schiff, *Improvisation*, 8.
76 Eliphalet Dyer to Joseph Trumbull, January 1, 1776, in Smith, *Letters*, 3:5.
77 Silas Deane to Elizabeth Deane, November 26, 1775, in *ibid.*, 2:392.
78 Eliphalet Dyer to Joseph Trumbull, January 1, 1776, in *ibid.*, 3:5.
79 Committee of Correspondence to Silas Deane, March 3, 1776, in Jared Sparks, ed., *The Diplomatic Correspondence of the American Revolution*. Vol. 1 (Boston: N. Hale and Gray & Bowen, 1829), 6.
80 Committee of Correspondence to Silas Deane, March 3, 1776, in *ibid.*, 1:6–7.
81 Committee of Correspondence to Silas Deane, March 3, 1776, in *ibid.*, 1:7.
82 Paul, *Unlikely Allies*, 126–27.

Chapter 14: Motives of Glory as Well as Interest

1 Anderson, *Fourteenth*, 291.
2 John Adams to James Warren, February 18, 1776, in Smith, *Letters*, 3:275.
3 Diary of John Adams, September 15, 1775, in Butterfield, *Adams Papers*, Diary and Autobiography, 2:172–73.
4 John Adams to James Warren, February 18, 1776, in Smith, *Letters*, 3:275.
5 Samuel Chase to John Adams, January 12, 1776, in Taylor, *Adams Papers*, Papers of John Adams, 3:400–1.
6 Anderson, *Fourteenth*, 293.
7 Samuel Chase to John Adams, January 12, 1776, in Taylor, *Adams Papers*, Papers of John Adams, 3:400–1.
8 Anderson, *Fourteenth*, 293–94.
9 Ford, *Journals*, 4:98–99, March 20, 1776.
10 Anderson, *Fourteenth*, 297.
11 Robert McConnell Hatch, *Thrust for Canada: The American Attempt on Quebec in 1775–1776* (Boston: Houghton Mifflin Company, 1979), 190.
12 Journal of Charles Carroll of Carrollton, April 7, 1776, in Lewis A. Leonard, *Life of Charles Carroll of Carrollton* (New York: Moffat, Yard and Company, 1918), 282.
13 Benjamin Franklin to Josiah Quincy, Sr., April 15, 1776, in William B. Willcox, ed., *The Papers of Benjamin Franklin*. Vol. 22, March 23, 1775, through October 27, 1776 (New Haven, CT: Yale University Press, 1982), 400–2.
14 Benjamin Franklin to John Hancock, April 13, 1776, in *ibid.*, 22:400.
15 Ford, *Journals*, 3:445, December 22, 1775.
16 Deming, *Boston*, 404.
17 George Washington to John Hancock, January 4, 1776, in Chase, *Washington*, 3:18–21.
18 Deming, *Boston*, 416.
19 Joseph Hewes to Samuel Johnston, March 20, 1776, in Smith, *Letters*, 3:416–17.
20 Oliver Wolcott to Laura Wolcott, April 17, 1776, in *ibid.*, 3:555.

21. Robert Morris to Horatio Gates, April 6, 1776, in *ibid.*, 3:495.
22. Ford, *Journals*, 4:230–32, March 23, 1776.
23. *Ibid.*, 4:258, April 6, 1776.
24. John Adams to James Warren, April 20, 1776, in Robert J. Taylor, ed., *The Adams Papers*, Papers of John Adams. Vol. 4, February–August 1776 (Cambridge, MA: Harvard University Press, 1979), 130–33.
25. John Adams, "Thoughts on Government," April 1776, in Rakove, *Founding*, 79.
26. Gordon S. Wood, *The Creation of the American Republic, 1776–1787* (Chapel Hill, NC: University of North Carolina Press, 1969), 133.
27. John Adams, "Thoughts on Government," April 1776, in Rakove, *Founding*, 86.
28. Journal of Charles Carroll of Carrollton, April 27, 1776, in Leonard, *Carroll*, 305.
29. Commissioners to Canada to John Hancock, May 1, 1776, in Smith, *Letters*, 3:611.
30. Journal of Charles Carroll of Carrollton, April 29, 1776, in Leonard, *Carroll*, 305.
31. John Carroll to his mother, in John Gilmary Shea, *Life and Times of the Most Rev. John Carroll* (New York: John G. Shea, 1888), 149.
32. *Ibid.*, 150–51.
33. Commissioners to Canada to [John Hancock], May 8, 1776, in Willcox, *Franklin*, 22:424–26.
34. Anderson, *Fourteenth*, 235, 240.
35. Commissioners to Canada to [John Hancock], May 8, 1776, in Willcox, *Franklin*, 22:424–26. Emphasis in original.
36. *Ibid.*
37. Riddell, *Franklin*, 39.

Chapter 15: We Cannot Make Events

1. Carter Braxton to Landon Carter, April 14, 1776, in Smith, *Letters*, 3:522–23.
2. *Ibid.*, 3:523.
3. Samuel Adams to Samuel Cooper, April 30, 1776, in *ibid.*, 3:601.
4. Richard Alan Ryerson, *The Revolution Is Now Begun: The Radical Committees of Philadelphia, 1765–1776* (Philadelphia: University of Pennsylvania Press, 1978), 12.
5. William Hogeland, *Declaration: The Nine Tumultuous Weeks When America Became Independent, May 1–July 4, 1776* (New York: Simon & Schuster, 2010), 22.
6. *Ibid.*, 23.
7. *Ibid.*, 21.
8. Steven Rosswurm, *Arms, Country, and Class: The Philadelphia Militia and the "Lower Sort" during the American Revolution* (New Brunswick, NJ: Rutgers University Press, 1987), 67.
9. Hogeland, *Declaration*, 24.
10. Rosswurm, *Arms*, 67, 69–70, 89.
11. Hogeland, *Declaration*, 25.
12. Rosswurm, *Arms*, 79.
13. *Ibid.*
14. John Adams to James Warren, March 21, 1776, in Taylor, *Adams Papers*, Papers of John Adams, 4:56–58.
15. Caesar Rodney to Thomas Rodney, May 1, 1776, in Smith, *Letters*, 3:616.
16. Robert Treat Paine's Diary, May 1, 1776, in *ibid.*, 3:615.
17. Hogeland, *Declaration*, 10.
18. *Ibid.*, 11, 13–14, 17.
19. *Ibid.*, 84, 94.
20. *Ibid.*, 38–39.
21. *Ibid.*, 39.
22. Josiah Bartlett to Mary Bartlett, May 18, 1776, in Smith, *Letters*, 4:33.
23. Narrative of Captain Andrew Snape Hamond, May 5–9, 1776, in William James Morgan, ed., *Naval Documents of the American Revolution*. Vol. 5 (Washington, DC: US Government Printing Office, 1970), 13, 15.
24. Account Book of James Wood, in *ibid.*, 5:13.
25. Hogeland, *Declaration*, 40–41.
26. Diary of Christopher Marshall, May 9, 1776, in Morgan, *Naval Documents*, 5:14.
27. Thomas Paine, "Forester Letter IV," *Pennsylvania Journal*, May 8, 1776.
28. Ford, *Journals*, 4:342, May 10, 1776.
29. Caesar Rodney to John Haslet, May 14, 1776, in Smith, *Letters*, 3:674.
30. Beeman, *Lives*, 347.
31. David Hawke, *In the Midst of a Revolution* (Philadelphia: University of Pennsylvania Press, 1961), 119–21.
32. Ford, *Journals*, 4:358, May 15, 1776.
33. Montross, *Reluctant Rebels*, 137.
34. John Adams' Notes of Debates, May 13, 1776, in Butterfield, *Adams Papers*, Diary and Autobiography, 2:238–41.
35. John Adams' Notes of Debates, May 13, 1776, in *ibid.*
36. Montross, *Reluctant Rebels*, 138.
37. Burnett, *Continental Congress*, 160.
38. James Duane to John Jay, May 18, 1776, in Smith, *Letters*, 4:34.
39. John Adams to James Warren, May 15, 1776, in *ibid.*, 3:676.

40 Caesar Rodney to Thomas Rodney, May 17, 1776, in *ibid.*, 4:30.
41 Beeman, *Lives*, 385
42 Maier, *Scripture*, 47.
43 David Freeman Hawke, *A Transaction of Free Men: The Birth and Course of the Declaration of Independence* (New York: Da Capo Press, 1964), 5–6.
44 Thomas Jefferson to Thomas Nelson, May 16, 1776, in Smith, *Letters*, 4:13.
45 *Ibid.*, 4:14, footnote 3.

Chapter 16: Knaves Imposing upon Fools

1 John Adams to James Warren, May 20, 1776, in Smith, *Letters*, 4:41.
2 James Clitherall, "Extracts from the Diary of Dr. James Clitherall, 1776," *The Pennsylvania Magazine of History and Biography* 22, no. 4 (1898): 470, May 13, 1776.
3 John Adams to James Warren, May 18, 1776, in Smith, *Letters*, 4:32.
4 William Whipple to John Langdon, May 18, 1776, in *ibid.*, 4:38.
5 Joseph Hewes to James Iredell, May 17, 1776, in *ibid.*, 4:27.
6 James Benjamin Wilbur, *Ira Allen: Founder of Vermont*. Vol. 1 (Boston: Houghton Mifflin Company, 1928), 80.
7 Marston, *King*, 247.
8 Ford, *Journals*, 4:405, May 30, 1776.
9 E. P. Walton, ed., *Records of the Governor and Council of the State of Vermont*. Vol. 1 (Montpelier, VT: J. & J. M. Poland, 1873), 19–20.
10 Caesar Rodney to Thomas Rodney, May 18, 1776, in Smith, *Letters*, 4:37.
11 Anderson, *Fourteenth*, 313.
12 Commissioners to Canada to John Hancock, May 10, 1776, in Willcox, *Franklin*, 22:426–27.
13 Anderson, *Fourteenth*, 314.
14 Thomas Jefferson to Thomas Nelson, May 19, 1776, in Smith, *Letters*, 4:40.
15 Boatner, *Encyclopedia*, 1220.
16 Ford, *Journals*, 4:388, May 24, 1776.
17 Elbridge Gerry to James Warren, May 20, 1776, in Smith, *Letters*, 4:42.
18 John Adams to James Warren, May 20, 1776, in Taylor, *Adams Papers*, Papers of John Adams, 4:195–97.
19 Virginia, "Transcription: Virginia's Fifth Revolutionary Convention Called for Independence," May 15, 1776, *Convention, General Correspondence, Minutes, and Journals,* *1774–1776*, Accession 30003 (Richmond, VA: Library of Virginia).
20 Stillé, *Dickinson*, 186.
21 *Ibid.*, 186–88.
22 John Adams to Patrick Henry, June 3, 1776, in Taylor, *Adams Papers*, Papers of John Adams, 4:234–35.
23 *Ibid.*
24 Samuel Adams to James Warren, June 6, 1776, in Smith, *Letters*, 4:150.
25 Ford, *Journals*, 5:425, June 7, 1776.
26 *Ibid.*
27 Beeman, *Lives*, 352.
28 Notes of Proceedings in the Continental Congress, June 7–August 1, 1776, in Julian P. Boyd, *The Papers of Thomas Jefferson*. Vol. 1, 1760–1776 (Princeton, NJ: Princeton University Press, 1950), 299–329.
29 *Ibid.*
30 *Ibid.*
31 *Ibid.*
32 *Ibid.*
33 *Ibid.*
34 Matthew Tilghman, Thomas Stone, John Rogers to Maryland Council of Safety, June 11, 1776, in Smith, *Letters*, 4:193.
35 Benjamin Franklin to Charles Carroll and Samuel Chase, May 27, 1776, in Willcox, *Franklin*, 22:439–40.
36 Commissioners to Canada to John Hancock, May 17, 1776, in Smith, *Letters*, 4:23.
37 Commissioners to Canada to John Hancock, May 27, 1776, in *ibid.*, 4:82.
38 Commissioners to Canada to John Hancock, May 27, 1776, in *ibid.*
39 Hatch, *Thrust*, 209.
40 John Lacey, Joseph Chapman, and Anthony Wayne, "Memoirs of Brigadier John Lacey, of Pennsylvania (Continued)," *The Pennsylvania Magazine of History and Biography* 25, no. 2 (1901): 194.
41 John Sullivan to George Washington, June 6, 1776, in Chase, *Washington*, 4:440–45.
42 Anderson, *Fourteenth*, 326.
43 John Sullivan to George Washington, June 6, 1776, in Chase, *Washington*, 4:440–45.
44 John Hancock to the Commissioners in Canada, May 24, 1776, in Smith, *Letters*, 4:66.
45 John Sullivan to George Washington, June 6, 1776, in Philander Chase, ed, *The Papers of George Washington*, Revolutionary War Series. Vol. 4, 1 April 1776–15 June 1776 (Charlottesville, VA: University Press of Virginia, 1991), 440–45.

46 Hatch, *Thrust*, 217.
47 Anderson, *Fourteenth*, 329.
48 Colonel Wait to Colonel Hurd, July 20, 1776, in Peter Force, ed., *American Archives, Fifth Series*. Vol. 1 (Washington, DC: M. St. Clair Clarke and Peter Force, 1848), 479–80.
49 Notes of Proceedings in the Continental Congress, June 7–August 1, 1776, in Boyd, *Jefferson*, 1:299–329.
50 *Ibid.*
51 Ford, *Journals*, 5:433, June 12, 1776.
52 William Pierce, "Characters in the Convention of the States Held at Philadelphia, May 1787," *American Historical Review* 3 (1898): 326.
53 Beeman, *Lives*, 390.
54 Ferling, *Leap*, 170.
55 Beeman, *Lives*, 390.
56 Montross, *Reluctant Rebels*, 143, 146.
57 McGaughy, *Lee*, 121–22.
58 Montross, *Reluctant Rebels*, 146.
59 Thomas Jefferson's Anecdotes of Benjamin Franklin, [*ca.* 4 December 1818], in J. Jefferson Looney, ed., *The Papers of Thomas Jefferson*, Retirement Series. Vol. 13, 22 April 1818 to 31 January 1819 (Princeton, NJ: Princeton University Press, 2016), 462–65.
60 John Adams to Timothy Pickering, August 6, 1822, in Charles Francis Adams, ed., *The Works of John Adams, Second President of the United States*. Vol. 2 (Boston: Little, Brown, and Company, 1865), 512.
61 Diary of John Adams [In Congress, May–July 1776], in Butterfield, *Adams Papers*, Diary and Autobiography, 3:335–37.
62 Thomas Jefferson to James Madison, August 30, 1823, in Paul Leicester Ford, ed., *The Writings of Thomas Jefferson*. Vol. 10 (New York: G. P. Putnam's Sons, 1899), 267.
63 Diary of John Adams [In Congress, May–July 1776], in Butterfield, *Adams Papers*, Diary and Autobiography. 3:335–37.
64 John Adams to Timothy Pickering, August 6, 1822, in Adams, *Works*, 2:512.
65 *Ibid.*
66 Meacham, *Jefferson*, 99, 103.
67 Beeman, *Lives*, 392.
68 Lawrence M. Small, "Mr. Jefferson's Writing Box," *Smithsonian Magazine*, February 2001.
69 Thomas Jefferson to Henry Lee, May 8, 1825, in Paul Leicester Ford, ed., *The Writings of Thomas Jefferson*. Vol. 12 (New York: G. P. Putnam's Sons, 1905); Ford, *Jefferson*, 409.
70 Montross, *Reluctant Rebels*, 146.
71 Ford, *Journals*, 5:430, 5:443, 5:465, 5:475–76, 5:483, June 11, 14, 19, 24, 26, 1776.
72 *Ibid.*, 5:464, June 18, 1776.
73 *Ibid.*, 5:434, June 12, 1776.
74 *Ibid.*, 5:434–35, June 12, 1776.
75 *Ibid.*, 5:466–67, June 19, 1776.

Chapter 17: Comfort and Cheer the Spirits

1 Nicholas Cooke to Stephen Hopkins, May 7, 1776, in William R. Staples, *Rhode Island in the Continental Congress* (Providence, RI: Providence Press Company, 1870), 68.
2 Maier, *Scripture*, 61
3 *Ibid.*, 48–49.
4 John Adams to James Warren, April 22, 1776, in Smith, *Letters*, 3:569.
5 Marston, *King*, 272.
6 South Carolina, *Journal of the Provincial Congress of South Carolina, 1776* (London: J. Almon, 1776), 97, March 23, 1776.
7 Merrill Jensen, *The Founding of a Nation: A History of the American Revolution, 1763–1776* (New York: Oxford University Press, 1968), 678.
8 North Carolina, *The Journal of the Proceedings of the Provincial Congress of North Carolina, Held at Halifax, on the Fourth Day of April, 1776* (Raleigh, NC: Lawrence & Lemay, 1831), 12, April 4, 1776.
9 John Russell Bartlett, ed., *Records of the Colony of Rhode Island and Providence Plantations in New England*. Vol. 7 (Providence, RI: A. Crawford Greene, 1862), 523.
10 Bartlett, *Rhode Island*, 7:526–27.
11 Nicholas Cooke to Stephen Hopkins, May 7, 1776, in Staples, *Rhode Island*, 68.
12 Jonathan Trumbull to Virginia Convention, June 14, 1776, in Peter Force, ed., *American Archives, Fourth Series*. Vol. 6 (Washington, DC: M. St. Clair Clarke and Peter Force, 1846), 902.
13 Connecticut Assembly, June 14, 1776, in *ibid.*, 6:868. Emphasis in original.
14 Maier, *Scripture*, 63.
15 Connecticut Assembly, June 14, 1776, in Force, *American Archives, Fourth Series*, 6:868.
16 Committee of Both Houses, June 13, 1776, in *ibid.*, 6:1030.
17 Marston, *King*, 290.
18 Quoted in George Herbert Ryden, ed., *Letters to and from Caesar Rodney, 1756–1784* (Philadelphia: Historical Society of Delaware, 1933), 11.
19 Marston, *King*, 291.

20 Skemp, *Franklin*, 184, 191, 202.
21 Marston, *King*, 291.
22 Skemp, *Franklin*, 202.
23 New Jersey Provincial Congress, June 16, 1776, in Force, *American Archives, Fourth Series*, 6:1621–22.
24 William Franklin to the Legislature of New Jersey, June 17, 1776, in Ricord, *New Jersey*, 10:721.
25 Nathanial Heard to Samuel Tucker, June 18, 1776, in Force, *American Archives, Fourth Series*, 6:1623.
26 New Jersey Provincial Congress Order for Letter from Samuel Tucker to John Hancock, June 17, 1776, in *ibid.*, 6:1624. Emphasis in original.
27 Instructions to New Jersey Delegates to Congress, June 22, 1776, in *ibid.*, 6:1628–29.
28 New Jersey Provincial Congress, June 21, 1776, in *ibid.*, 6:1627.
29 Ford, *Journals*, 5:473, June 24, 1776.
30 Skemp, *Franklin*, 214.
31 *Ibid.*, 216, 333.
32 Beeman, *Lives*, 360.
33 Stillé, *Dickinson*, 189.
34 Beeman, *Lives*, 363.
35 John Adams to James Warren, May 20, 1776, in Taylor, *Adams Papers*, Papers of John Adams, 4:195–97.
36 Maryland State Archives, "Writing It All Down: The Art of Constitution Making for the State & the Nation, 1776–1833."
37 Extracts from the Proceedings of the Convention of Maryland, May 15, 1776, in Force, *American Archives, Fourth Series*, 6:462. Emphasis in original.
38 Extracts from the Proceedings of the Convention of Maryland, May 15, 1776, in *ibid.*, 6:463.
39 Samuel Chase to John Adams, June 21, 1776, in Taylor, *Adams Papers*, Papers of John Adams, 4:322–23.
40 Frederick County (Maryland) Committee, June 17, 1776, in Force, *American Archives, Fourth Series*, 6:933.
41 Samuel Chase to John Adams, June 28, 1776, in Taylor, *Adams Papers*, Papers of John Adams, 4:351. Emphasis in original.
42 Marston, *King*, 292–93.
43 *Ibid.*, 293, 295.
44 Ford, *Journals*, 2:15–16, May 11, 1775.
45 New-York Congress to Their Delegates in Continental Congress, June 11, 1776, in Force, *American Archives, Fourth Series*, 6:814.
46 *Ibid.*

Chapter 18: Boots and Spurs

1 Maier, *Scripture*, 103.
2 *Ibid.*, 52, 104.
3 The Avalon Project, "English Bill of Rights 1689" (Yale Law School).
4 Bill of Rights, December 15, 1791, in Rakove, *Founding*, 639.
5 Maier, *Scripture*, 51, 54.
6 Avalon, "English Bill of Rights."
7 Declaration of Independence, July 4, 1776, in Rakove, *Founding*, 138.
8 Maier, *Scripture*, 126.
9 Richard Labunski, *James Madison and the Struggle for the Bill of Rights* (Oxford, UK: Oxford University Press, 2006), 163.
10 The Constitution of Virginia, in Francis Newton Thorpe, ed., T*he Federal and State Constitutions Colonial Charters, and Other Organic Laws of the States, Territories, and Colonies Now or Heretofore Forming the United States of America* (Washington, DC: Government Printing Office, 1909), 3812, footnote.
11 Maier, *Scripture*, 126.
12 Virginia Declaration of Rights, June 12, 1776, in Rakove, *Founding*, 88.
13 Declaration of Independence, July 4, 1776, in *ibid.*, 136.
14 Beeman, *Lives*, 422.
15 *Ibid.*, 407.
16 *Ibid.*, 370.
17 Ford, *Journals*, 5:504, July 1, 1776.
18 Beeman, *Lives*, 370.
19 *Ibid.*
20 *Ibid.*
21 John Dickinson and J. H. Powell, "Notes and Documents: Speech of John Dickinson Opposing the Declaration of Independence," *The Pennsylvania Magazine of History and Biography* 65, no. 4 (1941): 468–69.
22 *Ibid.*, 473.
23 *Ibid.*, 475, 478.
24 *Ibid.*, 480.
25 Diary of John Adams, [July 1, 1776], in Butterfield, *Adams Papers*, Diary and Autobiography, 3:395–98.
26 McCullough, *Adams*, 127.
27 Diary of John Adams, [July 1, 1776], in Butterfield, *Adams Papers*, Diary and Autobiography, 3:395–98.
28 *Ibid.*
29 McCullough, *Adams*, 128.
30 John Adams to Samuel Chase, July 1, 1776, in Smith, *Letters*, 4:347.

31 Beeman, *Lives*, 375.
32 Maier, *Scripture*, 45.
33 Beeman, *Lives*, 375.
34 Francis Lightfoot Lee to Richard Henry Lee, June 30, 1776, in Smith, *Letters*, 5:343.
35 Jefferson's "original Rough draught" of the Declaration of Independence, June 11–July 4, 1776, in Boyd, *Jefferson*, 1:423–28. Emphasis in original.
36 John Ferling, *Independence: The Struggle to Set America Free* (New York: Bloomsbury Press, 2011), 333.
37 Thomas McKean to Cesar A. Rodney, September 22, 1813, in Smith, *Letters*, 4:388, footnote 1.
38 Ferling, *Independence*, 328.
39 Beeman, *Lives*, 377
40 Thomas McKean to Cesar A. Rodney, September 22, 1813, in Smith, *Letters*, 4:388, footnote 1.
41 Caesar Rodney to Thomas Rodney, July 4, 1776, in *ibid.*, 4:388.
42 Ford, *Journals*, 5:50, July 2, 1776.
43 John Adams to Abigail Adams, July 23, 1775, in Butterfield, *Adams Papers*, Family Correspondence, 1:252–54.
44 Ferling, *Independence*, 331.
45 *Ibid.*, 332.
46 Letter from Robert Whitehill, June 10, 1776, in Smith, *Letters*, 4:274, footnote 1.
47 James Wilson's Conduct in Congress, June 20, 1776, in *ibid.*, 4:223.
48 John Adams to Abigail Adams, July 3, 1776, in Lyman H. Butterfield, ed, *The Adams Papers*, Adams Family Correspondence. Vol. 2, June 1776–March 1778 (Cambridge, MA: Harvard University Press, 1963), 29–33.

Chapter 19: Singular and Delicate

1 George Clinton, John Alsop, Henry Wisner, William Floyd, and Francis Lewis to the New York Provincial Congress, July 2, 1776, in Smith, *Letters*, 4:372.
2 Joseph Hewes to Samuel Purviance, Jr., July 2, 1776, in *ibid.*, 4:370.
3 Ferling, *Leap*, 184.
4 *Ibid.*
5 *Ibid.*
6 *Ibid.*
7 Carl Lotus Becker, *History of Political Parties in the Province of New York, 1760 to 1776* (Madison, WI: University of Wisconsin, 1909), 264–65.
8 Becker, *New York*, 273–74.
9 Notes of Proceedings in the Continental Congress, June 7–August 1, 1776, in Boyd, *Jefferson*, 1:299–329.
10 *Ibid.*
11 *Ibid.*
12 *Ibid.*
13 Hawke, *Transaction*, 203.
14 Thomas Jefferson to Richard Henry Lee, July 8, 1776, in Smith, *Letters*, 4:412.
15 Abigail Adams to John Adams, July 13, 1776, in Butterfield, *Adams Papers*, Family Correspondence, 2:45–49.
16 Beeman, *Lives*, 413.
17 *Ibid.*, 415.
18 Burnett, *Continental Congress*, 187.
19 Robert Treat Paine to Joseph Palmer, July 6, 1776, in Smith, *Letters*, 4:399.
20 Ford, *Journals*, 5:516, July 4, 1776.
21 Burnett, *Continental Congress*, 194.
22 United States, Continental Congress, *Secret Journals of the Acts and Proceedings of Congress*, Vol. 1 (Boston: Thomas B. Wait, 1820), 46.
23 Charles Warren, "Fourth of July Myths," *The William and Mary Quarterly* 2, no. 3 (1945): 246.
24 *Ibid.*
25 *Ibid.*
26 Elbridge Gerry to Samuel and John Adams, July 21, 1776, in Taylor, *Adams Papers*, Papers of John Adams, 4:398–404.
27 Warren, "Myths," 246.
28 John Adams to Samuel Chase, July 9, 1776, in Smith, *Letters*, 4:414.
29 Hawke, *Transaction*, 198.
30 *Ibid.*, 199.
31 *Ibid.*, 207.
32 Maier, *Scripture*, 130.
33 *Ibid.*, 131.
34 *Ibid.*, 130.
35 Beeman, *Lives*, 417.
36 John Hancock to the New Jersey Convention, July 5, 1776, in Smith, *Letters*, 4:392.
37 William Whipple to Joshua Brackett, July 8, 1776, in *ibid.*, 4:413.
38 Elbridge Gerry to James Warren, July 5, 1776, in *ibid.*, 4:392.
39 Samuel Adams to John Pitts, July 9, 1776, in *ibid.*, 4:417.
40 John Adams to Mary Palmer, July 5, 1776, in *ibid.*, 4:389.
41 John Adams to Samuel Chase, July 9, 1776, in *ibid.*, 414.
42 John Adams to Abigail Adams, July 7, 1776, in *ibid.*, 4:400.
43 General Orders, July 9, 1776, in Chase, *Washington*, 5:245–47.

44 Diary of Christopher Marshall, July 6, 8, 1776, in William Duane, Jr., ed., *Passages from the Remembrancer of Christopher Marshall* (Philadelphia: J. Crissy, 1839), 93–94.
45 Maier, *Scripture*, 157–59.
46 *Virginia Gazette* (Purdie), July 19, 1776.
47 Ibid., 160.
48 Charles S. Desbler, "How the Declaration Was Declared in the Old Thirteen," *Harpers New Monthly Magazine* 85 (1892): 174.
49 Maier, *Scripture*, 157.
50 Account from Worcester, Massachusetts, July 22, 1776, in Desbler, "Declaration," 174.
51 Rev. Dr. Inglis to Rev. Dr. Hind, October 31, 1776, in *ibid.*, 172–73.
52 Ibid., 173.
53 Ibid., 172.
54 Maier, *Scripture*, 157–58.
55 Desbler, "Declaration," 170.
56 Ibid., 177.
57 Joseph Barton to Henry Wisner, July 9, 1776, or later, in *ibid.*, 169.
58 George Johnstone, Member of Parliament, according to John Wilkes, in John Wilkes, *Speeches of Mr. Wilkes in the House of Commons* (London: 1786), 89.
59 Malcolm Freiberg, ed., *Thomas Hutchinson's Strictures upon the Declaration of the Congress at Philadelphia; in a Letter to a Noble Lord, &c.* (Boston: The Old South Association), 11. Emphasis in original.
60 Ibid., 22.
61 Serle, *Journal*, 31, July 13, 1776.
62 Maier, *Scripture*, 162.
63 Ford, *Journals*, 5:560, July 15, 1776.
64 Diary of John Adams, August 22, 1774, in Butterfield, *Adams Papers*, Diary and Autobiography, 2:105–8.
65 John Alsop to the New York Provincial Congress, July 16, 1776, in Smith, *Letters*, 4:468.
66 Ford, *Journals*, 5:590–91, July 19, 1776.

Chapter 20: Perfidy & Tyranny

1 Abraham Clark to Elias Dayton, August 6, 1776, in Smith, *Letters*, 4:628.
2 Joseph Hewes to Samuel Johnston, July 8, 1776, in *ibid.*, 4:411.
3 Montross, *Reluctant Rebels*, 161.
4 Boatner, *Encyclopedia*, 694.
5 Quoted in Stillé, *Dickinson*, 204.
6 Quoted in *ibid.*, 206.
7 John Adams to Horatio Gates, April 27, 1776, in Taylor, *Adams Papers*, Papers of John Adams, 4:146–48.
8 Robert Morris to Joseph Reed, July 20, 1776, in Smith, *Letters*, 4:511–12.
9 Beeman, *Lives*, 418.
10 Ira D. Gruber, *The Howe Brothers in the American Revolution* (New York: Atheneum, 1972), 45.
11 Ibid., 52.
12 Stephen Brumwell, "Band of Brothers," *History Today* 58, issue 6 (2008).
13 Ibid.
14 Gruber, *Howe Brothers*, 71.
15 Ibid., 77–78.
16 Ibid., 77.
17 Ibid., 89–90.
18 Ibid., 92–93.
19 Joseph Reed to Charles Pettit, July 15, 1776, in Reed, *Reed*, 1:204.
20 Ford, *Journals*, 5:536, July 10, 1776.
21 George C. Daughan, *Revolution on the Hudson: New York City and the Hudson River Valley in the American War of Independence* (New York: W. W. Norton & Company, 2016), 58.
22 Gruber, *Howe Brothers*, 95.
23 Ibid.
24 Memorandum of an Interview with James Paterson, July 20, 1776, in Philander Chase, ed., *The Papers of George Washington*, Revolutionary War Series. Vol. 5, 16 June 1776–12 August 1776 (Charlottesville, VA: University Press of Virginia, 1993), 398–403.
25 Memorandum of an Interview with James Paterson, July 20, 1776, in *ibid.*, 5:398–403.
26 Ford, *Journals*, 5:592–93, July 19, 1776.
27 Charles Carroll to Charles Carroll, Sr.?, July 20, 1776, in Smith, *Letters*, 4:496.
28 Benjamin Franklin to Richard Howe, July 20, 1776, in *ibid.*, 4:499.
29 Robert Morris to Joseph Reed, July 20, 1776, in *ibid.*, 4:511.
30 Mary Lynn Ritzenthaler and Catherine Nicholson, "The Declaration of Independence and the Hand of Time," *Prologue Magazine* 48, no. 3 (2016).
31 Montross, *Reluctant Rebels*, 164.
32 Benjamin Rush to John Adams, July 20, 1811, in L. H. Butterfield, ed., *Letters of Benjamin Rush*. Vol. 2, 1793–1813 (Princeton, NJ: Princeton University Press, 1951), 1090.
33 Boatner, *Encyclopedia*, 1007.
34 Montross, *Reluctant Rebels*, 165.
35 Ibid.
36 Ibid., 166–67.
37 Ford, *Journals*, 5:602, July 23, 1776.
38 Burnett, *Continental Congress*, 218.

39 Montross, *Reluctant Rebels*, 174.
40 Merrill Jensen, *The New Nation: A History of the United States During the Confederation, 1781–1789* (Boston: Northeastern University Press, 1981), 24.
41 Ford, *Journals*, 5:551, July 12, 1776.
42 Why South Sea? Why not West Sea? Blame explorer Vasco Núñez de Balboa, who gave it that name when he saw it for the first time after crossing what is now Panama from north to south. He was facing south when he saw the Pacific Ocean. From his perspective, the name South Sea seemed apt.
43 Jensen, *New Nation*, 8–9.
44 Josiah Bartlett to John Langdon, July 29, 1776, in Smith, *Letters*, 4:557.
45 Joseph Hewes to Samuel Johnston, July 28, 1776, in *ibid.*, 4:555.
46 John Adams' Notes of Debates, July 25, 1776, in *ibid.*, 4:539.
47 John Adams' Notes of Debates, August 1, 1776, in *ibid.*, 4:592.
48 Burnett, *Continental Congress*, 221, 226.
49 *Ibid.*, 222.
50 John Adams' Notes of Debates, August 2, 1776, in Smith, *Letters*, 4:603.
51 Samuel Chase to Richard Henry Lee, July 30, 1776, in *ibid.*, 4:571.
52 William Williams to Joseph Trumbull, August 7, 1776, in *ibid.*, 4:637–38.
53 Burnett, *Continental Congress*, 219.
54 Edward Rutledge to Robert R. Livingston, August 20, 1776, in Smith, *Letters*, 5:27.
55 Burnett, *Continental Congress*, 228.
56 *Ibid.*, 206–7.
57 Ford, *Journals*, 5:556, July 18, 1776.
58 Burnett, *Continental Congress*, 207.
59 Richard S. Patterson and Richardson Dougall, *The Eagle and the Shield: A History of the Great Seal of the United States* (Washington, DC: Office of the Historian, Bureau of Public Affairs, Department of State, 1976), 14–16.
60 *Ibid.*, 10–11.
61 *Ibid.*, 12.
62 *Ibid.*, 22–23.
63 *Ibid.*, 25
64 *Ibid.*, 14.
65 Ford, *Journals*, 5:464, June 14, 1777.
66 Richard P. McCormick, "Ambiguous Authority: The Ordinances of the Confederation Congress, 1781–1789," *The American Journal of Legal History* 41, no. 4 (1997): 419.
67 *Ibid.*, 413.

Chapter 21: The Most Silent Man in France

1 Clark, *Deane*, 44
2 Words of Pierre Augustin Caron de Beaumarchais, quoted in *ibid.*
3 *Ibid.*, 49.
4 *Ibid.*, 44.
5 *Ibid.*, 49.
6 Silas Deane to the Committee of Secret Correspondence, August 2, 1776, in Sparks, *Diplomatic Correspondence*, 1:27–28
7 McCullough, *Adams*, 151.
8 David Hackett Fischer, *Washington's Crossing* (Oxford, UK: Oxford University Press, 2004), 90–93.
9 *Ibid.*, 88
10 McCullough, *Adams*, 152.
11 *Ibid.*
12 *Ibid.*
13 Ford, *Journals*, 5:730, September 3, 1776.
14 Josiah Bartlett to William Whipple, September 3, 1776, in Smith, *Letters*, 5:94.
15 John Adams to James Warren, September 8, 1776, in Robert J. Taylor, ed., *The Adams Papers*, Papers of John Adams. Vol. 5, August 1776–March 1778 (Cambridge, MA: Harvard University Press, 1983), 20–21.
16 McCullough, *Adams*, 154.
17 John Adams to James Warren, September 4, 1776, in Smith, *Letters*, 5:102.
18 John Adams to Samuel Cooper, September 4, 1776, in *ibid.*
19 *Ibid.*
20 John Hancock to Certain States, September 3, 1776, in *ibid.*, 5:96–97.
21 Ford, *Journals*, 5:733, September 3, 1776.
22 McCullough, *Adams*, 154.
23 John Adams to James Warren, September 8, 1776, in Taylor, *Adams Papers*, Papers of John Adams, 5:20–21.
24 Smith, *Adams*, 1:301.
25 John Adams Autobiography, September 3–9, 1776, in Butterfield, *Adams Papers*, Diary and Autobiography, 3:417–20.
26 McCullough, *Adams*, 155.
27 John Adams Autobiography, September 3–9, 1776, in Butterfield, *Adams Papers*, Diary and Autobiography, 3:417–20.
28 *Ibid.*
29 McCullough, *Adams*, 155.
30 John Adams Autobiography, September 3–9, 1776, in Butterfield, *Adams Papers*, Diary and Autobiography, 3:417–20.

31 John Adams Autobiography, September 3–9, 1776, in *ibid.*
32 *Ibid.*
33 Serle, *Journal*, 101, September 13, 1776.
34 John Adams Autobiography, September 17, 1776, in Butterfield, *Adams Papers*, Diary and Autobiography, 3:420–31.
35 John Adams Autobiography, September 3–9, 1776, in *ibid.*
36 McCullough, *Adams*, 158.
37 John Adams Autobiography, September 3–9, 1776, in Butterfield, *Adams Papers*, Diary and Autobiography, 3:417–20.
38 *Ibid.*
39 McCullough, *Adams*, 158–59.
40 George Washington to John Hancock, September 16, 1776, in Philander Chase and Frank E. Grizzard, Jr., eds., *The Papers of George Washington*, Revolutionary War Series. Vol. 6, 13 August 1776–20 October 1776 (Charlottesville, VA: University Press of Virginia, 1994), 313–17.
41 William Heath, *Heath's Memoirs of the American War* (New York: A. Wessels Company, 1904), 70.
42 Colonel Smallwood to Maryland Convention, October 12, 1776, in Peter Force, ed., *American Archives, Fifth Series*. Vol. 2 (Washington, DC: M. St. Clair Clarke and Peter Force, 1851), 1013.
43 George Washington to John Hancock, September 16, 1776, in Chase, *Washington*, 6:313–17.
44 George Washington to Nicholas Cooke, September 17, 1776, in *ibid.*, 6:321–26.
45 George Washington to John Hancock, September 18, 1776, in *ibid.*, 6:331–37.
46 George Washington to Lund Washington, September 30, 1776, in *ibid.*, 6:440–43.

Chapter 22: Too Many Members to Keep Secrets

1 William Hooper to Samuel Johnston, September 26, 1776, in Smith, *Letters*, 5:247.
2 Ford, *Journals*, 5:762–63, September 16, 1776.
3 Diary of John Adams, [May 16, 1776], in Butterfield, *Adams Papers*, Diary and Autobiography, 3:386–88.
4 Flexner, *Washington*, 135.
5 Benjamin Rush to Richard Henry Lee, December 21, 1776, in Smith, *Letters*, 5:639–40.
6 Ford, *Journals*, 5:827, September 26, 1776.
7 Meachum, *Jefferson*, 109.
8 Thomas Jefferson to Richard Henry Lee, July 29, 1776, in Smith, *Letters*, 4:561.
9 Benjamin Rush to Thomas Morris, October 22, 1776, in *ibid.*, 6:365.
10 Committee of Secret Correspondence Statement, October 1, 1776, in *ibid.*, 5:273.
11 *Ibid.*
12 *Ibid.*
13 Julian P. Boyd, "Silas Deane: Death by Kindly Teacher of Treason?," *The William and Mary Quarterly* 16, nos. 2–4 (1959): 176, 178–81.
14 Diary of John Adams, [April 21, 1778], in L. H. Butterfield, ed., *The Adams Papers*, Diary and Autobiography of John Adams. Vol. 4, Autobiography, Parts Two and Three, 1777–1780 (Cambridge, MA: Harvard University Press, 1961), 67–77.
15 Boyd, "Deane," 181.
16 *Ibid.*, 182–83.
17 *Ibid.*, 184.
18 Schiff, *Improvisation*, 61.
19 Boyd, "Deane," 322.
20 *Ibid.*, 323–24.
21 *Ibid.*, 326.
22 Charles Rappleye, *Robert Morris: Financier of the American Revolution* (New York: Simon & Schuster, 2010), 97.
23 *Ibid.*, 11, 14, 23, 79; Robert Morris to Silas Deane, August 11, 1776, in Smith, *Letters*, 4:656–57.
24 Rappleye, *Morris*, 97.
25 Robert Morris to Thomas Morris, January 31, 1777, in Smith, *Letters*, 6:180.
26 Rappleye, *Morris*, 99.
27 Boyd, "Deane," 327.
28 Editors of Encyclopaedia Britannica, "Pierre-Augustin Caron de Beaumarchais," *Encyclopedia Britannica*.
29 Augur, *Secret*, 115.
30 Gary Kates, "The Transgendered World of the Chevalier/Chevalière d'Eon," *The Journal of Modern History* 67, no. 3 (1995): 558.
31 Louis Leonard de Loménie, *Beaumarchais and His Times*, translated by Henry Sutherland Edwards (New York: Harper & Brothers, 1857), 243.
32 James Lander, "A Tale of Two Hoaxes in Britain and France in 1775," *The Historical Journal* 49, no. 4 (2006): 996.
33 Boatner, *Encyclopedia*, 515.
34 Augur, *Secret*, 120.

35 Boatner, *Encyclopedia*, 515.
36 Augur, *Secret*, 122.
37 Boatner, *Encyclopedia*, 515.
38 Kite, *Beaumarchais*, 2:82.
39 Augur, *Secret*, 129, 140.
40 Boatner, *Encyclopedia*, 516.
41 Robert Morris to John Jay, September 23, 1776, in Smith, *Letters*, 5:224.
42 Meacham, *Jefferson*, 119–20.
43 Richard Henry Lee to Thomas Jefferson, November 3, 1776, in James Curtis Ballagh, ed., *The Letters of Richard Henry Lee*. Vol. 1 (New York: The Macmillan Company, 1911), 222.
44 Boatner, *Encyclopedia*, 603–4.
45 Augur, *Secret*, 116.
46 Paul, *Unlikely Allies*, 139.
47 H. James Henderson, "Congressional Factionalism and the Attempt to Recall Benjamin Franklin," *The William and Mary Quarterly* 27, no. 2 (1970): 247.
48 Paul, *Unlikely Allies*, 137.
49 Augur, *Secret*, 118–19.
50 Boatner, *Encyclopedia*, 605.
51 Secret Committee to Thomas Morris, October 25, 1776, in Smith, *Letters*, 5:388.
52 Augur, *Secret*, 127.
53 Ford, *Journals*, 5:815, September 24, 1776.
54 Burnett, *Continental Congress*, 208.
55 Ford, *Journals*, 5:815–16, September 24, 1776.
56 *Ibid.*, 5:816, September 24, 1776.

Chapter 23: Excrement of Expiring Genius & Political Phrenzy

1 Wood, *Creation*, 133; Jackson Turner Main, *The Sovereign States, 1775–1783* (New York: New Viewpoints, 1973), 144–45.
2 Wood, *Creation*, 133.
3 *Ibid.*
4 *Ibid.*
5 *Ibid.*
6 *Ibid.*, 134, 137, 139, 142, 148, 193.
7 Article XXIV, Georgia Constitution of 1777, University System of Georgia, "Georgia Archives: Virtual Vault."
8 Wood, *Creation*, 163, 214.
9 *Ibid.*, 166–68.
10 "To the Inhabitants of Great Britain," September 1774, in Don Higginbotham, ed., *The Papers of James Iredell*. Vol. 1 (Raleigh, NC: State Library of North Carolina, 1976), 257.
11 The Avalon Project, "Constitution of Pennsylvania—September 28, 1776" (Yale Law School): Section 32.
12 Wood, *Creation*, 170.
13 Main, *Sovereign*, 152–53.
14 Hawke, *Revolution*, 188–89.
15 The Avalon Project, "Constitution of Pennsylvania": Section 10.
16 William Hooper to Samuel Johnston, September 26, 1776, in Smith, *Letters*, 5:248–49.
17 John Adams to Abigail Adams, October 4, 1776, in Butterfield, *Adams Papers*, Family Correspondence, 2:137–38.
18 Boatner, *Encyclopedia*, 799, 802.
19 George Washington to Lund Washington, October 6, 1776, in Chase, *Washington*, 6:493–95.
20 Benjamin L. Carp, *The Great New York Fire of 1776: A Lost Story of the American Revolution* (New Haven, CT: Yale University Press, 2023), 243.
21 Serle, *Journal*, 111, September 21, 1776.
22 Ferling, *Leap*, 186.
23 Flexner, *Washington*, 138.
24 Boatner, *Encyclopedia*, 197–206.
25 David McCullough, *1776* (New York: Simon & Schuster, 2005), 230–31.
26 Flexner, *Washington*, 148.
27 Montross, *Reluctant Rebels*, 188.
28 Willard Sterne Randall, *Benedict Arnold: Patriot and Traitor* (New York: William Morrow and Company, 1990), 283.
29 Boatner, *Encyclopedia*, 1136.
30 Fischer, *Crossing*, 111.
31 Boatner, *Encyclopedia*, 801.
32 Fischer, *Crossing*, 111.
33 Flexner, *Washington*, 142.
34 McCullough, *1776*, 234–35.
35 *Ibid.*, 236.
36 John Ferling, *Whirlwind: The American Revolution and the War that Won It* (New York: Bloomsbury Press, 2015), 175.
37 *Ibid.*, 176.
38 John Buchanan, *The Road to Charleston: Nathanael Greene and the American Revolution* (Charlottesville, VA: University of Virginia Press, 2019), 31.
39 Ferling, *Whirlwind*, 176.
40 Fischer, *Crossing*, 111.
41 Flexner, *Washington*, 147.
42 Ferling, *Whirlwind*, 176.
43 McCullough, *1776*, 243.
44 Ferling, *Winning*, 28.
45 Fischer, *Crossing*, 113.
46 Washington Irving, *Life of George Washington*. Vol. 2 (New York: G. P. Putnam & Co., 1856), 398.

47 Boatner, *Encyclopedia*, 381.
48 McCullough, *1776*, 247–48.
49 *Ibid.*, 254.
50 *Ibid.*, 249–50.
51 Charles Lee to Joseph Reed, November 24, 1776, in Charles Lee, *The Lee Papers*. Vol. 2, 1776–1778 (New York: New-York Historical Society, 1872), 307–8.
52 George Washington to Joseph Reed, November 30, 1776, in Philander Chase, ed., *The Papers of George Washington*, Revolutionary War Series. Vol. 7, 21 October 1776–5 January 1777 (Charlottesville, VA: University Press of Virginia, 1997), 237–39.
53 McCullough, *1776*, 256.
54 *Ibid.*
55 *Ibid.*, 257.
56 George Washington to Lund Washington, December 10–17, 1776, in Chase, *Washington*, 7:289–92.

Chapter 24: Our Little Handfull

1 Samuel Adams to James Warren, December 12, 1776, in Smith, *Letters*, 5:600.
2 William Young, "Journal of William Young," *The Pennsylvania Magazine of History and Biography* 8, no. 3 (1884): 255–56, editor's note.
3 Fischer, *Crossing*, 136.
4 Oliver Wolcott to Laura Wolcott, December 11, 1776, in Smith, *Letters*, 5:600.
5 Samuel Adams to James Warren, December 12, 1776, in *ibid.*, 5:601.
6 Fischer, *Crossing*, 137.
7 Ford, *Journals*, 6:1020, December 10, 1776.
8 *Ibid.*, 6:1022, December 11, 1776.
9 *Ibid.*, 6:1023, December 11, 1776.
10 George Washington to John Hancock, December 12, 1776, in Chase, *Washington*, 7:309–12.
11 Ford, *Journals*, 6:1027, December 12, 1776.
12 Boatner, *Encyclopedia*, 202.
13 Benson Bobrick, *Angel in the Whirlwind: The Triumph of the American Revolution* (New York: Penguin, 1997), 224–25.
14 James Wilkinson, *Memoirs of My Own Times*. Vol. 1 (Philadelphia: Abraham Small, 1816), 102.
15 McCullough, *1776*, 264.
16 George Washington to Lund Washington, December 10–17, 1776, in Chase, *Washington*, 7:289–92.
17 Charles Lee to Horatio Gates, December 13, 1776, in Henry Steele Commager and Richard B. Morris, *The Spirit of 'Seventy-Six: The Story of the American Revolution as Told by Participants* (New York: Harper & Row, 1967), 500.
18 Wilkinson, *Memoirs*, 1:105.
19 McCullough, *1776*, 265.
20 Banastre Tarleton to his mother, December 18, 1776, in Commager, *Spirit*, 502.
21 McCullough, *1776*, 265.
22 Wilkinson, *Memoirs*, 1:106.
23 Silas Deane to John Jay, December 3, 1776, in Deane, "Deane," 1:395.
24 Benjamin Franklin to Jacques Barbeu-Dubourg, December 4, 1776, in William B. Willcox, ed., *The Papers of Benjamin Franklin*. Vol. 23, October 27, 1776, through April 30, 1777 (New Haven, CT: Yale University Press, 1983), 23–25.
25 Benjamin Franklin to Silas Deane, December 7, 1776, in *ibid.*, 23:28–30.
26 Schiff, *Improvisation*, 28.
27 Dull, *Franklin*, 71.
28 Schiff, *Improvisation*, xii, 50–51.
29 Dull, *Franklin*, 71.
30 Schiff, *Improvisation*, 91.
31 *Ibid.*, 38–39, 91.
32 *Ibid.*, 40.
33 *Ibid.*, 40, 42.
34 *Ibid.*, 43, 86.
35 *Ibid.*, 55.
36 Robert Morris to Silas Deane, August 11, 1776, in Smith, *Letters*, 4:657.
37 Louis W. Potts, *Arthur Lee: A Virtuous Revolutionary* (Baton Rouge, LA: Louisiana State University Press, 1981), 161–62.
38 *Ibid.*, 164–66, 174.
39 Dull, *Franklin*, 69.
40 Schiff, *Improvisation*, 31.
41 Dull, *Franklin*, 69.
42 *Ibid.*, 70.

Chapter 25: Dismal & Melancoly

1 Richard Howe and William Howe, "Proclamation of Admiral Howe and General Howe, November 30, 1776," Naval Documents of the American Revolution Digital Edition.
2 Joseph E. Wroblewski, "Winning Hearts and Minds: Pardons and Oaths of Allegiance," *Journal of the American Revolution*, January 3, 2023.
3 George Washington to Lund Washington, December 10–17, 1776, in Chase, *Washington*, 7:289–92.
4 Boatner, *Encyclopedia*, 1060.

5. George Corner, ed., *The Autobiography of Benjamin Rush: His 'Travels through Life' together with his Commonplace Book* (Westport, CT: Greenwood Press, 1970), 147.
6. Boatner, *Encyclopedia*, 1061.
7. Fischer, *Crossing*, 164.
8. Boatner, *Encyclopedia*, 1061.
9. Fischer, *Crossing*, 164.
10. Corner, *Rush*, 147.
11. Ford, *Journals*, 6:1027, December 12, 1776.
12. Oliver Wolcott to Laura Wolcott, December 13, 1776, in Smith, *Letters*, 5:606.
13. Montross, *Reluctant Rebels*, 191.
14. Rappleye, *Morris*, 90–91.
15. Robert Morris to Silas Deane, December 20, 1776, in Smith, *Letters*, 5:622.
16. Nelson, *Paine*, 102.
17. Fischer, *Crossing*, 140.
18. Thomas Paine to Henry Laurens, January 14, 1779, Thomas Paine National Historical Association (New Rochelle, NY).
19. Thomas Paine to Benjamin Franklin, June 20, 1777, in *ibid.*
20. John Hancock to Robert Treat Paine, January 13, 1777, in Smith, *Letters*, 6:91.
21. Edith Rossiter Bevan, "The Continental Congress in Baltimore, Dec. 20, 1776 to Feb. 27, 1777," *Maryland Historical Magazine* 42, no. 1 (1947): 22.
22. Oliver Wolcott to Laura Wolcott, January 2, 1777, in Smith, *Letters*, 6:14.
23. William Hooper to Robert Morris, December 28, 1776, in *ibid.*, 5:689.
24. William Ellery to Nickolas Cooke, January 4, 1777, in *ibid.*, 6:30–31.
25. John Hancock to Robert Morris, January 2, 1777, in *ibid.*, 6:22.
26. John Hancock to Robert Treat Paine, January 13, 1777, in *ibid.*, 6:91.
27. James Smith to Eleanor Smith, December 31, 1776, in *ibid.*, 5:715.
28. John Adams to Abigail Adams, February 2, 1777, in Butterfield, *Adams Papers*, Family Correspondence, 2:151–52.
29. John Adams to Abigail Adams, February 3, 1777, in *ibid.*, 2:152–53.
30. John Adams to Abigail Adams, February 2, 1777, in *ibid.*, 2:151–52.
31. Diary of John Adams, February 6, 1777, in Smith, *Letters*, 6:224.
32. Bevan, "Baltimore," 23.
33. Diary of John Adams, February 6, 1777, in Smith, *Letters*, 6:224.
34. Rappleye, *Morris*, 91.
35. Robert Morris to John Hancock, December 16, 1776, in Smith, *Letters*, 5:611–12.
36. Fischer, *Crossing*, 128, 136.
37. *Ibid.*, 160.
38. *Ibid.*, 116, 137.
39. Ferling, *Winning*, 33.
40. Bobrick, *Angel*, 230.
41. William Whipple to Josiah Bartlett, December 23, 1776, in Smith, *Letters*, 5:652.
42. Ford, *Journals*, 6:1032, December 21, 1776.
43. Rappleye, *Morris*, 91.
44. Robert Morris to John Hancock, December 21, 1776, in Smith, *Letters*, 5:636–37.
45. Robert Morris to Silas Deane, December 20, 1776, in *ibid.*, 5:626.
46. Ford, *Journals*, 6:1041, December 26, 1776.
47. *Ibid.*, 6:1031, December 21, 1776.
48. George Washington to John Hancock, December 20, 1776, in Chase, *Washington*, 7:381–89.
49. Nathanael Greene to John Hancock, December 21, 1776, in Fischer, *Crossing*, 144.
50. Bobrick, *Angel*, 229; Ferling, *Whirlwind*, 185; Ford, *Journals*, 6:1045–46, December 27, 1776.
51. Ford, *Journals*, 6:1053, December 30, 1776.
52. William Whipple to Josiah Bartlett, December 31, 1776, in Smith, *Letters*, 5:715–16.
53. Samuel Adams to James Warren, January 1, 1777, in *ibid.*, 6:3.
54. John Adams to Abigail Adams, April 6, 1777, in Butterfield, *Adams Papers*, Family Correspondence, 2:199–201.
55. Ferling, *Whirlwind*, 179.
56. Bobrick, *Angel*, 229.
57. Joseph Reed to George Washington, December 22, 1776, in Chase, *Washington*, 7:414–17.
58. Fischer, *Crossing*, 151.
59. *Ibid.*, 126, 174.
60. Journal of Charles Willson Peale, December 27, 1776, in Horace Wells Sellers and C. W. Peale, "Charles Willson Peale, Artist-Soldier," *The Pennsylvania Magazine of History and Biography* 38, no. 3 (1914): 277.
61. Fischer, *Crossing*, 174, 178–79, 181.
62. Bobrick, *Angel*, 230.
63. Fischer, *Crossing*, 193, 195.
64. Bobrick, *Angel*, 230.

Chapter 26: Violent, Seditious, Treasonable

1. Nelson, *Paine*, 108.
2. Diary of Sarah Logan Fisher, January 1, 1777, in Nicholas B. Wainwright and Sarah Logan

2 Fisher, "'A Diary of Trifling Occurrences': Philadelphia, 1776–1778," *The Pennsylvania Magazine of History and Biography* 82, no. 4 (1958): 420.
3 Fischer, *Crossing*, 142.
4 Thomas Paine, "The Crisis I," *Pennsylvania Packet*, December 27, 1776, January 4, 1777. Emphasis in original.
5 Bobrick, *Angel*, 230.
6 Ferling, *Whirlwind*, 180–81.
7 Bobrick, *Angel*, 231–32.
8 Ferling, *Whirlwind*, 181.
9 Fischer, *Crossing*, 205.
10 Bobrick, *Angel*, 232.
11 Fischer, *Crossing*, 205.
12 Bobrick, *Angel*, 233.
13 Boatner, *Encyclopedia*, 1115.
14 George Washington to John Hancock, December 27, 1776, in Chase, *Washington*, 7:454–61, footnote 14.
15 James Smith to Eleanor Smith, December 31, 1776, in Smith, *Letters*, 5:714.
16 William Ellery to Nicholas Cooke, December 31, 1776, in *ibid.*, 5:711.
17 George Clymer and George Walton to John Hancock, December 30, 1776, in *ibid.*, 5:700.
18 Ferling, *Whirlwind*, 181.
19 Boatner, *Encyclopedia*, 785.
20 Bobrick, *Angel*, 234.
21 *Ibid.*, 31–32, 234.
22 *Ibid.*, 234.
23 Ferling, *Whirlwind*, 182.
24 *Ibid.*
25 Boatner, *Encyclopedia*, 925.
26 Ferling, *Whirlwind*, 183.
27 Boatner, *Encyclopedia*, 746.
28 Bobrick, *Angel*, 235.
29 Boatner, *Encyclopedia*, 746.
30 William Hooper to Robert Morris, February 1, 1777, in Smith, *Letters*, 6:191.
31 Farley Grubb, *The Continental Dollar: How the American Revolution Was Financed with Paper Money* (Chicago: University of Chicago Press, 2023), Table C.I.
32 Ferguson, *Power*, 30.
33 Ralph Volney Harlow, "Aspects of Revolutionary Finance, 1775–1783," *The American Historical Review* 35, no. 1 (1929): 47.
34 Ferguson, *Power*, 30.
35 *Ibid.*
36 Robert Morris to the Commissioners in France, December 21, 1776, in Commager, *Spirit*, 789.
37 *Ibid.*, 790.
38 *Ibid.*
39 Benjamin Rush to Robert Morris, February 22, 1777, in Smith, *Letters*, 6:346.
40 Grubb, *Dollar*, 87.
41 *Ibid.*, 91.
42 Lucius Wilmerding, Jr., "The United States Lottery," *The New-York Historical Society Quarterly* 47, no. 1 (1963): 8–9.
43 *Ibid.*, 9–10.
44 McGaughy, *Lee*, 57.
45 Ferguson, *Power*, 35.
46 Wilmerding, "Lottery," 36.
47 Ford, *Journals*, 6:1036–37, December 23, 1776.
48 Jonathan Grossman, "Wage and Price Controls During the American Revolution," *Monthly Labor Review* 96, no. 9 (1973): 4.
49 E. M. Coleman, "New England Convention: December 25, 1776, to January 2, 1777: An Illustration of Early American Particularism," *The Historian* 4, no. 1 (1941): 44.
50 *Ibid.*, 45.
51 Charles J. Hoadly, *The Public Records of the State of Connecticut, from October, 1776, to February, 1778, Inclusive*. Vol. 1 (Hartford, CT: Case, Lockwood & Brainard Company, 1894), 585.
52 Providence Convention, December 27, 1776, in *ibid.*, 1:589.
53 Governor Trumbull to the President of Congress, December 23, 1776, in Peter Force, ed., *American Archives, Fifth Series*. Vol. 3 (Washington, DC: M. St. Clair Clarke and Peter Force, 1853), 1389.
54 Providence Convention, December 26–31, 1776, in Hoadly, *Connecticut*, 1:589–90, 1:592–93, 1:595.
55 Providence Convention, January 1, 1777, in *ibid.*, 1:598.
56 Benjamin Rush's Notes of Debates, February 14, 1777, in Smith, *Letters*, 6:275.
57 *Ibid.*, 6:274–75.
58 *Ibid.*, 6:276.
59 Ford, *Journals*, 7:124, February 15, 1777.
60 *Ibid.*, 7:124–25, February 15, 1777; Coleman, "Convention," 52.
61 Grossman, "Wage," 5.

Chapter 27: Great and Interesting Consequences

1 Montross, *Reluctant Rebels*, 198.
2 William Hooper to Robert Morris, February 1, 1777, in Smith, *Letters*, 6:192.
3 Ford, *Journals*, 7:61, January 24, 1777.
4 Smith, *Letters*, 6:175, footnote 4.

5   Benjamin Rush's Notes of Debates, February 4, 1777, in *ibid.*, 6:218.
6   *Ibid.*, 6:217–18.
7   Samuel Adams to John Adams, January 9, 1777, in *ibid.*, 6:64.
8   Robert Morris to John Jay, February 4, 1777, in *ibid.*, 6:216.
9   William Hooper to Robert Morris, December 28, 1776, in Stan V. Henkels, ed., *The Confidential Correspondence of Robert Morris* (Philadelphia: Stan V. Henkels, 1917), 23.
10 John Hancock to Robert Morris, January 14, 1777, in Smith, *Letters*, 6:99.
11 Rossie, *Politics*, 61.
12 *Ibid.*, 61–63, 70.
13 *Ibid.*, 73.
14 Elbridge Gerry to Horatio Gates, September 27, 1776, in Smith, *Letters*, 5:254.
15 Rossie, *Politics*, 135.
16 *Ibid.*, 138.
17 Ford, *Journals*, 7:133, February 19, 1777.
18 Thomas Burke's Notes of Debates, February 12–9, 1777, in Smith, *Letters*, 6:264.
19 Boatner, *Encyclopedia*, 26.
20 Anderson, *Fourteenth*, 330.
21 Wilkinson, *Memoirs*, 1:54–55.
22 Boatner, *Encyclopedia*, 1136.
23 Randall, *Arnold*, 323–24.
24 *Ibid.*, 326–28.
25 Barry K. Wilson, *Benedict Arnold: A Traitor in Our Midst* (Montreal: McGill-Queen's University Press, 2001), 135.
26 Benedict Arnold to George Washington, March 11, 1777, in Frank E. Grizzard, ed., *The Papers of George Washington*, Revolutionary War Series. Vol. 8, 6 January 1777–27 March 1777 (Charlottesville, VA: University Press of Virginia, 1998), 551–53.
27 Benedict Arnold to George Washington, March 26, 1777, in *ibid.*, 8:634–35.
28 George Washington to Benedict Arnold, April 2, 1777, in Philander Chase, ed., *The Papers of George Washington*, Revolutionary War Series. Vol. 9, 28 March 1777–10 June 1777 (Charlottesville, VA: University Press of Virginia, 1999), 45–46.
29 Nathaniel Philbrick, *Valiant Ambition: George Washington, Benedict Arnold, and the Fate of the American Revolution* (New York: Viking, 2016), 91.
30 Benedict Arnold to Horatio Gates, March 25, 1777, in *ibid.*, 91.

Chapter 28: Worst of All Possible Places

1   William Hooper to Robert Morris, February 1, 1777, in Smith, *Letters*, 6:191.
2   Abraham Clark to James Caldwell, February 4, 1777, in *ibid.*, 6:210.
3   William Whipple to Josiah Bartlett, February 7, 1777, in *ibid.*, 6:237.
4   Benjamin Rush to Robert Morris, February 8, 1777, in *ibid.*, 6:245.
5   Richard Henry Lee to Arthur Lee, February 17, 1777, in *ibid.*, 6:309.
6   Jonathan Dickinson Sergeant to John Hart, February 5, 1777, in *ibid.*, 6:224.
7   Samuel Adams to Elizabeth Adams, January 29, 1777, in *ibid.*, 6:157.
8   Oliver Wolcott to Laura Wolcott, January 22, 1777, in *ibid.*, 6:129.
9   Montross, *Reluctant Rebels*, 200.
10 John Hancock to Dorothy Hancock, March 5, 1777, in Smith, *Letters*, 6:397.
11 Montross, *Reluctant Rebels*, 200–1.
12 *Ibid.*, 200.
13 John Adams to Abigail Adams, March 7, 1777, in Butterfield, *Adams Papers*, Family Correspondence, 2:169–70.
14 Mann Page to George Weedon, March 5, 1777, in Smith, *Letters*, 6:388.
15 Montross, *Reluctant Rebels*, 200.
16 Fischer, *Crossing*, 347–48.
17 John Adams to Abigail Adams, February 17, 1777, in Butterfield, *Adams Papers*, Family Correspondence, 2:162–63.
18 Fischer, *Crossing*, 348, 355.
19 Robert Morris to George Washington, February 27, 1777, in Grizzard, *Washington*, 8:456–58.
20 Richard Henry Lee to George Washington, February 27, 1777, in Smith, *Letters*, 6:384.
21 John Adams to James Warren, June 11, 1777, in *ibid.*, 7:182.
22 Fischer, *Crossing*, 359.
23 Potts, *Lee*, 167.
24 John Adams to Robert R. Livingston, February 21, 1782, in Gregg L. Lint, Richard Alan Ryerson, Anne Decker Cecere, C. James Taylor, Jennifer Shea, Celeste Walker, and Margaret A. Hogan, eds., *The Adams Papers*, Papers of John Adams. Vol. 12, October 1781–April 1782 (Cambridge, MA: Harvard University Press, 2004), 250–59.
25 James H. Hutson, *John Adams and the Diplomacy of the American Revolution* (Lexington, KY: University Press of Kentucky, 1980), 153.

26 James Wilson to Robert Morris, January 14, 1777, in Smith, *Letters*, 6:104.
27 Benjamin Franklin to Arthur Lee, March 21, 1777, in Willcox, *Franklin*, 23:508–11.
28 Potts, *Lee*, 167.
29 Ibid.
30 Ibid., 169.
31 Ibid., 169–70.
32 Ibid., 169.
33 Ibid., 170.
34 Ibid., 171.
35 Boatner, *Encyclopedia*, 853–54.
36 Robert Morris to George Washington, February 27, 1777, in Smith, *Letters*, 6:389.
37 Thomas Burke to Richard Caswell, March 11, 1777, in *ibid.*, 6:430.
38 William Whipple to Josiah Bartlett, February 7, 1777, in *ibid.*, 6:236.
39 Jennings B. Sanders, "Thomas Burke in the Continental Congress," *The North Carolina Historical Review* 9, no. 1 (1932): 22.
40 Elisha P. Douglass, "Thomas Burke, Disillusioned Democrat," *The North Carolina Historical Review* 6, no. 2 (April 1949): 151, 154.
41 John S. Watterson, "Thomas Burke, Paradoxical Patriot," *The Historian* 41, no. 4 (1979): 674.
42 Sanders, "Burke," 22.
43 Thomas Burke's Notes of Debates, February 7, 1777, in Smith, *Letters*, 6:231.
44 Watterson, "Paradoxical," 668.
45 Thomas Burke's Notes of Debates, February 25, 1777, in Smith, *Letters*, 6:356–57.
46 Ford, *Journals*, 7:154, February 25, 1777.
47 Montross, *Reluctant Rebels*, 202.
48 Ford, *Journals*, 5:547, July 12, 1776.
49 Thomas Burke to Richard Caswell, April 29, 1777, in Smith, *Letters*, 6:672.
50 Burnett, *Continental Congress*, 238.
51 Thomas Burke to Richard Caswell, April 29, 1777, in Smith, *Letters*, 6:672.
52 Montross, *Reluctant Rebels*, 202–3.
53 Articles as Approved, November 15, 1777, in Rakove, *Founding*, 160–61; Watterson, "Paradoxical," 668.
54 Seth Lipsky, *The Citizen's Constitution: An Annotated Guide* (New York: Basic Books, 2009), 244.
55 The Bill of Rights, Amendment X, in Rakove, *Founding*, 639.
56 Thomas Burke to Richard Caswell, May 2, 1777, in Smith, *Letters*, 7:14.

Chapter 29: Laying the Foundation of Future Evils

1 Burnett, *Continental Congress*, 239.
2 Watterson, "Paradoxical," 669.
3 Thomas Burke to Richard Caswell, May 23, 1777, in Smith, *Letters*, 7:109.
4 Charles Carroll to Benjamin Franklin, August 12, 1777, in William B. Willcox, ed., *The Papers of Benjamin Franklin*. Vol. 24, May 1 through September 30, 1777 (New Haven, CT: Yale University Press, 1984), 417–21.
5 Ford, *Journals*, 8:704, September 2, 1777.
6 Schiff, *Improvisation*, 146.
7 William Lee to Richard Henry Lee, January 9, 1778, in Worthington Chauncey Ford, ed., *Letters of William Lee*. Vol. 1 (Brooklyn, NY: Historical Printing Club, 1891), 335.
8 William Lee to Richard Henry Lee, January 2, 1778, in *ibid.*, 1:315.
9 Jonathan Singerton, *The American Revolution and the Habsburg Monarchy* (Charlottesville, VA: University of Virginia Press, 2021), 101–2.
10 Potts, *Lee*, 169.
11 Ibid., 180–81.
12 Singerton, *Habsburg*, 102–3.
13 Schiff, *Improvisation*, 72.
14 Samuel Flagg Bemis, "British Secret Service and French–American Alliance," *The American Historical Review* 29, no. 3 (1924): 480–81.
15 William Eden to George III, October 20, 1777, in *ibid.*, 481.
16 Schiff, *Improvisation*, 70.
17 Montross, *Reluctant Rebels*, 427.
18 William Lee to Richard Henry Lee, March 23, 1778, in Worthington Chauncey Ford, ed., *Letters of William Lee*. Vol. 2. (Brooklyn, NY: Historical Printing Club, 1891), 409.
19 Bemis, "Secret," 474–75.
20 Potts, *Lee*, 180, 201–2.
21 Ibid., 175.
22 Arthur Lee to Benjamin Franklin and Silas Deane, May 27, 1777, in Willcox, *Franklin*, 24:91.
23 Singerton, *Habsburg*, 101.
24 Schiff, *Improvisation*, 73.
25 Potts, *Lee*, 176.
26 Schiff, *Improvisation*, 77, 80.
27 Ibid., 36, 86–90, 107.
28 William Temple Franklin to Jonathan Williams, Sr., May 27, 1777, in *ibid.*, 90.
29 Ferguson, *Power*, 85.

30 Schiff, *Improvisation*, 60.
31 *Ibid.*, 96, 101.
32 Boatner, *Encyclopedia*, 315.
33 Philbrick, *Valiant Ambition*, 95, 97.
34 John Adams to Abigail Adams, April 30, 1777, in Smith, *Letters*, 6:687.
35 Philbrick, *Valiant Ambition*, 96, 98.
36 John Adams to Abigail Adams, May 2, 1777, in Smith, *Letters*, 7:12.
37 John Adams to Nathanael Greene, May 9, 1777, in *ibid.*, 7:48.
38 Ford, *Journals*, 8:382, May 23, 1777.
39 *Ibid.*, 7:372, May 20, 1777.
40 Thomas Burke to Richard Caswell, April 29, 1777, in Smith, *Letters*, 6:671.
41 Wilbur, *Allen*, 91.
42 William Slade, *Vermont State Papers* (Middlebury, VT: J. W. Copeland, 1823), 70.
43 Ford, *Journals*, 4:342, May 10, 1776.
44 Wilbur, *Allen*, 92.
45 William Whipple to Josiah Bartlett, April 7, 1777, in Smith, *Letters*, 6:550.
46 Thomas Burke to Richard Caswell, May 23, 1777, in *ibid.*, 7:109.
47 Ford, *Journals*, 7:671–72, April 29, 1777.
48 Thomas Burke to Richard Caswell, May 23, 1777, in Smith, *Letters*, 7:109.
49 Abraham Ten Broeck to John Hancock, March 1, 1777, in Slade, *Vermont*, 75.
50 Abraham Ten Broeck to John Hancock, January 20, 1777, in *ibid.*, 73.
51 William Whipple to Josiah Bartlett, April 7, 1777, in Smith, *Letters*, 6:550.
52 Samuel Adams to Richard Henry Lee, June 29, 1777, in *ibid.*, 7:264.
53 Ford, *Journals*, 8:509, June 30, 1777.
54 Slade, *Vermont*, 79.
55 Randall, *Allen*, 444–45.

Chapter 30: A Great Expenditure of Liquor, Powder &c

1 Ford, *Journals*, 8:518, July 1, 1777.
2 *Ibid.*, 8:519, July 1, 1777.
3 *Ibid.*, 8:520, July 1, 1777.
4 Boatner, *Encyclopedia*, 546–47.
5 Singerton, *Habsburg*, 99.
6 *Ibid.*
7 *Ibid.*, 100.
8 Silas Deane to John Jay, December 3, 1776, in Deane, "Deane," 1:396.
9 Singerton, *Habsburg*, 100.
10 Silas Deane to John Jay, December 3, 1776, in Deane, "Deane," 1:396.
11 John Adams to Abigail Adams 2d, July 5, 1777, in Butterfield, *Adams Papers*, Family Correspondence, 2:274–75.
12 *Ibid.*
13 William Williams to Jonathan Trumbull, Sr., July 5, 1777, in Smith, *Letters*, 7:303.
14 Diary of Sarah Logan Fisher, July 4, 1777, in Wainwright, "Diary," 437–38.
15 William H. Gaines, Jr., "The Continental Congress Considers the Publication of a Bible, 1777," *Studies in Bibliography* 3 (1950): 276–77.
16 Philadelphia Printers, *ca.* July 7, 1777, in Smith, *Letters*, 7:311.
17 Gaines, "Bible," 276.
18 Philadelphia Printers, *ca.* July 7, 1777, in Smith, *Letters*, 7:312.
19 David Duncan Wallace, *The Life of Henry Laurens* (New York: G. P. Putnam's Sons, 1915), 5–7, 9, 13.
20 *Ibid.*, 15, 17.
21 Joseph P. Kelly, "Henry Laurens: The Southern Man of Conscience in History," *The South Carolina Historical Magazine* 107, no. 2 (2006): 106.
22 Wallace, *Laurens*, 47.
23 Kelly, "Laurens," 112.
24 Wallace, *Laurens*, 90.
25 Kelly, "Laurens," 107; Wallace, *Laurens*, 76.
26 Kelly, "Laurens," 104, 106.
27 Wallace, *Laurens*, 76
28 *Ibid.*, 57–59.
29 Henry Laurens to James Habersham, October 1, 1770, in *ibid.*, 181.
30 *Ibid.*, 60.
31 *Ibid.*, 96, 130.
32 Philip M. Hamer, "Henry Laurens of South Carolina: The Man and His Papers," *Proceedings of the Massachusetts Historical Society* 77 (1965): 4.
33 Wallace, *Laurens*, 95, 109.
34 *Ibid.*, 122, 148.
35 *Ibid.*, 179.
36 *Ibid.*, 182–83.
37 *Ibid.*, 185.
38 *Ibid.*, 197, 199, 205.
39 *Ibid.*, 226, 468.
40 *Ibid.*, 213, 221.
41 Henry Laurens letter, February 1776, in *ibid.*, 225.
42 *Ibid.*, 224.
43 Kelly, "Laurens," 91.
44 Henry Laurens to John Laurens, August 14, 1776, in Commager, *Spirit*, 405.
45 Wallace, *Laurens*, 45.

46 Henry Laurens to John Laurens, August 14, 1776, in Commager, *Spirit*, 405.
47 Kelly, "Laurens," 88.
48 Gregory D. Massey, "The Limits of Antislavery Thought in the Revolutionary Lower South: John Laurens and Henry Laurens," *The Journal of Southern History* 63, no. 3 (1997): 529.
49 Wallace, *Laurens*, 226–27.
50 Henry Laurens to William Brisbane, August 14, 1777, in Smith, *Letters*, 7:480.
51 Henry Laurens to John Lewis Gervais, August 9, 1777, in *ibid.*, 7:444.
52 Henry Laurens to Gebriel Manigault, August 15, 1777, in *ibid.*, 7:487.
53 Henry Laurens to John Lewis Gervais, August 9, 1777, in *ibid.*, 7:444.
54 Henry Laurens to John Rutledge, August 12, 1777, in *ibid.*, 7:466.
55 Henry O. Robertson, "Tories or Patriots? The Mississippi River Planters during the American Revolution," *Louisiana History: The Journal of the Louisiana Historical Association* 40, no. 4 (1999): 446.
56 *Ibid.*, 453.
57 Henry Laurens to John Rutledge, August 12, 1777, in Smith, *Letters*, 7:467.
58 *Ibid.*
59 Robertson, "Tories," 462.
60 Henry Laurens to John Rutledge, August 12, 1777, in Smith, *Letters*, 7:468.
61 Henry Laurens to John Lewis Gervais, September 5, 1777, in *ibid.*, 7:607–8.
62 Henry Laurens to John Lewis Gervais, September 8, 1777, in *ibid.*, 7:634.
63 Henry Laurens to John Lewis Gervais, September 5, 1777, in *ibid.*, 7:607.
64 Henry Laurens to John Lewis Gervais, September 8, 1777, in *ibid.*, 7:634.
65 John Adams to Abigail Adams, July 10, 1777, in Butterfield, *Adams Papers*, Family Correspondence, 2:278.
66 Abigail Adams to John Adams, July 16, 1777, in *ibid.*, 2:282–83.
67 John Adams to Abigail Adams, July 28, 1777, in *ibid.*, 2:292.
68 John Adams to Abigail Adams, August 3, 1777, in *ibid.*, 2:298–99.
69 John Adams to Abigail Adams, August 19, 1777, in *ibid.*, 2:319–20.
70 Wallace, *Laurens*, 229.

Chapter 31: A Painful Dilemma

1 Burnett, *Continental Congress*, 241.
2 Eric Spall, "Foreigners in the Highest Trust: American Perceptions of European Mercenary Officers in the Continental Army," *Early American Studies* 12, no. 2 (2014): 339, 346–47.
3 Thomas Jefferson to John Page, July 30, 1776, in Smith, *Letters*, 4:579.
4 Josiah Bartlett to John Langdon, October 19, 1776, in *ibid.*, 5:354.
5 Robert Morris to William Bingham, February 16, 1777, in *ibid.*, 6:301.
6 Ford, *Journals*, 7:174, March 13, 1777.
7 Henry Laurens to John Lewis Gervais, August 5, 1777, in Smith, *Letters*, 7:421.
8 Boatner, *Encyclopedia*, 1117.
9 Spall, "Foreigners," 360.
10 Silas Deane to Secret Committee of Congress, November 28, 1776, in Deane, "Deane," 1:377.
11 Edward E. Hale and Edward E. Hale, Jr., *Franklin in France* (Boston: Roberts Brothers, 1887), 47.
12 Letter from Pierre Augustin Caron de Beaumarchais, January 22, 1777, in John Durand, *New Materials for the History of the American Revolution* (New York: Henry Holt and Company, 1889), 106.
13 Hale, *Franklin*, 48.
14 George Washington to William Heath, June 1, 1777, in Chase, *Washington*, 9:579.
15 "The Continental Congress at Mass—Two Te Deums and Two Requiems. Washington at Catholic Burial Service," *The American Catholic Historical Researches* 6, no. 2 (1889): 53.
16 Elizabeth S. Kite, "General Washington and the French Engineers Duportail and Companions," *Record of the American Catholic Historical Society of Philadelphia* 43, no. 1 (1932): 4–5.
17 James Lovell to William Whipple, June 30, 1777, in Smith, *Letters*, 7:275.
18 John Adams to Nathanael Greene, June 2, 1777, in *ibid.*, 7:163.
19 John Adams to James Warren, June 19, 1777, in *ibid.*, 7:221.
20 Eliphalet Dyer to Joseph Trumbull, July 7, 1777, in *ibid.*, 7:313.
21 John Adams to Nathanael Greene, July 7, 1777, in *ibid.*, 7:306–7.
22 Ford, *Journals*, 8:537, July 7, 1777.
23 "Congress at Mass," 50.
24 Burnett, *Continental Congress*, 243.
25 Boatner, *Encyclopedia*, 1117.
26 Kite, "Washington," 6.
27 Diary of John Adams, September 18, 1777, in Butterfield, *Adams Papers*, Diary and Autobiography of John Adams, 2:263–64.

28. Kite, "Washington," 6.
29. Henry Laurens to John Rutledge, August 12, 1777, in Smith, *Letters*, 7:470.
30. Gonzague Saint Bris, *Lafayette: Hero of the American Revolution*, translated by George Holoch (New York: Pegasus Books, 2010), 19, 26–27, 30.
31. Bobrick, *Angel*, 293.
32. Marie Joseph Paul Yves Roch Gilbert Du Motier, Marquis de Lafayette, *Memoirs, Correspondence and Manuscripts of General Lafayette*. Vol. 1 (New York: Saunders and Otley, 1837), 7.
33. Laura Auricchio, *The Marquis: Lafayette Reconsidered* (New York: Alfred A. Knopf, 2014), 30.
34. Boatner, *Encyclopedia*, 570.
35. Lafayette, *Memoirs*, 8.
36. Ibid.
37. Saint Bris, *Lafayette*, 45, 79.
38. Agreement with General Lafayette, December 7, 1776, in Deane, "Deane," 1:410.
39. Auricchio, *Marquis*, 33.
40. Lafayette, *Memoirs*, 13.
41. Auricchio, *Marquis*, 39, 44–45.
42. Ibid., 45.
43. Ford, *Journals*, 8:592–3, July 31, 1777.
44. Henry Laurens to John Lewis Gervais, August 5, 1777, in Smith, *Letters*, 7:421–22.
45. Auricchio, *Marquis*, 47.
46. Ibid., 49.
47. George Washington to William Heath, July 27, 1777, in Frank E. Grizzard, ed., *The Papers of George Washington*, Revolutionary War Series. Vol. 10, 11 June 1777–18 August 1777 (Charlottesville, VA: University Press of Virginia, 2000), 437–38.
48. George Washington to Benjamin Harrison, August 19, 1777, in Philander Chase and Edward G. Lengel, eds., *The Papers of George Washington*, Revolutionary War Series. Vol. 11, 19 August 1777–25 October 1777 (Charlottesville, VA: University Press of Virginia, 2001), 4–5.
49. Benjamin Harrison to George Washington, August 20, 1777, in *ibid.*, 11:13–14.

Chapter 32: The Wretched Spectator of a Ruin'd Army

1. Bobrick, *Angel*, 243.
2. Richard M. Ketchum, *Saratoga: Turning Point of America's Revolutionary War* (New York: Henry Holt and Company, 1997), 85.
3. Rossie, *Politics*, 148, 152.
4. Ibid., 38, 60.
5. Boatner, *Encyclopedia*, 991.
6. Ferling, *Leap*, 201.
7. Rossie, *Politics*, 59–60, 100, 168.
8. William Duer to John Jay, May 28, 1777, in Smith, *Letters*, 7:139.
9. McGaughy, *Lee*, 130–32.
10. William Duer to Robert R. Livingston, July 9, 1777, in Smith, *Letters*, 7:327–28.
11. Boatner, *Encyclopedia*, 412.
12. Ketchum, *Saratoga*, 52.
13. Boatner, *Encyclopedia*, 412.
14. Thomas Fleming, *Washington's Secret War: The Hidden History of Valley Forge* (New York: Smithsonian Books, 2006), 109.
15. Dean Snow, *1777: Tipping Point at Saratoga* (New York: Oxford University Press, 2016), 11.
16. Bernard Knollenberg, "The Correspondence of John Adams and Horatio Gates," *Proceedings of the Massachusetts Historical Society* 67 (1941): 136.
17. Diary of John Adams, [May 16, 1776], in Butterfield, *Adams Papers*, Diary and Autobiography, 3:386–88.
18. John Adams to Horatio Gates, April 27, 1776, in Taylor, *Adams Papers*, Papers of John Adams, 4:146–48.
19. Ford, *Journals*, 4:359, May 16, 1776.
20. Ibid., 5:448, June 17, 1776.
21. Benson J. Lossing, *The Life and Times of Philip Schuyler*. Vol. 2 (New York: Sheldon & Company, 1873), 98.
22. Ford, *Journals*, 5:526, July 8, 1776.
23. Rossie, *Politics*, 110.
24. Ibid., 111, 127.
25. Philip Schuyler to George Washington, July 17, 1776, in Chase, *Washington*, 5:367–68.
26. Horatio Gates to John Adams, July 17, 1776, in Taylor, *Adams Papers*, Papers of John Adams, 4:388–89.
27. Rossie, *Politics*, 122.
28. Ibid., 122–25.
29. Edward Rutledge to Robert R. Livingston, September 23, 1776, in Smith, *Letters*, 5:227.
30. William Williams to Joseph Trumbull, September 28, 1776, in *ibid.*, 5:260.
31. Ford, *Journals*, 5:841, October 2, 1776.
32. Ibid., 7:24, January 9, 1777.
33. Boatner, *Encyclopedia*, 992.
34. Ford, *Journals*, 7:180, March 15, 1777.
35. Samuel Adams to John Adams, January 9, 1777, in Smith, *Letters*, 6:65.
36. John Hancock to Horatio Gates, March 25, 1777, in *ibid.*, 6:486.
37. Lossing, *Schuyler*, 2:169.

38 *Ibid.*, 2:167–68.
39 Rossie, *Politics*, 147.
40 New York Delegates to the New York Convention, May 9, 1777, in Smith, *Letters*, 7:51.
41 Rossie, *Politics*, 147.
42 *Ibid.*
43 Ford, *Journals*, 7:364, May 15, 1777.
44 William Duer to Robert Livingston, May 28, 1777, James Lovell to Oliver Wolcott, June 7, 1777, Samuel Adams to James Warren, July 31, 1777, in Smith, *Letters*, 7:140, 7:173, 7:396.
45 James Lovell to Horatio Gates, May 22, 1777, in *ibid.*, 7:106.
46 William Duer to Philip Schuyler, June 19, 1777, in *ibid.*, 7:228.
47 Horatio Gates' Notes for a Speech to Congress, June 18, 1777, in *ibid.*, 7:214.
48 William Duer to Philip Schuyler, June 19, 1777, in *ibid.*, 7:229.
49 James Duane to Robert R. Livingston, July 8, 1777, in *ibid.*, 7:321.
50 Ford, *Journals*, 8:540, July 8, 1777.
51 Rossie, *Politics*, 153.

Chapter 33: Marks of Deliberation & Design

1 Bobrick, *Angel*, 248.
2 Snow, *1777*, 8.
3 Bobrick, *Angel*, 249.
4 George Washington to Philip Schuyler, March 12, 1777, in Grizzard, *Washington*, 8:560–63.
5 Bobrick, *Angel*, 250; Rossie, *Politics*, 154.
6 John Ferling, *Almost a Miracle: The American Victory in the War of Independence* (Oxford, UK: Oxford University Press, 2007), 219.
7 Ketchum, *Saratoga*, 118.
8 *Ibid.*, 116.
9 *Ibid.*, 118.
10 *Ibid.*, 117.
11 *Ibid.*, 163.
12 *Ibid.*, 182.
13 Bobrick, *Angel*, 252.
14 Journal of Horace Walpole, August 22, 1777, in Horace Walpole, *Journal of the Reign of King George the Third*. Vol. 2, from the Year 1781–1783 (London: Richard Bentley, 1859), 131.
15 Eliphalet Dyer to Joseph Trumbull, July 15, 1777, in Smith, *Letters*, 7:346.
16 Henry Marchant to Nicholas Cooke, July 13, 1777, in *ibid.*, 7:340.
17 Henry Laurens to Solomon Legare, August 27, 1777, in *ibid.*, 7:565.
18 John Adams to Abigail Adams, August 19, 1777, in *ibid.*, 7:505.
19 Samuel Adams to James Warren, August 1, 1777, in *ibid.*, 7:401.
20 Samuel Adams to Richard Henry Lee, July 15, 1777, in *ibid.*, 7:344.
21 George Washington to John Hancock, July 10, 1777, in Grizzard, *Washington*, 10:240–41.
22 Philbrick, *Valiant Ambition*, 196.
23 Ford, *Journals*, 8:545, July 11, 1777.
24 Philbrick, *Valiant Ambition*, 133.
25 Bobrick, *Angel*, 259.
26 Philbrick, *Valiant Ambition*, 133.
27 Rossie, *Politics*, 167.
28 Philip Schuyler to George Washington, July 26–27, 1777, in Grizzard, *Washington*, 10:430–32.
29 Rossie, *Politics*, 162.
30 Charles Thomson's Notes of Debates, July 26, 1777, in Smith, *Letters*, 7:382.
31 William Duer to Philip Schuyler, July 29, 1777, in *ibid.*, 7:389.
32 Philip Livingston, James Duane, and William Duer to New York Council of Safety, July 29, 1777, in *ibid.*, 7:394.
33 James Duane to Philip Schuyler, August 23, 1777, in *ibid.*, 7:535.
34 James Kirby Martin, *Benedict Arnold, Revolutionary Hero: An American Warrior Reconsidered* (New York: New York University Press, 1997), 354.
35 Ford, *Journals*, 8:596, August 1, 1777; Rossie, *Politics*, 164.
36 New England Delegates to George Washington, August 2, 1777, in Smith, *Letters*, 7:405.
37 George Washington to John Hancock, August 3, 1777, in Grizzard, *Washington*, 10:492–93.
38 Ford, *Journals*, 8:604, August 4, 1777.
39 Henry Laurens to William Brisbane, August 14, 1777, in Smith, *Letters*, 7:482.
40 John Adams to Abigail Adams, August 11, 1777, in Butterfield, *Adams Papers*, Family Correspondence, 2:305–6.
41 George Washington to James Mease, June 13, 1777, in Grizzard, *Washington*, 10:30–31.
42 Flexner, *Washington*, 212–13.

Chapter 34: Calculated to Deceive

1 Bobrick, *Angel*, 262–63.
2 David G. Martin, *The Philadelphia Campaign: June 1777–July 1778* (Conshohocken, PA: Combined Books, Inc., 1993), 29.
3 Henry Laurens to John Loveday, August 11, 1777, in Smith, *Letters*, 7:449.

4. Connecticut Delegates to Jonathan Trumbull, Sr., August 19, 1777, in *ibid.*, 7:509.
5. John Adams to Abigail Adams, August 21, 1777, in Butterfield, *Adams Papers*, Family Correspondence, 2:321–22.
6. Benjamin Harrison to George Washington, August 20, 1777, in Philander Chase and Edward G. Lengel, eds., *The Papers of George Washington*, Revolutionary War Series. Vol. 11, 19 August 1777–25 October 1777 (Charlottesville, VA: University Press of Virginia, 2001), 13–14.
7. John Adams to Abigail Adams, August 11, 1777, in Butterfield, *Adams Papers*, Family Correspondence, 2:305–6.
8. John Adams to Abigail Adams, August 21, 1777, in *ibid.*, 2:321–22.
9. John Adams to Abigail Adams, August 20, 1777, in *ibid.*, 2:320–21.
10. Ford, *Journals*, 8:660, August 21, 1777.
11. George Washington to the President of Congress, August 21, 1777, in Chase, *Washington*, 11:21–24.
12. John Hancock to George Washington, August 22, 1777, in *ibid.*, 11:41–42.
13. Ford, *Journals*, 8:666, August 22, 1777.
14. George Washington to Israel Putnam, August 22, 1777, in Chase, *Washington*, 11:46.
15. Martin, *Philadelphia*, 37.
16. Flexner, *Washington*, 216.
17. John Adams to Abigail Adams, August 23, 1777, in Smith, *Letters*, 7:533.
18. James Lovell to Oliver Wolcott, August 25, 1777, in *ibid.*, 7:553.
19. George Washington to John Hancock, August 23, 1777, in Chase, *Washington*, 11:52–54.
20. General Orders, August 23, 1777, in *ibid.*, 11:49–51. Emphasis in original.
21. Martin, *Philadelphia*, 35–36.
22. Henry Marchant to Nicholas Cooke, August 24, 1777, in Smith, *Letters*, 7:541.
23. John Adams to Abigail Adams, August 24, 1777, in *ibid.*, 7:539.
24. Martin, *Philadelphia*, 36.
25. Ferling, *Miracle*, 245.
26. Martin, *Philadelphia*, 40.
27. *Ibid.*, 39.
28. Ford, *Journals*, 8:678–79, August 26, 1777.
29. *Ibid.*, 8:694, August 28, 1777.
30. Robert F. Oaks, "Philadelphians in Exile: The Problem of Loyalty during the American Revolution," *The Pennsylvania Magazine of History and Biography* 96, no. 3 (1972): 300–1.
31. Edward Rutledge to Robert R. Livingston, October 2, 1776, in Smith, *Letters*, 5:295.
32. Oaks, "Philadelphians," 301.
33. *Ibid.*, 302.
34. Ford, *Journals*, 8:694, August 28, 1777.
35. Oaks, "Philadelphians," 303.
36. Ford, *Journals*, 8:694, August 28, 1777.
37. *Ibid.*
38. *Ibid.*
39. Oaks, "Philadelphians," 303.
40. Wainwright, "Diary," 412.
41. Diary of Sarah Logan Fisher, January 23, 1777, in *ibid.*, 426.
42. Diary of Sarah Logan Fisher, September 2, 1777, in *ibid.*, 444.
43. Oaks, "Philadelphians," 305.
44. Ford, *Journals*, 8:719, September 7, 1777.
45. *Ibid.*, 8:722–23, September 8, 1777.
46. Israel Pemberton, "The Remonstrance of the Subscribers, Citizens of Philadelphia" (Philadelphia: Robert Bell, 1777), 33.
47. Ford, *Journals*, 8:723, September 8, 1777.
48. Henry Laurens to John Henry Gervais, September 5, 1777, in Smith, *Letters*, 7:612, 7:614.
49. Richard Henry Lee to Patrick Henry, September 8, 1777, in *ibid.*, 7:637.
50. John Adams to Abigail Adams, September 8, 1777, in *ibid.*, 7:627.
51. Sullivan, *Disaffected*, 76–79.
52. *Ibid.*, 81–82.
53. Oaks, "Philadelphians," 308–9.
54. Bobrick, *Angel*, 264–65.
55. *Ibid.*, 265.
56. *Ibid.*
57. Boatner, *Encyclopedia*, 592.
58. Thomas Burke to Richard Caswell, September 17, 1777, in Smith, *Letters*, 7:679.
59. Boatner, *Encyclopedia*, 1071.
60. Thomas Burke to Richard Caswell, September 17, 1777, in Smith, *Letters*, 7:680.
61. Ford, *Journals*, 8:742, September 14, 1777.
62. George Washington to John Hancock, September 15, 1777, in Chase, *Washington*, 11:236–38.
63. Ford, *Journals*, 8:749, September 16, 1777.
64. William Williams to Jonathan Trumbull, Sr., September 13, 1777, in Smith, *Letters*, 7:659.
65. Elias Boudinot to Elisha Boudinot, September 23, 1777, in Sullivan, *Disaffected*, 55.
66. Timothy Pickering to his brother, September 25, 1777, in *ibid.*

67 George Washington to Thomas Wharton, Jr., October 17–18, 1777, in Chase, Washington, 11:539–41.
68 Sullivan, Disaffected, 56–57.
69 Ford, Journals, 8:754, September 18, 1777.
70 Ibid., 8:741, September 14, 1777.
71 Boudreau, Independence, 351.
72 Diary of John Adams, September 16, 1777, in Butterfield, Adams Papers, Diary and Autobiography, 2:263.

Chapter 35: Women Running, Children Crying, Delegates Flying

1 Hoffman Nickerson, *The Turning Point of the Revolution: Or Burgoyne in America*. Vol. 1 (Port Washington, NY: Kennikat Press, 1967), 183–84.
2 Ketchum, Saratoga, 275.
3 Nickerson, Turning, 1:184–85.
4 Philbrick, Valiant Ambition, 125.
5 Nickerson, Turning, 1:185.
6 Jeremy Engels and Greg Goodale, "'Our Battle Cry Will Be: Remember Jenny McCrea': A Précis of the Rhetoric of Revenge," *American Quarterly* 61, no. 1 (March 2009): 98.
7 Massachusettensis, "To the Inhabitants of Massachusetts Bay," *The Independent Chronicle and Universal Advertiser*, August 14, 1777, in Engels, "Revenge," 99.
8 Ketchum, Saratoga, 275.
9 Horatio Gates to John Burgoyne, September 2, 1777, in Commager, Spirit, 560.
10 Bobrick, Angel, 254.
11 Ibid., 260.
12 Ketchum, Saratoga, 282, 330.
13 Ibid., 110, 281.
14 James Thomas Flexner, "How a Madman Helped Save the Colonies," *American Heritage Magazine* 7, no. 2 (1956).
15 Catherine S. Crary, *The Price of Loyalty: Tory Writings from the Revolutionary Era* (New York: McGraw-Hill Book Company, 1973), 244.
16 Flexner, "Madman."
17 Ketchum, Saratoga, 334–35.
18 Ibid., 353–54.
19 James Duane to George Clinton, September 16, 1777, in Smith, Letters, 7:670–61.
20 Ford, Journals, 8:751–52, September 17, 1777.
21 William Williams to Jonathan Trumbull, Sr., September 17, 1777, in Smith, Letters, 7:692.
22 Henry Laurens to George Galphin, September 16, 1777, in ibid., 7:674.
23 Henry Laurens to John Lewis Gervais, September 18, 1777, in ibid., 7:695.
24 William Williams to Jonathan Trumbull, Sr., September 13, 1777, in ibid., 7:659.
25 Ford, Journals, 8:754, September 18, 1777.
26 Thomas Paine to Benjamin Franklin: two letters, May 16, 1778, in William B. Willcox, ed., *The Papers of Benjamin Franklin*. Vol. 26, March 1 through June 30, 1778 (New Haven, CT: Yale University Press, 1987), 478–89.
27 Diary of Sarah Logan Fisher, September 21, 1777, in Wainwright, "Diary," 448.
28 Thomas Burke to Richard Caswell, September 20, 1777, in Smith, Letters, 8:6.
29 James McClure, "The Continental Congress in York Town," *Pennsylvania Legacies* 3, no. 1 (2003): 6.
30 Henry Laurens to Robert Howe, October 20, 1777, in Smith, Letters, 8:149.
31 Henry Laurens to John Lewis Gervais, October 8, 1777, in ibid., 8:80.
32 James Lovell to Robert Treat Paine, September 24, 1777, in ibid., 8:14.
33 James Lovell to William Whipple (?), September 20, 1777, in ibid., 8:6.
34 James Lovell to Elbridge Gerry, September 19, 1777, in ibid., 8:4.
35 James Lovell to Joseph Trumbull, September 23, 1777, in ibid., 8:12.
36 Bobrick, Angel, 266.
37 James Lovell to Horatio Gates, October 5, 1777, in Smith, Letters, 8:58.
38 Fleming, Secret, 75.
39 Ibid., 75–76.
40 Ibid., 75.
41 Diary of Sarah Logan Fisher, September 25–26, 1777, in Wainwright, "Diary," 450.

Chapter 36: A Dead Weight on Us

1 John Adams to Abigail Adams, September 30, 1777, in Smith, Letters, 8:27.
2 Diary of John Adams, September 24, 1777, in Butterfield, Adams Papers, Diary and Autobiography, 2:266–67.
3 James Duane to George Clinton, October 3, 1777, in Smith, Letters, 8:46.
4 McClure, "York Town," 6.
5 Montross, Reluctant Rebels, 209.
6 Henry Laurens to Robert Howe, October 20, 1777, in Smith, Letters, 8:149.
7 Robert Fortenbaugh, "York as the Continental Capital: September 30, 1777–June 27, 1778,"

Pennsylvania History: A Journal of Mid-Atlantic Studies 20, no. 4 (1953): 399.
8   John Adams to Abigail Adams, October 28, 1777, in Butterfield, *Adams Papers*, Family Correspondence, 2:361–62.
9   Fortenbaugh, "York," 400.
10 Fortenbaugh, "York," 401–3; Montross, *Reluctant Rebels*, 201.
11 John Hancock to Dorothy Hancock, October 1, 1777, in Smith, *Letters*, 8:38–39, 8:41.
12 John Hancock to Dorothy Hancock, October 8, 1777, in *ibid.*, 8:77.
13 James Duane to George Clinton, October 3, 1777, in *ibid.*, 8:46.
14 Eliphalet Dyer to Joseph Trumbull, September 28, 1777, in *ibid.*, 8:24.
15 Charles Carroll of Carrollton to Charles Carroll, Sr., September 29, 1777, in *ibid.*, 8:26.
16 John Adams to Abigail Adams, September 30, 1777, in *ibid.*, 8:27.
17 William Williams to Jonathan Trumbull, Sr., September 30, 1777, in *ibid.*, 8:35.
18 James Duane to George Clinton, October 3, 1777, in *ibid.*, 8:47.
19 Council of Safety of the Commonwealth of Pennsylvania, "Proclamation," October 13, 1777, in Samuel Hazard, ed., *Hazard's Register of Pennsylvania*. Vol. 3 (Philadelphia: F. W. Geddes, 1829), 200.
20 Sullivan, *Disaffected*, 69–70.
21 John Harvie to Thomas Jefferson, October 18, 1777, in Smith, *Letters*, 8:139.
22 Ford, *Journals*, 9:784, October 8, 1777.
23 Sullivan, *Disaffected*, 68.
24 Ford, *Journals*, 9:784, October 8, 1777.
25 John Adams to Abigail Adams, September 30, 1777, in Smith, *Letters*, 8:27.
26 Ketchum, *Saratoga*, 355.
27 *Ibid.*, 352–53, 356, 360.
28 *Ibid.*, 362, 366, 368.
29 Charles Carroll of Carrollton to Charles Carroll, Sr., October 5, 1777, in Smith, *Letters*, 8:50.
30 Rakove, *Beginnings*, 163, 178.
31 Ford, *Journals*, 9:779–81, October 7, 1777.
32 *Ibid.*, 9:782, October 7, 1777.
33 Burnett, *Continental Congress*, 249.
34 Henry Laurens to John Laurens, October 10, 1777, in Smith, *Letters*, 8:100.
35 Rakove, *Beginnings*, 179.
36 Burnett, *Continental Congress*, 250.
37 Bobrick, *Angel*, 267.
38 Boatner, *Encyclopedia*, 426.
39 Bobrick, *Angel*, 267–68.
40 *Ibid.*, 268.
41 Ford, *Journals*, 9:785, October 8, 1777.
42 Richard Henry Lee to Patrick Henry, October 8, 1777, in Smith, *Letters*, 8:82.
43 Charles Carroll of Carrollton to Charles Carroll, Sr., October 9, 1777, in *ibid.*, 8:86–87.
44 Ketchum, *Saratoga*, 385–87.

Chapter 37: Very Curious and Extraordinary

1   George Washington to John Hancock, October 16, 1777, in Chase, *Washington*, 11:527–28.
2   Jacob Duché to George Washington, October 8, 1777, in *ibid.*, 11:430–37.
3   George Washington to John Hancock, October 16, 1777, in *ibid.*, 11:527–28.
4   Henry Laurens to Robert Howe, October 20, 1777, in Smith, *Letters*, 8:150.
5   William Williams to Jonathan Trumbull, Sr., October 23, 1777, in *ibid.*, 8:169.
6   John Penn and Cornelius Harnett to Richard Caswell, October 20, 1777, in *ibid.*, 8:155.
7   John Harvie to Thomas Jefferson, October 25, 1777, in *ibid.*, 8:183.
8   John Adam to Abigail Adams, October 25, 1777, in *ibid.*, 8:179.
9   Nathanial Folsom to Josiah Bartlett, October 30, 1777, in *ibid.*, 8:213.
10 Henry Laurens to William Brisbane, October 17, 1777, in *ibid.*, 8:134.
11 John Adams to James Warren, October 24, 1777, in *ibid.*, 8:171.
12 Elbridge Gerry to Thomas Gerry, October 21, 1777, in *ibid.*, 8:156.
13 Richard Henry Lee to Patrick Henry, October 25, 1777, in *ibid.*, 8:185.
14 Burnett, *Continental Congress*, 260.
15 *Ibid.*, 261.
16 Montross, *Reluctant Rebels*, 216.
17 Ketchum, *Saratoga*, 439.
18 George Washington to Richard Henry Lee, October 28, 1777, in Frank E. Grizzard and David R. Hoth, eds., *The Papers of George Washington*, Revolutionary War Series. Vol. 12, 26 October 1777–25 December 1777 (Charlottesville, VA: University Press of Virginia, 2002), 40–42.
19 Horatio Gates to George Washington, November 2, 1777, in *ibid.*, 12:93–94.
20 Charles Thomson to George Washington, October 31, 1777, in *ibid.*, 12:71–72.
21 Ketchum, *Saratoga*, 374–76, 389, 393.
22 Bobrick, *Angel*, 277.
23 Ketchum, *Saratoga*, 394.
24 Ebeneezer Matoon to Philip Schuyler, October 7, 1835, in Commager, *Spirit*, 594.

25 Ketchum, *Saratoga*, 395, 399, 403–4.
26 Boatner, *Encyclopedia*, 978.
27 Snow, *1777*, 335.
28 Montross, *Reluctant Rebels*, 216–17.
29 Ketchum, *Saratoga*, 409.
30 *Ibid.*, 407, 410.
31 Snow, *1777*, 300.
32 Ketchum, *Saratoga*, 415.
33 Snow, *1777*, 322, 330–31.
34 Ketchum, *Saratoga*, 417.
35 Snow, *1777*, 348.
36 John Burgoyne to Horatio Gates, October 13, 1777, in *ibid.*, 348.
37 *Ibid.*, 371.
38 Ketchum, *Saratoga*, 422.
39 Snow, *1777*, 371, 374.
40 Horatio Gates to Elizabeth Gates, October 1777, in Frank Moore, ed., *Diary of the American Revolution*. Vol. 1 (New York: Charles Scribner, 1860), 511.
41 Ferling, *Winning*, xviii.

Chapter 38: Essential to Our Very Existence

1   Ford, *Journals*, 9:855, November 1, 1777.
2   Ketchum, *Saratoga*, 435.
3   *Ibid.*, 422.
4   Ford, *Journals*, 9:856–57, November 3, 1777.
5   *Ibid.*, 9:862, November 4, 1777.
6   Henry Laurens to Horatio Gates, November 5, 1777, in Smith, *Letters*, 8:235.
7   Eliphalet Dyer to Horatio Gates, November 5, 1777, in *ibid.*, 8:234.
8   Ketchum, *Saratoga*, 435.
9   Ford, *Journals*, 9:871, November 6, 1777.
10 George Washington to Richard Henry Lee, October 28, 1777, in Grizzard, *Washington*, 12:40–42.
11 Ford, *Journals*, 9:852, October 31, 1777.
12 Henry Laurens to the Carlisle Committee, November 4, 1777, in Smith, *Letters*, 8:239.
13 Henry Laurens to John Lewis Gervais, October 16, 1777, in *ibid.*, 8:124.
14 Ford, *Journals*, 9:853, October 31, 1777.
15 Samuel Adams to James Warren, November 4, 1777, in Smith, *Letters*, 8:226.
16 Samuel Adams to James Warren, October 30, 1777, in *ibid.*, 8:212.
17 *Independent Chronicle*, Nov. 27 and Dec. 4, 1777, in Herbert S. Allan, *John Hancock: Patriot in Purple* (New York: The MacMillan Company, 1948), 266.
18 Burnett, *Continental Congress*, 254.
19 Allan, *Hancock*, 266.
20 Elbridge Gerry to James Warren, November 13, 1777, in Smith, *Letters*, 8:254.
21 Burnett, *Continental Congress*, 251.
22 Cornelius Harnett to William Wilkinson, November 2, 1777, in Smith, *Letters*, 8:222.
23 Cornelius Harnett to Thomas Burke, November 13, 1777, in *ibid.*, 8:255.
24 Cornelius Harnett to William Wilkinson, November 20, 1777, in *ibid.*, 8:292.
25 Cornelius Harnett to Thomas Burke, November 20, 1777, in *ibid.*, 8:291.
26 Daniel Roberdeau to Timothy Matlack, November 1, 1777, in *ibid.*, 8:222.
27 James Lovell to William Whipple, November 3, 1777, in *ibid.*, 8:225.
28 Ford, *Journals*, 9:844, November 1, 1777.
29 Henry Laurens to John Laurens, November 15, 1777, in Smith, *Letters*, 8:271.
30 Rakove, *Beginnings*, 181.
31 Ford, *Journals*, 9:928, November 15, 1777.
32 Jonathan Dickinson Sergeant to James Lovell, November 20, 1777, in Smith, *Letters*, 8:296.
33 Ford, *Journals*, 9:928, footnote 2, November 15, 1777.
34 Burnett, *Continental Congress*, 256.
35 Ford, *Journals*, 9:933–34, November 17, 1777.
36 James Duane to Robert R. Livingston, December 2, 1777, in Smith, *Letters*, 8:370.
37 Cornelius Harnett to Thomas Burke, November 13, 1777, in *ibid.*, 8:254.
38 Ferling, *Leap*, 180.
39 *Ibid.*, 179.
40 Articles as Approved, November 17, 1777, Article V, in Rakove, *Founding*, 161–62.
41 Articles as Approved, November 17, 1777, Article IX, in *ibid.*, 166.
42 Merrill Jensen, *The Articles of Confederation: An Interpretation of the Social-Constitutional History of the American Revolution, 1774–1781* (Madison, WI: The University of Wisconsin Press, 1966), 242.
43 Articles as Approved, November 17, 1777, Article XI, in Rakove, *Founding*, 168.
44 Britannica, Editors of Encyclopaedia, "Articles of Confederation," *Encyclopedia Britannica*.
45 Jensen, *Articles*, 242.
46 *Ibid.*, 239.

Chapter 39: Men Cursing, Women Shrieking, Children Squalling

1   Thomas Fleming, "Gentleman Johnny's Wandering Army," *American Heritage* 24, no. 1 (1972).
2   Thomas Anburey, *Travels Through the Interior Parts of America*. Vol. 2 (Boston: Houghton Mifflin Company, 1923), 33.

3. Fleming, "Gentleman."
4. Janet Beroth, "The Convention of Saratoga," *The Quarterly Journal of the New York State Historical Society* 8, no. 3 (1927): 257.
5. Anburey, *Travels*, 2:39.
6. Helga B. Doblin and Mary C. Lynn, "A Brunswick Grenadier With Burgoyne: The Journal of Johann Bense, 1776–1783," *New York History* 66, no. 4 (1985): 434.
7. Beroth, "Convention," 258; William L. Stone, translator, *Letters of Brunswick and Hessian Officers during the American Revolution* (Albany, NY: Munsell, 1891), 135.
8. Fleming, "Gentleman."
9. Friederike Charlotte Luise (von Massow) Riedesel, *Baroness von Riedesel and the American Revolution* (Chapel Hill, NC: University of North Carolina Press, 1965), 66.
10. "A Private Letter from New England" to "My Dear Friends," December 18, 1777, in Stone, *Letters*, 147.
11. Richard J. Hargrove, Jr., *General John Burgoyne* (East Brunswick, NJ: Associated University Presses, 1983), 207.
12. Anburey, *Travels*, 2:35, 2:53–54.
13. *Ibid.*, 2:41–42.
14. "A Private Letter from New England" to "My Dear Friends," December 18, 1777, in Stone, *Letters*, 139.
15. *Ibid.*, 140.
16. Charles Ramsdell Lingley, "The Treatment of Burgoyne's Troops under the Saratoga Convention," *Political Science Quarterly* 22, no. 3 (1907): 446.
17. Hannah Winthrop to Mercy Warren, November 11, 1777, in Commager, *Spirit*, 867.
18. Anbury, *Travels*, 2:37.
19. Doblin, "Grenadier," 436.
20. Riedesel, *Baroness*, 72.
21. Quoted in Fleming, "Gentleman."
22. *Ibid.*
23. Riedesel, *Baroness*, 70.
24. F. J. Hudleston, *Gentleman Johnny Burgoyne: Misadventures of an English General in the Revolution* (Indianapolis, IN: Bobbs-Merrill, 1927), 260.
25. Anbury, *Travels*, 2:47.
26. Fleming, "Gentleman."
27. John Burgoyne to Horatio Gates, November 14, 1777, New York Public Library Digital Collections.
28. Hargrove, *Burgoyne*, 209.
29. Ford, *Journals*, 9:982, December 1, 1777.
30. Bobrick, *Angel*, 269.
31. Boatner, *Encyclopedia*, 861.
32. Bobrick, *Angel*, 270.
33. Boatner, *Encyclopedia*, 862.
34. McCullough, *Adams*, 174.
35. *Ibid.*
36. Abigail Adams to James Lovell, December 15, 1777, in Butterfield, *Adams Papers*, Family Correspondence, 2:370–71.
37. McCullough, *Adams*, 174, 176, 178.
38. Rakove, *Beginnings*, 251.
39. Jonathan Sewall to Joseph Lee, September 21, 1787, in Butterfield, *Adams Papers*, Family Correspondence, 1:137, footnote 5.
40. Ketchum, *Saratoga*, 445.
41. "The American Commissioners: A Public Announcement, 4 December 1777," in William B. Willcox, ed., *The Papers of Benjamin Franklin*. Vol. 25, October 1, 1777, through February 28, 1778 (New Haven, CT: Yale University Press, 1986), 234–36.
42. William Lee to Francis Lightfoot Lee, January 4, 1778, in Ford, *Lee*, 1:328–29.
43. Ketchum, *Saratoga*, 446.
44. Schiff, *Improvisation*, 120.
45. *Ibid.*, 132.
46. Jules A. Baisnée and John J. Meng, "Philadelphia and the Revolution: French Diplomacy in the United States, 1778–1779," *Records of the American Catholic Historical Society of Philadelphia* 56, no. 4 (1945): 307.
47. Schiff, *Improvisation*, 132.
48. *Ibid.*, 135, 139.
49. *Ibid.*, 136–37.
50. *Ibid.*, 141–42, 150.
51. *Ibid.*, 151.
52. *Ibid.*, 152.
53. Arthur Lee to Benjamin Franklin, April 2, 1778, in Willcox, *Franklin*, 26:220–22.
54. Benjamin Franklin to Arthur Lee, April 3, 1778, in *ibid.*, 26:223, footnote 6.
55. Benjamin Franklin to Arthur Lee, April 3, 1778, in *ibid.*, 26:223.
56. McCullough, *Adams*, 190.
57. Schiff, *Improvisation*, 155.
58. *Ibid.*, 163.
59. Autobiography of John Adams, [May 2, 1778], in Butterfield, *Adams Papers*, Diary and Autobiography, 4:85–88.
60. Schiff, *Improvisation*, 157.
61. John Adams to Abigail Adams, April 25, 1778, in L. H. Butterfield and Marc Friedlaender, eds., *The Adams Papers*, Adams Family

Correspondence. Vol. 3, April 1778–September 1780 (Cambridge, MA: Harvard University Press, 1973), 17.

Chapter 40: We Must Change Our Mode of Conduct

1. Jennings B. Sanders, *Evolution of Executive Departments of the Continental Congress, 1774–1789* (Chapel Hill, NC: The University of North Carolina Press, 1935), 6–8.
2. *Ibid.*, 9–10.
3. Kenneth Schaffel, "The American Board of War, 1776–1781," *Military Affairs* 50, no. 4 (1986): 185.
4. *Ibid.*
5. Samuel Chase to John Sullivan, December 24, 1776, in Smith, *Letters*, 6:186.
6. Flexner, *Washington*, 256.
7. Montross, *Reluctant Rebels*, 224.
8. Sanders, *Executive*, 45.
9. Montross, *Reluctant Rebels*, 224.
10. Kenneth R. Rossman, "Thomas Mifflin—Revolutionary Patriot," *Pennsylvania History: A Journal of Mid-Atlantic Studies* 15, no. 1 (1948): 9.
11. Flexner, *Washington*, 253.
12. Rossman, "Revolutionary Patriot," 14.
13. *Ibid.*
14. Flexner, *Washington*, 253.
15. Rossman, "Revolutionary Patriot," 15.
16. Flexner, *Washington*, 256.
17. *Ibid.*
18. Rossman, "Revolutionary Patriot," 16.
19. Flexner, *Washington*, 255–56.
20. Rossman, "Revolutionary Patriot," 17, 20.
21. Schaffel, "Board," 186–87.
22. Rossman, "Revolutionary Patriot," 16.
23. George Washington to Henry Laurens, December 23, 1777, in Grizzard, *Washington*, 12:683–87.
24. Boatner, *Encyclopedia*, 276.
25. Rossie, *Politics*, 189.
26. Gloria E. Brenneman, "The Conway Cabal: Myth or Reality," *Pennsylvania History: A Journal of Mid-Atlantic Studies* 40, no. 2 (1973): 170.
27. George Washington to John Hancock, May 9, 1777, in Chase, *Washington*, 9:370–71.
28. Flexner, *Washington*, 196.
29. Bernard Knollenberg, *Washington and the Revolution, a Reappraisal: Gates, Conway, and the Continental Congress* (Hamden, CT: Archon Books, 1968), 43.
30. Flexner, *Washington*, 241.
31. Rossie, *Politics*, 189.
32. *Ibid.*, 189–90.
33. *Ibid.*, 190–91.
34. George Washington to Richard Henry Lee, October 16, 1777, in Chase, *Washington*, 11:529–30.
35. Richard Henry Lee to George Washington, October 20, 1777, in *ibid.*, 11:562–63.
36. Ford, *Journals*, 9:762, October 3, 1777.
37. Rossie, *Politics*, 190–91.
38. William Alexander ("Stirling") to George Washington, November 3, 1777, in Grizzard, *Washington*, 12:110–11.
39. Bobrick, *Angel*, 297.
40. George Washington to Thomas Conway, November 5, 1777, in Grizzard, *Washington*, 12:129–30.
41. Thomas Conway to George Washington, November 5, 1777, in *ibid.*, 12:130–31.
42. Horatio Gates to George Washington, January 23, 1778, in Edward G. Lengel, ed., *The Papers of George Washington*, Revolutionary War Series. Vol. 13, 26 December 1777–28 February 1778 (Charlottesville, VA: University of Virginia Press, 2003), 319–22.
43. Quoted in Rossie, *Politics*, 197.
44. Footnote 3 under letter from John Fitzgerald to George Washington, February 16, 1778, in Lengel, *Washington*, 13:555–56.
45. Quoted in Rossie, *Politics*, 192.
46. Thomas Conway to George Washington, November 16, 1777, in Grizzard, *Washington*, 12:276–77.
47. George Washington to Thomas Conway, November 16, 1777, in *ibid.*, 12:277.
48. Ford, *Journals*, 9:1024, December 13, 1777.
49. Flexner, *Washington*, 259.
50. George Washington to Horatio Gates, January 4, 1778, in Lengel, *Washington*, 13:138–40.

Chapter 41: Too Important to Be Trifled With

1. Bobrick, *Angel*, 286.
2. Ford, *Journals*, 9:972, November 28, 1777.
3. Nathanael Greene to George Washington, November 24, 1777, in Grizzard, *Washington*, 12:376–79.
4. Ferling, *Miracle*, 257.
5. Bobrick, *Angel*, 286.
6. Ferling, *Miracle*, 257–58.
7. Bobrick, *Angel*, 287.
8. Ferling, *Miracle*, 275.
9. Bobrick, *Angel*, 287.
10. Diary of Albigence Waldo, December 14, 1777, in Albigence Waldo, "Valley Forge, 1777–1778."

Diary of Surgeon Albigence Waldo, of the Connecticut Line," *The Pennsylvania Magazine of History and Biography* 21, no. 3 (1897): 307.
11 General Orders, December 18, 1777, in Grizzard, *Washington*, 12:626–28.
12 Flexner, *Washington*, 260.
13 General Orders, December 18, 1777, in Grizzard, *Washington*, 12:626–28.
14 Thomas Paine to Benjamin Franklin, May 16, 1778, in Willcox, *Franklin*, 26:478–89.
15 Bobrick, *Angel*, 287; Bruce Chadwick, *The First American Army* (Naperville, IL: Sourcebooks, 2007), 218.
16 Fleming, *Secret*, 140–43.
17 Ferling, *Miracle*, 329.
18 Fleming, *Secret*, 143–44.
19 Ferling, *Winning*, 51.
20 Fleming, *Secret*, 88.
21 Ibid.
22 Ibid.
23 Ibid.
24 E. Wayne Carp, *To Starve the Army at Pleasure* (Chapel Hill, NC: University of North Carolina Press, 1984), 42.
25 Fleming, *Secret*, 88.
26 Ferling, *Miracle*, 278.
27 Fleming, *Secret*, 92.
28 Ferling, *Miracle*, 279.
29 Ibid., 279–80.
30 Ferling, *Miracle*, 279.
31 Burnett, *Continental Congress*, 270–71.
32 Ferling, *Miracle*, 281.
33 George Washington to Henry Laurens, December 14–15, 1777, in Grizzard, *Washington*, 12:604–7.
34 George Washington to Henry Laurens, December 23, 1777, in *ibid.*, 12:683–87.
35 Ferling, *Miracle*, 277.
36 George Washington to Henry Laurens, January 2, 1778, in Lengel, *Washington*, 13:119–20.
37 Thomas Conway to George Washington, December 29, 1777, in *ibid.*, 13:40–41.
38 George Washington to Thomas Conway, December 30, 1777, in *ibid.*, 13:66–67.
39 Thomas Conway to George Washington, December 31, 1777, in *ibid.*, 13:77–79.
40 George Washington to Horatio Gates, January 4, 1778, in *ibid.*, 13:138–40.

Chapter 42: My Heart Is Full, My Eyes Overflow

1 Diary of Rev. George Neisser, February 20, 1778, in Richard Peters, "Incidents in the History of York, Pennsylvania, 1778," *The Pennsylvania Magazine of History and Biography* 16, No. 4 (1893): 433.
2 Diary of Rev. George Neisser, May 27, 1778, in *ibid.*, 436.
3 Henry Laurens to John Rutledge, March 11, 1778, in Smith, *Letters*, 9:271.
4 Diary of Rev. George Neisser, March 19, 1778, in Peters, "Incidents," 433.
5 Francis Lightfoot Lee to Samuel Adams, December 22, 1777, in Smith, *Letters*, 8:460.
6 Cornelius Harnett to Thomas Burke, December 16, 1777, in *ibid.*, 8:425–26.
7 Cornelius Harnett to William Wilkinson, December 28, 1777, in *ibid.*, 8:490.
8 Henry Laurens to William Livingston, December 30, 1777, in *ibid.*, 8:505–6.
9 Wallace, *Laurens*, 29–30.
10 Henry Laurens to John Lewis Gervais. December 30, 1777, in Smith, *Letters*, 8:502.
11 Ford, *Journals*, 9:1056, December 27, 1777.
12 Bobrick, *Angel*, 288.
13 Henry Laurens to John Lewis Gervais, December 30, 1777, in Smith, *Letters*, 8:502–5.
14 *Ibid.*, 8:503.
15 Eliphalet Dyer to Jonathan Trumbull, Sr., January 5, 1778, in *ibid.*, 8:527.
16 Henry Laurens to William Heath, December 27, 1777, in *ibid.*, 8:485.
17 "John Witherspoon," *Dictionary of American Biography* (Charles Scribner's Sons, 1936), Gale In Context: Biography.
18 Princeton University, "The Presidents of Princeton University: John Witherspoon."
19 "Witherspoon," *Dictionary of American Biography*.
20 Lingley, "Treatment," 466; Riedesel, *Baroness*, 72.
21 John Witherspoon, *The Works of John Witherspoon*. Vol. 9 (Edinburgh: J. Ogle, 1815), 113–14.
22 Ford, *Journals*, 10:35, January 8, 1778.
23 *Ibid.*, January 8, 1778.
24 Montross, *Reluctant Rebels*, 221; Ferling, *Miracle*, 271.
25 Henry Laurens to John Henry Gervais, December 30, 1777, in Smith, *Letters*, 8:503.
26 William Ellery to Nicholas Cooke, January 14, 1778, in *ibid.*, 8:585.
27 William Howe to Henry Clinton, November 16, 1777, in Jane Clark, "The Convention Troops and the Perfidy of Sir William Howe," *The American Historical Review* 37, no. 4 (1932): 722–23.
28 John Adams to Abigail Adams, October 26, 1777, in Butterfield, *Adams Papers*, Family Correspondence, 2:360–61.

29 Stephen Fried, *Rush: Revolution, Madness & the Visionary Doctor Who Became a Founding Father* (New York: Crown, 2018), 138–39.
30 *Ibid.*, 6.
31 *Ibid.*, 220.
32 Benjamin Rush to John Adams, October 1, 1777, in Butterfield, *Rush*, 1:156.
33 Benjamin Rush to John Adams, October 1, 1777, in *ibid.*, 1:155–57.
34 Benjamin Rush to John Adams, October 13, 1777, in *ibid.*, 1:158. Emphasis in original.
35 Benjamin Rush to John Adams, October 21, 1777, in *ibid.*, 1:159–60.
36 Benjamin Rush to Patrick Henry, January 12, 1778, in *ibid.*, 1:183. Emphasis in original.
37 Jonathan Dickinson Sergeant to James Lovell, November 20, 1777, in Smith, *Letters*, 8:296.
38 Flexner, *Washington*, 247.
39 James Lovell to Horatio Gates, November 17, 1777, in Rossie, *Politics*, 183.
40 James Lovell to Horatio Gates, November 27, 1777, in Smith, *Letters*, 8:229.
41 Rossie, *Politics*, 197.
42 McGaughy, *Lee*, 138.
43 *Ibid.*, 139.
44 Richard Henry Lee to George Washington, January 2, 1778, in Lengel, *Washington*, 13:120–22.
45 The Marquis de Lafayette to George Washington, December 30, 1777, in *ibid.*, 13:68–72.
46 Knollenberg, *Reappraisal*, 67.
47 Eliphalet Dyer to William Williams, March 10, 1778, in Smith, *Letters*, 9:257.
48 Henry Laurens to the Marquis de Lafayette, January 12, 1778, in *ibid.*, 8:571.
49 Henry Laurens to Isaac Motte, January 26, 1778, in *ibid.*, 8:654.
50 Henry Laurens to George Washington, January 27, 1778, in Lengel, *Washington*, 13:364–66.
51 George Washington to Henry Laurens, January 31, 1778, in *ibid.*, 13:420–21.
52 Burnett, *Continental Congress*, 287.
53 Footnote 1 under letter from Henry Laurens to George Washington, January 27, 1778, in Lengel, *Washington*, 13:364–66.
54 George Washington to Patrick Henry, November 13, 1777, in Grizzard, *Washington*, 12:242–43.

Chapter 43: A Most Shameful Deficiency

1 Henry Laurens to William Livingston, January 27, 1778, in Smith, *Letters*, 8:663–65.
2 Hazlehurst Smith Beezer, "John Mathews: Delegate to Congress from South Carolina, 1778–1782," *The South Carolina Historical Magazine* 103, no. 2 (2002): 153, 171.
3 John Mathews to Thomas Bee, July 7, 1778, in Smith, *Letters*, 10:236.
4 John Mathews to Thomas Bee, September 22, 1778, in *ibid.*, 10:682–83.
5 Ferling, *Winning*, 39.
6 George Washington to Henry Laurens, December 23, 1777, in Grizzard, *Washington*, 12:683–87.
7 Fleming, *Secret*, 153.
8 Benjamin Rush to Julia Rush, January 15, 1778, in Butterfield, *Rush*, 1:185.
9 Henry Laurens to John Laurens, February 3, 1778, in Smith, *Letters*, 9:18.
10 Richard Brookhiser, *Gentleman Revolutionary: Gouverneur Morris, the Rake Who Wrote the Constitution* (New York: Free Press, 2003), 1, 23, 25, 42.
11 *Ibid.*, 25–26.
12 *Ibid.*, 10–11, 42.
13 Gouverneur Morris to Robert R. Livingstone, February 5, 1778, in Smith, *Letters*, 9:35.
14 William Duer to Robert R. Livingston, July 9, 1777, in *ibid.*, 7:328.
15 Henry Laurens to the Marquis de Lafayette, January 28, 1778, in *ibid.*, 8:677.
16 Remark in a letter from Robert Morris, quoted in Brookhiser, *Morris*, 42.
17 Fleming, *Secret*, 164.
18 Gouverneur Morris to John Jay, February 1, 1778, in Smith, *Letters*, 9:4.
19 Fleming, *Secret*, 164.
20 *Ibid.*, 174.
21 *Ibid.*
22 Boatner, *Encyclopedia*, 477.
23 Joseph A. Murray, *Alexander Hamilton: America's Forgotten Founder* (New York: Algora, 2007), 9.
24 Ferling, *Leap*, 243; Murray, *Hamilton*, 10.
25 Boatner, *Encyclopedia*, 477.
26 James Thomas Flexner, *The Young Hamilton: A Biography* (New York: Fordham University Press, 1997), 34.
27 Murray, *Hamilton*, 16, 21, 25.
28 Flexner, *Hamilton*, 66, 77.
29 Boatner, *Encyclopedia*, 478.
30 Flexner, *Hamilton*, 122, 127.
31 *Ibid.*, 135–36.
32 Murray, *Hamilton*, 45.
33 *Ibid.*, 57.
34 Flexner, *Hamilton*, 195, 205–6.
35 George Washington to a Continental Congress Camp Committee, January 29, 1778, in Lengel, *Washington*, 13:376–409.

36 Ferling, *Miracle*, 284.
37 Burnett, *Continental Congress*, 311.
38 George Washington to a Continental Congress Camp Committee, January 29, 1778, in Lengel, *Washington*, 13:376–409.
39 Fleming, *Secret*, 177.
40 George Washington to a Continental Congress Camp Committee, January 29, 1778, in Lengel, *Washington*, 13:376–409.

Chapter 44: I Schall Be Laughed At

1 Ford, *Journals*, 10:84, January 22, 1778.
2 Ferling, *Miracle*, 290.
3 Footnote 2 under letter from Henry Laurens to the Marquis de LaFayette, January 22, 1778, in Smith, *Letters*, 8:635.
4 Ferling, *Miracle*, 291.
5 Henry Laurens to John Rutledge, March 11, 1778, in Smith, *Letters*, 9:270.
6 Ferling, *Miracle*, 292; Eliphalet Dyer to William Williams, February 17, 1778, in Smith, *Letters*, 9:115.
7 Ford, *Journals*, 10:87, January 23, 1778.
8 George Washington to Thomas Nelson, Jr., February 8, 1778, in Lengel, *Washington*, 13:480–82.
9 Ferling, *Miracle*, 291.
10 Gouverneur Morris to Henry Laurens, January 26, 1778, in Smith, *Letters*, 8:658.
11 The Marquis de Lafayette to Henry Laurens, January 26, 1778, in Marie Joseph Paul Yves Roch Gilbert Du Motier, Marquis de Lafayette, "Letters from the Marquis de Lafayette to Hon. Henry Laurens, 1777–1780 (Continued)," *The South Carolina Historical and Genealogical Magazine* 7, no. 3 (1906): 126.
12 Ferling, *Miracle*, 292.
13 Henry Laurens to John Rutledge, February 3, 1778, in Smith, *Letters*, 9:19.
14 *Ibid*.
15 Flexner, *Washington*, 268.
16 Ferling, *Miracle*, 292.
17 Burnett, *Continental Congress*, 294.
18 The Marquis de Lafayette to George Washington, February 19, 1778, in Lengel, *Washington*, 13:594–97.
19 Burnett, *Continental Congress*, 294.
20 The Marquis de Lafayette to George Washington, February 19, 1778, in Lengel, *Washington*, 13:594–97.
21 Ford, *Journals*, 10:253, March 13, 1778.
22 Footnote 3 under letter from Henry Laurens to George Washington, April 28, 1778, in Smith, *Letters*, 9:517; Henry Laurens to the Marquis de Lafayette, June 5, 1778, in Smith, *Letters*, 10:27.
23 Flexner, *Washington*, 268.
24 Footnote 3 under letter from Henry Laurens to George Washington, April 28, 1778, in Smith, *Letters*, 9:517.
25 Henry Laurens to the Marquis de Lafayette, June 5, 1778, in *ibid.*, 10:27.
26 The Marquis de Lafayette to Henry Laurens, June 1, 1778, in Marie Joseph Paul Yves Roch Gilbert Du Motier, Marquis de Lafayette, "Letters from the Marquis de Lafayette to Hon. Henry Laurens, 1777–1780," *The South Carolina Historical and Genealogical Magazine* 8, no. 4 (1907): 182.
27 Rossie, *Politics*, 206.
28 Boatner, *Encyclopedia*, 277.
29 Richard Henry Lee to Francis Lightfoot Lee, July 5, 1778, in Smith, *Letters*, 10:223.
30 *Ibid*.
31 Henry Laurens to John Laurens, July 6, 1778, in *ibid.*, 10:231.
32 Thomas Conway to George Washington, July 23, 1778, in David R. Hoth, ed., *The Papers of George Washington*, Revolutionary War Series. Vol. 16, 1 July–14 September 1778 (Charlottesville, VA: University of Virginia Press, 2006), 140.
33 Horatio Gates to George Washington, February 19, 1778, in Lengel, *Washington*, 13:590.
34 George Washington to John Fitzgerald, February 28, 1778, in *ibid.*, 13:694–95.
35 Henry Laurens to John Rutledge, March 11, 1778, in Smith, *Letters*, 9:269.
36 Rossie, *Politics*, 206.
37 *Ibid*.
38 Fleming, *Secret*, 230, 281.
39 George Washington to Gouverneur Morris, May 18, 1778, in Edward G. Lengel, ed. *The Papers of George Washington*, Revolutionary War Series. Vol. 15, May–June 1778 (Charlottesville, VA: University of Virginia Press, 2006.), 156–57.
40 Henry Laurens to Rawlins Lowndes, June 12, 1778, in Smith, *Letters*, 10:80.
41 Ford, *Journals*, 591, June 11, 1778.
42 Henry Laurens to Rawlins Lowndes, June 12, 1778, in Smith, *Letters*, 11:80.
43 Fleming, *Secret*, 303.
44 Ferling, *Winning*, 76.
45 Robert Morris to Richard Peters, January 25, 1778, in Smith, *Letters*, 8:649–50.
46 Ford, *Journals*, 9:1069, December 30, 1777.

47 Ford, *Journals*, 10:295, March 30, 1778.
48 George Washington to Henry Laurens, April 4, 1778, in David R. Hoth, ed., *The Papers of George Washington*, Revolutionary War Series. Vol. 14, 1 March 1778–30 April 1778 (Charlottesville, VA: University of Virginia Press, 2004), 401–4.
49 Thomas Burke to Richard Caswell, April 9, 1778, in Smith, *Letters*, 9:393–94.
50 Ford, *Journals*, 10:334, April 10, 1778.
51 Burnett, *Continental Congress*, 308.
52 Thomas Burke to Richard Caswell, April 29, 1778, in Smith, *Letters*, 9:525.
53 Burnett, *Continental Congress*, 308.
54 *Ibid.*, 306.
55 Ford, *Journals*, 10:334, April 10, 1778.
56 *Ibid.*, 10:336, April 11, 1778.
57 *Ibid.*, April 11, 1778.
58 *Ibid.*, April 11, 1778.
59 Burnett, *Continental Congress*, 309–10.
60 Henry Laurens to George Washington, April 14, 1778, in Hoth, *Washington*, 14:509–13.
61 Henry Laurens to George Washington, April 14, 1778, in *ibid.*
62 George Washington to Henry Laurens, April 18, 1778, in *ibid.*, 14:546–48.
63 Burnett, *Continental Congress*, 309.

Chapter 45: Fire Cake & Water

1 Fleming, *Secret*, 60.
2 *Ibid.*
3 *Ibid.*
4 *Ibid.*, 61.
5 George Washington to William Howe, January 13, 1777, in Grizzard, *Washington*, 8:59–61.
6 Fleming, *Secret*, 61–62.
7 *Ibid.*, 129.
8 Chadwick, *First*, 219.
9 Ferling, *Miracle*, 280.
10 Bobrick, *Angel*, 288.
11 Diary of Albigence Waldo, December 22, 1777, in Waldo, "Valley Forge," 310.
12 Ferling, *Miracle*, 280.
13 *Ibid.*
14 Bobrick, *Angel*, 291; Chadwick, *First*, 220.
15 Fleming, *Secret*, 135.
16 Ferling, *Miracle*, 280.
17 Bobrick, *Angel*, 291.
18 Ferling, *Miracle*, 280.
19 Fleming, *Secret*, 278–80.
20 Ferling, *Miracle*, 297.
21 John Richard Alden, *General Charles Lee, Traitor or Patriot?* (Baton Rouge, LA: Louisiana State University Press, 1951), 165.
22 Ferling, *Miracle*, 297.
23 Alden, *Lee*, 169.
24 Thomas Burke's Notes of Debates, Feb. 21, 1777, in Smith, *Letters*, 6:336.
25 George Washington to William Howe, January 13, 1777, in Grizzard, *Washington*, 8:59–61.
26 Ferling, *Miracle*, 298.
27 Alden, *Lee*, 168–69.
28 Ferling, *Miracle*, 297.
29 Alden, *Lee*, 167, 183.
30 *Ibid.*, 183.
31 Henry Laurens to John Lewis Gervais, August 5, 1777, in Smith, *Letters*, 7:419.
32 Boatner, *Encyclopedia*, 886.
33 Serle, *Journal*, 238, July 14, 1777.
34 Alden, *Lee*, 185.
35 Ferling, *Miracle*, 298.
36 Alden, *Lee*, 184–85.
37 *Ibid.*, 187.
38 Fleming, *Secret*, 45; Darlene Emmert Fisher, "Social Life in Philadelphia During the British Occupation," *Pennsylvania History: A Journal of Mid-Atlantic Studies* 37, no. 3 (July 1970): 249.
39 Charles Lee to Benjamin Rush, June 4, 1778, in Ferling, *Miracle*, 298.
40 Alden, *Lee*, 188.
41 Elias Boudinot, *Journal or Historical Recollections of American Events during the Revolutionary War* (Philadelphia: F. Bourquin, 1894), 78.
42 Sullivan, *Disaffected*, 87–88.
43 *Ibid.*, 88.
44 *Ibid.*, 91, 104.
45 *Ibid.*, 106–7.
46 *Ibid.*, 93.
47 Walter Stewart to George Washington, January 18, 1778, in Lengel, *Washington*, 13:276–78.
48 Sullivan, *Disaffected*, 98.
49 Walter Stewart to George Washington, January 28, 1778, in Lengel, *Washington*, 13:371–73.
50 Nathanael Greene to George Washington, February 15, 1778, in *ibid.*, 13:546–48.
51 Nathanael Greene to George Washington, February 16, 1778, in *ibid*, 13:557–58.
52 Sullivan, *Disaffected*, 111.
53 Anthony Wayne to George Washington, February 26, 1778, in Lengel, *Washington*, 13:677–78.
54 Sullivan, *Disaffected*, 109, 113.
55 *Ibid.*, 130–31.
56 Boatner, *Encyclopedia*, 409.
57 Sullivan, *Disaffected*, 131.
58 Fleming, *Secret*, 59.
59 Serle, *Journal*, 200.
60 Fleming, *Secret*, 17.

61. Sullivan, *Disaffected*, 142–43.
62. *Ibid.*, 141–42.
63. *Ibid.*, 131, 146, 165.
64. Drinker, *Extracts*, 81, January 10, 1778.
65. Fisher, "Social Life," 245.
66. Ferling, *Miracle*, 290.
67. Fisher, "Social Life," 244.
68. Irvin, "Streets," 24.
69. Fleming, *Secret*, 36.
70. Rebecca Franks to Anne Harrison Paca, February 26, 1778, in Rebecca Franks, "A Letter of Miss Rebecca Franks, 1778," *The Pennsylvania Magazine of History and Biography* 16, no. 2 (1892): 216–17.
71. Sullivan, *Disaffected*, 132.
72. *Ibid.*, 150.
73. John Clark, Jr., to George Washington, December 3, 1777, in Grizzard, *Washington*, 12:510–11.
74. Robert Proud to John Proud, "Anno 10th," 1778, in Robert Proud, "Letters of Robert Proud," *The Pennsylvania Magazine of History and Biography* 34, no. 1 (1910): 71.
75. Sullivan, *Disaffected*, 152–53.
76. *Ibid.*, 154.
77. *Ibid.*, 155.
78. *Ibid.*, 170.
79. *Ibid.*, 171.

Chapter 46: Most Wicked, Diabolical Baseness

1. Singerton, *Habsburg*, 103.
2. William Lee to Francis Lightfoot Lee, November 11, 1777, in Ford, *Lee*, 1:264–65.
3. William Lee to the President of Congress, in *ibid.*, 1:345.
4. Karl A. Roider, Jr., "William Lee, Our First Envoy in Vienna," *The Virginia Magazine of History and Biography* 86, no. 2 (1978): 164.
5. Singerton, *Habsburg*, 104, 109–10.
6. *Ibid.*, 110–11.
7. Roider, "Lee," 166–67.
8. Singerton, *Habsburg*, 118.
9. Roider, "Lee," 168.
10. *Ibid.*, 165.
11. Singerton, *Habsburg*, 1.
12. *Ibid.*, 118.
13. Alonzo T. Dill, *William Lee, Militia Diplomat* (Williamsburg, VA: Virginia Independence Bicentennial Commission, 1976).
14. Dill, *Lee*.
15. Samuel Flagg Bemis, *The Diplomacy of the American Revolution* (Bloomington, IN: Indiana University Press, 1957), 158.
16. Dill, *Lee*.
17. The Fourth Anglo–Dutch War of 1780–84, which broke out after the document was found in the effects of former delegate Henry Laurens when he was captured by the British in 1780 on his way to Amsterdam.
18. *Ibid.*
19. William Lee to Francis Lightfoot Lee, May 20, 1779, in Ford, *Lee*, 2:639.
20. George Washington to Henry Laurens, April 18, 1778, in Hoth, *Washington*, 14:546–48.
21. Burnett, *Continental Congress*, 324.
22. George Washington to Henry Laurens, April 18, 1778, in Hoth, *Washington*, 16:546–48.
23. Henry Laurens to James Duane, April 20, 1778, in Smith, *Letters*, 9:457.
24. George Washington to John Banister, April 21, 1778, in Hoth, *Washington*, 14:573–79.
25. Ferling, *Miracle*, 264.
26. John Henry to Thomas Johnson, April 20, 1778, in Smith, *Letters*, 9:454.
27. Burnett, *Continental Congress*, 324.
28. Ford, *Journals*, 10:379, April 22, 1778.
29. Burnett, *Continental Congress*, 325.
30. Thomas McKean to Caesar Rodney, April 28, 1778, in Smith, *Letters*, 9:521.
31. Burnett, *Continental Congress*, 313.
32. Thomas Burke to Richard Caswell, April 9, 1778, in Smith, *Letters*, 9:395.
33. Burnett, *Continental Congress*, 313.
34. Henry Laurens to James Duane, April 7, 1778, in Smith, *Letters*, 9:381.
35. James Lovell to Samuel Adams, January 13, 1778, in *ibid.*, 8:581.
36. Burnett, *Continental Congress*, 314.
37. George Washington to Henry Laurens, April 10, 1778, in Hoth, *Washington*, 14:459–64.
38. George Washington to John Banister, April 21, 1778, in *ibid.*, 14:573–79.
39. H. James Henderson, *Party Politics in the Continental Congress* (New York: McGraw-Hill, 1974), 122.
40. Burnett, *Continental Congress*, 314–15.
41. Ferling, *Miracle*, 285.
42. Henry Laurens to Rawlins Lowndes, May 17, 1778, in Smith, *Letters*, 9:702.
43. Connecticut Delegates to Jonathan Trumbull, Sr., May 18, 1778, in *ibid.*, 9:707–8.
44. Ferling, *Winning*, 80.
45. Fleming, *Secret*, 197–98.
46. *Ibid.*, 198.
47. Nathanael Greene to George Washington, April 24, 1779, in Lengel, *Washington*, 20:186–89.

48 Fleming, *Secret*, 199–200.
49 Bob Drury and Tom Clavin, *Valley Forge* (New York: Simon & Schuster, 2018), 264–65.
50 Fleming, *Secret*, 277.
51 Rappleye, *Morris*, 146.
52 Footnote 1 under letter from Henry Laurens to Robert Morris, April 27, 1778, in Smith, *Letters*, 9:505.
53 Rappleye, *Morris*, 146.
54 Footnote 1 under letter from Henry Laurens to Robert Morris, April 27, 1778, in Smith, *Letters*, 9:505.
55 Burnett, *Continental Congress*, 330.
56 James Lovell to American Diplomats in France, April 30, 1778, in Smith, *Letters*, 9:547.
57 Burnett, *Continental Congress*, 331.
58 Montross, *Reluctant Rebels*, 235.
59 Footnote 1 under letter from Simeon Deane to the Commissioners, April 16, 1778, in Robert J. Taylor, ed., *The Adams Papers*, Papers of John Adams. Vol. 6, March–August 1778 (Cambridge, MA: Harvard University Press, 1983), 35–36.
60 Burnett, *Continental Congress*, 333.
61 Virginia Delegates to Patrick Henry, May 3, 1778, in Smith, *Letters*, 9:593.
62 Quoted in Burnett, *Continental Congress*, 332.
63 George Washington to Henry Laurens, May 4, 1778, in Lengel, *Washington*, 15:32
64 George Ewing, *The Military Journal of George Ewing (1754–1824), a Soldier of Valley Forge* (Yonkers, NY: T. Ewing, 1928), 47.
65 Ferling, *Miracle*, 294.
66 Douglas Southall Freeman, *George Washington: A Biography*. Vol. 5 (New York: Charles Scribner's Sons, 1952), 2.
67 Ferling, *Miracle*, 294.
68 Ford, *Journals*, 11:469, May 6, 1778.
69 *Ibid.*, 11:478, May 8, 1778.
70 Flexner, *Washington*, 286.
71 Bobrick, *Angel*, 332.
72 *Ibid.*, 332–33.
73 John McAuley Palmer, *General Von Steuben* (New Haven, CT: Yale University Press, 1937), 124.
74 Flexner, *Washington*, 287.
75 Bobrick, *Angel*, 333.
76 Ashbel Greene to A., February 15, 1841, in Joseph H. Jones, *The Life of Ashbel Greene, V. D. M.* (New York: Robert Carter and Brothers, 1849), 109.
77 Flexner, *Washington*, 288.
78 Bobrick, *Angel*, 334.
79 Baron Steuben to von Gaudy, in Palmer, *Steuben*, 157.
80 Henry Laurens to James Duane, April 7, 1778, in Smith, *Letters*, 9:380.
81 Bobrick, *Angel*, 336.

Chapter 47: Ridiculous, Undeserved and Unmerited

1 Sullivan, *Disaffected*, 178–79.
2 Ferling, *Miracle*, 267.
3 Bobrick, *Angel*, 341.
4 Richard B. Morris, ed., *The American Revolution by George Trevelyan: A Condensation into One Volume of the Original Six-Volume Work* (New York: David McKay Company, 1964), 294, 361.
5 Ferling, *Miracle*, 267–68.
6 *Ibid.*, 269.
7 *Ibid.*, 268–69.
8 *Ibid.*, 266, 289.
9 Bobrick, *Angel*, 341.
10 Ferling, *Miracle*, 269.
11 Ferling, *Miracle*, 294–95; Sullivan, *Disaffected*, 178.
12 Sullivan, *Disaffected*, 180.
13 James Lovell to Horatio Gates, June 9, 1778, in Smith, *Letters*, 10:56.
14 Benson J. Lossing, *The Two Spies: Nathan Hale and John André* (New York: D. Appleton and Company, 1897), 47, 49, 53, 55; Bobrick, *Angel*, 342.
15 John André to Miss Seward, May 23, 1778, in Lossing, *Spies*, 58.
16 *Ibid.*, 59.
17 Thomas Jones, *History of New York during the Revolutionary War*, Vol. 1 (New York: New York Historical Society, 1879), 261.
18 Serle, *Journal*, 293–94, May 18, 1778.
19 Sullivan, *Disaffected*, 181.
20 Serle, *Journal*, 306–7, June 6, 1778.
21 Weldon A. Brown, *Empire or Independence: A Study in the Failure of Reconciliation, 1774–1783* (Port Washington, NY: Kennikat Press, 1966), 245.
22 *Ibid.*, 245.
23 Carl Van Doren, *Secret History of the American Revolution* (Garden City, NY: Garden City Publishing, 1941), 66; Boatner, *Encyclopedia*, 844.
24 Bobrick, *Angel*, 340.
25 Ferling, *Miracle*, 263.
26 Van Doren, *Secret*, 73.
27 Brown, *Empire*, 246–47.

28 Quoted in Van Doren, *Secret*, 69.
29 *Ibid.*, 83–84.
30 Ferling, *Miracle*, 265.
31 Boatner, *Encyclopedia*, 844.
32 Van Doren, *Secret*, 69–70, 88.
33 *Ibid.*, 90.
34 Ferling, *Miracle*, 272; Sullivan, *Disaffected*, 188.
35 Van Doren, *Secret*, 90.
36 Earl of Carlisle to Rev. Ekins, in Brown, *Empire*, 261.
37 Quoted in *ibid.*, 263.
38 *Ibid.*, 264.
39 *Ibid.*
40 *Ibid.*, 264–65.
41 Henry Laurens to Horatio Gates, June 13, 1778, in Smith, *Letters*, 10:87.
42 Ford, *Journals*, 11:605–6, June 13, 1778.
43 *Ibid.*, June 13, 1778.
44 Burnett, *Continental Congress*, 336–37.
45 Gouverneur Morris to John Jay, June 23, 1778, in Smith, *Letters*, 10:186.
46 Van Doren, *Secret*, 94.
47 Richard Henry Lee to Thomas Jefferson, June 16, 1778, in Smith, *Letters*, 10:106.
48 Brown, *Empire*, 268.
49 Ford, *Journals*, 11:615, June 17, 1778.
50 Brown, *Empire*, 269.
51 Van Doren, *Secret*, 74, 97.
52 Henry Laurens to Horatio Gates, June 13, 1778, in Smith, *Letters*, 10:87.
53 Montross, *Reluctant Rebels*, 239.
54 George Johnstone to Robert Morris, June 16, 1778, in Francis Wharton, ed., *The Revolutionary Diplomatic Correspondence of the United States*. Vol. 2. (Washington, DC: Government Printing Office, 1889), 616.
55 Thomas McKean to Caesar Rodney, June 17, 1778, in Smith, *Letters*, 10:129.
56 Henry Laurens to George Washington, June 18, 1778, in Lengel, *Washington*, 15:451–57.
57 Burnett, *Continental Congress*, 339.
58 Henry Laurens to George Washington, June 18, 1778, in Lengel, *Washington*, 15:451–57.
59 Rivington's New York *Royal Gazette*, June 3, 1778, in Brown, *Empire*, 255.

Chapter 48: You Damned Poltroon

1 Van Doren, *Secret*, 91–92.
2 Serle, *Journal*, 295, May 21, 1778.
3 Ewald, *Diary*, 130.
4 Serle, *Journal*, 296, May 22, 1778.
5 Sullivan, *Disaffected*, 182–83.
6 Ferling, *Miracle*, 300.
7 Bobrick, *Angel*, 336.

8 Richard Henry Lee to John Adams, June 20, 1778, in Smith, *Letters*, 10:154.
9 Joseph Reed to Henry Laurens, June 15, 1778, in *ibid.*, 10:101.
10 Alden, *Lee*, 190–92, 194; Ferling, *Miracle*, 299
11 Boudinot, *Journal*, 79.
12 Ferling, *Miracle*, 296–97.
13 *Ibid.*, 296.
14 *Ibid.*
15 Van Doren, *Secret*, 93.
16 Ferling, *Winning*, 89.
17 Bobrick, *Angel*, 343.
18 Ferling, *Winning*, 89.
19 Robert Middlekauff, *The Glorious Cause: The American Revolution, 1763–1789* (New York: Oxford University Press, 1985), 421.
20 Ferling, *Miracle*, 301.
21 *Ibid.*, 300.
22 Bobrick, *Angel*, 344.
23 Henry Armitt Brown, *The Battle of Monmouth* (Philadelphia: Christopher Sower Company, 1913), 46.
24 Ferling, *Miracle*, 304.
25 Boatner, *Encyclopedia*, 719.
26 Ferling, *Miracle*, 304.
27 Flexner, *Washington*, 303–4.
28 Quoted in Bobrick, *Angel*, 345.
29 Flexner, *Washington*, 305.
30 Quoted in *ibid.*
31 *Ibid.*, 306.
32 *Ibid.*
33 *Ibid.*, 308.
34 Ferling, *Miracle*, 305.
35 *Ibid.*, 306.
36 *Ibid.*
37 Alden, *Lee*, 229.
38 Ferling, *Miracle*, 307.
39 Ford, *Journals*, 12:1195, December 5, 1778.
40 Dominick Mazzagetti, *Charles Lee: Self Before Country* (New Brunswick, NJ: Rutgers University Press, 2013), 191.
41 Fleming, *Secret*, 339.

Chapter 49: The Sluttish Manner of Washing Our Linnen

1 Randall, *Arnold*, 408.
2 Bobrick, *Angel*, 407.
3 Randall, *Arnold*, 406.
4 Sullivan, *Disaffected*, 213.
5 Boudreau, *Independence*, 287.
6 Bobrick, *Angel*, 407.
7 Stephen Brumwell, *Turncoat: Benedict Arnold and the Crisis of American Liberty* (New Haven, CT: Yale University Press, 2018), 131.

8   Randall, *Arnold*, 408.
9   Fleming, *Secret*, 261, 331.
10 Sullivan, *Disaffected*, 202.
11 Fleming, *Secret*, 262.
12 Randall, *Arnold*, 408.
13 Van Doren, *Secret*, 91.
14 Montross, *Reluctant*, 240.
15 Sullivan, *Disaffected*, 191.
16 Van Doren, *Secret*, 92–93.
17 Beverley Baxter, "Grace Growden Galloway: Survival of a Loyalist, 1778–1779," *Frontiers: A Journal of Women's Studies* 3, no. 1 (1978): 63.
18 Josiah Bartlett to Mary Bartlett, June 21, 1778, in Smith, *Letters*, 10:167.
19 Joseph Reed to Esther Reed, June 15, 1778, in *ibid.*, 10:102.
20 John Hancock to Dorothy Hancock, June 23, 1778, in *ibid.*, 10:178–79.
21 Burnett, *Continental Congress*, 340.
22 *Ibid.*, 341.
23 *Ibid.*
24 Ford, *Journals*, 11:632, June 22, 1778.
25 Rakove, *Beginnings*, 188.
26 *Ibid.*, 187–88.
27 Burnett, *Continental Congress*, 343.
28 Rakove, *Beginnings*, 188.
29 Richard Henry Lee to John Adams, June 20, 1778, in Smith, *Letters*, 10:153.
30 Burnett, *Continental Congress*, 343.
31 Josiah Bartlett to Mary Bartlett, June 21, 1778, in Smith, *Letters*, 10:167.
32 Samuel Holten's Diary, [June 24–25, 1778], in *ibid.*, 10:186.

Chapter 50: Preventing Every Wish of My Heart

1   Boudreau, *Independence*, 201.
2   Fleming, *Secret*, 261.
3   Henry Laurens to Rawlins Lowndes, July 15, 1778, in Smith, *Letters*, 10:284.
4   Fleming, *Secret*, 331.
5   Irvin, "Streets," 27.
6   Samuel Holten's Diary, [July 4, 1778], in Smith, *Letters*, 10:221.
7   Diary of William Ellery, June 28–July 23, 1778, footnote 1 under entry from Samuel Holten's Diary, [July 4, 1778], in *ibid.*, 10:221.
8   *Pennsylvania Packet*, supplement, July 6, 1778, footnote 1 under entry from Samuel Holten's Diary, [July 4, 1778], in *ibid.*, 10:222.
9   *Pennsylvania Packet*, supplement, July 6, 1778, footnote 1 under entry from Samuel Holten's Diary, [July 4, 1778], in *ibid.*; Irvin, *Clothed*, 184.
10 Thomas McKean to William Atlee, July 7, 1778, in Smith, *Letters*, 10:236.
11 Diary of William Ellery, June 28–July 23, 1778, footnote 1 under entry from Samuel Holten's Diary, [July 4, 1778], in *ibid.*, 10:221–22.
12 Richard Henry Lee to Francis Lightfoot Lee, July 5, 1778, in *ibid.*, 10:224.
13 Burnett, *Continental Congress*, 344.
14 *Ibid.*, 343.
15 Henry Laurens to Rawlins Lowndes, July 15, 1778, in Smith, *Letters*, 10:284.
16 "The Early Years: The Charity School Academy and College of Philadelphia" (Philadelphia: University of Pennsylvania, 1972).
17 Nathaniel Scudder to John Hart, July 13, 1778, in Smith, *Letters*, 10:272.
18 John Mathews to Thomas Bee, July 7, 1778, in *ibid.*, 10:235.
19 Ferling, *Miracle*, 315.
20 John J. Meng, "Philadelphia Welcomes America's First Foreign Representatives," *Records of the American Catholic Historical Society of Philadelphia* 45, no. 1 (1934): 53.
21 Irvin, *Clothed*, 169.
22 Quoted in Elizabeth S. Kite, "Reports of Conrad Alexandre Gérard, Minister Plenipotentiary to America, 1778–1779, from His Most Christian Majesty, Louis XVI, King of France (Continued)," *Records of the American Catholic Historical Society of Philadelphia* 33, no. 1 (1922): 276.
23 Ford, *Journals*, 11:688, July 14, 1778.
24 Samuel Adams to James Warren, July 15, 1778, in Smith, *Letters*, 10:280.
25 Burnett, *Continental Congress*, 348.
26 *Ibid.*
27 *Ibid.*, 348–49.
28 Irvin, *Clothed*, 172, 174–75.
29 Burnett, *Continental Congress*, 349.
30 *Ibid.*, 346.
31 Samuel Adams to James Warren, July 15, 1778, in Smith, *Letters*, 10:280.
32 Burnett, *Continental Congress*, 349.
33 Irvin, *Clothed*, 174–75.
34 *Ibid.*, 176.
35 Andrew Adams to Oliver Wolcott, July 22, 1788, in Smith, *Letters*, 10:336.
36 Quoted in Durand, *Materials*, 170.
37 Fleming, *Secret*, 333–34.
38 Sullivan, *Disaffected*, 201.
39 Baxter, "Galloway," 62; Grace Growden Galloway and Raymond C. Werner, "The Diary of Grace Growden Galloway," *The Pennsylvania Magazine of History and Biography* 55, no. 1 (1931): 33.

40 Galloway, "Diary,", 41, July 22, 1778.
41 Baxter, "Galloway," 64.
42 Galloway, "Diary," 44, August 2, 1778.
43 *Ibid.*, 49, August 13, 1778.
44 *Ibid.*, August 14, 1778.
45 Irvin, "Streets," 35.
46 Ferling, *Miracle*, 404
47 Galloway, "Diary," 41, July 21, 1778.
48 *Ibid.*, 33.
49 *Ibid.*, 52, August 20, 1778.
50 *Ibid.*, 56, November 5, 1778.
51 *Ibid.*, 57, November 13, 1778.
52 *Ibid.*, 59–60, November 25, 1778.
53 Schiff, *Improvisation*, 163, 171.
54 *Ibid.*, 190.
55 *Ibid.*, 184–85.

Acknowledgments

I thank my wife, Carol Damioli, for her careful copyediting of the text and for her support over the years in completing this project. I also thank my brother Stuart for reading a portion of the draft and for his encouragement.

I thank Farley Grubb of the University of Delaware for explaining through emails issues concerning the Continental dollar, a subject that was more complex than I anticipated.

I thank Jane Calvert of the University of Kentucky for her help in pinning down the source of a quote of John Dickinson.

I thank April C. Armstrong of Princeton University for clarifying by email facts about the history of Nassau Hall.

For my research, I am grateful for many online resources, especially those of the Toronto Public Library, the Library of Congress, and the United States National Archives.

Bibliography

Note: hyperlinks referenced in this bibliography were accessed between January 2014 and December 2024.

Abbot, W. W. *The Papers of George Washington*, Colonial Series. Vol. 1, 7 July 1748–14 August 1755. Charlottesville, VA: University Press of Virginia, 1983. https://founders.archives.gov/.
Abbot, W. W. *The Papers of George Washington*, Colonial Series. Vol. 2, 14 August 1755–15 April 1756. Charlottesville, VA: University Press of Virginia, 1983. https://founders.archives.gov/.
Abbot, W. W. *The Papers of George Washington*, Colonial Series. Vol. 4, 9 November 1756–24 October 1757. Charlottesville, VA: University Press of Virginia, 1984. https://founders.archives.gov/.
Abbot, W. W. *The Papers of George Washington*, Colonial Series. Vol. 6, 4 September 1758–26 December 1760. Charlottesville, VA: University Press of Virginia, 1988. https://founders.archives.gov/.
Abbot, W. W., and Dorothy Twohig. *The Papers of George Washington*, Colonial Series. Vol. 10, 21 March 1774–15 June 1775. Charlottesville, VA: University Press of Virginia, 1995. https://founders.archives.gov/.
Adams, Charles Francis, ed. *The Works of John Adams, Second President of the United States*. Vol. 2. Boston: Little, Brown, and Company, 1865. https://babel.hathitrust.org/cgi/pt?id=uc2.ark:/13960/t59c6sc8b&seq=11.
Adams Papers: Digital Edition. Boston, MA: Massachusetts Historical Society, 2023. https://www.masshist.org/.
Alden, John Richard. *General Charles Lee, Traitor or Patriot?* Baton Rouge, LA: Louisiana State University Press, 1951.
Allan, Herbert S. *John Hancock: Patriot in Purple*. New York: The MacMillan Company, 1948.
Allen, Ethan. *A Narrative of Col. Ethan Allen's Captivity*. Burlington, VT: C. Goodrich, 1846. https://archive.org/details/narrativeofcolet00alle2/page/n7/mode/2up.
American Archives: Documents of the American Revolutionary Period. http://amarch.lib.niu.edu/islandora/object/niu-amarch%3A101937.
Ammerman, David. *In the Common Cause: American Response to the Coercive Acts of 1774*. Charlottesville, VA: University Press of Virginia, 1974.
Anburey, Thomas. *Travels Through the Interior Parts of America*. Vol. 2. Boston: Houghton Mifflin Company, 1923. https://archive.org/details/travelsthroughin02anbu/page/30/mode/2up.
Anderson, Fred. *Crucible of War: The Seven Years' War and the Fate of Empire in British North America*. New York: Alfred A. Knopf, 2000.
Anderson, Fred W. "The Hinge of the Revolution: George Washington Confronts a People's Army." *Massachusetts Historical Review* 1 (1999): 20–48. http://www.jstor.org/stable/25081140.
Anderson, Mark R. *The Battle for the Fourteenth Colony: America's War of Liberation in Canada, 1774–1776*. London: University Press of New England, 2013.
Augur, Helen. *The Secret War of Independence*. New York: Dull, Sloan and Pearce, 1955.
Auricchio, Laura. *The Marquis: Lafayette Reconsidered*. New York: Alfred A. Knopf, 2014.
The Avalon Project. "Constitution of Pennsylvania—September 28, 1776." Yale Law School. https://avalon.law.yale.edu/18th_century/pa08.asp.
The Avalon Project. "English Bill of Rights 1689." Yale Law School. https://avalon.law.yale.edu/17th_century/england.asp.

BIBLIOGRAPHY • 445

Baisnée, Jules A., and John J. Meng. "Philadelphia and the Revolution: French Diplomacy in the United States, 1778–1779." *Records of the American Catholic Historical Society of Philadelphia* 56, no. 4 (1945): 307–28. http://www.jstor.org/stable/44209823.

Balch, Thomas, ed. *The Examination of Joseph Galloway, Esq., by a Committee of the House of Commons*. Philadelphia: The Seventy-Six Society, 1855. https://archive.org/details/cu31924095644773/page/n5/mode/2up.

Ballagh, James Curtis, ed. *The Letters of Richard Henry Lee*. Vol. 1. New York: The Macmillan Company, 1911. https://archive.org/details/richhenryleelet01richrich/page/n9/mode/2up.

Bartlett, John Russell, ed. *Records of the Colony of Rhode Island and Providence Plantations in New England*. Vol. 7. Providence, RI: A. Crawford Greene, 1862. https://archive.org/details/recordsofcolonyo07rhod/page/n5/mode/2up.

Baxter, Beverley. "Grace Growden Galloway: Survival of a Loyalist, 1778–1779." *Frontiers: A Journal of Women's Studies* 3, no. 1 (1978): 62–67. https://doi.org/10.2307/3345995.

Becker, Carl Lotus. *History of Political Parties in the Province of New York, 1760 to 1776*. Madison, WI: University of Wisconsin, 1909. https://archive.org/details/historypolitica05beckgoog/page/n4/mode/2up.

Beeman, Richard R. *Our Lives, Our Fortunes, and Our Sacred Honor: The Forging of American Independence, 1774–1776*. New York: Basic, 2013.

Beezer, Hazlehurst Smith. "John Mathews: Delegate to Congress from South Carolina, 1778–1782." *The South Carolina Historical Magazine* 103, no. 2 (2002): 153–72. http://www.jstor.org/stable/27570564.

Benedict, William A. *History of the Town of Sutton, Massachusetts*. Worcester, MA: Sanford & Company, 1878. https://archive.org/details/historytownsutt00benegoog/page/n12/mode/2up.

Bemis, Samuel Flagg. "British Secret Service and French–American Alliance." *The American Historical Review* 29, no. 3 (1924): 474–95. https://doi.org/10.2307/1836521.

Bemis, Samuel Flagg. *The Diplomacy of the American Revolution*. Bloomington, IN: Indiana University Press, 1957. https://archive.org/details/TheDiplomacyOfTheAmericanRevolution/page/n3/mode/2up.

Benson, Mark. "The Unfortunate Captain Death of the Terrible Privateer." *Royal Museums Greenwich*. https://www.rmg.co.uk/stories/blog/library-archive/unfortunate-captain-death-terrible-privateer.

Beroth, Janet. "The Convention of Saratoga." *The Quarterly Journal of the New York State Historical Society* 8, no. 3 (1927): 257–80. http://www.jstor.org/stable/43553888.

Bevan, Edith Rossiter. "The Continental Congress in Baltimore, Dec. 20, 1776 to Feb. 27, 1777." *Maryland Historical Magazine* 42, no. 1 (1947). https://mdhs.msa.maryland.gov/pages/Viewer.aspx?speccol=5881&Series=1&Item=165.

Boatner, Mark Mayo III. *Encyclopedia of the American Revolution*. New York: David McKay Company, 1974.

Bobrick, Benson. *Angel in the Whirlwind: The Triumph of the American Revolution*. New York: Penguin, 1997.

Botkin, B. A. *A Treasury of New England Folklore*. New York: Bonanza Books, 1947.

Boudinot, Elias. *Journal or Historical Recollections of American Events during the Revolutionary War*. Philadelphia: F. Bourquin, 1894. https://archive.org/details/journalorhistori00boud/page/n3/mode/2up.

Boudreau, George W. *Independence: A Guide to Historic Philadelphia*. Yardley, PA: Westholme, 2016.

Boyd, Julian P., ed. *The Papers of Thomas Jefferson*. Vol. 1, 1760–1776. Princeton, NJ: Princeton University Press, 1950. https://founders.archives.gov/.

Boyd, Julian P., ed. *The Papers of Thomas Jefferson*. Vol. 10, 22 June–31 December 1786. Princeton, NJ: Princeton University Press, 1954. https://founders.archives.gov/.

Boyd, Julian P. "Silas Deane: Death by Kindly Teacher of Treason?" *The William and Mary Quarterly* 16, nos. 2–4 (1959): 165–87; 319–42; 515–50. https://doi.org/10.2307/1916821; https://doi.org/10.2307/1916948; https://doi.org/10.2307/1916948.

Brady, Patricia. *Martha Washington, An American Life*. New York: Viking, 2005.

Bradley, A. G. *The Fight with France for North America*. New York: E. P. Dutton and Company, 1900. https://archive.org/details/fightwithfranc00brad/page/n7/mode/2up.

Breen, T. H. *American Insurgents, American Patriots: The Revolution of the People*. New York: Hill and Wang, 2010.

Brenneman, Gloria E. "The Conway Cabal: Myth or Reality." *Pennsylvania History: A Journal of Mid-Atlantic Studies* 40, no. 2 (1973): 168–77. http://www.jstor.org/stable/27772111.

Britannica, Editors of Encyclopaedia. "Pierre-Augustin Caron de Beaumarchais." *Encyclopedia Britannica*, May 14, 2023. https://www.britannica.com/biography/Pierre-Augustin-Caron-de-Beaumarchais.

Britannica, Editors of Encyclopaedia. "Articles of Confederation." *Encyclopedia Britannica*, December 8, 2023. https://www.britannica.com/topic/Articles-of-Confederation.

Brookhiser, Richard. *Gentleman Revolutionary: Gouverneur Morris, the Rake Who Wrote the Constitution*. New York: Free Press, 2003.

Brown, Abram English. *John Hancock, His Book*. Boston: Lee and Shepard, 1898. https://archive.org/details/johnhancock00browrich/page/n5/mode/2up.

Brown, Weldon A. *Empire or Independence: A Study in the Failure of Reconciliation, 1774–1783*. Port Washington, NY: Kennikat Press, 1966.

Brumwell, Stephen. "Band of Brothers." *History Today* 58, issue 6 (2008). https://www.historytoday.com/archive/band-brothers.

Brumwell, Stephen. *Turncoat: Benedict Arnold and the Crisis of American Liberty*. New Haven, CT: Yale University Press, 2018.

Buchanan, John. *The Road to Charleston: Nathanael Greene and the American Revolution*. Charlottesville, VA: University of Virginia Press, 2019.

Burnett, Edmund Cody. *The Continental Congress*. New York: W. W. Norton & Company, Inc., 1964.

Butterfield, L. H., ed. *Letters of Benjamin Rush*. Vol. 1, 1761–1792. Princeton, NJ: Princeton University Press, 1951. https://archive.org/details/in.ernet.dli.2015.475745/page/n5/mode/2up.

Butterfield, L. H., ed. *Letters of Benjamin Rush*. Vol. 2, 1793–1813. Princeton, NJ: Princeton University Press, 1951.

Butterfield, Lyman H., ed. *The Adams Papers*, Adams Family Correspondence, Vol. 1, December 1761–May 1776. Cambridge, MA: Harvard University Press, 1963. https://www.masshist.org/publications/adams-papers/index.php/volume/ADMS-04-01.

Butterfield, Lyman H., ed. *The Adams Papers*, Adams Family Correspondence. Vol. 2, June 1776–March 1778. Cambridge, MA: Harvard University Press, 1963. https://www.masshist.org/publications/adams-papers/index.php/volume/ADMS-04-02.

Butterfield, L. H., and Marc Friedlaender, eds. *The Adams Papers*, Adams Family Correspondence. Vol. 3. April 1778–September 1780. Cambridge, MA: Harvard University Press, 1973. https://www.masshist.org/publications/adams-papers/index.php/volume/ADMS-04-03.

Butterfield, L. H., ed. *The Adams Papers*. Diary and Autobiography of John Adams. Vol. 2. Cambridge, MA: The Belknap Press of Harvard University Press, 1962. https://founders.archives.gov/.

Butterfield, L. H., ed. *The Adams Papers*. Diary and Autobiography of John Adams. Vol. 3, Diary, 1782–1804; Autobiography, Part One to October 1776. Cambridge, MA: The Belknap Press of Harvard University Press, 1961. https://founders.archives.gov/.

Butterfield, L. H., ed. *The Adams Papers*. Diary and Autobiography of John Adams. Vol. 4, Autobiography, Parts Two and Three, 1777–1780. Cambridge, MA: Harvard University Press, 1961. https://founders.archives.gov/.

Calhoon, Robert M. "'I Have Deduced Your Rights': Joseph Galloway's Concept of His Role, 1774–1775." *Pennsylvania History: A Journal of Mid-Atlantic Studies* 35, no. 4 (1968): 356–78. https://journals.psu.edu/phj/article/view/23328/23097.

Calvert, Jane E. *Quaker Constitutionalism and the Political Thought of John Dickinson*. Cambridge, UK: Cambridge University Press, 2009.

Carp, Benjamin L. *The Great New York Fire of 1776: A Lost Story of the American Revolution*. New Haven, CT: Yale University Press, 2023.

Carp, E. Wayne. *To Starve the Army at Pleasure*. Chapel Hill, NC: University of North Carolina Press, 1984.

Carpenters' Company of Philadelphia. *Carpenters' Hall: Meeting Place of History*. Philadelphia: Carpenters' Company of Philadelphia, 2006.

Chadwick, Bruce. *The First American Army*. Naperville, IL: Sourcebooks, 2007.
Chandler, Thomas Bradbury. *A Friendly Address to All Reasonable Americans on the Subject of Our Political Confusions*. New York, 1774. https://archive.org/details/cihm_20462.
Chandler, Thomas Bradbury. *What Think Ye of the Congress Now? Or, An Enquiry, How Far the Americans are Bound to Abide by, and Execute the Decisions of, the Late Congress?* New York: James Rivington, 1775. https://quod.lib.umich.edu/cgi/t/text/text-idx?c=evans;idno=N10953.0001.001;rgn=div1;view=text;cc=evans;node=N10953.0001.001:2.
Chase, Philander, ed. *The Papers of George Washington*, Revolutionary War Series. Vol. 1, June 1775–15 September 1775. Charlottesville, VA: University Press of Virginia, 1985. https://founders.archives.gov/.
Chase, Philander, ed. *The Papers of George Washington*, Revolutionary War Series. Vol. 2, 16 September 1775–31 December 1775. Charlottesville, VA: University Press of Virginia, 1987. https://founders.archives.gov/
Chase, Philander, ed. *The Papers of George Washington*, Revolutionary War Series. Vol. 3, 1 January 1776–31 March 1776. Charlottesville, VA: University Press of Virginia, 1988. https://founders.archives.gov/.
Chase, Philander, ed. *The Papers of George Washington*, Revolutionary War Series. Vol. 4, 1 April 1776–15 June 1776. Charlottesville, VA: University Press of Virginia, 1991. https://founders.archives.gov/.
Chase, Philander, ed. *The Papers of George Washington*, Revolutionary War Series. Vol. 5, 16 June 1776–12 August 1776. Charlottesville, VA: University Press of Virginia, 1993. https://founders.archives.gov/.
Chase, Philander, and Frank E. Grizzard, Jr., eds. *The Papers of George Washington*, Revolutionary War Series. Vol. 6, 13 August 1776–20 October 1776. Charlottesville, VA: University Press of Virginia, 1994. https://founders.archives.gov/.
Chase, Philander, ed. *The Papers of George Washington*, Revolutionary War Series. Vol. 7, 21 October 1776–5 January 1777. Charlottesville, VA: University Press of Virginia, 1997. https://founders.archives.gov/.
Chase, Philander, ed. *The Papers of George Washington*, Revolutionary War Series. Vol. 9, 28 March 1777–10 June 1777. Charlottesville, VA: University Press of Virginia, 1999. https://founders.archives.gov/.
Chase, Philander, and Edward G. Lengel, eds. *The Papers of George Washington*, Revolutionary War Series. Vol. 11, 19 August 1777–25 October 1777. Charlottesville, VA: University Press of Virginia, 2001. https://founders.archives.gov/.
Chernow, Ron. *Washington: A Life*. New York: The Penguin Press, 2010.
Clark, George L. *Silas Deane: A Connecticut Leader in the American Revolution*. New York: G. P. Putnam's Sons, 1913. https://archive.org/details/silasdeane00clar/page/n9/mode/2up.
Clark, Jane. "The Convention Troops and the Perfidy of Sir William Howe." *The American Historical Review* 37, no. 4 (1932): 721–30. https://doi.org/10.2307/1843337.
Clitherall, James. "Extracts from the Diary of Dr. James Clitherall, 1776." *The Pennsylvania Magazine of History and Biography* 22, no. 4 (1898): 468–74.
Coleman, E. M. "New England Convention: December 25, 1776, to January 2, 1777: An Illustration of Early American Particularism." *The Historian* 4, no. 1 (1941): 43–55. http://www.jstor.org/stable/24435939.
Collections of the Connecticut Historical Society. Vol. 2. Hartford, CT: Connecticut Historical Society, 1870. https://archive.org/details/collectionsofcon02conn_0/page/n11/mode/2up.
Collections of the New-York Historical Society for the Year 1878. New York: New-York Historical Society, 1879. https://archive.org/details/collectionsofnewv11newy/page/n7/mode/2up.
Commager, Henry Steele, and Richard B. Morris. *The Spirit of 'Seventy-Six: The Story of the American Revolution as Told by Participants*. New York: Harper & Row, 1967.
"The Continental Congress at Mass—Two Te Deums and Two Requiems. Washington at Catholic Burial Service." *The American Catholic Historical Researches* 6, no. 2 (1889): 50–55. http://www.jstor.org/stable/44373622.
Corner, George, ed. *The Autobiography of Benjamin Rush: His "Travels through Life" Together with His Commonplace Book*. Westport, CT: Greenwood Press, 1970.
Crary, Catherine S. *The Price of Loyalty: Tory Writings from the Revolutionary Era*. New York: McGraw-Hill Book Company, 1973.

Cresswell, Nicholas. "'I Am Now in an Enemy's Country': Travel Journal of Nicholas Cresswell, November 1, 1774." *Making the Revolution: America, 1763–1791*. National Humanities Center, Research Triangle Park, NC. http://americainclass.org/sources/makingrevolution/rebellion/text3/vacresswell.pdf.

Cushing, Harry Alonzo, ed. *The Writings of Samuel Adams*. Vol. 3, 1773–1777. New York: G. P. Putnam's Sons, 1907. https://archive.org/details/writingssam03adamuoft/page/n7/mode/2up.

Daughan, George C. *Revolution on the Hudson: New York City and the Hudson River Valley in the American War of Independence*. New York: W. W. Norton & Company, 2016.

Davies, Samuel, and Publishing Committee. *Memoir of the Rev. Samuel Davies*. Boston: Massachusetts Sabbath School Union, 1832. https://babel.hathitrust.org/cgi/pt?id=hvd.hn59z5&seq=3.

Deane, Silas. "The Deane Papers. Vol. 1. 1774–1777." *Collections of the New-York Historical Society for the Year 1886*. New York: New-York Historical Society, 1887. https://archive.org/stream/collectionsforye19newyuoft.

Decatur, Stephen, Jr. *Private Affairs of George Washington, from the Records and Accounts of Tobias Lear, Esquire, His Secretary*. Boston: The Riverside Press, 1933. https://archive.org/details/privateaffairsof0000deca.

Deming, Brian. *Boston and the Dawn of American Independence*. Yardley, PA: Westholme, 2013.

Desbler, Charles S. "How the Declaration Was Declared in the Old Thirteen." *Harpers New Monthly Magazine* 85 (1892): 165–87. https://babel.hathitrust.org/cgi/pt?id=mdp.39015056081600&seq=1.

Dickinson, John. *The Late Regulations, Respecting the British Colonies on the Continent of America Considered*. London: J. Almon, 1765. https://archive.org/details/cihm_20384/page/n5/mode/2up.

Dickinson, John, and J. H. Powell. "Notes and Documents: Speech of John Dickinson Opposing the Declaration of Independence." *The Pennsylvania Magazine of History and Biography* 65, no. 4 (1941): 458–81. http://www.jstor.org/stable/20087418.

Dill, Alonzo T. *William Lee, Militia Diplomat*. Williamsburg, VA: Virginia Independence Bicentennial Commission, 1976. https://leefamilyarchive.org/reference/books/dill-wl/index.html.

Doblin, Helga B., and Mary C. Lynn. "A Brunswick Grenadier With Burgoyne: The Journal of Johann Bense, 1776–1783." *New York History* 66, no. 4 (1985): 420–44. http://www.jstor.org/stable/23174811.

Dolin, Eric Jay. *Rebels at Sea: Privateering in the American Revolution*. New York: Liveright Publishing Corporation, 2022.

Douglass, Elisha P. "Thomas Burke, Disillusioned Democrat." *The North Carolina Historical Review* 6, no. 2 (April 1949): 150–86. http://www.jstor.org/stable/23514902.

Drury, Bob, and Tom Clavin. *Valley Forge*. New York: Simon & Schuster, 2018.

Duane, William, Jr., ed. *Passages from the Remembrancer of Christopher Marshall*. Philadelphia: J. Crissy, 1839. https://archive.org/details/passagesfromrem00marsgoog/page/n2/mode/2up.

Dull, Jonathan R. *Benjamin Franklin and the American Revolution*. Lincoln, NE: University of Nebraska Press, 2010.

Durand, John. *New Materials for the History of the American Revolution*. New York: Henry Holt and Company, 1889. https://babel.hathitrust.org/cgi/pt?id=hvd.32044086255882&seq=9.

"The Early Years: The Charity School Academy and College of Philadelphia." Philadelphia: University of Pennsylvania, 1972. https://archives.upenn.edu/digitized-resources/docs-pubs/early-years-1972/.

Engels, Jeremy, and Greg Goodale. "'Our Battle Cry Will Be: Remember Jenny McCrea': A Précis of the Rhetoric of Revenge." *American Quarterly* 61, no. 1 (March 2009): 93–112. http://www.jstor.org/stable/27734977.

Ewald, Johann. Edited and translated by Joseph P. Tustin. *Diary of the American War: A Hessian Journal*. New Haven, CT: Yale University Press, 1979. https://ia800804.us.archive.org/30/items/EwaldsDIARYOFTHEAMERICANWAR/Ewalds%20DIARY%20OF%20THE%20AMERICAN%20WAR.pdf.

Ewing, George. *The Military Journal of George Ewing (1754–1824), a Soldier of Valley Forge*. Yonkers, NY: T. Ewing, 1928. https://babel.hathitrust.org/cgi/pt?id=mdp.39015002381377&num=1&seq=7&view=1up.

Ferguson, E. James. *The Power of the Purse: A History of American Public Finance, 1776–1790*. Chapel Hill, NC: University of North Carolina Press, 1961.

Ferguson, Robert A. "The Commonalities of *Common Sense*." *The William and Mary Quarterly* 57, no. 3 (July 2000): 465–504. https://doi.org/10.2307/2674263.
Ferling, John. *Almost a Miracle: The American Victory in the War of Independence*. Oxford, UK: Oxford University Press, 2007.
Ferling, John. "Compromise or Conflict: The Rejection of the Galloway Alternative to Rebellion." *Pennsylvania History: A Journal of Mid-Atlantic Studies* 43, no. 1 (January 1976): 4–20. http://www.jstor.org/stable/27772320.
Ferling, John. *Independence: The Struggle to Set America Free*. New York: Bloomsbury Press, 2011.
Ferling, John. *A Leap in the Dark: The Struggle to Create the American Republic*. Oxford, UK: Oxford University Press, 2003.
Ferling, John. *Whirlwind: The American Revolution and the War that Won It*. New York: Bloomsbury Press, 2015.
Ferling, John. *Winning Independence: The Decisive Years of the Revolutionary War, 1778–1781*. New York: Bloomsbury Publishing, 2021.
Fields, Joseph E., compiler. *"Worthy Partner": The Papers of Martha Washington*. Westport, CT: Greenwood Press, 1994.
Fischer, David Hackett. *Washington's Crossing*. Oxford, UK: Oxford University Press, 2004.
Fisher, Daniel, and Mrs. Conway Robinson Howard. "Extracts from the Diary of Daniel Fisher, 1755." *The Pennsylvania Magazine of History and Biography* 17, no. 3 (1893): 263–78. http://www.jstor.org/stable/20083545.
Fisher, Darlene Emmert. "Social Life in Philadelphia During the British Occupation." *Pennsylvania History: A Journal of Mid-Atlantic Studies* 37, no. 3 (July 1970): 237–60. http://www.jstor.org/stable/27771875.
Flanders, Henry. *The Lives and Times of the Chief Justices of the Supreme Court*. Vol. 1. New York: James Cockcroft & Company, 1875. https://archive.org/details/livesandtimesch00flangoog/page/n2/mode/2up.
Fleming, Thomas. "Gentleman Johnny's Wandering Army." *American Heritage* 24, no. 1 (1972). https://www.americanheritage.com/gentleman-johnnys-wandering-army.
Fleming, Thomas. *Washington's Secret War: The Hidden History of Valley Forge*. New York: Smithsonian Books, 2006.
Flexner, James Thomas. *George Washington in the American Revolution (1775–1783)*. Boston: Little, Brown and Company, 1968.
Flexner, James Thomas. "How a Madman Helped Save the Colonies." *American Heritage Magazine* 7, no. 2 (1956). https://www.americanheritage.com/how-madman-helped-save-colonies.
Flexner, James Thomas. *The Young Hamilton: A Biography*. New York: Fordham University Press, 1997.
Force, Peter, ed. *American Archives, Fifth Series*. Vol. 1. Washington, DC: M. St. Clair Clarke and Peter Force, 1848. https://archive.org/details/americanarchives51forc/page/n7/mode/2up.
Force, Peter, ed. *American Archives, Fifth Series*. Vol. 2. Washington, DC: M. St. Clair Clarke and Peter Force, 1851. https://archive.org/details/americanarchive052forc/page/n9/mode/2up.
Force, Peter, ed. *American Archives, Fifth Series*. Vol. 3. Washington, DC: M. St. Clair Clarke and Peter Force, 1853. https://archive.org/details/americanarchives53forc/page/n7/mode/2up.
Force, Peter, ed. *American Archives, Fourth Series*. Vol. 2. Washington, DC: M. St. Clair Clarke and Peter Force, 1839. https://archive.org/details/americanarchives42forc/page/n9/mode/2up.
Force, Peter, ed. *American Archives, Fourth Series*. Vol. 3. Washington, DC: M. St. Clair Clarke and Peter Force, 1840. https://archive.org/details/americanarchive043forc/page/n9/mode/2up.
Force, Peter, ed. *American Archives, Fourth Series*. Vol. 6. Washington, DC: M. St. Clair Clarke and Peter Force, 1846. https://archive.org/details/americanarchivea46forc/page/n11/mode/2up.
Ford, Paul Leicester, ed. *The Writings of Thomas Jefferson*. Vol. 10. New York: G. P. Putnam's Sons, 1899. https://oll.libertyfund.org/title/ford-the-works-vol-10-correspondence-and-papers-1803-1807.
Ford, Paul Leicester, ed. *The Writings of Thomas Jefferson*. Vol. 12. New York: G. P. Putnam's Sons, 1905. https://oll-resources.s3.us-east-2.amazonaws.com/oll3/store/titles/808/0054-12_Bk.pdf.
Ford, Worthington Chauncey, ed. *Journals of the Continental Congress: 1774–1789*. 34 vols. Washington, DC: Government Printing Office, 1904–1937. https://www.loc.gov/item/05000059/.

Ford, Worthington Chauncey, ed. *Letters of William Lee*. Vol. 1. Brooklyn, NY: Historical Printing Club, 1891. https://babel.hathitrust.org/cgi/pt?id=hvd.32044011630894&seq=341 https://archive.org/details/cu31924092886153/page/n17/mode/2up.

Ford, Worthington Chauncey, ed. *Letters of William Lee*. Vol. 2. Brooklyn, NY: Historical Printing Club, 1891. https://babel.hathitrust.org/cgi/pt?id=hvd.32044011630977&seq=5.

Fortenbaugh, Robert. "York as the Continental Capital: September 30, 1777–June 27, 1778." *Pennsylvania History: A Journal of Mid-Atlantic Studies* 20, no. 4 (1953): 399–408. http://www.jstor.org/stable/27769456.

Fortescu J., ed. *Correspondence of King George the Third, From 1760 to December 1783*. Vol. 3, July 1773–December 1777. London: MacMillan and Co., Limited, 1928. https://babel.hathitrust.org/cgi/pt?id=mdp.39015011495382&seq=7.

Franklin, Benjamin. *The Autobiography of Benjamin Franklin*. New Haven, CT: Yale University Press, 2003. https://archive.org/details/autobiographyofb0000fran_b4c4/page/70/mode/2up.

Franks, Rebecca. "A Letter of Miss Rebecca Franks, 1778." *The Pennsylvania Magazine of History and Biography* 16, no. 2 (1892): 216–18. http://www.jstor.org/stable/20083480.

Freeman, Douglas Southall. *George Washington: A Biography*. Vol. 5. New York: Charles Scribner's Sons, 1952.

Freiberg, Malcolm, ed. *Thomas Hutchinson's Strictures upon the Declaration of the Congress at Philadelphia; in a Letter to a Noble Lord, &c*. Boston: The Old South Association. https://ia802800.us.archive.org/23/items/thomashutchinson00hutc/thomashutchinson00hutc.pdf.

French, Allen. "November Meeting. The First George Washington Scandal." *Proceedings of the Massachusetts Historical Society* 65 (1932): 460–74. http://www.jstor.org/stable/25080304.

Fried, Stephen. *Rush: Revolution, Madness & the Visionary Doctor Who Became a Founding Father*. New York: Crown, 2018.

Fruchtman, Jack, Jr. *Thomas Paine: Apostle of Freedom*. New York: Four Walls Eight Windows, 1994.

Furtado, Peter. *Quakers*. Oxford, UK: Shire Publications, 2013.

Gaines, William H., Jr. "The Continental Congress Considers the Publication of a Bible, 1777." *Studies in Bibliography* 3 (1950): 274–81. http://www.jstor.org/stable/40381894.

Galloway, Grace Growden, and Raymond C. Werner. "The Diary of Grace Growden Galloway." *The Pennsylvania Magazine of History and Biography* 55, no. 1 (1931): 32–94. http://www.jstor.org/stable/20086760.

Galloway, Joseph. *The Examination of Joseph Galloway, Esq; Late Speaker of the House of Assembly of Pennsylvania. Before the House of Commons, in a Committee on the American Papers*. London: J. Wilkie, 1779. https://archive.org/stream/examinationjose00gallgoog#page/n8/mode/2up.

Galloway, Joseph. *Reflections on the Rise and Progress of the American Rebellion*. London: J. Paralmore, 1780. https://archive.org/details/bim_eighteenth-century_reflections-on-the-rise-_galloway-joseph_1780.

Gillingham, Harrold E., and Solomon Drowne. "Dr. Solomon Drowne." *The Pennsylvania Magazine of History and Biography* 48, no. 3 (1924): 227–50. http://www.jstor.org/stable/20086541.

Graydon, Alexander. *Memoirs of His Own Time: With Reminiscences of the Men and Events of the Revolution*. Philadelphia: Lindsay & Blakiston, 1846. https://archive.org/details/memoirsofhisownt00gray/page/n5/mode/2up.

Great Britain. *A Collection of All the Statutes Now in Force Relating to the Revenue and Officers of the Customs in Great Britain and the Plantations*. Vol. 2. London: C. Eyre and W. Strahan, 1780. https://catalog.hathitrust.org/Record/009805820.

Greene, Jack P., ed. *The Diary of Colonel Landon Carter of Sabine Hall*. Vol. 2, 1752–78. Charlottesville, VA: The University Press of Virginia, 1965.

Grizzard, Frank E., ed. *The Papers of George Washington*, Revolutionary War Series. Vol. 8, 6 January 1777–27 March 1777. Charlottesville, VA: University Press of Virginia, 1998. https://founders.archives.gov/.

Grizzard, Frank E., ed. *The Papers of George Washington*, Revolutionary War Series. Vol. 10, *11 June 1777–18 August 1777*. Charlottesville, VA: University Press of Virginia, 2000. https://founders.archives.gov/.

Grizzard, Frank E., and David R. Hoth, eds. *The Papers of George Washington*, Revolutionary War Series. Vol. 12, 26 October 1777–25 December 1777. Charlottesville, VA: University Press of Virginia, 2002. https://founders.archives.gov/.

BIBLIOGRAPHY • 451

Grossman, Jonathan. "Wage and Price Controls During the American Revolution." *Monthly Labor Review* 96, no. 9 (1973): 3–10. http://www.jstor.org/stable/41839092.

Grubb, Farley. *The Continental Dollar: How the American Revolution Was Financed with Paper Money.* Chicago: University of Chicago Press, 2023.

Gruber, Ira D. *The Howe Brothers in the American Revolution.* New York: Atheneum, 1972.

Hale, Edward E. and Edward E. Hale, Jr. *Franklin in France.* Boston: Roberts Brothers, 1887.

Hamer, Philip M. "Henry Laurens of South Carolina: The Man and His Papers." *Proceedings of the Massachusetts Historical Society* 77 (1965): 3–14. http://www.jstor.org/stable/25080598.

Hargrove, Richard J., Jr. *General John Burgoyne.* East Brunswick, NJ: Associated University Presses, 1983.

Harley, Lewis R. *Life of Charles Thomson.* Philadelphia: George W. Jacobs & Co., 1900. https://archive.org/details/thomsonsecretary00harlrich/page/n7/mode/2up.

Harlow, Ralph Volney. "Aspects of Revolutionary Finance, 1775–1783." *The American Historical Review* 35, no. 1 (1929): 45–68. https://doi.org/10.2307/1838471.

Hatch, Robert McConnell. *Thrust for Canada: The American Attempt on Quebec in 1775–1776.* Boston: Houghton Mifflin Company, 1979.

Haw, James. "The Rutledges, the Continental Congress, and Independence." *The South Carolina Historical Magazine* 94, no. 4 (1993): 232–51. http://www.jstor.org/stable/27569960.

Hawes, Lilla Mills, ed. *The Journal of the Reverend John Joachim Zubly, A.M., D.D., March 5, 1770 through June 22, 1781.* Savannah, GA: Georgia Historical Society, 1989. https://dlg.usg.edu/record/g-hi_g-hiia_collectionsofgeo21zubl?canvas=1&x=2206&y=1722&w=9127.

Hawke, David. *In the Midst of a Revolution.* Philadelphia: University of Pennsylvania Press, 1961.

Hawke, David Freeman. *A Transaction of Free Men: The Birth and Course of the Declaration of Independence.* New York: Da Capo Press, 1964.

Hayes, Kevin J. *The Road to Monticello: The Life and Mind of Thomas Jefferson.* Oxford, UK: Oxford University Press, 2008.

Hazard, Samuel, ed. *Hazard's Register of Pennsylvania.* Vol. 3. Philadelphia: F. W. Geddes, 1829. https://babel.hathitrust.org/cgi/pt?id=hvd.32044098898331&seq=5.

Heath, William. *Heath's Memoirs of the American War.* New York: A. Wessels Company, 1904. https://tile.loc.gov/storage-services/public/gdcmassbookdig/heathsmemoirsofa01heat/heathsmemoirsofa01heat.pdf.

Henderson, H. James. "Congressional Factionalism and the Attempt to Recall Benjamin Franklin." *The William and Mary Quarterly* 27, no. 2 (1970): 246–67. https://doi.org/10.2307/1918652.

Henderson, H. James. *Party Politics in the Continental Congress.* New York: McGraw-Hill, 1974.

Henkels, Stan V., ed. *The Confidential Correspondence of Robert Morris.* Philadelphia: Stan V. Henkels, 1917. https://archive.org/details/cu31924029561390/page/n11/mode/2up.

Higginbotham, Don, ed. *The Papers of James Iredell.* Vol. 1. Raleigh, NC: State Library of North Carolina, 1976. https://digital.ncdcr.gov/Documents/Detail/papers-of-james-iredell-vol.-1/2149018?item=2236880.

Hillstrom, Lauries Collier, Lawrence W. Baker, and Kevin Hillstrom, eds. "Events Leading to the French and Indian War." *French and Indian War.* Vol. 1. Detroit: UXL, 2003. 3–11. *Gale Virtual Reference Library.* January 22, 2015. http://go.galegroup.com.ezproxy.torontopubliclibrary.ca/ps/i.do?id=GALE%7CCX-3411000013&v=2.1&u=tplmain_z&it=r&p=GVRL&sw=w&asid=a2f57f743e40ff7e7cc14b4e4a96b31b

Hoadly, Charles J. *The Public Records of the State of Connecticut, from October, 1776, to February, 1778, Inclusive.* Vol. 1. Hartford, CT: Case, Lockwood & Brainard Company, 1894. https://babel.hathitrust.org/cgi/pt?id=wu.89067359620&seq=13.

Hoban, Charles F., ed. *Pennsylvania Archives, Eighth Series.* Vol. 8. January 7, 1771–September 26, 1776. Harrisburg, PA: Pennsylvania Archives, 1935. https://babel.hathitrust.org/cgi/pt?id=hvd.32044032309098&seq=5.

Hogeland, William. *Declaration: The Nine Tumultuous Weeks When America Became Independent, May 1–July 4, 1776.* New York: Simon & Schuster, 2010.

Hoth, David R., ed. *The Papers of George Washington,* Revolutionary War Series. Vol. 14, 1 March 1778–30 April 1778. Charlottesville, VA: University of Virginia Press, 2004. https://founders.archives.gov/.

Hoth, David R., ed. *The Papers of George Washington*, Revolutionary War Series. Vol. 16, 1 July–14 September 1778. Charlottesville, VA: University of Virginia Press, 2006. https://founders.archives.gov/.

Howe, Richard, and William Howe. "Proclamation of Admiral Howe and General Howe, November 30, 1776." *Naval Documents of the American Revolution Digital Edition*. https://ndar-history.org/?q=node/9244.

Hudleston, F. J. *Gentleman Johnny Burgoyne: Misadventures of an English General in the Revolution*. Indianapolis, IN: Bobbs-Merrill, 1927. https://archive.org/details/gentlemanjohnnyb00hudl_0/page/n7/mode/2up.

Humphreys, David. *The Life and Heroic Exploits of Israel Putnam*. New York: E. Strong, 1834. https://archive.org/details/lifeheroicexploi00hump/page/n9/mode/2up.

Hutchinson, Thomas, and Andrew Oliver. "Copy of Letters Sent to Great-Britain by His Excellency Thomas Hutchinson, the Hon. Andrew Oliver, and Several Other Persons." Boston: Edes and Gill, 1773. https://gutenberg.org/cache/epub/48819/pg48819-images.html.

Hutchinson, Peter Orlando. *The Diary and Letters of His Excellency Thomas Hutchinson, Esq.* Vol. 2. Boston: Houghton, Mifflin, & Co., 1886. https://archive.org/details/cu31924080796950/page/n7/mode/2up.

Hutson, James H., ed. *A Decent Respect to the Opinions of Mankind: Congressional State Papers, 1774–1776*. Washington, DC: Library of Congress, 1975. https://babel.hathitrust.org/cgi/pt?id=mdp.49015000217522&seq=1.

Hutson, James H. *John Adams and the Diplomacy of the American Revolution*. Lexington, KY: University Press of Kentucky, 1980.

Irvin, Benjamin. *Clothed in the Robes of Sovereignty: The Continental Congress and the People Out of Doors*. Oxford, UK: Oxford University Press, 2011.

Irvin, Benjamin H. "The Streets of Philadelphia: Crowds, Congress, and the Political Culture of Revolution, 1774–1783." *The Pennsylvania Magazine of History and Biography* 129, no. 1 (2005): 7–44. http://www.jstor.org/stable/20093763.

Irving, Washington. *Life of George Washington*. Vol. 2. New York: G. P. Putnam & Co., 1856. https://babel.hathitrust.org/cgi/pt?id=uc2.ark:/13960/t1sf2mc4r&seq=11.

Isaacson, Walter. *Benjamin Franklin: An American Life*. New York: Simon & Schuster, 2004.

Jacobson, David L. "John Dickinson's Fight against Royal Government, 1764." *The William and Mary Quarterly* 19, no. 1 (1962): 64–85. https://doi.org/10.2307/1919958.

Janney, Samuel M. *The Life of William Penn*. Philadelphia: Hogan, Perkins & Co., 1852. https://archive.org/details/lifeofwilliampen1852jann/page/n171/mode/2up.

Jay, William. *The Life of John Jay: With Selections from His Correspondence*. Vol. 1. New York: J. & J. Harper, 1833. https://archive.org/details/lifeofjohnjaywith01jayw/page/n11/mode/2up.

Jefferson, Thomas. *Autobiography of Thomas Jefferson: 1743–1790*. New York: G. P. Putnam's Sons, 1914. https://archive.org/details/autobiographyoft00jeff/page/n5/mode/2up.

Jensen, Merrill. *The Articles of Confederation: An Interpretation of the Social-Constitutional History of the American Revolution, 1774–1781*. Madison, WI: The University of Wisconsin Press, 1966.

Jensen, Merrill. *The Founding of a Nation: A History of the American Revolution, 1763–1776*. New York: Oxford University Press, 1968.

Jensen, Merrill. *The New Nation: A History of the United States During the Confederation, 1781–1789*. Boston: Northeastern University Press, 1981.

"John Witherspoon." *Dictionary of American Biography*, Charles Scribner's Sons, 1936. *Gale In Context: Biography*. https://link-gale-com.ezproxy.torontopubliclibrary.ca/apps/doc/BT2310000358/BIC?u=tplmain&sid=BIC&xid=e2ac26a2.

Jones, Joseph H. *The Life of Ashbel Greene, V.D.M.* New York: Robert Carter and Brothers, 1849. https://archive.org/details/lifeofashbelgreen00gree/page/n5/mode/2up.

Jones, Thomas. *History of New York during the Revolutionary War*. Vol. 1. New York: New York Historical Society, 1879. https://archive.org/details/historynewyorkd03jonegoog/page/n14/mode/2up.

Kashatus, William C. III. *Historic Philadelphia: The City, Symbols & Patriots, 1681–1800*. Lanham, MD: University Press of America, 1992.

Kates, Gary. "The Transgendered World of the Chevalier/Chevalière d'Eon." *The Journal of Modern History* 67, no. 3 (1995): 558–94. http://www.jstor.org/stable/2124220.

Kelly, Joseph P. "Henry Laurens: The Southern Man of Conscience in History." *The South Carolina Historical Magazine* 107, no. 2 (2006): 82–123. http://www.jstor.org/stable/27570804.

Ketchum, Richard M. *Divided Loyalties: How the American Revolution Came to New York*. New York: Henry Holt and Company, 2002.

Ketchum, Richard M. *Saratoga: Turning Point of America's Revolutionary War*. New York: Henry Holt and Company, 1997.

Kidd, Thomas S. *Patrick Henry: First among Patriots*. New York: Basic Books, 2011.

King George III. "His Majesty's Most Gracious Speech." October 27, 1775. Library of Congress. https://tile.loc.gov/storage-services/service/rbc/rbpe/rbpe10/rbpe108/10803800/10803800.pdf.

Kite, Elizabeth Sarah. *Beaumarchais and the War of Independence*. Vol. 2. Boston: R. G. Badger, 1918. https://babel.hathitrust.org/cgi/pt?id=mdp.39015033154652&seq=9.

Kite, Elizabeth S. "Conrad Alexandre Gerard and American Independence." *Records of the American Catholic Historical Society of Philadelphia* 32, no. 4 (1921): 274–94. http://www.jstor.org/stable/44208561.

Kite, Elizabeth S. "General Washington and the French Engineers Duportail and Companions." *Record of the American Catholic Historical Society of Philadelphia* 43, no. 1 (1932): 1–33. http://www.jstor.org/stable/44209134.

Kite, Elizabeth S. "Reports of Conrad Alexandre Gérard, Minister Plenipotentiary to America, 1778–1779, from His Most Christian Majesty, Louis XVI, King of France (Continued)." *Records of the American Catholic Historical Society of Philadelphia* 33, no. 1 (1922): 54–91. http://www.jstor.org/stable/44208569.

Knollenberg, Bernard. "The Correspondence of John Adams and Horatio Gates." *Proceedings of the Massachusetts Historical Society* 67 (1941): 135–51. http://www.jstor.org/stable/25080351.

Knollenberg, Bernard. *Washington and the Revolution, a Reappraisal: Gates, Conway, and the Continental Congress*. Hamden, CT: Archon Books, 1968. https://archive.org/details/washingtonrevolu0000knol/page/n5/mode/2up.

Labaree, Leonard W., ed. *The Papers of Benjamin Franklin*. Vol. 1, January 6, 1706, through December 31, 1734. New Haven, CT: Yale University Press, 1959. https://founders.archives.gov/.

Labaree, Leonard W., ed. *The Papers of Benjamin Franklin*. Vol. 3, January 1, 1745, through June 30, 1750. New Haven, CT: Yale University Press, 1961. https://founders.archives.gov/.

Labaree, Leonard W., ed. *The Papers of Benjamin Franklin*. Vol. 4, July 1, 1750, through June 30, 1753. New Haven, CT: Yale University Press, 1961. https://founders.archives.gov/.

Labaree, Leonard W., ed. *The Papers of Benjamin Franklin*. Vol. 6, April 1, 1755, through September 30, 1756. New Haven, CT: Yale University Press, 1963. https://founders.archives.gov/.

Labaree, Leonard W., ed. *The Papers of Benjamin Franklin*. Vol. 7, October 1, 1756, through March 31, 1758. New Haven, CT: Yale University Press, 1963. https://founders.archives.gov/.

Labaree, Leonard W., ed. *The Papers of Benjamin Franklin*. Vol. 9, January 1, 1760, through December 31, 1761. New Haven, CT: Yale University Press, 1966. https://founders.archives.gov/.

Labaree, Leonard W., ed. *The Papers of Benjamin Franklin*. Vol. 10, January 1, 1762, through December 31, 1763. New Haven, CT: Yale University Press, 1959. https://founders.archives.gov/.

Labunski, Richard. *James Madison and the Struggle for the Bill of Rights*. Oxford, UK: Oxford University Press, 2006.

Lacey, John, Joseph Chapman, and Anthony Wayne. "Memoirs of Brigadier John Lacey, of Pennsylvania (Continued)." *The Pennsylvania Magazine of History and Biography* 25, no. 2 (1901): 191–207. http://www.jstor.org/stable/20085965.

Lafayette, Marie Joseph Paul Yves Roch Gilbert Du Motier, Marquis de. "Letters from the Marquis de Lafayette to Hon. Henry Laurens, 1777–1780 (Continued)." *The South Carolina Historical and Genealogical Magazine* 7, no. 3 (1906): 115–29. https://www.carolana.com/SC/eBooks/SCHGM/The_South_Carolina_Historical_and_Genealogical_Magazine_Volume_VII.pdf.

Lafayette, Marie Joseph Paul Yves Roch Gilbert Du Motier, Marquis de. "Letters from the Marquis de Lafayette to Hon. Henry Laurens, 1777–1780." *The South Carolina Historical and Genealogical Magazine* 8, no. 4 (1907): 181–88. https://www.carolana.com/SC/eBooks/SCHGM/The_South_Carolina_Historical_and_Genealogical_Magazine_Volume_VIII.pdf.

Lafayette, Marie Joseph Paul Yves Roch Gilbert Du Motier, Marquis de. *Memoirs, Correspondence and Manuscripts of General Lafayette*. Vol. 1. New York: Saunders and Otley, 1837. https://archive.org/details/memoirscorrespon00lafarich/page/n5/mode/2up.

Lander, James. "A Tale of Two Hoaxes in Britain and France in 1775." *The Historical Journal* 49, no. 4 (2006): 995–1024. http://www.jstor.org/stable/4140148.

Lee, Charles. *The Lee Papers*. Vol. 2. 1776–1778. New York: New-York Historical Society, 1872. https://archive.org/details/leepapers00leegoog/page/n16/mode/2up.

Lee, Charles. *Life and Memoirs of Major General Lee*. New York: Richard Scott, 1813. https://babel.hathitrust.org/cgi/pt?id=nyp.33433082353545&seq=11.

Lee, Edmund Jennings. *Lee of Virginia, 1642–1892*. Philadelphia: Franklin Printing Company, 1895. https://archive.org/details/leeofvirginia16400inleee/page/n5/mode/2up.

Lengel, Edward G., ed. *The Papers of George Washington*, Revolutionary War Series. Vol. 13, 26 December 1777–28 February 1778. Charlottesville, VA: University of Virginia Press, 2003. https://founders.archives.gov/.

Lengel, Edward G., ed. *The Papers of George Washington*, Revolutionary War Series. Vol. 15, May–June 1778. Charlottesville, VA: University of Virginia Press, 2006. https://founders.archives.gov/.

Lengel, Edward G., ed. *The Papers of George Washington*, Revolutionary War Series. Vol. 20, 8 April–31 May 1779. Charlottesville, VA: University of Virginia Press, 2010. https://founders.archives.gov/.

Leonard, Lewis A. *Life of Charles Carroll of Carrollton*. New York: Moffat, Yard and Company, 1918. https://archive.org/details/lifeofcharlescar00leonuoft/page/n7/mode/2up.

Liell, Scott. *46 Pages: Thomas Paine, Common Sense, and the Turning Point to American Independence*. Philadelphia: Running Press, 2003.

Lingley, Charles Ramsdell, "The Treatment of Burgoyne's Troops under the Saratoga Convention." *Political Science Quarterly* 22, no. 3 (1907): 440–59. https://doi.org/10.2307/2141057.

Lint, Gregg L., Richard Alan Ryerson, Anne Decker Cecere, C. James Taylor, Jennifer Shea, Celeste Walker, and Margaret A. Hogan, eds. *The Adams Papers*, Papers of John Adams. Vol. 12, October 1781–April 1782. Cambridge, MA: Harvard University Press, 2004. https://founders.archives.gov/.

Lipsky, Seth. *The Citizen's Constitution: An Annotated Guide*. New York: Basic Books, 2009.

Loménie, Louis Leonard de. *Beaumarchais and His Times*. Translated by Henry Sutherland Edwards. New York: Harper & Brothers, 1857. https://archive.org/details/beaumarchaishist00lomeiala/page/n7/mode/2up.

Looney, J. Jefferson, ed. *The Papers of Thomas Jefferson*, Retirement Series. Vol. 13, 22 April 1818 to 31 January 1819. Princeton, NJ: Princeton University Press, 2016.

Lossing, Benson J. *The Life and Times of Philip Schuyler*. Vol. 2. New York: Sheldon & Company, 1873. https://archive.org/details/lifeandtimesphi00lossgoog/page/2/mode/2up.

Lossing, Benson J., *The Two Spies: Nathan Hale and John André*. New York: D. Appleton and Company, 1897. https://www.gutenberg.org/cache/epub/63119/pg63119-images.html.

MacDonald, William, ed. *Documentary Source Book of American History*. New York: The MacMillan Company, 1916. https://tile.loc.gov/storage-services/public/gdcmassbookdig/documentarysourc00mac/documentarysourc00mac.pdf.

Mackenzie, Frederick. *A British Fusilier in Revolutionary Boston*. Cambridge, MA: Harvard University Press, 1926. https://archive.org/details/ABritishFusilierInRevolutionaryBoston_392/ABritishFusilierInRevolutionaryBoston1775/mode/2up.

Maier, Pauline. *American Scripture: Making the Declaration of Independence*. New York: Alfred A. Knopf, 1998.

Main, Jackson Turner. *The Sovereign States, 1775–1783*. New York: New Viewpoints, 1973.

Mansfield, Isaac. *A Sermon, Preached in the Camp at Roxbury, November 23, 1775*. Boston: S. Hall, 1776. https://archive.org/details/wsb5f8_images/wsb5f8.pdf.

Manuscripts and Archives Division, The New York Public Library. "Letter from John Burgoyne to Horatio Gates." New York Public Library Digital Collections. https://digitalcollections.nypl.org/items/cd951680-1bb1-0134-b162-00505686a51c.

Marshall, Christopher. *Extracts from the Diary of Christopher Marshall: Kept at Philadelphia and Lancaster During the American Revolution, 1774–1781*. Albany, NY: Joel Munsell, 1877. https://babel.hathitrust.org/cgi/pt?id=hvd.32044036966869&view=1up&seq=11.

Marston, Jerrilyn Greene. *King and Congress: The Transfer of Political Legitimacy, 1774–1776*. Princeton, NJ: Princeton University Press, 1987.

Martin, David G. *The Philadelphia Campaign: June 1777–July 1778*. Conshohocken, PA: Combined Books, Inc., 1993.

Martin, James Kirby. *Benedict Arnold, Revolutionary Hero: An American Warrior Reconsidered*. New York: New York University Press, 1997.

Maryland State Archives. "Writing It All Down: The Art of Constitution Making for the State & the Nation, 1776–1833." https://msa.maryland.gov/msa/speccol/sc2200/sc2221/000004/000000/html/00000004.html.

Massachusetts Historical Society Collections, Fifth Series. Vol. 4. Boston: Massachusetts Historical Society, 1878.

Massey, Gregory D. "The Limits of Antislavery Thought in the Revolutionary Lower South: John Laurens and Henry Laurens." *The Journal of Southern History* 63, no. 3 (1997): 495–530. https://doi.org/10.2307/2211648.

Mazzagetti, Dominick. *Charles Lee: Self Before Country*. New Brunswick, NJ: Rutgers University Press, 2013. https://archive.org/details/charlesleeselfbe0000mazz/page/n5/mode/2up.

McClure, James. "The Continental Congress in York Town." *Pennsylvania Legacies* 3, no. 1 (2003): 6–10. http://www.jstor.org/stable/27764868.

McCormick, Richard P. "Ambiguous Authority: The Ordinances of the Confederation Congress, 1781–1789." *The American Journal of Legal History* 41, no. 4 (1997).

McCullough, David. *1776*. New York: Simon & Schuster, 2005.

McCullough, David. *John Adams*. New York: Simon & Schuster, 2001.

McDonald, Forrest. *Empire and Nation*. Englewood Cliffs, NJ: Prentice-Hall, Inc., 1999. https://oll-resources.s3.us-east-2.amazonaws.com/oll3/store/titles/690/Mcdonald_0010.html.

McGaughy, J. Kent. *Richard Henry Lee of Virginia: A Portrait of an American Revolutionary*. London: Rowman & Littlefield Publishers, Inc., 2004.

McWilliams, John. "The Faces of Ethan Allen." *The New England Quarterly* 49, no. 2 (1976): 257–82. https://doi.org/10.2307/364502.

Meacham, Jon. *Thomas Jefferson: The Art of Power*. New York: Random House, 2012.

Meade, Robert Douthat. *Patrick Henry: Patriot in the Making*. Philadelphia: J. B. Lippincott Co., 1957.

Meng, John J. "Philadelphia Welcomes America's First Foreign Representatives." *Records of the American Catholic Historical Society of Philadelphia* 45, no. 1 (1934): 51–67. http://www.jstor.org/stable/44209162.

Michener, Ron. "Money in the American Colonies." Economic History Association. http://eh.net/encyclopedia/money-in-the-american-colonies/.

Middlekauff, Robert. *The Glorious Cause: The American Revolution, 1763–1789*. New York: Oxford University Press, 1985.

Miller, John C. *Sam Adams: Pioneer in Propaganda*. Stanford, CA: Stanford University Press, 1964.

Mires, Charlene. *Independence Hall in American Memory*. Philadelphia: University of Pennsylvania Press, 2002.

Montross, Lynn. *The Reluctant Rebels: The Story of the Continental Congress, 1774–1789*. New York: Harper & Brothers Publishers, 1950.

Moore, Frank, ed. *Diary of the American Revolution*. Vol. 1. New York: Charles Scribner, 1860. https://babel.hathitrust.org/cgi/pt?id=iau.31858021665421&seq=11.

Moore, Frank. *Songs and Ballads of the American Revolution*. New York: D. Appleton and Company, 1856. https://archive.org/details/mooresongsball00franrich/page/n11/mode/2up.

Morgan, Edmund S. *Benjamin Franklin*. New Haven, CT: Yale University Press, 2002.

Morgan, William James, ed. *Naval Documents of the American Revolution*. Vol. 5. Washington, D.C.: US Government Printing Office, 1970. https://www.history.navy.mil/content/dam/nhhc/research/publications/naval-documents-of-the-american-revolution/NDARVolume5.pdf.

Morison, Samuel Eliot. *Oxford History of the American People*. New York: Oxford University Press, 1965.

Morris, Richard B., ed. *The American Revolution by George Trevelyan: A Condensation into One Volume of the Original Six-Volume Work*. New York: David McKay Company, 1964.

Murchison, William. *The Cost of Liberty: The Life of John Dickinson*. Wilmington, DE: ISI Books, 2013.

Murray, Joseph A. *Alexander Hamilton: America's Forgotten Founder*. New York: Algora, 2007.
National Archives, *Founders Online*. https://founders.archives.gov/.
National Archives. "The Founding Fathers—Connecticut." https://www.archives.gov/founding-docs/founding-fathers-connecticut.
National Park Service. "Interior Architecture of Independence Hall." https://www.nps.gov/inde/learn/historyculture/places-independencehall-architecture-interior.htm.
National Park Service. "The Liberty Bell." https://www.nps.gov/inde/learn/historyculture/stories-libertybell.htm.
Nelson, Craig. *Thomas Paine: Enlightenment, Revolution, and the Birth of Modern Nations*. New York: Viking, 2006.
Nelson, William, and Frederick William Ricord, eds. *Documents Relating to the Colonial History of the State of New Jersey, 1631–1776*. Vol. 10. Newark, NJ: New Jersey Council, 1890. https://www.loc.gov/resource/gdcmassbookdig.documentsrelatin19whit/?sp=2&st=image
New Jersey. *Votes and Proceedings of the General Assembly of the Province of New Jersey. 1772–76*. Philadelphia: Andrew Bradford, 1772–1776. https://archive.org/details/votesproceedings1772newj/page/20/mode/2up.
Nickerson, Hoffman. *The Turning Point of the Revolution: Or Burgoyne in America*. Vol. 1. Port Washington, NY: Kennikat Press, 1967. https://babel.hathitrust.org/cgi/pt?id=mdp.39015027011082&seq=7.
North Carolina. *The Journal of the Proceedings of the Provincial Congress of North Carolina, Held at Halifax, on the Fourth Day of April, 1776*. Raleigh, NC: Lawrence & Lemay, 1831. https://digital.ncdcr.gov/Documents/Detail/journal-of-the-proceedings-of-the-provincial-congress-north-carolina-held-at-halifax-on-the-fourth-day-of-april-1776/2689737?item=2747250.
Oaks, Robert F. "Philadelphians in Exile: The Problem of Loyalty during the American Revolution." *The Pennsylvania Magazine of History and Biography* 96, no. 3 (1972): 298–325. http://www.jstor.org/stable/20090650.
Olson, Gary D. "Loyalists and the American Revolution: Thomas Brown and the South Carolina Backcountry, 1775–1776 (Continued)." *The South Carolina Historical Magazine* 68, no. 4 (1967): 201–19. http://www.jstor.org/stable/27566842.
Ousterhout, Anne M., "Frontier Vengeance: Connecticut Yankees vs. Pennamites in the Wyoming Valley." *Pennsylvania History: A Journal of Mid-Atlantic Studies* 62, no. 3 (1995): 330–63. http://www.jstor.org/stable/27773826.
Paine, Thomas. "Forester Letter IV," *Pennsylvania Journal*, May 8, 1776. http://thomaspaine.org/essays/american-revolution/the-forester-s-letters.html.
Paine, Thomas. "The Crisis I." *Pennsylvania Packet*, December 27, 1776–January 4, 1777. http://thomaspaine.org/major-works/american-crisis/crisis-1.html.
Paine, Thomas. *Rights of Man; Common Sense*. New York: Alfred A. Knopf, 1994.
Palmer, John McAuley. *General Von Steuben*. New Haven, CT: Yale University Press, 1937. https://archive.org/details/generalvonsteube0000john/page/n9/mode/2up.
Patterson, Richard S., and Richardson Dougall. *The Eagle and the Shield: A History of the Great Seal of the United States*. Washington, DC: Office of the Historian, Bureau of Public Affairs, Department of State, 1976.
Paul, Joel Richard. *Unlikely Allies: How a Merchant, a Playwright, and a Spy Saved the American Revolution*. New York: Riverhead Press, 2009.
Pemberton, Israel. "The Remonstrance of the Subscribers, Citizens of Philadelphia." Philadelphia: Robert Bell, 1777. digitalhistory.hsp.org/pafrm/doc/remonstrance-subscribers-citizens-philadelphia-september-5-1777.
Pemberton, W. Baring. *Lord North*. London: Longmans, Green and Co., 1938.
Peters, Richard. "Incidents in the History of York, Pennsylvania, 1778." *The Pennsylvania Magazine of History and Biography* 16, No. 4 (1893): 433–38. http://www.jstor.org/stable/20083508.
Peterson, Charles E. "Carpenters' Hall." *Transactions of the American Philosophical Society* 43, no. 1 (1953): 96–128. https://doi.org/10.2307/1005666.
Philbrick, Nathaniel. *Valiant Ambition: George Washington, Benedict Arnold, and the Fate of the American Revolution*. New York: Viking, 2016.

Phillips, Kevin. *1775: A Good Year for Revolution.* New York: Viking, 2012.
Pierce, William. "Characters in the Convention of the States Held at Philadelphia, May 1787." *American Historical Review* 3 (1898): 325–34. https://lawlibrary.wm.edu/wythepedia/images/5/53/NotesOfMajorWilliamPierceAmericanHistoricalReviewJanuary1898.pdf.
Platt, John David Ronalds. *Independence City Tavern.* Denver, CO: Denver Service Center, National Park Service, 1973. https://catalog.hathitrust.org/Record/006807106.
Potts, Louis W. *Arthur Lee: A Virtuous Revolutionary.* Baton Rouge, LA: Louisiana State University Press, 1981.
Princeton University. "The Presidents of Princeton University: John Witherspoon." https://pr.princeton.edu/pub/presidents/witherspoon/.
Proud, Robert. "Letters of Robert Proud." *The Pennsylvania Magazine of History and Biography* 34, no. 1 (1910): 62–73. http://www.jstor.org/stable/20085498.
"Publisher's Preface," *Pennsylvania Magazine* 1. Philadelphia: R. Aitken, 1775. https://archive.org/stream/pennsylvaniamaga11775phil#page/n7/mode/2up.
Quarles, Benjamin. "Lord Dunmore as Liberator." *The William and Mary Quarterly* 15, no. 4 (1958): 494–507. https://doi.org/10.2307/2936904.
Rakove, Jack, ed. *Founding America: Documents from the Revolution to the Bill of Rights.* New York: Barnes & Noble Classics, 2006.
Rakove, Jack N. *The Beginnings of National Politics: An Interpretive History of the Continental Congress.* New York: Alfred A. Knopf, 1979.
Randall, Willard Sterne. *Benedict Arnold: Patriot and Traitor.* New York: William Morrow and Company, 1990.
Randall, Willard Sterne. *Ethan Allen: His Life and Times.* New York: W. W. Norton & Company, 2011.
Rappleye, Charles. *Robert Morris: Financier of the American Revolution.* New York: Simon & Schuster, 2010.
Reed, William B., ed. *Life and Correspondence of Joseph Reed.* Vol. 1. Philadelphia: Lindsay and Blakiston, 1847. https://archive.org/details/lifecorresponden01reed/page/n11/mode/2up?view=theater.
Ricord, Frederick W., and William Nelson, eds. *Documents Related to the Colonial History of the State of New Jersey.* Vol. 10. Newark, NJ: Daily Advertiser Printing House, 1886. https://www.loc.gov/resource/gdcmassbookdig.documentsrelatin18whit/?sp=7&r=-1.077,-0.032,3.153,1.789,0.
Riddell, William Renwick. *Benjamin Franklin and Canada: Benjamin Franklin's Mission to Canada and the Causes of Its Failure.* Toronto: 1923. https://archive.org/details/benjaminfranklin00ridduoft/page/n3/mode/2up.
Riedesel, Friederike Charlotte Luise (von Massow). *Baroness von Riedesel and the American Revolution.* Chapel Hill, NC: University of North Carolina Press, 1965.
Rife, Clarence W. "Ethan Allen, An Interpretation." *The New England Quarterly* 2, no. 4 (1929): 561–84. https://doi.org/10.2307/359168.
Ritzenthaler, Mary Lynn, and Catherine Nicholson. "The Declaration of Independence and the Hand of Time." *Prologue Magazine* 48, no. 3 (2016). https://www.archives.gov/publications/prologue/2016/fall/declaration#:~:text=Timothy%20Matlack%2C%20a%20clerk%20in,of%20the%20document%20for%20signatures.
Robertson, Henry O. "Tories or Patriots? The Mississippi River Planters during the American Revolution." *Louisiana History: The Journal of the Louisiana Historical Association* 40, no. 4 (1999): 445–62. http://www.jstor.org/stable/4233616.
Robinson, Rowland Evans. *Vermont: A Study of Independence.* Boston: Houghton, Mifflin and Company, 1892. https://www.gutenberg.org/cache/epub/35573/pg35573-images.html.
Roider, Karl A., Jr. "William Lee, Our First Envoy in Vienna." *The Virginia Magazine of History and Biography* 86, no. 2 (1978): 163–68. http://www.jstor.org/stable/4248202.
Rossie, Jonathan Gregory. *The Politics of Command in the American Revolution.* Syracuse, NY: Syracuse University Press, 1975.
Rossman, Kenneth R. "Thomas Mifflin—Revolutionary Patriot." *Pennsylvania History: A Journal of Mid-Atlantic Studies* 15, no. 1 (1948): 9–23. http://www.jstor.org/stable/27766855.
Rosswurm, Steven. *Arms, Country, and Class: The Philadelphia Militia and the "Lower Sort" during the American Revolution.* New Brunswick, NJ: Rutgers University Press, 1987.

Ryden, George Herbert, ed. "Letters to and from Caesar Rodney, 1756–1784." Philadelphia: Historical Society of Delaware, 1933. https://babel.hathitrust.org/cgi/pt?id=mdp.39015016868930&seq=1&q1=safety.

Ryerson, Richard Alan. *The Revolution Is Now Begun: The Radical Committees of Philadelphia, 1765–1776*. Philadelphia: University of Pennsylvania Press, 1978.

Saint Bris, Gonzague. *Lafayette: Hero of the American Revolution*. Translated by George Holoch. New York: Pegasus Books, 2010. https://archive.org/details/lafayetteheroofa0000sain/page/n5/mode/2up.

Sanders, Jennings B. *Evolution of Executive Departments of the Continental Congress, 1774–1789*. Chapel Hill, NC: The University of North Carolina Press, 1935.

Sanders, Jennings B. "Thomas Burke in the Continental Congress." *The North Carolina Historical Review* 9, no. 1 (1932): 22–37. http://www.jstor.org/stable/23514880.

Saunders, William L. *The Colonial Records of North Carolina*. Vol. 9. Raleigh, NC: Josephus Daniels, 1890. https://archive.org/details/colonialrecordso09nort/page/n5/mode/2up.

Schaffel, Kenneth. "The American Board of War, 1776–1781." *Military Affairs* 50, no. 4 (1986): 185–89. https://doi.org/10.2307/1988008.

Schaw, Janet. *Journal of a Lady of Quality*. New Haven, CT: Yale University Press, 1923. https://babel.hathitrust.org/cgi/pt?id=uc2.ark:/13960/t02z15h83&seq=7.

Schiff, Stacy. *A Great Improvisation: Franklin, France, and the Birth of America*. New York: Henry Holt and Company, 2005.

Schmidt, Jim. "John J. Zubly." *New Georgia Encyclopedia*. https://www.georgiaencyclopedia.org/articles/history-archaeology/john-j-zubly-1724-1781/.

Seabury, Samuel. *Thoughts on the Proceedings of the Continental Congress*. New York: Richardson and Urquhart, 1775. https://archive.org/details/cihm_20488/page/n7/mode/2up.

Selesky, Harold E., ed. *Encyclopedia of the American Revolution: Library of Military History*. Detroit, MI: Charles Scribner's Sons, 2006. Gale eBooks, link.gale.com/apps/pub/0SGQ/GVRL?u=tplmain&sid=gale_marc.

Sellers, Horace Wells, and C. W. Peale. "Charles Willson Peale, Artist-Soldier." *The Pennsylvania Magazine of History and Biography* 38, no. 3 (1914): 257–86. www.jstor.org/stable/20086174.

Serle, Ambrose (Edward H. Tatum, Jr., ed.). *The American Journal of Ambrose Serle, Secretary to Lord Howe, 1776–1778*. San Marino, CA: The Huntington Library, 1940. https://archive.org/details/americanjournalo0000ambr/page/n7/mode/2up.

Shaw, John. "Affidavit of John Shaw." *Colonial Records of South Carolina: Documents Relating to Indian Affairs, Series 2, 1754–1765*. Columbia, SC: South Carolina Department of Archives & History, 1970: 3–7. https://scdah.sc.gov/documents-relating-indian-affairs-1754-1760.

Shea, John Gilmary. *Life and Times of the Most Rev. John Carroll*. New York: John G. Shea, 1888. https://archive.org/details/lifeandtimesmos00sheagoog/page/n10/mode/2up.

Singerton, Jonathan. *The American Revolution and the Habsburg Monarchy*. Charlottesville, VA: University of Virginia Press, 2021. https://doi.org/10.52156/m.5768.

Skemp, Sheila L. *William Franklin: Son of a Patriot, Servant of a King*. New York: Oxford University Press, 1990.

Slade, William. *Vermont State Papers*. Middlebury, VT: J. W. Copeland, 1823. https://babel.hathitrust.org/cgi/pt?id=mdp.39015001989071&seq=5.

Small, Lawrence M. "Mr. Jefferson's Writing Box." *Smithsonian Magazine*, February 2001. http://www.smithsonianmag.com/history/mr-jeffersons-writing-box-37204074/.

Smith, Page. *John Adams*. Vols. 1–2. Garden City, NY: Doubleday & Company, Inc., 1962.

Smith, Paul H., et al., eds. *Letters of Delegates to Congress, 1774–1789*. 25 volumes. Washington, DC: Library of Congress, 1976–2000. https://memory.loc.gov/ammem/amlaw/lwdg.html.

Snow, Dean. *1777: Tipping Point at Saratoga*. New York: Oxford University Press, 2016.

South Carolina. *Journal of the Provincial Congress of South Carolina, 1776*. London: J. Almon, 1776. https://archive.org/details/bim_eighteenth-century_journal-of-the-provincia_south-carolina_1776/mode/2up.

Spall, Eric. "Foreigners in the Highest Trust: American Perceptions of European Mercenary Officers in the Continental Army." *Early American Studies* 12, no. 2 (2014): 338–65. http://www.jstor.org/stable/24474884.

Sparks, Jared. *Life of Gouverneur Morris*. Vol. 1. Boston: Gray & Bowen, 1832. https://babel.hathitrust.org/cgi/pt?id=hvd.32044072029663&seq=21.

Sparks, Jared, ed. *The Diplomatic Correspondence of the American Revolution.* Vol. 1. Boston: N. Hale and Gray & Bowen, 1829. https://ia803100.us.archive.org/2/items/diplomaticcorres01sparuoft/diplomaticcorres01sparuoft.pdf.
Stahr, Walter. *John Jay: Founding Father.* New York: Hambledon and London, 2005.
Staples, William R. *Rhode Island in the Continental Congress.* Providence, RI: Providence Press Company, 1870. https://babel.hathitrust.org/cgi/pt?id=miun.aqj4219.0001.001&seq=3.
Stillé, Charles J. *The Life and Times of John Dickinson, 1732–1808.* Philadelphia: The Historical Society of Philadelphia, 1891. https://archive.org/details/lifetimesofjohnd13stil/page/n15/mode/2up.
Stone, William L., translator. *Letters of Brunswick and Hessian Officers during the American Revolution.* Albany, NY: Munsell, 1891. https://catalog.hathitrust.org/Record/000364743.
Sullivan, Aaron. *The Disaffected: Britain's Occupation of Philadelphia during the American Revolution.* Philadelphia: University of Pennsylvania Press, 2009.
Taylor, Robert J., ed. *The Adams Papers*, Papers of John Adams. Vol. 3, May 1775–January 1776. Cambridge, MA: Harvard University Press, 1979. https://founders.archives.gov/.
Taylor, Robert J., ed. *The Adams Papers*, Papers of John Adams. Vol. 4, February–August 1776. Cambridge, MA: Harvard University Press, 1979. https://founders.archives.gov/.
Taylor, Robert J., ed. *The Adams Papers*, Papers of John Adams. Vol. 5, August 1776–March 1778. Cambridge, MA: Harvard University Press, 1983. https://founders.archives.gov/.
Taylor, Robert J., ed. *The Adams Papers*, Papers of John Adams. Vol. 6, March–August 1778. Cambridge, MA: Harvard University Press, 1983. https://founders.archives.gov/.
Thomas Paine National Historical Association, New Rochelle, NY. https://www.thomaspaine.org/pages/about-us.html.
Thorpe, Francis Newton, ed. T*he Federal and State Constitutions Colonial Charters, and Other Organic Laws of the States, Territories, and Colonies Now or Heretofore Forming the United States of America.* Washington, DC: Government Printing Office, 1909. https://archive.org/details/federalstatecons07thor/page/3818/mode/2up.
Tinkcom, Harry M. "The Revolutionary City, 1765–1783." *Philadelphia: A 300-Year History* New York: W. W. Norton & Company, 1982.
Trinity Church Wall Street. "The General and the Monument." https://trinitywallstreet.org/stories-news/general-and-monument.
Tuckerman, Bayard. *Life of General Philip Schuyler, 1733–1804.* New York: Dodd, Mead and Company, 1903.
United States, Continental Congress. *Secret Journals of the Acts and Proceedings of Congress.* Vol. 1. Boston: Thomas B. Wait, 1820. https://archive.org/details/secretjournals01unit/page/n5/mode/2up.
University System of Georgia. "Georgia Archives: Virtual Vault." https://vault.georgiaarchives.org/.
Van Doren, Carl. *Secret History of the American Revolution.* Garden City, NY: Garden City Publishing, 1941. https://openlibrary.org/works/OL4459887W/Secret_history_of_the_American_Revolution.
Virginia Gazette (Purdie), July 19, 1776. https://research.colonialwilliamsburg.org/DigitalLibrary/va-gazettes/VGSinglePage.cfm?issueIDNo=76.P.50.
Virginia, "Transcription: Virginia's Fifth Revolutionary Convention Called for Independence," May 15, 1776. *Convention, General Correspondence, Minutes, and Journals, 1774–1776*, Accession 30003, Library of Virginia, Richmond, VA. http://www.virginiamemory.com/docs/05-15-1776_trans_ck.pdf.
Wainwright, Nicholas B., and Sarah Logan Fisher. "'A Diary of Trifling Occurrences': Philadelphia, 1776–1778." *The Pennsylvania Magazine of History and Biography* 82, no. 4 (1958): 411–65. http://www.jstor.org/stable/20089127.
Waldo, Albigence. "Valley Forge, 1777–1778. Diary of Surgeon Albigence Waldo, of the Connecticut Line." *The Pennsylvania Magazine of History and Biography* 21, no. 3 (1897): 299–323. http://www.jstor.org/stable/20085750.
Wallace, David Duncan. *The Life of Henry Laurens.* New York: G. P. Putnam's Sons, 1915. https://archive.org/details/in.ernet.dli.2015.171269/page/n1/mode/2up.
Walpole, Horace. *Journal of the Reign of King George the Third.* Vol. 2, from the Year 1781–1783. London: Richard Bentley, 1859. https://babel.hathitrust.org/cgi/pt?id=hvd.hx14a2&seq=9.

Walton, E. P., ed. *Records of the Governor and Council of the State of Vermont.* Vol. 1. Montpelier, VT: J. & J. M. Poland, 1873. https://babel.hathitrust.org/cgi/pt?id=uc2.ark:/13960/t91834q5z&seq=9.

Warren, Charles. "Fourth of July Myths." *The William and Mary Quarterly* 2, no. 3 (1945): 237–72. https://doi.org/10.2307/1921451.

Watterson, John S. "Thomas Burke, Paradoxical Patriot." *The Historian* 41, no. 4 (1979): 664–81. http://www.jstor.org/stable/24443529.

Weaver., Emily P. "Nova Scotia and New England during the Revolution." *The American Historical Review* 10, no. 1 (1904): 52–71. https://doi.org/10.2307/1833814.

Wharton, Francis, ed. *The Revolutionary Diplomatic Correspondence of the United States.* Vol. 1. Washington, DC: Government Printing Office, 1889. https://babel.hathitrust.org/cgi/pt?id=mdp.35112102334887&seq=7.

Wharton, Francis, ed. *The Revolutionary Diplomatic Correspondence of the United States.* Vol. 2. Washington, DC: Government Printing Office, 1889. https://babel.hathitrust.org/cgi/pt?id=hvd.32044074367285&seq=7.

Wilbur, James Benjamin. *Ira Allen: Founder of Vermont.* Vol. 1. Boston: Houghton Mifflin Company, 1928. https://archive.org/details/iraallenfoundero0001jame/page/n9/mode/2up.

Wilkes, John. *Speeches of Mr. Wilkes in the House of Commons.* London: 1786. https://archive.org/details/speechesmrwilke00wilkgoog/page/n6/mode/2up.

Wilkinson, James. *Memoirs of My Own Times.* Vol. 1. Philadelphia: Abraham Small, 1816. https://archive.org/details/memoirsofmyownti01wilk/page/n5/mode/2up.

Willcox, William B., ed. *The Papers of Benjamin Franklin.* Vol. 20, January 1 through December 31, 1773. New Haven, CT: Yale University Press, 1976. https://founders.archives.gov/.

Willcox, William B., ed. *The Papers of Benjamin Franklin.* Vol. 21, January 1, 1774, through March 22, 1775. New Haven, CT: Yale University Press, 1978. https://founders.archives.gov/.

Willcox, William B., ed. *The Papers of Benjamin Franklin.* Vol. 22, March 23, 1775, through October 27, 1776. New Haven, CT: Yale University Press, 1982. https://founders.archives.gov/.

Willcox, William B., ed. *The Papers of Benjamin Franklin.* Vol. 23, October 27, 1776, through April 30, 1777. New Haven, CT: Yale University Press, 1983. https://founders.archives.gov/.

Willcox, William B., ed. *The Papers of Benjamin Franklin.* Vol. 24, May 1 through September 30, 1777. New Haven, CT: Yale University Press, 1984. https://founders.archives.gov/.

Willcox, William B., ed. *The Papers of Benjamin Franklin.* Vol. 25, October 1, 1777, through February 28, 1778. New Haven, CT: Yale University Press, 1986. https://founders.archives.gov/.

Willcox, William B., ed. *The Papers of Benjamin Franklin.* Vol. 26, March 1 through June 30, 1778. New Haven, CT: Yale University Press, 1987. https://founders.archives.gov/.

Wilmerding, Lucius, Jr. "The United States Lottery." *The New-York Historical Society Quarterly* 47, no. 1 (1963): 5–22. https://digitalcollections.nyhistory.org/islandora/object/islandora%3A15521#page/1/mode/2up.

Wilson, Barry K. *Benedict Arnold: A Traitor in Our Midst.* Montreal: McGill-Queen's University Press, 2001.

Witherspoon, John. *The Works of John Witherspoon.* Vol. 9. Edinburgh: J. Ogle, 1815. https://babel.hathitrust.org/cgi/pt?id=umn.319510020365902&seq=7.

Wolf, Edwin. "The Authorship of the 1774 Address to the King Restudied." *The William and Mary Quarterly* 22, no. 2 (1965): 190–224. https://doi.org/10.2307/1920696.

Wood, Gordon S. *The Americanization of Benjamin Franklin.* New York: The Penguin Press, 2004.

Wood, Gordon S. *The Creation of the American Republic, 1776–1787.* Chapel Hill, NC: University of North Carolina Press, 1969.

Wroblewski, Joseph E. "Winning Hearts and Minds: Pardons and Oaths of Allegiance." *Journal of the American Revolution*, January 3, 2023. https://allthingsliberty.com/2023/01/winning-hearts-and-minds-pardons-and-oaths-of-allegiance/.

Young, William, "Journal of William Young." *The Pennsylvania Magazine of History and Biography* 8, no. 3 (1884). http://www.jstor.org/stable/20084659.

Index

Adams, Abigail, 13, 28, 86, 95, 109, 120–21, 164, 167, 169, 215, 237, 258, 313
Adams, John, 12–13, 16, 18, 20, 27–28, 30–31, 36–37, 39, 45–46, 58–59, 66, 76–77, 86, 91, 94–96, 107–10, 120–23, 127, 130, 135, 136–39, 140–48, 150, 159, 161, 164, 167–68, 182–83, 187–91, 202, 215, 237–39, 248, 252–53, 261–62, 268, 276, 278, 280, 285, 292, 300, 307, 309, 313–14, 316, 317, 334, 392
Adams, John Quincy, 46, 105, 314, 316
Adams, Samuel, 19, 27–28, 32, 45–46, 111, 121–23, 134–39, 150, 197–98, 207, 220, 232, 237, 250, 270, 274, 306–7, 330, 382, 388–89
Africans, 171, 254
Aitken, Robert, 118–19
Albany, 32, 41, 100, 128, 131, 144, 165, 266–67, 270, 272, 274–75, 276, 286, 288, 302–3, 310, 323, 347
alcohol *see* liquor
Allegheny Mountains, 180–81
Allen, Ethan, 63–65, 136, 141, 233
Allen, Heman, 141
Alsop, John, 172
American Crisis, The, 223
American Grand Council, 33
American Revolution, 17, 35, 48, 79, 83, 90, 120, 169, 171–72, 175, 178, 193, 197, 201, 241–42, 252, 255, 267–68, 295, 304, 334, 343, 363
Amphitrite, 196, 260–61
Amsterdam, 246, 363
Andrea Doria, 97
Anglican, 15–16, 32, 40, 117, 299, 373
Annapolis, 31, 81, 127, 155
Army
    barracks, 62, 204, 311, 387
    British, 4, 7, 61, 73, 87, 99, 127, 165, 177, 187, 207, 266, 268, 278, 280, 283, 288–89, 295, 298, 300, 303, 305, 312, 327, 353, 366 *see also* Redcoat
    Continental, 67, 70, 89, 97, 99, 101, 185, 188, 199, 214, 217, 226, 228, 232, 242, 275, 318, 358, 369, 378, 380–81
    Convention Army, 310–12, 331–33
    German, 112, 189, 221, 311–12, 359
    light infantry, 46, 111, 307
    Middlesex County's First Battalion, 153
    militia, 29, 37, 44–47, 62–63, 65, 67, 86, 88, 95, 97, 105, 114, 135, 152–53, 162, 173, 175, 190, 191, 202, 207, 220–22, 224, 229, 232, 238–39, 248, 274–76, 280, 285, 287, 294, 318, 326, 338–39, 342, 344, 357–58
    Northern Army, 88, 146, 152, 232, 266–68, 270–71, 272, 275, 279, 287
    Patriot army, 68, 95 *see also* Patriot
    Queen's Loyal Rangers, 287
    Riflemen, 68, 238, 303
    Rogers's Rangers, 78
Arnold, Benedict, 233–35, 287–88, 296, 298, 301–3, 347, 383, 387–88, 391
Articles of Confederation, 92, 180, 242, 293, 297, 307, 385
assemblies, 11, 33, 40, 44, 104, 150, 168, 220, 340, 376
Baltimore, 214, 252, 270, 318, 379
Bancroft, Edward, 193–94, 246
Bartlett, Josiah, 119, 180, 187, 259, 384, 386
Beaumarchais, Pierre Augustin Caron de, 195–97, 261
Board of War and Ordinance, 149
Bennington, 250, 275, 286–87
Berlin, 246–47, 251–52, 362–63
Bermuda, 92
Bible, 18, 49, 120, 253 *see also* Old Testament
Bill of Rights
    "Jefferson's," 79
    American, 157–58, 243

blasphemy, 65, 136
Board of War, 149, 317–19, 323, 328, 341, 346–50
Bonvouloir, Julien-Alexandre Archard de, 124–25
Boston, 1, 4–5, 7–8, 13, 19–20, 22, 27–29, 31–32, 34, 38, 44–46, 50, 56–57, 61–62, 67, 69, 77–78, 85–86, 89, 92–95, 97, 101, 106, 115, 129, 136, 148, 165, 176, 183, 204, 237, 286, 290, 294, 305, 310–12, 314, 331, 337, 366, 368, 370, 384
    Harbor, 1, 6, 38, 57, 66, 133
    Massacre, 5–6, 13, 366
    Port Act, 6, 81
    Tea Party, 1, 6, 13, 19, 22, 32, 57, 75, 78, 81, 118
Braddock, Major General Edward, 72–73, 268
Braintree, 45, 94, 313
Braxton, Carter, 133, 147
Bristol, 254, 289
British constitution, 100, 119
British Empire, 6, 11, 53, 56, 94
Brown, Philip, 176
Bulloch, Archibald, 95
Bunker Hill, 86, 90–91, 175, 186, 205, 275
Burgoyne, General John, 266, 272–76, 278, 286–88, 296, 300–4, 305, 310, 312, 314, 332–33, 337, 339, 346
Burke, Thomas, 241, 284, 289, 308, 350–52
Burlington, 114–15, 152–53, 217
Burwell, Rebecca, 80
Cabot, 97
Cambridge, 28, 61, 102, 105, 311–12
Canada, 4, 6, 38, 63, 87–88, 99–100, 105–6, 115, 121–24, 127–28, 131, 133, 141–46, 149, 155, 170, 176, 178, 203–4, 208, 234, 249, 266, 268–69, 272–73, 274, 287–88, 315, 346–47 *see also* Quebec
Cannon, James, 135–36
Capitol, 26, 48, 159, 216
Caribbean, 192, 372
Carlisle, 163, 283, 381
Carlton, Guy, 205
Carpenters' Hall, 2, 3, 19, 23, 26–27, 30, 35–36, 47, 124, 154, 360
Carroll, Charles, 127–28, 131, 144–45, 177, 205, 244–45, 294, 296
Catholic, 6, 38, 87, 100, 127–28, 131–32, 372
Charleston, 5, 12, 83, 178, 203, 209, 230, 252, 254–55, 263, 278–79, 340
Charlottesville, 80

Chase, Samuel, 31, 97, 99, 104, 127–28, 144–45, 155, 180–81, 229, 318
Cherokee, 91, 255, 345
Chestnut Street, 81, 95, 110
Church, Benjamin, 101–2
City Tavern, 1, 13, 14, 39, 111, 387
civil war, 40, 119, 250
Clinton, Henry, 305, 333, 373, 375–76, 378–81, 384
Clymer, George, 218, 225, 263
coffee, 1, 41, 47, 76, 87, 109, 118, 185, 228–29, 254
coins, 68, 82–84, 101, 131, 183, 309, 311, 352
College of William & Mary, 80
Committee of Commerce, 113 *see also* Secret Committee
Committee of Privates, 135
Common Sense, 117, 119–21, 214, 223, 334
Concord, 44–46, 57–58, 61, 63, 65, 78, 118, 129, 135, 147, 156, 232, 248, 285
Confederation Congress, 24
Congregationalist, 27
Connecticut, 1–2, 8, 11–14, 23, 25, 29, 40, 46, 60, 64–65, 67, 76–78, 87, 91, 86, 100, 102–3, 111, 116, 125, 133, 147, 151–54, 158, 170–71, 180–81, 193, 200, 207, 214, 215, 228–29, 233–34, 237, 248–49, 253, 269, 273, 285, 287, 289, 297, 331–32, 356, 367, 385, 390
    River, 91
Continental Congress, 1, 3, 7, 9, 14, 18–24, 25, 38, 40–43, 48, 62–63, 67, 70, 76, 78, 81, 93, 87, 94, 97, 114, 126–27, 134, 141, 151–54, 156–57, 166, 172, 174, 179, 184, 214, 228–29, 249, 256, 293, 332 *see also* Confederation Congress
    First, 1, 3, 7, 9, 14, 19–20, 23–24, 25–26, 37, 43, 57, 61, 70, 78, 81, 331
    Second, 24, 44, 45, 49, 58, 60–61
Continental dollar, 83–85, 131, 207, 226–28, 297, 286, 311–12, 327, 353, 360, 365
conventions, 44, 104, 107, 239, 251
Conway, Thomas, 320–23, 328–29, 335–37, 346–48, 369
Cornwallis, Charles, 225
Coudray, Phillippe Charles Jean Baptiste Tronson de, 259–62, 264
Council of Safety, 108, 295
courthouse, 170, 216, 238, 292–93, 368, 380
court-martial, 89, 295
Court of France, 197, 199

crime, 101, 169, 215, 235, 281
Crown, 17, 38, 112–13, 119, 138, 143, 155, 250, 298, 365 *see also* monarchy
Crown Point, 38, 64, 178
currency, 22, 68, 82–85, 100–2, 132, 149, 179, 182, 226–29, 267, 281, 285, 353, 360 *see also* Continental dollar
Cushing, Thomas, 4, 46
Custis, Martha (later Martha Washington), 74 *see also* Martha Washington
Daymon, Francis, 124
Deane, Silas, 12–15, 25, 28, 30–31, 37, 40, 47, 60, 66, 69, 77, 97, 109, 125–26, 143, 185, 192–98, 210–12, 240, 245–47, 252, 260–61, 263–64, 308, 313–16, 320, 368, 370, 392
Declaration of Independence, 34, 48, 90, 143, 154, 159–60, 163, 167, 170–71, 200, 213, 249, 253, 309, 360, 387
Declaration of Rights, 157–58
  English, 157
  Virginia, 158
Delaware, 3, 8, 15–16, 27, 29–30, 35, 51, 65, 134, 137–38, 152, 160–62, 170, 173, 180, 200–1, 206, 209, 214, 217, 221, 224–25, 231, 244, 279–80, 283, 297, 313, 334–35, 343, 357, 360–61, 365, 373, 375, 378–79, 385, 388 *see also* Dover
  Convention, 152
  River, 15, 136–37, 217, 223, 298, 313, 375
D'Eon, Chevalier, 196
Detroit, 96
Dickinson, John, 16–18, 19, 23, 35, 38, 40, 55, 66, 89–90, 95, 109, 113, 115, 121, 138, 142–43, 148, 160–61, 163, 173–74, 179–80, 207, 236, 240, 242, 297, 308, 336, 384 *see also Letters from a Pennsylvania Farmer*
diplomatic mission, 127, 254, 362
disease, 42, 132, 145, 219, 326, 354 *see also* dysentery, smallpox
Dover, 118, 162, 170
Duane, James, 23, 31–32, 34, 60, 139, 170, 240, 266, 271, 275, 288, 294–95, 308
Duché, Jacob, 27–28, 61, 299–300, 362
Dunlap, John, 168–69
Dunmore, Earl of (John Murray), 104–5, 109, 112, 155
Du Simitière, Pierre Eugène, 183
Dyer, Eliphalet, 67, 76–78, 96, 111, 116, 233, 261, 273, 294, 305, 332, 337, 346

dysentery, 13, 73–74, 264, 354
Eagle, 176–77
East India, 5–6, 37, 130
  Company, 5–6
  Tea, 5, 37, 130
East River, 186
education, 12, 14, 19–20, 25, 31, 50, 70, 76, 80, 85, 193, 254–55, 233, 343
electricity, 52
Ellery, William, 215, 333
England, 5, 15, 20, 22, 40, 49, 53–58, 68, 83, 87, 105, 107, 112, 117, 119, 157, 166, 183, 193, 211, 215, 236, 245–46, 251–52, 254–55, 304, 306, 312, 355, 373–75, 392
English Channel, 117, 124, 193
English constitution, 34
enslavement *see* slavery
E Pluribus Unum, 183 *see also* Great Seal of the United States
Fairfax, Sally, 74
Falmouth, 105, 137
flag, 159, 183, 304, 332, 376, 387
Flanders, 54, 127
Florida, 4, 39, 62, 92, 143, 240, 257, 372
food, 22, 122, 205, 226, 238, 272, 288, 313, 326–27, 331, 343, 354, 357, 360–61, 367
Fort Constitution, 203
Fort Necessity, 72
Fort Pitt, 74
Fort St. Jean, 88, 99, 105
Fort Ticonderoga, 63, 88, 203, 272, 383
Fort Washington, 203–4
Founding Fathers, 32
France, 4, 52, 71, 78, 117, 123–28, 143, 157, 160, 168–69, 182, 185, 192–99, 210, 228, 239–40, 245–47, 252, 260–62, 264, 297, 314–16, 320–22, 329, 331, 347, 362–64, 367–70, 372, 375–76, 385, 388, 390, 392 *see also* Court of France, Paris
Franklin, Benjamin, 11, 33, 49, 50–59, 85, 90, 92–93, 96, 110, 113, 118, 124–28, 144, 146–47, 152–54, 158–59, 163, 167–68, 175, 177, 179, 182–83, 188–89, 192–94, 196–98, 210–12, 240, 245–47, 289, 308, 314–16, 370, 391–92
Franklin, William, 11, 44, 58, 113–15, 152–54
Frederick County, 155
French and Indian War, 38, 53, 68, 70, 72, 75, 78, 91, 175, 327
Gage, General Thomas, 44

Galloway, Joseph, 2, 9–11, 16–20, 23, 30–31, 33–35, 37, 39–40, 43, 47, 58, 60, 358–59, 361, 372, 378, 384, 391
Gates, General Horatio, 77, 111, 178, 235, 266, 269–71, 274, 276–77, 278, 285–86, 296, 298, 300–4, 305, 309, 312, 319, 321–23, 332, 334–37, 339, 341, 344, 348–49
George III, King, 3, 54, 68, 116, 172, 174, 252, 263, 273, 374
Georgia, 3, 39–40, 49, 56, 62, 94, 109, 114, 158, 166, 170, 180, 183, 200–1, 218, 255–56, 278, 388, 393
Gérard, Conrad Alexandre, 314, 388–90
Germany, 183, 252, 341, 362–63 see also Berlin
Gerry, Elbridge, 142, 168–69, 178, 300
gold, 82, 84, 100–1, 131, 196, 305, 311, 315, 353, 360
Graves, Admiral Samuel, 105
Gravier, Charles, Count of Vergennes, 125, 185, 194, 196, 212, 247, 315
Great Britain, 1, 4, 9, 11–12, 30–31, 40, 60, 63, 67, 90, 92, 94, 108, 112–13, 116, 121, 125, 128–30, 138, 143, 155–56, 163, 172, 174, 189, 250–51, 270, 314, 333, 365, 368, 377, 392 see also England
Great Seal of the United States, 182 see also E Pluribus Unum
Greek and Roman mythology, 183, 236
Greene, Nathanael, 204–5, 220, 261, 324, 344, 349, 358, 367
Green Mountain Boys, 65, 141, 249–50
Green Mountains, 64, 136, 310
Gulf Stream, 210, 217
Habsburgs, 251–52, 363 see also Joseph II
Hamilton, Alexander, 343–44
Hancock, John, 19, 45–46, 49, 65, 85, 91, 95, 100, 105, 111, 121, 128, 148, 158–59, 163, 167, 169, 187, 208, 214–16, 218, 225, 229, 231–32, 237, 250, 254, 264, 293, 299, 306–7, 370, 384–85, 389
hanging, 55, 65, 73, 86, 166, 178, 194, 221, 281, 330, 356, 359, 390
Harlem Heights, 189, 203
Harrison, Benjamin, 26, 95, 111, 147, 158, 178, 181, 265, 275, 278
Harvard, 12, 19, 50, 52, 312
Hawes, Joseph, 85
Heard, Colonel Nathaniel, 153
Henry, Patrick, 25, 95, 143, 337, 339, 368
Hewes, Joseph, 112, 120, 129, 141, 165, 173, 180
Hichborn, Benjamin, 95

Holland, 54, 253, 363
Hooper, William, 40, 65, 112, 130, 191, 202, 215, 226, 231–32, 236
House of Burgesses, 8, 21, 23, 25, 65, 72–75, 81
House of Commons, 14, 33, 55, 368
House of Representatives
    Connecticut, 8
    Massachusetts, 8, 20, 56, 61
    New Hampshire, 200
    South Carolina, 340
    United States, 181, 244
Howe, Admiral Lord Richard, 174–77, 187–89, 203, 217, 298, 301, 375
Howe, General William, 174–75, 217, 221, 266, 278–79, 284, 290, 295, 312–13, 324, 330, 333, 339, 350, 352, 353, 355–56, 358–60, 364, 373–76, 383, 384
Hudson River, 31–32, 87, 128, 165, 203–5, 266, 274, 278–79, 287–88, 231, 305, 349
Huguenot, 32, 254, 342–43
Hutchinson, Thomas, 56–57, 171
Hynson, Joseph, 246
Independence Hall, 2, 48–49, 159 see also Pennsylvania State House
indigenous people, 3, 53, 55, 73–74, 78, 88–89, 91–92, 103–4, 108, 176, 253, 286–88, 302–3, 309, 341, 345 see also Cherokee, Iroquois, Mohawk
Iredell, James, 201
Ireland, 113, 183, 241, 253, 320
Iroquois, 91, 148
Intolerable Act, 6, 31, 34
Jamaica, 93
Jay, John, 23, 31–32, 113, 198, 210, 240, 252, 266
Jefferson, Thomas, 78–81, 82, 89, 92, 104, 139, 142, 144, 147–48, 157–59, 162–63, 166, 168, 170–71, 180, 182–83, 192, 240, 252, 259 see also Summary View of the Rights of British America
Jehovah, 63
Joseph II, Emperor, 252, 362
July 4, 167–69, 171, 200, 348
Kennebec River, 99, 106
Lake Champlain, 62–63, 87–88, 100, 131, 178, 203–4, 234–35, 266, 269, 346–47, 383
Lake George, 131, 274
Laurens, Henry, 254–58, 260, 264, 273, 276, 278, 283, 289–90, 292, 297, 300, 305–7, 322, 328, 330–33, 338, 340–50, 356, 364–65, 367, 371, 376–78, 382, 385, 387–90

lawmaker, 2, 5–6, 8–9, 20, 23, 33, 48, 65, 74, 103, 114–15, 134, 136–37, 142, 150–53, 166, 168, 175, 201, 255, 308, 328, 388, 391
Lee, Arthur, 21, 197, 210, 236, 239–40, 245–46, 251, 314–16, 363, 392
Lee, Charles, 68–69, 77, 94, 203–4, 206, 209–10, 213, 336–37, 355–56
Lee, Francis Lightfoot, 21, 109, 123, 161, 197, 245, 330, 382
Lee, Richard Henry, 20–21, 29, 105, 109–10, 120, 130, 143–44, 147, 167, 192, 197–98, 232, 236, 238, 267–68, 283, 292, 298, 308, 318, 320–21, 331, 337, 376, 378–82, 387, 389
Lee, William, 245–46, 251, 314–16, 362–64
Letters from a Pennsylvania Farmer, 17 see also Dickinson, John
Lewis, Francis, 178
Lexington, 44–46, 57–58, 61, 63, 65, 78, 115, 118, 135, 147, 156, 232, 248, 285
liberties of America, 7, 104, 154, 339
Liberty Bell, 49, 285
"Liberty Song," 17
Library Company of Philadelphia, 2, 27
liquor, 89, 118, 251, 253, 288, 303, 331, 369
Liverpool, 75, 254
Livingston, Philip, 23, 266
Livingston, Robert, 31, 143, 147, 159
Livingston, William, 23
London, 5, 10, 14–16, 23, 33, 38, 40, 46, 50–58, 64, 68, 71–75, 79, 93, 117–18, 123–25, 175, 183, 193, 195, 197–98, 228, 245–46, 251, 254, 340, 355, 362, 364, 375, 377, 379
Long Island, 165, 186–87, 225, 343
Louis XV, King, 52
Louis XVI, King, 239, 315, 369
Lovell, James, 261, 264, 271, 279, 290, 307, 313, 336–37, 366, 368, 373, 382
Loyalist, 7, 11, 28, 40, 54, 57, 60, 95, 104, 108–9, 113–14, 116, 118, 129, 136–38, 152, 162, 166, 173, 176, 209, 217–18, 221, 239, 257, 270, 279, 286–87, 289–91, 302, 337, 342–43, 350–52, 356, 360, 373–74, 377–78, 383–84, 387, 390–91
Lynch, Thomas, 12, 14, 96, 106, 122
Maine, 2–3, 99, 105–6, 122, 137, 233, 368
Manhattan, 165, 186, 189, 202–4, 269, 318, 356
Marie Antoinette, 263, 363

Marshall, Christopher, 111, 136
Maryland, 3, 8, 14, 16, 31, 40–41, 51, 68, 81, 97, 99, 104–5, 116, 121, 127, 133–34, 139, 143, 155–56, 158, 171, 177, 180–81, 200, 229, 231, 244, 246, 270–80, 283, 318, 360, 364, 372, 374, 377, 378, 385–86, 388
Convention, 155, 180
Mason, George, 158
Masons, 51, 282
May 15 resolution, 139, 140, 152–53, 156
McCrea, Jane "Jenny," 286–87
McKean, Thomas, 162, 173, 365, 377
McPherson, John, 102
Middle Atlantic colonies/states, 3, 14, 134, 143–44, 197, 226, 349, 373, 393 see also Delaware, New Jersey, New York, Pennsylvania
Middlesex County, 153
Middleton, Henry, 4, 14, 37, 65
Mississippi River, 4, 257, 373, 385
Mohawk, 5, 266, 287–88
monarchy, 119, 157, 252
money see coins, Continental dollar, currency
Montgomery, Brigadier-General Richard, 100–1, 105, 115, 121–23, 142
Montreal, 4, 87–88, 97, 99, 105, 110, 115, 122, 131, 144–46
Morris, Robert, 126, 163, 174, 177, 192–95, 197, 211, 214, 216–18, 227, 232, 238, 240, 245, 259, 264, 342, 346–50, 365, 368–69, 374, 377
Mount Vernon, 74–76, 104, 189
Murray, John see Dunmore, Earl of
Nantes, 195, 240, 245, 314
Navy, 97–98, 130, 178, 203, 207, 234, 300
British/Royal, 1, 137, 186–87, 217, 246
French, 212
Marine Committee, 98
New Brunswick, 170, 188, 205–6, 224
New England, 3, 12, 14, 26, 28–29, 37, 40, 43, 45–47, 62, 64–65, 67–69, 76–77, 83, 93, 101–6, 122, 134, 165, 191–92, 197, 203–4, 207, 217, 226, 228–30, 231–33, 249, 252, 267–69, 272–77, 285, 293, 297, 299, 311, 318, 333, 337, 339, 342, 346, 349, 366–67, 372–73, 393 see also Connecticut, Maine, Massachusetts, New Hampshire, Rhode Island, Vermont
Convention, 228, 230–32

New Hampshire, 3, 8, 10, 42–43, 60, 64, 99, 107–9, 116, 119, 130, 136–37, 141, 152, 158, 169, 178, 180, 183, 187, 196, 200, 218, 220, 228, 236–37, 241, 246, 249–50, 259, 261, 275, 289, 297, 313, 242, 370, 384–85

New Hampshire Grants, 64, 141, 249–50 *see also* Vermont

New Haven, 12–13, 248, 293

New Jersey, 8, 11, 23, 40, 44, 46, 51, 55–58, 93, 113–18, 130, 134, 143, 152–54, 160–61, 169–71, 173, 178, 180, 188, 200, 203–9, 213–18, 220–21, 224–26, 230, 236, 238–39, 261, 271, 275, 281, 290, 297, 324, 328, 332, 336–37, 343, 354, 356, 358, 378–80, 385–86, 388

New York

  City, 5, 7, 10, 31–32, 40–41, 46–47, 83, 86, 144, 156, 165–66, 169–70, 172–73, 176–78, 186–87, 189, 193, 202, 204–5, 209, 217–18, 226, 239, 252, 254, 266, 278, 306, 313, 318, 326, 333, 342–43, 355, 373, 377, 379–81, 384

  colony/state, 3, 9–10, 30, 32, 40–41, 62, 64–65, 68, 77–78, 88, 100, 103–4, 114, 133–34, 136, 139, 141, 143, 147, 156, 161–62, 164–67, 172, 180, 200, 204, 214, 218, 231, 249–50, 266, 268, 269–71, 275–77, 287, 297, 339, 342, 346, 347, 349, 354, 365, 385

  Convention, 172, 250, 270

  Harbor, 165, 355

North Carolina, 3, 8, 10, 14, 40, 42, 47, 65, 85–86, 112, 120, 129–30, 141, 151, 158, 165, 173, 180, 191, 200–2, 215, 226, 231–32, 241, 249, 263, 278, 284, 297, 307–8, 330, 350, 352, 388

Northern Department, 88, 267, 269–70, 276, 278, 287, 339, 349

Nova Scotia, 39, 62, 92, 106, 129

Ohio River, 6, 53, 71

Old Testament, 182–83

Pacific Ocean, 180, 297, 385 *see also* South Sea

pacifism, 3, 15, 18, 134, 180, 281–82, 318, 327

Paine, Thomas, 46, 117–21, 137, 167, 214, 223, 289, 318, 334

Paris, 15, 58, 185, 313–16, 362–64, 368, 375, 392

Patriot, 7–9, 11–13, 17, 19, 30, 34, 37, 44–47, 57, 62–65, 67–68, 78–79, 87–88, 94, 95, 101–2, 104, 108–9, 111, 114, 122, 127, 129, 136, 140–42, 147, 149–56, 166, 174, 268, 270, 274–75, 281–82, 286–88, 301–3, 322, 331, 342–44, 353, 357–59, 361, 364, 366, 384, 387

Patterson, Lieutenant Colonel James, 177

Pennsylvania, 3, 8–10, 15–16, 30, 35, 39, 47, 50, 52–53, 54–56, 58, 66, 68, 71–72, 83, 90, 93, 101–4, 109, 114, 116, 133–40, 142–43, 145, 154–55, 160–64, 169, 173–74, 178, 180, 200–2, 206–7, 214–15, 217–18, 221, 224–25, 230, 236, 238, 241, 280, 282, 285, 288, 290, 292, 294–95, 297, 299, 318, 324, 328, 337–38, 342, 357–58, 360–61, 372, 378, 381, 385, 389–91

Convention, 135, 138, 140, 174

Pennsylvania Assembly, 2, 6, 48–49, 51, 54–55, 58, 60, 134, 136, 138, 142

Pennsylvania Gazette, 51, 137, 158

Pennsylvania Magazine, 118

Pennsylvania State House, 2, 47–48, 67, 116, 136, 140, 146, 159, 242, 354 *see also* Independence Hall

Penn, Governor John, 130, 134

Penn, Thomas, 53–55

Penn, William, 15–16, 53–55

Perth Amboy, 114, 152–54, 176, 188

Pickering, Timothy, 319, 341

Plain Truth, 121, 334

police, 107, 152, 242, 359

Portsmouth, 42, 107, 196, 261, 370

Potomac River, 20, 21, 47, 74, 104

Presbyterian, 27, 94, 136, 215, 253, 332

Prince Edward Island, 39, 62

Princeton, 153, 213, 224–25, 275, 318, 332, 334

prison, 18, 136, 205, 282, 387

prisoner, 43, 103, 117, 123, 149, 157, 176–77, 188, 214, 224–26, 239, 254, 282–83, 300, 303, 310–14, 317, 331, 344, 350–52, 353, 355, 361, 369, 379, 383

Privy Council, 57

Proclamation of Rebellion, 112

Prohibitory Act, 123, 130

Protestant, 6, 27, 106, 128, 157, 254

Prussia, 246, 251–52, 363, 370

Putnam, Israel, 78

Quakerism, 3, 8–9, 15–18, 27–28, 47, 53, 67, 117, 134–35, 173, 214, 237, 253, 281–83, 291, 295, 318, 327, 359, 361, 372, 390

Quebec, 4, 6, 22, 38, 62–63, 87–88, 91–92, 96, 99, 106, 110, 115, 120–22, 127, 132, 142, 145–46, 233–34, 267, 302

radical, 1, 7, 9–12, 16, 20–23, 25, 31, 33–34, 57, 135–36, 147–48, 201, 227, 245
Randolph, Peyton, 23–24, 37, 61, 65, 78–80, 101
rebels, 34, 44, 64, 86, 112, 121, 123, 176, 196, 263, 306, 358, 375, 378
Redcoat, 4, 8, 61–62, 67, 97, 191, 226, 256, 296, 373, 380
Reed, Joseph, 176, 205–6, 220, 225, 337, 342, 377–78, 384, 390
Religious Society of Friends, 15 see also Quakerism
Reprisal, 198, 210
Revolutionary leaders, 108, 201, 259
Revolutionary War, 48
Rhode Island, 3, 8, 10, 30, 36, 40, 60, 78, 95, 97, 101, 116, 150–52, 158, 180, 200, 204, 215, 217, 218, 228–29, 239, 244, 271, 273, 297, 312, 326, 331, 333, 356, 385
Riedesel, Baroness Friederike von, 310–11
Rodney, Cesar, 28–30, 136, 138–39, 162, 365
Roebuck, 137
Rush, Benjamin, 136, 178, 229, 231, 236, 334–37, 341
Rutledge, Edward, 14, 23, 30, 33, 37, 62, 96, 143, 161–62, 182, 188–89, 269, 281
Saratoga, 128, 144, 267, 293, 300–1, 303–4, 305–6, 309, 312, 314, 319, 323–24, 331–34, 344
  Convention, 304, 306, 309, 331–33
Savannah, 94, 170
Schuyler, Philip, 32, 78, 88, 96, 99–101, 106, 110, 128, 232, 266–72, 274–76, 286–88, 303, 310, 312, 337, 347, 367
Schuylkill River, 15, 110, 262, 324
Scotland, 54, 163, 183, 253, 332
Secret Committee, 96, 113 see also Committee of Commerce
settlers, 15, 64–65, 102–3, 108, 134, 141, 183, 249
Seven Years' War, 70, 124, 370
Shadwell, 80–81
Sherman, Roger, 13–14, 96, 147, 159, 181
slavery, 22, 27, 37, 79, 119, 136, 162, 171, 197, 241, 256
smallpox, 132, 354
snow, 5, 122, 128, 223, 310, 325, 328, 354, 366
South, the, 31, 104, 134, 178, 207, 230, 372–73, 381 see also Georgia, Maryland, North Carolina, South Carolina, Virginia

South Carolina, 2, 4, 8, 12, 14, 23, 28, 31, 33, 36–37, 62, 65, 96, 106, 108–9, 116, 122, 130, 137, 143–44, 151, 160–62, 166, 180, 200–3, 230, 237, 254–58, 263, 269, 276, 278, 307, 331, 340, 365, 367, 388
South Sea, 179–81, 385 see also Pacific Ocean
Spain, 82, 143, 185, 195, 239–40, 256, 251, 315, 372
Stamp Act, 4, 12, 17, 22–23, 25, 37, 55, 75, 94, 175, 255
Stark, John, 275
state constitutions, 107, 200–2
  Delaware, 200
  Georgia, 200–1
  Maryland, 200
  Massachusetts, 200
  New Hampshire, 131, 200
  New Jersey, 200
  New York, 156, 200
  North Carolina, 200–1
  Pennsylvania, 174, 200–2, 295
  South Carolina, 131, 151, 200, 256
  Vermont, 250
  Virginia, 139, 147, 157–58, 200
Staten Island, 176, 187–88
Steuben, Lieutenant General Frederick William Augustus Henry Ferdinand Baron von, 370–71, 382
St. Clair, General Arthur, 272–73, 275–76
St. Lawrence River, 87, 106, 122, 146
Stockton, Richard, 213
Strahan, William, 58
Stratford Hall, 20–21
Suffolk Resolves, 29–31
sugar, 43, 82, 228, 273, 372
Sullivan, General John, 145, 187, 261, 284
Summary View of the Rights of British America, 78–79, 148
Supreme Court, 39, 49
Susquehanna River, 103, 292, 379
Tanaghrisson, 71–72
tax, 1, 4–5, 17, 19, 29, 33, 36, 42, 53–55, 68, 75, 84, 92–93, 107–8, 113, 118, 171, 179, 181–82, 201, 226–27, 229, 231, 255, 281–82, 297, 309, 377, 391
tea, 1, 6, 13, 37, 38, 41–42, 57, 66, 76, 78, 81, 110, 118, 130–31, 228, 391 see also Boston Tea Party
Terrible, 117–18
Thetford, 117–18
Thomson, Charles, 23, 61, 90, 158, 167, 384

Ticonderoga *see* Fort Ticonderoga
tobacco, 16, 20–22, 25, 31, 74–75, 82, 118, 125, 195–96, 212, 226, 245, 247, 267, 278, 372
Tories, 7, 149, 152–53, 156, 187, 202, 223, 251, 253, 282, 330, 387 *see also* Loyalist
Treaty of Amity and Commerce, 314, 368
Trinity Church, 170
Trois Rivières, 146
Trumbull, Governor Jonathan, 159, 229, 231, 267
Tryon, William, 86
Tuscany, 251–52, 316
tyranny, 75, 90, 173, 177, 200, 223, 251–52
United Colonies, 92, 128, 130, 142–43, 152, 155, 250
United States, 13, 123, 172, 179–80, 182–83, 190, 198–99, 203, 210, 220, 228–29, 242–43, 252, 260, 264, 272, 282–83, 295, 297, 308–9, 314–15, 326, 333, 363–65, 368, 373, 375, 387–88, 392
United States Constitution, 35, 48, 157–58, 181, 243–44, 308
   8th Amendment, 157
   10th Amendment, 243, 385
University of Pennsylvania, 53
University of St. Andrews, 54, 163
Vergennes, Count of *see* Gravier, Charles, Count of Vergennes
Vermont, 53, 64, 136, 141, 249–50, 267, 287 *see also* New Hampshire Grants Convention, 249
Vienna, 246, 251–52, 262, 362–63
Virginia, 2, 7–8, 11, 14, 20–23, 25–31, 35, 37, 40–43, 60, 65, 68–69, 70–81, 93, 95–96, 104–5, 109–14, 116, 123, 130, 133, 137, 139, 142–43, 147, 155, 157–58, 161, 170–71, 180–81, 190, 192, 197, 200–1, 237, 241–42, 244–45, 252, 259, 265, 267–68, 275, 278, 283, 295, 297, 299, 336, 342, 361, 368, 379, 385, 393
   Convention, 139, 142
Wadsworth, Jeremiah, 367
Ward, Artemis, 69, 77
Ward, Samuel, 36, 40, 78, 85, 101, 112, 116
Warren, James, 95, 143, 150
Warren, Joseph, 67
warship, 104, 108, 178, 185, 205, 212, 228, 370, 372, 374
Washington, George, 69, 70, 73, 75–77, 79, 86, 89, 93, 95–96, 99, 101–5, 110–11, 115, 120, 122, 129, 165–66, 169, 172–74, 176–79, 183–90, 191, 199, 202–10, 213–14, 217–22, 223–26, 233–34, 238, 240, 261, 264–65, 268–69, 271–77, 278–98, 299–301, 306, 312–13, 318–19, 321–23, 324–35, 327–39, 332–38, 340–45, 346–60, 364–71, 372–82, 383–84, 388
Washington, Lund, 189–90
Washington, Martha, 74, 104, 111, 135–36, 324, 356 *see also* Custis, Martha
Watertown, 62, 67
weapons
   artillery, 73, 102, 129, 146, 260–62, 372, 303, 313, 317, 343, 379, 381
   bayonet, 89, 188, 199, 205, 290, 380, 391
   cannon, 12, 32, 44, 63, 91, 122, 129, 131, 135–37, 141, 170, 196, 205, 212, 234, 253, 274, 303, 307, 313, 317, 369, 381, 387–88
   gunpowder, 28, 43, 67 68, 91, 93, 105, 113, 124–25, 196, 217
   musket, 72, 74–75, 78, 91, 129, 141 42, 174, 189, 199, 212, 214, 224, 248, 369
Wentworth, Benning, 64, 107
Wentworth, John, 107
Wentworth, Paul, 64, 246
West Indies, 4, 31, 51, 75, 92, 192, 226, 315, 343, 372
wheat, 75, 82, 146, 229, 267
Whipple, William, 141, 169, 218, 220, 236–37, 241, 250
White Plains, 166, 203–4
Wilkes, John, 245
Williamsburg, 8, 23, 72, 75, 79–81, 104, 197
Williams, William, 181, 253, 269, 285, 289, 295
Wilmington (Delaware), 279, 283
Wilmington (North Carolina), 42–43
Wolcott, Oliver, 207, 214–15, 237
women, 21, 51, 54, 62, 71, 110, 145, 221, 255, 272, 285–91, 292, 303, 310–15, 325, 340, 342, 357, 359–60, 373, 387
Wooster, Major General David, 142, 248, 269
Worcester, 41, 46, 170, 293
Wyeth, George, 80, 130
Wyoming Valley, 102
Yale, 12, 14, 52, 87, 152, 193
Yankee, 96, 103, 125, 311
Yorktown, 104
Zubly, John J., 94, 105, 109